Lecture Notes in Computer Science

Lecture Notes in Artificial Intelligence 16131
Founding Editor

Jörg Siekmann

Series Editors

Randy Goebel, *University of Alberta, Edmonton, Canada*
Wolfgang Wahlster, *DFKI, Berlin, Germany*
Zhi-Hua Zhou, *Nanjing University, Nanjing, China*

The series Lecture Notes in Artificial Intelligence (LNAI) was established in 1988 as a topical subseries of LNCS devoted to artificial intelligence.

The series publishes state-of-the-art research results at a high level. As with the LNCS mother series, the mission of the series is to serve the international R & D community by providing an invaluable service, mainly focused on the publication of conference and workshop proceedings and postproceedings.

Mariacarla Staffa · John-John Cabibihan ·
Bruno Siciliano · Shuzhi Sam Ge ·
Leon Bodenhagen · Adriana Tapus · Silvia Rossi ·
Filippo Cavallo · Laura Fiorini ·
Marco Matarese · Hongsheng He
Editors

Social Robotics + AI

17th International Conference, ICSR+AI 2025
Naples, Italy, September 10–12, 2025
Proceedings, Part I

Editors
Mariacarla Staffa
University of Naples Parthenope
Naples, Italy

Bruno Siciliano
University of Naples Federico II
Naples, Italy

Leon Bodenhagen
University of Southern Denmark
Odense, Denmark

Silvia Rossi
Università degli Studi di Napoli Federico II
Naples, Napoli, Italy

Laura Fiorini
University of Florence, Dipt di Ingegneria
Florence, Italy

Hongsheng He
The University of Alabama
Tuscaloosa, AL, USA

John-John Cabibihan
Qatar University
Doha, Qatar

Shuzhi Sam Ge
National University of Singapore
Queenstown, Singapore

Adriana Tapus
ENSTA
Palaiseau, France

Filippo Cavallo
University of Florence
Florence, Italy

Marco Matarese
Italian Institute of Technology
Genoa, Italy

ISSN 0302-9743 ISSN 1611-3349 (electronic)
Lecture Notes in Artificial Intelligence
ISBN 978-981-95-2378-8 ISBN 978-981-95-2379-5 (eBook)
https://doi.org/10.1007/978-981-95-2379-5

LNCS Sublibrary: SL7 – Artificial Intelligence

© The Editor(s) (if applicable) and The Author(s), under exclusive license
to Springer Nature Singapore Pte Ltd. 2026
Chapters ""Who Ignores You Matters" Asymmetrical Team Dynamics in Human-Robot Collaboration" and "When a Question Isn't Fair: Grounding Perceptions of Nonhuman Agents' (Un)Fairness in a Quiz Game Experience" are licensed under the terms of the Creative Commons Attribution 4.0 International License (http://creativecommons.org/licenses/by/4.0/). For further details see license information in the chapters.

This work is subject to copyright. All rights are solely and exclusively licensed by the Publisher, whether the whole or part of the material is concerned, specifically the rights of translation, reprinting, reuse of illustrations, recitation, broadcasting, reproduction on microfilms or in any other physical way, and transmission or information storage and retrieval, electronic adaptation, computer software, or by similar or dissimilar methodology now known or hereafter developed.
The use of general descriptive names, registered names, trademarks, service marks, etc. in this publication does not imply, even in the absence of a specific statement, that such names are exempt from the relevant protective laws and regulations and therefore free for general use.
The publisher, the authors and the editors are safe to assume that the advice and information in this book are believed to be true and accurate at the date of publication. Neither the publisher nor the authors or the editors give a warranty, expressed or implied, with respect to the material contained herein or for any errors or omissions that may have been made. The publisher remains neutral with regard to jurisdictional claims in published maps and institutional affiliations.

This Springer imprint is published by the registered company Springer Nature Singapore Pte Ltd.
The registered company address is: 152 Beach Road, #21-01/04 Gateway East, Singapore 189721, Singapore

If disposing of this product, please recycle the paper.

Preface

The 17th International Conference on Social Robotics (ICSR)+AI 2025 took place in Naples, Italy as an in-person event from September 10–12, 2025. ICSR+AI 2025 was hosted by the University of Naples Parthenope with the support of Global Robotics, Arts, and Science Synergies (GRASS).

These three LNCS volumes comprise the peer-reviewed proceedings of the conference. From a total of 276 submitted manuscripts that were single-blindly reviewed by an international team of program committee, associate editors, and reviewers, 117 regular papers and 57 short papers were selected for inclusion in the proceedings and presented during the technical sessions.

The theme of this year's conference was "Emotivation at the Core: Empowering Social Robots to Inspire and Connect". The conference featured 3 keynote speeches, 15 regular sessions, 5 Special Sessions, 2 poster sessions, 11 workshops, and 3 robot competitions. The first plenary speech was delivered by Dr. Daniela Rus, who is the Andrew (1956) and Erna Viterbi Professor of Electrical Engineering and Computer Science and Director of the Computer Science and Artificial Intelligence Laboratory (CSAIL) at Massachusetts Institute of Technology. The second plenary speech was delivered by Dr. Jérôme Monceaux, who is a co-founder of Aldebaran Robotics. The third plenary speech was delivered by Dr. Anouk Wipprecht, who is a pioneering Dutch fashion designer and innovator at the forefront of the FashionTech movement.

The conference brought together researchers and practitioners working on the interaction between humans and intelligent robots and on the integration of social robots into our society, including innovative ideas and concepts, new discoveries and improvements, novel applications based on the latest fundamental advances in the core technologies that form the backbone of social robotics, as well as distinguished studies and projects pertaining to social robotics and its interaction with and impact on our society.

We extend our sincere gratitude to all members of the organizing committee and the volunteers for their dedication, which made the conference a resounding success. We are also deeply indebted to the program committee, associate editors, and reviewers for their rigorous review of the papers. Finally, we are immensely grateful for the continued support from the authors, participants, and sponsors, without whom ICSR+AI 2025 would not have been possible.

September 2025

Mariacarla Staffa
John-John Cabibihan
Bruno Siciliano
Shuzhi Sam Ge
Leon Bodenhagen
Adriana Tapus
Silvia Rossi
Filippo Cavallo
Laura Fiorini
Marco Matarese
Hongsheng He

Organization

Honorary Chair

Bruno Siciliano — University of Naples Federico II, Italy

General Chair

Mariacarla Staffa — University of Naples Parthenope, Italy

General Co-chair

John-John Cabibihan — Qatar University, Qatar

Steering Committee Chair

Shuzhi Sam Ge — National University of Singapore, Singapore

Program Chairs

Leon Bodenhagen — University of Southern Denmark, Denmark
Adriana Tapus — ENSTA Paris, France
Silvia Rossi — University of Naples Federico II, Italy
Filippo Cavallo — University of Florence, Italy

Special Session Committee

Alessandra Sciutti — Italian Institute of Technology, Italy
Luisa Damiano — IULM University, Italy
Kerstin Sophie Haring — University of Denver, USA

Workshop Committee

Maryam Alimardani   Vrije Universiteit Amsterdam, Netherlands
Patrick Holthaus   University of Hertfordshire, UK
Alberto Pirni   Scuola Superiore Sant'Anna di Pisa, Italy

Short Papers Committee

Alessandra Sorrentino   University of Florence, Italy
Jauwairia Nasir   Universität Augsburg, Germany
Alessandro Umbrico   CNR, Italy

Young Leader Committee

Lorenzo D'Errico   University of Naples Federico II, Italy
Francesco Vigni   University of Naples Federico II, Italy
Tamara Siegmann   University of Applied Sciences and Arts
                         Northwestern Switzerland
Nihan Karatas   Nagoya University, Japan

Award Committee

Antonio Sgorbissa   University of Genoa, Italy
Abderrahmane Kheddar   LIRMM Montpellier, France and CNRS-AIST,
                         Japan
Vali Lalioti   University of the Arts London, UK

Art and Robotics Committee

Hooman Samani   University of the Arts London, UK
Vali Lalioti   University of the Arts London, UK

Women in Robotics Committee

Hatice Gunes	University of Cambridge, UK
Micol Spitale	Politecnico di Milano, Italy
Samira Rasouli	University of Waterloo, Canada
Natalia Calvo	Uppsala University, Sweden

Publication Committee

Hongsheng He	The University of Alabama, USA
Marco Matarese	Italian Institute of Technology, Italy
Laura Fiorini	University of Florence, Italy

Social Media Chair

Francesca Cocchella — Italian Institute of Technology, Italy

Press Office Chair

Daniela Passariello — University of Naples Federico II, Italy

Publicity Committee

Oliver Bendel	FHNW University of Applied Sciences and Arts Northwestern Switzerland
Antonio Andriella	Artificial Intelligence Research Institute (IIIA), Spain
Minsu Jang	Electronics and Telecommunications Research Institute, South Korea
Oskar Palinko	University of Southern Denmark, Denmark

Competition Chairs

Amit Kumar Pandey	Rovial Space, France
Alessandra Rossi	University of Naples Federico II, Italy
Luca Iocchi	Sapienza University of Rome, Italy

Local Arrangement Chairs

Diana di Luccio — University of Naples Parthenope, Italy

Sustainability Chairs

Elvira Buonocore — University of Naples Parthenope, Italy
Franziska Kirstein — University of Southern Denmark, Denmark

Standing Committee

Oussama Khatib — Stanford University, USA
Maja Mataric — University of Southern California, USA
Haizhou Li — Chinese University of Hong Kong, China
Jong Hwan Kim — Korea Advanced Institute of Science and Technology, South Korea
Paolo Dario — Scuola Superiore Sant'Anna, Italy
Abderrahmane Kheddar — LIRMM Montpellier, France and CNRS-AIST, Japan
Tianmiao Wang — Beihang University, China

Associate Editors

Alessandra Rossi — University of Naples Federico II, Italy
Alessandra Sciutti — Italian Institute of Technology, Italy
Alessandra Sorrentino — University of Florence, Italy
Alessandro Umbrico — Centro Nazionale delle Ricerche, Italy
Antonio Andriella — Artificial Intelligence Research Institute (IIIA), Spain
Antonio Fleres — IULM University, Italy
Bipin Indurkhya — Jagiellonian University, Poland
Britta Wrede — University of Bielefeld, Germany
Cristina Gena — University of Turin, Italy
Eleonora Zedda — Centro Nazionale delle Ricerche, Italy
Ester Fuoco — IULM University/ISPF CNR, Italy
Filippo Cavallo — University of Florence, Italy
Francesca Cordella — University Campus Biomedico, Italy
Giacinto Barresi — University of the West of England, UK

Giulia Perugia	Eindhoven University of Technology, The Netherlands
Giuliana Vitiello	University of Salerno, Italy
Gökçe Nur Yılmaz	Ankara University, Turkey
Grazia D'Onofrio	IRCSS Ospedale Casa Sollievo della Sofferenza, Italy
Hongsheng He	University of Alabama, USA
Igor Farkaš	Comenius University Bratislava, Slovenia
Ilaria Alfieri	IULM University, Italy
Jauwairia Nasir	Universität Augsburg, Germany
John-John Cabibihan	Qatar University, Qatar
Kutluk Arikan	Ankara University, Turkey
Laura Fiorini	University of Florence, Italy
Lorenzo D'Errico	University of Naples Federico II, Italy
Luisa Damiano	IULM University, Italy
Marco Matarese	Italian Institute of Technology, Italy
Mariacarla Staffa	University of Naples Parthenope, Italy
Nele Russwinkel	University of Lübeck, Germany
Olive Bendel	University of Applied Sciences and Arts Northwestern Switzerland, Switzerland
Omar Eldardeer	Italian Institute of Technology, Italy
Oskar Palinko	University of Southern Denmark, Denmark
Patrick Holthaus	University of Hertfordshire, UK
Piotr Mirowski	Google DeepMind, UK
Rebecca Mannocci	IULM University, Italy
Thomas Sievers	University of Lübeck, Germany
Yue Hu	University of Waterloo, Canada

Contents

Emotion and Affective Interaction

Emotionally Adaptive Conversational Models for Long-Term
Human-Robot Interaction Using Proximal Policy Optimization 3
   Patrick Houman Jair and Chung Hyuk Park

Individual Differences in Social and Emotional Responses to Robotic
Dining Companions: Toward Personalized Interaction Design 16
   *Hunter Fong, Selim Soufargi, Yifei Li, Maurizio Mancini,
and Radoslaw Niewiadomski*

Affective Communication via Haptic Technology: A Usability Study
of a Huggable Device with Older Adults 33
   *Eleuda Nunez, Zuzanna Radosz-Knawa, Anna Kołbasa, Paulina Zguda,
Alicja Kamińska, Tymon Kukier, Masakazu Hirokawa, Kenji Suzuki,
and Bipin Indurkhya*

Multimodal Framework for Adaptive HRI via Dynamic Engagement
and Affective Feedback 46
   *Gayathri Girijadevi Radhakrishnan, Olga Tveretina,
Farshid Amirabdollahian, and Diego Resende Faria*

User Concerns Regarding Social Robots for Mood Regulation: A Case
Study on the Sunday Blues 59
   *Zhuochao Peng, Jiaxin Xu, Jun Hu, Haian Xue, Laurens A. G. Kolks,
and Pieter M. A. Desmet*

Applications in Real-World Case Studies

Social Robot Assistive Intervention for Science Students to Prevent
Laboratory Accidents 83
   *Mohammad Nehal Hasnine, Yuhuan Wang, Yuya Sato, Bipin Indurkhya,
and Mahmoud Mohamed Hussien Ahmed*

Remote vs. Presence Laboratories in Human-Robot Interaction with Social
Robots: A Study on Task Performance 96
   *Christopher Peters, Kai M. Blum, Ibrahim Al Krad, Pablo Moraes,
Ricardo Bedin Grando, Reinhard Gerndt, and Tobias Doernbach*

Do Social Robots Motivate Students like Humans? 111
    Akshara Pande, Bethany Gosala, Manjari Gupta, and Deepti Mishra

More Than a Tool: A Multi Method Exploration of Contextual Social
Robot Roles in German Secondary Schools 126
    Nadine Jansen, Ann-Kathrin Kubullek, and Aysegül Dogangün

Children's Questions to Robots as an Educational Opportunity - Design
Implications 141
    Alicja Wróbel, Paulina Zguda, and Bipin Indurkhya

LLMs and Conversational/Verbal Interaction

AwaR(e)obot: Towards Designing and Generating Context-Aware
Companion Robot Behavior Using LLMs 159
    Eshtiak Ahmed, Juho Hamari, and Oğuz 'Oz' Buruk

Message for You: Observing the Effects of a Social Robot's Interruptions
During an Office Task 174
    Elisabeth Ganal, Sophia C. Steinhaeusser, Florian Niebling,
    and Birgit Lugrin

"Who Ignores You Matters" Asymmetrical Team Dynamics
in Human-Robot Collaboration 194
    Clarissa Sabrina Arlinghaus, Kennedy Mambilla, and Günter W. Maier

Exploring LLM-Generated Culture-Specific Affective Human-Robot
Tactile Interaction 211
    Qiaoqiao Ren and Tony Belpaeme

Knowledge-Based Design Requirements for Persuasive Generative Social
Robots in Eldercare 224
    Stephan Vonschallen, Ennio Zumthor, Markus Simon,
    Theresa Schmiedel, and Friederike Eyssel

Motion Control, Prosthetics and Functional Robotics

A Learning-Based Model Reference Adaptive Controller Implemented
on a Prosthetic Hand Wrist 243
    Shifa Sulaiman, Mohammad Gohari, Francesco Schetter,
    and Fanny Ficuciello

Design and Optimization of a Sliding Mode Controller for a Modified
EduExo Upper Limb Exoskeleton 256
  Hamidreza Heidari, Mohammad Gohari, and Fanny Ficuciello

Human–Robot Co-design for Cleaning: Leveraging Vision Language
Model and Multi-Objective Optimization for Adaptive Layouts 269
  *S. M. Bhagya P. Samarakoon, M. A. Viraj J. Muthugala,
  W. K. R. Sachinthana, and Mohan Rajesh Elara*

Efficient Path Planner via Predator Dominance and Prey Approach
for a Vector Surveillance Robot 281
  *Ash Yaw Sang, Veerajagadheswar Prabakaran, Mohan Rajesh Elara,
  and Anh Vu Le*

It's the Way You Move: Efficient Movement Shapes Robot Perception
Across Embodiments 295
  *Kristina Nikolovska, Jan Pohl, Bernhard Hommel, Francesco Maurelli,
  and Arvid Kappas*

Context Awareness and Explainability

Context Is Cue-Cial: Assessing the Interpretation of Social Signals
from Non-anthropomorphic Robots in Different Contexts 311
  *Aparajita Chowdhury, Ana Carrasco, Florian Müller, Aino Ahtinen,
  Kaisa Väänänen, Albrecht Schmidt, and Jan Leusmann*

I Can See All of You: Supporting User Awareness with Augmented
Field-of-View for Remote Collaborative Work 331
  *Ryota Suzuki, Mina Takao, Kosei Shino, Yoshinori Kobayashi,
  Kenji Iwata, Tomomi Satoh, Yutaka Satoh, Naoki Uchida,
  Akiko Yamazaki, Keiichi Yamazaki, Felix Bergmann, and Karola Pitsch*

A Bayesian Neural Network Approach for Spatial Relations Learning
in Human-Robot Collaboration 343
  Mark McCarthy, Mai Dao, and Fujian Yan

Social Robot Haru Imitating Human Gaze for Attention and Turn-Taking
Coordination in Multi-party Conversation 356
  *Liu Tian, Yang Chen, Mingyang Hu, Eric Nichols, Randy Gomez,
  and Guangliang Li*

Modeling Social Robot Navigation: From Human Observation
to Proxemics-Based Scenario Simulation 372
  Roni Burdman, Ehud Nahum, Yael Edan, and Tal Oron-Gilad

Ethics, Trust and Social Acceptability

Determinants of Attitudes Toward Social Robots: The Role of Contact
and Beliefs in Human Uniqueness 387
   Konrad Maj, Piotr Bekier, and Albert Łukasik

Exploring Mentalising Tendencies Toward a Non-Humanoid Robot
in Individuals with Autism Spectrum Disorder: A Pilot Study 399
   *Silvia Larghi, Cristina Liviana Caldiroli, Leonardo Lapomarda,
and Edoardo Datteri*

Gender and Technology Knowledge Role on Collaborative Human-Robot
Interaction 413
   *Marcos Maroto-Gómez, Sofía Álvarez-Arias, Sara Carrasco-Martínez,
Juan Rodríguez-Huelves, Arecia Segura-Bencomo,
and Álvaro Castro-González*

When Robots Say No: Temporal Trust Recovery Through Explanation 424
   *Nicola Webb, Zijun Huang, Sanja Milivojevic, Chris Baber,
and Edmund R. Hunt*

Short Papers Session 1

RoboTale: Leveraging Large Language Models for Generative Storytelling
and Gestural Interaction on a Humanoid Robot for Children's Hospitals 439
   *Pol Barrera Valls, John Allan Øllgaard, Tabea Sudermann,
Angelina Stoyanova Wolf, Ricki Kenn Rasmussen, Leon Bodenhagen,
and Oskar Palinko*

Rethinking the Evaluation of Non-stationary Dueling Bandits
for Human-Robot Interaction 450
   Sebastian Schneider

Cheerbot: A Socially Assistive Robot for Workplace Wellbeing 456
   *Helena Webb, Pepita Barnard, Praminda Calebsolly, Alfie Cameron,
Peter Craigon, Karen Lancaster, and Emma Mcclaughlin*

Wearable Social Robots in Space 462
   Tamara Siegmann and Oliver Bendel

Attitudes Toward AI: The Role of Gender, Age, and Smartwatch Ownership ... 470
   Kimmo J. Vänni, Erika Tanhua-Piiroinen, Antti Syvänen, and Jarmo Viteli

Social Robots for Pediatric Asthma Education: A Pilot Study 476
   Katarzyna Pasternak, Cynthia Foronda, Charles Downs, and Ubbo Visser

Scaffolding Reflection, not Generation: Exploring Non-Directive Social
Robot Interaction in Early-Stage Ideation 482
   Wisanukorn Boribun and Frank Heidmann

Facilitating the Emergence of Assistive Robots to Support Frailty:
Psychosocial and Environmental Realities 490
   *Angela Higgins, Stephen Potter, Mauro Dragone,
Mark Hawley, Farshid Amirabdollahian, Alessandro Di Nuovo,
and Praminda Caleb-Solly*

Examining the Legibility of Humanoid Robot Arm Movements
in a Pointing Task 499
   *Andrej Lúčny, Matilde Antonj, Carlo Mazzola, Hana Hornáčková,
Ana Farić, Kristína Malinovská, Ana Vavrečka, and Igor Farkaš*

AI Pedagogy: Dialogic Social Learning for Artificial Agents 508
   *Sabrina Patania, Luca Annese, Cansu Koyuturk, Azzurra Ruggeri,
and Dimitri Ognibene*

Beyond Detection - Orchestrating Human-Robot-Robot Assistance
via an Internet of Robotic Things Paradigm 516
   Joseph Hunt, Koyo Fujii, Aly Magassouba, and Praminda Caleb-Solly

Towards Expert Human-Robot Interactions Using Knowledge Graphs 524
   *Graham Wilcock, Kristiina Jokinen, Biju Thankachan,
and Markku Turunen*

LLMs and Humanoid Robot Diversity: The Pose Generation Challenge 531
   *Riccardo Catalini, Federico Biagi, Giacomo Salici, Guido Borghi,
Roberto Vezzani, and Luigi Biagiotti*

Identifying Public Engagement with Autonomous Art Through Human
Pose and Speed Detection 539
   Tianyuan Wang, Fanta Camara, Robert Woolley, and Darren Reed

A Cognitive Social Robot in Manufacturing 547
   Dimitra Anastasiou, Ben Gaffinet, and Yannick Naudet

Pitch Training with Furhat: Effects of a Social Robot in Entrepreneurship
Education 553
   Ilona Buchem, Yasmin Olteanu, and Georges Arnaud Kouayim Bonga

A Progressive Multimodal Robot System for Emotional Learning
in Autistic Children 559
   Yiyi Wu, Maninderjit Kaur, and Fengpei Yuan

Breathe with Me: A Breathing Exercise Guided by the Robot NAO
Reduces Stress 566
   Ilona Buchem, Katharina Kuehne, Martina Mauch, and Niklas Baecker

Come Closer: A Social Bench to Measure Children's Interaction
with Robots 572
   *Francesca Cocchella, Sara Mongile, Giulia Pusceddu,
Luca Andrighetto, Francesco Rea, and Alessandra Sciutti*

Conceptual Framework for Autonomous Coaching in Orthopaedic
Rehabilitation with Socially Assistive Robots 578
   *C. Tamantini, A. Umbrico, A. Fabrizio, A. Carnevale, E. Schena,
U. G. Longo, and A. Orlandini*

HRI-Based Interview Training Using the FurHat Robot 584
   Adam Jones and Roger K. Moore

Exploring New Vitality Forms in Human-Robot Interaction 590
   *Carlesso Serena, Abdul Kader Mohamed Ismail, Di Cesare Giuseppe,
Sciutti Alessandra, and Niewiadomski Radoslaw*

Impact of Gaze-Based Interaction and Augmentation on Human-Robot
Collaboration in Critical Tasks 598
   Ayesha Jena, Stefan Reitmann, and Elin Anna Topp

EMOROBCARE: A Low-Cost Social Robot for Supporting Children
with Autism in Therapeutic Settings 607
   *Sara Cooper, Bartomeu Pou, Arnau Mayoral-Macau, Alberto Redondo,
David Rios, and Raquel Ros*

When a Question Isn't Fair: Grounding Perceptions of Nonhuman Agents'
(Un)Fairness in a Quiz Game Experience 616
   August Bäckström, William Ekenberg, and Victor Kaptelinin

Diffusion of Responsibility in HRI: Reduction of Human Agency Does
not Occur When Sharing a Task with a Robotic Arm 625
   *Francesca Ciardo, Alessandra Fava, Paola Ricciardelli, Valeria Villani,
Cristina Iani, and Lorenzo Sabattini*

Exploring Emotional Support Through Interaction with a Social Robot
for Individuals with a Visual and Cognitive Impairment: a Pilot Study 632
   *Veerle L. N. F. Hobbelink, Dustin Lischer, Martijn van Zeeland,
Rick Gevaert, Victor van der Hout, and Matthijs H. J. Smakman*

A Path to Gradual Individual Experience and Recollection for Social
Robots Based on a Cognitive Architecture 641
   Thomas Sievers and Nele Russwinkel

SitBot: A Posture-Mimicking Robot to Reduce Slouching 648
   Chia-An Wang, Adam Wikström, Linus Pettersson, Anasha Sarker,
   Martina De Cet, Georgios Diapoulis, Mohammad Obaid, and Ilaria Torre

Author Index 655

Emotion and Affective Interaction

Emotionally Adaptive Conversational Models for Long-Term Human-Robot Interaction Using Proximal Policy Optimization

Patrick Houman Jair[✉] and Chung Hyuk Park

Assistive Robotics and Tele-Medicine (ART-Med) Lab., Department of Biomedical Engineering, School of Engineering and Applied Science, The George Washington University, Washington, DC, USA
{Jairpat530,chpark}@gwu.edu

Abstract. As socially assistive robots become increasingly integrated into everyday life, their ability to engage in emotionally intelligent interactions is essential for supporting long-term human-robot relationships. This work presents a reinforcement learning-based conversational model that dynamically adapts to the user's emotional state across multi-turn dialogues. Using Proximal Policy Optimization (PPO), the system selects appropriate response types based on emotion labels extracted from user speech. A pre-trained emotion classifier (DistilRoBERTa) processes speech-to-text input, and the selected response type guides a GPT-based response generator. The model is deployed on Pepper, a humanoid robot, and evaluated through a two-week longitudinal user study comparing static and adaptive dialogue systems. Results demonstrate that the PPO-powered adaptive model significantly improves user engagement and reduces stress levels over time. This study highlights the importance of reinforcement learning for sustained emotional coherence and opens pathways for emotionally adaptive robots in mental health, education, and social support applications.

Keywords: Human-Robot Interaction · Emotion Recognition · Reinforcement Learning · PPO · Conversational AI

1 Introduction

Robots are increasingly expected to communicate in emotionally intelligent ways. Socially assistive robots, in particular, must adapt to human emotions to provide effective support in healthcare, education, and companionship. This requires conversational models that go beyond single-turn sentiment detection and generate responses aligned with long-term emotional context [1].

While large language models like GPT have enabled fluid text generation [2], most existing systems rely on static or reactive strategies that fail to sustain emotional coherence [3]. In contrast, this paper presents a reinforcement learning (RL) framework that uses Proximal Policy Optimization (PPO) to dynamically select response types (e.g., empathetic, supportive) based on detected emotion and evolving user state.

The model is deployed on Pepper, a humanoid robot, and evaluated through a longitudinal user study. Results show improvements in stress reduction, emotional well-being, and engagement, confirming the value of adaptive strategies in real-world human-robot interaction (HRI).

2 Related Work

Our work draws from three research areas: emotion-aware dialogue systems, reinforcement learning for response optimization, and multi-turn dialogue systems in social robotics. We briefly review these areas and position our approach.

2.1 Emotion-Aware Dialogue Systems

Early emotion-aware systems like Breazeal's *Kismet* modeled affective cues to support interactive behaviors [4]. More recent methods use deep learning to classify user emotions from text and adapt responses accordingly [5,6]. However, most systems are reactive, without adapting to long-term emotional trends.

2.2 Reinforcement Learning in Dialogue

RL has been used to optimize dialogue policies for task success [7]. In social contexts, RL enables adaptive pacing and engagement [8]. Actor-critic methods and PPO have shown promise for aligning responses with user goals [9,10]. Yet few integrate emotion signals into the reward function or support repeated interactions.

2.3 Multi-Turn Dialogue in Social Robotics

Maintaining coherent, context-aware conversations is central to long-term HRI. Models like HRED [11] and DialoGPT [12] enable multi-turn generation. Breazeal [13], Matarić [14], and Mutlu [15] have advanced this in embodied agents. Still, most lack real-time adaptation to users' evolving emotional states.

2.4 Positioning Our Work

We bridge these domains by combining real-time emotion recognition, PPO-based response type selection, and multi-turn dialogue in a physical social robot. Unlike prior systems, our model is optimized not for task completion, but for sustaining emotional alignment over repeated interactions in a real-world HRI setting.

3 Methodology

Our system integrates real-time speech-to-text (STT), emotion classification, PPO-based response selection, and GPT-based language generation. It runs live on Pepper and adapts continuously to user input across multi-turn interactions (Fig. 1).

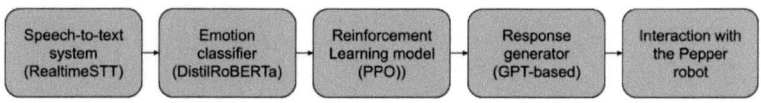

Fig. 1. System architecture. User input is transcribed, classified for emotion, then passed to a PPO model that selects a response type. GPT generates a response, which is spoken by Pepper.

3.1 Response Selection with PPO

Our PPO model operates in a Markov Decision Process (MDP) framework. The state space S includes a 7-dimensional one-hot encoded emotion label obtained from DistilRoBERTa and a context vector summarizing the user's previous utterance. The action space A consists of five discrete response types: {Empathetic, Supportive, Reassuring, Informative, Neutral}.

The PPO model uses an actor-critic architecture with two hidden layers (128 units each, ReLU activations). The actor outputs a probability distribution over response types, while the critic estimates the expected reward.

The reward function $R(s, a)$ is shaped as follows: +1 if the detected user emotion improves in the next turn, +0.5 if the emotion remains stable, and 1 if it worsens. This structure encourages emotionally supportive and coherent interactions over time (Figs. 2, 3 and 4).

3.2 Dataset and Training

To train the initial PPO policy, we used the DailyDialog dataset [16], a high-quality multi-turn conversation dataset containing diverse emotional content. For each conversation, even-numbered turns, representing responses, were labeled with one of five high-level response types (Inform, Empathetic, Supportive, Reassuring, or Neutral). These labels were generated using ChatGPT based on the emotional context of the preceding user utterance.

The PPO model was first pre-trained on this labeled dataset to learn an initial policy for selecting response types based on input emotion and dialogue context. During the user study, the model was further fine-tuned using interaction data collected from each participant in the experimental group. After each session, the conversations of the participants, the emotions detected, and the feedback of

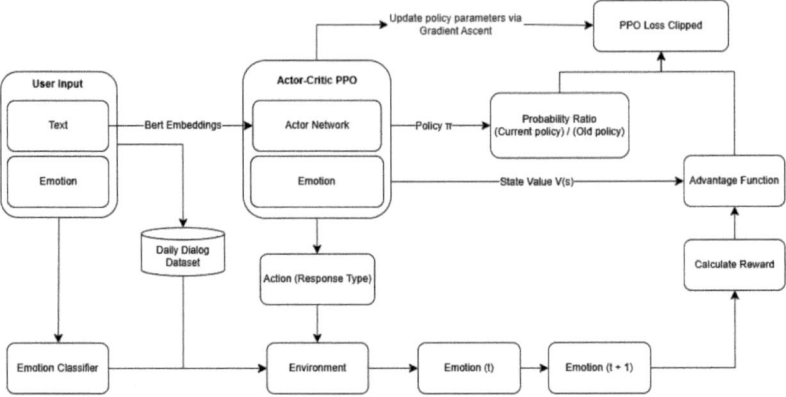

Fig. 2. Emotion-aware PPO architecture. The model processes emotion and dialogue context to select a response type.

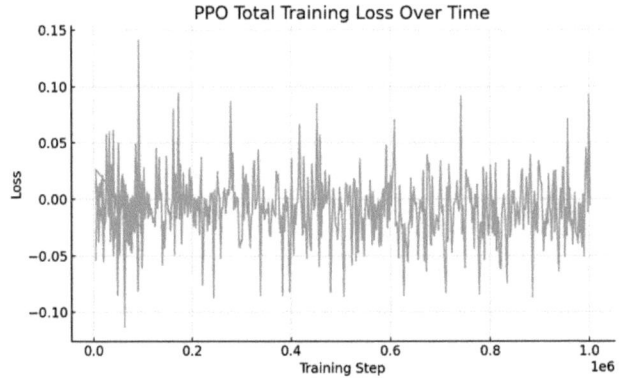

Fig. 3. PPO training loss over time. Convergence is observed.

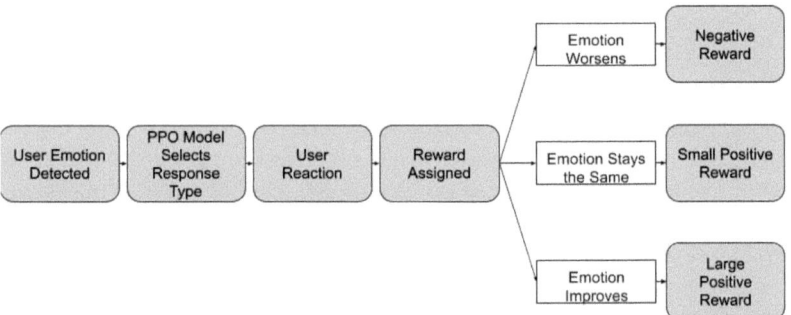

Fig. 4. Reward system: negative for worse emotion, small positive for stable, high positive for improvement.

rewards were used to adapt the policy, allowing personalized response strategies to evolve over time.

To better understand the performance of the PPO model, we also explored its behavior in relation to alternative reinforcement learning strategies. Specifically, we qualitatively examined the expected decision patterns of Deep Q-Network (DQN) and Advantage Actor-Critic (A2C) architectures using the same state and reward design as our PPO implementation. A rule-based (non-adaptive) baseline using fixed response types was also considered.

While these alternative agents were not fully trained or deployed on the robot, their inclusion helped guide our choice of PPO by highlighting its theoretical advantages in handling continuous adaptation, stability, and reward clipping under sparse emotional feedback. PPO was therefore selected as the primary policy optimization method for our real-world deployment.

4 Experiment

To evaluate the effectiveness of the emotionally adaptive conversational system, we conducted a two-week longitudinal user study involving 11 participants. Each participant completed five separate 10-min conversation sessions with the humanoid robot Pepper, scheduled across weekdays to simulate natural, repeated interaction.

Participants were randomly assigned to one of two groups. The experimental group (n = 7) interacted with Pepper equipped with the full adaptive system. This included real-time speech-to-text (STT) processing, emotion classification using DistilRoBERTa, response type selection via Proximal Policy Optimization (PPO), and GPT-based response generation tailored to the user's detected emotional state. The control group (n = 4) interacted with a non-adaptive version of Pepper that generated static GPT responses without emotion recognition or reinforcement learning.

Prior to the first session, all participants completed a demographic survey and a baseline well-being questionnaire. During each session, participants spoke naturally with Pepper about their day or current thoughts. The experimental group received emotionally adaptive responses, while the control group received generic GPT responses. At the beginning and end of each session, participants self-reported their stress levels using a 10-point Likert scale. After each session, they rated how engaging and natural the conversation felt and indicated whether their mood had improved, stayed the same, or worsened.

At the conclusion of the fifth session, participants completed a follow-up well-being survey to assess longitudinal emotional effects. All interaction data, including recognized text, predicted emotion, selected response type, and generated response, were recorded. For the experimental group, the PPO model was fine-tuned after each session using participant-specific interaction data to improve personalization over time.

This design supported both within-subject comparisons across sessions and between-group comparisons across all emotional and engagement measures.

4.1 Procedure

The participants were seated across from the humanoid robot Pepper in a private room and engaged in a natural conversation about their day. Each session lasted 10 min and was repeated on five separate days of the week.

Participants were seated in a quiet, distraction-free environment, with Pepper placed at table height directly facing the user to support natural eye contact and conversational flow. The study took place in the same room for all participants to maintain environmental consistency.

The participant pool included 11 individuals (6 male, 5 female), aged between 21 and 45 years (mean = 27.4, SD = 6.8). Participants were recruited from the university population, including both students and staff. They were randomly assigned to either the experimental group (n = 7), which interacted with the full emotionally adaptive system, or the control group (n = 4), which interacted with a non-adaptive version of Pepper providing static GPT-based responses.

Each participant completed five 10-min conversation sessions with Pepper across two weeks, scheduled on weekdays to simulate regular, short-term social contact. Before and after each session, participants rated their stress level on a 10-point Likert scale and reported whether their mood improved, stayed the same, or worsened. After each session, they also rated how engaging and natural the conversation felt. A final well-being survey was administered after the fifth session to assess longitudinal emotional impact (Figs. 5 and 10).

Fig. 5. Scenes from the experiment showing the humanoid robot Pepper engaging in conversation with participants in a controlled setting. The right image shows a session with a student participant, while the left image shows interaction with a faculty member, demonstrating the adaptability of the system across user types.

5 Discussion

The results of this study provide compelling evidence for the emotional and experiential benefits of long-term interaction with an emotionally adaptive robot. Across stress, well-being, engagement, and mood, the experimental group, which

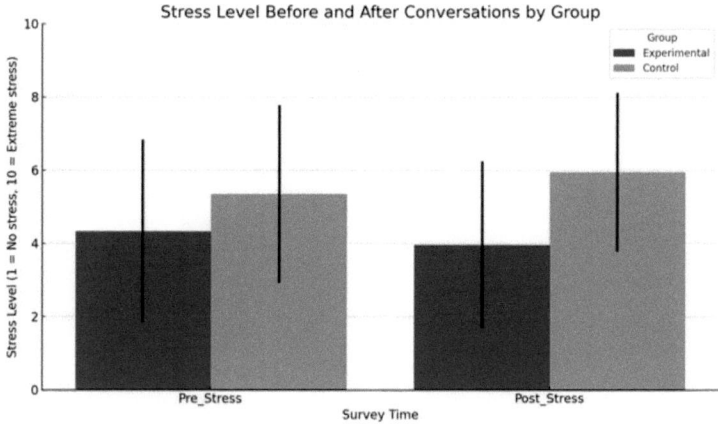

Fig. 6. Stress levels pre/post session. Experimental group: significant reduction ($p = 0.004$).

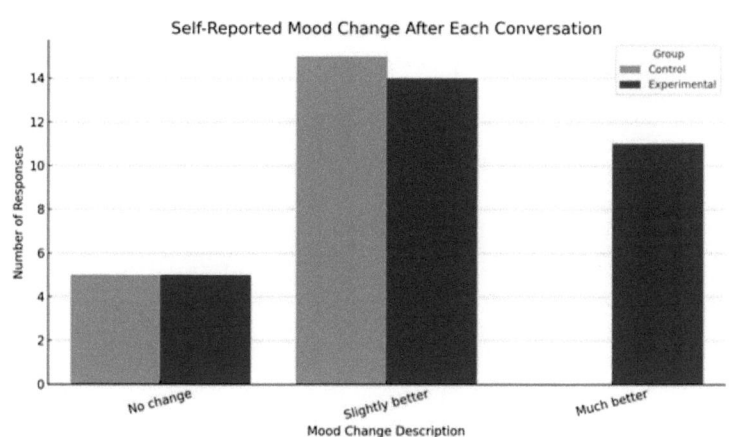

Fig. 7. Mood change after conversation. More "much better" reports from experimental group.

interacted with the adaptive PPO-powered version of Pepper, consistently outperformed the control group. This suggests that reinforcement learning-based emotional adaptation plays a key role in enhancing human-robot interaction.

5.1 Cumulative Stress Reduction Over Time

The strongest finding emerged in terms of stress reduction. As shown in Fig. 9, the experimental group exhibited a consistent decline in average stress levels over the five sessions, while the control group's levels fluctuated and ultimately

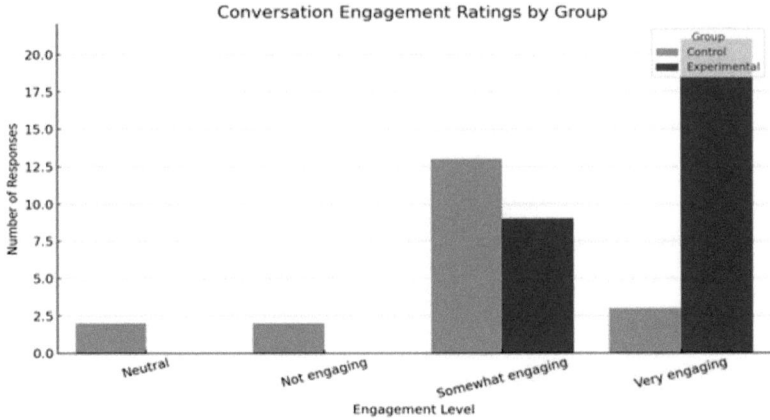

Fig. 8. Engagement ratings. Experimental group rated interactions more highly.

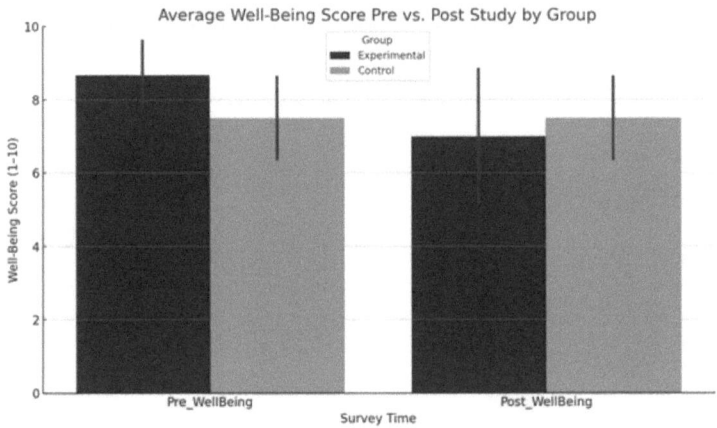

Fig. 9. Well-being over two weeks. Improvement for experimental group (not significant, $p = 0.153$).

returned near baseline. This cumulative effect indicates that emotionally adaptive interaction yields benefits that grow over time. Furthermore, the immediate pre- vs. post-session stress comparison (Fig. 6) shows a statistically significant decrease for the experimental group ($p = 0.004$), reinforcing the conclusion that adaptive systems effectively reduce short-term emotional burden.

5.2 Engagement and Perceived Naturalness

Engagement ratings (Fig. 8) further support the impact of the adaptive system. While both groups had responses in the "somewhat engaging" category, the experimental group received nearly double the number of "very engaging"

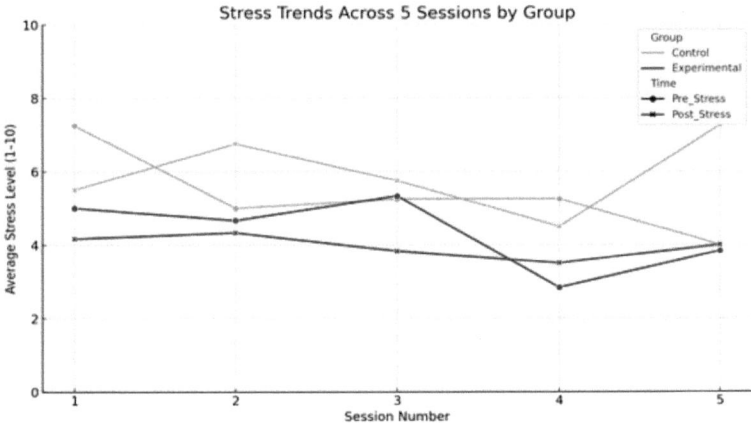

Fig. 10. Stress trend across 5 sessions. Experimental group showed consistent decline.

responses compared to the control group. This suggests that emotional responsiveness, as facilitated by PPO, contributed to a more immersive and natural interaction experience. Participants frequently noted that Pepper's responses felt more relevant and appropriately tuned to their emotional state.

5.3 Subjective Mood Improvements

In addition to stress reduction, subjective mood improvements were reported more frequently in the experimental group. Figure 7 shows that while both groups had similar "slightly better" responses, only the experimental group had a substantial number of "much better" responses after sessions. This supports the idea that emotional adaptation not only relieves stress but also fosters positive affect, particularly when the system maintains emotional coherence over the course of a conversation.

5.4 Well-Being Trends and Emotional Coherence

Figure 9 shows a modest upward trend in well-being for the experimental group and a flatter trajectory for the control group. Although the difference in post-study well-being scores was not statistically significant ($p = 0.153$), the trend direction, combined with mood reports, suggests that long-term emotional alignment has the potential to improve baseline emotional state. With a larger sample size or extended study period, this trend may yield stronger significance.

5.5 Interpreting Group Differences in Context

It is important to note that participants varied in emotional baseline, stress history, and lifestyle context. Despite this, the adaptive system produced consistent advantages, implying robustness across user variability. The personalization mechanism built into the PPO model likely played a key role in enabling tailored responses over time, helping users feel more heard and emotionally supported.

Overall, these findings support the hypothesis that reinforcement learning-based response selection enhances social robot interaction by improving affective alignment, perceived helpfulness, and emotional outcomes. By adjusting behavior based on real-time emotional context, the system strengthens user trust, satisfaction, and long-term engagement.

6 Limitations

While the findings from this study are promising, several limitations should be noted.

6.1 Technical Limitations

The system processes user input through a multi-stage pipeline-speech-to-text (STT), emotion classification, PPO-based response selection, and GPT-based response generation. This layered architecture introduces slight latency, which may impact conversational naturalness. Additionally, the STT system may misinterpret speech, particularly in the presence of accents, background noise, or unclear pronunciation, potentially leading to incorrect emotion classification.

Another constraint lies in the emotion recognition module, which relies solely on textual input and does not account for prosody, tone, or sarcasm. As a result, certain emotional nuances may be missed, reducing the system's ability to fully understand or respond to complex human affect.

6.2 Study Limitations

The participant pool in this study was relatively small ($n = 11$), which limits the statistical power and generalizability of the results. While trends were observed in stress and well-being improvements, a larger and more diverse sample would be necessary to confirm these effects at scale.

Furthermore, human emotions are inherently dynamic and context-dependent. The PPO model adapts based on recent emotional changes, but rapid or contradictory shifts in emotion may still lead to mismatched or inappropriate responses. Real-world deployment will require broader emotional datasets and additional robustness to handle these fluctuations effectively. Another limitation is the use of unimodal, text-only emotion recognition. The system does not account for prosodic cues, vocal tone, facial expressions, or body language, which are often critical in understanding nuanced emotional states. This may reduce the system's ability to fully align with user affect, especially in cases of sarcasm or mixed emotions.

Additionally, while the PPO model adapts based on emotional feedback, the reasoning behind its response selections remains opaque. Future work will explore explainable reinforcement learning approaches to improve transparency and user trust in emotionally adaptive decision-making.

7 Future Work

Building on the promising results of this study, several directions can be pursued to further enhance the system's capabilities and real-world applicability.

7.1 Technical Enhancements

Future iterations of the system will focus on optimizing processing efficiency to reduce response latency and improve conversational fluidity. This includes streamlining the pipeline from speech-to-text through emotion classification, PPO decision-making, and GPT response generation.

To improve emotional understanding, we plan to integrate multimodal emotion recognition that incorporates not only text but also vocal tone and facial expressions. This would allow the system to interpret a wider range of emotional cues and respond with greater accuracy. Additionally, future versions of the PPO model will explore more dynamic reinforcement learning approaches that can better adapt to highly variable user behaviors in real time.

Language support will also be expanded to accommodate multilingual users, ensuring broader accessibility and cultural relevance in emotionally adaptive human-robot interaction.

7.2 Study Expansion

To increase generalizability and statistical power, future studies will include a larger and more diverse participant pool. This will enable deeper insights into how emotionally adaptive systems affect users across different age groups, cultural backgrounds, and emotional baselines.

Longer-term studies will also help assess the durability of emotional improvement and engagement effects over time, as well as refine the personalization mechanisms that underpin user-specific adaptation.

8 Conclusion

This study presents a reinforcement learning-based conversational framework for enhancing long-term human-robot interaction through emotional adaptation. By leveraging Proximal Policy Optimization (PPO) to select response types based on the user's detected emotional state, the system delivered personalized and emotionally coherent dialogue through the humanoid robot Pepper.

Across five sessions over two weeks, participants in the experimental group, who interacted with the adaptive system, experienced significantly greater stress reduction ($p = 0.004$), higher engagement, and more frequent self-reported mood improvements compared to the control group. Although the increase in well-being scores was not statistically significant, the positive trend observed in the adaptive group suggests potential long-term benefits of emotionally responsive interaction.

These findings highlight the value of reinforcement learning in shaping emotionally intelligent robot behavior. The ability to continuously adapt responses based on evolving user emotion not only enhances user experience, but also fosters rapport and emotional support over time. This work contributes to the growing field of affective human-robot interaction and demonstrates that reinforcement learning can serve as a powerful tool for creating more empathetic and supportive conversational agents.

Future applications of this system may include therapeutic, educational, and companionship settings where emotional understanding and sustained engagement are essential. By expanding the framework to support multimodal emotion recognition and multilingual dialogue, emotionally adaptive systems like this one could become key components of socially assistive robotics in real-world contexts.

Acknowledgments. This research was partially supported by the NSF Grants #1846658 and #2348081 throughout the development of this project. The authors would like to thank Drs. Vesna Zderic and Victor Krauthamer for their support on this study with their facility.

References

1. Spezialetti, M., et al.: Emotion recognition for human-robot interaction: recent advances and future perspectives. In: Proceedings of IEEE International Conference on Systems, Man, and Cybernetics (SMC), pp. 3451–3457 (2020)
2. Yang, Y., Lin, Z., Liu, X., He, P., Chen, W., Gao, J.: A survey of large language models. arXiv preprint arXiv:2303.18223 (2024)
3. Zhao, T., Liu, W., Wang, D., Campbell, M., Potdar, S.: A survey of emotion-aware dialog systems. ACM Comput. Surv. **55**(12), 1–36 (2023)
4. Breazeal, C.: Emotion and sociable humanoid robots. Int. J. Hum. Comput. Stud. **59**(1–2), 119–155 (2003)
5. Saravia, E., Liu, H.C.T., Huang, Y.H., Wu, J., Cambria, E.: CARER: contextualized affect representations for emotion recognition. In: Proceedings of EMNLP, pp. 3687–3697 (2018)
6. Huang, C., Lu, Y.S., Chen, Y.S., Liu, H.Y.: EmotionBERT: improving emotion classification with pre-trained language models. arXiv preprint arXiv:2108.03529 (2021)
7. Li, J., Zhu, C., Liu, X., Zeng, M., Gao, J.: Reinforcement learning for dialogue generation: a review. In: Proceedings of 61st Annual Meeting of the Association for Computational Linguistics (ACL), pp. 1–17 (2023)
8. Mutlu, B., Forlizzi, J., Hodgins, J.K.: Conversational robots: building meaningful dialogue with context and personality. In: Proceedings of International Conference on Human-Robot Interaction (2013)
9. Jaques, N., Gu, S., Bahdanau, D., Brock, A., Kahou, S.S.E., Pineau, J.: Human-centric dialog training via off-policy reinforcement learning. arXiv preprint arXiv:1906.01622 (2020)
10. Schulman, J., Wolski, F., Dhariwal, P., Radford, A., Klimov, O.: Proximal policy optimization algorithms. arXiv preprint arXiv:1707.06347 (2017)

11. Serban, I.V., Sordoni, A., Bengio, Y., Courville, A., Pineau, J.: Building end-to-end dialogue systems using generative hierarchical neural network models. In: Proceedings of AAAI Conference on Artificial Intelligence, vol. 30, no. 1 (2016)
12. Zhang, Y., Sun, S., Galley, M., Chen, Y.C., Brockett, C., Gao, J.: DialoGPT: large-scale generative pre-training for conversational response generation. arXiv preprint arXiv:1911.00536 (2019)
13. Gordon, G., Spaulding, S., Breazeal, C.: Affective personalization of a social robot tutor for children's second language skills. In: Proceedings of AAAI Conference on Artificial Intelligence, vol. 30, no. 1 (2016)
14. Mataric, M.J.: Socially assistive robotics: human augmentation versus automation. Sci. Robot. (2016)
15. Mutlu, B., Forlizzi, J.: Designing robots for long-term social interaction. In: Proceedings of IEEE/RSJ International Conference on Intelligent Robots and Systems (IROS), pp. 1454–1459 (2012)
16. Li, Y., Su, H., Shen, X., Li, W., Cao, Z., Niu, S.: DailyDialog: a manually labelled multi-turn dialogue dataset. In: Proceedings of IJCNLP, pp. 986–995 (2017)
17. Rossi, S., Ferland, F., Tapus, A.: Adaptive human-robot interaction in social contexts. In: Proceedings of SIMPAR 2025 (2025). https://doi.org/10.1109/SIMPAR62925.2025.10979036
18. Mehta, V., Kim, J., et al.: Evaluating real-time adaptive behavior in humanoid tutors. In: CEUR Workshop Proceedings, vol. 3932. https://ceur-ws.org/Vol-3932/paper8.pdf

Individual Differences in Social and Emotional Responses to Robotic Dining Companions: Toward Personalized Interaction Design

Hunter Fong[1], Selim Soufargi[2], Yifei Li[2], Maurizio Mancini[2], and Radoslaw Niewiadomski[1](✉)

[1] Department of Informatics, Bioengineering, Robotics and Systems Engineering, University of Genoa, Genoa, Italy
{hunter.fong,radoslaw.niewiadomski}@unige.it
[2] Department of Computer Science, Sapienza University of Rome, Rome, Italy
{soufargi,li,m.mancini}@di.uniroma1.it

Abstract. This study investigates how affective and personality traits shape users' emotional and social responses to a robotic dining companion in a commensal context. The companion is a *NAO* robot, equipped with a GPT-based dialogue and a commensal activity visual detection module, able to engage in mealtime conversation and exhibit responsive nonverbal behaviors. Twenty-two participants shared a meal with the robot and completed pre- and post-interaction measures of personality, affect, commensality habits, enjoyment of the interaction, and perceived social connection. Results showed that participants high in openness reported greater enjoyment of the interaction and more positive situational affect, while those high in negative trait affect also reported high enjoyment of the interaction, suggesting that the robot provided value even for users who were not predisposed to feel good. Perceived social connection was predicted by negative affect, frequency of eating with others, and technology use during meals. Traits like extraversion and agreeableness were inversely related to connection—suggesting that artificial social agents may resonate most with emotionally sensitive users, rather than the most sociable ones. These findings suggest that commensal robotic companions may be particularly well-suited to users high in negative affect and openness, but also highlight the importance of adapting dialogue and behavioral strategies to users' personality traits.

Keywords: Human–robot interaction · Commensality · Emotion · Social robotics · Personalization · Individual differences · Social connection

1 Introduction

Commensality—eating together—has long been associated with mental health, mood, dietary habits [1,12,25,38,52], group cohesion [15,19,21,27,28], and the development of social identity [20]. Conversely, eating alone has been linked to negative health outcomes such as binge eating and poor nutrition [21]. Illness, social isolation, old age, or epidemic-related restrictions may compel individuals to dine alone [3,4,42,53]. Moreover, commensality with a human partner is not always satisfying, and may depend on individual preferences [49].

Recently, commensality has drawn interest in Human–Robot Interaction (HRI) [43]. In this context, we developed an artificial commensal companion (ACC) using a *NAO* robot capable of multimodal, socially plausible dining interaction—including gaze, gesture, speech, and adaptive prompts. Prior work suggests that such companions may benefit lonely eaters and provide some of the psychosocial advantages of human commensality [17,22,37,44].

In this paper, we investigate how individual differences shape emotional and social responses to robotic commensality. Drawing on theories of affective intensity [34], social withdrawal and approach motivation [6,58], and openness to novelty [41], we ask: (1) How do personality and affective traits influence emotional responses—such as enjoyment and situational affect—during an ACC interaction? (2) How do these traits shape perceived social connection with the robot? We focus on social connection because it is not only central to commensality, but also predicts HRI outcomes such as engagement, repeat use, and emotional benefit [2,11,36]. By identifying which individual traits predict more positive responses, we aim to inform future personalization strategies.

The study contributes empirical evidence linking user traits to enjoyment, situational affect, and perceived connection—particularly via partner responsiveness—and lays groundwork for tailoring ACC behaviors to individual user profiles.

2 Related Work

2.1 Commensality and Human–Robot Interaction

Several studies have explored the introduction of artificial agents into mealtime contexts, though relatively few have focused on their social or affective impact. For instance, [26] presented a speculative prototype, FoBo, designed to create playful and entertaining interactions during meals. [40] developed a socially assistive robot aimed at cognitively stimulating and engaging elderly users through gestures, greetings, and humor. Similarly, [47] modeled socially appropriate bite timing by analyzing video recordings of human triads dining together. [17] introduced a humanoid robot that simulates food consumption via mixed reality; users wearing headsets saw the robot eat in synchrony with them, and reported increased enjoyment of the experience. [18] explored multi-robot dining companions, finding that participants who frequently ate alone preferred dining with two robots over one. [44] proposed a toy robot that engaged nonverbally with diners to simulate social presence during meals.

While these systems highlight the feasibility of integrating agents into mealtime settings, questions remain about how user traits—such as personality, trait-level affect, mood, and commensality habits—shape these interactions. Our work addresses this gap by focusing explicitly on individual differences in response to robotic companionship during meals.

2.2 Individual Differences in HRI

Individual differences have long been recognized as influential in shaping how users engage with artificial agents. Prior work has explored adapting robot behavior based on inferred user personality—such as tailoring robot demeanor to user sociability in assistive and pedagogical contexts—to improve engagement and effectiveness [54]. Similarly, healthcare and well-being agents have shown variable outcomes depending on users' baseline affect and emotional needs [24].

When personality traits have been directly measured, studies have shown that traits like openness, agreeableness, and extraversion predict users' acceptance of and trust in domestic and assistive robots [8,55]. Affective tendencies such as anxiety, trust propensity, and loneliness have also been linked to perceived supportiveness and social bonding in long-term HRI [5].

Across these domains, personality and affective traits shape not only the interaction itself, but also whether users perceive artificial agents as emotionally supportive, trustworthy, or socially resonant [8].

Recent work by Laban and colleagues has advanced our understanding of how individual traits shape emotional disclosure and well-being in human–robot relationships. In a series of studies, they demonstrate that users' emotional states, disclosure tendencies, and long-term interaction trajectories significantly affect both subjective well-being and relationship formation with social robots [30–32]. For instance, emotional distress and the desire to cope predict increased self-disclosure to robots [32], while emotional expression during interaction can itself lead to improved affective outcomes [30]. Importantly, these effects vary over time and are shaped by user perceptions of trust, understanding, and social presence [31]. These findings underscore the need for trait-sensitive robot design and support our focus on how personality and affect influence users' responses to robotic companions in meaningful social settings such as commensal interaction.

In addition to personality-based adaptation, prior work has shown that verbal and paraverbal cues—such as empathetic phrasing, emotional mirroring, and prosodic modulation—can shape users' emotional and social responses in HRI. For example, empathetic or socially aligned dialogue styles have been found to improve rapport and affective support in long-term interactions [39,45,50]. Verbal strategies such as emotional disclosure, tailored prompting, and turn-taking sensitivity have also been shown to enhance users' feelings of being understood and supported [16,35]. These findings highlight the importance of not only what is said, but how and when it is delivered—particularly in socially meaningful contexts such as healthcare or companionship. While our current system uses only basic verbal fallback prompts and non-adaptive GPT responses, future ACC designs could incorporate real-time verbal alignment to strengthen social connection and partner responsiveness.

Yet despite this growing body of evidence, little attention has been paid to how these individual differences play out in one of the most socially loaded and emotionally meaningful domains: mealtimes. Unlike task-based or assistive HRI, commensality centers on emotional presence, affective resonance, and informal social norms. While previous work has focused on feasibility and user enjoyment in aggregate, ours is the first study to examine how trait affect and personality interact to shape emotional and social outcomes in this context. In doing so, we respond to recent calls to better understand user diversity in HRI, and offer the first empirical insight into individual differences in this emerging subfield. Importantly, this context introduces both opportunities and risks. While eating together can promote bonding and emotional well-being, prior research has shown that commensality is not universally positive: group tension, mismatched personalities, and unmet social expectations can diminish the benefits, or even create discomfort [15,19,21]. These findings highlight the importance of examining not just how robots behave, but *who they're interacting with*, and how user characteristics shape experience.

3 System Overview

To support emotionally and socially engaging mealtime interaction, we developed a multimodal artificial commensal companion (ACC) built around the *NAO* robot. The system integrates speech-based conversation with nonverbal behaviors—such as gaze and gesture—to simulate a socially plausible dining partner. Gaze behavior is used to orient toward the user during speech or silence, while simple arm gestures are triggered during greetings or conversational turns. These functions contribute to the robot's perceived responsiveness and friendly demeanor. A schematic of the full system is shown in Fig. 1.

The ACC integrates two core modules: a computer vision module and a speech interaction module. The vision module detects eating activity using pose, facial, and hand-tracking data. The speech module includes voice activity detection, speech recognition, and GPT-based language generation, enabling context-aware verbal responses.

Dialogue management is handled by a lightweight rule-based controller that monitors user engagement in real time. If extended silence (e.g., >10 s), gaze aversion, or eating gestures are detected, the robot attempts to re-engage the user through a verbal prompt. These prompts are drawn from a pre-curated set of socially appropriate conversation starters (e.g., "What kind of food do you like?", "Do you cook often?"), tailored to match typical mealtime small talk. Once a conversational trigger is activated, the GPT system generates a response using a natural language prompt (e.g., "Ask a friendly follow-up question about hobbies") while considering the user's previous input. This strategy allowed the system to deliver socially fluent phrasing with moderate variation, while remaining constrained in both topic and tone.

Despite the limited adaptiveness of the interaction given the strict system's prompt input forcing the robot to reply briefly, participants generally responded

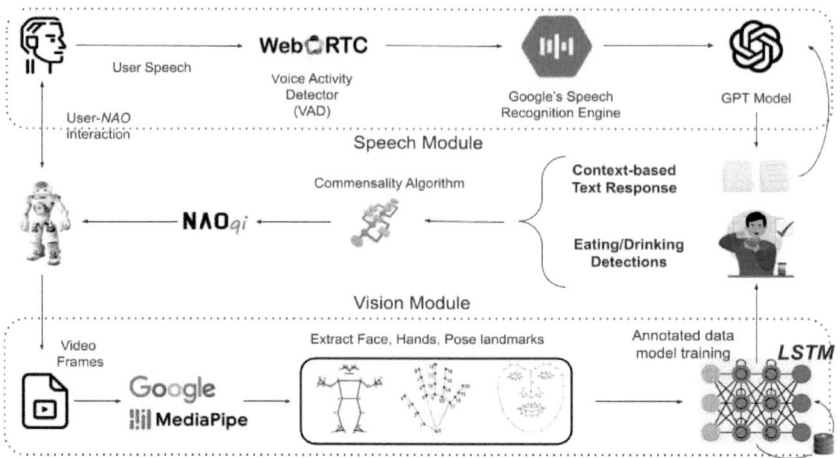

Fig. 1. Schematic diagram of our commensal companion. The left-to-right pipeline includes speech detection and recognition, GPT-based response generation, visual detection of eating activity, and robot-controlled speech, gaze, and gesture outputs. Static rule-based triggers and GPT-generated responses are both used in managing the conversation.

verbally, and the conversation advanced based on pauses, backchannels, and user speech activity. The robot also used head gaze, arm gestures, and idle motions to simulate attentiveness and presence. Details of the underlying interaction algorithm are described in [51].

The goal of the ACC is to become a socially appropriate mealtime companion using structured behaviors and accessible technologies—not to replicate a fully human dining partner. Prior work has emphasized that robotic agents can effectively support social engagement without fully mimicking human interaction, particularly when users are primed to treat the system as a companion rather than a person [10,14]. While the robot's responses are GPT-generated, the ACC does not dynamically adapt to individual users, and its affective responsiveness is limited to detecting basic disengagement cues.

4 Method

This study employed a within-subjects design to examine how individual differences—including personality and affective traits, technology use, and commensality habits—predict emotional and social responses to an ACC. Participants completed pre- and post-test surveys and shared a meal with the robot in a structured, laboratory-based lunchtime interaction.

4.1 Research Questions and Hypotheses

RQ1: How do individual differences influence participants' emotional responses to eating with an ACC?

H1a: Participants high in trait negative affect and loneliness will report greater enjoyment of the interaction, even if they do not report increased situational positivity. **H1b:** Participants high in openness to experience will report higher enjoyment of and situational positivity during the interaction. **H1c:** Participants high in neuroticism or conscientiousness are expected to report lower enjoyment of the interaction with an ACC.

RQ2: How do individual differences influence perceived social connection with an ACC?

H2a: Participants high in trait negative affect or loneliness will report stronger connection. **H2b:** Participants high in extraversion or agreeableness will report lower perceived connection. **H2c:** Frequency of eating with others and technology use during meals will positively predict perceived connection.

4.2 Measures

Participants completed standardized surveys both before and after the interaction to assess individual traits and responses to the robotic companion.

For clarity, we use "PANAS_Neg" and "PANAS_Pos" to refer to trait-level affect, and "PANASSIT_Neg" and "PANASSIT_Pos" to refer to situational affect measured after the interaction.

Pre-interaction: Online measures included Demographics, the Abridged Big Five Personality Test (BFI-S) [33], and a custom General Commensality Questionnaire composed of three subscales: Me and Commensality, Frequency of Eating, and Use of Technology—focused specifically on technology use during meals (adapted from [18,44,59]). To contextualize general digital habits, one additional item from the Orcatech Technology Use Survey [48] was included to assess overall frequency of device use for internet access. Additional measures included the Positive and Negative Affect Schedule—General (PANAS-GEN) [57] and the Short Loneliness Scale (LON) [23].

Post-interaction: Administered in-lab, surveys included the Enjoyment of Interaction scale (adapted from [18,44]), the PANAS-SIT (a modified version of PANAS-GEN to assess situational affect), and the Connection During Conversations Scale (CDCS), which includes four subscales: Shared Reality, Partner Responsiveness, Participant Interest, and Affective Experience [46].

4.3 Materials and Procedure

The experimental setup included: (1) a *NAO* robot, (2) a control computer for the robot system, (3) a laptop for system monitoring, (4–5) two video cameras (facing the robot and the participant), (6) one microphone.

The procedure is illustrated in Fig. 2. Participants brought their own food and completed the study during a typical lunchtime period. Upon arrival, participants signed a written consent form. Participants sat at a table facing the *NAO* robot, which greeted them and initiated a conversation. Dialogue was partially GPT-generated, with fallback prompts used during disengagement. Following

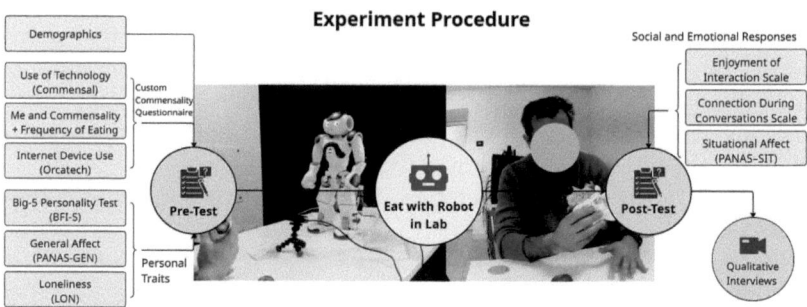

Fig. 2. Experiment procedure is depicted in the Figure.

the interaction, participants completed post-test surveys. A full debriefing was conducted at the end of the session.

5 Results

Twenty-two volunteers participated in the study (18 male; ages 19–62), most of whom were university students. Eligibility criteria included being at least 18 years old and fluent in English.

Within-group analyses using correlational and regression-based approaches were used to examine how individual differences predicted emotional and social responses to ACC. Due to the homogeneity of the sample in terms of age, gender, and cultural background comparisons were not pursued. Analyses are organized by research question.

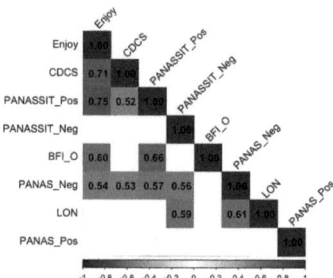

Fig. 3. Correlation matrix showing statistically significant ($p < .05$) relationships between enjoyment, affective measures (PANAS, PANASSIT), connection (CDCS), and key individual difference variables. Darker cells indicate stronger correlations.

Table 1. Descriptive statistics for primary outcome and predictor variables. All items were rated on 5-point or 7-point Likert scales unless otherwise noted. Higher values indicate greater endorsement or intensity.

Variable	Mean	SD	Min	Max
Enjoyment	3.37	0.69	2.29	4.76
PANASSIT_Pos (situational pos. affect)	3.13	0.77	1.60	4.60
PANASSIT_Neg (situational neg. affect)	1.44	0.40	1.00	2.50
CDCS (perceived connection)	3.91	1.03	2.43	6.14
PANAS_Neg (trait neg. affect)	2.03	0.77	1.00	3.40
PANAS_Pos (trait pos. affect)	3.57	0.64	2.00	4.60
BFI_O (Openness)	5.50	0.89	4.00	7.00
BFI_A (Agreeableness)	5.26	1.36	2.00	7.00
BFI_E (Extraversion)	4.24	1.58	1.67	7.00
BFI_C (Conscientiousness)	4.96	0.88	3.33	6.33
BFI_N (Neuroticism)	3.54	1.41	1.67	5.33
LON (Loneliness)	1.81	0.79	1.00	4.00
Comm (Commensality Habits)	3.94	0.64	2.50	5.00
Techeat (Tech Use During Meals)	4.20	0.52	3.54	5.41

5.1 RQ1: Emotional Impact

Descriptive and Correlational Analysis. Descriptive statistics for all primary outcome and predictor variables can be found in Table 1.

Enjoyment was positively correlated with i) Perceived connection (CDCS; $r = .71$, $p < .001$), ii) Situational positive affect (PANASSIT_Pos; $r = .75$, $p < .001$), iii) Openness to Experience (BFI_O; $r = .60$, $p < .01$), and iv) Trait negative affect (PANAS_Neg; $r = .54$, $p < .05$). A weak negative correlation was observed with Agreeableness (BFI_A; $r = -.22$), but this was not statistically significant. No notable relationships were found between enjoyment and loneliness, extraversion, commensality habits, or technology use (all $r < .25$).

All correlations were computed using Pearson's r (see Fig. 3), as the variables were continuous and approximately normally distributed. Spearman's rank correlations yielded similar patterns.

Regression Analysis. A multiple regression predicting enjoyment from pretest variables revealed that Openness to Experience ($\beta = .40$, $p = .014$) and trait negative affect (PANAS_Neg; $\beta = .69$, $p = .010$) were significant positive predictors. Trait positive affect (PANAS_Pos) was not significant ($\beta = -.36$, $p = .123$), but may have acted as a suppressor due to its overlap with other predictors. Loneliness showed a small negative trend ($\beta = -.25$, $p = .190$), while the "Frequency of Eating with Others" subscale from the commensality questionnaire showed a modest positive trend ($\beta = .38$, $p = .105$). The final model explained 65% of the variance in enjoyment (Adj. $R^2 = .50$).

Trait–State Affective Dynamics. To explore how stable affective traits influence in-the-moment experience, we examined relationships between trait (PANAS) and state (PANASSIT) affect.

Trait–State correlations were as follows: i) PANAS_Neg → PANASSIT_Neg: $r = .56$, $p = .017$, ii) PANAS_Pos → PANASSIT_Pos: $r = .45$, $p = .060$. These results suggest that trait negative affect carries more consistently into situational experience, while trait positivity is more context-dependent.

We then tested whether trait or state affect better predicted reported enjoyment of the interaction. A regression including both PANAS_Neg and PANASSIT_Neg revealed that only trait negative affect remained significant ($\beta = .59$, $p = .013$), while state negative affect did not ($\beta = -.50$, $p = .278$). This indicates that participants high in negative affect may derive value from the interaction, even if they experience some momentary discomfort. We also found that Openness to Experience significantly predicted PANASSIT_Pos ($\beta = .53$, $p = .003$, $R^2 = .44$), suggesting that participants with certain personality traits may enjoy the interaction more because they feel more positive during it.

5.2 RQ2: Social Impact

Correlational and Regression Analyses. CDCS (composite) scores were positively associated with Enjoyment ($r = .71$, $p < .001$), PANASSIT_Pos ($r = .52$, $p < .05$), and PANAS_Neg ($r = .53$, $p < .05$).

A stepwise multiple regression predicting CDCS revealed five predictors, explaining 61% of the variance (Adj. $R^2 = .41$, $p = .061$):

PANAS_Neg ($\beta = .81$, $p = .012$): High trait negative affect predicted stronger connection.
FreqComm ($\beta = .89$, $p = .061$): Frequent commensality predicted higher connection.
Techeat ($\beta = 1.72$, $p = .099$): Tech use during meals showed a positive trend.
BFI_E ($\beta = -.53$, $p = .071$): Higher extraversion predicted lower connection.
BFI_A ($\beta = -.38$, $p = .224$): Lower agreeableness showed a non-significant trend.

These results suggest that perceived connection with the ACC was shaped less by traits traditionally associated with social warmth—such as extraversion and agreeableness—and more by emotional sensitivity (e.g., PANAS_Neg) and habitual dining contexts (e.g., FreqComm, Techeat).

CDCS Subscale Analysis (Exploratory). To examine whether predictors of overall connection also applied to specific connection types, we tested models for each CDCS subscale. While patterns generally aligned with the composite model, results varied in strength and direction. The three subscales—Shared Reality, Participant Interest, and Affective Experience—generally reflected similar trends as the composite score, especially with PANAS_Neg and commensality measures.

However, only CDCS_PR (Partner Responsiveness) stood out as statistically and conceptually distinct.

Unlike other subscales, Partner Responsiveness (CDCS_PR) was not significantly predicted by any individual difference variables. This suggests that perceptions of the robot's responsiveness may have been driven more by the robot's behavior than by user traits (e.g., PANAS_Neg, Extraversion, or FreqComm). Notably, CDCS_PR was positively correlated with Enjoyment and Affective Experience, indicating that feeling understood may still play an important role in satisfaction with the interaction.

The subscale-level differences suggest that distinct components of connection—such as emotional resonance versus responsiveness—may be shaped by distinct underlying mechanisms.

6 Discussion

This study examined how individual differences shape emotional and social responses to an ACC. Trait negative affect and openness to experience predicted both enjoyment and perceived connection, suggesting that affective sensitivity and openness—rather than sociability—may drive positive HRI experiences. These findings extend prior work on personality and robot acceptance [8,54] and offer new insight into commensal HRI contexts.

6.1 Emotional Responses to an ACC

Participants high in trait negative affect and openness reported greater enjoyment of the interaction (H1a/H1b). This aligns with theories of affective intensity and emotional variability [29,34] and prior HRI studies on individual engagement [8,54]. Notably, trait negative affect remained a significant predictor of enjoyment even when controlling for PANASSIT_Neg (H1d). This suggests users high in negative affect may not feel "better" in the moment but still find the structure and neutrality of the ACC socially rewarding. Prior work has similarly shown that structured interactions reduce pressure for emotionally sensitive users [2,5]. While openness did not significantly predict enjoyment in the final model, it strongly predicted positive situational affect (PANASSIT_Pos). This supports the view that openness may amplify real-time engagement through novelty-seeking or flexibility [9,41], even if it doesn't translate to retrospective enjoyment.

Contrary to H1c, neither neuroticism nor conscientiousness predicted lower enjoyment. These traits may operate differently in HRI or be moderated by affective context [7,13,54]. Future work could examine their interaction with robot design or environment.

Several trait-based hypotheses were not supported, including those involving loneliness, conscientiousness, and neuroticism. While prior work has linked loneliness to increased receptivity toward social robots, our null findings may reflect differences in how loneliness was operationalized (as a stable trait vs. a situational feeling) or the short, low-stakes nature of the interaction. It is also possible that loneliness alone does not predict enjoyment unless paired with other traits like openness or emotional sensitivity. Likewise, conscientiousness and neuroticism may only influence HRI outcomes when the interaction involves greater behavioral demands, task performance, or accountability—conditions that were largely absent in our informal, socially neutral setup. These patterns highlight that not all personality traits exert equal influence in every context, and that trait effects may depend on environmental structure, task salience, and user expectations.

6.2 Social Connection with an ACC

Perceived connection (CDCS) was predicted by trait negative affect, commensality frequency, and tech use (H2a/H2c), while extraversion and agreeableness were negatively associated (H2b). These results challenge assumptions that sociability enhances HRI outcomes [7] and suggest instead that emotional sensitivity and routine digital commensality may foster stronger social responses.

Agreeableness may reflect willingness to participate politely without deeper engagement [2,13]. Similarly, participants who frequently ate with others reported lower enjoyment—perhaps because the ACC offered less richness than their typical meals.

Overall, ACCs may be particularly well-suited to users who seek connection but prefer structure and reduced social pressure. Aligning design with affective disposition may prove more fruitful than simulating human-like sociability.

6.3 Perceptions of Responsiveness

Unlike other connection subscales, CDCS_PR (Partner Responsiveness) was unrelated to trait variables, but positively correlated with Enjoyment and Affective Experience. This suggests that responsiveness was likely shaped by system behavior (e.g., latency, gestures) rather than user disposition. This supports recent findings that behavioral synchrony and affective alignment—rather than co-presence alone—drive connection in HRI dining contexts [56]. While CDCS_PR (Partner Responsiveness) was not predicted by personality or affective traits, its strong correlations with enjoyment and affective experience suggest that participants valued perceived responsiveness—even when it was system-driven. This highlights a design opportunity: improving the robot's timing, non-verbal feedback, or backchanneling may boost perceived responsiveness without requiring true personalization. Future iterations of the ACC could incorporate simple synchrony-enhancing behaviors, such as brief nods, verbal acknowledgments ("I see," "That's interesting"), or more responsive gaze shifts, to strengthen the illusion of social attunement. These cues may increase engagement even for users not dispositionally inclined to connect. Responsiveness may operate independently of broader emotional resonance, highlighting the layered nature of human–robot connection.

6.4 Trait–State Dynamics

Trait negative affect significantly predicted situational negative affect (PANAS-SIT_Neg), while trait positive affect only marginally predicted PANASSIT_Pos. This asymmetry reflects established patterns in affective science: negative affect tends to be more stable and harder to override than positive affect, which is more context-sensitive [9,29].

Importantly, PANAS_Neg remained a significant predictor of enjoyment even when controlling for PANASSIT_Neg. This supports H1d and illustrates what we describe as "affective override"—where users high in trait negativity still appraised the ACC experience positively. The robot's structured, low-pressure format may have offered emotional safety or predictability, aligning with prior findings that users high in negative affect prefer nonjudgmental interaction partners [2,5,58]. Openness to Experience did not significantly predict enjoyment (contrary to H1b), but did predict higher situational positivity (PANAS-SIT_Pos). This suggests that openness may amplify real-time affective engagement through curiosity and novelty-seeking, even when this doesn't translate to retrospective evaluation. Similar trait–state dynamics have been observed in pedagogical and healthcare HRI contexts [24,54].

Together, these findings support the relevance of trait–state interaction models in affective HRI—particularly in socially ambiguous or novel settings like commensal robotics.

7 Conclusions

As eating alone becomes increasingly common-due to aging, lifestyle, or social isolation-socially assistive robots offer a potential source of emotional and interpersonal support. This study demonstrates that individuals do not respond to artificial companionship uniformly. Rather, users' affective traits, particularly negative affect and Openness to Experience, shaped their enjoyment and perceived connection with a robotic dining companion.

For HRI designers, this highlights the value of tuning social robots to internal states. Emotional attunement is important to fostering connection, especially for users who are prone to negative feelings.

Limitations. This was a short-term, single-session study with a small, relatively homogeneous sample. Although promising, results may not generalize to repeated or long-term interaction, where novelty effects could diminish. The robot was used in a controlled lab setting, which may not reflect how users would respond in real-world environments. Additionally, our loneliness measure was brief and assessed only as a stable trait. Including state loneliness or post-interaction follow-up could better capture momentary changes.

Importantly, the sample consisted primarily of young adult male university students, limiting generalizability across age, gender, and cultural backgrounds. Prior research on robotic dining companions has emphasized elderly or socially isolated populations as target users, and further studies are needed to validate whether our findings—particularly the benefits for users high in negative affect or openness—extend to these groups. Moreover, while the sample size was adequate to detect large effects, it lacked the statistical power to reliably detect smaller but potentially meaningful associations. These limitations underscore the need for larger, more diverse samples in future work to confirm the stability and scope of trait-based effects.

Future Work. Future studies should explore how ACCs function across more diverse contexts—such as group meals or home environments—and test repeated interactions over time to examine novelty decay and sustained engagement. Ongoing work will also investigate real-time affect modeling using behavioral signals (e.g., eating pace, gaze, vocal prosody).

This system appeared particularly well-suited for individuals high in negative affect or openness—likely due to its structured, low-pressure style. Conversely, users high in extraversion or agreeableness showed weaker connection, suggesting that a single interaction style may not suit all users equally well. Our findings support a need for personalization: future ACCs should adapt dialogue tone, pacing, and content to user traits such as openness, affect, or commensality habits. One promising direction involves using pre-survey data (e.g., PANAS, BFI, commensality habits) to assign personality parameters to the robot. Ultimately, aligning conversational behavior with individual dispositions may enable ACCs not only to support emotional well-being, but to actively motivate social engagement—meeting users where they are, and nudging them toward meaningful connection.

Finally, future work should prioritize broader demographic representation. Our sample was primarily composed of young adult university students, but artificial commensal companions have been proposed for diverse user populations, including older adults, individuals with disabilities, adolescents, and culturally varied diners. Older adults, in particular, are frequently cited as target users for socially assistive agents, yet their engagement patterns, affective needs, and technology attitudes may differ significantly. Expanding to these groups will be essential not only for validating generalizability, but for tailoring interaction strategies—such as conversational pacing, topic relevance, or multimodal expressivity—to distinct user expectations and social norms.

Acknowledgments. This work is supported by the PRIN 2022 project COCOA, PRIN 2022T8ZNNM, funded by the European Union - Next Generation EU (NGEU) Programme.

Disclosure of Interests. The authors have no competing interests to declare that are relevant to the content of this article.

References

1. Apio Dr, E.O.: Food and commensality in non-state armed groups: the case of the lord's resistance army in northern Uganda, 1987–2008. Peace Conflict Stud. **30**(1), 2 (2023)
2. Bickmore, T., Picard, R.: Establishing and maintaining long-term human-computer relationships. ACM Trans. Comput.-Hum. Interact. (TOCHI) **12**(2), 293–327 (2005)
3. Björnwall, A., Sydner, Y.M., Koochek, A., Neuman, N.: Eating alone or together among community-living older people - a scoping review. Int. J. Environ. Res. Public Health **18**, 3495 (2021). https://doi.org/10.3390/ijerph18073495
4. Björnwall, A., Sydner, Y.M., Koochek, A., Neuman, N.: Perceptions and experiences of eating alone among community-living retired swedes: loss, routine and independence. Appetite **186**, 106570 (2023). https://doi.org/10.1016/j.appet.2023.106570. ISSN 0195-6663
5. Broadbent, E., Stafford, R., MacDonald, B.: Acceptance of healthcare robots for the older population: review and future directions. Int. J. Soc. Robot. **1**(4), 319–330 (2009). https://doi.org/10.1007/s12369-009-0030-6
6. Cheek, J.M., Buss, A.H.: Shyness and sociability. J. Pers. Soc. Psychol. **41**(2), 330–339 (1981)
7. Costa, P.T., McCrae, R.R.: Revised neo personality inventory (NEO PI-R) and neo five-factor inventory (NEO-FFI). Professional Manual (1992)
8. de Graaf, M.M.A., Allouch, S.B.: Exploring influencing variables for the acceptance of social robots. Robot. Auton. Syst. **61**(12), 1476–1486 (2013). https://doi.org/10.1016/j.robot.2013.07.007
9. Diener, E., Diener, M.: Most people are happy. Psychol. Sci. **7**(3), 181–185 (1996). https://doi.org/10.1111/j.1467-9280.1996.tb00354.x
10. Duffy, B.R.: Anthropomorphism and the social robot. Robot. Auton. Syst. **42**(3–4), 177–190 (2003)
11. Dunbar, R.I.M.: Breaking bread: the functions of social eating. Adapt. Hum. Behav. Physiol. **3**(3), 198–211 (2017)
12. Duplouy, A., Brock, R.W.: Defining Citizenship in Archaic Greece. Oxford University Press (2018)
13. Eyssel, F., Kuchenbrandt, D., Bobinger, S., De Ruiter, L., Hegel, F.: 'if you sound like me, you must be more human': on the interplay of robot and user features on human-robot acceptance and anthropomorphism, pp. 125–126 (2012). https://doi.org/10.1145/2157689.2157717
14. Fong, T., Nourbakhsh, I., Dautenhahn, K.: Survey of socially interactive robots. Robot. Auton. Syst. **42**(3–4), 143–166 (2003)
15. Freitas, R.M.S., Brandão, T.B.C., da Silveira, J.A.C., Oliveira, J.S., Longo-Silva, G., de Menezes, R.C.E.: Commensality and eating patterns in adolescents: an analysis from structural equation modeling. Appetite **178**, 106183 (2022)
16. Fu, D., Abawi, F., Allgeuer, P., Wermter, S.: Human impression of humanoid robots mirroring social cues, pp. 458–462 (2024). https://doi.org/10.1145/3610978.3640580
17. Fujii, A., Kochigami, K., Kitagawa, S., Okada, K., Inaba, M.: Development and evaluation of mixed reality co-eating system: sharing the behavior of eating food with a robot could improve our dining experience. In: 2020 29th IEEE International Conference on Robot and Human Interactive Communication (RO-MAN), pp. 357–362 (2020). https://doi.org/10.1109/RO-MAN47096.2020.9223518

18. Fujii, A., Okada, K., Inaba, M.: A basic study for acceptance of robots as meal partners: number of robots during mealtime, frequency of solitary eating, and past experience with robots. In: 2021 30th IEEE International Conference on Robot & Human Interactive Communication (RO-MAN), pp. 73–80 (2021). https://doi.org/10.1109/RO-MAN50785.2021.9515451
19. Giacoman, C.: The dimensions and role of commensality: a theoretical model drawn from the significance of communal eating among adults in Santiago, Chile. Appetite **107**, 460–470 (2016)
20. Grevet, C., Tang, A., Mynatt, E.: Eating alone, together: new forms of commensality. In: Proceedings of the 17th ACM International Conference on Supporting Group Work, pp. 103–106. ACM (2012)
21. Hetherington, M.M., Anderson, A.S., Norton, G.N., Newson, L.: Situational effects on meal intake: a comparison of eating alone and eating with others. Physiol. Behav. **88**(4–5), 498–505 (2006)
22. Hoxha, A., Fong, H., Niewiadomski, R.: Do we need artificial dining companions? Exploring human attitudes toward robots in commensality settings. In: Companion Proceedings of 26th ACM International Conference on Multimodal Interaction (2024). https://doi.org/10.1145/3686215.3686220
23. Hughes, M.E., Waite, L.J., Hawkley, L.C., Cacioppo, J.T.: A short scale for measuring loneliness in large surveys: results from two population-based studies. Res. Aging **26**(6), 655–672 (2004). https://doi.org/10.1177/0164027504268574
24. Io, H.N., Lee, C.B.: Chatbots and conversational agents: a bibliometric analysis. In: 2017 IEEE International Conference on Industrial Engineering and Engineering Management (IEEM), pp. 215–219 (2017). https://doi.org/10.1109/IEEM.2017.8289883
25. Jong, J., Porter, J., Palermo, C., Ottrey, E.: Meals beyond the bedside: an ethnographic exploration of staffs' perspectives and experiences of communal dining in subacute care. Nurs. Health Sci. **23**(2), 372–380 (2021)
26. Khot, R.A., Arza, E.S., Kurra, H., Wang, Y. Fobo: towards designing a robotic companion for solo dining. In: Extended Abstracts of the 2019 CHI Conference on Human Factors in Computing Systems, CHI EA 2019, pp. LBW1617:1–LBW1617:6, New York, NY, USA. ACM (2019). ISBN 978-1-4503-5971-9. https://doi.org/10.1145/3290607.3313069
27. Klataske, R.T., Ramos, A.K.: Commensality, ritual, and reciprocity: cattle feedyard managers' perspectives on safety culture. Anthropol. Notebooks **29**(2), 86–100 (2023)
28. Kniffin, K.M., Wansink, B., Devine, C.M., Sobal, J.: Eating together at the firehouse: how workplace commensality relates to the performance of firefighters. Hum. Perform. **28**(4), 281–306 (2015). https://doi.org/10.1080/08959285.2015.1021049. PMID: 27226698
29. Kuppens, P., Oravecz, Z., Tuerlinckx, F.: Feelings change: accounting for individual differences in the temporal dynamics of affect. J. Pers. Soc. Psychol. **99**(6), 1042–1060 (2010). https://doi.org/10.1037/a0020962
30. Laban, G., Cross, E.S.: Sharing our emotions with robots: why do we do it and how does it make us feel? IEEE Trans. Affect. Comput. 1–18 (2024). https://doi.org/10.1109/TAFFC.2024.3470984
31. Laban, G., Kappas, A., Morrison, V., Cross, E.S.: Building long-term human-robot relationships: examining disclosure, perception and well-being across time. Int. J. Soc. Robot. **16**(5), 1–27 (2024)

32. Laban, G., Morrison, V., Kappas, A., Cross, E.S.: Coping with emotional distress via self-disclosure to robots: an intervention with caregivers. Int. J. Soc. Robot. 1–34 (2025)
33. Lang, F.R., John, D., Lüdtke, O., Schupp, J., Wagner, G.G.: Short assessment of the big five: robust across survey methods except telephone interviewing. Behav. Res. Methods **43**, 548–567 (2011)
34. Larsen, R.J., Diener, E.: Affect intensity as an individual difference characteristic: a review. J. Res. Pers. **21**(1), 1–39 (1987). https://doi.org/10.1016/0092-6566(87)90023-7
35. Lee, Y.K., Jung, Y., Kang, G., Hahn, S.: Developing social robots with empathetic non-verbal cues using large language models. arXiv preprint arXiv:2308.16529 (2023)
36. Leite, I., Martinho, C., Paiva, A.: Social robots for long-term interaction: a survey. Int. J. Soc. Robot. **5**(2), 291–308 (2013). https://doi.org/10.1007/s12369-013-0178-y
37. Liu, R., Inoue, T.: Application of an anthropomorphic dining agent to idea generation. In: Proceedings of the 2014 ACM International Joint Conference on Pervasive and Ubiquitous Computing: Adjunct Publication, UbiComp 2014 Adjunct, pp. 607–612, New York, NY, USA. ACM (2014). ISBN 978-1-4503-3047-3. https://doi.org/10.1145/2638728.2641342
38. Mancini, M., Niewiadomski, R., De Lucia, G., Longobardi, F.M.: A virtual agent as a commensal companion. In: Proceedings of the 24th ACM International Conference on Intelligent Virtual Agents, IVA 2024, New York, NY, USA. Association for Computing Machinery (2024). ISBN 9798400706257. https://doi.org/10.1145/3652988.3673963
39. Martelaro, N., Nneji, V. C., Ju, W., Hinds, P.: Tell me more designing HRI to encourage more trust, disclosure, and companionship. In: 2016 11th ACM/IEEE International Conference on Human-Robot Interaction (HRI), pp. 181–188 (2016). https://doi.org/10.1109/HRI.2016.7451750
40. McColl, D., Nejat, G.: Meal-time with a socially assistive robot and older adults at a long-term care facility. J. Hum.-Robot Interact. **2**(1), 152–171 (2013). https://doi.org/10.5898/JHRI.2.1.McColl. ISSN 2163-0364
41. McCrae, R.R., et al.: Personality trait structure as a human universal. Am. Psychol. **52**(5), 509–516 (1997)
42. Mensah, D.O., Tuomainen, H.: Exploring university students' eating patterns before and during the covid-19 pandemic. Food Foodways **32**(2), 163–185 (2024). https://doi.org/10.1080/07409710.2024.2333119
43. Niewiadomski, R., Ceccaldi, E., Huisman, G., Volpe, G., Mancini, M.: Computational commensality: from theories to computational models for social food preparation and consumption in HCI. Front. Robot. AI **6**, 119 (2019). https://doi.org/10.3389/frobt.2019.00119. ISSN 2296-9144
44. Niewiadomski, R., Bruijnes, M., Huisman, G., Gallagher, C.P., Mancini, M.: Social robots as eating companions. Front. Comput. Sci. **4**, 909844 (2022). https://doi.org/10.3389/fcomp.2022.909844. ISSN 2624-9898
45. Novikova, J., Dondrup, C., Papaioannou, I., Lemon, O.: Sympathy begins with a smile, intelligence begins with a word: use of multimodal features in spoken human-robot interaction, pp. 86–94 (2017). https://doi.org/10.18653/v1/W17-2811
46. Okabe-Miyamoto, K., Walsh, L.C., Ozer, D., Lyubomirsky, S.: Measuring the experience of social connection within specific social interactions: the connection during conversations scale (CDCS). PLoS ONE **19**(1), e0286408 (2024). https://doi.org/10.1371/journal.pone.0286408

47. Ondras, J., et al.: Human-robot commensality: bite timing prediction for robot-assisted feeding in groups. In: 6th Annual Conference on Robot Learning (2022)
48. Orcatech. Orcatech technology use survey 2020 (2021). https://ohsuorcatech.az1.qualtrics.com/Q/EditSection/Blocks/Ajax/GetSurveyPrintPreview?ContextSurveyID=SV_0vmBalYJxyr5z9z&ContextLibraryI
49. Salvy, Sarah-Jeanne., Jarrin, Denise, Paluch, Rocco, Irfan, Numrah, Pliner, Patricia: Effects of social influence on eating in couples, friends and strangers. Appetite **49**, 92–9 (2007). https://doi.org/10.1016/j.appet.2006.12.004
50. Skantze, G.: Turn-taking in conversational systems and human-robot interaction: a review. Comput. Speech Lang. **67**, 101178 (2021). https://doi.org/10.1016/j.csl.2020.101178
51. Soufargi, S., Niewiadomski, R., Fong, H., Mancini, M.: A social robot companion for individuals eating alone. In: Companion Proceedings of the 30th International Conference on Intelligent User Interfaces, IUI 2025 Companion, pp. 5–8, New York, NY, USA. Association for Computing Machinery (2025). ISBN 9798400714092. https://doi.org/10.1145/3708557.3716340
52. Sudkamp, K.M.: Clear, Hold, Eat: Commensality, Community, and Survival in the Post-9/11 Deployment Experience. Ph.D. thesis, Chatham University (2018)
53. Tani, Y., Sasaki, Y., Haseda, M., Kondo, K., Kondo, N.: Eating alone and depression in older men and women by cohabitation status: the JAGES longitudinal survey. Age Ageing **44**, 1019–1026 (2015). https://doi.org/10.1093/ageing/afv145
54. Tapus, A., Mataric, M.J., Scassellati, B.: User-robot personality matching and assistive robot behavior adaptation for post-stroke rehabilitation therapy. Intell. Serv. Robot. **1**(2), 169–183 (2008). https://doi.org/10.1007/s11370-008-0017-4
55. Tay, B., Jung, Y., Park, T.: When stereotypes meet robots: the double-edge sword of robot gender and personality in human-robot interaction. Comput. Hum. Behav. **38**, 75–84 (2014). https://doi.org/10.1016/j.chb.2014.05.014. ISSN 0747-5632
56. Wang, J.-Y., Inoue, T.: The similarity of virtual meal of a co-eating agent affects human participant. In: Takada, H., Marutschke, D.M., Alvarez, C., Inoue, T., Hayashi, Y., Hernandez-Leo, D. (eds.) Collaboration Technologies and Social Computing, pp. 115–132. Springer, Cham (2023). https://doi.org/10.1007/978-3-031-42141-9_8
57. Watson, D., Clark, L.A., Tellegen, A.: Development and validation of brief measures of positive and negative affect: the PANAS scales. J. Pers. Soc. Psychol. **54**, 1063–1070 (1988)
58. Watson, D., Clark, L.A., McIntyre, C.W., Hamaker, S.: Affect, personality, and social activity. J. Pers. Soc. Psychol. **63**(6), 1011–1025 (1992)
59. Yazgi, K., Beyan, C., Mancini, M., Niewiadomski, R.: Automatic recognition of commensal activities in co-located and online settings. In: Companion Proceedings of 26th ACM International Conference on Multimodal Interaction (2024). https://doi.org/10.1145/3686215.3686219

Affective Communication via Haptic Technology: A Usability Study of a Huggable Device with Older Adults

Eleuda Nunez[1](✉) , Zuzanna Radosz-Knawa[2] , Anna Kołbasa[2],
Paulina Zguda[2] , Alicja Kamińska[2] , Tymon Kukier[2] ,
Masakazu Hirokawa[3] , Kenji Suzuki[1] , and Bipin Indurkhya[2]

[1] University of Tsukuba, Tsukuba, Japan
eleuda@ai.iit.tsukuba.ac.jp
[2] Jagiellonian University, Krakow, Poland
[3] Data Science Laboratories, NEC Corporation, Kawasaki, Japan

Abstract. Loneliness among older adults is a growing concern with significant implications for mental and physical health. Although traditional communication technologies often lack the emotional richness of physical touch, recent advances in haptic interfaces offer new possibilities to improve remote social interactions. This study evaluates HugBits, a huggable communication device designed to connect users through shared hugging experiences, with a focus on its usability and emotional impact among older residents in a care facility. Using a mixed methods approach, we conducted a usability study with 16 participants (aged 65+), combining surveys, physiological measures, and qualitative interviews. The results show that while HugBits improved the experience of communication and was generally well received, it did not lead to significant reductions in loneliness or physiological stress markers. Participants valued the simplicity and emotional potential of the device, but highlighted the need for more immersive features, such as warmth or vibration. The findings underscore the promise of haptic communication for emotional support in older adults and underscore the importance of co-design in developing acceptable and meaningful interaction paradigms.

Keywords: Participatory design · Older adults · Computer-mediated communication · Haptic interfaces

1 Introduction

Loneliness among older adults is a growing social and psychological problem with significant consequences for both mental and physical health. Social isolation has been associated with depression, cognitive decline, and increased mortality rates [13]. As the global population continues to age, addressing loneliness through

---
E. Nunez and Z. Radosz-Knawa—Contributed equally to this work.

innovative communication methods has become increasingly urgent. Older adults are particularly vulnerable to chronic loneliness, often due to loss of loved ones, reduced mobility, and social withdrawal due to health limitations. Those living alone or in assisted care facilities face even greater risks of prolonged isolation [7]. The COVID-19 pandemic further intensified these challenges, as physical distancing measures severely limited contact with older adults, leaving many of them feeling disconnected and emotionally unsupported [11].

A promising approach to mitigating these effects lies in affective haptics, a field that explores how touch-based technologies can be used to communicate and evoke emotions [4]. Physical touch plays a crucial role in human emotional well-being: affectionate gestures such as hugs and holding of hands are known to lower cortisol levels [14], reduce stress, and promote feelings of social bonding [6]. Individuals who regularly experience such contact report lower levels of anxiety and depression compared to those who do not [7]. Recognizing the importance of touch, researchers have begun integrating haptic technologies into communication tools. When effectively designed, these systems can help bridge the gap created by physical distance, offering some of the emotional benefits of real-life interactions [16]. However, replicating the nuanced experience of human touch remains a design challenge. To be truly effective, affective haptic systems must be personalized and user-centered, as emotional responses to touch are highly individual and culturally specific [4].

In this context, robotic systems and physically embodied interfaces present new opportunities for touch-based communication. For example, socially assistive robots have been found to improve engagement and foster positive emotions among older people with cognitive impairments. A study demonstrated that socially assistive robots that provide personalized cognitive therapies can maintain attention and participation in people with dementia through social interaction [15]. Similarly, a different group reported that companion robots such as Paro and Aibo can reduce loneliness and improve mood, although the evidence remains largely qualitative due to small sample sizes and methodological limitations [2]. Devices like PARO the seal, a robotic pet designed for dementia patients, demonstrated that tactile interaction could reduce stress and improve emotional states [12]. More recent research tells a similar story. A study quantitatively assesses the immediate emotional reactions of people with dementia to multisensory stimuli presented by socially assistive robots, suggesting that such interactions can effectively generate positive emotions [10]. In addition, the effects of SAR on the health and well-being of older adults, indicating potential benefits such as reduced loneliness, improved social interaction, and increased positive affect [3]. Regarding design choices, it was emphasized that robot acceptance among older adults is strongly influenced by appearance: older users tended to reject overly humanoid robots and instead preferred smaller, less anthropomorphic designs that were seen as "cute" or "non-threatening" [19]. Furthermore, it was stressed that successful adoption depends on aligning robot roles, behaviors, and appearances with the cognitive, physical, and emotional profiles of the users.

In addition to the physicality that naturally supports touch interaction and the strong present of a physical embodiment, keeping older users closer to their peers or their loved ones seems to be a straightforward approach to mitigate loneliness. During COVID-19 lockdown, a study explored how loneliness influences the relationship between computer-mediated communication (CMC) usage, online social capital, and well-being, finding that high levels of online communication can mitigate the negative effects of loneliness [5]. This research investigates how older adults use CMC for social support and coping strategies, highlighting the role of online communication in enhancing social connection and providing avenues for emotional support [18]. Despite ongoing progress, significant challenges persist to accommodate sensory decline, respect cultural sensitivities, and ensure usability within the daily contexts of older adults. In response, researchers have explored the integration of communication technologies into familiar physical artifacts. An example is SnowGlobe, an ambient communication device that promotes social connectedness by allowing users to sense the presence of others through subtle light and touch signals, thus promoting emotional closeness through low-bandwidth interaction [17]. Similarly, the implementation of a simplified communication device in nursing home settings demonstrated that technologies designed with user-specific needs in mind can effectively support meaningful social interactions, even among individuals with limited technological proficiency [1].

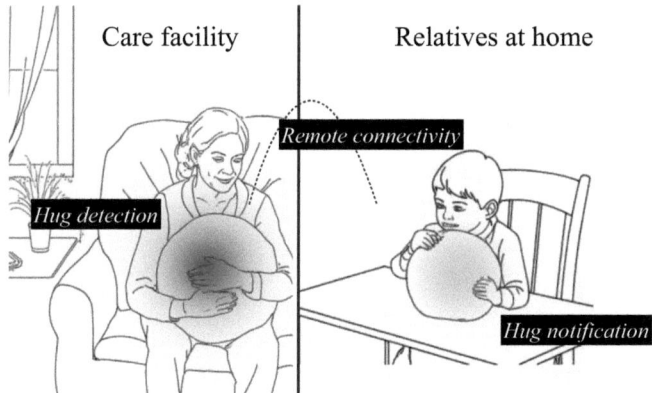

Fig. 1. HugBits is envisioned as a communication tool for older adults living in care homes, helping them stay connected with family members and loved ones who live far away.

Building on these insights, the present study evaluates HugBits, a huggable communication interface designed to integrate affective haptics into remote social interaction for older adults. HugBits combines two key strategies: It serves as a tangible, physically embodied interface that becomes part of the user's personal environment, while also facilitating emotional connectivity with distant loved ones. The device takes the form of a soft cushion-shaped object that enables users to send and receive simulated hugs through visual and tactile signals, fostering a sense of emotional closeness and social presence [8]. It is particularly suited for older residents in care homes, offering a comforting and accessible alternative to conventional communication technologies (see Fig. 1). The objective of this study is to investigate the potential of HugBits as a therapeutic communication tool - specifically, its effectiveness in improving the communication experience and alleviating feelings of loneliness and stress among older adults. In addition, we assess the usability and overall impact of the device in the care home environment. The study addresses two key research questions:

1. Can HugBits be used effectively to promote emotional well-being and mitigate loneliness in older adults?
2. How do older adults perceive the usability and role of HugBits in their daily lives?

Through this investigation, the study adds to ongoing research on emotion-aware technologies aimed at supporting older adults in care homes. It provides valuable guidance on how affective haptic systems can be thoughtfully designed and embedded in daily routines to enhance emotional well-being and foster meaningful social connections supported by technology.

2 HugBits

HugBits was conceived as a tool to promote emotional well-being by embedding the act of hugging, a universally recognized form of comfort, into CMC. As discussed in Sect. 1, existing research underscores the potential of incorporating affective touch into digital interactions to foster emotional connection and social presence. The design philosophy of HugBits centers on conveying presence through ambiguous, non-verbal signals. Rather than transmitting explicit messages, it focuses on the emotional quality of the interaction itself, using tactile input and minimal visual output to evoke a sense of intimacy. Each interaction carries the symbolic gesture of a hug, allowing users to interpret the message contextually. An important feature of HugBits is its ability to support synchronized gestures, allowing users to feel as though they are hugging each other at the same time, even from a distance.

2.1 Adapting HugBits for Older Adults

While initial studies explored HugBits in controlled laboratory settings - showing effects on stress reduction [9] and enhanced social presence [8]-this work marks the first time HugBits is being evaluated in one of its intended real-world applications: residential care homes for older adults. This study examines how older adults in Polish care facilities perceive and experience the use of HugBits. To enhance accessibility, the system was simplified based on previous user feedback. The vibration channel was removed, leaving only visual cues, as previous testing

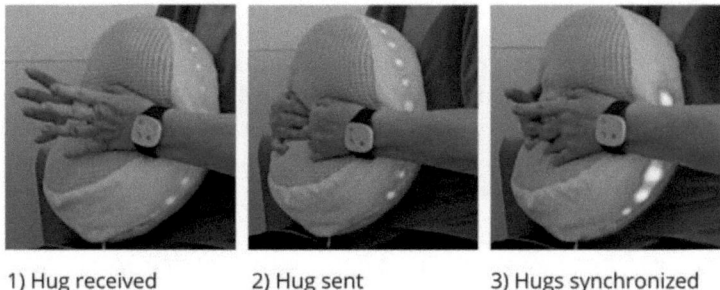

1) Hug received 2) Hug sent 3) Hugs synchronized

Fig. 2. HugBits detects hug gestures and translate them into color signals: red for hug detected, blue for hug received, and purple for synchronized hugs. (Color figure online)

indicated that multimodal feedback could be confusing. Physical design was also modified to better suit the care home environment: the original spherical form was replaced with a flat, circular cushion and plain, neutral-colored fabrics were used to improve the visibility of LED and create a more subtle, age-appropriate appearance (Fig. 2). HugBits functions by detecting physical gestures and providing visual feedback. When a hug is detected, an embedded LED strip displays color-coded light signals to indicate:

- Asynchronous events: red glow when a hug is sent and blue glow when a message (hug) is received.
- Synchronous events: a circulating purple light indicates that both users are hugging their devices at the same time.

3 Methodology

The study followed a mixed-method approach that included both qualitative and quantitative analyzes. Participants interacted with HugBits in a controlled remote communication scenario. The methodology aimed to assess user engagement, effectiveness, and emotional impact.

3.1 Participants

Sixteen participants (65 years and older) were selected based on specific criteria, ensuring diversity in age, previous technological exposure, and social background. All participants were residents of the Krakow Municipal Care Center, Poland (https://www.mco.krakow.pl/). The participants had different levels of experience using digital communication tools. They were part of the daycare ward, stayed in the center during the day and returned home at the end of the day. Before the study, the participants provided their informed consent. The study was approved by the Ethics Committee of the Faculty of Philosophy at Jagiellonian University (Application No. 221.0042.72_2023).

3.2 Measurements

To address the first research question, we measured stress levels and perceived loneliness using physiological data and standardized self-report scales. To explore the second research question, we used a short questionnaire to assess the quality of the interaction experience, complemented by a semi-structured interview to gather in-depth qualitative feedback.

Loneliness. The Revised UCLA Loneliness Scale (R-UCLA) is a widely used self-report instrument designed to measure subjective feelings of loneliness and social isolation [13]. It consists of 20 items rated on a four-point Likert scale, assessing both the frequency and intensity of experiences related to loneliness. The scale has shown strong psychometric properties and is commonly used in studies involving older adults due to its sensitivity to capture variations in perceived social connection.

Stress Levels. Measuring stress provides an objective indicator of emotional and physiological response, making it a valuable method to assess the effectiveness of HugBits. Since the device is designed to promote comfort, emotional connection, and well-being through affective touch, a reduction in stress levels among users suggests that the interaction is meaningful and beneficial. For that purpose, we used a pulse oximeter to record the physiological data of the participants, including heart rate and oxygen saturation before and after the interaction.

Quality of the Experience. To assess participants' perceptions of the quality of the interaction, we administered a custom 12-item questionnaire using a 5-point Likert scale. The questions concerned both behavioral and affective dimensions of the communication, including perceived emotional closeness, attention, and engagement of the conversation partner, as well as the perceived influence of the HugBits device on the overall experience. The elements were designed to explore whether the presence and use of the device enhanced or detracted from the interpersonal dynamics of the conversation.

- Q1: My conversation partner did not seem interested in our conversation.
- Q2: My conversation partner created a sense of emotional distance.
- Q3: My conversation partner communicated in a cold and distant manner.
- Q4: My conversation partner appeared unfocused during our conversation.
- Q5: Did the presence of the device positively influence your overall experience of the conversation?
- Q6: Did the use of the pillow make you perceive your conversation partner more positively?
- Q7: How would you generally rate the quality of the conversation when using the HugBits pillow?

- Q8: Would you recommend this device to someone who wishes to communicate with loved ones remotely?
- Q9: My conversation partner was enthusiastic in a way that was appropriate for the topic of discussion.
- Q10: My conversation partner nurtured a sense of emotional closeness.
- Q11: My conversation partner was very engaged during our interaction.
- Q12: My conversation partner was attentive and interested throughout the interaction.

3.3 Experiment Setup

The experiment was carried out in two separate rooms to simulate a remote interaction scenario (Fig. 3). The participants were already familiar with the facility and its daily routines, which created a comfortable environment to introduce the HugBits device. This familiarity also enabled us to observe the interactions within a semi-naturalistic social context. Each room was equipped with a HugBits device and a laptop. In addition, Room 1 had a camera installed to record the behavior of the participant for later analysis. The two participants were connected through the HugBits system, allowing them to exchange hug-based messages through the devices. They also communicated via video call using the laptops provided in each room.

3.4 Experiment Procedure

Participants were first given general information about the experiment and asked to sign a consent form to confirm their voluntary participation. Once consent was obtained, the session began with the participant complete the R-UCLA loneliness questionnaire and attaching a wristband to collect physiological data. Baseline measurements of heart rate and oxygen saturation were recorded. The participant was then introduced to the HugBits device. The functions and concept of HugBits were explained and the participant was given time to explore the device until they felt comfortable using it.

The interactive phase of the experiment then began. Although HugBits was originally designed to facilitate communication with loved ones, for practical reasons, participants were asked to test the interface while interacting with caregivers from the care center. Each participant was paired with a caregiver who took one HugBits device and moved from Room 1 to Room 2 to simulate a remote interaction scenario. To help them acclimatize to the new situation, both the participant and the caregiver simultaneously watched a short scene (approximately 3 min) from a well-known Polish film. During this viewing they freely interacted through HugBits. Following the film, they transitioned to a video call, during which they were asked to discuss the movie or discuss any other film of their choice. HugBits remained active during the video call and could be used at any time to send or receive hugs. In this phase, HugBits functioned as a complementary channel to video communication. The call lasted approximately 10 min.

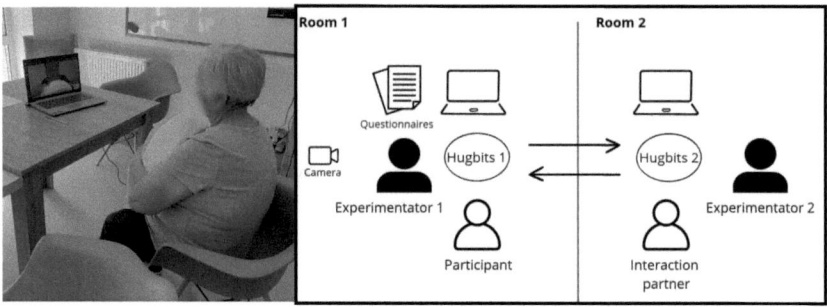

Fig. 3. (Left) Participant during Interaction Phase. (Right) Physical setup of the experiment.

After the conversation, the participants completed the R-UCLA questionnaire again and a second set of physiological measurements was collected. They then evaluated their experience using the Quality of the experience questionnaire (Sect. 3.2). The session ended with a semi-structured interview aimed at gathering additional impressions and feedback from the participants.

4 Results

4.1 Qualitative Results

The participants generally responded positively to the HugBits device, describing it as 'interesting' and 'amusing.' Many appreciated its soft and huggable qualities, which were perceived as comforting and emotionally engaging. Several users indicated that tactile interaction fosters a sense of bonding, suggesting the potential of the device to support affective connection in remote communication. However, some participants also identified areas for improvement. Reports of delayed connectivity and occasional technical malfunctions highlighted the need for greater system stability. In addition, some participants recommended enhancing sensory feedback by incorporating auditory or vibratory signals, as some perceived current visual only feedback as insufficient to convey emotional nuance. Some participants also said that they had expected the technology to be more impressive or 'cool', suggesting a mismatch between expectations and actual experience.

The responses to the appearance of the device were mixed. Although some participants found the form factor attractive, others suggested modifications to better align with user preferences. Recommendations included the use of brighter or more playful colors, heart-shaped designs, or increased softness for added tactile appeal. In contrast, some favored more subdued, neutral tones (e.g., cream or beige), which were considered more appropriate for adult users and improved the visibility of the LED lighting. One participant expressed concern that the LED color scheme evoked associations with emergency lights, detracting from the calming intent of the device. Further comments addressed the broader applicability of HugBits. Several participants believed that the device could be beneficial for a wide range of users, including children. Although some users felt that the device improved emotional connection, others emphasized that the quality of the underlying relationship with the communication partner played a more decisive role.

4.2 Quantitative Results

Loneliness. Contrary to expectations, the results of the post-test of the R-UCLA Loneliness Scale did not indicate a statistically significant reduction in loneliness scores [13]. The mean pre-test loneliness score was M = 42.8 (SD = 8.3), while the mean post-test score was M = 44.1 (SD = 7.9), indicating a slight increase in perceived loneliness. A Wilcoxon Signed-Rank test was performed to compare pre-test and post-test loneliness scores, which revealed no significant differences (W = 47.0, p = 0.591). Some participants even reported slightly higher levels of loneliness after the experiment. This finding suggests that, while Hugbits may enhance social presence, it does not necessarily replace the benefits of human interaction in person [11].

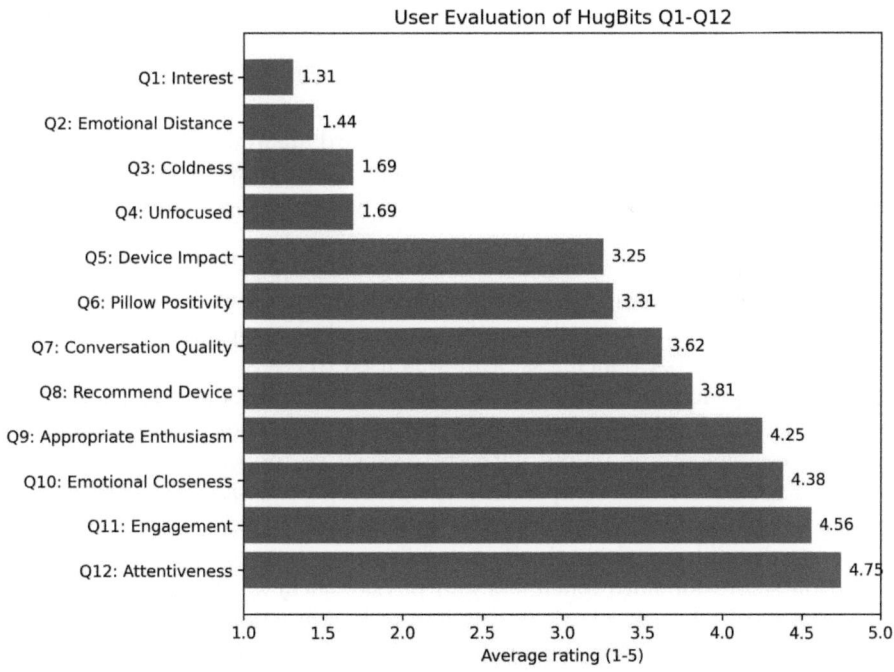

Fig. 4. Average ratings for survey items assessing the quality of the communication experience using HugBits.

Stress Levels. The physiological data collected included measurements of heart rate and oxygen saturation taken before and after the interaction. The Shapiro-Wilk test was used to assess the normality of the dataset, revealing that the distribution of differences in heart rate values deviated from normality ($p = 0.004$). Consequently, a nonparametric Wilcoxon signed rank test was applied instead of a paired t-test to compare heart rate values before and after the test. The results did not show statistically significant differences ($W = 26.0$, $p = 0.878$), indicating that the interaction with Hugbits did not produce a measurable effect on the physiological states of the participants. The mean level of oxygen saturation prior to the test was $M = 96.8\%$ ($SD = 1.2$), and the post-test mean was $M = 96.6\%$ ($SD = 1.3$). Statistical analysis using the Wilcoxon Signed Rank test revealed no significant differences between the pre- and post-test values ($W = 26.0$, $p = 0.878$).

Quality of the Experience. The results of the Quality of Experience questionnaire are presented in Fig. 4. Participants responded to 12 items evaluating their interaction experience (Sect. 3.2).

5 Discussion

This study aimed to explore the potential of HugBits as a therapeutic solution for the population of older adults. Specifically, we asked: Can HugBits promote well-being, particularly by reducing loneliness and fostering feelings of connectedness? This study represents an initial step toward answering that question. To that end, we designed a controlled experiment that allowed us to observe the target user interacting with HugBits first-hand and to identify both its strengths and areas for improvement.

Evaluating the impact of HugBits on emotional or physical well-being within a single session is inherently challenging. We addressed this by collecting multimodal data, including subjective self-reports and physiological measurements. Although the R-UCLA Loneliness Scale was used to assess changes in perceived loneliness, it is primarily intended to measure more stable long-term experiences. Although it can be applied in short-term exploratory studies, it is recommended that such assessments be paired with state-sensitive tools or physiological and behavioral indicators. To complement the self-report data, we recorded heart rate and oxygen saturation as objective indicators of stress.

The results did not show significant differences between the pre and post-interaction scores for both loneliness and physiological stress. Although we initially hypothesized that physical contact and interaction with the huggable device, along with the emotional symbolism of sharing a hug, could reduce stress or loneliness, several important limitations were observed. First, although heart rate and oxygen saturation are frequently used as physiological indicators, their reliability in assessing psychological stress in older adults is limited. Age-related changes in autonomic function can alter cardiovascular responses to stress, making HR a less sensitive marker in this population. In addition, common age-related comorbidities and medications can further confuse both heart rate and oxygen saturation readings. Since we did not collect detailed health background information, future studies could benefit from mapping the physiological responses of users to their self-reported physical condition. Second, while we assumed that participating in the experiment might induce a mild stress baseline, thus allowing us to detect reductions after interaction, this may not have occurred. The participants were very familiar with their environment and the people around them, which likely reduced any sense of novelty-related stress.

Regarding the second question in this study: How do older adults perceive the usability and role of HugBits in their daily lives? The questionnaire evaluating the quality of the experience provided more insight into the role of technology in shaping the interaction. The results indicated a generally positive user experience in multiple dimensions (Fig. 4). Most of the participants gave high ratings (above 4 on average) on items related to emotional engagement and communication quality. They described the conversation as enjoyable and emotionally meaningful, and many reported that the presence of HugBits positively influenced their perception of the conversation partner.

Participants also indicated that HugBits helped foster a sense of emotional closeness. Conversation partners were seen as engaged, enthusiastic, and attentive. In contrast, negative descriptors, such as emotional distance, coldness, or disinterest, received very low scores. In particular, the item asking whether participants would recommend the device to others received one of the highest ratings, indicating a high overall satisfaction. However, the ratings for the item related to whether the device improved the conversation experience itself were somewhat lower, suggesting that while the device supported emotional perception, it may not have fundamentally altered the nature of the conversation for all users. Several participants noted that Hugbits could be particularly useful in long-distance relationships, where physical contact is not possible. This supports previous studies on the importance of mediated touch in maintaining emotional bonds [16]. However, others expressed concerns about the accessibility of the technology, highlighting the need for intuitive and easy-to-use interfaces geared to older adults.

Finally, this study presents several limitations that should be addressed in future research. First, the small sample size limits the generalizability of the findings, highlighting the need for larger and more diverse grouping of participants. Second, the short-term nature of the study prevents conclusions about long-term effects, underscoring the importance of longitudinal investigations to assess sustained impacts on loneliness. Third, the current prototype lacks advanced haptic features; incorporating additional modalities such as vibration or temperature feedback could enhance realism and emotional resonance. Comparative studies with other haptic communication devices are also necessary to evaluate the relative efficacy of HugBits. In addition, integrating multisensory feedback-including auditory or olfactory cues-may improve the user experience. Finally, exploring personalization options, such as adjustable haptic intensity or user-specific pairing, could further enhance engagement and emotional relevance.

Lessons Learned and Design Considerations. Drawing from the results of the questionnaire and the feedback from the interview, we highlight several key insights and directions for the design of similar technologies aimed at older users.

1. Tactile Interaction Is Valuable but Needs Depth: participants appreciated the huggable, soft nature of HugBits, emphasizing the emotional power of physical comfort and the symbolic act of hugging. However, many suggested that the experience could be made more immersive through multisensory feedback, such as vibration or sound, to increase the emotional richness of the interaction.
2. Simplicity Supports Usability, but Customization Matters: the simplified version of HugBits, which consists only of visual cues, was generally well received, especially by older adults less familiar with complex technology. At the same time, users expressed various preferences regarding aesthetic design, highlighting the need for customizable features (e.g., color, shape, texture) to align with individual taste and age-appropriate contexts.
3. Technical Reliability Is Crucial for Trust and Acceptance: Although not widespread, reports of delayed connectivity and occasional malfunctions underscore the importance of technical robustness. Even minor disruptions can negatively affect emotional engagement and reduce trust in the device, especially in emotionally sensitive settings like elder care.
4. Emotional Connection Is Shaped by Context, Not Just Technology: several participants noted that the emotional quality of the interaction depended more on their relationship with the communication partner than on the device itself. This suggests that HugBits should be viewed as a facilitator of emotional connection, rather than a substitute for relational depth.

6 Conclusions

This study investigated the potential of HugBits to enhance emotional well-being in older adults through mediated tactile interaction. Although no significant changes in physiological stress or perceived loneliness were observed, participants reported a positive and emotionally engaging experience with the device. The usability study provided valuable information on how older adults perceive the comfort, responsiveness, and communicative potential of a huggable interface. These findings highlight the importance of designing emotionally resonant and easy-to-use technologies that support the affective connection in aging populations. Future work should build on these results through long-term studies and iterative refinements based on user feedback.

Acknowledgments. We thank the participants in this study. This research was partially supported by JST CREST Social Signals (No. JPMJCR19A2).

Disclosure of Interests. The authors have no competing interests to declare that are relevant to the content of this article.

References

1. Akhtar, S.A.: Socially connected while apart: the use of technology to increase social connection between nursing home residents and their relatives. Front. Public Health **12**, 1296524 (2024)
2. Broekens, J., Heerink, M., Rosendal, H., et al.: Assistive social robots in elderly care: a review. Gerontechnology **8**(2), 94–103 (2009)
3. Carnevale, A., et al.: Exploring the impact of socially assistive robots in rehabilitation scenarios. Bioengineering **12**(2), 204 (2025)
4. Eid, M.A., Al Osman, H.: Affective haptics: current research and future directions. IEEE Access **4**, 26–40 (2015)
5. Fahy, M., Barry, M.: Investigating the interplay of loneliness, computer-mediated communication, online social capital, and well-being: insights from a covid-19 lockdown study. Front. Digit. Health **6**, 1289451 (2024)
6. Forsell, L.M., Åström, J.A.: Meanings of hugging: from greeting behavior to touching implications. Compr. Psychol. **1**, 02–17 (2012)
7. Morrison, I.: Keep calm and cuddle on: social touch as a stress buffer. Adapt. Hum. Behav. Physiol. **2**, 344–362 (2016)
8. Nunez, E., Hirokawa, M., Hautasaari, A., Suzuki, K.: Remote communication via huggable interfaces-behavior synchronization and social presence. In: CHI Conference on Human Factors in Computing Systems Extended Abstracts, pp. 1–7 (2022)
9. Nunez, E., Hirokawa, M., Perusquia-Hernandez, M., Suzuki, K.: Effect on social connectedness and stress levels by using a huggable interface in remote communication. In: 2019 8th International Conference on Affective Computing and Intelligent Interaction (ACII), pp. 1–7. IEEE (2019)
10. Otaka, E., et al.: Positive emotional responses to socially assistive robots in people with dementia: pilot study. JMIR Aging **7**(1), e52443 (2024)
11. Rettie, R.: Connectedness, awareness and social presence (2003)
12. Robinson, H., MacDonald, B., Broadbent, E.: Physiological effects of a companion robot on blood pressure of older people in residential care facility: a pilot study. Australas. J. Ageing **34**(1), 27–32 (2015)
13. Russell, D., Peplau, L.A., Cutrona, C.E.: The revised UCLA loneliness scale: concurrent and discriminant validity evidence. J. Pers. Soc. Psychol. **39**(3), 472 (1980)
14. Sumioka, H., Nakae, A., Kanai, R., Ishiguro, H.: Huggable communication medium decreases cortisol levels. Sci. Rep. **3**, 3034 (2013). https://doi.org/10.1038/srep03034
15. Tapus, A., Tapus, C., Mataric, M.J.: The use of socially assistive robots in the design of intelligent cognitive therapies for people with dementia. In: 2009 IEEE International Conference on Rehabilitation Robotics, pp. 924–929. IEEE (2009)
16. Tsetserukou, D., Neviarouskaya, A., Prendinger, H., Kawakami, N., Tachi, S.: Affective haptics in emotional communication. In: 2009 3rd International Conference on Affective Computing and Intelligent Interaction and Workshops, pp. 1–6. IEEE (2009)
17. Visser, T., Vastenburg, M.H., Keyson, D.V.: Designing to support social connectedness: the case of snowglobe. Int. J. Des. **5**(3) (2011)
18. Wright, K.: Computer-mediated social support, older adults, and coping. J. Commun. **50**(3), 100–118 (2000)
19. Wu, Y.H., Fassert, C., Rigaud, A.S.: Designing robots for the elderly: appearance issue and beyond. Arch. Gerontol. Geriatr. **54**(1), 121–126 (2012)

Multimodal Framework for Adaptive HRI via Dynamic Engagement and Affective Feedback

Gayathri Girijadevi Radhakrishnan[1]($\boxtimes$), Olga Tveretina[1], Farshid Amirabdollahian[1], and Diego Resende Faria[1,2]

[1] University of Hertfordshire, Hatfield, UK
{g.girijadevi-radhakrishnan,o.tveretina,f.amirabdollahian2,
d.resende-faria}@herts.ac.uk, d.resende-faria@lboro.ac.uk
g.girijadevi-radhakrishnan@herts.ac.uk , o.tveretina@herts.ac.uk ,
f.amirabdollahian2@herts.ac.uk,
d.resende-faria@herts.ac.uk,d.resende-faria@lboro.ac.uk
[2] Loughborough University, Loughborough, UK

Abstract. In this work, we propose a multimodal affective communication framework to enhance human-robot interaction (HRI) by dynamically assessing user engagement through biophysiological responses. The system fuses facial expression analysis, speech emotion recognition, and text sentiment analysis to compute an engagement score, which informs adaptive robot behavior. Each modality is processed independently and contributes to a composite score categorized into low, medium, or high engagement levels. A key contribution of this study is a Bayesian-based engagement estimation mechanism, where the weight of each modality is dynamically adjusted based on its reliability, quantified via normalized inverse entropy. This probabilistic approach enables the robot to prioritize the most stable and informative signals, enhancing robustness in real-world environments. Additionally, the robot uses a Bayesian strategy to optimize predefined behavioral stimuli, learning over time which responses most effectively promote user engagement. The proposed framework supports personalized and context-aware real-time adaptation, with promising applications in assistive robotics, socially interactive systems, and long-term HRI.

Keywords: Human-Robot Interaction · Affective Computing · Multimodal Emotion Recognition · Socially Assistive Robotics · Engagement Estimation

1 Introduction

Emotions are integral to daily human experience, shaping our perception, behavior, and interactions with the world. They influence decision-making, interpersonal relationships, and overall well-being. Effectively understanding and managing emotions is thus critical to maintaining mental health and enhancing quality of life [5,6].

Recent studies have explored the use of digital technologies—including mobile apps, chatbots, and social robots—for promoting mental well-being across diverse populations [2,8,14]. Among these, human-robot interaction (HRI) has shown significant promise for emotion regulation interventions. Social robots can offer immersive, personalized experiences by emulating human-like behavior, thereby enhancing user comfort and emotional engagement [13]. Multimodal interaction—leveraging speech, facial expressions, gestures, and touch—has become a cornerstone of effective HRI. The integration of these cues, often referred to as multimodal fusion, supports more natural and adaptive communication between humans and robots [1].

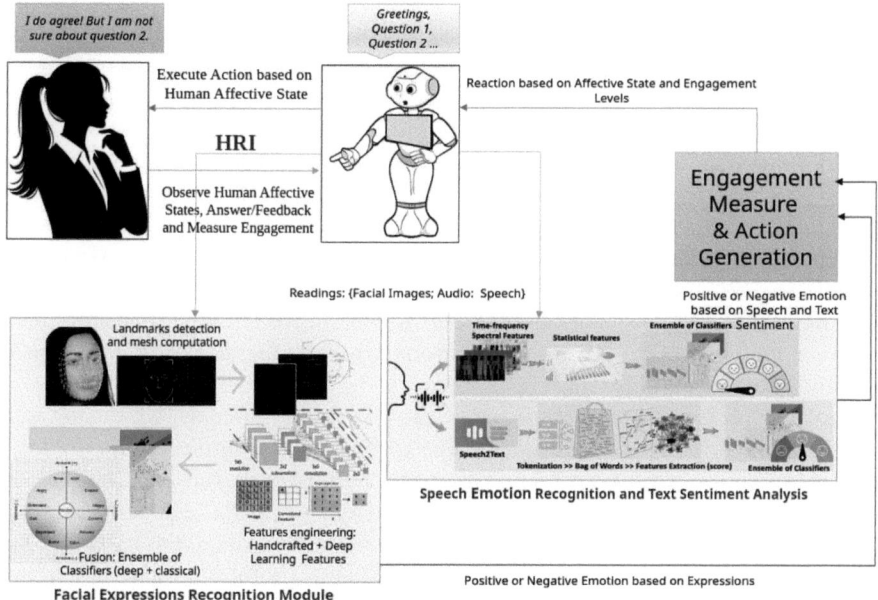

Fig. 1. Overview of the proposed multimodal affective framework for enhancing HRI.

In this study, we present a novel framework that explores the role of multisensory perception in human-robot interaction (HRI) for emotion regulation, as shown in Fig. 1. Our multimodal system integrates facial expression analysis, speech emotion recognition, and sentiment analysis to classify emotions into three categories: positive, neutral, and negative. Initially, seven facial expressions—angry, disgust, fear, happy, neutral, sad, and surprise—are recognized and grouped as positive (happy, surprise), neutral, and negative (angry, disgust, sad). Speech emotion is similarly processed, mapping four emotions—angry, happy, sad, and surprise—into the same categories. This simplified structure supports early cross-modality fusion and reduces computational load, while enabling future refinement into finer affective states. The resulting emotional classification informs an engagement score that guides adaptive robot behavior. A pilot study with a small sample demonstrates feasibility in real-time adaptive HRI.

The paper is structured as follows: Sect. 2 reviews related work; Sect. 3 describes the methodology, including multimodal emotion recognition, engagement evaluation, and adaptive Bayesian mechanisms; Sect. 4 presents experimental results; and Sect. 5 concludes with future directions.

2 Related Work

In psychology, affective computing, and human-computer interaction, several models have been developed to classify and analyze emotional states. Ekman's model originally included seven basic emotions—fear, anger, happiness, sadness, neutral, disgust, and surprise—but was later revised to six by removing the neutral category [3]. Plutchik's "Wheel of Emotions" identifies eight basic emotions, varying in intensity and capable of combining into complex affective states [11]. Russell's dimensional model represents emotions in a two-dimensional valence-arousal space, where valence reflects emotional polarity and arousal indicates intensity [12]. This model delineates four quadrants: High-arousal/Positive (e.g., excitement, happiness), High-arousal/Negative (e.g., anger, frustration), Low-arousal/Negative (e.g., depression, boredom), and Low-arousal/Positive (e.g., calm, neutral). Affective computing plays a central role in HRI, enabling robots to detect and respond to human emotions through facial expressions, speech, and physiological signals, thereby improving user engagement [7,15,16].

Recent developments include embodied systems such as UGotMe, which enable real-time multimodal emotion recognition in dynamic settings, addressing environmental noise and responsiveness challenges [9,16]. Studies have also shown that robots conveying affective narratives—particularly vulnerability—can elicit empathy, increasing user willingness to engage and assist [4,15]. Despite these advances, current systems often rely on static emotion models that struggle with noisy biophysical data, individual differences, and fluctuating engagement. Most multimodal frameworks remain reactive, lacking real-time adaptation. In contrast, our framework incorporates dynamic Bayesian adaptation and personalized feedback mechanisms to continuously update engagement estimates and contextually select interaction strategies. This approach enhances personalization, robustness, and sustained user engagement.

3 Methodology

This section presents a framework for HRI that uses multimodal inputs to estimate users' emotional states and adapt robot behavior in real time to enhance engagement. The framework consists of three core modules: (1) Multimodal Emotion Recognition, (2) Engagement Measurement, and (3) Action Generation.

Emotional states are detected through facial expressions, speech, and textual sentiment, each independently classified as positive, neutral, or negative. These outputs are fused with attentional cues to compute a dynamic engagement score. A Bayesian inference mechanism is used to update this score and select appropriate robot behavior. If user engagement is low, the system iteratively presents stimuli—such as gestures, speech, or visual cues—until engagement improves. Effective responses are stored for future use, enabling personalized, emotionally intelligent interaction that evolves over time.

3.1 Face Emotion Recognition

We evaluated several machine learning classifiers for facial emotion recognition using the Karolinska Directed Emotional Faces (KDEF) dataset [10], which includes seven emotion classes: angry, disgust, fear, happy, neutral, sad, and

---

Algorithm 1. Algorithm used for Facial Emotion Recognition

1: **Input:** Face image of size 224×224
2: **Output:** Predicted Emotional State
3: **Step 1: Preprocessing the Image**
4: Detect facial landmarks using a pretrained landmark detector(68 from DLib).
5: Convert the input image to grayscale.
6: Resize the image to 224×224 (input size for VGG16).
7: **Step 2: Feature Extraction**
8: *Handcrafted Geometric Features:*
9: Extract Pairwise Distances between selected facial landmarks.
10: Compute Angles by triangular points within facial regions.
11: Calculate Log-Covariance of Landmark Distances.
12: Compute Euclidean distances between all landmark points.
13: Extract HoG features over the face image.
14: *Deep Learning Features (VGG16):*
15: Pass the preprocessed image through the VGG16 model (pretrained) and extract features from its fully connected layers.
16: **Step 3: Feature Fusion**
17: Concatenate all extracted features into a single feature vector:
18: $F = \mathrm{Concat}(F_{\mathrm{geo}}, F_{\mathrm{HoG}}, F_{\mathrm{VGG16}})$ where:
19: F_{geo} are the geometric features,
20: F_{HoG} are the HoG features,
21: F_{VGG16} are the VGG16 deep learning features.
22: **Step 4: Train SVM-Linear and Logistic Regression Classifiers**
23: *Train Support Vector Machine (SVM-Linear kernel):*
24: $\min_{\mathbf{w},b} \frac{1}{2}\|\mathbf{w}\|^2$ subject to $y_i(\mathbf{w}\cdot\mathbf{x}_i + b) \geq 1 \quad \forall i$
25: *Train Logistic Regression:*
26: $h_\theta(\mathbf{x}) = \frac{1}{1+e^{-\theta^T \mathbf{x}}}$
27: **Step 5: Individual Predictions by SVM and Logistic Regression**
28: Predict with SVM:
29: $\hat{y}_{\mathrm{SVM\text{-}linear}} = \mathrm{SVM\text{-}linear}(F_{\mathrm{selected}})$
30: Predict with Logistic Regression:
31: $\hat{y}_{\mathrm{LR}} = \mathrm{LR}(F_{\mathrm{selected}})$
32: **Return:** Final predicted emotion class.

surprise. To capture both localized and high-level facial features, we employed a hybrid feature extraction approach combining handcrafted and deep learning representations.

Handcrafted features included geometric descriptors such as pairwise landmark distances, angles between facial regions, log-covariance metrics, and histogram of oriented gradients (HoG). For deep features, we used the pretrained VGG16 model to extract representations from fully connected layers.

To enhance classification performance, we used an ensemble of Support Vector Machine (SVM) with a linear kernel and Logistic Regression. This ensemble model was deployed in real-time within the Multimodal Emotion Recognition module to ensure robust facial emotion inference during HRI. The detailed process is described in Algorithm 1.

Algorithm 2. Algorithm used for Speech Emotion Recognition

1: **Input:** Audio signal of emotional speech
2: **Output:** Predicted emotion class
3: **Step 1: Feature Extraction**
4: Extract audio features and Statistical features .
5: Normalize the features
6: **Step 2: Train and Predict the Classifiers**
7: 1DCNN
8:    Input: Reshaped features
9:    Input Layer: Conv1D layer with kernel size 3
10:   Hidden Layer 1: MaxPooling1D layer with pool size 2
11:   Hidden Layer 2: Flatten layer
12:   Output Layer: Dense layer with softmax activation
13:   Predict:$\hat{y}_{\text{CNN}} = \arg\max(\text{softmax}(\mathbf{W}_{\text{CNN}} \cdot \text{Flatten}(\text{Conv1D}(\mathbf{x}_{\text{reshaped}})) + \mathbf{b}_{\text{CNN}}))$
14: Support Vector Machine (SVM):
15:   $\min_{\mathbf{w},b} \frac{1}{2}\|\mathbf{w}\|^2$ subject to $y_i(\mathbf{w} \cdot \mathbf{x}_i + b) \geq 1, \quad \forall i$
16: Random Forest classifier
17: Gaussian Naive Bayes
18: MLP Classifier
19:   Input Layer: Flattened features
20:   Hidden Layer 1: 320 neurons with ReLU activation
21:   Hidden Layer 2: 192 neurons with ReLU activation
22:   Output Layer: Softmax over class neurons
23:   Predict:$\hat{y}_{\text{MLP}} = \arg\max(\text{softmax}(f(x)))$, where $f(x) = W_2 \cdot \text{ReLU}(W_1 \cdot x + b_1) + b_2$
24: **Step 7: Train and Predict Ensemble Model (Voting Classifier)**
25:   Combine classifiers:
26:   Each classifier f_i produces a predicted class label:
27:     $y_i = f_i(\mathbf{x}), \quad i \in \{1, 2, 3\}$
28:   Final prediction by majority voting:
29:     $\hat{y}_{\text{ensemble}} = \arg\max_{c \in C} \sum_{i=1}^{3} \mathbb{1}\,[y_i = c]$
30: **Return:** Final predicted emotion class

3.2 Speech Emotion Recognition

For speech emotion recognition, we evaluated several classifiers using the Emotional Speech Database (ESD), which includes five emotion categories: neutral, happy, angry, sad, and surprise. Audio features were extracted using both time- and frequency-domain techniques, including Mel-frequency cepstral coefficients (MFCCs), Mel spectrogram, Chroma, Tonnetz, Pitch, Energy, Zero Crossing Rate, RMS energy, and statistical descriptors. These features were used to train classifiers such as SVM, Random Forest, 1D-CNN, Gaussian Naive Bayes (GNB), and Multilayer Perceptron (MLP). To enhance accuracy and ensure robustness in real-time scenarios, an ensemble method was applied, combining predictions from the top-performing models (1D-CNN and MLP). The complete algorithm is shown in Algorithm 2.

Algorithm 3. Algorithm used for Text Sentiment Analysis

1: **Input:** Text data
2: **Output:** Predicted polarity
3: **Step 1: Logistic Regression Model**
4:     Vectorize the sentences using TF-IDF
5:     Train a Logistic Regression model using TF-IDF features
6:     Predict sentiment on test data
7: **Step 2: SVM Model**
8:     Vectorize the sentences using TF-IDF
9:     Train an SVM model using TF-IDF features
10:    Predict sentiment on test data
11: **Step 3: Random Forest Model**
12:    Vectorize the sentences using TF-IDF
13:    Train a Random Forest model using TF-IDF features
14:    Predict sentiment on test data
15: **Step 4: MLP Model**
16:    Vectorize the sentences using TF-IDF
17:    Train a Multi-Layer Perceptron (MLP) model using TF-IDF features
18:    Predict sentiment on test data
19: **Step 5: 1D-CNN Model**
20:    Tokenize sentences using a Keras Tokenizer
21:    Convert text to sequences
22:    Convert sentiment labels to one-hot encoded format
23:    Train a 1D-CNN model on text sequences
24:    Predict sentiment on test data
25: **Return:** Final predicted polarity

3.3 Sentiment Analysis

For sentiment analysis, we evaluated multiple machine learning classifiers using an extended version of the Emotional Speech Database (ESD) [17]. To enhance the dataset and improve model generalization, data augmentation was performed by generating over 3,000 additional everyday sentences using OpenAI ChatGPT, covering positive, neutral, and negative sentiment classes. This enriched dataset was subsequently used to train and evaluate various classifiers, including SVM, Random Forest, Logistic Regression, as well as transformer-based models such as BERT and GPT-2, as detailed in Algorithm 3.

3.4 Attentional Mechanism

The attentional mechanism estimates the user's focus level during interaction, providing a binary classification of either focused or distracted to support the Engagement Measurement module. Unlike the emotion and sentiment recognition components, this mechanism does not rely on machine learning models. Instead, it employs a lightweight, real-time approach based on facial landmark analysis. Facial orientation is used to infer attention: when the user's face is directed toward the robot (i.e., in a frontal position), the system classifies the user as focused. Conversely, if the user's head is turned upwards, downwards, or to the side for an extended period, they are considered distracted. This rule-based method offers computational efficiency and contextual insight, contributing an additional modality to the engagement estimation process and supporting adaptive behavior generation.

3.5 Engagement Score Evaluation

The proposed engagement score offers a quantitative framework for assessing the effectiveness of HRI, encompassing emotional and behavioral dimensions. It acts as an integrative marker of how well the an individual engages with the robot.

By analyzing multimodal sensor and behavioral data, the score facilitates a structured evaluation of interaction quality. Elevated scores reflect attentional stability, positive affect, and active involvement, while diminished scores suggest disengagement or negative responses, triggering adaptive interventions.

Multi-modal Factors and Adaptive Bayesian Weighting. Engagement is computed using a range of behavioral and emotional metrics observed during HRI. Each modality is scored from 1 (low) to 5 (high), depending on its contextual relevance. The considered modalities include: Facial Expression (F), Speech Emotion (S), Attention (A), Text Sentiment Feedback (T). These inputs form the basis of the global engagement score:

$$E = \sum_{i=1}^{n} w_i \cdot m_i, \tag{1}$$

where E is the overall engagement score computed as a weighted sum; m_i is the observed score for a specific modality i (ranging from 1 to 5); w_i is the confidence-based weight assigned to modality i; n represents the total number of modalities. The weights are normalized to ensure $\sum w_i = 1$.

Bayesian Update of Weights with Normalized Inverse Entropy. Weights are dynamically updated over time using Bayesian inference. Initially, each modality is considered equally reliable, so uniform prior is assumed, $P(w_i) = \frac{1}{n}$. The likelihood is given by the normalized inverse entropy as Confidence-based Likelihood. Given the empirical distribution of weights over time (based on previous observations of normalized modality scores), the entropy for each modality i is computed as $H(w_i) = -\sum_x p(m_i) \log p(m_i)$, where $p(m_i)$ represents the empirical probability distribution (e.g., histogram) of score values over time for modality i (e.g., A, S, F, T). $H(w_i)$: is the Shannon entropy, quantifying uncertainty or variability in the modality. The entropy is then normalized using the maximum entropy for K discrete bins, $H_{\max} = \log_2(K)$. Using this, the confidence is calculated as:

$$\text{Confidence}(m_i) = 1 - \frac{H(m_i)}{H_{\max}}, \tag{2}$$

where $\text{Confidence}(m_i)$ is the estimated reliability of modality i. Higher values indicate more stable, trustworthy modality readings. The confidence value serves as the likelihood in the Bayesian update, $P(D_t|w_i) = \text{Confidence}(m_i)$, where D_t is the observed data score history up to time t for modality i. The posterior is updated recursively using Bayes' rule:

$$P(w_i|D_t) = \frac{P(D_t|w_i)P(w_i)}{\sum_{j=1}^{n} P(D_t|w_j)P(w_j)}, \tag{3}$$

where $P(w_i|D_t)$ is the updated (posterior) weight for modality i, reflecting current confidence. The denominator ensures normalization across all n modalities. These posterior values are used as the final weights in the engagement score, giving more influence to the most informative modalities over time.

Bayesian Estimation of Optimal Stimuli to Improve Engagement. When the engagement score E is classified as low or medium, the robot selects from a predefined set of stimuli—such as gestures, spoken prompts, or visual feedback—to enhance user interaction. It sequentially delivers each stimulus from the set, monitoring the engagement score after each attempt. If a stimulus does not yield a noticeable increase in engagement, the system proceeds to the next one. Once a stimulus produces a positive shift, it is recorded as the most effective response for that specific interaction type and user profile. Over time, this adaptive strategy enables the robot to build a memory of which stimuli are most effective in different emotional or engagement contexts. When a similar low-engagement state is encountered again, the robot first attempts the previously successful stimulus. If engagement still does not improve, it resumes exploring other options in the sequence. Let s_k denote the k-th predefined stimulus. The system tracks each stimulus's effectiveness by computing a reward signal $r_k(t)$, which represents the positive change in engagement resulting from stimulus s_k at time t. The cumulative historical impact of each stimulus is defined as:

$$H(s_k) = \sum_t r_k(t), \tag{4}$$

where $H(s_k)$ denotes the accumulated engagement gain associated with stimulus s_k. The Bayesian posterior probability that a given stimulus s_k is optimal for the current engagement context is calculated as:

$$P(s_k|E) = \frac{P(E|s_k)P(s_k)}{\sum_j P(E|s_j)P(s_j)}, \tag{5}$$

where $P(E|s_k) \propto H(s_k)$ represents the likelihood of increased engagement from s_k, and $P(s_k)$ is the prior, typically uniform in the absence of prior knowledge. Finally, the robot selects the action with the highest posterior probability $s^* = \arg\max_{s_k} P(s_k|E)$, ensuring it progressively learns and prioritizes the most effective behavior to enhance the quality of interaction.

4 Results

4.1 Emotional Expressions Performance on Datasets

Facial Emotion Recognition. We evaluated the facial emotion recognition approach using the Karolinska Directed Emotional Faces (KDEF) dataset [10], which consists of 4,900 images representing seven distinct emotions: anger, disgust, fear, happiness, neutrality, sadness, and surprise. An 80% training and 20% testing data split was used for model training and evaluation. Among the classifiers tested, the SVM with a linear kernel achieved the highest accuracy at 84.83%, closely followed by Logistic Regression at 83.62%. Random Forest achieved 68.10%, while the SVM with an RBF kernel demonstrated the lowest accuracy at 51.90%.

Speech Emotion Recognition. Experiments were conducted on the Emotional Speech Database (ESD) [17], using the subset of native English speakers. The dataset was split into 80% training and 20% testing data. Several classifiers were evaluated, including SVM, Random Forest, 1D-CNN, GNB, and MLP. The MLP classifier achieved the highest accuracy at 93.19%, outperforming all other models. The 1D-CNN achieved 88.37%, while Random Forest and SVM obtained 85.28% and 82.91%, respectively. GNB showed the lowest performance, with an accuracy of 40.94%.

Sentiment Analysis. For sentiment analysis, we used the Emotional Speech Dataset (ESD) by converting audio to text transcripts and augmenting the data with over 3,000 everyday sentences to enhance model generalization. We evaluated multiple machine learning and deep learning models, including Logistic Regression, SVM, Random Forest, MLP, 1D-CNN, and pre-trained transformer-based models such as GPT-2 and BERT. The MLP classifier achieved the highest accuracy at 98.6%, closely followed by SVM (98.4%), Logistic Regression

(98.3%), and Random Forest (98.1%). BERT performed similarly well, with an accuracy of 98%. In contrast, the 1D-CNN and GPT-2 models had lower accuracies of 80.3% and 81%, respectively, indicating that traditional machine learning classifiers and transformer-based models were more effective for this task.

4.2 Performance Evaluation in Real-Time HRI

Experimental Setup and Protocol. The experimental setup involved two robots—Pepper and JD—alongside an HD camera (60 Hz) and a microphone (48kHz) for facial and speech emotion recognition (Fig. 2). Pepper served as the primary social agent, engaging in conversation with participants, while JD provided stimuli through gestures and short dance routines to enhance engagement. Each participant participated in 1-minute interactive trials (3 to 5 trials in total), during which Pepper initiated dialogue with questions such as: "Hello! I'm Pepper. What's your name, and how are you feeling today?"; "How has your week been so far?"; "Is there anything you're working on that excites or stresses you?"; and "What do you enjoy doing on your day off?".

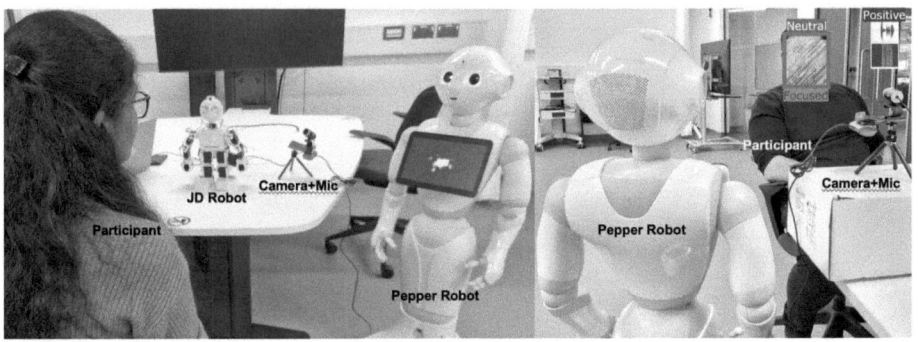

Fig. 2. Experimental setup for HRI trials, featuring the Pepper and JD robots.

During and after each response, Pepper analyzed the participant's emotional state and engagement score. Based on the detected engagement, it provided empathetic responses—such as "That's great to hear!", "I'm sorry to hear that," or "Thanks for sharing"—and triggered a sequence of stimuli (verbal cues, visuals, or support from JD) aimed at boosting engagement. Engagement levels were continuously computed using multimodal fusion, with the robot adaptively selecting future stimuli based on real-time feedback. The primary goals of the study were to (i) assess the impact of multimodal robot-led emotion regulation and (ii) evaluate real-time adaptation based on affective signals in human-robot interaction.

Four adults (1 male, 3 female) participated in the experiment. All participants were informed about the study and their role in interacting with the robot. The study adhered to ethical guidelines and data privacy regulations. During the sessions, a dataset was collected containing biophysical characteristics and engagement scores.

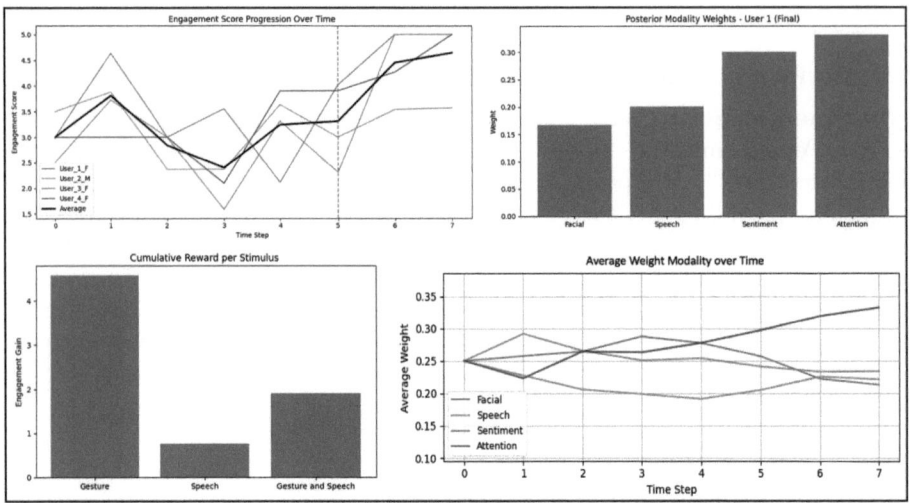

Fig. 3. Experimental results from HRI trials. From left to right, top to bottom: (1) Engagement score progression over time across participants; (2) Posterior modality weights for Participant 1; (3) Cumulative engagement gain by stimulus type; (4) Time-evolving average modality weights across all participants.

Figure 3 presents the results. The first subplot shows the Engagement Score Progression Over Time for all four participants, along with the overall average. A noticeable increase in engagement occurs after time step 5 (marked by the dashed line), suggesting that the adaptive mechanism and stimulus strategy positively influenced user engagement. This post-intervention trend implies the robot successfully adapted to individual affective responses over time.

The second subplot displays the Posterior Modality Weights for participant 1 at the final time step, highlighting the relevance of each modality. Attention was the most influential, followed by sentiment and speech, with facial expressions contributing the least—underscoring the role of attentional signals in sustaining engagement and supporting dynamic modality weighting.

The third subplot shows the Cumulative Reward per Stimulus. Gestures alone led to the highest engagement gain, outperforming both speech and the combined gesture-speech stimulus. This indicates that visual, embodied cues were more effective than verbal stimuli in this setup.

Finally, the fourth subplot presents the Average Time-Evolving Modality Weights across participants. Attention consistently gained importance across sessions, while facial and speech cues fluctuated. Sentiment and attention either maintained or improved their contributions. These trends confirm a shift toward attention-dominant weighting over time.

Overall, the results demonstrate that the adaptive engagement framework effectively leverages multimodal affective cues, with attention and gesture-based stimuli playing a key role in maximizing user engagement during our HRI experiments.

5 Conclusion and Future Work

In this paper, we presented a novel multimodal affective communication framework for adaptive HRI, integrating facial expression recognition, speech emotion analysis, sentiment analysis, and attention tracking to compute dynamic engagement scores. A key innovation is the use of Bayesian inference to adjust modality weights over time, allowing the robot to prioritize the most reliable affective cues. Additionally, the system employs engagement-driven reward learning to guide adaptive stimulus selection. Experimental results from real-time HRI scenarios demonstrate a significant increase in user engagement, with gestures proving to be the most effective stimulus. The dynamic weight adaptation mechanism also highlighted the growing importance of attention throughout the interaction. This pilot study lays the foundation for broader evaluations, offering key insights into adaptability and engagement that will guide future experiments with larger and more diverse samples. Next steps include integrating physiological data (e.g., EEG) for cognitive state detection and real-time speech analysis using transformer models.

References

1. D'Mello, S.K., Kory, J.M.: A review and meta-analysis of multimodal affect detection systems. ACM Comput. Surv. **47**(3), 43:1–43:36 (2015). https://doi.org/10.1145/2682899
2. Edwards, A., Edwards, C., Abendschein, B., Espinosa, J., Scherger, J., Vander, P.: Using robot animal companions in the academic library to mitigate student stress. Lib. Hi Tech **40**(4), 878–893 (2022)
3. Ekman, P.: An argument for basic emotions. Cogn. Emotion, **6**, 169–200 (1992)
4. Frederiksen, M.R., Fischer, K., Mataric, M.J.: Robot vulnerability and the elicitation of user empathy. CoRR **abs/2401.02684** (2024). https://doi.org/10.48550/arXiv.2401.02684
5. Fredrickson, B.L.: The role of positive emotions in positive psychology: the broaden-and-build theory of positive emotions. Am. Psychol. **56**(3), 218–226 (2001)
6. Gross, J.J., John, O.P.: Individual differences in two emotion regulation processes: implications for affect, relationships, and well-being. J. Pers. Soc. Psychol. **85**(2), 348–362 (2003)
7. Gunes, H., Churamani, N.: Affective computing for human-robot interaction research: Four critical lessons for the hitchhiker. In: 32nd IEEE International Conference on Robot and Human Interactive Communication, RO-MAN 2023, Busan, Republic of Korea, August 28-31, 2023, pp. 1565–1572. IEEE (2023). https://doi.org/10.1109/RO-MAN57019.2023.10309450

8. Jeong, S., et al.: A robotic positive psychology coach to improve college students' wellbeing. In: 29th IEEE International Conference on Robot and Human Interactive Communication, RO-MAN 2020, Naples, Italy, August 31 - September 4, 2020, pp. 187–194. IEEE (2020). https://doi.org/10.1109/RO-MAN47096.2020.9223588
9. Li, P., Cao, L., Wu, X., Yu, X., Yang, R.: UGotMe: An embodied system for affective human-robot interaction. CoRR (2024). https://doi.org/10.48550/arXiv.2410.18373
10. Lundqvist, D., Flykt, A., Öhman, A.: The Karolinska Directed Emotional Faces–KDEF (CD ROM). Karolinska Institute, Department of Clinical Neuroscience, Psychology Section, Stockholm (1998)
11. Plutchik, R.: Emotion: a Psychoevolutionary Synthesis. Longman Higher Education (1980)
12. Russell, J.A.: A circumplex model of affect. J. Pers. Soc. Psychol. **39**(6), 1161–1178 (1980)
13. Scoglio, A.A.J., Reilly, E.D., Gorman, J.A., Drebing, C.E.: Use of social robots in mental health and well-being research: Systematic review. J. Med. Internet Res. **21**(7), e13322 (2019)
14. Spitale, M., Axelsson, M., Gunes, H.: Robotic mental well-being coaches for the workplace: an in-the-wild study on form. In: Castellano, G., Riek, L.D., Cakmak, M., Leite, I. (eds.) Proceedings of the 2023 ACM/IEEE International Conference on Human-Robot Interaction, HRI 2023, Stockholm, Sweden, March 13-16, 2023, pp. 301–310. ACM (2023). https://doi.org/10.1145/3568162.3577003
15. Spitale, M., et al.: Past, present, and future: a survey of the evolution of affective robotics for well-being. CoRR **abs/2407.02957** (2024). https://doi.org/10.48550/arXiv.2407.02957
16. Tzes, A.: Human-robot interactions using affective computing. In: Drakopoulos, G., Kafeza, E. (eds.) Proceedings of the CIKM 2022 Workshops co-located with 31st ACM International Conference on Information and Knowledge Management (CIKM 2022), Atlanta, USA, October 17-21, 2022. CEUR Workshop Proceedings, vol. 3318. CEUR-WS.org (2022). https://ceur-ws.org/Vol-3318/keynote1.pdf
17. Zhou, K., Sisman, B., Liu, R., Li, H.: Emotional voice conversion: theory, databases and ESD. Speech Commun. **137**, 1–18 (2022). https://doi.org/10.1016/j.specom.2021.11.006

User Concerns Regarding Social Robots for Mood Regulation: A Case Study on the "Sunday Blues"

Zhuochao Peng[1(✉)], Jiaxin Xu[2], Jun Hu[2], Haian Xue[3], Laurens A. G. Kolks[1], and Pieter M. A. Desmet[1]

[1] Delft University of Technology, Delft, The Netherlands
{z.peng,l.a.g.kolks,p.m.a.desmet}@tudelft.nl
[2] Eindhoven University of Technology, Eindhoven, The Netherlands
{j.xu2,j.hu}@tue.nl
[3] Tongji University, Shanghai, China
haianxue@tongji.edu.cn

Abstract. While recent research highlights the potential of social robots to support mood regulation, little is known about how prospective users view their integration into everyday life. To explore this, we conducted an exploratory case study that used a speculative robot concept—Mora—to provoke reflection and facilitate meaningful discussion about using social robots to manage subtle, day-to-day emotional experiences. We focused on the "Sunday Blues," a common dip in mood that occurs at the end of the weekend, as a relatable context in which to explore individuals' insights. Using a video prototype and a co-constructing stories method, we engaged 15 participants in imagining interactions with Mora and discussing their expectations, doubts, and concerns. The study surfaced a range of nuanced reflections around the attributes of social robots like empathy, intervention effectiveness, and ethical boundaries, which we translated into design considerations for future research and development in human-robot interaction.

Keywords: Design consideration · Human-robot interaction · Mental health and well-being · Mood regulation · Social robots

1 Introduction

The use of social robots to support mental health and well-being has been explored across domains. However, it is only in recent years that this topic has emerged as a clearly defined area in human-robot interaction (HRI) [1]. In response to this growing interest, several recent systematic reviews have analyzed existing studies on the subject [2–5]. These reviews suggest that most current research focuses on addressing severe emotional distress (e.g., depression or stress/anxiety disorders), primarily in therapeutic or clinical settings (e.g., mental healthcare facilities), or among vulnerable populations (e.g., children or older adults with/without dementia). In contrast, the idea that social robots could help manage everyday mood fluctuations—the subtle shifts in emotional state that many people experience as part of daily life—remains largely underexplored within the HRI community.

Human moods fluctuate, like the ever-changing weather—sometimes bright with happiness, other times clouded by sadness. Moods are low-intensity, diffuse feeling states that typically persist for hours [6]. They are always present, gradually evolving, and often operating below conscious awareness [7]. Despite their subtle nature, moods directly influence subjective well-being. When people experience a positive mood, they tend to evaluate their overall life as more satisfying and fulfilling, and they are more likely to recall positive life events compared to when they are experiencing a negative mood [8]. Furthermore, moods can significantly impact overall health. Persistent negative moods can contribute to mental health problems such as affective disorders [9] and increase the risk of physical health issues like heart disease [10]. Additionally, moods influence daily functioning and performance by affecting individuals' perceptions, judgments, and decision-making [11]. Given these profound effects mood has on individuals, effective mood regulation becomes essential in daily life [12,13].

Looking toward a future where social robots become part of people's personal lives as close companions, they hold promise for supporting everyday mood regulation. These robots could encourage people to open up and express their feelings through empathetic, non-judgmental communication [14]. They might also offer personalized, context-aware suggestions to promote self-care practices [15]. Compared to disembodied agents like chatbots, social robots can leverage additional communication channels, including proxemics [16], oculesics [17], and physical contact [18]. Utilizing these channels can enhance emotional exchanges and make interactions with robots feel more comforting [19], engaging [20], and helpful [21]. Additionally, the heightened social presence of robots can facilitate rapport building, providing not only immediate but also sustained company and support [22].

Recent research in HRI has begun exploring the use of social robots for everyday mood regulation. For instance, Jeong et al. [23] designed a social robot intervention for college students living in dormitories, where the robot helped with everyday tasks and engaged students through casual conversation. Their results indicated that interactions with the robot positively influenced students' overall moods. Similarly, Laban et al. [24] investigated the effects of self-disclosure to a social robot on caregivers, a group often experiencing distress. Their study found that participants who shared their thoughts and feelings with the robot reported improved moods and perceived the robot as increasingly comforting over time. Despite these promising findings, integrating social robots into daily life can raise significant concerns. Studies have identified such user concerns in various contexts. For instance, in early childhood education, teachers worry about their limited knowledge about robots, safety risks, and potential distractions for children [25]. Similarly, implementing social robots for people with dementia faces challenges such as their unfamiliarity with technology, fear of robots, and privacy issues [26]. This suggests that while social robots have the potential to support everyday mood regulation, they may also introduce major problems that hinder user acceptance and robot employment. However, existing research on social robots for mood regulation has only briefly touched upon these user concerns (e.g., [27]). Given the rapid advancements in social robotics, especially with large language models enabling more sophisticated social interactions, understanding users' concerns is just as crucial, if not more so, than exploring their benefits.

Hence, this study aims to address a key research question: *What concerns do users have about integrating social robots into their daily lives for mood regulation, particularly for managing everyday subtle mood fluctuations?* To achieve this aim, we conducted an exploratory case study investigating prospective users' attitudes and opinions on using a social robot to manage the "Sunday Blues"—a common negative mood state experienced during the transition from the weekend to the workweek. Insights from this case study provide a foundation for understanding end-user expectations and concerns, offering design recommendations for future applications of social robots in mood regulation.

2 Method

2.1 The Case Study

We selected the Sunday Blues as the focus of our case study—a mood characterized by anxiety, sadness, or regret as the weekend concludes and the new workweek approaches [28]. Its typical causes include the loss of leisure time, unmet weekend expectations, and anticipation of upcoming workloads and challenges [29]. A recent survey suggests this mood issue is widespread among employees, with 80% of respondents reporting frequent experiences of it [30]. Given its prevalence and impact on employees' mental health and well-being [31,32], the Sunday Blues has gained significant attention in popular culture, with numerous blogs and podcasts addressing the topic and suggesting coping strategies (e.g., [33,34]). Despite this, the phenomenon remains largely unexplored in academic research, including within the HRI research community, highlighting an opportunity to explore potential solutions based on social robots. Leveraging the Sunday Blues as a relatable context, we designed a robot aimed at helping individuals manage or alleviate this negative mood.

To illustrate the robot's functionality, we developed a video prototype depicting key interactions between users and the robot. We chose *video prototyping* to elicit feedback on a concept that is not yet technically feasible in the form envisioned. This method allowed participants to immerse themselves in a realistic scenario and reflect on how the robot might fit into their own routines. Video-based scenarios are a common method in early-stage HRI research (e.g., [35–37]), particularly when exploring emotionally sensitive topics or future-use contexts, as they avoid the ethical and practical constraints of live deployment while still enabling rich user engagement [38,39].

To facilitate discussions with potential users, we employed the method of *co-constructing stories*, engaging participants in direct dialogue to envision and articulate their thoughts about a novel design based on personal lived experiences [40]. This method has proven helpful in eliciting in-depth user feedback and suggestions in various design contexts (e.g., [41–43]). It is important to emphasize that the purpose of this study was not to evaluate a functional product, but to open up a design-led inquiry into the emerging space of social robots for everyday mood regulation. By presenting a speculative concept, we sought to provoke reflection and facilitate meaningful discussion with prospective users. Through these conversations, we explored how participants imagine living with a mood-regulating social robot, what expectations, hopes, and concerns this raises, and what these reflections teach us about the broader challenges of designing emotionally supportive technologies for everyday life.

In the following sections, we describe our design and video prototyping process, participant recruitment, co-constructing stories sessions, and data analysis.

2.2 Design and Video Prototyping

Design Concept. We conceptualized *Mora* (short for "Mood Regulation Assistant"), a social robot designed to function both as an everyday companion and as a personal assistant within home environments. Mora's primary goal is to monitor users' mood fluctuations and provide timely emotional support. One key focus of Mora is helping users cope with the Sunday Blues during the transitional period from the weekend to the weekdays. Specifically, once detecting signs of anxiety, sadness, or unease emerging on Sunday evenings or nights, Mora approaches users and offers conversation-based interventions to alleviate their negative feelings. This concept is inspired by recent HRI research, which highlights the mood-regulatory benefits of sharing thoughts and feelings with a social robot (e.g., [24, 44, 45]). Mora's intervention approach incorporates the following three evidence-based psychological strategies for mood regulation.

The first strategy is *venting* [46]. To interrupt and prevent a potential emotional spiral, Mora initiates conversations and encourages users to openly express their feelings. Throughout these interactions, Mora actively acknowledges and validates users' thoughts and feelings, creating a safe and supportive conversational environment that facilitates emotional relief.

Positive Thinking is another strategy [47]. Users experiencing the Sunday Blues often dwell on frustrations or disappointments from the weekend. Mora addresses this by encouraging users to reflect on their positive weekend experiences, highlighting enjoyable moments or personal achievements to foster feelings of gratitude and contentment. Additionally, Mora nudges users to plan relaxing or entertainment activities for the upcoming weekdays, guiding them to anticipate these pleasurable experiences, thus easing their transition into the workweek.

Finally, Mora integrates the strategy of *problem solving* [48]. Returning to work after a restful weekend can lead users to feel overwhelmed by upcoming tasks and responsibilities. Mora addresses this by guiding users to organize their thoughts, prioritize tasks, and formulate clear action plans, enabling them to approach the upcoming workweek with confidence, clarity, and reduced anxiety regarding workload and challenges.

Video Prototype. To develop the prototype for Mora, we utilized the *Misty II robot*, an open robotics platform for research and educational purposes [49]. We chose Misty II because it can be programmed to display various verbal and non-verbal behaviors aligned with Mora's intended functions. Moreover, its small size makes it well-suited for home use.

Following Markopoulos's guidelines for video prototyping [50], we filmed authentic user interactions with Mora within the intended context of use (i.e., Sunday evenings at home), allowing users to immerse themselves deeply in the envisioned experience. Additionally, drawing upon animation techniques [51], we designed and synchronized Mora's facial expressions and body movements with its speech to ensure users understand Mora's emotions and motives, facilitating a more intuitive user-robot interaction.

The resulting video introduces Mora and presents two scenarios demonstrating how Mora helps a user to manage the Sunday Blues. In Scenario 1, Mora detects the user's low mood on Sunday evening and initiates a supportive conversation. After discovering the user's disappointment over an unproductive weekend, Mora comforts them by highlighting rest as an essential aspect of productivity. To further reduce the user's negative thinking, Mora suggests preparing their bag for the following day, fostering a sense of preparedness. Similarly, in Scenario 2, Mora proactively engages with the user during a period of anxiety related to upcoming heavy workload. Mora assists with identifying and organizing stressors, planning a manageable task for Monday morning, and scheduling a rewarding self-care activity during the day. To conclude, Mora plays a relaxing playlist to help the user unwind and ease into sleep. Figure 1 presents several snapshots and dialogue snippets of these scenarios, and the full video can be accessed through the provided link (https://vimeo.com/1063895899/31a69169f0).

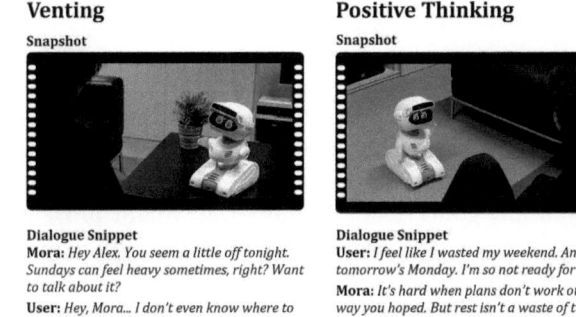

Fig. 1. Snapshots and dialogue snippets of the video prototype instantiating three mood regulation strategies.

2.3 Participants

Fifteen participants (aged 24-34; 7 female, 8 male), predominantly researchers from higher education and technology sectors, were recruited through convenience sampling. All participants were employed, typically started their workweek on Monday, and frequently experienced or had previously experienced the Sunday Blues. The sample size was determined following guidance from Hennink and Kaiser [52], who suggest that 9 to 17 interviews are generally sufficient to reach data saturation. Each participant received a five-euro voucher as compensation, and the study was approved by the Human Research Ethics Committee at the Delft University of Technology (reference number 5088).

2.4 Co-constructing Stories

Based on Buskermolen and Terken's framework [40], each co-constructing stories session was structured into two phases: (1) *sensitization*, aimed at eliciting participants' past experiences, and (2) *envisioning*, which encouraged participants to relate these experiences to the design concept and envision future contexts of use.

In the sensitization phase, participants were first asked to describe their typical weekend routines and how they usually felt on Sunday nights. They then watched a short sensitizing video (available at https://vimeo.com/1064033409/d19fe0b5e2), which depicted a scenario of someone experiencing the Sunday Blues. To ensure a consistent narrative across phases, this video featured the same character and home environment as the subsequent Mora video prototype. After watching the sensitizing video, participants reflected on their personal experiences related to the scenario. They shared their own encounters with the Sunday Blues and discussed strategies they had developed to manage these feelings.

The envisioning phase started with participants watching the Mora video prototype, which presented a fictional story about how a social robot assisted a user in dealing with the Sunday Blues. After viewing, participants shared their overall impressions of the design concept, pointing out what they liked or disliked in the story. Next, they were asked to imagine themselves as the main character in the video. They described how they would respond in a similar situation, what actions they would take, and any concerns or barriers that might prevent them from using Mora as a coping tool. Finally, participants connected their earlier shared experiences with the Sunday Blues to the design concept, offering suggestions for how it could be improved or adapted to better fit their personal contexts and needs.

Each co-constructing stories session lasted approximately 30 min, with all discussions audio-recorded for subsequent analysis.

2.5 Data Analysis

All audio recordings were transcribed, and thematic analysis was conducted based on Braun and Clarke's framework [53]. The process involved six steps:

(1) familiarization with the data, (2) coding, (3) generating initial themes, (4) reviewing and developing themes, (5) refining themes, and (6) reporting the results. To ensure reliability, two researchers collaborated throughout the process [54]. Familiarization occurred naturally during transcription, so the first author began by independently coding all transcripts and generating initial themes, which produced a preliminary codebook. The second author then independently applied this codebook to the transcripts, critically evaluating the existing codes and themes while suggesting modifications and/or additions. Next, the two researchers discussed discrepancies and refined the categories until they reached a consensus, resulting in a more accurate and comprehensive set of codes and themes. Finally, this refined collection was reviewed and finalized by all authors when reporting the results. Our final coding scheme included 3 themes and 20 codes, presented in Tables 1, 2, and 3, and further elaborated in the results section.

3 Results

3.1 User Concerns Regarding the Social Robot

Participants expressed five key concerns regarding Mora as a social robot, specifically focusing on its capabilities and attributes required in the context of mood regulation (Table 1).

Limited Humanness in Conversation. Participants found conversations with Mora unnatural compared to human interactions. They noted that those conversations felt rigid, following a predetermined structure. Additionally, they perceived Mora's communication style as "sterile" and suggested that Mora should exhibit a more distinctive personality, express more emotions, and occasionally incorporate humor to create a more authentic conversational experience.

Lack of Genuine Empathy. Participants acknowledged that Mora's responses felt supportive and empathetic. They even pointed out that such expressed empathy could be greater than that of humans in certain cases, especially given recent advancements in artificial intelligence. However, deep down inside, participants believed that Mora could not genuinely empathize with them or truly understand their thoughts and feelings, as the robot lacks lived experiences and personal situations similar to their own.

Limited Social Sensitivity. Participants raised concerns about Mora's level of social sensitivity, i.e., its ability to accurately interpret and appropriately respond to users' social cues and context. They stressed that Mora should be highly sensitive in recognizing when a conversation is unwanted or inappropriate. For instance, Mora should disengage when a user shows little interest, or refrain from initiating a conversation if a user is already occupied, even though early signs of the Sunday Blues are detected.

Lack of Genuine Rapport with Users. Participants expressed doubts about Mora's ability to develop a genuine rapport with users. They were particularly skeptical about whether Mora could intuitively determine when a user desires company or conversation versus when they prefer solitude to process their thoughts and emotions. One participant emphasized this by describing the complex and subtle nature of human rapport: a close friend realizes when to step back and leave someone alone, but also knows precisely when to reapproach to provide comfort and support, even if it temporarily overrides personal autonomy.

Potential Replaceability. Some participants questioned the unique value of a social robot like Mora for conversation-based interventions. One participant specifically mentioned that an embodied conversational agent integrated into a smartwatch could be equally effective. Another participant, who regularly practices gratitude journaling via a mobile application, felt Mora's functions were already met by existing tools, making the presence of a physical robot potentially unnecessary.

3.2 User Concerns Regarding Intervention Effectiveness

Participants expressed ten main concerns regarding Mora's effectiveness, highlighting various factors that could impact how it functions in real-life situations (Table 2).

Intangibility of Mood Participants questioned Mora's ability to accurately detect the Sunday Blues, as it is a subtle and intangible feeling state that may not manifest through obvious facial or bodily expressions. They also noted that individuals may experience a mix of moods on Sunday night, such as the joy of the weekend alongside anxiety about the upcoming week, making the detection of the Sunday Blues even more challenging.

Unresolvable Causes of Mood Participants mentioned that the Sunday Blues could stem from multiple causes, some of which might be difficult or even impossible to resolve. For example, one participant felt that a heavy workload in the upcoming week was sometimes inevitable, while another believed that the unfavorable social relationships at work contributing to their Sunday Blues could not be effectively addressed.

Machine Communication Reluctance. Several participants expressed a general reluctance to communicate with Mora, perceiving it as a "machine" that lacks genuine care and understanding. They felt that conversations with such a "fabricated" entity would induce feelings of awkwardness and discomfort. Additionally, unlike human interactions, where social norms create an obligation to respond, participants perceived communication with Mora as entirely optional, further discouraging engagement.

Table 1. User concerns regarding the social robot.

Code	Example participant quote
Limited humanness in conversation	"It's now a one-way kind of interaction. Like, Mora is asking me questions. I'm replying to Mora. It's asking me questions again. I think there needs to be more of a dialogue that happens as well as a dialogue with some personality." (P11)
Lack of genuine empathy	"It's not a real person or real living who can really accompany you, really understand you, because it couldn't experience all the things you're doing." (P10)
Limited social sensitivity	"If you're having a conversation with friends on the phone, or if you're in this important part of your Netflix series or your book, then I would actually be a bit annoyed. So, it would need to know when to talk to you and when not ... so, when you can be interrupted and when not, I guess." (P4)
Lack of genuine rapport with users	"I think the robot should sense in some way that, 'Okay, now, enough of venting, I can just leave her some time.' So, I think that transition needs to happen ... that we talk, and once I know I'm now good and grounded, then I also need to be by myself for some time. I think it would be very similar to talking to a friend." (P8)
Potential replaceability	"I don't see that much value that it's being physical now. I could still imagine, for instance, your watch saying, 'Hey, you're stressed, why don't you want to have this call with whatever?' And then a kind of avatar or something else could do the same." (P4)

Social Withdrawal Tendency. Participants reported that experiencing Sunday Blues often led to a tendency to withdraw from or reduce engagement in social interactions. They explained that when they were not feeling well, explaining their feelings to others could feel rather taxing and exhausting. Additionally, they expressed a need for solitude during these moments, preferring to process and reflect on their negative thoughts and feelings privately.

Environmental Intricacies. Participants pointed out the complexities of their home environments, where the presence of roommates, family members, or pets could influence their interactions with Mora. For instance, one participant anticipated providing inauthentic responses to Mora when a roommate was nearby to maintain privacy. Another participant envisioned that their child might interfere in the conversation, making it difficult to stay engaged.

Dependence on Human-Robot Bonds. Participants believed that the depth of their conversations with Mora would largely depend on the relationship they developed with it. They explained that they would only feel comfortable sharing their negative emotions and vulnerabilities if they knew that Mora understood them and their context well. Participants emphasized that building this closer, friendship-like bond with Mora would require a prolonged period of acclimatization and consistently satisfying interactions.

Potential Counterproductive Effects. Participants expressed concerns that Mora might unintentionally worsen the Sunday Blues. They explained that individuals are not always conscious of their negative feelings or the underlying reasons. In such cases, Mora's intervention could inadvertently draw attention to their negativity, as well as Monday's approach, potentially intensifying their distress. Additionally, participants worried that Mora's suggestions might be too generic to address their complex personal situations involving life, work, and relationships. If the advice felt repetitive or similar to what they had heard many times before, it could lead to frustration or dissatisfaction rather than relief.

Potential Loss of Interest. Participants expressed concerns about sustaining long-term engagement with Mora. They felt that after some weeks, the conversations might become repetitive, leading to boredom and a decline in motivation to continue using Mora.

Real-Time Intervention Versus Prevention. Participants noted that Mora's in-the-moment intervention on Sunday evening or night might be ineffective due to time constraints. For instance, users may not have sufficient time to engage in a suggested mood-regulation activity late at night. Instead, several participants proposed a preventive approach, where Mora could provide support throughout the whole weekend by actively checking in on their feelings and influencing their plans and activities. By ensuring a fulfilling and enjoyable weekend, Mora could help foster a lasting sense of contentment that extends into Sunday night, potentially reducing the intensity of the Sunday Blues.

Long-Term Mood Resilience. Some participants noted that while Mora provided comfort and relief, the effects felt temporary. Instead, they emphasized the importance of fostering self-regulation, hoping interactions with Mora would encourage self-reflection and help them recognize effective mood regulation strategies. Ideally, they aimed to develop independent coping mechanisms to manage the Sunday Blues without relying on Mora.

3.3 User Concerns Regarding Ethics

Participants raised five ethical concerns regarding using Mora for mood regulation in home environments (Table 3).

Violation of Privacy. Participants expressed concerns about Mora's constant monitoring and analysis of their mood states, feeling a sense of surveillance in their own homes. They also worried about data security and privacy, fearing that unauthorized individuals might gain access to their personal lives through Mora's data, which could include sensitive information about their work, relationships, and other private details.

Deprivation of Autonomy. Participants felt a potential loss of control over their own emotional states due to Mora's constant mood detection and active intervention. They were also concerned that Mora's frequent suggestions might limit their own reflection and decision making. They described Mora's approach as "paternalistic," feeling it repeatedly directed their thoughts and actions, without fully respecting their ability to take responsibility for themselves.

Overemphasis on Positivity. Many participants felt that the Sunday Blues was not a severe mood issue, regarding it as a normal part of their weekly rhythms. They expressed concerns that Mora and its approach might place too much emphasis on positivity, potentially leading users to perceive the Sunday Blues as a more serious problem than they previously had. This, in turn, could overshadow the value of accepting negative feelings as a natural part of the human experience.

Risk of Technology Attachment. While some participants acknowledged the promising potential of Mora, they also expressed concerns about becoming emotionally attached to it. They envisioned that as Mora became more familiar with their preferences or behaviors, they might feel increasingly inclined to interact with it and rely on its suggestions or interventions. This potential attachment to technology made them feel uneasy and even dreaded.

Risk of Undermining Human Relationships. Participants worried that relying on Mora for mood regulation could undermine their relationships with

Table 2. User concerns regarding intervention effectiveness.

Code	Example participant quote
Intangibility of mood	"I think if someone is in a not good mood, they might not have very clear facial expressions, or they just want to lie down on the sofa ... with no bodily language. And if Mora incorrectly detects this and classifies this as the Sunday Blues, then I think the user probably feels kind of annoyed." (P8)
Unresolvable causes of mood	"[What] if I don't want to see a colleague in the office? Actually, this is not about work itself, it's about the relationship in the office." (P14)
Machine communication reluctance	"I always wonder in real situations, would you have those kinds of conversations with the machine while you're cognitively knowing this is a machine?" (P3)
Social withdrawal tendency	"Sometimes if you are in the Sunday Blues ... you probably just want to lock your mind and want to self-digest your negative mood. So, in that case, the user probably will gonna refuse to continue the chat with Mora." (P13)
Environmental intricacies	"For example, you're living with someone else. You also don't want to share your thoughts or problems with that person. So, if Mora is there and comes to ask you, you may just give them some wrong answers." (P5)
Dependence on human-robot bonds	"You would still not, like, start talking about your feelings immediately unless you already had that kind of relationship." (P11)
Potential counterproductive effects	"Sometimes even though I feel my weekend is wasted, or I feel very reluctant to start my new week ... it's not that obvious. If somebody just mentioned to me, 'You look like depressed,' then it reminds me, 'Okay, tomorrow is Monday,' and probably it's like reinforcing the bad mood." (P2)
Potential loss of interest	"In the first weeks, you might think it's a good conversation. But after a few weeks, you [might] realize why there is always a fixed routine, and I can imagine what you are gonna say next. Right? So, I might feel a bit bored." (P6)
Real-time intervention versus prevention	"I'm thinking that Mora probably can do one step ahead. Like, instead of fixing it after the problem happened, they can prevent this even before this happened. ... Like, on Sunday, [Mora] can just give users some advice, saying, 'Hey, it seems you didn't do much today, or it seems you are not going out or not having fun today, I suggest you can have some activities or have some fun, since this is the last day of the weekend.' (P13)
Long-term mood resilience	"I think a more sustainable way is that the users can learn those strategies, and they can adopt them when they feel depressed during weekends. ... I want to have some technology [that] can help me reflect and can help me do better for the next time after all of this." (P2)

loved ones. They emphasized that there is a positive side of experiencing negative feelings—it creates opportunities to seek social support and strengthen connections with others. If Mora consistently helped manage their moods, they feared it might reduce their motivation to engage with friends and family.

Table 3. User concerns regarding ethics.

Code	Example participant quote
Violation of privacy	"It's keeping track of your emotional state ... I would be wary of it, with regards to privacy." (P7)
Deprivation of autonomy	"When it started giving kind of proper tasks, like, 'You could do this or this.' I think in that case I would maybe feel like losing autonomy in a way, like, Mora is starting to make the decision for you." (P7)
Overemphasis on positivity	"This kind of always being positive could be annoying ... so, it's like, sometimes when you take this role of being the positive one, then you don't give the other person space to be negative." (P10)
Risk of technology attachment	"It feels it would learn [about me] over time ... probably after a while, I could get attached to that, because I'm more curious about it. I don't know if I would actually want that, because then I would be scared to get too attached." (P10)
Risk of undermining human relationships	"I would be worried that it would work a little bit, and therefore my need to share my feelings with a friend or with my partner would go down. Therefore, I wouldn't do that. ... So, I feel like, when you're not feeling well, it's kind of an opportunity to share that with other people. And it could be a shame if you don't do it." (P10)

4 Discussion

4.1 Implications for Designing Social Robots for Mood Regulation

In this section, we discuss the implications of our findings for designing social robots to support everyday mood regulation. We highlight four design considerations (DC1 to DC4) translated from the study results that HRI practitioners could consider to promote user acceptance and mood intervention effectiveness.

DC1 – Design Robots with Honest Identities. Our findings show that participants were clearly aware of the robot's artificial essence. Although they generally appreciated the social interactions, they still recognized robots as machines lacking genuine understanding and empathy. This aligns with Alač's argument that while people may engage with robots *as if* they were sentient beings, they ultimately perceive them as material objects [55]. This insight leads to an important design takeaway: robots should be designed with *honest identities*. Designers should avoid overstating robots' emotional capabilities—for example, by claiming that robots truly "understand" or "feel" emotions—as this may lead to user disappointment or distrust. Even though recent advances in large language models have enabled robots to simulate human conversation with remarkable fluency, it is equally important that the interaction remains consistent with the robot's inherent machine identity to ensure an authentic user experience.

DC2 – Prioritize Social Bonding. Our findings suggest that despite participants' awareness of robots' inherent machineness, they remained open to forming relationships with robots, implying that establishing a bond is critical for them to feel comfortable opening up about personal mood-related issues. This indicates that, for everyday mood regulation, it is not sufficient for robots to merely deliver professional advice (like a coach); they should also serve as meaningful *social companions*. Without this social bond, users may hesitate to disclose deeper feelings, view robots as easily replaceable, or quickly lose interest. We, therefore, encourage designers of mood-regulating robots to actively integrate relationship-building strategies, such as creating engaging shared activities [56], enabling robots to maintain persistent memories over time [57], or considering the matching between human and robot personalities [58].

DC3 – Be Mindful of Social Norm Violations. Our findings indicate that social robot interventions designed for mood regulation were perceived as prone to making social errors. These may include intervening at inappropriate times, incorrectly recognizing user mood states, or intruding on users' personal spaces. Such errors can significantly undermine users' perceptions of the robot's social-affective competence, reduce user willingness to accept interventions, and even provoke social conflict [59]. These challenges highlight the importance of designing social robots to be sensitive to both explicit and implicit social norms. This sensitivity may involve enabling robots to proactively solicit users' willingness to interact, while also accurately interpreting unspoken social signals—such as facial expressions or bodily gestures [60,61]—to assess users' openness to interaction and thus avoid unintended intrusions.

DC4 – Set Intervention Boundaries. Our findings underscore several ethical challenges. Participants frequently expressed concerns about privacy and loss of control. Some also warned that interacting with robots could distance them from real human relationships—a concern previously raised in HRI research [62]. These challenges must be addressed with care. First, mood-related data collection should be under user control, and robots must clearly communicate what data is being collected and how it is stored [27]. Second, robots should encourage users to maintain connections with the real world. While designing social robots to support human well-being is a valuable goal, it is equally important to establish clear boundaries for intervention and avoid fostering overdependence.

4.2 Implications for Designing for Mood Regulation

Beyond informing the design of social robots, our findings contribute to the broader discourse on designing emotionally supportive technologies within the human-computer interaction (HCI) community [63–65]. We outline four key design considerations (DC5 to DC8) that apply both specifically to social robots and more generally to technologies aimed at supporting mood regulation.

DC5 – Balance Mood Regulation and Other Fundamental Needs. Our findings reveal that while interventions may effectively support mood regulation, they may also inadvertently undermine users' other fundamental needs such as privacy, autonomy, socialization, and personal development, as observed in our case study. To mitigate this risk, we recommend that HCI practitioners proactively investigate and understand these core needs during the early design phase and thoughtfully integrate these considerations into the design process to ensure both intervention effectiveness and user experience.

DC6 – Tailor Strategies to Mood's Multifaceted Causes. Our findings reveal that a single mood-regulation intervention may not effectively address all the underlying causes of a negative mood, especially when these causes stem from broader, more complex problems. To enhance effectiveness, we recommend that HCI practitioners adopt a holistic approach incorporating diverse strategies tailored to different types of stressors. For example, an intervention could facilitate avoidance or suggest direct resolution for identifiable and manageable stressors, while offering relief or distractions for stressors that cannot be easily resolved.

DC7 – Combine Preventive and Intervening Approaches. Our findings suggest that real-time interventions may be ineffective for mood regulation due to time and contextual constraints on Sunday evenings or nights. To address this, we found the preventive approach proposed by our participants particularly insightful, where interventions proactively reduce the likelihood of negative moods arising rather than only responding once they occur. We recommend integrating both preventive and intervening strategies: prevention to minimize stressors in advance, and intervention to address or mitigate them when they still arise. This combined approach better aligns with the elusive and long-lasting nature of human mood, ultimately enhancing the effectiveness of mood-regulation interventions.

DC8 – Respect the Acceptance of Negative Moods. Our findings indicate that individuals may perceive the Sunday Blues as a normal part of their weekly experience rather than a problem requiring intervention. In such cases, introducing a mood-regulation solution could inadvertently increase awareness of the issue, potentially reframing it as more serious than previously perceived. This shift might lead users to replace their existing, comfortable ways of coping with a new approach focusing on pursuing positivity at all costs. Over time, this could disrupt their natural mood equilibrium, hindering their ability to accept and navigate negative moods in the long term. Hence, we suggest HCI practitioners exercise caution when offering mood-regulation interventions, ensuring they do not overshadow the value of accepting negative feelings as a part of the human experience.

4.3 Limitations of This Study

Our exploratory study has several limitations. First, our participants were drawn from a local research community, with most having backgrounds in design and HCI. Their familiarity with emerging technologies may have influenced how they perceived and evaluated Mora. For example, prior HRI studies have shown that individuals with more experience with robots tend to hold less negative attitudes toward them (e.g., [66]). Future studies should aim to include more experientially diverse populations to capture a broader range of perspectives. Second, participants only viewed a video prototype rather than interacting with a real robot. While the video-based co-constructing story method can be useful for eliciting rich reflections, it may fall short in stimulating the more complex affective responses (e.g., caring and bonding [67]) that are associated with physical embodied interactions. Future studies should explore interactions with functional robot prototypes in naturalistic settings to uncover more diverse and ecologically valid user experiences and concerns. Third, our findings are purely qualitative. While we gained a broad overview of user concerns, we did not collect quantitative data to test specific hypotheses. We encourage future HRI research to build on our findings by examining potential statistical relationships between user concern factors, which could help clarify the underlying psychological mechanisms involved in social robots for mood regulation.

5 Conclusion

This article presents a study that explores user concerns regarding social robots designed for mood regulation, specifically focusing on alleviating the "Sunday Blues." The findings reveal that users expect these robots to possess specific attributes, such as empathy and social sensitivity. Participants also expressed concerns about factors that could affect the effectiveness of robot-based interventions, including reluctance in machine communication and potential counterproductive effects. Additionally, users emphasized ethical considerations regarding the integration of social robots into daily life. Based on these insights, we derive eight design considerations to guide researchers and practitioners in the HRI and HCI communities in developing more effective and ethically sound mood regulation interventions. While the study is limited by its use of video prototyping, it contributes valuable, user-centered empirical knowledge to inform future design practices in social robots for mood regulation, and it opens up opportunities for further exploration of high-fidelity robotic prototypes in real-world settings.

Acknowledgments. This study was funded by the China Scholarship Council (CSC), grant number 202106130007, and the MaGW VICI, grant number 453-16-009, of the Netherlands Organization for Scientific Research (NWO), awarded to Pieter M. A. Desmet.

Disclosure of Interests. The authors have no competing interests to declare that are relevant to the content of this article.

References

1. Laban, G., Morrison, V., Cross, E.S.: Social robots for health psychology: A new frontier for improving human health and well-being. Eur. Health Psychol. **23**(1), 1095–1102 (2024). https://www.ehps.net/ehp/index.php/contents/article/view/3442
2. Scoglio, A.A., Reilly, E.D., Gorman, J.A., Drebing, C.E.: Use of social robots in mental health and well-being research: systematic review. J. Med. Internet Res. **21**(7), e13322 (2019). https://doi.org/10.2196/13322
3. Robinson, N.L., Cottier, T.V., Kavanagh, D.J.: Psychosocial health interventions by social robots: systematic review of randomized controlled trials. J. Med. Internet Res. **21**(5), e13203 (2019). https://doi.org/10.2196/13203
4. Nichol, B., et al.: Exploring the impact of socially assistive robots on health and wellbeing across the lifespan: an umbrella review and meta-analysis. Int. J. Nursing Stud. **153**, 104730 (2024). https://doi.org/10.1016/j.ijnurstu.2024.104730
5. Ghafurian, M., Chandra, S., Hutchinson, R., Lim, A., Baliyan, I., Rhim, J., Gupta, G., Aroyo, A.M., Rasouli, S., Dautenhahn, K.: Systematic review of social robots for health and wellbeing: a personal healthcare journey lens. ACM Trans. Human-Rob. Interaction **14**(1), 1–48 (2025). https://doi.org/10.1145/3700446
6. Morris, W.N.: Mood: The frame of mind. Springer, New York (1989)
7. Watson, D., Clark, L.A.: Emotions, moods, traits, and temperaments: Conceptual distinctions and empirical findings. In: Ekman, P.E., Davidson, R.J. (eds.) The Nature of Emotion: Fundamental Questions, pp. 89–93. Oxford University Press, New York (1994)
8. Morris, W.N.: A functional analysis of the role of mood in affective systems. In: Clark, M.S. (ed.) Emotion (The Review of Personality and Social Psychology), pp. 256–293. SAGE Publications, Thousand Oaks (1992)

9. Peeters, F., Berkhof, J., Delespaul, P., Rottenberg, J., Nicolson, N.A.: Diurnal mood variation in major depressive disorder. Emotion **6**(3), 383–391 (2006). https://doi.org/10.1037/1528-3542.6.3.383
10. Cohen, B.E., Edmondson, D., Kronish, I.M.: State of the art review: Depression, stress, anxiety, and cardiovascular disease. American J. Hyper. **28**, 1295–1302 (2015). https://doi.org/10.1093/ajh/hpv047
11. Forgas, J.P.: Mood and judgment: the affect infusion model (AIM). Psychol. Bull. **117**(1), 39–66 (1995). https://doi.org/10.1037/0033-2909.117.1.39
12. Larsen, R.J.: Toward a science of mood regulation. Psychol. Inq. **11**(3), 129–141 (2000). https://doi.org/10.1207/S15327965PLI1103_01
13. Parkinson, B., Totterdell, P., Briner, R.B., Reynolds, S.: Changing Moods: The Psychology of Mood and Mood Regulation. Longman, Detroit (1996)
14. Laban, G., Kappas, A., Morrison, V., Cross, E.S.: Building long-term human–robot relationships: Examining disclosure, perception and well-being across time. Int. J. Soc. Rob. **16**(5), 1–27 (2024). https://doi.org/10.1007/s12369-023-01076-z
15. Arango, J.A.R., Marco-Detchart, C., Inglada, V.J.J.: Personalized cognitive support via social robots. Sensors **25**(3), 888 (2025). https://doi.org/10.3390/s25030888
16. Takayama, L., Pantofaru, C.: Influences on proxemic behaviors in human-robot interaction. In: Proceedings of the IEEE/RSJ International Conference on Intelligent Robots and Systems, pp. 5495–5502. IEEE (2009)
17. Mutlu, B., Kanda, T., Forlizzi, J., Hodgins, J., Ishiguro, H.: Conversational gaze mechanisms for humanlike robots. ACM Trans. Inter. Intell. Syst. (TiiS) **1**, 1–33 (2012). https://doi.org/10.1145/2070719.2070725
18. Willemse, C.J., Van Erp, J.B.: Social touch in human–robot interaction: Robot-initiated touches can induce positive responses without extensive prior bonding. Int. J. Soc. Rob. **11**, 285–304 (2019https://doi.org/10.1007/s12369-018-0500-9
19. Bates, D.P., Dudek, S.Y., Berzuk, J.M., González, A.L., Young, J.E.: SnuggleBot the companion: exploring in-home robot interaction strategies to support coping with loneliness. In: Proceedings of the 2024 ACM Designing Interactive Systems Conference, pp. 2972–2986 (2024)
20. Kidd, C.D., Breazeal, C.: Effect of a robot on user perceptions. In: Proceedings of the 2014 IEEE/RSJ International Conference on Intelligent Robots and Systems (IROS), pp. 3559–3564. IEEE (2004)
21. Fasola, J., Matarić, M.J.: A socially assistive robot exercise coach for the elderly. J. Human-Rob. Inter. **2**, 3–32 (2013). https://doi.org/10.5898/JHRI.2.2.Fasola
22. Deng, E., Mutlu, B., Mataric, M.J., others: Embodiment in socially interactive robots. Found. Trends® Rob. **7**, 251–356 (2019). https://doi.org/10.1561/2300000056
23. Jeong, S., et al.: A robotic positive psychology coach to improve college students wellbeing. In: Proceedings of the 29th IEEE International Conference on Robot and Human Interactive Communication (RO-MAN), pp. 187–194. IEEE (2020)
24. Laban, G., Morrison, V., Kappas, A., Cross, E.S.: Coping with emotional distress via self-disclosure to robots: intervention with caregivers (2023). https://doi.org/10.31234/osf.io/gbk2j
25. Neumann, M.M., Calteaux, I., Reilly, D., Neumann, D.L.: Exploring teachers' perspectives on the benefits and barriers of using social robots in early childhood education. Early Child Develop. Care **193**(13-14), 1503–1516 (2023). https://doi.org/10.1080/03004430.2023.2257000

26. Koh, W.Q., Felding, S.A., Budak, K.B., Toomey, E., Casey, D.: Barriers and facilitators to the implementation of social robots for older adults and people with dementia: a scoping review. BMC Geriatr. **21**(1), 351 (2021). https://doi.org/10.1186/s12877-021-02277-9
27. Axelsson, M., Spitale, M., Gunes, H.: Robots as mental well-being coaches: design and ethical recommendations. ACM Trans. Human-Rob. Inter. **13**(2), 1–55 (2024). https://doi.org/10.1145/3643457
28. Zuzanek, J.: Sunday Blues: have sunday time use and its emotional connotations changed over the past two decades? Time Soc. **23**(1), 6–27 (2014). https://doi.org/10.1177/0961463X12441173
29. Tufvesson, A.: Feeling blue. LSJ: Law Soc. J. **86**, 50—51 (2022). https://search.informit.org/doi/abs/10.3316/informit.20220321063973
30. Heitmann, B.: Your guide to winning @work: Decoding the Sunday Scaries. https://blog.linkedin.com/2018/september/28/your-guide-to-winning-work-decoding-the-sunday-scaries. Accessed 2025/03/28
31. Akay, A., Martinsson, P.: Sundays are blue: Aren't they? The day-of-the-week effect on subjective well-being and socio-economic status. IZA Discussion, 4563 (2009). https://doi.org/10.2139/ssrn.1506315
32. Mihalcea, R., Liu, H.: A corpus-based approach to finding happiness. In: Proceedings of the AAAI Spring Symposium: Computational Approaches to Analyzing Weblogs, pp. 139—144 (2006). https://digital.library.unt.edu/ark:/67531/metadc30980/
33. Headspace: How to beat the sunday night blues and the sunday scaries work anxiety. https://www.headspace.com/articles/sunday-anxiety. Accessed 2025/03/28
34. Calm: Sunday Scaries: 10 ways to settle Sunday evening anxiety. https://www.calm.com/blog/sunday-scaries. Accessed 2025/03/28
35. Albers, R., Dörrenbächer, J., Weigel, M., Ruiken, D., Weisswange, T., Goerick, C., Hassenzahl, M.: Meaningful telerobots in informal care: a conceptual design case. In: Proceedings of Nordic Human-Computer Interaction Conference (NordiCHI'22), pp. 1–11. ACM, New York (2022)
36. Syrdal, D.S., Koay, K.L., Gácsi, M., Walters, M.L., Dautenhahn, K.: Video prototyping of dog-inspired non-verbal affective communication for an appearance constrained robot. In: Proceedings of the 19th International Symposium in Robot and Human Interactive Communication (RO-MAN), pp. 632–637. IEEE (2010)
37. Xu, J., Zhang, C., Cuijpers, R.H., IJsselsteijn, W.A.: Affective and cognitive reactions to robot-initiated social control of health behaviors. In: Proceedings of the 2024 ACM/IEEE International Conference on Human-Robot Interaction (HRI'24), pp. 810–819. ACM, New York (2024)
38. Zamfirescu-Pereira, J., et al.: Fake it to make it: exploratory prototyping in HRI. In: Companion of the 2021 ACM/IEEE International Conference on Human-Robot Interaction (HRI'21 Companion), pp. 19–28. ACM, New York (2021)
39. Syrdal, D.S., Otero, N., Dautenhahn, K.: Video prototyping in human-robot interaction: results from a qualitative study. In: Proceedings of the 15th European Conference on Cognitive Ergonomics: The Ergonomics of Cool Interaction, pp. 1–8. ACM, New York (2008)
40. Buskermolen, D.Ö., Terken, J.: Co-constructing stories: a participatory design technique to elicit in-depth user feedback and suggestions about design concepts. In: Proceedings of the 12th Participatory Design Conference: Exploratory Papers, Workshop Descriptions, Industry Cases, pp. 33–36. ACM, New York (2012)

41. Christiansen, M.B., Rafsanjani, A., Jørgensen, J.: It brings the good vibes: exploring biomorphic aesthetics in the design of soft personal robots. Int. J. Soc. Robot. **16**(5), 835–855 (2024). https://doi.org/10.1007/s12369-023-01037-6
42. Xue, M., et al.: Co-constructing stories based on users lived experiences to investigate visualization design for collective stress management. In: Proceedings of the 2023 ACM Designing Interactive Systems Conference, pp. 652–663. ACM, New York (2023)
43. Davis, K., Feijs, L., Hu, J., Marcenaro, L., Regazzoni, C.: Improving awareness and social connectedness through the social hue: Insights and perspectives. In: Proceedings of the International Symposium on Interactive Technology and Ageing Populations, pp. 12–23. ACM, New York (2016)
44. Akiyoshi, T., Nakanishi, J., Ishiguro, H., Sumioka, H., Shiomi, M.: A robot that encourages self-disclosure to reduce anger mood. IEEE Rob. Autom. Lett. **6**(4), 7925–7932 (2021). https://doi.org/10.1109/LRA.2021.3102326
45. Duan, Y., Yoon, M., Liang, Z., Hoorn, J.F.: Self-disclosure to a robot: only for those who suffer the most. Robotics **10**(3), 98 (2021). https://doi.org/10.3390/robotics10030098
46. Zech, E., Rimé, B.: Is talking about an emotional experience helpful? Effects on emotional recovery and perceived benefits. Clin. Psychol. Psych. Int. J. Theor. Practice **12**(4), 270–287 (2005). https://doi.org/10.1002/cpp.460
47. Lightsey, O.R.: Thinking positive as a stress buffer: the role of positive automatic cognitions in depression and happiness. J. Couns. Psychol. **41**(3), 325 (1994). https://doi.org/10.1037/0022-0167.41.3.325
48. D'Zurilla, T.J., Nezu, A.M.: Problem-solving therapy. In: Dobson, K.S. (ed.) Handbook of Cognitive-Behavioral Therapies, pp. 197–225. The Guilford Press, New York (2010)
49. Misty Robotics. https://www.mistyrobotics.com/misty-ii. Accessed 2025/03/28
50. Markopoulos, P.: Using video for early interaction design. In: Collaboration in Creative Design: Methods and Tools, pp. 271–293. Springer (2016)
51. Schulz, T., Torresen, J., Herstad, J.: Animation techniques in human-robot interaction user studies: a systematic literature review. ACM Trans. Human-Rob. Inter. **8**(2), 1–22 (2019). https://doi.org/10.1145/3317325
52. Hennink, M., Kaiser, B.N.: Sample sizes for saturation in qualitative research: A systematic review of empirical tests. Soc. Sci. Med. **292**, 1–10 (2021). https://doi.org/10.1016/j.socscimed.2021.114523
53. Braun, V., Clarke, V.: Using thematic analysis in psychology. Qual. Res. Psychol. **3**(2), 77–101 (2006). https://doi.org/10.1191/1478088706qp063oa
54. Clarke, V., Braun, V.: Successful Qualitative Research: a Practical Guide for Beginners. SAGE Publications (2013)
55. Alač, M.: Social robots: Things or agents? AI Soc **31**, 519–535 (2016). https://doi.org/10.1007/s00146-015-0631-6
56. Gaggioli, A., Chirico, A., Lernia, D.D., Maggioni, M.A., Malighetti, C., Manzi, F., Marchetti, A., Massaro, D., Rea, F., Rossignoli, D., Sandini, G., Villani, D., Wiederhold, B.K., Riva, G., Sciutti, A.: Machines like us and people like you: toward human–robot shared experience. Cyberpsychol. Behav. Soc. Netw. **24**(5), 357–361 (2021). https://doi.org/10.1089/cyber.2021.29216.aga
57. Fox, J., Gambino, A.: Relationship development with humanoid social robots: Applying interpersonal theories to human–robot interaction. Cyberpsychol. Behavior Soc. Netw. **24**, 294–299 (2021). https://doi.org/10.1089/cyber.2020.0181

58. Lei, X., Liu, F.: How service robots facilitate user self-disclosure: The roles of personality, animacy, and automated social presence. Int. J. Human–Comput. Inter. **41**, 2135–2148 (2025). https://doi.org/10.1080/10447318.2024.2316368
59. Tian, L., Oviatt, S.: A taxonomy of social errors in human-robot interaction. ACM Trans. Human-Rob. Inter. (THRI) **10**, 1–32 (2021). https://doi.org/10.1145/3439720
60. Sartori, L., Becchio, C., Castiello, U.: Cues to intention: The role of movement information. Cognition **119**, 242–252 (2011). https://doi.org/10.1016/j.cognition.2011.01.014
61. Giuliani, M., Mirnig, N., Stollnberger, G., Stadler, S., Buchner, R., Tscheligi, M.: Systematic analysis of video data from different human–robot interaction studies: A categorization of social signals during error situations. Front. Psychol **6**, 931, (2015). https://doi.org/10.3389/fpsyg.2015.00931
62. Friedman, C.: Ethical concerns with replacing human relations with humanoid robots: an ubuntu perspective. AI Ethics **3**, 527–538 (2023). https://doi.org/10.1007/s43681-022-00186-0
63. Peng, Z., Lin, Q., Hu, J., Xue, H., Desmet, P.M.A.: Design considerations for mood-regulation interventions: Insights from a case study on the Sunday Blues. Proyecta56, Indus. Design J. **5**(1), 8–22 (2025). https://doi.org/10.24310/p56-idj.5.1.2025.21571
64. Peng, Z., Desmet, P.M.A., Xue, H.: Mood in experience design: a scoping review. She Ji: J. Design Econ. Innov. **9**(3), 330–378 (2023). https://doi.org/10.1016/j.sheji.2023.09.001
65. Desmet, P.M.A.: Design for mood: Twenty activity-based opportunities to design for mood regulation. Int. J. Design **9**(2), 1–19 (2015). http://www.ijdesign.org/index.php/IJDesign/article/view/2167/691
66. Rosén, J., Lindblom, J., Lamb, M., Billing, E.: Previous experience matters: an in-person investigation of expectations in human–robot interaction. Int. J. Soc. Robot. **16**(3), 447–460 (2024). https://doi.org/10.1007/s12369-024-01107-3
67. Xu, J., Zhang, C., Cuijpers, R. H., IJsselsteijn, W. A.: Does care lead to bonds? Exploring the relationship between human caregiving for robots and human-robot bonding. In Proceedings of the 2025 CHI Conference on Human Factors in Computing Systems, pp. 1–15. ACM, New York (2025)

Applications in Real-World Case Studies

Social Robot Assistive Intervention for Science Students to Prevent Laboratory Accidents

Mohammad Nehal Hasnine[1](✉) , Yuhuan Wang[1], Yuya Sato[1], Bipin Indurkhya[2] ,
and Mahmoud Mohamed Hussien Ahmed[3]

[1] Hosei University, Tokyo 184-8584, Japan
nehal.hasnine.79@hosei.ac.jp
[2] Jagiellonian University, 30-060 Kraków, Poland
[3] South Valley University, Qena 83523, Egypt

Abstract. In science laboratories, accidents happen due to human errors, including carelessness and negligence of laboratory guidelines by the students, resulting in personal injuries and damaged assets. The lab supervisor (hereafter, the teacher) sets certain laboratory protocols for the students to follow to ensure the safety of the laboratory's experimental conditions and avoid potential accidents. One of the first rules students need to follow daily is to wear appropriate personal protective equipment, such as aprons, goggles, and gloves, before conducting an experiment. However, it is time-consuming for the teacher to check them daily. Therefore, this process needs to be automated. To address this research issue, we proposed the Laboratory Safety Assistant (LSA) framework, a robot-assisted learning framework to detect students' behaviors that could lead to accidents and cause personal injuries during experiments. The LSA framework comprises Misty II Plus, a social robot as a social companion, a Behavior Detection and Analysis (BDA) server, and an intervention decision-making dashboard. We prepared a 'Lab Objects' dataset for this study containing 1288 images and 2295 objects grouped into 7 classes. We used this dataset to develop a new object detection model trained on a pre-trained YoloV8 model that could analyze image and video data captured by Misty II Plus. In addition, we developed an educational intervention for the teachers who lead science laboratories. Using this intervention, the teacher assesses students' in-lab behaviors, identify their areas of support, and guide them in addressing the areas of need.

Keywords: Social Robot · Robot-assisted Intervention · Educational Technology · Science Laboratory · Laboratory Accidents · Wellbeing in Laboratory · Social Robot as a Companion

1 Introduction

Science laboratories are where scientific research, teaching, engineering training, and experimental research occur [1]. Students and teachers often refer to them as science labs or simply labs. In recent years, science laboratories have become important in the university as new scientific and technological ideas are innovated and tested in various laboratory settings. The increasing number of science laboratories in universities also creates safety issues because students and teachers must handle many hazardous chemicals: If not handled properly, they cause potential safety risks and laboratory accidents.

Laboratory accidents are gaining more and more attention in higher education. According to the Occupational Safety and Health Administration (OSHA) report, about 10,000 laboratory accidents were reported in science laboratories in 2005 [2]. The report also suggests that 2 out of 100 researchers got injured due to laboratory accidents. A study on laboratory accidents in the context of Chinese universities reported that the time periods with the highest frequency, number of injuries, and number of fatalities were 10:01–12:00, 14:01–16:00, and 08:01–10:00, respectively [3]. They [3] identified human factors as the leading direct cause of those laboratory accidents between 2011 and 2021. In this line, several studies [1, 4] aimed to understand the root causes for laboratory accidents. According to [1], direct causes behind laboratory accidents include: forgetting to turn off the power, unsafe operation, violating operating procedures, burning of flammable items, protection measures are not in place, not wearing protective gear, and insufficient protection measures. Some indirect causes are overload operation, leakage of flammable and explosive materials, equipment failures, aging equipment, leakage of toxic substances, and complex operating procedures [1]. To avoid them, laboratories set safety measures, protocols, and guidelines for the students. One common rule in various science laboratories is to wear protective measures when conducting experiments, for example, wearing aprons, goggles, and protective gloves, and not talking over the phone while experimenting. These could minimize the risk of human injuries and decrease potential risks.

Social robots are designed to interact with humans. They can communicate with humans naturally like other human beings with their verbal and non-verbal communication abilities. They are designed to understand human intelligence and behavior, including affective, cognitive, physical, and social factors. Therefore, they are easy to pair with humans to solve complex social problems. In recent years, they have shown positive outcomes in diverse applications such as health, entertainment, collaborative teamwork, education, and communication [5]. Some popular social robots are Misty, MiRo-E, and Pepper. They have different shapes and physical structures (Fig. 1). Some social robots come in the shape of humans; some are pet-like. Therefore, they are easy to interact with and can provide a sense of companionship.

Social robots have been used in education to increase the students' cognitive and affective outcomes, as tutoring agents, as peer learners, and to understand students' learning processes [6, 7]. However, they have not been used much to address the issues related to science laboratories, for example, to prevent laboratory accidents, lower human injuries, and increase well-being in laboratory environments. This paper presents a social robot assistive intervention technology for teachers to prevent laboratory accidents. Its novelty is that it explores the potential of social robots in designing and developing educational technology for science laboratories.

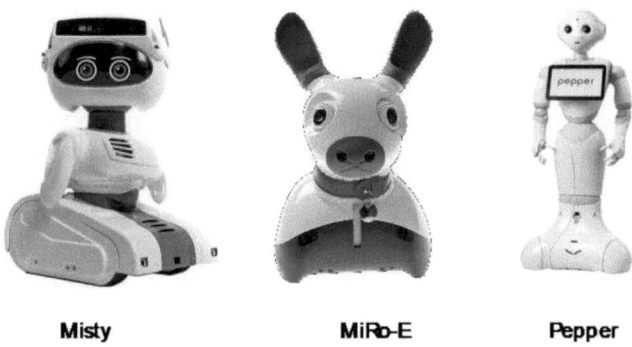

Fig. 1. Social robots.

2 Literature Review

Social robots are used to develop various intervention technologies. They are used as clinical interventions for children with Autistic Spectrum Disorders (ASD) and dementia [8, 9]. Studies [8, 9] found that social robots can effectively engage users and contribute to improvements in their mental health, such as improving their mood, increasing perceived social support, and enhancing the quality of life. Social robots have been used for psychological intervention [10] to reduce social anxiety [11]. They have been used for an image-guided intervention for medical science [12–14], to improve learning performance of elementary school children with learning disorders and were found to be effective [15]. Social robots are used to support the process of learning with different roles. They are used as companions, co-learners, assistants, and real-time feedback tools. Various aspects of education and learning are researched using social robots. However, with the presence of a social robot, the mental and wellbeing factors of students while conducting experiments in a science laboratory are yet to be explored, and we did not find any study where social robots are used as an intervention for science laboratories to prevent laboratory accidents.

We developed a robot-assisted intervention system for the teachers who lead science laboratories in life science, chemistry, or biology. This intervention is an integrated component of the Laboratory Safety Assistant (LSA) framework [16]. This framework is designed to detect student behaviors that could lead to accidents during laboratory experiments. This framework comprises a socially assistive robot, including advanced sensors and dashboards that enable interventions. In designing the framework, a user-centered co-design approach is taken into consideration. The framework aims to meet three user requirements, namely monitoring, assisting, and social companionship.

3 Methodology

The design is carried out in seven steps (Fig. 2). 1) Design a dashboard using a user-centered co-design approach that will work as an intervention in a science lab. 2) Prepare a dataset for training a detection model. 3) Develop multiple detection models, analyze their detection accuracies, and determine the best model. 4) Develop new skills for Misty. 5) Develop a dashboard for the teacher to be used as an intervention system. 6) Develop a pipeline by which Misty's sensor data including video data could be integrated with the detection model and dashboard. 7) Create a simulated science laboratory environment in our research facility to check the overall performance of the intervention system. This section provides a detailed description of the design methodology.

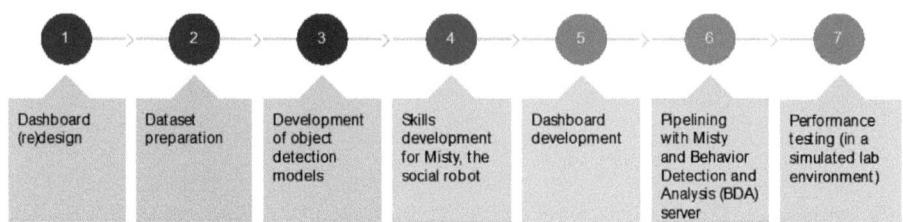

Fig. 2. Design Methodology.

3.1 Dashboard (Re)design

The Laboratory Safety Framework (LSA) consists of three dashboards those were designed based on a set of user requirements [16]. These dashboards were designed using a co-design approach to help in understanding users' specific needs, increase engagements, promote human-to-robot interaction, and promote human-to-intervention interaction [16]. The current work focuses on developing an intervention system for the teacher consisting of one responsive and real-time dashboard. We have followed a co-design method to redesign one dashboard (Fig. 3) that shares the initial design components of Intervention 1 and Intervention 2. This method is iterative and consists of four phases: contextual inquiries, consultation with teachers and students, participatory design, and dashboard design. This dashboard will be used as a robot-assistive intervention technology for detecting five safely measures in a science laboratory. The dashboard is to perform the following five tasks when a student is experimenting: A) check if a student is wearing goggles when experimenting with hazardous items such as toxic chemicals, toxic gas, acids, neurotoxins, microscopes, beakers, bunsen burners, magnetic stirrers, and reagent bottles. B) check if a student is wearing hand gloves when conducting an experiment with hazardous items. C) check if a student is wearing lab-specific shoes when in the lab. D) check if a student is wearing an apron when conducting an experiment with hazardous items, and E) check if a student is using a mobile phone, including talking or playing games when an experiment is in progress.

3.2 Dataset Preparation

We prepared a dataset called Lab Objects (Fig. 4) containing 1288 images, and 2295 objects grouped in seven classes, which represent gloves, glasses, shirts, goggles, phones, aprons, and shoes. Among the 1288 images, there are 395 gloves, 349 glasses, 339 shirts,

337 goggles, 313 phones, 302 aprons, and 261 pairs of shoes. These 1288 images were selected from Google image search engine. We annotated the objects in these images using the object annotation method. A total of 2295 objects were annotated. The median image ratio is 710 x 578.

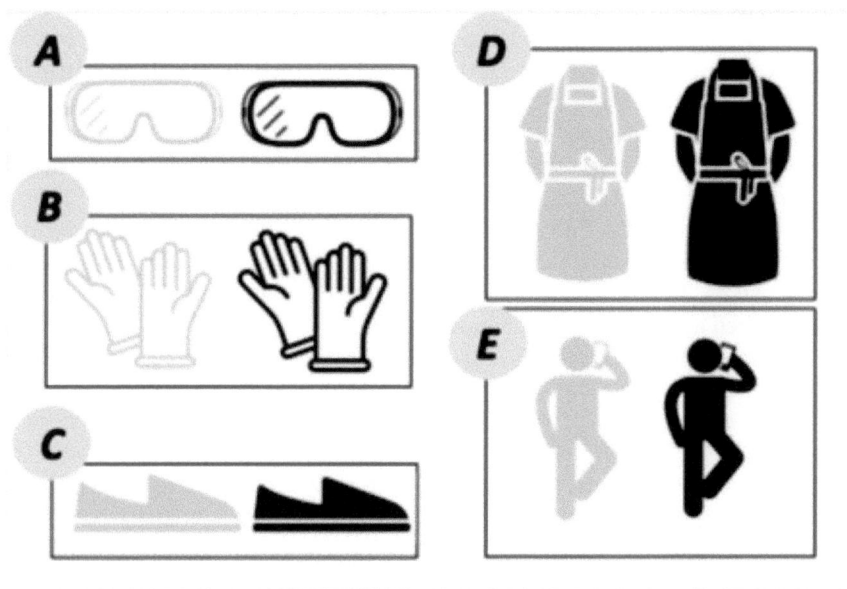

Fig. 3. The design of the dashboard.

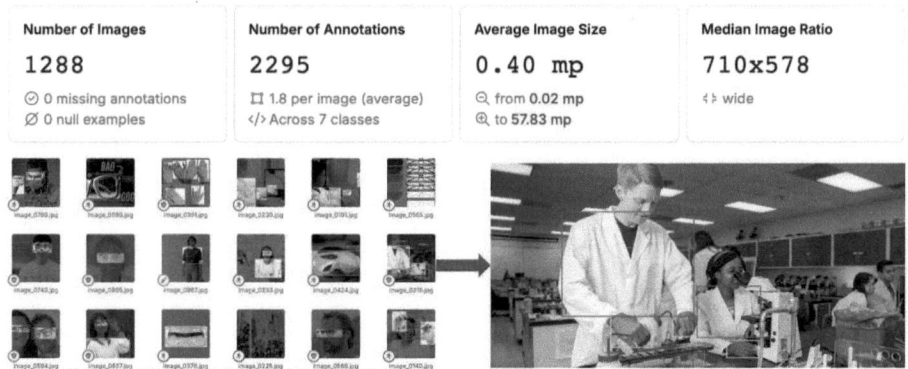

Fig. 4. The Lab Objects dataset.

3.3 Object Detection Models

Next, we developed object detection models to determine whether students are following safety measures such as wearing lab aprons, lab goggles, lab gloves, and lab shoes.

In computer vision, other approaches, such as image classification, are used to identify objects. However, we chose to develop an object detection model because image classification for multiple targets in the same image reduces performance. Also, the classification model cannot determine who is wearing what in real time. Furthermore, deploying an image classification model with a social robot is complex. So, in our approach we decided to use a pre-trained object detection model.

To develop and determine the most appropriate object detection model for our robot Misty II Plus, we trained the Lab Objects dataset on four object detection models, namely Roboflow 3.0 [17], YOLO-NAS [18], YOLOv5 [19], and YOLOv8 [20]. As stated earlier, our dataset has 1288 images and 2295 objects of seven classes. The average image size is 0.40 MP, and the central image ratio is 710 x 578. For the pre-processing of the dataset, the training data, validation data, and test data in a ratio of 7:2:1 (that is, 70%, 20%, and 10%) were prepared (Fig. 5). Then, auto orient and resizing (to 640x640) are performed. Finally, we flipped them horizontally and vertically to enlarge the data. This results in 3096 pieces of data. The four models were trained on a computer with an RTX3090 GPU. We have analyzed and compared each model's "mAP," "Precision," and "Recall." From the results of testing the four models (Fig. 6) one by one with the prepared images and live cameras-feed, YOLOv8 has the strongest performance. YOLOv8 obtained 86.6% mAP, 84.3% Precision and 81.1% Recall. The YOLOv8 training took 0.695 h for 146 epochs on a single RTX3090 GPU. Therefore, we have chosen the YOLOv8 model. Once the appropriate detection model (the YOLOv8 model) was determined, the loss function analysis and the confusion matrix were executed to evaluate the model's performance and normalize the data.

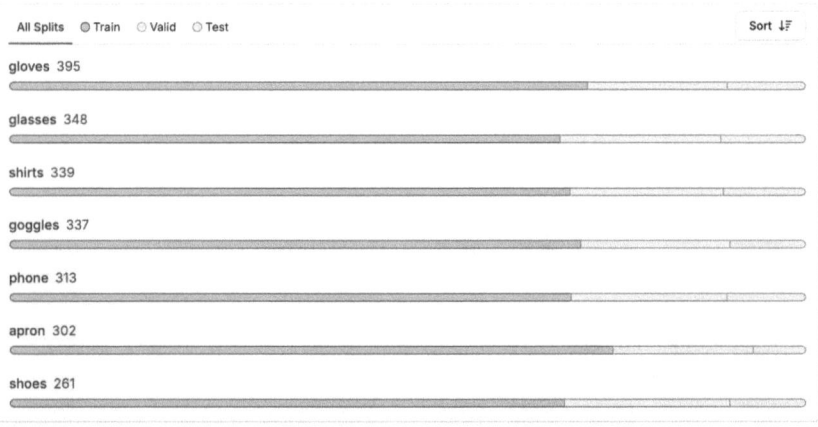

Fig. 5. Training, validation, and test sets.

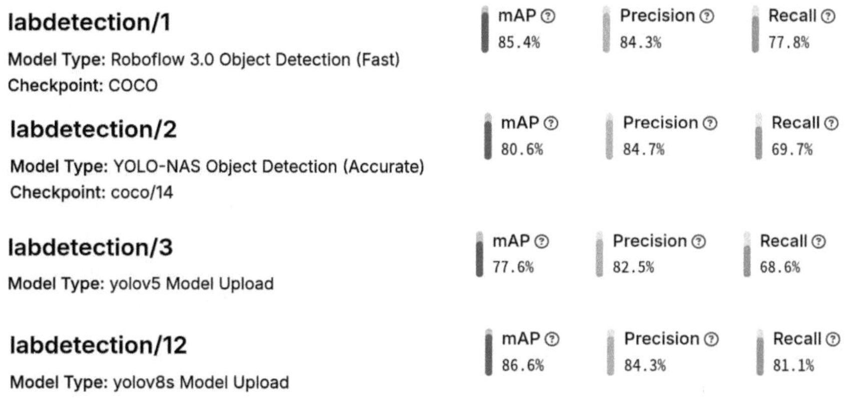

	mAP	Precision	Recall
labdetection/1 Model Type: Roboflow 3.0 Object Detection (Fast) Checkpoint: COCO	85.4%	84.3%	77.8%
labdetection/2 Model Type: YOLO-NAS Object Detection (Accurate) Checkpoint: coco/14	80.6%	84.7%	69.7%
labdetection/3 Model Type: yolov5 Model Upload	77.6%	82.5%	68.6%
labdetection/12 Model Type: yolov8s Model Upload	86.6%	84.3%	81.1%

Fig. 6. Result comparisons of the four models.

3.4 Developing Skills for Misty

We developed many new skills for our social robot, Misty II Plus to develop the intervention system, as explained below.

Voice. Misty is equipped with a microphone and a speaker. It can recognize English speech and read out over 50 languages and dialects. This allows us processing voice data, such as performing certain actions when key phrases are heard or calling out to people. Interacting with people in Misty by incorporating natural language processing is also possible. However, as streaming of voice only is not supported, it is necessary to record the voice, save it in Misty, and send it to a PC.

Capturing Images and Videos Using Misty's Camera. Misty is equipped with a camera that can take photos and record video. It uses a Sony IMX 214, a 13-megapixel camera with a maximum resolution of 3840 × 2880 pixels. We use Misty's Web API to take photos and record videos. It is also possible to download images and videos stored on Misty to a PC. Misty also functions with AV streaming functions that simultaneously stream camera video and audio.

Movement and Parts Operation. We implemented functions for Misty to move backward and forward, change direction, and move her head and hands. This allows the robot to move freely. The angle of view on the camera can be adjusted via the direction and tilt of the head. Emotions can be expressed by moving the head and hands. Several capacitive touch sensors are built into the head and neck, which can detect when a person touches Misty and performs specific actions.

LED. Our Misty is equipped with LEDs on its chest. These LEDs can specify a total of 16,777,216 colors with 8 bits for each RGB color channel. A mechanism is built in by default to light up in a specific color in certain states, such as blue during voice recording, orange during charging, etc. By changing the color of the LEDs according to Misty's state, it is possible to visually express Misty's state. It is also possible to express emotions by combining them with voice and part movements.

Real-time Video Streaming. We developed a function that obtains information from Misty's camera in real time and processes the images accordingly. This is achieved using WebSocket: the camera streams from Misty via WebSocket, and the PC receives the binary data from WebSocket and converts it to *numpy* data. This enables the camera image at each frame to be acquired in real time. Based on this mechanism, we built a system to detect and identify people and objects reflected in the camera, to track their faces when they appear, and to change the direction of Misty's body and face as appropriate so that the camera can continue to capture human faces. In addition, using capacitance sensors, a mechanism was constructed to express different emotions when Misty's head or chin is touched, depending on the location of the touch.

Path Navigation in Complex Surroundings. Misty II does not have features such as environmental mapping or automatic navigation by default. However, it can drive in complex environments by combining cameras, distance, and bump sensors. When Misty detects that it is moving towards a cliff or elevated region, it automatically stops bumping into it. It has a built-in function to stop itself to ensure its safety: it stops if the bump sensor detects an obstacle while driving. Misty has three distance sensors on the front and one on the rear to provide information on the distance to obstacles, the intensity of reflected light, and light dispersion. When the distance is measured correctly, the reflected light is stronger, and the light dispersion is lower. We set a confidence level for the information by setting thresholds for reflected light intensity and light dispersion. When the confidence level is low, it can be determined that there are no obstacles in front. If the sensor on the left side of the three sensors on the front detects an obstacle and the sensor on the right side does not, it can be assumed that there is an obstacle only on the left side or an obstacle at an angle to Misty. Thus, the system considers all possible situations based on the distance and reliability received from the three sensors and decides whether to continue moving, stop moving, or change direction. In addition, we expect to improve the accuracy of the movement further by incorporating the processing of camera images into the current mechanism. It can easily understand its nearby environment by analyzing camera information, such as detecting objects and people and estimating depth maps from camera information.

Path Navigation under Poor Light Condition and Dark Areas. We used distance sensors to develop functions so that the robot could find its path even under poor light and dark areas of the laboratory. Distance sensors are called ToF sensors, which emit infrared light and measure the distance from the time it is reflected back. This is less affected by ambient light and can measure distances in dark environments. This allows the robot to avoid obstacles in darkness. The intensity of the ambient light can be measured by analyzing the camera images. As Misty is equipped with a flashlight, we built a system to switch on the flashlight when the environment is deemed dark, which improves the images that appear on the camera in dark environments.

Emotions. Misty can show various facial expressions on the display. We use this for emotional expression and interaction. For example, if a student asks Misty to 'tell me the weather tomorrow,' it can show tomorrow's weather on the display while also announcing the weather with a voice and the color of the LED lights.

3.5 Dashboard

We developed a robot-assisted dashboard called Lab Detection Dashboard (LDD) for teachers to visualize behavioral traces of students in real-time (Fig. 7). This can be used by teachers as an intervention system to determine which students need support, such as guidance or warning. We chose this design as research shows that a dashboard increases the motivation, autonomy, effectiveness, and efficiency of the learners and teachers [21]. LDD provides two functions for the teachers.

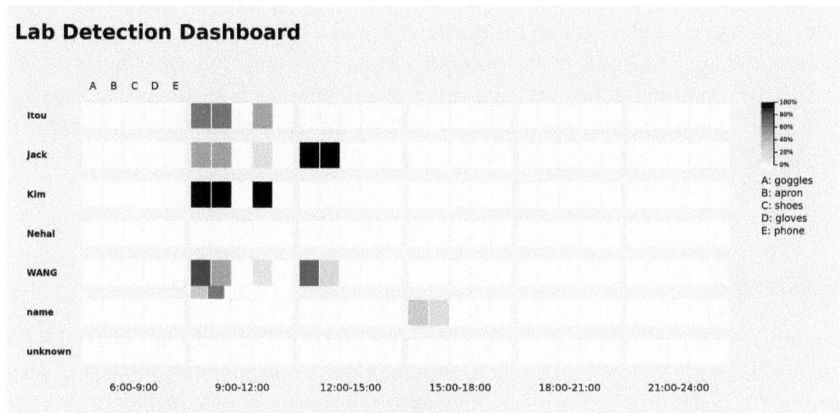

Lab View

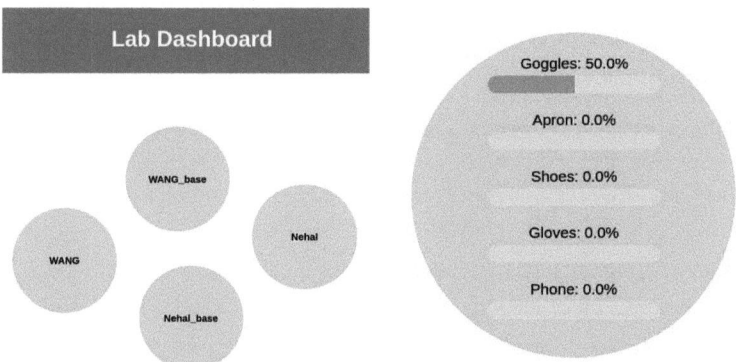

Tell Me More

Fig. 7. The dashboard for teacher.

Lab View. This displays various data tracked by Misty from the science laboratory environment. 1) Information about whether a student is wearing goggles, an apron, laboratory-specific shoes, and gloves while experimenting. 2) Information about whether a student is talking over the phone while an experiment is in progress. The robot moves across the laboratory every 30 min, collects various data using its sensors, and sends them to the BDA server for analysis. We implemented this feature to make our design a trust-based system, where the operation and functionality depend on a high level of trust between the users involved. Trust-based systems incorporate explicit and implicit trust relationships between the users to generate insights. A teacher can get an overall glimpse of the laboratory using the lab view. Hovering the mouse on the dashboard allows a teacher to see more details on whether or not students are wearing protective equipment, such as aprons, goggles, and gloves.

Tell Me More. This visualization allows a teacher to get more information about a specific student who might need assistance. This dashboard can be used to track students who often violate laboratory protocols such as not wearing protective gears or talking over the phone while conducting an experiment. For example (Fig. 7), the teacher clicks on a student, 'Wang,' to know more about his behaviors and finds that he is wearing goggles 50% of the time but not wearing other safety gear such as an apron, shoes, and goggles, but he is not talking over phone. Based on this information, the teacher could intervene by advising or warning him or checking whether the safety measures he is not following are required for his experiments.

3.6 Pipelining

After implementing the dashboard, we pipelined it with a GPU-enabled (NVIDIA RTX 3090 and NVIDIA RTX 2080Ti) PC, the Behavior Detection and Analysis (BDA) server, and the robot for faster processing. The aim was to send a variety of sensor data, including video, images, and audio, captured by Misty to the BDA server for analysis and to display results on the Lab Detection Dashboard (LDD) in real-time.

3.7 Performance Testing

We simulated several science laboratory environments in our research facilities to test the performance. The purpose of registering students' faces in the model is so that the dashboard produces accurate information. We also conducted a precheck testing session. The robot checks a student when s/he starts his/her day at the lab.

Face Registration and Detection. A face detection model called 'YuNet' is used to register a student's face, and a face recognition model called 'SFace' is used to recognize the student later. We first store the *numpy* data of the faces a teacher wants to register to achieve this. Then, when Misty II runs the program and transfers the photo, it first detects the face and then decides whether the detected facial features match the registered facial features. If, a face cannot be judged is addressed as the 'Unknown'.

Precheck. In the precheck step (Fig. 8), students are asked to sit in front of the robot before they start their day, ideally in the morning when they come to the lab for the first time. The robot scans them and guides them on their safety measures. The precheck could also increase students' attention and awareness of the laboratory safety guidelines. This could also give students a sense of companionship that could increase their well-being in the lab.

Fig. 8. Precheck in a simulated environment.

4 Use Case

Our proposed social robot-assisted intervention can be used in controllable experimental setups, including chemistry lab, biology lab, and life science laboratory (Fig. 9). With the help of social robots, data between students with robots and teachers with robots can be collected. By evaluating this data, behavioral patterns can be created, areas of human errors can be identified, and human-assisted and robot-assisted interventions can be generated. The proposed dashboards allow the teachers and the students to get insights into their behaviors that may be missed by humans. In addition, a robot can provide a whole new way of interacting with those students who are introverted and shy. With the help of dashboards, advanced sensors, and human-robot interaction data, teachers can promote safe behaviors in their students more effectively.

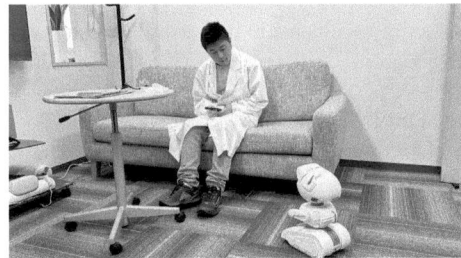 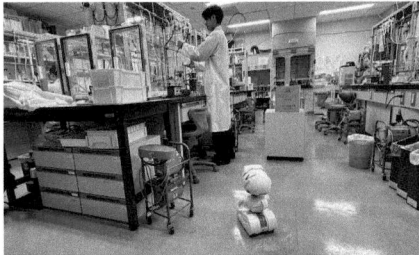

Social companionship during the break *Behavior and activity surveillance*

Fig. 9. A science laboratory.

5 Conclusion

In recent years, many institutions have used humanoid robot NAO for interventions, such as supporting autistic patients. A few studies utilized social robots such as Misty or MiRo-E to develop intervention technologies, but their potential is yet to be exploited in broader contexts. This project aimed to explore the potential of social robots for guiding students in following proper safety measures while conducting experiments with dangerous chemical compounds.

We introduced a socially assistive intervention system for the teachers who lead science laboratories. This intervention supports the Laboratory Safety Assistant (LSA) framework initiative. The intervention comes in the form of a Lab Detection Dashboard (LDD). A teacher leading a science lab can track in-lab behaviors of students, identify which rule a student is violating, and when to intervene (provide assistance). In addition, the presence of a social robot (in our case, a Misty II Plus) can provide a sense of companionship. It can also provide a relatively safe and relaxed laboratory experience to the students as they can avoid direct interaction with their superiors (such as the teacher or the lab administrator) for general questions, which could reduce their stress and anxiety levels.

6 Disclosure of Interests.

The authors have no competing interests to declare that are relevant to the content of this article.

Acknowledgments. We would like to thank Professor Kawachi Atsushi of Faculty of Bioscience and Applied Chemistry, Department of Chemical Science and Technology, Hosei University for allowing us to create a simulated experimental environment at his laboratory. Bipin Indurkhya was supported by the National Science Centre, Poland under the OPUS call in the Weave programme under the project number 2021/43/I/ST6/02489.

References

1. Kong, S., et al.: Analysis of characteristics of safety accidents in university laboratory and research on the causes of accidents. In: E3S Web of Conferences, EDP Sciences, 2021, p. 03050. Accessed 07 May 2025
2. Coghlan, K.: Investigating laboratory accidents. Prof. Saf. **53**(1), 56 (2008)
3. Lv, P., Zhu, S., Pang, L.: Statistical analysis of laboratory accidents in Chinese universities from 2011 to 2021. Process Saf. Prog. **42**(4), 712–728 (2023). https://doi.org/10.1002/prs.12479
4. Yang, Q.-Z., Deng, X.-L., Yang, S.-Y.: Laboratory explosion accidents: case analysis and preventive measures. ACS Chem. Health Saf. **30**(2), 72–82 (2023). https://doi.org/10.1021/acs.chas.2c00083
5. Breazeal, C., Dautenhahn, K., Kanda, T.: Social robotics. In: Siciliano, B., Khatib, O. (eds.) Springer Handbook of Robotics, pp. 1935–1972. Springer, Cham (2016). https://doi.org/10.1007/978-3-319-32552-1_72
6. Belpaeme, T., Kennedy, J., Ramachandran, A., Scassellati, B., Tanaka, F.: Social robots for education: a review. Sci. Robot. **3**(21), eaat5954 (2018). https://doi.org/10.1126/scirobotics.aat5954
7. Lampropoulos, G.: Social robots in education: current trends and future perspectives. Information **16**(1), 29 (2025)
8. Wood, L.J., Zaraki, A., Robins, B., Dautenhahn, K.: Developing Kaspar: a humanoid robot for children with Autism. Int J of Soc Robotics **13**(3), 491–508 (2021). https://doi.org/10.1007/s12369-019-00563-6

9. Vanderborght, B., et al.: Using the social robot probo as a social story telling agent for children with ASD, IS, vol. 13, no. 3, pp. 348–372, Dec. 2012. https://doi.org/10.1075/is.13.3.02van
10. Robins, B., Dautenhahn, K., Boekhorst, R.T., Billard, A.: Robotic assistants in therapy and education of children with autism: can a small humanoid robot help encourage social interaction skills? Univ. Access Inf. Soc. **4**, 105–120 (2005)
11. Rasouli, S., Gupta, G., Nilsen, E., Dautenhahn, K.: Potential applications of social robots in robot-assisted interventions for social anxiety. Int. J. Soc. Robot. **14**(5), 1–32 (2022). https://doi.org/10.1007/s12369-021-00851-0
12. Simaan, N., Yasin, R.M., Wang, L.: Medical technologies and challenges of robot-assisted minimally invasive intervention and diagnostics. Annu. Rev. Control Robot. Auton. Syst. **1**(1), 465–490 (2018). https://doi.org/10.1146/annurev-control-060117-104956
13. Unger, M., Berger, J., Melzer, A.: Robot-assisted image-guided interventions. Front. Robot. AI **8**, 664622 (2021)
14. Lau, Y., Chee, D.G.H., Chow, X.P., Wong, S.H., Cheng, L.J., Lau, S.T.: Humanoid robot-assisted interventions among children with diabetes: a systematic scoping review. Int. J. Nurs. Stud. **111**, 103749 (2020). https://doi.org/10.1016/j.ijnurstu.2020.103749
15. Papadopoulou, M.T., et al.: Efficacy of a robot-assisted intervention in improving learning performance of elementary school children with specific learning disorders. Children **9**(8), 1155 (2022)
16. Hasnine, M.N., Indurkhya, B., Ahmed, M.M.H.: Socially assistive robot as laboratory safety assistant for science students. In: 2024 IEEE International Conference on Advanced Robotics and Its Social Impacts (ARSO), IEEE, 2024, pp. 37–42. Accessed: Apr. 22, 2025
17. "Roboflow," GitHub. https://github.com/roboflow
18. Ultralytics, "YOLO-NAS (Neural Architecture Search)." https://docs.ultralytics.com/models/yolo-nas
19. Ultralytics, "YOLOv5." https://docs.ultralytics.com/models/yolov5
20. Ultralytics, "YOLOv8." https://docs.ultralytics.com/models/yolov8
21. Verbert, K., Duval, E., Klerkx, J., Govaerts, S., Santos, J.L.: Learning analytics dashboard applications. Am. Behav. Sci. **57**(10), 1500–1509 (2013). https://doi.org/10.1177/0002764213479363

Remote vs. Presence Laboratories in Human-Robot Interaction with Social Robots: A Study on Task Performance

Christopher Peters[1], Kai M. Blum[1], Ibrahim Al Krad[1], Pablo Moraes[2], Ricardo Bedin Grando[2], Reinhard Gerndt[1], and Tobias Doernbach[1](✉)

[1] Human-Centered Robotics Lab, Ostfalia University of Applied Sciences, Wolfenbuettel, Germany
t.doernbach@ostfalia.de
[2] Robotics and AI Lab, Universidad Tecnológica, Rivera, Uruguay
ricardo.bedin@utec.edu.uy

Abstract. A remote laboratory provides users with remote access to real physical experiments, enhancing accessibility and offering greater flexibility in time management. Yet, the application of remote labs in Human-Robot Interaction (HRI) research and teaching working with social robots introduces unique challenges. This study examines both perceived and objective task performance of a typical undergraduate HRI laboratory task, comparing remote and presence laboratory settings. We developed a remote lab setup that enables users to visually and verbally communicate with a humanoid robot. To investigate potential differences in task performance between these conditions, a user study was conducted at two universities, with 24 participants in total. Our study indicates that perceived task performance and usability are lower in remote laboratory settings compared to in-person setups. In addition, objective performance metrics—such as task duration and the number of questions asked—also favored the presence lab. However, there was no notable difference in grading outcomes. Overall, the observed differences are subtle and only partially statistically significant. We suggest further research into usability and training efforts in order to enable the potential of remote labs for enriching HRI research and teaching between physically distinct sites.

Keywords: Human-Robot Interaction · Remote Laboratory · Task Performance

1 Introduction

Remote laboratories have gained significant attention already in the early 2000s [Scanlon et al. (2004), Gomes and Bogosyan (2009)] as a means to enhance accessibility and flexibility in engineering and robotics education. These systems allow students and researchers to conduct real-world experiments remotely, as opposed to remote executed simulated experiments of virtual laboratories. Remote Laboratories can eliminate constraints related to space, scheduling, and resource availability. Normally, one of the key benefits of remote labs lies in eliminating the human as a source of error. In the context of a remote HRI lab, however, this specific advantage becomes less relevant, as the human is not merely a variable to be controlled, but rather a central subject of study. Consequently, the typical added value of reducing human error is significantly diminished in this context. Particularly in the field of Human-Robot Interaction (HRI), remote labs can facilitate global collaboration and experimentation with expensive robotic systems without requiring physical presence. However, despite these advantages, concerns remain regarding their effectiveness compared to traditional hands-on laboratories in HRI, especially because of the differences of HRI research and teaching in comparison to fields such as mechanical or electrical engineering [Riso and Adascalitei (2024)].

Existing research on remote labs has primarily focused on their applicability in traditional engineering disciplines, such as control systems and robotic courses [Heradio et al. (2016), Reid et al. (2022), Pang et al. (2022)]. Studies comparing hands-on and remote labs generally suggest that learning outcomes are similar [Tzafestas et al. (2006), Ogot et al. (2003)] and that students acceptance is high [Scanlon et al. (2004), Pang et al. (2022)]. However, the field of HRI presents unique challenges due to its considerations of "human factors". Even more so for social robots, which are designed to interact and communicate socially. [Riso and Adascalitei (2024)] Most existing studies [Liang et al. (2023), Gittens (2021), Liang and Nejat (2022)] in the field of remote HRI focus on application of robotic telepresence in an assistive field rather than on laboratory-based HRI work. The impact of remote lab conditions on laboratory work with social robots remains underexplored.

To address this gap, this study investigates the impact of remote lab conditions on task performance and frustration in a HRI context. Specifically, we examine this research question: *To what extent, if any, is work on a social robot in a remote lab comparable to or inferior to work in a presence laboratory in the context of Human-Robot Interaction?*

Our research is based on a controlled within-subjects user study conducted across two institutions (Universidad Tecnológica (UTEC) in Rivera, Uruguay and Ostfalia University of Applied Sciences in Wolfenbuettel, Germany), using the social humanoid robots Pepper and NAO. Participants performed predefined visual programming tasks under different conditions: *presence* and *remote*. The study integrates both subjective and objective metrics to evaluate subjective task performance, objective task performance comprehensively.

The results show a tendency of lower perceived task performance in the remote lab. This is supported by a decrease of usability and subtle but non-significant increase of frustration. However, only a small part of this differences were significant. While a noticeable increased task duration and tendencies of increased questions indicate lower objective task performance, assessed grades remained similar. Therefore, our findings indicate that task performance loss in the remote laboratory with a social robot in the context of HRI exists but is subtle. Especially the quality of results produced in such an environment might be comparable. Therefore, the loss of task performance has potential to be reduced with further research.

2 Related Work

2.1 Remote Laboratories

According to the criteria defined by [Gomes and Bogosyan (2009)], a Remote Lab is an experimental setup involving physical devices-such as robots-that are operated by users from a different geographical location. It is important to emphasize that this work does not focus on laboratories based on simulated experiment models, commonly referred to as *Virtual Labs* [Heradio et al. (2016)].

Incorporating remote labs in education and research can offer significant advantages. They provide flexibility by eliminating constraints related to space and scheduling. This flexibility allows remote labs to complement or replace traditional assignments, enhancing accessibility for diverse learning needs [Gomes and Bogosyan (2009), Heradio et al. (2016), Gravier et al. (2008)]. The high cost and limited availability of robotic equipment make remote labs beneficial for optimizing resource usage and scheduling. Shared resources also facilitate global collaboration, enabling institutions and individuals to work on the same hardware [Gomes and Bogosyan (2009), Heradio et al. (2016)]. Furthermore, the COVID-19 pandemic has highlighted the utility of being able to conduct research and education in HRI remotely [Gittens (2021), Feil-Seifer et al. (2021)].

2.2 Current Remote Labs in Robotics

Research on remote labs exists for a long time; [Tzafestas et al. (2006)] already compared presence, remote and virtual labs with a test. The results showed that in general there was no significant difference, although "low-level" mistakes (like e.g. pressing a wrong button) appeared more often in the remote context. [Lopes et al. (2017)] developed a remote lab which was used in an programming introduction course to program and test live online with a line follower robot. They concluded that they see potential to be used in an educational context. They also concluded that their platform improved academic performance, although it was not compared against an in-presence course. [Bunse and Wieck (2022)] conducted a pre-study where students used a "distance" robotics lab, which included camera streams and an online IDE for programming Turtle Bots with high student acceptance. However, HRI is a different field than traditional engineering and robotics, since it includes human factors of interaction.

2.3 Remote Human-Robot Interaction

The terms "remote lab", "HRI" and "social robots" seem to not appear often together in literature. Yet, the term "remote HRI" frequently describes applied social robotics in a remote context. For example, [Liang et al. (2023)] found that a Pepper robot facilitating dancing of elderly people in long-term care situations in a live video stream to be as good as with being physically present. Although this study has components of a remote lab for HRI (video and audio modalities), it bases on one-way communication only.

[Gittens (2021)] conducted a study about the acceptance of an ASUS Zenbot in a different context than laboratory work. They reported an increased mental demand in the remote setting compared to presence. [Teng et al. (2024)] let students remotely solve tasks of an undergraduate robot programming course, but their focus was on finding out how collaboration with other students affected learning outcomes. The meta analysis of [Liang and Nejat (2022)] compared multiple constructs between the conditions "in-person" and "remote", namely Positive Experience, Perceptions and Attitudes towards the robots and Efficacy (including task performance). All variables, except for Positive Experience, showed a significant decrease in the remote condition. Yet, their analysis focused on social robots deployed in real scenarios rather than a lab context which often includes programming tasks with higher levels of computer mediation.

Based on previous literature, we identified *perceived* and *objective task performance* as key constructs research on work in remote labs, including usability and frustration assessment as well. Our research is positioned at the intersection of remote lab work in undergraduate university education and remote Human-Robot Interaction (HRI) with social robots, aiming to assess the challenges involved in integrating the well-documented benefits of remote labs into future research and educational settings.

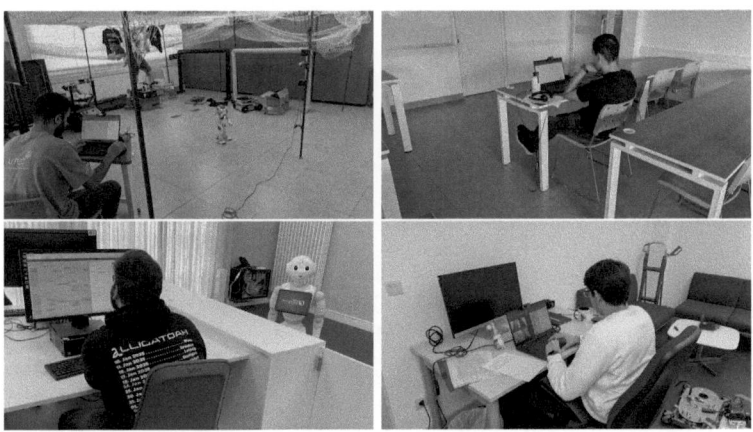

Fig. 1. Comparative photos of study environments "presence" (left) and "remote" (right) at UTEC, Uruguay (top) and Ostfalia, Germany (bottom)

3 Methodology

3.1 Study Design

The study follows a randomized laboratory within-subjects design. Two experimental setups at different universities with nearly identical conditions were implemented to increase variance in the collected data. These setups were located in Uruguay (UTEC, Rivera, see Fig. 1) and Germany (Ostfalia University, Wolfenbuettel), ensuring diverse participant samples and environmental conditions.

A pilot study was conducted with 3 students at each university. The primary goal of the pilot study was to validate and refine the task descriptions, questionnaires, and tutorial material. In particular, it provided valuable insights for improving the overall study script and streamlining the study process.

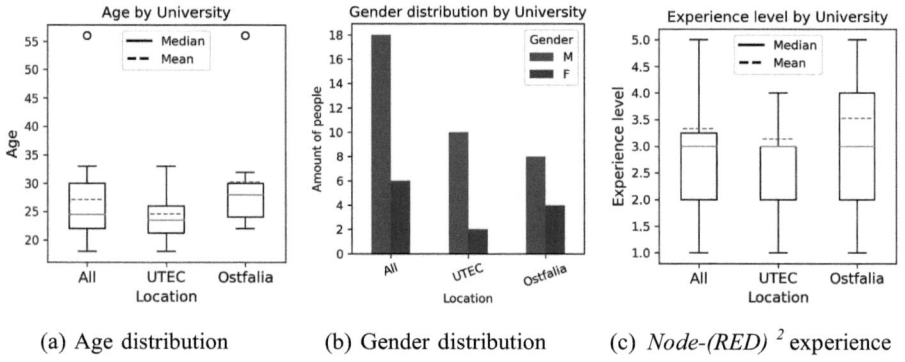

(a) Age distribution (b) Gender distribution (c) *Node-(RED)* [2] experience

Fig. 2. Participants' demographic statistics and previous experience

3.2 Participants

The study included 24 participants (UTEC: $n = 12$, Ostfalia: $n = 12$) with a mean age 26.68 ± 7.72 years (Mdn $= 24.5$, see Fig. 2a). When comparing the subgroups, UTEC participants were slightly younger (24.08 ± 4.64, Mdn $= 23.5$) than Ostfalia participants (29.8 ± 9.45, Mdn $= 28.0$). Notably, Ostfalia showed considerably higher age variation. All in all, the participants were slightly older than the typical graduation age in Germany, which was 23.5 in 2023 (Median). The gender distribution analysis (Fig. 2b) showed a clear predominance of male participants ($n = 18$) compared to female participants ($n = 6$), with a male-to-female ratio of 3:1. This gender imbalance was present in both institutions, with UTEC having a more pronounced disparity (10:2) compared to Ostfalia (8:4). Regarding experience levels (see Fig. 2), participants reported an overall mean of 2.83 ± 1.02 (Mdn $= 3.0$). The subgroup comparison revealed that Ostfalia participants reported marginally higher experience levels (3.03 ± 1.06, Mdn = 3.0) compared to UTEC participants (2.64 ± 0.96, Mdn = 3.0). Participants at UTEC were recruited from the five-year Automation and Control Engineering program where Ostfalia participants had various academic backgrounds within the CS department with most of them studying Computer Science.

The participants signed up voluntarily and were provided written informed consent with respect to data privacy, study structure, as well as their right to interrupt and exit the study anytime on their wish. Prior ethical approval was obtained from the ethics committees of Ostfalia and UTEC to ensure compliance with institutional research guidelines.

In this study, an existing remote lab platform developed internally at Ostfalia University was utilized. This platform includes a booking system and a web interface where participants can access live camera feeds and talk to the robot. As illustrated in Fig. 3, the setup consisted of multiple peripheral devices: two separate webcams, a microphone, and a speaker. The same infrastructure was set up at Ostfalia as well.

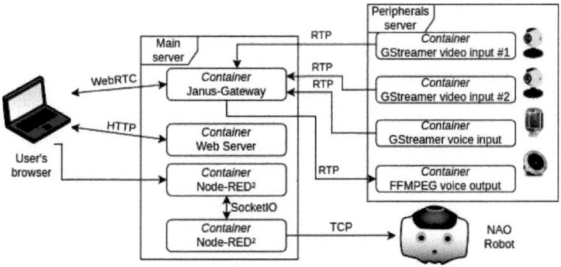

Fig. 3. "Remote Lab" setup at UTEC, Uruguay

3.3 Experimental Setup

The participants, in any setup, accessed these streams through a web interface on a laptop browser, as can be seen in Fig. 4. The research objects were two commonly used humanoid social robots in HRI: Pepper (Ostfalia) and NAO (UTEC). Both robots were controlled using *Node-(RED)^2* [Weike et al. (2024)], a customized extension of the popular Node-RED visual programming tool. This adapted version ensured compatibility with both robots by providing an identical subset of control nodes and allowed users to control robots through a flow-based programming interface.

The study consists of three components: a short tutorial followed by 2 study phases (see Fig. 5). The tutorial began with an explanation of the purpose and structure of *Node-(RED)^2*. Subsequently, the relevant nodes were introduced,

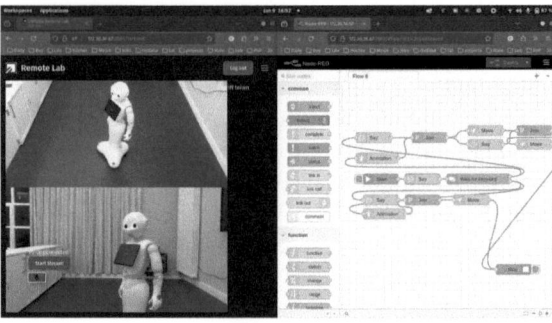

Fig. 4. Screenshot of participants' desktop after a "remote" study phase. Left: Remote Lab platform, Right: *Node-(RED)²*

and the execution of a basic flow was demonstrated. The two study phases contained both study conditions, where "presence" represented a traditional laboratory programming task in HRI and "remote" represented the same but conducted in a remote lab environment. To ensure comparability, two similar tasks were designed, each applicable to both conditions. To minimize learning effects, the order of laboratory types (Presence/Remote) was counterbalanced across participants. To reduce the influence of task type (Restaurant/Amusement Park) on the results, task assignments were also counterbalanced. Consequently, the total number of participants had to be a multiple of 4 to maintain a balanced study design. The total duration of the study for each participant was approximately 50 min.

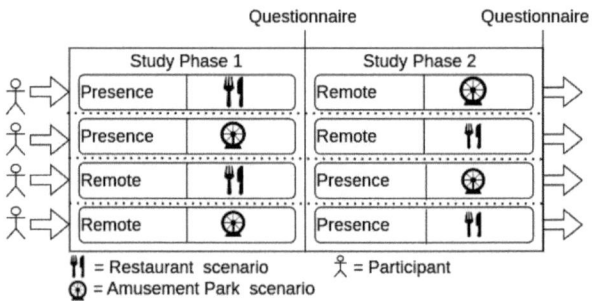

Fig. 5. Study structure for four example participants

The tasks were designed to be related to actual undergraduate HRI course tasks where participants get confronted with programming an interaction with Pepper through *Node-(RED)²*. More specific, those created for "presence vs. remote" were thematically distinct but had similar technical requirements. This approach ensured comparability while preventing participant frustration from performing the same implementation twice. Each task included a sequential description of the expected robot behavior, provided in both German and Spanish. This ensured applicability to both universities.

The contents of the two tasks were set as follows:

Restaurant Task

1. Robot greets the person using speech output.
2. Robot asks whether a reservation exists.
   yes: 1. Robot asks for the reservation name (any chosen name), 2. Robot moves to the imaginary reserved table.
   no: Robot apologizes and states that a prior reservation is required. Simultaneously performs a gesture.

Amusement Park Task

1. Robot detects a person (e.g. via speech recognition) and greets them using speech output.
2. Robot asks if the person wants to ride the roller coaster.
   yes: Robot asks the person to follow and leads them to the roller coaster.
   no: Robot recommends trying the haunted house instead.

3.4 Metrics and Operationalization

Regarding the research question about whether work is equal or inferior when using social robots in remote labs in the context of HRI, the construct of "work" was divided into "perceived task performance" and "objective task performance" to differentiate between users' subjective assessments and objective performance metrics. This distinction led to the formulation of the following hypotheses:

- H_1: The perceived task performance in a remote lab with a social robot is equal or inferior compared to a presence lab in the context of HRI
- H_2: The objective task performance in a remote lab with a social robot is equal or inferior compared to a remote lab in the context of HRI

In general, data related to H_1 and H_2 were collected using two well-established standardized questionnaires: The 4-item "Usability Metric for User Experience" (UMUX) [Finstad (2010)] with a 7-point Likert scale and the six item "NASA Task Load Index" (NASA TLX) [Hart (2006)] with a 21-point Likert scale.

The System Usability Scale (SUS) is one of the most widely used usability questionnaires. However, since the questionnaire consists of 10 items, combining it with the NASA-TLX was considered too demanding, especially because the questionnaire was administered 2 times during the study (directly after each study phase).

To address this, we used the two-item UMUX-Lite questionnaire [Lewis (2019)], which only uses the two positive UMUX items "*[This system's] capabilities meet my requirements*" (Ease) and "*[This system] is easy to use*" (Useful) to estimate a SUS score:

$$\left(\frac{\text{UMUX Ease} + \text{UMUX Useful}}{2} - 1\right) \cdot \frac{100}{6} = \text{SUS}_{\text{Estimated}}$$

This estimation facilitates easier comparison with other systems in the literature and future studies. We assessed demographic information such as age and gender in the questionnaire together with previous experience on a 5-point Likert scale.

For $\mathbf{H_1}$, perceived performance was assessed via Question 4 of the NASA TLX. The SUS approximation supported overall usability comparison. Free-text comments and supervisor observations provided qualitative insights.

For $\mathbf{H_2}$, which focused on objective task performance, several key metrics were recorded. Based on the framework by [Steinfeld et al. (2006)], task completion time was used as a measure of participant efficiency. General questions were counted to assess task clarity and participant confidence. We also recorded the number of *Node-(RED)²*-related questions asked, as an indicator of confidence in each condition. Finally, each participant's final implementation was video-recorded and rated by a professor on a 5-point scale (1 = poor, 5 = excellent).

The questionnaire concluded with two open-ended questions to gather qualitative feedback beyond the predefined questionnaire items:

1. *"What aspects did you find most frustrating?"*
2. *"Which additional comments would you like to give?"*

These metrics formed the basis for the subsequent analysis of participants' perceived task performance, as detailed in the following section.

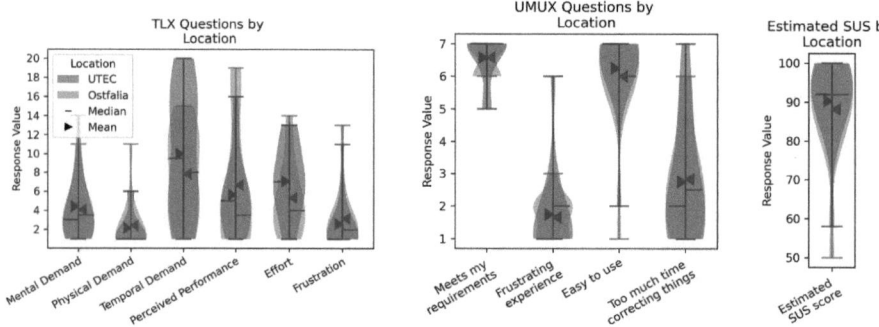

Fig. 6. Questionnaire results in violin plots "UTEC vs. Ostfalia (in presence)": (Left to right) NASA TLX (21 ≡ *highest*, inverted for Perceived Performance), UMUX (7 ≡ *highest*), Estimated SUS score (100 ≡ *highest*)

4 Results

Descriptive statistics were first computed. As none of the samples met the normality assumption (Shapiro–Wilk test), two-sided Wilcoxon signed-rank tests were used to compare conditions. Figure 6 shows median and mean differences between the UTEC and Ostfalia samples, though generally subtle.

4.1 Comparison of Perceived Task Performance

To investigate on this topic, we defined H_1 "The perceived task performance in a remote lab with a social robot is equal or inferior compared to a presence lab in the context of HRI". To test this hypothesis, we analyzed the estimated SUS score, UMUX item 2 "Using [this system] is a frustrating experience", as well as NASA TLX items 4 "How successful were you in accomplishing what you were asked to do?" and 6 "How insecure, discouraged, irritated, stressed, and annoyed were you?" by comparing the conditions "presence" and "remote".

As can be seen in Fig. 7, participants reported high usability for both conditions, with a marginal preference for the presence setting (**Estimated SUS**: presence 89.29 ± 12.51, remote 87.17 ± 12.87), noted as a statistically significant effect with the Wilcoxon Signed-Rank Test. The test statistics W (Table 1) were below the critical values of 81 for the joined sample ($n = 24, \alpha = 0.05$) and 13 for an individual sample ($n = 12, \alpha = 0.05$) across all groups as well (All: $p = 0.007, W = 58.0$; UTEC: $p = 0.021, W = 10.0$; Ostfalia: $p = 0.151, W = 19.5$). Regarding **TLX Perceived Performance**, the remote condition scored slightly lower on average (7.12 ± 3.84) compared to the presence condition (6.21 ± 3.88), with statistical significance nearly achieved in the Ostfalia sample and W being below the critical value ($p = 0.064, W = 12.0$). The measurements of **UMUX Frustrating experience** and **TLX Frustration** indicated a lower level of frustration in the presence setting (UMUX: presence 1.71 ± 1.12, remote 2.04 ± 1.3; TLX: presence 2.88 ± 3.22, remote 3.75 ± 3.42). In these metrics, no significant effect could be observed.

Table 1. Wilcoxon Signed-Rank test results for relevant variables of H_1. Significance p and test statistic W are highlighted according to $\alpha = 0.05$

Item	All		UTEC		Ostfalia	
	p	W	p	W	p	W
Estimated SUS score	**0.007**	**58.0**	**0.021**	**10.0**	0.151	19.5
UX Frustrating experience	0.966	**70.0**	0.569	19.0	0.622	17.0
TLX Performance	0.208	99.0	0.85	35.0	0.064	**12.0**
TLX Frustration	0.277	83.0	0.569	21.0	0.47	23.0

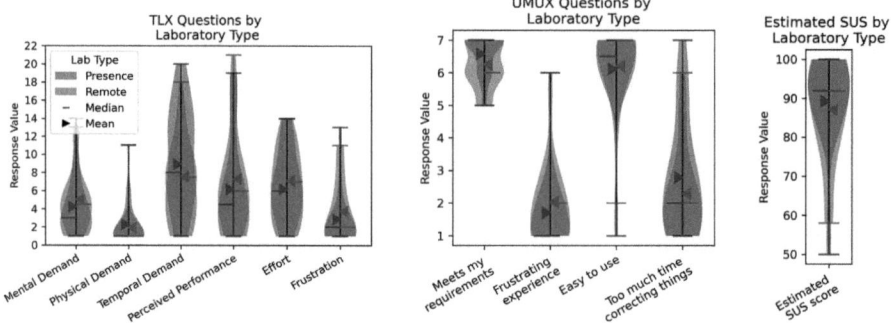

Fig. 7. Questionnaire results in violin plots "Presence vs. Remote": (Left to right) NASA TLX (21 ≡ *highest*, inverted for Perceived Performance), UMUX (7 ≡ *highest*), Estimated SUS score (100 ≡ *highest*)

Qualitative feedback revealed that participants primarily directed criticism toward the robot or occasionally *Node-(RED)²* in both conditions, while some remote participants specifically criticized the remote lab user interface. One participant specifically noted the limited workspace in *Node-(RED)²* resulting in reduced overview capabilities, an observation that aligns with concerns previously identified regarding the study design. An insecurity was observed at some points with controlling the robot in the remote setting, as highlighted by a participant's reluctance to test his developed scenario, citing, "I cannot estimate depth with the system [Remote Lab]" .

4.2 Comparison of Objective Task Performance

To examine this matter, we formulated H_2 as "The objective task performance in a remote lab with a social robot is equal or inferior compared to a remote lab in the context of HRI". To test this hypothesis, we compared the assessed grades and the measured task completion time, as well as the count of general questions and the count of questions only related to *Node-(RED)²*. These metrics were considered for the conditions "presence" and "remote" (Table 2 and Fig. 8).

For **Grade**, both conditions displayed identical mean and median values (4.17±0.87 for presence, 4.17±0.76 for remote), indicating that grading remained consistent across lab settings. This consistency is supported by the lack of statistical significant difference in all samples. **Duration** of tasks was longer in remote sessions, where a remote task was on average around 47 (∼ 9.8%) and regarding medians 75 s (∼ 15.6%) longer than a presence task. This difference approached statistical significance and W passed the critical values in the combined sample and as well as in the UTEC sample, but not in the Ostfalia group (All: $p = 0.0787, W = 78$; UTEC: $p = 0.0425, W = 10$). The average amount of **General Questions** was nearly double in remote sessions (1.92 ± 1.67 vs. 1.0 ± 0.88), although medians for both conditions were equal at 1.0. This sug-

Table 2. Wilcoxon Signed-Rank test results for relevant variables of H_2. Significance p and test statistic W are highlighted according to $\alpha = 0.05$

Item	All		UTEC		Ostfalia	
	p	W	p	W	p	W
Grade	0.439	112.5	0.677	**11.5**	0.129	18.5
Duration	0.079	**78.0**	**0.042**	**10.0**	0.677	29.5
General Questions	**0.039**	**50.0**	0.064	13.5	0.519	**8.5**
Node-(RED)^2 related questions	0.456	**57.0**	0.424	18.0	1.0	**10.5**

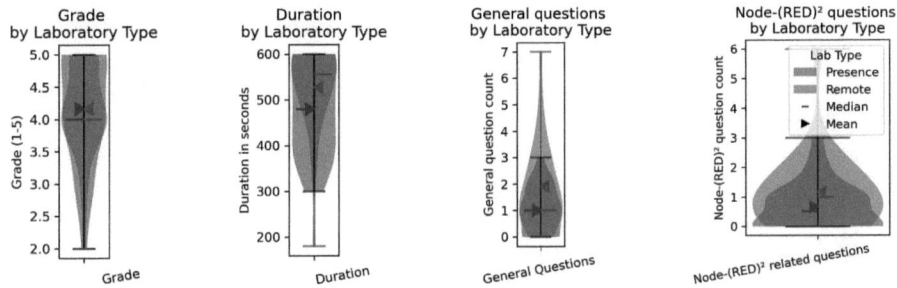

Fig. 8. Objective measurements "Presence vs. Remote": (Left to Right) Grade (1-5, 5 is the best), Task duration in seconds (time limit was $600s$), Count of asked questions in general, Count of questions related to *Node-(RED)^2*

gests that while the quantity of questions was comparable for many participants, some in remote sessions often required more assistance. The significance of these findings is confirmed in the combined and nearly for the UTEC sample, but not in the Ostfalia sample, hinting potential disparities in study conditions (All: $p = 0.039, W = 50$; UTEC: $p = 0.063, W = 13.5$). A different pattern was observed for **Node-(RED)^2-related questions**, with mean and median being both doubled in remote sessions (1.17 ± 1.34 vs. 0.67 ± 0.82), despite the median values being 1.0 vs. 0.5. However, the observed differences were not statistically significant.

5 Discussion

5.1 Hypotheses

Participants rated the usability significantly lower in the remote setting. Also, there was a noticeable decrease in perceived task performance in the Ostfalia sample for the remote lab. This observation was not supported by the UTEC nor the combined datasets. These tendencies are reinforced by the trend in both frustration metrics towards higher frustration in the remote context, although without significance. Participants also highlighted usability issues with the remote setup, particularly the website and the shared screen with *Node-(RED)*[2] in the remote setup. A sense of insecurity while controlling the robot through the remote lab was both reported and observed. Based on these observations, we conclude that H_1 is accepted, although the differences were subtle. Therefore, they recognize potential for adjustments that could equalize the differences of the perceived task performances in the future. For that, further investigation is required to enhance usability in remote labs in the context of HRI and to address the observed insecurities in robot control.

The analysis showed that grades remained consistent across groups, with no significant differences observed. This suggests parity in academic performance regardless of the setting. In contrast, the remote sample partly had significantly longer study execution times and some participants needed more clarification. However, questions specific to the tool showed no significant change. Collectively, these findings provide sufficient evidence to challenge hypothesis H_2, although the increased study execution times and number of questions may simply be symptoms of adapting to a new environment. We see potential of reducing the difference in objective task performance with future research.

Key limitations of this study include the small sample size per experimental condition and the use of low-complexity tasks. Most participants interacted with the robot only during the final testing phase, which may have constrained the depth of their engagement. The study also focused solely on audio and visual communication modalities, excluding others such as haptic interaction.

6 Conclusion and Future Work

Remote labs offer several advantages, such as increased flexibility and accessibility, and have been successfully implemented in various fields, including mechanical engineering and robotics. This study investigated whether similar concepts could be applied to Human-Robot Interaction (HRI) by conducting a within-subject laboratory experiment at two universities: Ostfalia University in Wolfenbüttel, Germany and UTEC in Rivera, Uruguay. During the study, participants programmed flow-based the humanoid social robots Pepper and NAO.

The findings indicate that task performance in a remote lab is decreased, although not as severe as expected. Regarding perceived task performance, direct ratings and rated usability decreased, while measured frustration only increased slightly. However, these differences were not significant across all samples, therefore only displaying a trend. The compared objective task performance is mixed. While the assessed grades remained consistent, task completion time and the number of clarification questions in the remote condition increased. However, except for a median increase of 15.6% in task duration, the other differences were subtle and mostly not significant. Yet, combined, the results display a trend towards decreased object task performance as well. However, we see potential to minimize these differences for both perceived and objective task performance further with future research.

Future research should focus on improving usability and enhancing participants' sense of control over the robot, building on previous research. The sample size per study should be increased, for example by collecting data when using it in an actual HRI class using a social robot. More complex tasks with extended interaction time should be introduced to evaluate whether increased familiarity with the system leads to improved performance. Integrating additional common social robot communication and perception modalities, such as the face detection capabilities of Pepper and NAO, should be considered for remote lab applications to enable their potential and better understand the challenges in this area.

Acknowledgements. The authors would like to thank Matheus Pereira, Mónica Rodríguez and Larissa Sprigade for their technical support in conducting this user study.

References

Alam, A., Lwin, M., Khan, A., Mubin, O.: Impact of robot size and number on human-robot persuasion. Information **15**(12), 782 (2024). https://doi.org/10.3390/info15120782

Bunse, C., Wieck, T.: Experiences in developing and using a remote lab in teaching robotics. In: IEEE German Education Conference (GeCon), pp. 1–6. IEEE (2022). https://doi.org/10.1109/GeCon55699.2022.9942749

Feil-Seifer, D., Haring, K.S., Rossi, S., Wagner, A.R., Williams, T.: Where to next? The impact of COVID-19 on human-robot interaction research. ACM Trans. Hum.-Robot Interact. **10**(1), 1–7 (2021). https://doi.org/10.1145/3405450

Finstad, K.: The usability metric for user experience. Interact. Comput. **22**(5), 323–327 (2010). https://doi.org/10.1016/j.intcom.2010.04.004

Gittens, C.L.: Remote HRI: a methodology for maintaining COVID-19 physical distancing and human interaction requirements in HRI studies. Inf. Syst. Front. 1–16 (2021). https://doi.org/10.1007/s10796-021-10162-4

Gomes, L., Bogosyan, S.: Current trends in remote laboratories. IEEE Trans. Ind. Electron. **56**(12), 4744–4756 (2009). https://doi.org/10.1109/TIE.2009.2033293

Gravier, C., Fayolle, J., Bayard, B., Ates, M., Lardon, J.: State of the art about remote laboratories paradigms-foundations of ongoing mutations. Int. J. Online Eng. **4**(1) (2008). https://doi.org/10.3991/ijoe.v4i1.480

Hart, S.G.: Nasa-task load index (NASA-TLX); 20 years later. Proc. Hum. Factors Ergon. Soc. Annu. Meet. **50**(9), 904–908 (2006). https://doi.org/10.1177/154193120605000909

Heradio, R., De La Torre, L., Galan, D., Cabrerizo, F.J., Herrera-Viedma, E., Dormido, S.: Virtual and remote labs in education: a bibliometric analysis. Comput. Educ. **98**, 14–38 (2016). https://doi.org/10.1016/j.compedu.2016.03.010

Lewis, J.R.: Measuring perceived usability: SUS, UMUX, and CSUQ ratings for four everyday products. Int. J. Hum.-Comput. Interact. **35**(15), 1404–1419 (2019). https://doi.org/10.1080/10447318.2018.1533152

Liang, N., Li, Y., Nejat, G.: In-person vs remote HRI: a comparative study of robot facilitated dance with older adults in long-term care. In: International Conference on Humanoid Robots (Humanoids), pp. 1–7 (2023). https://doi.org/10.1109/Humanoids57100.2023.10375155

Liang, N., Nejat, G.: A meta-analysis on remote HRI and in-person HRI: what is a socially assistive robot to do? Sensors **22**(19), 7155 (2022). https://doi.org/10.3390/s22197155

Lopes, M.S., Gomes, I.P., Trindade, R., da Silva, A., Lima, A.: Web environment for programming and control of a mobile robot in a remote laboratory. IEEE Trans. Learn. Technol. **10**(4), 526–531 (2017). https://doi.org/10.1109/TLT.2016.2627565

Ogot, M., Elliott, G., Glumac, N.: An assessment of in-person and remotely operated laboratories. J. Eng. Educ. **92**(1), 57–64 (2003). https://doi.org/10.1002/j.2168-9830.2003.tb00738.x

Pang, Dangfeng, Cui, Shigang, Yang, Genghuang: Remote laboratory as an educational tool in robotics experimental course. Int. J. Emerg. Technol. Learn. (iJET) **17**(21), 230–245 (2022). https://doi.org/10.3991/ijet.v17i21.33791

Reid, David, Burridge, Joshua, Lowe, David, Drysdale, Timothy: Open-source remote laboratory experiments for controls engineering education. Int. J. Mech. Eng. Educ. **50**(4), 828–848 (2022). https://doi.org/10.1177/03064190221081451

Riso, S., Adascalitei, D.: Human-robot interaction: what changes in the workplace? (2024). https://doi.org/10.2806/67956

Scanlon, Eileen, Colwell, Chetz, Cooper, Martyn, Di Paolo, Terry: Remote experiments, re-versioning and re-thinking science learning. Comput. Educ. **43**(1–2), 153–163 (2004). https://doi.org/10.1016/j.compedu.2003.12.010

Steinfeld, A., et al.: Common metrics for human-robot interaction. In: SIGCHI/SIGART Conference on Human-Robot Interaction, pp. 33–40 (2006). https://doi.org/10.1145/1121241.1121249

Teng, L., Tang, Y.M., Wu, R.P., Tsui, G.C., Tsang, Y.P., Tang, C.Y.: Exploring the efficacy of collaborative learning in a remote robotics laboratory: a comparative analysis of performance and pedagogical approaches. Smart Learn. Environ. **11**(1), 15 (2024). https://doi.org/10.1186/s40561-024-00305-w

Tzafestas, C., Palaiologou, N., Alifragis, M.: Virtual and remote robotic laboratory: comparative experimental evaluation. IEEE Trans. Educ. **49**(3), 360–369 (2006). https://doi.org/10.1109/TE.2006.879255

Weike, M., Ruske, K., Gerndt, R., Doernbach, T.: Enabling untrained users to shape real-world robot behavior using an intuitive visual programming tool in human-robot interaction scenarios. In: International Symposium on Technological Advances in Human-Robot Interaction (2024). https://doi.org/10.1145/3648536.3648541

Do Social Robots Motivate Students like Humans?

Akshara Pande[1], Bethany Gosala[2], Manjari Gupta[2,3], and Deepti Mishra[1(✉)]

[1] Intelligent Systems and Analytics Group, Department of Computer Science (IDI), Norwegian University of Science and Technology (NTNU), Gjøvik, Norway
deepti.mishra@ntnu.no.com
[2] DST-CIMS, Institute of Science, Banaras Hindu University, Varanasi, India
[3] Department of Computer Science, Banaras Hindu University, Varanasi, India

Abstract. The application of artificial intelligence tools provides the opportunity for improvements in several sectors, including education. A companion providing constant motivation can help students towards advanced engagement, learning and performance. In this direction, the present study explores the importance of feedback by considering many factors together, such as feedback provider, feedback type and feedback sequence on students' visual attention and performance. An experiment was performed with two feedback providers, a social robot Pepper and a human companion; during the task, they provided three types of feedback: negative, neutral and positive. The task was to search for an object in the specified image within a certain time. Furthermore, four scenarios were formed to observe the impact of the feedback provider and the order of feedback provided. The participants were equipped with wearable eye trackers, Tobii Pro glasses 3, to collect their eye movement data. The aim of the paper is to evaluate the effectiveness of Pepper's feedback in comparison to human feedback in motivating users to enhance their visual attention and performance. The findings of the present study indicate the comparable influence of both robot and human feedback on participants' visual attention and performance, possibly more so with feedback from Pepper. Thus, it suggests that social robots have the potential to inspire participants as human companions and can be utilized as teaching assistants. However, it is important to explore this further with a diverse and increased number of participants in real settings.

Keywords: Eye tracking · Human companion · Robot companion · Artificial Intelligence · FFD · TFD

1 Introduction

The rapid progression of technology has led to major developments in the education field. The incorporation of Artificial Intelligence (AI) – based tools in the education domain is not only useful for enhancing the learning experience and evaluating performance but also for providing fruitful outcomes in terms of increased motivation, learning, engagement, and performance [1]. Similarly, Kavitha et al. [2] also emphasized learners' experience through the proper utilization of AI in the field of e-learning. Furthermore, AI-based tools are useful in collaborative contexts as well by incorporating theories related to education and learning, as well as supporting instructors [3]. The integration of AI with eye tracking provides the facility to predict students' performance through their gaze behaviours [4]. Eye trackers are suitable for school environments with many characteristics, such as portability and have the potential to measure the attention and engagement of students [5]. Eye tracking devices are mainly of two types: Screen-based and wearable eye trackers; the difference between them is how they capture person's gaze. Screen-based eye trackers are limited to computer screen-related experiments, whereas wearable eye trackers are capable of tracking anything in which direction a person's head is moving [6]. However, Hooge et al. [7] suggested that the accuracy of wearable eye trackers decreases with varied movements.

Feedback plays an important role in influencing the performance of the users, which could be reflected through the eye movements. Hu et al. [8] performed an experiment where subjects were provided with three kinds of automatic feedback by computer: positive, negative, and no feedback while watching videos. The movement of participants' eyes was recorded using Tobii 1750. Further, they demonstrated that the performances were better when positive feedback was provided. Additionally, the authors also considered self-efficacy and showed that people with low self-efficacy were more susceptible to negative feedback. Ahmed et al. [9] compared the influence of feedback on students' performance when human tutor and automated adaptive feedback provided feedback for correcting flawed programs. Further, the author suggested that automated feedback impacts performance more. These studies motivate us to evaluate whether feedback from social robots with human-like appearances can inspire users' visual attention and performance similar to human feedback.

Social robots, due to their capabilities, are increasingly employed in the education sector as educational assistants [10] or learning assistants [11]. The presence of general AI capabilities such as facial, emotion and speech recognition in social robots [12], makes them suitable for learning environments. Previous studies showed that the presence of a physical entity, such as a social robot, is useful for improvement in learning [13, 14] and cognition [15]. Furthermore, the inclusion of social robots in education can impact the learning outcomes [16].

The present study includes two feedback providers, a social robot, Pepper, and a human companion, as indicated in Fig. 1. It is assumed that they represent teaching assistants or lab assistants. During the experiment, participants wore Tobii Pro wearable glass and received continuous feedback from a robot or a human companion. The aim is to investigate the impact of positive, neutral and negative feedback on users' performance while they were engaged in the given task. Furthermore, four scenarios were considered to conduct the experiment. The first and second scenarios were initiated by the feedback (from Pepper and human, respectively) in the sequence of negative, neutral, and positive comments to the participants undertaking the tasks. The third and fourth scenarios started again with comments (from Pepper and human, respectively), but the order was different: positive, neutral and negative feedback. The main objective is to identify whether a social robot can be similar to a human companion to motivate humans to perform various tasks requiring attention. To achieve this, the overall goal is divided into the following research questions:

RQ1: Does feedback and its sequence from a social robot influence the attention of users in the same way as feedback from a human companion?

RQ2: Which companion's feedback - Social robot or human - impacts the average performance of the users? Does the order of feedback matter?

Fig. 1. Robot and human companions providing negative, neutral and positive feedback to participant (wearing tobii eye glass) in between the tasks

The paper is organized as follows: Sect. 2 describes previously done research work, Sect. 3 illustrates the methodology adopted, Sect. 4 shows results, Sect. 5 contains a discussion, and Sect. 6 states conclusions and future work.

2 Related Works

The increasing advancement of technology brings advantages in various fields, including education. One such technology is an eye tracker, which helps capture students' behaviour through their gazes for understanding students' efficiencies in handling the given tasks [5] and evaluating their learning styles [17–20]. The Tobii eye-tracking platforms, encompassing their applications as screen-based systems and wearable glass, play a significant role in this direction. Both eye-tracking platforms contain modules such as eye cameras, illuminators, a facility to identify images using the processing unit, 3D eye models and algorithms for gaze mapping [21]. However, they differ in various aspects including portability, mobility and scope of capturing.

The inclusion of AI tools has both positive and negative impacts on education. Cai et al. [22] reviewed the influence of AI tools on higher education and suggested that they are beneficial for enhancing engagement, motivation, support for learning, the development of collaborative learning settings, and better communication. Furthermore, Chen et al. [23] illustrated in their review the application of AI for education and suggested that

AI integration with other technologies, such as robots, could efficiently advance the learning experience. In the same line, Pande et al. [10] integrated Pepper's speech recognition system with the speech-to-text conversion tool, Whisper, to evaluate the performance of Pepper as an educational assistant in both online and offline environments.

With different types of feedback, there is scope for improvement in learners' characteristics, including performance [24], self-regulation [25], emotions, motivations, and learning [26]. A previous study [26] indicated that the incorporation of other AI tools, such as ChatGPT, could be beneficial for students in improving computational thinking, self-efficacy, and encouragement. However, on the other side, the integration of ChatGPT could potentially negatively influence students' emotional intelligence [27]. Escalante et al. [28] compared the difference between human tutor feedback and Chatgpt-generated feedback on the writing skills of students learning English as a new language. Through the experiment, the authors found similar learning outcomes in both cases. Further, the authors also evaluated the perceptions of participants and revealed that participants preferred both feedbacks equally. Moreover, they suggested the use of blending human tutor feedback and AI-generated feedback to reduce the burden on teachers.

3 Methodology

The experiment was conducted with 15 participants in the laboratory environment. The participants were primarily students and researchers aged 16 to 40. The present study received approval from the Sikt-Norwegian Agency for Shared Services in Education and Research for ethically handling sensitive and personal information. Additionally, before the experiment, consent forms were signed by participants to collect their eye movement data from the wearable eye tracker Tobii pro glasses 3. Tobii pro glasses 3 is a recently launched wearable eye tracker for gathering human gaze information [29]. It contains 16 illuminators, four eye cameras in wearable lenses and built-in microphones, which help capture sound from the environment. There is a facility to analyze the captured data with Tobii Pro Lab [30] by utilizing different AI algorithms such as gaze estimation algorithms, identification of SCR in GSR data by applying SCR detection algorithm, eye movement classification with Gaze Filter and Tobii I-VT Fixation Filter [31].

3.1 Task Details

The participants were asked to find an object in the given image. The images were displayed on a computer screen within a controlled laboratory setting, ensuring minimum ambient light in the room. Each image was presented before them for 10 seconds. While searching for an object, participants received feedback from robot and human companions (Fig. 1).

3.2 Scenarios for Providing Feedback

The feedback contains three kinds of comments: positive, neutral and negative from both robot and human in different orders. The authors carefully finalized the statements for positive, neutral, and negative feedback through a collaborative discussion. A human companion stated all feedback included in the paper, while the Pepper robot was programmed to provide the feedback through speech by utilizing a text-to-speech method. The few examples of feedback are as follows: Positive- 'You are doing well', 'Keep going', 'Do not give up'; Neutral - 'Lets move to the next', 'That is interesting', 'Onto the next one'; Negative - 'You seem distracted', 'Others did better', 'Is, this your best?'. Four scenarios were considered for the experiment; each scenario contained all three types of feedback while the participants tried to find the object in the given image.

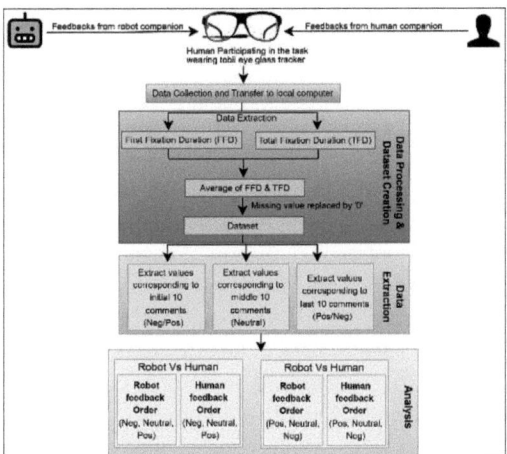

Fig. 2. An overview of data collection and analysis to evaluate the impact of companions' feedback on participants' performance

An overview of data collection and analysis has been shown in Fig. 2. A total of 30 images were displayed on the screen, 10 images each for all three types of feedback in each scenario. The type of feedback was given for ten consecutive images, but with different statements each time. It was assumed that all the images had the same level of complexity. For each scenario, a total of 30 pieces of feedback were given by the companions, irrespective of the participants' performance. More details about the four scenarios are discussed below:

- **Scenario 1**: In this scenario, a social robot was selected as a companion for providing feedback to the participant in the sequence of negative, followed by neutral and followed by positive comments (R_{Neg} -> R_{Neu} -> R_{Pos})
- **Scenario 2**: In this scenario, a human was selected as a companion for providing feedback to the participant in the sequence of negative, followed by neutral and followed by positive comments (H_{Neg} -> H_{Neu} -> H_{Pos})
- **Scenario 3**: In this scenario, a social robot was selected as a companion for providing feedback to the participant in the sequence of positive, followed by neutral and followed by negative comments (R_{Pos} -> R_{Neu} -> R_{Neg})
- **Scenario 4**: In this scenario, a human was selected as a companion for providing feedback to the participant in the sequence of positive, followed by neutral and followed by negative comments (H_{Pos} -> H_{Neu} -> H_{Neg})

3.3 Data Processing and Dataset Creation

We first uploaded the snapshots of the images in which the participant had to find the object to the Tobii Pro Lab software. We then used the AOI tool to create the area of interest (AOI) for the objects in each snapshot image. AOI plays a very important role in the calculation of various metrics. Tobii Pro Lab software was further used for initial preprocessing and to obtain metrics such as First Fixation Duration (FFD), Total Fixation Duration (TFD), etc. We then created secondary data by exporting these metrics in the form of an Excel file. A secondary analysis of the experiments was done on this exported data. The average of FFD and TFD were considered for further analysis. Additionally, missing values were replaced by '0', and a new dataset was created.

3.4 Data Extraction and Analysis

We assumed that all the images had the same complexity level. The values of the FFD and TFD for the negative comments were extracted and averaged to get a single value. Furthermore, a threshold value of '2' was assumed to indicate that any value exceeding this value would suggest successful identification (denoted by 1) of the object in the given image; otherwise, it would be considered an unsuccessful identification (denoted by 0). Additionally, the averages for successful and unsuccessful identifications corresponding to negative, neutral, and positive comments were also calculated. Likewise, the same process was repeated for neutral and positive comments for each of the four scenarios. Moreover, these values were considered to observe the effect of feedback provided by robots and human companions.

4 Results

Thirty images were displayed before the participants for each of the four scenarios. The task was to find a given object inside the image in the presence of continuous comments provided by both companions. One such image with scan paths of eye movements is illustrated in Fig. 3. Tobii Pro Lab was used to observe the scan path of all the participants' gazes. The color of a circle is different for each of the 15 participants, the number inside the circle is the gaze point number, and the size of the circle presents the duration of focus of the participant; the bigger the circle, the bigger the gaze point focus duration. We instructed all the participants before the experiment to focus on the object if they found it in the image, so the bigger the size of the circle, the higher the chance that the participant might have found the object inside the image that they were searching for.

In all the scenarios, participants were asked to focus their gaze once they found the object in the given picture. Scenario 1 (R_{Neg} -> R_{Neu} -> R_{Pos}) and Scenario 2 (H_{Neg} -> H_{Neu} -> H_{Pos}) started with negative feedback provided by the robot and human, respectively. Scenario 3 (R_{Pos} -> R_{Neu} -> R_{Neg}) and Scenario 4 (H_{Pos} -> H_{Neu} -> H_{Neg}) began with positive feedback provided by the robot and human, respectively. Table 1 denotes the average values corresponding to the successful and unsuccessful identification of objects in the given image for all the feedback. Furthermore, this table is explored for a better understanding of these attained values.

Fig. 3. Scan-path created using Tobii Pro Lab for all the participants' eye-movement while searching for an object

Figure 4 shows the comparison of extracted average values progressing from negative comments, followed by neutral and concluding with positive comments from both the companions. The higher value indicates the participants' strong attention and focus during the task. For instance, the influence of the robot-provided feedback could be observed for participant 10, who has the lowest value for negative comments and the highest value for positive comments and as far as neutral comments are concerned, the value lies between the two. However, for the same participant, Fig. 4 suggests the values gained with human-provided feedback are similar in all the cases (negative, neutral and positive feedback) and less than robot-provided feedback. The same trend of values gained could be visualized for participant 17 with a robot companion. However, there was no impact from any of the human-provided feedback.

Further, the maximum values for robot-provided feedback are found for participant 25, with higher values for neutral and positive comments in comparison to negative comments. Additionally, for the same participant, the value obtained with negative comments from human companion is lower in comparison to neutral and positive comments of human feedback provider. There is a very slight difference between the values attained for negative comments from human and robot companions, with a slightly higher value gained with human companion's comment. However, for the same participant 25, the value achieved with negative and neutral comments from the robot were more than the similar kind of comments provided by the human companion. On the other hand, Fig. 4 indicates that the values obtained for participant 16, participant 24 and participant 9 were usually high with human feedback rather than robot feedback. One interesting thing could be noted that for participant 7 only value obtained with human positive feedback; otherwise, it is absent in all the above-mentioned situations.

To summarize, with respect to scenario 1 and scenario 2, the obtained results are mixed which shows that participants' focus can be influenced by the feedback provided by both social robot and human companion.

In Fig. 5, the sequence of comments provided by both companions is opposite to the previous cases. It starts with positive comments, moving to neutral comments and finally ending with negative comments. It can be observed that in Fig. 5, similar to Fig. 4, the

Table 1. Average Performance of participants in finding an object inside image

Participants	Scenario 1: $R_{Neg} \to R_{Neu} \to R_{Pos}$			Scenario 2: $H_{Neg} \to H_{Neu} \to H_{Pos}$			Scenario 3: $R_{Pos} \to R_{Neu} \to R_{Neg}$			Scenario 4: $H_{Pos} \to H_{Neu} \to H_{Neg}$		
	Avg Neg	Avg Neu	Avg Pos	Avg Neg	Avg Neu	Avg Pos	Avg Pos	Avg Neu	Avg Neg	Avg Pos	Avg Neu	Avg Neg
P10	0.5	0.7	0.8	0.4	0.4	0.4	0.6	0.8	0.4	0.3	0.1	0.3
P12	0.08	0	0.1	0	0	0	0.1	0.2	0.1	0	0.1	0.1
P15	0.08	0	0.2	0.1	0.1	0.4	0.3	0.6	0.7	0.7	0.6	0.8
P16	0.42	0.2	0.6	0.7	0.5	0.6	0.7	0.8	0.5	1	0.7	0.9
P17	0.58	0.7	0.8	0	0	0	0.6	0.9	0.6	0.2	0	0.2
P19	0.25	0.2	0.2	0.2	0	0.2	0.4	0.2	0	0.4	0.2	0.3
P2	0.67	0.5	0.6	0	0.3	0.4	0.8	0.5	0.4	0.4	0.2	0.6
P23	0.17	0.3	0.3	0	0	0.1	0.8	0.9	1	0.8	0.5	0.8
P24	0.33	0.3	0.3	0.7	0.5	0.6	0.6	0.5	0.7	0.8	0.4	0.3
P25	0.5	0.9	0.9	0.6	0.8	0.7	0.8	0.8	0.7	0.8	0.4	0.8
P29	0.58	0.4	0.4	0.3	0.3	0.4	0.3	0.1	0.1	0.1	0	0.1
P30	0.58	0.8	0.6	0.6	0.1	0.6	0.4	0.5	0.6	0.5	0.3	0.4
P7	0	0	0	0	0	0.1	0	0	0	0	0	0
P8	0.5	0.6	0.6	0.5	0.4	0.6	0.7	0.8	0.7	0.6	0.8	0.9
P9	0.5	0.6	0.6	0.7	0.7	0.6	0.7	0.9	0.5	0.6	0.5	0.5

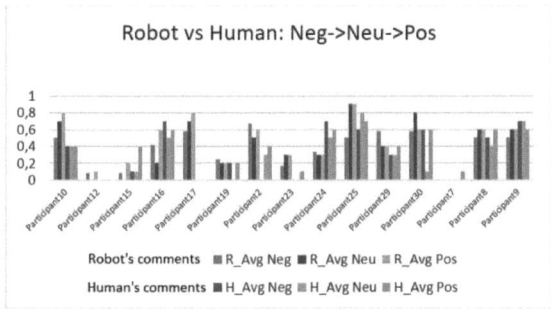

Fig. 4. Visual attention of participants when feedback was provided by robot and human companion during scenario 1 and scenario 2

values attained for participant 10 with the robot companion's comments are higher than the human companion's comments. However, with neutral feedback from the robot, the value is highest, whereas with human's neutral feedback, the value is lowest. But the interesting insight is that participants pay more visual attention to positive comments than to negative comments by a robot. Similarly, the gained values are relatively higher for participant 17, participant 23 and participant 9 with the robot companion's feedback in comparison to the human companion's feedback. Further, the highest obtained values for participant 17 and participant 9 are with neutral comments, whereas for participant 23, it is with negative comments of the robot. On the other hand, the values achieved for participant 15 and participant 16 are relatively higher for positive and negative comments provided by human companion. Interestingly, the visualization of Fig. 5 indicates the slightly higher values obtained for participant 2 and participant 8 with positive comments of the robot in comparison to human comments. However, for the same participants, with negative comments of human companion the values are higher with respect to robot's negative comments.

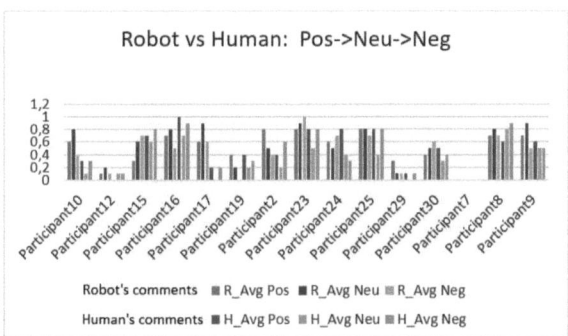

Fig. 5. Visual attention of participants when feedback was provided by robot and human companion during scenario 3 and scenario 4

To summarize, with respect to scenario 3 and scenario 4, similar to the previous results, it also led to mixed results indicating the similar impact of robot and human companions on the focus of participants.

As far as order of feedback (Neg-> Neu-> Pos) is concerned, it is observed that participants' visual attention increased in case of some participants (participants 10, 17, 23, 25, 8, and 9), with the robot companion's comments. However, this was not the case for other participants. Similarly, we found a lack of a consistent pattern with human companion's feedback. Some cases (with participants 16, 19, 24, and 30) were identified where there is a drop in visual attention when moving from negative to neutral comments and then again enhanced by positive comments.

With respect to the order of feedback (Pos-> Neu-> Neg), the impact of the robot's comments is most evident in the increased visual attention of participants, with the highest rise observed during neutral comments. This was followed by, for some participants (9, 10, and 16), positive and then negative comments, whereas, for others (participants 8, 12, and 17), the same level of attention was achieved for both positive and negative comments. With regard to human companion's feedback, five cases (with participants 10, 7, 23, 25 and 29) are noticeable, having similar influence on visual attention with positive and negative comments, but with a drop with neutral comments.

It should be noted that, in general, no consistent pattern in terms of achieving visual attention was found when the order of feedback was changed.

To explore the effectiveness of the robot and human companion's feedback, aggregated group analyses are done for participants' performance. Figure 6 suggests that the average performance of participants is always higher with all three kinds of feedback from the robot companion. Furthermore, a noticeable trend is that the average performance of participants increases as the robot's comments move from negative to neutral to positive. However, it can be observed with feedback from the human companion that the average performance is the least with neutral comments and highest with positive comments.

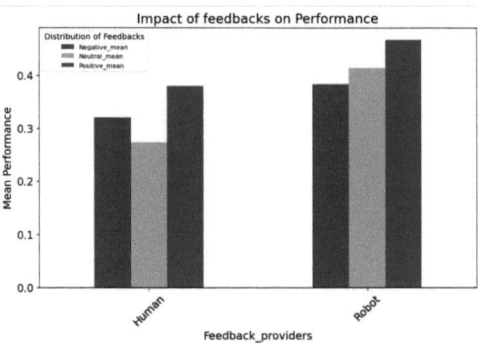

Fig. 6. Average Performance of Participants in case of scenario 1 and scenario 2

Figure 7 illustrates the comparison between the average performances of participants when the feedback provided by companions are in order of positive comments, neutral comments and negative comments. It could be visualized from the figure that average performance is comparatively higher with positive and neutral comments with robot companion. Furthermore, moving from positive to neutral comments from human feedback-provider, the average performance drops, but again increases for negative comments. Whereas in the case of shifting from positive to neutral comments from the robot companion, there is a slight increase in average performance and a sudden drop with negative comments. On the other hand, with negative comments from both the companions, the average performance is exactly the same.

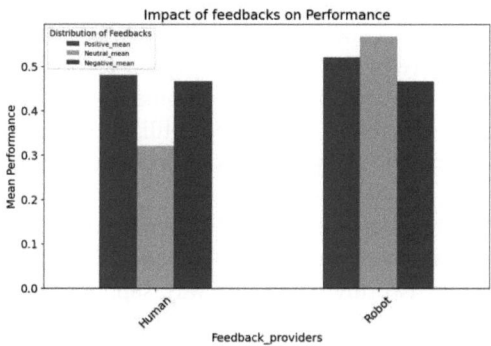

Fig. 7. Average Performance of Participants in case of scenario 3 and scenario 4

With respect to all four scenarios, the results from aggregated group analysis suggested that most of the time, there is an increase in average performance when the feedback provider is a robot. However, this increase in average performance is not substantial compared to human feedback. It should be noted that there is always a drop in performance with neutral comments of human companion, irrespective of initiation with positive or negative comments. Conversely, neutral comments from a robot companion consistently led to an increase in performance compared to the starting comment, regardless of whether it was positive or negative. Neutral feedback yields the best performance when preceded by a positive comment, while when negative feedback comes first, it ranks between the two with the highest for positive feedback.

5 Discussions

The present study explores whether feedback from the robot and human companions influences participants' focus and performance. The feedback contains negative, neutral and positive comments. Concerning RQ1, the findings suggest the mixed impact of feedback on participants' visual attention. The reason behind it might be due to the personality of individuals and how the feedback motivates and demotivates them. Further, it can be seen from the analysis that when the feedback started with negative comments followed by neutral and ended with positive comments (i.e. scenario 1 and scenario 2), participants' visual attention was mostly higher for positive and neutral comments by the robot companion. It suggests that participants were motivated by the feedback of the robot companion more in the case of neutral and positive comments. In a similar way, the higher impact on visual attention of positive comments by human companion could be observed, although this impact is lesser than the impact of the robot's positive comments. Therefore, this study suggests participants were more motivated by positive comments (when feedback started with negative comments) irrespective of who the feedback provider was – robot or human. When feedback began with positive comments (i.e. scenario 3 and scenario 4), the mixed outcomes were received again with mostly higher visual attention with the robot's neutral comments. The reason could be that the initial positive comments inspired the participants, and this inspiration was sustained when the positive feedback shifted to neutral comments. However, overall, with regard to RQ1, the results indicate that social robot feedback was able to influence the visual attention of participants more or was similar to human feedback. Furthermore, it also suggests that social robots can be utilized in environments with the purpose of inspiring individuals to work more efficiently. Such robot utilization will not only help reduce the burden of individuals but also help in terms of dependency and availability of other people.

Previous studies have indicated the impact of feedback on users. Ruwe et al. [32] demonstrated the comparison between AI and human feedback providers and found AI-mediated feedback more trustworthy, which, in a way, supports the findings of the present study. Furthermore, Leite et al. [33] showed that students understood the concepts of AI and programming better with human-written feedback than with computer-generated feedback. This is a bit contrary to the outcome of the present study although the context is different. Lee et al. [34] described the importance of feedback and showed that the learners focused more on the next item when they received negative feedback on the previous item and vice versa. The findings concerning visual attention demonstrate inconsistency in relation to the sequence of feedback. In our case, it is also possible that feedback provided for the previous image does carry an influence on the next. However, we did not explore that in the present paper, which will be the focus of future work.

With regard to RQ2, the present study's results from the analysis of the aggregate group demonstrated that the participants achieved higher average performance with all kinds of feedback provided by the robot compared to a human, except when negative comments were provided at the end. However, the average performance gained was the same, with negative comments from both the robot and human companion. This indicates that, in most cases, the influence of the robot companion on average performance is greater than that of a human companion. Additionally, it can be inferred from the study's outcomes that the order of feedback given also matters, with an increase in average performance resulting from neutral comments by the robot companion. In the case when feedback is initiated with the robot's positive comments, neutral feedback is the most impactful. In contrast, beginning with negative comments results in an improvement from negative to neutral, and then to positive comments. On the other hand, there is always a drop in performance with neutral comments of human, relative to the negative and positive comments, no matter what order they are in. Similar to our study, past research [35] demonstrated that negative feedback from human and computer could influence performance and induce stress. However, Ahmed et al. [36] suggested no significant impact of various feedback from non-humanoid robot on task performance. The outcomes of aggregated group analysis relating to each of the four scenarios indicated that the increase in average performance was majorly with the feedback of the robot. Nevertheless, it is not noticeably higher than human feedback.

6 Conclusion

The present study focused on exploring the impact of three kinds of feedback provided by Pepper and human companions on participants with the help of eye movement data. The task was presented to participants to find a given object in a series of images. The findings of the present study with respect to RQ1 illustrate that, similar to human companion, robot companion feedback also has an influence on participants' visual attention, indicating the possibility of social robots as potential assistants in various professions where there is a need for inspiring users. However, concerning the sequence of feedback, the results obtained were inconclusive for both feedback providers – robot and human. There is still a question about the trustworthiness of robots. In the future, we will explore this feasibility by including more characteristics such as empathy, speech, gestures and context-awareness in the robots. Concerning RQ2, the results mostly favoured the robot's feedback, as participants performed well with all kinds of feedback provided by the robot, rather than a human. Moreover, the order of feedback impacts participants' average performance, regardless the initiation by positive or negative feedback, resulting in a decrease in performance with neutral comments from a human companion and an increase in performance with neutral comments from a robot companion. It should be noted that the results should be taken into consideration in view of the sample size. In the present study, the target sample size was small and in the future, we will select a larger sample size and participants with more variations. The present study is a pilot investigation that will act as a prototype for designing experiments with the selection of the right participants in the future. Further, findings obtained and lessons learnt from present analyses can help us to get more precise results.

Further, the experiments were performed in laboratory settings within a controlled environment. The feedback comments were already defined and not generated in real time. Moreover, the images shown to participants were considered to be of the same difficulty level. There were some technical issues encountered during the experiment since Pepper sometimes did not respond in the manner it was programmed to because of environmental interference due to its built-in AI intelligence. Therefore, in the future, experiments could be designed to provide real-time feedback from human and robot to improve students' motivation and performance.

The present study findings suggest that a social robot can be used as an assistive tool in different settings to provide feedback and motivate individuals, just like humans. Moreover, with the physical embodiment of the robot, students may feel more comfortable with the robot companion and receive feedback from it in comparison to other digital tools. Sometimes, participants might be hesitant to share information, ask questions, and accept feedback from other human beings, and in those cases, a robot assistant can be a viable alternative, as per the result of this preliminary study. Furthermore, the integration of social robots will reduce the workload for educators, allowing them to handle the classes more efficiently and focus on other important responsibilities. Besides this, robot employment might contribute towards minimizing dependency and the availability of other human beings.

Disclosure of Interests. The authors have no competing interests to declare that are relevant to the content of this article.

References

1. Xu, Z.: AI in education: enhancing learning experiences and student outcomes. Appl. Comput. Eng. **51**(1), 104–111 (2024)
2. Kavitha, V., Lohani, R.: A critical study on the use of artificial intelligence, e-Learning technology and tools to enhance the learners experience. Clust. Comput. **22**(3), 6985–6989 (2019)
3. Ouyang, F., Zhang, L.: AI-driven learning analytics applications and tools in computer-supported collaborative learning: a systematic review. Educ. Res. Rev. **44**, 100616 (2024)
4. Sharma, K., Giannakos, M., Dillenbourg, P.: Eye-tracking and artificial intelligence to enhance motivation and learning. Smart Learn. Environ. **7**(1), 13 (2020)
5. da Silva Soares, R., et al.: Chapter Three - Exploring the potential of eye tracking on personalized learning and real-time feedback in modern education, in Progress in Brain Research, M. Gomides, I. Starling-Alves, and F.H. Santos, Editors. Elsevier, pp. 49–70 (2023)
6. Jongerius, C., et al.: Eye-tracking glasses in face-to-face interactions: Manual versus automated assessment of areas-of-interest. Behav. Res. Methods **53**(5), 2037–2048 (2021)
7. Hooge, I.T.C., et al.: How robust are wearable eye trackers to slow and fast head and body movements? Behav. Res. Methods **55**(8), 4128–4142 (2023)
8. Hu, J., et al.: How feedback intervention affects the performance of self-efficacy: an eye movement study. In: 2009 Second International Conference on Education Technology and Training. IEEE (2009)
9. Ahmed, U.Z., et al.: Characterizing the pedagogical benefits of adaptive feedback for compilation errors by novice programmers. In: Proceedings of the ACM/IEEE 42nd International Conference on Software Engineering: Software Engineering Education and Training (2020)
10. Pande, A., Mishra, D.: Humanoid robot as an educational assistant – insights of speech recognition for online and offline mode of teaching. Behav. Inf. Technol., 1–18
11. Tilden, S., et al.: Humanoid Robots as Learning Assistants? Useability Perspectives of Grade 6 Students. Technology, Knowledge and Learning (2024)
12. Robert, L.P., et al.: Social robotics business and computing. Inf. Syst. Front. **26**(1), 1–8 (2024)
13. Kennedy, J., Baxter, P., Belpaeme, T.: The robot who tried too hard: Social behaviour of a robot tutor can negatively affect child learning. In: Proceedings of the Tenth Annual ACM/IEEE International Conference on Human-Robot Interaction (2015)
14. Li, J.: The benefit of being physically present: a survey of experimental works comparing copresent robots, telepresent robots and virtual agents. Int. J. Hum Comput. Stud. **77**, 23–37 (2015)
15. Leyzberg, D., et al.: The physical presence of a robot tutor increases cognitive learning gains. In: Proceedings of the Annual Meeting of the Cognitive Science Society (2012)
16. Belpaeme, T., et al.: Social robots for education: A review. Science Robotics **3**(21) (2018)
17. Höffler, T.N., Koć-Janutcha, M., Leutner, D.: More evidence for three types of cognitive style: validating the object-spatial imagery and verbal questionnaire using eye tracking when learning with texts and pictures. Appl. Cogn. Psychol. **31**(1), 109–115 (2017)

18. Luo, Z., O'Steen, B., Brown, C.: The use of eye-tracking technology to identify visualisers and verbalisers: accuracy and contributing factors. Interactive Technol. Smart Educat. **17**(2), 229–247 (2020)
19. Luo, Z., Wang, Y.: Eye-tracking technology in identifying visualizers and verbalizers: data on eye-movement differences and detection accuracy. Data Brief **26**, 104447 (2019)
20. Raptis, G.E., et al.: Using eye gaze data and visual activities to infer human cognitive styles: method and feasibility studies. In: Proceedings of the 25th Conference on User Modeling, Adaptation and Personalization (2017)
21. Tobii eye trackers web page. https://connect.tobii.com/s/article/How-do-Tobii-eye-trackers-work?language=en_US. Assessed 12th Jan 2025
22. Cai, L., Msafiri, M.M., Kangwa, D.: Exploring the impact of integrating AI tools in higher education using the Zone of Proximal Development. Educ. Inf. Technol., 1–74 (2024)
23. Chen, L., Chen, P., Lin, Z.: Artificial intelligence in education: a review. IEEE Access **8**, 75264–75278 (2020)
24. Aucejo, E.M., Wong, K.: The effect of feedback on student performance. J. Public Econ. **241**, 105274 (2025)
25. Brown, G.T., Peterson, E.R., Yao, E.S.: Student conceptions of feedback: impact on self-regulation, self-efficacy, and academic achievement. Br. J. Educ. Psychol. **86**(4), 606–629 (2016)
26. Mandouit, L., Hattie, J.: Revisiting "The Power of Feedback" from the perspective of the learner. Learn. Instr. **84**, 101718 (2023)
27. Jammeli, H., et al.: The Impact of AI Tools in Education Environment. In: 2024 12th International Conference on Information and Education Technology (ICIET). IEEE (2024)
28. Escalante, J., Pack, A., Barrett, A.: AI-generated feedback on writing: insights into efficacy and ENL student preference. Int. J. Educ. Technol. High. Educ. **20**(1), 57 (2023)
29. Tobii webpag. https://www.tobii.com/products/eye-trackers/wearables/tobii-pro-glasses-3. Accessed 17 Dec 2024
30. Tobii Pro Lab webpage. https://www.tobii.com/products/software/behavior-research-software/tobii-pro-lab. Accessed 17 Dec 2024
31. Tobii Pro Lab User's Manual. http://www.vinis.co.kr/TPL_manual.pdf. Accessed 14 Jan 2025
32. Ruwe, T., Mayweg-Paus, E.: "Your argumentation is good", says the AI vs humans – The role of feedback providers and personalised language for feedback effectiveness. Comput. Educ. Artif. Intell. **5**, 100189 (2023)
33. Leite, A., Blanco, S.A.: Effects of human vs. automatic feedback on students' understanding of AI concepts and programming style. In: Proceedings of the 51st ACM Technical Symposium on Computer Science Education (2020)
34. Lee, J.F., Doherty, S.: The effects of implicit positive and negative feedback on processing subsequent linguistic target items: an eye-tracking study. In: The Routledge handbook of second language research in classroom learning, pp. 361–374. Routledge (2019)
35. Thuillard, S., et al.: When humans and computers induce social stress through negative feedback: Effects on performance and subjective state. Comput. Hum. Behav. **133**, 107270 (2022)
36. Ahmed, M.S., Giuliani, M., Bremner, P.: Influencing Human Performance: Investigating the Effect of Non-humanoid Robot Feedback on Task Performance. In: Companion of the 2024 ACM/IEEE International Conference on Human-Robot Interaction (2024)

More Than a Tool: A Multi Method Exploration of Contextual Social Robot Roles in German Secondary Schools

Nadine Jansen(✉), Ann-Kathrin Kubullek, and Aysegül Dogangün

Ruhr West University of Applied Sciences, Bottrop, Germany
{nadine.jansen,ann-kathrin.kubullek,ayseguel.doganguen}@hs-ruhrwest.de

Abstract. Social robots, understood as autonomous, physically embodied systems designed to engage in social interaction with humans, are increasingly explored for use in educational settings, are being explored as support tools in education, yet their roles beyond instruction remain under-researched. This study investigates how students and professionals envision acceptable uses for robots in secondary schools. Using a multi-method approach—including a participatory workshop, student observations, and expert interviews—we identify key expectations and role preferences. Findings suggest that acceptance hinges on role clarity, contextual fit, and non-authoritative behavior. Social robots are most accepted when designed to assist rather than supervise. The study offers design implications for socially embedded robots and highlights the value of participatory development.

Keywords: Social robots · Education · Role design · Human-robot interaction

1 Introduction

The shortage of skilled workers is also affecting teaching staff in Germany, leading to increasingly overcrowded classrooms. Recent estimates indicate that Germany is currently facing a shortage of 25,000 teachers [31], with projections suggesting that this gap could increase to 85,000 by 2030 [14]. As the demands on teachers are increasing, opportunities for individual support and personalized learning often diminish. This situation raises important questions about how technological innovations could help maintain and even improve educational quality despite limited human resources. One promising avenue is the integration of social robots into everyday school life.

The study is informed by two theoretical frameworks: the Technology Acceptance Model (TAM) and Role Theory. TAM highlights perceived usefulness and ease of use as drivers of acceptance, while Role Theory analyzes how actors—human or robotic—gain legitimacy through socially expected behaviors.

The present study investigates how social robots can be meaningfully integrated into everyday secondary school life. Adopting a multi-method approach, including a participatory workshop with students, a student-led observational study, and expert interviews, we examine user needs, expectations, and potential challenges related to the deployment of social robots in schools.

In the student workshop, we employed the Jobs-to-be-Done (JTBD) method [5,17,36], a user-centered framework from innovation and product development that focuses on the underlying goals people seek to accomplish in specific situations. Rather than starting with technology features, JTBD emphasizes the desired outcomes of users, both functional and emotional, which makes it particularly valuable for identifying context-sensitive expectations in educational settings.

To complement these insights, a group of trained students conducted a structured observational study within their own school environment. Drawing on ethnographic techniques, the observations focused on everyday routines, organizational bottlenecks, and social dynamics where robots might offer meaningful support.

Finally, we conducted semi-structured expert interviews with educators and researchers in the field of educational technology and social robotics. These interviews provided system-level perspectives on technical feasibility, ethical concerns, and long-term visions for the use of robots in schools.

2 Related Work

2.1 Social Robots in Educational Context

Social robots have been increasingly investigated in educational contexts [12]. Research has explored their use as tutor-like or peer-like learning companions [3], particularly in structured instructional settings such as STEM education [23] and second language learning [13]. A recent meta-analysis further supports the overall learning benefits of social robots, while highlighting that the outcomes are strongly shaped by the way robots are integrated into instructional settings and by the type of control conditions used [40]. However, most studies focus on curricular applications, while everyday aspects of school life—such as transitions, recess, cafeteria interactions, or administrative tasks—remain largely unexplored.

2.2 Role-Specific Acceptance of Social Robots in Schools

The acceptance of social robots in educational settings has been shown to depend strongly on their perceived role, social behavior, and contextual fit. While robots are generally evaluated more positively when taking on supportive roles—such as tutor, assistant, or peer-like companion—acceptance tends to decline when robots are perceived as enforcers of rules or authority figures. This distinction is particularly relevant in school environments, where trust and perceived social appropriateness play key roles in shaping user attitudes [12]. Empirical studies further demonstrate that students and teachers are more likely to accept robots that exhibit socially appropriate behavior, emotional sensitivity, and clearly defined, non-threatening roles [25,26]. Perceived usefulness, technological reliability, and ease of use are also consistently identified as major predictors of acceptance [11]. In contexts where robots are expected to support rather than replace human actors, acceptance is higher—especially when users are involved in the design or implementation process [39]. Within informal and administrative school settings—such as hallways, recess areas, or school offices—these factors become even more critical. Here, robots are not just instructional aids but part of everyday social dynamics. As such, their social roles need to be clearly communicated and aligned with user expectations to foster legitimacy and integration. The importance of role clarity and user-centered design is echoed in systematic reviews that emphasize the need for transparency, contextual sensitivity, and adaptability in educational robots [21,28]. These findings underscore that successful implementation of social robots in schools hinges not only on technical capabilities but also on social framing, emotional resonance, and participatory development processes—particularly in settings where human-robot interaction occurs beyond structured instructional tasks.

2.3 Participatory Approaches in Educational Robotics Design

Participatory design has become an important methodology in the development of social robots, particularly to ensure that technologies meet the expectations, needs, and values of diverse user groups. Studies consistently emphasize that using multi-methods approaches and including multiple stakeholders early in the design process can lead to more robust, socially acceptable, and context-appropriate robotic systems [27]. Research involving older adults has shown that participatory processes are crucial for maximizing the acceptance and utility of social robots, as they help identify specific user needs related to autonomy, social connection, and interaction styles [27]. Similarly, long-term participatory research with primary school children highlights the importance of demystifying robots' capabilities: children often have overly high or unrealistic expectations of what robots can do, which can distort the co-design process if not properly managed [2]. In educational contexts, participatory design has also been applied to support culturally and linguistically diverse learners. Louie et al. [18] demonstrated that gathering stakeholder beliefs and expectations is essential when designing culturally responsive social robots for multilingual children. By systematically integrating the perspectives of students, teachers, and community members, robots can be better tailored to support engagement and learning. Finally, participatory approaches have proven particularly promising in identifying critical design features such as social role, appearance, personality, and voice of social robots. A study by Pnevmatikos et al. [24] showed that direct user involvement helped developers to align robot attributes more closely with stakeholder expectations, ultimately fostering higher acceptance and usability in educational settings. Taken together, these findings underline that participatory design is not only beneficial but necessary to create educational robots that are socially embedded, culturally sensitive, and technically effective.

3 Methodology

3.1 Participatory Workshop

We adopted a participatory design approach, which involves end users early and actively in the development process to ensure that technologies align with their needs, values, and everyday contexts. To implement this, we conducted a structured participatory workshop with upper secondary school students (N = 12; 4 female, 8 male; age range: 16–18 years; M = 17.25, SD = 0.8) Participants received a short introduction to the capabilities and limitations of current social robots, including examples and ethical considerations (e.g. privacy, autonomy, and emotional dependency). They also had the opportunity to interact with a robot (Naval), allowing them to gain a hands-on impression of current technological possibilities and constraints. All participants were informed about the goals, procedures, and voluntary nature of the study prior to participation. They were made aware that they could withdraw at any point without negative consequences. Written consent was obtained from all participants. In the case of underage students, parental consent was also collected and documented in accordance with ethical research standards. The workshop took place at the Fraunhofer Institute IMS and lasted approximately 90 min. It was designed to explore students' needs, ideas, and expectations regarding the use of social robots in everyday school contexts, using a structured Jobs-to-be-Done (JTBD) approach [5,17,36]. To promote inclusive participation and minimize groupthink or dominance by extroverted individuals, the Diverge-and-Converge technique [22] was applied. In the divergent phase, participants independently developed robot use-case scenarios using a sentence template: "When I [situation], I want to [goal], so I can [benefit]." In the convergent phase, they shared and clustered their ideas, discussed them collaboratively, and refined robot roles for various school situations, such as classroom learning, breaks, or interactions in administrative areas. This combination of individual and group-based ideation ensured both depth and diversity in the results. Due to the open and exploratory nature of the workshop, participants' responses were not quantified systematically. However, thematic saturation was reached across the developed scenarios (Fig. 1).

3.2 Observational Study

To complement the participatory workshop, we conducted a student-led observational study aimed at identifying everyday challenges and potential areas for robot assistance within school contexts. The observational approach was grounded in educational ethnography and systematic fieldwork techniques [1,35]. Twelve upper secondary school students who had also participated in the workshop took part in the study after receiving targeted training in observation methodology, including the use of a structured observation sheet developed for the project. The training emphasized the importance of objective, non-judgmental note taking and a clear separation between description and interpretation [6].

Fig. 1. Students participating in the workshop attach Post-it notes during the ideation phase.

3.3 Expert Interviews

To complement the perspectives gathered in workshops and observations, eight semi - structured interviews were conducted. The sample included eight experts (6 female, 2 male), aged 30 to 63 years. Their backgrounds covered education, human-computer interaction, educational science, informatics, mechanical engineering, and the philosophy of technology. The group comprised teachers, university researchers, a postdoctoral scholar, and a retired teacher. Several participants had experience with educational robots (e.g., BeeBots, Dash), while others had conducted research on robotic systems or participated in digitalization initiatives at schools. Professional experience ranged from 5 to 30 years. The interviews explored attitudes, potentials, challenges, and future visions for social robots in schools, including expected roles (e.g., tutor, assistant), key functions (e.g., feedback, navigation), and desired traits (e.g., reliability, empathy). The interviews lasted 30 to 45 min and were conducted via videoconferencing. Participants were informed about the purpose of the study and their rights; consent was documented. Transcripts were pseudonymized and analyzed using qualitative content analysis [20]. Citations such as "(I13)" refer to anonymized expert interviews conducted as part of the study.

To explore professional.

3.4 Data Analysis

The data collected from the participatory workshop, observational study, and expert interviews were analyzed using qualitative content analysis [20]. For each method, a two - stage procedure was followed: (1) open coding to identify relevant units of meaning, and (2) thematic clustering to extract cross-cutting categories and roles for educational robots. Workshop and observation data were analyzed inductively based on participants' own formulations, using thematic grouping to identify recurring patterns in use case scenarios and situational challenges. Observation protocols were coded line by line to extract insights related to spatial, social, and pedagogical dynamics, as well as robot-relevant intervention points. The expert interview transcripts were analyzed using a deductive inductive coding approach. A preliminary codebook was developed based on the interview guide, and refined iteratively to accommodate emergent themes [20]. Findings across all data sources were synthesized through methodological triangulation [8], allowing for the comparison of roles and expectations across different stakeholder perspectives and contexts.

4 Results

4.1 Participatory Workshop

In the participatory workshop, eight secondary school students articulated specific needs, expectations, and ideas for how robots could support their everyday school life. The resulting responses were clustered and analyzed thematically. A central finding was the strong emphasis on individualized learning support. Students envisioned robots assisting in various subjects, such as English, French, Mathematics, Philosophy, and Chemistry, by providing targeted feedback on written assignments, helping with vocabulary, giving step - by - step explanations of complex content, and supporting safe experimentation. Robots were also imagined as helpful in preparing for major exams, such as the high school diploma, by identifying individual weaknesses and offering tailored review strategies. Another prominent area was organizational and administrative support. The participants suggested that robots could assist teachers by printing materials, retrieving equipment, or temporarily supervising a class when the teacher is occupied. In administrative contexts, robots were expected to handle routine tasks in the school office, such as registering absences, or support students in navigating the school building, particularly on their first day. Safety and emergency assistance also emerged as a key theme. Robots were imagined as monitoring hallways, de-escalating fights, or alerting medical personnel in case of injury. Some of the ideas-such as emergency response or supervision-suggest that students are aware of and responsive to safety-related challenges in school environments. In terms of social roles, students and teachers emphasized that robots could act as companions, especially for students with disabilities or those who feel isolated. They could interact with students during breaks, facilitate games or creative activities, and contribute to a more inclusive social environment.

Finally, several context-specific roles were described. These included robots as digital librarians, providing help with book searches and recommendations; as cafeteria assistants, speeding up the food distribution process; and as interactive knowledge providers in subjects like geography, where robots might tell stories or simulate travel experiences to enhance student engagement. Across all scenarios, robots were attributed with diverse social roles such as tutor, assistant, supervisor, companion, or even temporary teacher. Participants emphasized that these robots should possess certain traits, including empathy, adaptability, reliability, and user-friendliness, as well as functional abilities such as language processing, spatial navigation, feedback generation, and visual interaction. Overall, the results of the workshop highlight that students and educators do not merely see robots as technical tools, but rather as socially embedded agents capable of supporting both the instructional and interpersonal dimensions of school life.

4.2 Observational Study

In a two - week observational phase, trained students conducted systematic observations in various school settings to explore potential roles and application areas for social robots. The observations followed a structured protocol and occurred at different times and locations within the school, such as classrooms, stairs, cafeterias, and recreation areas. The type of observation was predominantly non-participant, covert, and third person, with one instance of participant observation. Across all sessions, over 50 individuals (students and teachers) were observed. The observations revealed a range of everyday challenges that informed ideas for robotic support. These findings were clustered into five thematic categories: **1. Pedagogical Support and Tutoring.** In several classroom settings, observers noted situations where students lacked timely help, particularly during individual learning phases or oral exam preparation. Robots were therefore envisioned as tutors or mentors, capable of giving feedback, simulating exam situations, or helping students with homework and independent study tasks. **2. Supervision and Rule Enforcement**: In locations such as stairs, cafeterias, and break rooms, students often failed to follow rules (e.g., keeping to the right on stairs or refraining from using mobile phones). Teachers were either absent or unable to enforce rules effectively due to spatial constraints. In these contexts, robots were imagined as supervisory agents, reminding students of behavioral norms, or stepping in temporarily during teacher absences. **3. Safety and Emergency Response** Situations involving crowding, loud noise, or minor conflicts, especially in cafeterias and stairs, exposed a need for fast, responsive support. Robots were imagined as emergency assistants that could autonomously recognize critical situations (e.g., fights or injuries) and trigger alerts or notify human personnel. **4. Social Observation and Inclusion** The students also suggested that robots could support the analysis of social dynamics, for example, by observing interactions during breaks and identifying patterns of exclusion or group formation. These insights could then help teachers address social challenges more effectively. **5. Organizational and Logistical Assistance** In multiple classroom observations, valuable instruction time was lost due to routine administrative tasks, such as attendance taking, worksheet distribution, or leaving the classroom to retrieve materials. Robots were therefore imagined as organizational assistants capable of automating such tasks, thereby helping teachers remain present and focused on pedagogy. Across all observed scenarios, the perceived usefulness of robotic support ranged from moderate to high. Particularly in the cafeteria and during transitions (e.g. breaks or teacher changes), robots were seen as capable of improving structure, communication, and safety. However, challenges such as acceptance of the robot as an authority figure, its technical robustness, and vulnerability to vandalism were also recognized. The observational study generated nuanced, practice - oriented insights into the school environment and helped identify where and how robots could offer meaningful support, not just in educational tasks, but also in terms of supervision, social interaction, and administrative relief.

4.3 Expert Interviews

Despite the different backgrounds, the interviewees shared several core views. While direct experience with robots in schools was limited among most participants, many had worked with digital media, programming tools such as Dash or NAO, or had backgrounds in telepresence robotics and human - robot interaction research. This practical and researchoriented knowledge informed nuanced, often critical reflections on robot integration in education. **Attitudes toward Robots in Schools.** Most experts expressed cautious optimism regarding the use of social robots in education. While none supported the idea of replacing teachers with robots, many considered robots useful as supportive tools-particularly in areas such as differentiated learning, language support, or administrative assistance. One participant described their attitude as "very positive" (I1), another noted: "If robots become part of everyday life, then they also belong in schools" (I15). However, skepticism remained about robots' abilities to replace key interpersonal or pedagogical functions. For example, one interviewee argued: "Robots can't replace human contact" (I18), and another stated: "That would require a kind of human consciousness-a heart, various ways of thinking" (I13). **Perceived Potentials and Applications.** Interviewees highlighted several promising application areas, including individualized learning support, administrative relief, and support for students with special needs. Robots were imagined as tutors or assistants that could provide feedback, help with vocabulary, or guide students through exercises. One interviewee emphasized the potential to foster skill development (I16), while another mentioned that robots could enable remote participation: "They can help students be physically present in the classroom from a distance" (I18). Administrative use cases were also mentioned, such as printing materials or navigating the school building (I15). These roles align with broader trends in educational robotics research, which suggest that robots can serve as companions or scaffolds in both formal and informal learning contexts [3]. **Social Roles and Functions.** Most participants agreed that robots in schools should not act as authority figures but rather as assistants, learning companions, or coaches. Their role was seen as supplementary-helping both students and teachers without taking control. Several experts emphasized the importance of role clarity to foster acceptance and avoid unrealistic expectations. They also linked role clarity to the issue of trust: robots were seen as more likely to be accepted when they followed socially expected support roles. One interviewee warned: "Should a machine be allowed to exercise authority over humans?" (I20), while another noted that students might try to sabotage robots they do not respect (I21). These reflections suggest that trust in robots is not only technical, but also strongly shaped by the perceived appropriateness of their social role. In line with this, one expert emphasized: "Robots can't replace social pedagogues-that would require a kind of human consciousness" (I13). **Desired Characteristics and Capabilities.** Interviewees consistently stressed the need for high reliability, simple operation, and empathic, understandable interaction. One participant noted that "the robot must work reliably out of the box" (I21), while another emphasized: "Children are sad when [robots] are no longer there" (I18), highlighting the emotional component of reliability. Robots should be robust, culturally adaptive, and capable of responding to students' emotional or educational needs. Features such as speech recognition, intuitive interfaces, and context-awareness were seen as essential for successful school deployment. **Challenges and Concerns.** Key concerns included data privacy, technical reliability, maintenance, and the risk of social isolation if students were to rely too heavily on robot interaction. One expert raised the question: "What happens if someone hacks the robot?" (I18), while another warned that "no jobs should be replaced" and stressed the importance of maintaining human contact (I21). Acceptance by teachers, students, and parents was considered a decisive factor for successful implementation. The lack of infrastructure and financial resources-particularly in public schools-was named as a major obstacle. One interviewee remarked: "I don't know any school that uses such a thing-it's just not realistic yet" (I13). **Implementation Strategies.** To increase acceptance, experts recommended pilot projects, demonstrations, and targeted training sessions. One interviewee suggested: "You need to show how it works in practice-otherwise no one will take it seriously" (I1). Transparency regarding robot capabilities, limitations, and data use was considered critical. As one expert put it: "We need to make it clear what the robot can and cannot do-and who has access to the data" (I18). Interviewees also called for inclusive design processes involving all school stakeholders to ensure need-based development and meaningful integration. **Future Perspectives.** Longterm, experts envisioned robots playing a growing role in education, particularly in well-equipped schools and hybrid learning models. As one interviewee stated: "If robots become part of everyday life, then they also belong in schools" (I15). However, most anticipated only incremental change in the next 5–10 years due to structural, financial, and ethical challenges. One expert noted: "I've never really thought about it, since I don't know any school that uses such a thing" (I13), indicating skepticism about short-term feasibility. Some expressed interest in alternative robot forms (e.g., four-legged robots) over humanoid designs, due to lower expectations and maintenance needs.

4.4 Integrated Synthesis and Triangulated Insights

A synthesis of findings from the participatory workshop, the observational study, and expert interviews revealed both overlapping and complementary perspectives on the roles of social robots in schools. Several core functions – such as tutor, assistant, and provider of individualized support – emerged consistently across all methods. These shared roles indicate a robust cross - perspective consensus on the supportive and relational potential of educational robots. At the same time, each method contributed unique insights: students emphasized imaginative and comfort-enhancing scenarios; observations highlighted discipline - related and logistical challenges; and experts offered future-oriented, systemic perspectives. This methodological triangulation strengthened the empirical foundation of the study. The combination of stakeholder-driven ideas with grounded observations and expert foresight provided a robust basis for identifying feasible and relevant robotic roles in schools. This multi-method approach also helped identify overlaps and gaps between imagined, observed, and systemically plausible applications. The combination of stakeholder-driven ideas with grounded observations and expert foresight provided a robust basis for identifying feasible and relevant robotic roles in schools. This multi-method approach also helped identify overlaps and gaps between imagined, observed, and systemically plausible applications

5 Discussion

5.1 Summary and Interpretation of Key Findings

This exploratory study identified various potential roles for social robots in secondary school settings based on three distinct methodological perspectives—students, peer observers, and experts. Despite the differences in access and framing, consistent patterns emerged regarding the core functions of educational robots: tutor, assistant, organizer, and social companion. These roles are consistent with previous typologies. Belpaeme et al. (2018) [3] describe robots in educational settings as tutors, peers, and companions, while Scaradozzi et al. (2019) [30] highlight functions such as learning organization, cognitive support, and motivation. The assistant role identified in this study overlaps with these functions but also reflects a more pragmatic, task-oriented support role emphasized by participants. The Jobs-to-be-Done methodology further revealed that students frame these roles not merely in terms of instrumental utility but also as responses to emotional and interpersonal needs—particularly regarding personalized learning, school logistics, and social belonging. These findings support the view that students experience social robots as emotionally responsive technologies, which can foster social presence, engagement, and perceived support [16]. Recent reviews emphasize the growing relevance of affective and empathic functions in educational robotics, including emotional scaffolding and peer-like companionship [15, 29]. The observational study added a grounded, ecological perspective. A key insight was the need for behavioral regulation and oversight in informal school spaces, such as stairways or cafeterias. In these situations, robots were imagined as extensions of the teacher, tasked with maintaining order or offering guidance. However, students also voiced concerns about whether such robots would be accepted as legitimate authority figures or be capable of responding appropriately in dynamic, unpredictable environments. These reflections echo existing research that highlights ethical and pedagogical tensions when robots assume roles traditionally associated with human authority. The importance of teacher accountability and legitimacy becomes especially evident when classroom responsibilities are delegated to robotic systems [37]. Similarly, the introduction of social robots in educational contexts—particularly in areas involving behavioral control and supervision—raises concerns about the fragility of trust and the need for social acceptance [34]. Expert interviews supported many of the student-generated ideas while adding a structural perspective. They emphasized longterm implementation challenges such as data privacy, infrastructure limitations, and funding constraints. These concerns align with broader research on institutional and organizational barriers to adopting educational robotics—particularly in public education systems. Studies show that both external factors (e.g., lack of resources, unclear policy frameworks) and internal factors (e.g., limited digital competencies among teachers) can hinder sustainable integration [10,19].

These findings can be further interpreted through the lens of technology acceptance models and role theory. From a TAM/UTAUT perspective [7,38], participants' emphasis on usefulness, reliability, and ease of use reflects the core dimensions of acceptance in educational settings. However, our data suggest that social appropriateness and clarity of the robot's role may outweigh purely instrumental considerations. This insight aligns closely with role theory [4,9], which posits that legitimacy and acceptance of actors—human or artificial—depend on how well their behavior conforms to socially expected role scripts. When robots are perceived as tutors, assistants, or companions, rather than as authority figures or enforcers, their integration into school life becomes more acceptable. This highlights the importance of role congruence and contextual fit in human-robot interaction design. Our findings underscore that successful implementation of educational robots depends not only on technical capabilities, but also on aligning robot behavior with socially intelligible and institutionally appropriate roles.

5.2 Limitations

Some limitations must be acknowledged. The workshop and observational samples were small and context - specific, which limits generalizability. Observations were confined to a single school, and most expert participants had limited direct experience with social robots in everyday classrooms. The deployment of social robots in educational environments raises a range of ethical, legal, and social considerations that are increasingly recognized in the literature. Core concerns include data privacy, emotional dependency, autonomy, surveillance, and the shifting boundaries of pedagogical responsibility, particularly when robots interact with minors in socially meaningful ways [32,33]. Although our study did not focus explicitly on ethical aspects, several themes, such as robot authority, technical robustness, or potential misuse, emerged indirectly through interviews and observations. These reflections highlight the need for future research to systematically explore ethical and practical boundaries of robotic deployment in school settings.

5.3 Implications for Research and Practice

Our findings suggest that social robots in schools should be designed as assistive and relational tools, not as replacements for human educators. Across all stakeholder groups, there was a strong emphasis on social embeddedness, empathetic interaction, and the ability to respond appropriately to students' needs in diverse school situations. Two key recommendations emerge for future design and implementation: User-centered and participatory design processes should be integrated from the outset to ensure relevance, acceptance, and context-fit. Research has shown that involving end users in the design phase leads to more suitable and accepted robot characteristics. For example, Reich-Stiebert et al. (2020) [26] found that students strongly preferred robots with specific features, such as machine-like appearance, minimal facial design, speech based interaction, and socially appropriate personality traits, when they were actively engaged in the design process. Similarly, Weidmann et al. (2024) [39] demonstrated that higher levels of user participation significantly increased utilitarian and hedonic attitudes as well as intention to use the robot. These studies underscore the value of co-creation with students and school staff when designing educational robots. Technical simplicity and robustness are just as critical as socially responsive capabilities, such as natural language interaction, empathy, and contextual awareness. In practical terms, this means robots should operate reliably "out of the box," without requiring users to adjust settings, handle technical breakdowns, or troubleshoot errors. Particularly in school environments, where staff time and technical support are limited, this expectation is non - negotiable. As de Graaf, Ben Allouch, and van Dijk (2013) [11] emphasize, long - term use of social robots in realworld contexts like homes—or by extension, schools—requires a baseline level of technical reliability. Without that, even socially sophisticated robots will fail to integrate meaningfully into users' daily routines. Together, these implications suggest that educational robots must be designed not only for functionality and interaction quality, but also for practical, low-maintenance deployment in everyday educational settings. Only then can they realistically support and enrich the social and instructional dynamics of school life.

6 Conclusion

This study expands the current discourse on educational social robots by exploring how diverse stakeholders envision context-specific, socially appropriate roles beyond instructional settings. While existing research has demonstrated the value of social robots in structured learning environments such as STEM and language education [3,13,23], our findings suggest that their potential extends meaningfully into everyday school life, particularly when designed to act as assistants, companions, or logistical aids. The importance of role clarity, contextual fit, and participatory development processes, as highlighted in prior work [21,26,39], was echoed across all user groups in our study.

Building on insights from technology acceptance frameworks [7,38], we found that usefulness and usability remain important for acceptance, but must be complemented by social and emotional resonance. Role theory [4,9] proved to be a helpful analytical lens, as it clarified why roles that align with school - specific expectations (e.g., assistant rather than supervisor) fostered trust and legitimacy. Moreover, participatory methods enabled stakeholders to articulate nuanced expectations around emotional support, authority, and contextual adaptability, extending existing findings on the value of user-centered design in HRI [2,24].

Taken together, this study reinforces the notion that social robots are more than instructional tools: they are envisioned as social actors by participants, based on imagined interactions and perceived role expectations. Future research should further explore how dynamic role assignment, emotional intelligence, and ethical safeguards can support the long-term integration of social robots in educational institutions.

This study was supported by the PAROL project funded by the University of Applied Sciences Bottrop.

References

1. Angrosino, M.: Doing Ethnographic and Observational Research. Sage (2007)
2. Barendregt, W., Ekström, S., Kiesewetter, S., Pareto, L., Serholt, S.: Demystifying robots in the co-design of a tutee robot with primary school children. Int. Des. Archit. J. IxD&A (44), 109–128 (2020)
3. Belpaeme, T., Kennedy, J., Ramachandran, A., Scassellati, B., Tanaka, F.: Social robots for education: a review. Sci. Robot. **3**(21) (2018). https://doi.org/10.1126/scirobotics.aat5954
4. Biddle, B.J., Thomas, E.J.: Role Theory: Concepts and Research. Wiley, New York (1966)
5. Christensen, C.M., Hall, T., Dillon, K., Duncan, D.S.: Competing against Luck: The Story of Innovation and Customer Choice. HarperBusiness, New York (2016)
6. Cohen, L., Manion, L., Morrison, K.: Research Methods in Education, 8th edn. Routledge (2018)
7. Davis, F.D., Bagozzi, R.P., Warshaw, P.R.: User acceptance of computer technology: a comparison of two theoretical models. Manage. Sci. **35**(8), 982–1003 (1989). https://doi.org/10.1287/mnsc.35.8.982
8. Flick, U.: Mantras and myths: the disenchantment of mixed-methods research and revisiting triangulation as a perspective. Qual. Inq. **23**(1), 46–57 (2017). https://doi.org/10.1177/1077800416655827

9. Goffman, E.: The Presentation of Self in Everyday Life. Doubleday, New York (1956)
10. Gonzales, M.C., Andal, E.Z., Ching, D.A., Gaffud, M.P., Tabo, E.C.: Assessing the efficacy of roboteach extension project on public school teachers. Int. J. Educ. Manag. Dev. Stud. **2**(3), 78–100 (2021). https://doi.org/10.53378/348742
11. de Graaf, M.M.A., Ben Allouch, S.: Exploring influencing variables for the acceptance of social robots. Robot. Auton. Syst. **61**(12), 1476–1486 (2013). https://doi.org/10.1016/j.robot.2013.07.007
12. Guggemos, J., Seufert, S., Sonderegger, S., Burkhard, M.: Social robots in education: conceptual overview and case study of use. In: Ifenthaler, D., Isaías, P., Sampson, D.G. (eds.) Orchestration of Learning Environments in the Digital World. CELDA, pp. 173–195. Springer, Cham (2022). https://doi.org/10.1007/978-3-030-90944-4_10
13. Kennedy, J., Baxter, P., Senft, E., Belpaeme, T.: Social robot tutoring for child second language learning. In: Proceedings of the 11th ACM/IEEE International Conference on Human-Robot Interaction (HRI 2016), pp. 231–238. IEEE (2016). https://doi.org/10.1109/HRI.2016.7451757
14. Klemm, K.: Entwicklung von Lehrkräftebedarf und -angebot in Deutschland bis 2030: Expertise im Auftrag des VBE. Essen (2022)
15. Lampropoulos, G.: Social robots in education: current trends and future perspectives. Information **16**(1), 29 (2025). https://doi.org/10.3390/info16010029
16. Leite, I., Castellano, G., Pereira, A., Martinho, C., Paiva, A.: Empathic robots for long-term interaction: evaluating social presence, engagement and perceived support in children. Int. J. Soc. Robot. **6**, 329–341 (2014). https://doi.org/10.1007/s12369-014-0227-1
17. Lewrick, M., Link, P., Leifer, L.: Das Design Thinking Toolbook: Die besten Werkzeuge & Methoden. Vahlen, München (2020), in Gemeinschaft mit Versus Verlag, Zürich
18. Louie, B., Björling, E.A., Kuo, A.C., Alves-Oliveira, P.: Designing for culturally responsive social robots: an application of a participatory framework. Front. Robot. AI **9**, 983408 (2022). https://doi.org/10.3389/frobt.2022.983408
19. Vasou, M., Kyprianou, G., Amanatiadis, A., Chatzichristofis, S.A.: Transforming education with AI and robotics: potential and challenges. In: Lecture Notes in Business Information Processing, vol. 535. Springer, Cham (2025). https://doi.org/10.1007/978-3-031-81322-1_1
20. Mayring, P.: Qualitative Inhaltsanalyse: Grundlagen und Techniken, 12th edn. Beltz, Weinheim und Basel (2014)
21. Naneva, S., Sarda Gou, M., Webb, T.L., Prescott, T.J.: A systematic review of attitudes, anxiety, acceptance, and trust towards social robots. Int. J. Soc. Robot. **12**, 1179–1201 (2020). https://doi.org/10.1007/s12369-020-00659-4
22. Nielsen Norman Group: Diverge and converge: Understanding the dynamics of group collaboration (2020). https://www.nngroup.com/articles/diverge-converge/. Accessed 28 Apr 2025
23. Ouyang, F., Xu, W.: The effects of educational robotics in stem education: a multilevel meta-analysis. Int. J. STEM Educ. **11**(7) (2024). https://doi.org/10.1186/s40594-024-00469-4
24. Pnevmatikos, D., Christodoulou, P., Fachantidis, N.: Designing a socially assistive robot for education through a participatory design approach: pivotal principles for developers. Int. J. Soc. Robot. **14**, 763–788 (2022). https://doi.org/10.1007/s12369-021-00826-1

25. Rosenthal-von der Pütten, A.M., Krämer, N.C., Hoffmann, L., Sobieraj, S., Eimler, S.C.: An experimental study on emotional reactions towards a robot. Int. J. Soc. Robot. **5**, 17–34 (2013). https://doi.org/10.1007/s12369-012-0173-8
26. Reich-Stiebert, N., Eyssel, F., Hohnemann, C.: Exploring university students' preferences for educational robot design by means of a user-centered design approach. Int. J. Soc. Robot. **12**(1), 227–237 (2020). https://doi.org/10.1007/s12369-019-00554-7
27. Rogers, W.A., Kadylak, T., Bayles, M.A.: Maximizing the benefits of participatory design for human–robot interaction research with older adults. Hum. Factors (2022). https://doi.org/10.1177/00187208221075885
28. Rossi, S., Dhamija, D., Ivaldi, S.: Scrita 2023: understanding human-robot relationships and trust. arXiv preprint (2023). https://arxiv.org/abs/2311.05401
29. Ružić, I., Balaban, I.: El uso de robots sociales como asistentes docentes en las escuelas: implicaciones para la investigación y la práctica. Revista de Educación a Distancia (RED) **24**(78) (2024). https://doi.org/10.6018/red.600771
30. Schön, S., Ebner, M., Grandl, M.: Designing a makerspace for children – let's do it. In: Moro, M., Alimisis, D., Iocchi, L. (eds.) Edurobotics 2018. AISC, vol. 946, pp. 3–15. Springer, Cham (2020). https://doi.org/10.1007/978-3-030-18141-3_1
31. Sekretariat der Ständigen Konferenz der Kultusminister der Länder: Lehrkräfteeinstellungsbedarf und -angebot in der bundesrepublik deutschland 2024–2035 (2025), dokumentation Nr. 2, Februar 2025
32. Serholt, S., et al.: The case of classroom robots: teachers' deliberations on the ethical tensions. AI Soc. **32**, 613–631 (2017). https://doi.org/10.1007/s00146-016-0667-2
33. Sharkey, A.J.C.: Should we welcome robot teachers? Ethics Inf. Technol. **18**(4), 283–297 (2016). https://doi.org/10.1007/s10676-016-9387-z
34. Smakman, M., Vogt, P., Konijn, E.A.: Moral considerations on social robots in education: a multi-stakeholder perspective. Comput. Educ. **174**, 104317 (2021). https://doi.org/10.1016/j.compedu.2021.104317 104317 104317
35. Spradley, J.P.: Participant Observation. Holt, Rinehart and Winston (1980)
36. Ulwick, A.W.: What Customers Want: Using Outcome-Driven Innovation to Create Breakthrough Products and Services. McGraw-Hill (2005)
37. Vasalou, A., Kontopoulou, M., Joinson, A.: Technological limitations and pedagogical implications of ethical classroom robot design. AI Soc. **31**(4), 519–529 (2016). https://doi.org/10.1007/s00146-016-0667-2
38. Venkatesh, V., Morris, M.G., Davis, G.B., Davis, F.D.: User acceptance of information technology: toward a unified view. MIS Q. **27**(3), 425–478 (2003)
39. Weidmann, C., Roesler, E., Wiese, E.: Designing social educational robots: how user participation shapes acceptance. In: Companion of the ACM/IEEE International Conference on Human-Robot Interaction, pp. 1114–1118 (2024). https://doi.org/10.1145/3610978.3640601
40. de Winter, J.C.F., Dodou, D., Moorlag, F., Broekens, J.: Social robots: a meta-analysis of learning outcomes. PsyArXiv preprint (2024). [Preprint]

Children's Questions to Robots as an Educational Opportunity - Design Implications

Alicja Wróbel[1], Paulina Zguda[2](✉)[ID], and Bipin Indurkhya[3][ID]

[1] Jagiellonian University, Kraków, Poland
[2] Doctoral School in the Humanities, Jagiellonian University, Kraków, Poland
paulina.zguda@doctoral.uj.edu.pl
[3] Centre for Cognitive Science, Jagiellonian University, Kraków, Poland
bipin.indurkhya@uj.edu.pl

Abstract. We examine the role of spontaneous questions from children directed at or about social robots, specifically NAO and Misty, within educational settings. Focusing on children aged 3 to 6, the study compares different age groups to explore how their inquiries and behaviors reflect their understanding of and relationship with robots. The analysis combines quantitative data, based on the number of questions asked to robots and adults, with qualitative insights into the content of the questions and the broader behavioral trends across age groups. The results show that as children grow older, their interactions become more expressive, both verbally and physically. 6-year-olds, in particular, demonstrated increased physical engagement and more abstract or imaginative questioning. In contrast, younger children tended to initiate conversations grounded in familiar topics such as food or family. These developmental differences suggest a shift toward more complex and socially nuanced interactions with age. Based on these findings, the article proposes age-sensitive design guidelines to support interaction designers in creating more responsive and developmentally appropriate robotic systems for young users.

Keywords: Child-Robot Interaction · In-the-wild · Questions-making and a Robot

1 Introduction

In the era of advanced social robotics, child-robot interactions are becoming increasingly common. These interactions require more detailed planning than those with adults due to the unique needs of young users, such as shorter attention spans [1,19], the need for safe and predictable environments [25], and the importance of maintaining engagement throughout the interaction [28].

A. Wróbel and P. Zguda—Contributed equally to this work.

However, the challenges posed by these needs can also be valuable assets. The work by [16] suggests that children, compared to adults, are more likely to participate in interactions, and the shorter durations of these interactions may offer unique research opportunities.

In addition, the inherent curiosity and imagination of children lead to more spontaneous and expressive responses, providing valuable insights into the social and emotional aspects of human-robot interaction. Their openness to anthropomorphizing robotic agents facilitates stronger emotional bonds, which are beneficial when designing robots for education, therapy, or companionship.

When designing social robots for CRI, it is essential to consider children's cognitive and emotional development across age groups. Preschool children typically exhibit shorter attention spans and higher levels of distraction, relying more heavily on human facilitators during robot interactions. Therefore, robots targeting this demographic should incorporate frequent engagement cues and potentially integrate adult mediation to maintain focus and engagement [2]. In contrast, older children (ages 6–11) demonstrate greater sustained engagement and can participate in more complex interactions. They also show differentiated affective responses and preferences based on the personality traits of the robot [2,12]. These emotional responses vary even among older children, as 6–7 years old respond differently to robot attributes than their older peers, highlighting the importance of age-sensitive emotional design [12]. Proximity preferences also evolve with age: while younger children may prefer close physical interaction with robots, older children tend to tolerate or even prefer greater interpersonal distance [21]. From a developmental point of view, the complexity of robot behaviors and tasks should be tailored to match the cognitive capabilities of the target age group to avoid overwhelming younger users while still engaging older ones [27]. Robots designed for educational contexts should act as peer partners who motivate and support learning, incorporating features such as joint attention, meaningful gestures, and appropriate feedback mechanisms to build trust and scaffold cognitive development [24]. Furthermore, children's interpretations of unexpected robot behaviors, such as malfunctions or expressions of personality and identity, are also shaped by their developmental stage, suggesting that designers must anticipate diverse responses and adapt accordingly [26].

1.1 Questions as a Useful Tool in the Recognition of Children's Mental State

The ability to ask questions plays a critical role in the cognitive and linguistic development of children. Children not only learn the structural aspects of asking questions, but also the appropriate contexts in which to ask them, reflecting the functional use of language in social interaction [11]. Early questioning often serves multiple purposes, ranging from playful verbal exploration to seeking confirmation or new information. In their second and third years, children predominantly ask questions about objects in their immediate environment, gradually extending their inquiries to absent or non-perceptible entities, thus indicating the emergence of mental representations [4]. Moreover, preschoolers' questions are thought to play a vital role in cognitive development by addressing gaps, ambiguities, or inconsistencies in their knowledge, allowing them to obtain targeted information precisely when they are most receptive to it. This process, conceptualized as the Information Requesting Mechanism (IRM), highlights how children's active information-seeking behaviors, including verbal questions and other communicative acts, support the refinement of their knowledge structures toward more adult-like forms. For questions to effectively contribute to cognitive development, children must ask relevant and purposeful questions, receive informative answers, and use the acquired information to update their understanding. Despite its importance, the role of question asking in child cognitive growth has been relatively underexplored [6].

In this study, we focus on children's questions as a window into their mental states, using them to explore how children at different developmental stages (3–6 yrs) perceive social robots during naturalistic interactions.

2 Related Research

2.1 Age Differences in CRI Engagement

Although the literature on CRI is extensive, most studies focus on children in their early school years and older. Although there are studies with 3-year-old participants [8], there is a lack of research examining how children's response to robots evolve within a narrowly defined developmental window, especially within the in-the-wild paradigm [18]. The present study addresses this gap by focusing on children between the ages of three and six. This age range is particularly interesting due to the emergence and intensification of developmental differences, even between children only a year apart, such as between 4- and 5-year-olds.

Despite the limited number of studies directly comparing children's responses to robots within this specific age range, there are reports that shed light on how children of different ages react to robotic agents. For example, 5-year-olds treat a humanoid robot with more gentleness than 3-year-olds and are more likely to attribute lifelikeness to it [20]. Moreover, [12] compared children aged 6 to 11 years who were asked to recognize a change in the personality of the robot and to identify their own emotional states after interacting with two different robots. Their findings suggest that younger children (6–7 yrs) had more difficulty noticing the change in robot personality compared to older children. This may imply that such cues, related to personality traits, need to be more exaggerated or explicit for younger children to recognize them. Furthermore, the same age group appeared to be more forgiving of the negative behaviors displayed by robots and more tolerant of uncooperative robots, while older children showed less preference for such traits. This aligns with the suggestion of [16] that younger children are naturally more inclined to engage with robots and tend to have lower initial expectations of them compared to their older peers.

These studies show that the distinctions between the perception of the robot can be noticed even within a small age difference between children, which might be reflected in the questions they pose to or about social robots.

2.2 Preschoolers' Mental Representations of Robots

One way to understand the mental representations of a robot by preschoolers is by analyzing their drawings [13,17]. Analyzing drawings of preschoolers (3–6 yrs), before and after briefly interacting with a robot, [17] found that robots should have a flexible appearance that allows imaginative play, while expressive features (such as heart-shaped eyes and blushing cheeks) are especially engaging for younger children (3–4 yrs). In contrast, 5- to 6-year-olds prioritize understanding how the robot works and how to control it, suggesting that functionality becomes more important with age. In another work, [13] studied the views of children (3–6 yrs) about robots through drawings and interviews. Initially, 64% of the drawings were human-like; after interviews, this dropped to 54%, suggesting a shift toward more technical understanding. Some children mentioned sensors or human control, reflecting a growing conceptual awareness. Although the original study used a human researcher to facilitate this shift in understanding, in our study, the robot itself assumed the role of facilitator, which could influence how children conceptualized robotic agency and function.

Another way of studying preschooler's understanding of social robots is analyzing the questions they pose towards them and about them. A study by [15] showed that children (3–6 yrs) were more inclined to ask robots questions in certain domains, suggesting that they perceive robots as knowledgeable entities in specific contexts. This suggested that preschool children want to interact with social robots but rely more on a human facilitator. This context is important in the classroom: the robot might be a useful tool and be treated as an enhancement of educational process, but it will not replace the moderation from the teacher.

Another study [3] used the method of analyzing spontaneous questions from children during interactions with a humanoid robot to study their perceptions of robot animacy. It was found that younger children (5–6 yrs) were more likely than older ones (7–8 yrs) to treat the robot as animate, suggesting that children often hold naive animacy beliefs, attributing intentionality to non-living entities, and these perceptions tend to become more mechanistic with age. Similarly, [5] observed that 5–6-year-olds asked Zenbo robot questions about its daily life, capabilities, and knowledge. This suggests that children are mostly interested in a robot's ability to maintain general daily conversations about topics such as family, age, home, its preferences, and about its abilities and functions.

The works of [3] and [5] found interesting patterns in children asking questions to the robot. However, the most common and extensively studied procedure in child-robot interaction involves the robot asking questions to children. The researchers then examine how this questioning influences the behavior of children [14,23], as well as whether it encourages them to ask robots questions about a specific topic [22].

Our study aims to explore how children between the ages of 3 and 6 years form unprompted questions during interactions with a social robot. Specifically, we seek to address the following research questions.

- How the behavior towards the robot differs between age groups 3, 4, 5 and 6 years old?
- What questions (topics) are dominant in different age groups?
- How does the number of questions asked differ between different age groups?
- Who is the recipient of questions about the robot: the robot itself or the human moderator? - How is this different in different age groups?

Furthermore, the study provides design implications for future child-robot interaction.

3 Methodology

3.1 In-the-Wild Setting

In-the-wild studies, conducted in natural settings such as classrooms or homes, are key to understanding how children interact with robots in real life. Unlike lab studies, they capture more natural and spontaneous behavior, offering better insight into how social context (such as the presence of peers or teachers) affects children's responses to robots [18,28].

Such studies include more diverse participants and settings, helping to design robots that fit real-world needs [7,9]. They reveal practical challenges and user reactions that might not appear in controlled environments, making the findings more relevant and applicable [10].

We used an in-the-wild setting to explore how children of different ages interact with robots. This approach allows us to observe more natural and authentic behaviors in their responses to robots.

3.2 Participants

The study involved 70 children from a single preschool in Kraków, Poland, all of whom spoke Polish during the interactions. The participants were divided into four age groups: 3 yrs (15: 10F, 5M); 4 yrs (20: 13F, 7M); 5 yrs (19: 15F, 4M); 6 yrs (16: 10F, 6M). The robot interaction sessions took place over two days: the 3- and 4-year-olds participated on the first day, and the 5- and 6-year-olds on the second. All children in each age group were invited to participate. None of the children had previous experience with robots in the laboratory. Participation was voluntary and the children were free to withdraw at any time. Parental consent was obtained for participation and for video/audio recording, and parents were assured that the children's faces would not be published.

3.3 Materials

Two robots were used in the study:

- **NAO** is a humanoid robot capable of full body movement, including gestures with its arms and legs. It can speak, make gestures, take various poses, dance, and play various sounds. During our study, NAO introduced itself to children, engaged in simple conversations asking and answering questions, and demonstrated dance moves. It also performed several poses, such as pretending to be different vehicles or animals, and played different sounds to support the play activities.
- **Misty** is a robot with a more machine-like appearance. It has a head with a screen that displays animated eyes to show different emotions, as well as movable arms. Instead of legs, it moves using a wheeled base, similar to a small vehicle. During the interaction, Misty did not speak, but communicated by displaying various facial expressions on its screen. It also moved around the room a little using its wheeled base.

Each robot in the study was controlled remotely by a different researcher using the Wizard-of-Oz technique. The robots are visible in Fig. 1.

3.4 Setup and Procedure

This study was conducted as part of a robotics workshop designed to engage children in interactive games with social robots. The children were divided into four groups according to their age, and each group interacted with the robots separately. Each workshop consisted of two parts: *Introduction to the robots NAO and Misty* and *Playtime with the robots*. The average duration of the workshops was 26.22 min (SD = 3.27).

During the study, the children stayed in their regular classroom. They sat together on a carpet, forming a circle around the robot. In the conversation and play sessions, the robots were placed on a table on one side of the carpet and the children could easily walk up to them. The setup of the study is shown in Fig. 2.

At the beginning of the workshop, the robots introduced themselves to the children and invited them to play. During the same time, the human facilitator (one of the researchers) explained the structure of the event. During the free play session, children were encouraged to interact with the robots by asking questions, approaching to touch or pat them, and engaging in playful activities. The robots demonstrated their movements and capabilities.

Each session was supported by a team of adults: two researchers were present to operate and control the robots, one researcher facilitated the interaction by explaining the activities to the children, and two preschool teachers, who normally work with the children, were also present to support the group.

Fig. 1. Misty II (left) is a compact social robot with an expressive LCD screen, depth camera, and microphones. NAO (right) is a larger humanoid robot with articulated joints, cameras, microphones, and LEDs for expressive communication.

Fig. 2. Setup of the study. NAO is placed on a table, while Misty is positioned on the floor to allow it to move around the room. The study facilitator is sitting to the left of the table.

4 Analysis and Results

4.1 Quantitative Analysis of Children Questions

Quantitative analysis was performed by manually annotating the videos by a single researcher using MAXQDA software. Two codes were applied during the annotation process. When a child directed a question to the NAO or Misty robot, it was tagged as 'Question to a robot'. When a child asked a question to an adult, either a teacher or researcher, about one of the robots or robots in general, it was tagged as 'Question to an adult'.

Descriptive Analysis of Distribution of the Questions. A descriptive analysis revealed age-related differences in the number and distribution of questions directed at a robot versus at an adult, as shown in Table 1 and visualized on a graph in Fig. 3. We can see that 4-year-olds showed the strongest preference for addressing the robot directly, while 3-year-olds relied more on adults. The 5- and 6-year-olds showed a more balanced approach, and the 6-year-olds slightly favor the direct interaction with the robot.

Statistic Analysis of Distribution of the Questions. To examine whether the way children directed their questions (to a robot or to an adult) dif-

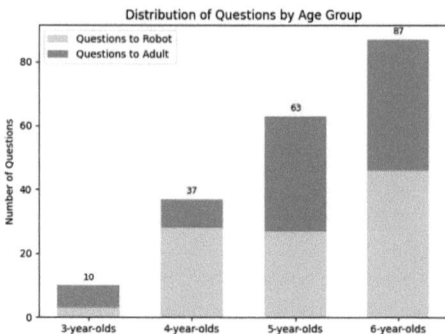

Fig. 3. Graph showing the distribution of questions to a robot and to an adult about a robot by age group.

Table 1. Distribution of questions addressed to a robot and to an adult across age groups.

Age Group	Questions to Robot	Questions to Adult	Total Questions
3-year-olds	3 (30.0%)	7 (70.0%)	10
4-year-olds	28 (75.7%)	9 (24.3%)	37
5-year-olds	27 (42.9%)	36 (57.1%)	63
6-year-olds	46 (52.9%)	41 (47.1%)	87

fered between age groups, a chi-square independence test was performed, which revealed a significant difference between age groups ($\chi^2(3) = 12.35$, $p = .006$).

To examine whether children in each age group showed a significant preference for directing their questions to a robot versus to an adult, binomial tests were performed. The results indicated that the 3-year-olds asked significantly more questions to an adult than to a robot (p < .001), despite the small sample size (N = 10). This finding should be interpreted with caution, as the low number of observed questions increases the sensitivity of the test and limits the generalizability of the result. In contrast, 4-year-olds showed a strong tendency to direct their questions to a robot (28 out of 37), but this difference did not reach statistical significance (p = 0.991), probably due to the influence of the sample size on the sensitivity of the test. For 5- and 6-year-olds, the differences in the question distribution were statistically significant (p < .001), with both groups exhibiting a more balanced yet differentiated pattern: 5-year-olds asked more questions to an adult, while 6-year-olds showed a slight preference for a robot.

To investigate whether age predicted the total number of questions asked by children during robot interaction sessions, a linear regression analysis was performed, which revealed a statistically significant positive relationship between age and the total number of questions asked ($\beta = 26.33$, $p = .005$). Specifically, the number of questions increased by approximately 26 for each additional year of age. This trend indicates that older children were progressively more likely to engage verbally with robots and adult facilitators. Despite the limited number of age groups, the strength of the association suggests a clear developmental progression in children's willingness and ability to formulate and express questions in a social-robotic context.

4.2 Qualitative Analysis of Children's Behavior Towards Robots

The qualitative analysis was performed by a single researcher and focused on identifying general patterns in children's behavior toward robots that could not be captured by individual codes. This included watching video recordings of the sessions to closely observe the behavior of the children toward the robots, and transcribing the children's questions and verbal expressions directed at the robots to explore common conversational themes. The analysis specifically looked at general behavioral trends, instances of physical proximity (such as touching or approaching the robot), and recurring types of question asked by the children. The children spoke Polish during the interactions, and the comments quoted in this article have been translated into English.

3-Year-Olds. The 3-year-olds showed varied participation, with an initial hesitation to speak directly to the robot, often responding only after asking. They displayed interest through gestures, echoed the robot's phrases playfully, and expressed enjoyment of its actions like dancing and flying, though their verbal contributions were frequently self-referential or directed at the facilitator rather than the robot. Their questions presented a variety of themes.

- Functional: "What can he do?"
- Emotions and relationships: "Does he like to hug mom and dad?"
- Preferences on food: "Does he like meatballs/still water/lollipops?"

4-Year-Olds. The 4-year-olds actively greeted the robot, introduced themselves, and responded with laughter and excitement, especially when the robot repeated their names. They moved closer during activities, gathered around the robot during a playful protest, and expressed affection verbally. The children raised their hands to ask questions, often repeated questions, gave commands to the robot, and occasionally shared unrelated personal information. Their questions displayed the following themes.

- Physicality and functionality: "Can you slip?"/"Can you jump?"
- Preferences: "How do you like to play?"
- Imaginative: "Was he ever attacked by a monster?"

5-Year-Olds. The 5-year-olds actively introduced themselves, responded spontaneously to robots' actions, and remained seated while engaging verbally throughout the session. They asked numerous questions, maintained topical relevance, built on each other's questions, and showed a high interest in physical interaction by lining up to touch the robots and returning for additional turns. The themes of their questions were more varied compared to younger age groups.

- Identity and personal characteristics: "Where was the little robot born?"
- Physical structure and functionality: "Do you hear from your ears or speak from them?"
- Emotions, relationships, and family: "Do you have parents?"/"Where are your parents?"/"Do you live with them at home?"
- Preferences and experiences: "Do you have insects in your country? Because we do."
- Language, understanding, and correctness: "Can you say 'How are you?' in English?"
- Various and humorous comments: "He fell in love with us?"

6-Year-Olds. The 6-year-olds showed the highest levels of verbal expression, physical closeness, and emotional engagement, often surrounding robots, petting them, and using affectionate language. They responded with loud exclamations, laughter, and repeated requests for robots to perform actions, frequently interpreting robot behavior in emotional terms (e.g., 'He's crying'). Social interaction was strong within the group, and the children discussed robot behavior among themselves and frequently issued direct commands. Their questions were the most diverse and imaginative across all age groups, though their excitement sometimes disrupted turn-taking and structure. The following themes were evidenced in their questions.

- Action-oriented/Command-like questions: "Can you do karate for us?"
- Functionality and capabilities: "Do you have a phone?"
- Identity and personal characteristics: "How old are you?"
- Emotions: "Is he shy?", "Is he angry?"
- Language, understanding, and correctness: "Can you say 'how are you'?"
- Inventive and playful hypotheticals: "Do you have fires in your legs that you can use to fly?", "Have you been to Mars?"

5 Discussion

The quantitative analysis provided several insights into how children interact with social robots. The differences in the number of questions directed to the robot versus those addressed to the adult, along with the statistically significant results of the chi-square test, suggest that children's interaction patterns with the robot vary across age groups from 3 to 6 years old. Specifically, age appears to influence whether children treat the robot as a direct conversational partner or rely on adults to mediate their communication. [22] suggests that the robot may be perceived as a non-judgmental and approachable source of information, possibly lowering social inhibitions associated with authority questioning - our research supports these claims.

The differences in the number of questions directed to the robot versus the adult, combined with the binomial test results, reveal a developmental shift in children's preferences rather than a simple linear trend. Specifically, 3-year-olds clearly preferred asking questions to the adult, 4-year-olds showed a tendency to ask more questions to the robot (though not statistically significant), 5-year-olds again preferred the adult, and 6-year-olds slightly favored the robot. This pattern suggests a nonlinear trajectory-possibly a U-shaped or fluctuating pattern-in how children assign communicative and informational roles to robots versus humans. Rather than steadily increasing or decreasing with age, children's willingness to address robots appears to vary across developmental stages. This nuanced pattern partially aligns with previous findings by [15], who observed children's general tendency to rely more on humans for questions and answers. However, our results indicate that this dependency changes dynamically with age, possibly reflecting changes in factors related to cognitive, social, or novelty as children grow.

The total number of questions asked per group, together with the statistically significant results of the linear regression analysis, indicated that the number of questions increased with age between 3 and 6 years. However, this contradicts the finding of [3], where no significant differences were observed between the number of questions asked by the younger and the older children.

One possible reason for this difference is the way the studies were designed, especially how age groups and the interaction setting were defined. In our study, we looked at separate age groups (3-, 4-, 5-, and 6-year-olds), which helped us see gradual changes with age. In contrast, [3] used broader age groups (5–6 and 7–8 years), which may have hidden differences between 5- and 6-year-olds. It is also possible that the question asking increases only up to age 6 and stays stable afterward, which would match their result of no difference between older children. The studies also differed in setting and appearance of the robot. [3] was done in a lab with one robot that looked very humanlike in both face and body. Our study was carried out in a preschool classroom, using two robots that were more machine-like in appearance, although still somewhat human-like in posture. These differences in context and robot design could have influenced the number of children who engaged and asked questions.

The qualitative analysis of children's behavior across age groups revealed that as children age (between 3 and 6 years), they generally become more expressive toward robots, both verbally and physically. 6-year-olds, in particular, demonstrate significantly higher levels of physical engagement with robots, actively seeking touch and physical proximity, compared to younger children. This is consistent with [16]'s statement that younger children (up to 6 years old) are more likely to engage with robots. However, the current study expands this finding by showing that interest in interacting with robots increases with age (from 3 to 6 years), with the highest outcome observed at age 6.

Additionally, the analysis of the themes in questions asked by different age groups revealed that younger children (3–4 years old) show the greatest interest in the robot's functionality and preferences, particularly in relation to food and play. The limited number of question topics, along with the overall low number of questions, may align with [16]'s finding that younger children tend to have lower expectations of robots compared to their older peers. Our study also confirmed that younger children are more inclined to bond with the robot on simpler and more everyday life-related topics [16]. Moreover, supporting the claims of [3] (younger children are more interested in the robot if animate), we found that children's questions focused on functions and physical abilities. These questions were present in every age group in our study, and they appear earlier than the other categories: children expect robot to be animate and are interested in its physical performance. However, our results challenge the claims of [20], who suggest that 3-year-olds are less likely to attribute lifelike qualities to robots, as the content of their questions clearly indicates that they do.

In contrast, older children (5–6 years old) through their questions display a broader range of interests in robots, spanning from physical traits and preferences to abilities (such as language), identity (including age, nationality, and gender), emotional states (robot emotions and family relationships), and even more abstract or humorous concepts (like traveling to Mars or having fire-powered legs for flight). It corresponds to general research on question-asking behavior in children [4,6], suggesting that the ability to form more elaborate and abstract questions grows with age.

Moreover, the categories of questions asked by older children about the robot overlapped with categories brought up by [5], meaning that general daily conversations, robots' preferences, their family status and abilities are universally explored topics by children of this age.

Finally, although more research [14,23] explores the questions children are asked by the robot, the findings from [3] and the study described above also uncover an important trope in the use of social robots in education. For example, [13] found that children have a clearer mental representation of the robot after the interview with the researcher; in our study, the robot is able to clarify this by itself, facilitating the process.

6 Conclusions and Design Implications

Our findings highlight that children's reactions to robots vary significantly with age, reflecting the evolving cognitive, social, and emotional abilities in early childhood. Younger children (ages 3–4) engage more readily in simple, concrete interactions, favoring immediate, tangible feedback. As children mature (ages 5–6), their interactions become increasingly abstract, imaginative, and socially complex, accompanied by a growing curiosity about the robot's identity and social role.

Physical engagement, such as touch and proximity, also increases with age, suggesting that the physical responsiveness of robots plays an important role in maintaining interaction. Furthermore, children's preferences for engaging with robots versus adults do not follow a linear pattern, indicating that their perceptions of social roles are flexible and dependent on context. These findings emphasize the importance of designing robots that can dynamically adapt to the developmental stage, interests, and social expectations of the child users.

6.1 Design Implications

Based on our findings, we propose the following design implications for CRI. First, robot communication should be age-sensitive. For 3–4-year-olds, simple language and immediate, clear feedback (for example, "I like apples, do you?") are important. For 5- to 6-year-olds, robots should support more abstract and diverse dialogue, including open-ended questions and topics such as emotions or identity. This aligns with [26,27], emphasizing the importance of developmental sizing in CRI design.

As children's question-asking increases with age, robots should actively encourage curiosity. Older children, in particular, could benefit from responsive dialogue systems capable of handling various inquiries (e.g., "Where do you live?"). Adaptive prompts (for example, "What do you think I like to eat?") can sustain engagement and promote agency. In addition, as children become more expressive with age, robots should mirror this through gestures, facial expressions, and tone of voice. Responsive behaviors, such as nodding or sharing excitement, can foster participation. This aligns with [2] guidelines for the incorporation of frequent engagement cues in younger children to reduce their destruction.

With age, children show greater interest in physical contact with robots, underscoring the need for physical responsiveness. Robots should respond meaningfully to touch, such as hugging or handholding, through sensors and feedback (e.g., sounds, facial expressions, LEDs), reinforcing positive interactions. This is consistent with [21] findings that physical contact up to a certain age may be crucial for interaction.

The nonlinear, fluctuating trend of preferring robot vs. adult suggests that children's perception of social roles varies. Robots could flexibly adapt their social role, from a playful peer to a knowledgeable guide, depending on the context. Customizable interaction styles allow adults to calibrate the robot's demeanor to match specific needs. As older children show increasing interest in humor and imagination, robots could support these capacities through storytelling and scenario-based play (e.g., "Let's go to Mars"), responding creatively to fantastical input and encouraging pretend play.

Finally, as older children show interest in a robot's identity, robots should share consistent, personalized information (e.g., name, favorite activities) and allow children to co-construct its persona, enhancing connection and continuity over time.

In general, CRI design must recognize and embrace developmental diversity among young users. Adaptive, responsive, and expressive robot behaviors can better support meaningful engagement, encourage curiosity, and foster positive relational experiences.

Acknowledgements. This research was supported in part by a grant from the National Science Centre, Poland, under the OPUS call in the Weave Programme under the project number 2021/43/I/ST6/02489. We thank Julia Klimecka and Tymon Kukier for their help in organizing and conducting the workshops.

Disclosure of Interests. The authors have no competing interests to declare that are relevant to the content of this article.

References

1. Attamimi, M., Miyata, M., Yamada, T., Omori, T., Hida, R.: Attention estimation for child-robot interaction. In: Proceedings of the Fourth International Conference on Human Agent Interaction, pp. 267–271 (2016)
2. Baxter, P., De Jong, C., Aarts, R., de Haas, M., Vogt, P.: The effect of age on engagement in preschoolers' child-robot interactions. In: Proceedings of the Companion of the 2017 ACM/IEEE International Conference on Human-Robot Interaction, pp. 81–82 (2017)
3. Cameron, D., et al.: Children's age influences their use of biological and mechanical questions towards a humanoid. In: Gao, Y., Fallah, S., Jin, Y., Lekakou, C. (eds.) TAROS 2017. LNCS (LNAI), vol. 10454, pp. 290–299. Springer, Cham (2017). https://doi.org/10.1007/978-3-319-64107-2_23
4. Cazden, C.B.: Children's questions: their forms, functions and roles in education. Young Child. 202–220 (1970)
5. Chen, Y.: Preschoolers' reactions to a social robot in their first encounter: a pilot study. Int. J. Humanit. Soc. Sci. Educ. **5**, 32–38 (2018)
6. Chouinard, M.M., Harris, P.L., Maratsos, M.P.: Children's questions: a mechanism for cognitive development. In: Monographs of the Society for Research in Child Development, pp. i–129 (2007)
7. De Graaf, M.M., Allouch, S.B., Klamer, T.: Sharing a life with harvey: exploring the acceptance of and relationship-building with a social robot. Comput. Hum. Behav. **43**, 1–14 (2015)
8. Di Dio, C., et al.: Shall i trust you? From child-robot interaction to trusting relationships. Front. Psychol. **11**, 469 (2020)
9. Kennedy, J., Baxter, P., Belpaeme, T.: The robot who tried too hard: social behaviour of a robot tutor can negatively affect child learning. In: Proceedings of the Tenth Annual ACM/IEEE International Conference on Human-Robot Interaction, pp. 67–74 (2015)
10. Leite, I., Martinho, C., Paiva, A.: Social robots for long-term interaction: a survey. Int. J. Soc. Robot. **5**, 291–308 (2013)
11. Lewis, M.M.: Language, thought and personality in infancy and childhood (1964)
12. Martínez-Miranda, J., Pérez-Espinosa, H., Espinosa-Curiel, I., Avila-George, H., Rodríguez-Jacobo, J.: Age-based differences in preferences and affective reactions towards a robot's personality during interaction. Comput. Hum. Behav. **84**, 245–257 (2018)

13. Monaco, C., Mich, O., Ceol, T., Potrich, A.: Investigating mental representations about robots in preschool children. arXiv preprint arXiv:1806.03248 (2018)
14. Okanda, M., Taniguchi, K.: How do children answer questions from a physically present humanoid robot? Infant Child Dev. **31**(3), e2300 (2022)
15. Oranç, C., Küntay, A.C.: Children's perception of social robots as a source of information across different domains of knowledge. Cogn. Dev. **54**, 100875 (2020)
16. Ros, R., et al.: Child-robot interaction in the wild: advice to the aspiring experimenter. In: Proceedings of the 13th International Conference on Multimodal Interfaces, pp. 335–342 (2011)
17. Rudenko, I., et al.: Drawings for insight on preschoolers' perception of robots. In: Companion of the 2024 ACM/IEEE International Conference on Human-Robot Interaction, pp. 920–924 (2024)
18. Salter, T., Werry, I., Michaud, F.: Going into the wild in child-robot interaction studies: issues in social robotic development. Intel. Serv. Robot. **1**(2), 93–108 (2008)
19. Simon, A.J., et al.: Quantifying attention span across the lifespan. Front. Cogn. **2**, 1207428 (2023)
20. Taniguchi, K., Okanda, M.: Children's animistic beliefs toward a humanoid robot and other objects. J. Exp. Child Psychol. **244**, 105945 (2024)
21. Tokmurzina, D., Sagitzhan, N., Nurgaliyev, A., Sandygulova, A.: Exploring child-robot proxemics. In: Companion of the 2018 ACM/IEEE International Conference on Human-Robot Interaction, pp. 257–258 (2018)
22. Unlutabak, B., Barkana, E., et al.: Children's information search with social robots: a focus on children's question-asking behavior. Prof. Dr. Duygun, Children's Information Search with Social Robots: A Focus on Children's Question-Asking Behavior
23. van Straten, C.L., Peter, J., Kühne, R., Barco, A.: On sharing and caring: investigating the effects of a robot's self-disclosure and question-asking on children's robot perceptions and child-robot relationship formation. Comput. Hum. Behav. **129**, 107135 (2022)
24. Vogt, P., De Haas, M., De Jong, C., Baxter, P., Krahmer, E.: Child-robot interactions for second language tutoring to preschool children. Front. Hum. Neurosci. **11**, 73 (2017)
25. Westlund, J.M.K., Martinez, M., Archie, M., Das, M., Breazeal, C.: Effects of framing a robot as a social agent or as a machine on children's social behavior. In: 2016 25th IEEE International Symposium on Robot and Human Interactive Communication (RO-MAN), pp. 688–693. IEEE (2016)
26. Wróbel, A., Źróbek, K., Schaper, M.-M., Zguda, P., Indurkhya, B.: Age-appropriate robot design: in-the-wild child-robot interaction studies of perseverance styles and robot's unexpected behavior. In: 2023 32nd IEEE International Conference on Robot and Human Interactive Communication (RO-MAN), pp. 1451–1458. IEEE (2023)
27. Zaga, C., et al.: Growing-up hand in hand with robots: designing and evaluating child-robot interaction from a developmental perspective. In: Proceedings of the Companion of the 2017 ACM/IEEE International Conference on Human-Robot Interaction, pp. 429–430 (2017)
28. Zguda, P., Kołota, A., Venture, G., Sniezynski, B., Indurkhya, B.: Exploring the role of trust and expectations in cri using in-the-wild studies. Electronics **10**(3), 347 (2021)

LLMs and Conversational/Verbal Interaction

AwaR(e)obot: Towards Designing and Generating Context-Aware Companion Robot Behavior Using LLMs

Eshtiak Ahmed(✉) , Juho Hamari , and Oğuz 'Oz' Buruk

Faculty of ITC, Tampere University, Tampere, Finland
eshtiak.ahmed@tuni.fi

Abstract. As robots move beyond industrial and assistive roles into everyday human environments, the ability to communicate naturally and responsively becomes increasingly important. This paper presents a system that enables a quadruped robot, Boston Dynamics' Spot, to respond to human voice inputs with expressive, dog-like physical behaviors. By integrating voice recognition, large language models (LLMs), and a structured response mapping framework, the robot interprets conversational inputs and generates sequences of behavior markers aligned with its physical capabilities. The system defines a robot persona and prompts the LLM with contextual constraints, including movement affordances and limitations, to ensure realistic and semantically appropriate responses. Our study highlights the potential of using LLMs not only for dialogue generation but also for embodied interaction design. While the limited expressivity and subtlety of robotic movement pose challenges, this work demonstrates a promising step toward more intuitive and engaging human-robot interaction. We discuss the implications for generalizing this approach to different robot morphologies and outline future directions for expanding behavioral nuance, emotional interpretation, and multimodal engagement.

Keywords: LLM · Contextual Robot Reactions · Embodied Interaction

1 Introduction

Robots have become an integral part of modern life, transitioning from industrial applications to more personalized roles in homes, healthcare, education, and entertainment [1]. They are no longer limited to repetitive tasks but are evolving to engage with humans in increasingly sophisticated ways. In the current landscape of robots alongside humans, their importance lies in their ability to assist, complement, and augment human capabilities [2]. However, their ability to interpret and respond to human interventions, engage in meaningful interactions, and adapt to different social contexts has positioned them to potentially become companions to humans [3, 4]. As robots develop more advanced communication and behavioral capabilities, they are not just tools but entities that might have the ability to create meaningful agency with humans in daily life scenarios. One way to create and express agency is to respond contextually to human interaction cues, making the response meaningful to humans [5, 6].

Early approaches to robot response generation, especially in social contexts, often rely on pre-programmed scripts or limited sets of rules, which restrict adaptability and fail to capture the complexity of real-time, dynamic human-robot interactions [7–10]. Development in natural language processing paved the way for leveraging voice-based interaction with robots, which allowed for the creation of voice-based feedback mechanisms on robots [11]. However, the process stayed far from dynamic due to the shortcomings of natural language generation from the robot's perspective. The introduction of Large Language Models (LLMs) addresses a lot of these shortcomings, especially because it provides a more dynamic while still being controllable and predictable depending on how it is configured [12]. Also, Artificial Intelligence (AI), being the driving force of LLMs, makes it more adaptive and situated in diverse contexts. Through reasoning, LLMs can enable robots to understand the sentiment, intent, and context behind human speech [13, 14]. This study explores how LLMs can be integrated with robotic systems to understand voice-based inputs and then interpret them to create dynamic reactions from a robot.

In this study, we make an attempt to implement a system where voice inputs are analyzed by an LLM, generating a series of reactions on a four-legged mobile robot, Spot [15]. Our approach demonstrates the potential of LLMs to bridge the gap in dynamic reaction generation, offering a method for real-time, contextually appropriate robot responses. The initial system design can be used as a framework for generating dynamic robot reactions to human dialogue that can be adopted for any robot in any given context.

2 Background

2.1 Behavior Generation in HRI

Human-Robot Interaction (HRI) research has long focused on enabling robots to respond to human input through appropriate, context-sensitive behaviors. Early approaches to behavior generation were largely pre-programmed and rule-based, relying on predefined scripts that mapped specific inputs to specific outputs [3, 7, 8]. These methods were limited in flexibility and could not adapt well to novel or unexpected situations. As the field matured, learning-based approaches began to emerge. These systems employed machine learning algorithms, such as reinforcement learning or imitation learning, to generate behaviors through experience or demonstration [16, 17]. While more adaptable, these models often require large amounts of data and could be difficult to generalize across different tasks or environments.

Despite these advances, a significant gap remains in real-time and dynamic response generation, especially when it comes to social and affective interactions. Many systems still rely on static, pre-defined templates or dialogue trees, which limit their ability to respond naturally to the subtleties of human communication [18]. The challenge lies in creating systems that can not only understand the context of human inputs but also generate appropriate physical behaviors in response. Our system attempts to address both these limitations by introducing LLM as the brain of the process that provides context for the interaction scenario and tries to create reasoning for behavioral responses dynamically, without using predefined input structures.

2.2 Voice-Based Interaction in Robotics

Voice-based interaction is a natural and intuitive modality for communicating with robots. It has been widely studied in service robots, assistive technologies, and social robotics [19–21]. Voice input allows for hands-free and accessible control, making it suitable for a wide range of users and environments. However, most systems rely on limited voice command structures, often requiring specific keywords or phrases to trigger actions [7–10]. These systems typically produce static responses, failing to capture the emotional tone, intent, or subtlety of the speaker's message. Moreover, existing voice interaction models often struggle to handle ambiguous or open-ended input, further reducing the perceived intelligence and responsiveness of the robot [22].

As a result, many current voice-enabled robots lack the expressiveness and emotional depth required for naturalistic interaction. This limits their ability to function as social companions or emotionally supportive agents in human environments. We attempt to bridge this gap by incorporating dynamic responses that are generated in real-time by analyzing the interaction context and voice input in combination.

2.3 Use of LLMs in HRI

Recent advances in Large Language Models (LLMs), such as GPT-3 and GPT-4 [12], have opened new possibilities for robotic interactions. LLMs have demonstrated strong capabilities in contextual understanding, dialogue generation, and zero-shot reasoning, making them promising tools for generating robot responses from natural language input [23, 24]. In robotics, LLMs have been used to interpret instructions, plan high-level actions, and even generate code to control robotic systems [25, 26]. For example, the Code-as-Policies (CaP) framework leverages language models to output executable robot code from user commands, allowing for flexible and composable robot behavior [27]. More recently, LLMs have also been explored for embodied language understanding, where the model integrates sensory data and physical actions with conversational input [28]. These capabilities suggest that LLMs could play a critical role in enabling real-time, sentiment-sensitive robot behaviors, especially in social and affective contexts.

However, their application to direct behavior generation for emotionally expressive movements, particularly from unconstrained voice input, remains underexplored. This study aims to add valuable knowledge to this domain by leveraging LLMs to interpret human voice input and dynamically generate contextual robot movement responses.

3 System Design

This section presents the architecture and functioning of our system that enables real-time voice-based interaction between a human user and a robot using a Large Language Model (LLM) as an interpretive and generative intermediary. The design supports natural dialogue input from users, transforms it into behavior markers, and subsequently executes robot actions via a structured response generation pipeline. The system comprises three main components: Human Interface, LLM Module, and Robot Execution Layer. Figure 1 shows a high-level design of the system.

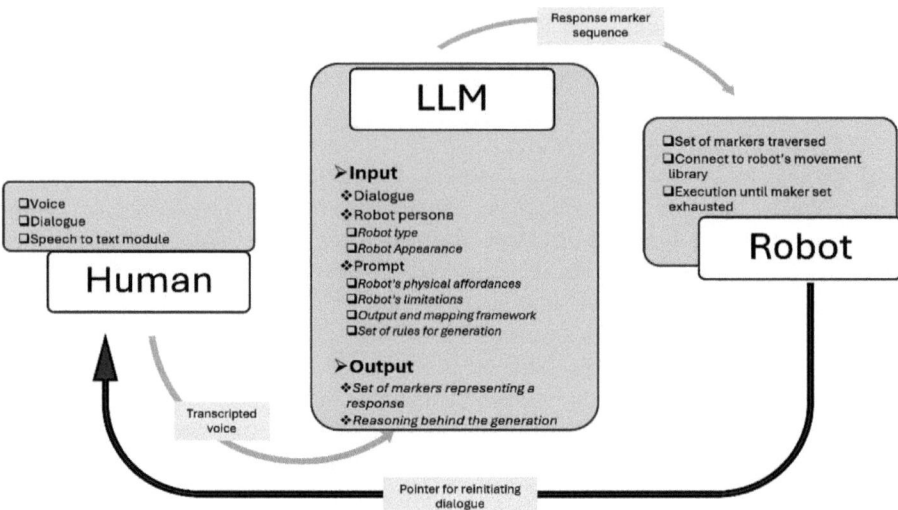

Fig. 1. System design including components.

3.1 Human Interface

The interaction begins with the human user providing voice input, which serves as the primary modality for initiating communication with the system. This input can vary widely in form and intent, ranging from explicit commands, such as *"follow me"*, *"sit down"*, or *"walk ahead"*, to more expressive and emotionally rich dialogue, like *"I feel tired today"* or *"this place feels a bit eerie"*. By accommodating this full spectrum of utterances, the system moves beyond traditional command-and-control paradigms and instead embraces a more conversational model of interaction. Supporting both directive and expressive speech opens up avenues for more nuanced human-robot relationships.

Once the voice is detected, it is transcribed into text using a speech-to-text module and immediately fed to the LLM module. The length of the voice input can be set either to 1) listen until the human keeps talking, allowing longer and more complex dialogs, or 2) listen for a finite amount of time, allowing for shorter interactions.

3.2 LLM Module

The core of the system is the Large Language Model (LLM), which acts as a bridge between the natural language and the robot execution layer. The primary aim of this module is to take the voice input as text, feed it to LLM along with the prompt, and then generate response markers as output. It also provides detailed reasoning for the response markers it produces.

Input Specifications. The LLM receives an input that comprises the robot's persona, its affordance profile, and response mapping framework along with the voice input.

Robot Persona. To guide appropriate and context-sensitive responses, the large language model (LLM) is provided with a clearly defined robot persona. This persona acts as a foundational prompt that influences the style, tone, and behavioral intent of the robot's generated responses. By instilling a consistent persona, the system ensures that the robot's interactions remain coherent, believable, and aligned with user expectations across varying scenarios. The persona is constructed using robot type and appearance. For instance, a quadruped robot like Boston Dynamics' Spot [15] is structurally and functionally different from a humanoid robot such as SoftBank's Pepper. The LLM is informed of the robot's morphological category, which constrains and defines the range of possible actions, postures, and gestures. For example: A quadruped robot might "wag its body" or "lower its stance" as an expressive gesture. A humanoid robot might "nod," "wave," or "tilt its head in curiosity."

Robot's Affordance Profile. LLM is also provided with a structured and explicit description of the robot's physical affordances and limitations. This component acts as a filter, ensuring that the behaviors generated are grounded in the robot's embodied reality. Affordances describe the actions the robot is physically capable of performing, such as walking, turning, bowing, or shaking its legs, movements that are derived from its mechanical structure, degrees of freedom, and actuation capabilities. By embedding these constraints into the prompt, the LLM is discouraged from generating responses that reference actions the robot cannot perform, thereby preventing unrealistic, confusing, or misleading interactions. This careful framing allows the LLM to remain both creative and grounded, synthesizing responses that are expressive and appropriate, yet always physically realizable by the robot's hardware.

Response Mapping Framework. To bridge the gap between the LLM's textual outputs and the robot's physical execution system, the architecture includes a Response Mapping Framework. It consists of micro-movements and behaviors that can form meaningful responses if performed subsequently, for example, looking up, or tilting the body, etc. These markers serve as an intermediate layer, working as conceptual tags that the robot can later interpret corresponding to parameterized routines in its movement library. In addition to the marker framework, the prompt includes a set of generation rules that determine how these markers can be composed and an output sequence structure that helps generate a set of sequence that is understandable for the execution layer. These rules encode temporal dynamics (e.g., certain gestures must follow or precede others), behavioral concurrency (e.g., walking and nodding can occur simultaneously, but bowing and turning cannot), and technical dynamics (e.g., consecutive sitting or standing movements are undesirable as they do not make any changes in response). This structuring ensures that the robot's behavior sequences are not just functional but also socially legible and believable, echoing human patterns of expression.

Output Generation. The system is designed so that the large language model (LLM) produces two distinct but complementary outputs: (1) a set of behavioral markers, and (2) a short reasoning text. Together, these outputs form a cohesive representation of the robot's intended response and its underlying rationale.

Behavioral Markers. The behavioral markers are structured codes or labels that serve as interpretable and executable instructions for the robot's behavior engine, obtained in the form of python lists. These markers are derived from the internal vocabulary defined in the system's response mapping framework and represent the robot's non-verbal, physical reactions to the user's voice input. Each movement marker is an alphabet representing a specific behavior of the robot, which is associated with a timeframe that ranges from 0.5 s to 2.0 s, which represents the amount of time that specific movement will be performed by the robot. For example, an output marker set of ["f,1.0", "q,1.2", "g,0.8", "u,1.5"] means the robot will perform the movement associated with f for 1 s, q for 1.2 s, g for .8 s and u for 1.5 s.

Generation Reasoning. The LLM provides a short reasoning text that explains the logic behind the chosen responses. This might include interpretations of the user's tone, or word choices, and justify why certain behavioral responses were selected. For instance, the reasoning might state: "The user initiated the interaction with a friendly tone, suggesting a casual greeting. The robot responds with a friendly motion sequence that includes moving toward the user, looking up to them, and acknowledging the mention". This reasoning layer adds a level of transparency and interpretability to the system, making it easier for developers to debug behavior generation pipelines and for researchers to analyze how and why certain robot actions are produced.

3.3 Robot Execution Layer

The Robot Execution Layer serves as the final stage in the system pipeline and is responsible for translating the high-level response markers generated by the LLM into tangible, physical movements performed by the robot. Once a sequence of behavioral markers is produced as a python list, they are processed sequentially, using an iterative loop to traverse each marker in the list. As each marker is encountered, it is passed through a mapping function that links it to a corresponding routine in the robot's movement library. These routines consist of predefined movement primitives such as *"walk forward"*, *"move backward"*, *"go belly up"*, or *"strafe left"*, etc. that are natively supported by the robot's hardware capabilities. This marker-to-movement translation operates via a lookup mechanism in a python method library that ensures every behavioral marker is matched to a physically feasible and safe motion routine.

3.4 Interaction Loop

Once the robot completes executing its full sequence of behavioral responses mapped from the user's prior voice input, it transitions back into a receptive state. To signal this shift and prompt the user for the next input, the robot emits a distinct sound marker, such as a short chime or mechanical tone, signifying that the robot is now actively listening and ready for further interaction.

4 Initial Testing

We have conducted some preliminary testing in the laboratory to understand how the system works, what results we get, and to overall obtain some insights into the system's feasibility as well as credibility.

4.1 Technical Specifications

We initially developed the system on the Boston Dynamics' Spot robot [15] (Firmware version 4.1.1), a quadruped robotic platform equipped with advanced mobility and sensor capabilities, hence, the initial testing was done on the same robot. For capturing user input, an external microphone was used to record voice commands, while a speaker was integrated to play auditory cues that signal the engagement prompt. On the software side, we implemented the system using Python (version 3.8), which handles input processing, communication between modules, and movement execution. The robot's behavioral logic and language understanding are powered by the OpenAI API (gpt-4o-mini) [12], which serves as the Large Language Model backend for generating context-aware responses based on voice input. The LLM and the python client was run on a windows 10 laptop which connected with the robot via the robot's own wireless network.

4.2 Prompt

Figure 2 shows the prompt we have used to test the initial implementation. It includes the response markers that have been defined for each robot behavior. The response generation framework here uses characters to define robot movements, making it more straightforward to execute them in the execution layer with method library mapping. As the robot in question is a four-legged mobile robot, we chose to generate behaviors that resemble a dog.

4.3 Results

Table 1 gives a summary of three iterations of voice input, their corresponding response sequence along with LLM's reasoning for generating the sequence. Figure 3 demonstrates the response sequence for the voice input *"Who wants a treat?!"*.

4.4 Preliminary Insights

Preliminary testing of our system with the Spot robot revealed several key insights that reflect both the potential and limitations of using Large Language Models (LLMs) for embodied behavior generation. These findings, though based on informal trials, provide useful direction for future refinement and formal evaluation of the system.

LLM Behavior is Bounded by Robot Affordances. While LLMs are powerful in generating diverse, semantically rich outputs, their expressive potential is inherently limited by what the robot can physically do. Spot's movement repertoire, though advanced for a quadruped robot, does not offer the same granularity or subtlety as human or animal behaviors, which restricts the fidelity of the behavioral mapping. This is a consideration for future developments where more advanced robotic systems might offer more freedom in generating responses with greater detail. Additionally, API and firmware level manipulation might open up more possibilities for generating more diversified responses.

The Spot robot has an appearance like a dog, and it is capable of some doglike movements. It is a mobile robot, so it can move forward, backward, sideways as well as tilting its body. We want the spot robot to show movement behaviours when we talk to it. We will take voice as input from the user, convert it to text, then analyse the text to create commands for the spot robot.

Keyboard keys are connected to different robot movements, aiming to replicate dog-like behaviours.

The following keys are mapped to specific actions for controlling the Spot robot:

v key: (SIT) Makes the robot sit.
b key: (GO UPSIDE DOWN) Makes the robot go belly up (like dogs play or seek belly rubs).
f key: (STAND) Makes the robot stand (like a dog getting ready to move or being attentive).
w key: (MOVE FORWARD) Moves the robot forward (like a dog walking or running forward).
s key: (MOVE BACKWARD) Moves the robot backward (like a dog stepping back or retreating).
a key: (MOVE TO LEFT) Moves the robot to the left (like a dog moving to its left side)
d key: (MOVE TO RIGHT) Moves robot to the right (like a dog moving to its right side).
q key: (TURN LEFT) Turns the robot to the left (like a dog looking or turning its body with changing head direction).
e key: (TURN RIGHT) Turns the robot to the right (similar to the left turn).
u key: (LOOK UP) Makes the robot look up (Similar to a dog sitting on its back).
j key: (LOOK DOWN) Makes the robot look down (Similar to a dog looking down to something on the surface)
n key: (LOOK LEFT) Makes the robot look left, without changing position (Similar to a dog looking to its left)
m key: (LOOK RIGHT) Makes the robot look right, without changing position (Similar to a dog looking to its right)
g key: (ROTATE BODY LEFT) Makes the robot rotate its body to the left (legs are stable, but body rotates to left)
h key: (ROTATE BODY RIGHT) Makes the robot rotate its body to the right (legs are stable, but body rotates to right)
z key: (NOD POSITIVELY) Makes the robot nod by moving its head up and down (positive agreeing gesture)
x key: (SHAKE HEAD NEGATIVELY) Makes the robot shake its head to show negative stance or disagreement (gesture for disagreement)
c key: (SHRUGGING/BODY SHAKING) Makes the robot shrug or shake its whole body (gesture to dry off excess moisture, or simply as a reflexive behaviour)

Create key commands that will make the robot move and behave like an actual dog would behave listening to the voice input. Based on what is said to the robot, generate complex movement commands that best represents a dog's response, including a mix of complex movements like moving and looking to different directions, nodding or shaking to show agreement or disagreement, and shrugging to show unique response.

Key Command Generation Rules:
- Only put key commands that are defined here.
- Never put consecutive sit (v) commands.
- Never put consecutive stand (f) commands.
- After a sit (v) command, always put a stand (f) command if it is not the last command of the sequence.
- After a belly up (b) command, always put a stand (f) command. So, every sequence with b will be followed by f.
- Use a mix of moving on different direction, turning, looking up, looking down, looking left or right, rotating, nodding, shaking, etc. to mimic dog behaviour.

Command sequence structure:
- The command sequence will be like a python list
- Each component of the list will be an action command key and float number that represents the number of seconds that command will run, separated by a comma, example: u,1.5 means the robot will look up for 1.5 seconds. Each symbol of the list will be a character.
- The time component can range from 0.5 seconds to 2.0 seconds, it can be any number between them
- An example list could be like this: ["f,1.0", "q,1.2", "g,0.8", "u,1.5"], this means the robot will stand for 1 second, turn left for 1.2 seconds, rotate its body to the left for .8 seconds and then look up for 1.5 seconds.

Now give the following things separated by a new line for the text at the end:
- A set of commands for the robot as a python list (no explanation, only the list, without commenting)
- In a new line, a short explanation justifying the set of commands that have been generated.

Fig. 2. Test prompt sent to LLM along with voice input.

Ambiguity in Movement Interpretation. In several instances, parts of the generated sequences of actions did not clearly convey a specific intent or emotional tone to human observers. For example, when the voice input was *"Who wants a treat?!"*, the robot stood up, then looked down, moved forward, turned right, looks left, nods positively, then looks right, moves backwards a little, and stays standing. While fragments of this response (e.g., looking down for a treat, or nodding to show positive intentions) might seem relevant for what has been said, parts of it might seem ambiguous. However, this ambiguity aligns interestingly with real-life dog behavior [29, 30], which is itself sometimes difficult to interpret. In this case, the robot's animal-like form might soften the impact of such uncertainty and make behaviors seem more playful or natural rather than flawed.

Limitations in Understanding Emotion. Since the system currently relies solely on textual transcription of voice input, it may miss critical vocal cues such as tone, emphasis, or affective nuance. The GPT version we have used here only works with textual data; hence it can't only detect word-semantics and tries to compensate for the lack of emotion-oriented knowledge by understanding the scenario and persona of the users. This can result in robot responses that feel mismatched or emotionally flat in comparison to what the human user intended, suggesting a future need for multimodal input processing. Additionally, newer LLM models with emotion detection capabilities from voice might work better in scenarios like this.

Spatial Considerations for Behavior Execution. One emergent challenge was to accommodate the space for occasionally generated long and dynamic behavior sequences. These can cause the robot to travel significantly from its starting location, making the robot prone to encounter obstacles, especially in confined or cluttered spaces. Because the responses are generated in real-time and not pre-evaluated for spatial feasibility, ensuring an open and safe interaction environment becomes a critical requirement for smooth operation.

These insights highlight both the promise and complexity of integrating LLMs with embodied robotic systems. They underscore the need for fine-tuning prompt structures, incorporating environmental awareness, and designing for better alignment between abstract reasoning and physical expression.

5 Discussion

This study explored the use of a large language models (LLMs) to generate behavior commands for the Spot robot [15] in response to human voice input. The results demonstrate a promising level of coherence and contextual appropriateness in the LLM's responses, with generated command sequences reflecting dog-like behaviors in reaction to a wide range of expressive and directive utterances.

One of the deeper implications of this work lies in its potential to serve as a generalized framework for robot behavior generation. The modular design, consisting of a voice-to-text layer, LLM-based semantic interpretation, behavior marker generation, and robot execution mapping, can be adapted across robotic platforms with different hardware specifications. By abstracting robot actions into semantic markers (e.g., "greet formally," "look playful") before mapping them to platform-specific movement primitives, the framework offers a flexible pipeline that separates social logic from physical implementation. This abstraction enables scalability and portability, provided that each target robot has an associated library of motion mappings that correspond to its specific embodiment. Robots like Spot, a quadruped with no facial expressions, speech, or arms, rely solely on locomotion and posture, whereas humanoid robots might convey intent

Table 1. Summary of three iterations of input and output.

Voice input	Response sequence	Reasoning
Good boy!	["f,1.0", "u,1.5", "g,0.8", "n,1.0", "x,1.0", "d,1.0", "b,1.5", "f,1.0", "q,1.0", "e,1.2", "m,1.0"]	The commands begin with the robot standing and looking up to acknowledge the user. It then rotates its body slightly while looking left and shakes its head negatively to mimic confusion or disagreement. After moving to the right, the robot goes belly up for playful interaction and subsequently stands again. Finally, it turns left, right, and looks towards the right, capturing a friendly and curious dog-like response.
It's so good to see you!	["f,1.0", "q,1.5", "n,1.2", "z,1.0", "b,1.5", "f,1.0", "w,1.0", "e,1.0", "m,1.2", "s,1.0", "x,1.0"]	The commands start with the robot standing and turning left while looking in that direction, indicating attentiveness and acknowledgment. Then it nods positively to show agreement. After that, it playfully goes belly up to engage, followed by standing up again. It then moves forward, turns right, looks right, moves backward while shaking its head to express a playful yet hesitant response to the idea of moving back, reflecting a dog's natural behavior in a social setting.
Who wants a treat?!	["f,1.0", "j,1.5", "w,1.0", "e,1.0", "n,1.0", "z,0.7", "m,1.0", "s,1.0", "f,1.0"]	The robot stands attentively, then looks down for a while as if observing a treat, moves forward, and then turns right. It then looks left and nods positively to show eagerness for the treat, looks right and moves backward to show cautiousness. Finally, the robot stands again to be ready for the next interaction.

through gestures, gaze, or spoken language [31, 32]. This disparity requires tailored prompt structures, marker vocabularies, and control logic for each robot type. Our study outlines an initial framework for aiding this shortcoming of the current systems.

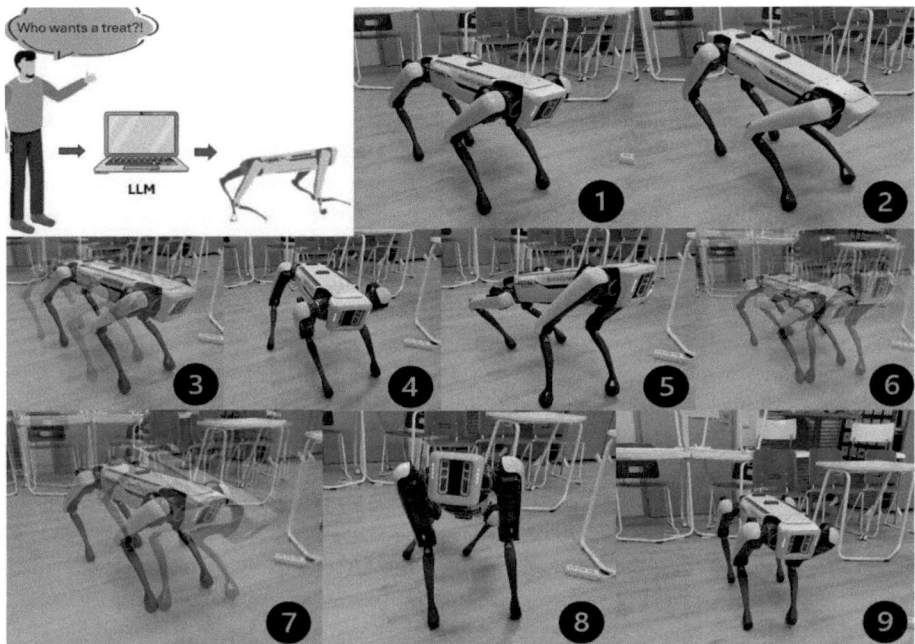

Fig. 3. Preliminary testing results for input *"Who wants a treat?!"*.

While generating basic control commands is relatively straightforward due to their finite and deterministic nature, crafting expressive, nuanced behaviors is far more complex [33]. Robots typically lack the subtle expressivity of humans, such as a raised eyebrow or slight tilt, which makes their actions more ambiguous and harder to interpret [34, 35]. This expressive gap, especially pronounced in simpler or non-humanoid robots, complicates user understanding and engagement [36]. Therefore, to ensure believability and emotional relevance, robots must align closely with a robot's physical capabilities, using carefully constrained behavioral mappings to avoid overgeneration or misinterpretation. We have attempted to bridge this gap by introducing a prompt structure that provides LLM with comprehensive knowledge about the actors of the interaction, the context, as well as the affordances of the robot. While the system can still improve, it can be considered as a starting point for further exploration.

LLMs are traditionally employed for generating natural language responses, but their capabilities extend far beyond dialogue. This work demonstrates that LLMs can serve as powerful tools for embodied interaction design, where the goal is to generate physical behaviors that align with semantic meaning and social context. By prompting LLMs with the robot's physical affordances, persona, and interaction goals, it can reason about how a robot should act, not just speak, based on a given input. This enables the creation of complex, multi-step behavior sequences that are contextually grounded and socially expressive. Rather than generating disembodied responses, the LLM functions as a semantic bridge between human intent and embodied robotic behavior, opening new avenues for designing robots that interact with the world in meaningful, situated ways.

6 Limitations and Future Work

Despite promising initial results, our current system presents several limitations that highlight important avenues for future development. First, while generating control commands for robots is relatively straightforward due to their finite action sets and deterministic execution, producing specific, expressive, and nuanced behaviors remains a significant challenge. This difficulty is largely rooted in the restricted movement affordances and limited degrees of freedom of robots like Spot. This expressive gap often leads to robot responses that, while technically correct, may appear repetitive, unnatural, or fail to convey the intended social or emotional message.

Technically, the system relies on a finite set of affordance-mapped actions, which constrains the expressive potential of the robot. Additionally, while the LLM provides a reasoning output for transparency, this component remains underutilized in the current implementation and could be leveraged more effectively for generating user-facing explanations or guiding interaction flow.

Another significant limitation is the lack of user evaluation. Although we have tested the system on the Spot robot and confirmed its operational viability, we have yet to assess how human users perceive these generated behaviors. A user study would provide critical insight into whether the robot's actions are interpreted as socially meaningful and would also help refine the mapping between voice input and physical actions and uncover hidden mismatches in behavior generation.

Looking ahead, we aim to explore integrating multi-modal inputs, combining voice with gesture, facial expression, or environmental cues, to generate more contextually rich and responsive robot behaviors as future works. Including learning mechanisms that adapt based on user feedback and interaction history would also improve personalization and long-term engagement. On the implementation side, moving away from finite control to direct API-level manipulation of Spot's SDK would enable finer control over timing and transitions, leading to numerous possible movements.

7 Conclusion

In this paper, we explored a novel framework that enables a quadruped robot, Spot, to engage in expressive, voice-based interactions using a large language model (LLM). By leveraging structured prompts that define the robot's persona, physical capabilities, and behavioral mappings, we enabled the system to generate coherent movement responses to natural human speech. Our results demonstrate the feasibility of using LLMs to bridge abstract human intentions with physical robot behaviors, even within the constraints of limited movement affordances. These interactions, while playful and engaging, also revealed challenges around expressivity, interpretation, and embodiment. Moving forward, our approach lays the groundwork for a generalized behavior generation system adaptable to various robot morphologies. As future work, we will focus on expanding behavioral repertoires, integrating multimodal feedback, and enhancing interpretability to support more meaningful and emotionally resonant human-robot relationships.

8   Disclosure of Interests.

There are no conflicting professional or financial interest to declare.

Acknowledgement. This research is funded by the Academy of Finland Flagship Programme (337653—Forest-Human-Machine Interplay (UNITE)).

References

1. Ahmed, E., 'Oz' Buruk, O., Hamari, J.: Human–robot companionship: current trends and future agenda. Int. J. Soc. Robot., July 2024. https://doi.org/10.1007/s12369-024-01160-y
2. Goodrich, M.A., Schultz, A.C.: Human-robot interaction: a survey. Found. Trends Hum.-Comput. Interact. **1**(3), 203–275 (2007). https://doi.org/10.1561/1100000005
3. Breazeal, C.: Toward sociable robots. Robot. Auton. Syst. **42**(3), 167–175 (2003). https://doi.org/10.1016/S0921-8890(02)00373-1
4. Fong, T., Nourbakhsh, I., Dautenhahn, K.: A survey of socially interactive robots. Robot. Auton. Syst. **42**, 143–166 (2003). https://doi.org/10.1016/S0921-8890(02)00372-X
5. Harrison, K., et al.: The imperfectly relatable robot: an interdisciplinary workshop on the role of failure in HRI. In: Companion of the 2023 ACM/IEEE International Conference on Human-Robot Interaction, in HRI '23. Association for Computing Machinery, New York, pp. 917–919, March 2023. https://doi.org/10.1145/3568294.3579952
6. Engwall, O., et al.: Editorial: Socially, culturally and contextually aware robots. Front. Robot. AI **10**, November 2023. https://doi.org/10.3389/frobt.2023.1232215
7. Kanda, T., Ishiguro, H., Ono, T., Imai, M., Nakatsu, R.: Development and evaluation of an interactive humanoid robot 'Robovie. In: Proceedings 2002 IEEE International Conference on Robotics and Automation (Cat. No.02CH37292), May 2002, pp. 1848–1855, vol. 2. https://doi.org/10.1109/ROBOT.2002.1014810
8. Surjeet, Gupta, N.: A novel voice controlled robotic vehicle for smart city applications. J. Phys.: Conf. Ser. **1817**(1), 012016 (2021).https://doi.org/10.1088/1742-6596/1817/1/012016
9. Foggia, P., Greco, A., Roberto, A., Saggese, A., Vento, M.: A social robot architecture for personalized real-time human-robot interaction. IEEE Internet Things J. **10**(24), 22427–22439 (2023). https://doi.org/10.1109/JIOT.2023.3303196
10. Alonso-Martín, F., M.A. and Salichs: Integration of a voice recognition system in a social robot. Cybern. Syst. **42**(4), 215–245, May 2011. https://doi.org/10.1080/01969722.2011.583593
11. Mavridis, N.: A review of verbal and non-verbal human–robot interactive communication. Robot. Auton. Syst. **63**, 22–35 (2015). https://doi.org/10.1016/j.robot.2014.09.031
12. OpenAI et al., "GPT-4 Technical Report," Mar. 04, 2024, *arXiv*: arXiv:2303.08774. https://doi.org/10.48550/arXiv.2303.08774
13. Brown, T., et al.: Language Models are Few-Shot Learners. In: Advances in Neural Information Processing Systems, Curran Associates, Inc., 2020, pp. 1877–1901. Accessed: Apr. 28, 2025. https://papers.nips.cc/paper/2020/hash/1457c0d6bfcb4967418bfb8ac142f64a-Abstract.html
14. Ouyang, L., et al.: Training language models to follow instructions with human feedback, Mar. 04, 2022, arXiv: arXiv:2203.02155. https://doi.org/10.48550/arXiv.2203.02155
15. "Spot® - The Agile Mobile Robot | Boston Dynamics." Accessed 08 Feb 2022. https://www.bostondynamics.com/products/spot

16. Argall, B.D., Chernova, S., Veloso, M., Browning, B.: A survey of robot learning from demonstration. Robot. Auton. Syst. **57**(5), 469–483 (2009). https://doi.org/10.1016/j.robot.2008.10.024
17. Kober, J., Bagnell, J.A., Peters, J.: Reinforcement learning in robotics: a survey. Int. J. Robot. Res. **32**(11), 1238–1274 (2013). https://doi.org/10.1177/0278364913495721
18. de Graaf, M.M.A., Allouch, S.B., Klamer, T.: Sharing a life with Harvey: exploring the acceptance of and relationship-building with a social robot. Comput. Hum. Behav. **43**, 1–14 (2015). https://doi.org/10.1016/j.chb.2014.10.030
19. Seaborn, K., Miyake, N.P., Pennefather, P., Otake-Matsuura, M.: Voice in human–agent interaction: a survey. ACM Comput. Surv. **54**(4), 81:1–81:43 (2021). https://doi.org/10.1145/3386867
20. Norberto Pires, J.: Robot-by-voice: experiments on commanding an industrial robot using the human voice. Ind. Robot Int. J. **32**(6), 505–511 (2005). https://doi.org/10.1108/01439910510629244
21. Li, S.-A., Liu, Y.-Y., Chen, Y.-C., Feng, H.-M., Shen, P.-K., Wu, Y.-C.: Voice interaction recognition design in real-life scenario mobile robot applications. Appl. Sci. **13**(5), Art. no. 5, January 2023. https://doi.org/10.3390/app13053359
22. Gockley, R., et al.: Designing robots for long-term social interaction. In: 2005 IEEE/RSJ International Conference on Intelligent Robots and Systems, Aug. 2005, pp. 1338–1343. https://doi.org/10.1109/IROS.2005.1545303
23. Ahn, M., et al.: Do As I Can, Not As I Say: Grounding Language in Robotic Affordances, 16 Aug 2022, arXiv: arXiv:2204.01691. https://doi.org/10.48550/arXiv.2204.01691
24. Huang, W., et al.: Inner Monologue: Embodied Reasoning through Planning with Language Models, 12 Jul 2022, arXiv: arXiv:2207.05608. https://doi.org/10.48550/arXiv.2207.05608
25. Singh, I., et al.: ProgPrompt: program generation for situated robot task planning using large language models. Auton. Robots **47**(8), 999–1012 (2023). https://doi.org/10.1007/s10514-023-10135-3
26. Mu, Y., et al.: RoboCodeX: Multimodal Code Generation for Robotic Behavior Synthesis, Feb. 25, 2024, arXiv: arXiv:2402.16117. https://doi.org/10.48550/arXiv.2402.16117
27. Liang, J., et al.: Code as policies: language model programs for embodied control. In: 2023 IEEE International Conference on Robotics and Automation (ICRA), May 2023, pp. 9493–9500. https://doi.org/10.1109/ICRA48891.2023.10160591
28. Shridhar, M., et al.: ALFRED: a benchmark for interpreting grounded instructions for everyday tasks. In: 2020 IEEE/CVF Conference on Computer Vision and Pattern Recognition (CVPR), Jun. 2020, pp. 10737–10746. https://doi.org/10.1109/CVPR42600.2020.01075
29. Topál, J., et al.: Chapter 3 The Dog as a Model for Understanding Human Social Behavior. In: Advances in the Study of Behavior, vol. 39, Academic Press, pp. 71–116 (2009). https://doi.org/10.1016/S0065-3454(09)39003-8
30. Lakestani, N.N., Donaldson, M., Waran, N.: Interpretation of dog behaviour by children and young adults. Anthrozoös **27**(1), 65–80 (2014). https://doi.org/10.2752/175303714X13837396326413
31. Manohar, V., Crandall, J.W.: Programming robots to express emotions: interaction paradigms, communication modalities, and context. IEEE Trans. Hum.-Mach. Syst. **44**(3), 362–373 (2014). https://doi.org/10.1109/THMS.2014.2309662
32. Danev, L., Hamann, M., Fricke, N., Hollarek, T., Paillacho, D.: Development of animated facial expressions to express emotions in a robot: RobotIcon. In: 2017 IEEE Second Ecuador Technical Chapters Meeting (ETCM), pp. 1–6, October 2017. https://doi.org/10.1109/ETCM.2017.8247472
33. Gomez Cubero, C., Pekarik, M., Rizzo, V., Jochum, E.: The robot is present: creative approaches for artistic expression with robots. Front. Robot. AI **8**, July 2021. https://doi.org/10.3389/frobt.2021.662249

34. Sheridan, T.B.: Human–robot interaction: status and challenges. Hum. Factors **58**(4), 525–532 (2016). https://doi.org/10.1177/0018720816644364
35. Ratajczyk, D.J.: Dominant or submissive? exploring social perceptions across the human-robot spectrum. In: Proceedings of the 2024 4th International Conference on Human-Machine Interaction. In: ICHMI '24. Association for Computing Machinery, New York, pp. 8–14, August 2024. https://doi.org/10.1145/3678429.3678431
36. Złotowski, J., Proudfoot, D., Yogeeswaran, K., Bartneck, C.: Anthropomorphism: opportunities and challenges in human-robot interaction. Int. J. Soc. Robotics **7**(3), 347–360 (2015). https://doi.org/10.1007/s12369-014-0267-6

Message for You: Observing the Effects of a Social Robot's Interruptions During an Office Task

Elisabeth Ganal[1(✉)], Sophia C. Steinhaeusser[1], Florian Niebling[2], and Birgit Lugrin[1]

[1] Socially Interactive Agents, University of Würzburg, Würzburg, Germany
`elisabeth.ganal@uni-wuerzburg.de`
[2] Advanced Media Institute, TH Köln, Köln, Germany

Abstract. Social robots and smart assistants are increasingly finding their way into our society. For social robots to be accepted in everyday life, it is essential that they adhere to social norms. The timing of message delivery is crucial, influenced by the message's urgency and context, as well as the user's current activity, to minimize distracting or disrupting the user. Vice versa, the timing can also affect how users perceive and evaluate a robotic assistant. In a user study, we investigated different timings of interruptions by a social robot during an office task, and how participants subsequently rate the robot's social capabilities. For this, we asked participants about the main task's workload, the stress level before and after the task, the social robot, and additional questions about the notifications. The subjective data is enhanced by objective measurements from log files and eye tracking recordings. The results show that the interruption timing can influence how participants perceive the notifications and the robot. This highlights the importance of context recognition and appropriate timing of interruptions in human-robot interaction.

Keywords: Social robot · Task interruption · Context-awareness

1 Introduction

The use of assistive technology can enable people to live in their homes with more comfort, safety, or, particularly important for older adults, with more independence [14,45]. The main uses of assistive technology and smart home devices are energy monitoring, integrating safety and surveillance systems, and controlling household appliances and multimedia systems [39,45]. The use and control of robotic household assistants in a smart home system emerges as well [45]. In a smart home an assistive system can use sensor data to assume an inhabitant's needs, and to support daily life activities through appropriate actions [13]. such as the communication (1) between the human user and the assistive system [37], and (2) between human individuals [43]. In both cases, the smart home system provides information to its user by either being the source or deliverer of a message or notification, which could be facilitated by including a social robot within the system [8,18,49,54]. Such a robot, connected to ambient sensors via a network, can exchange data from the environment and present them to users [8,19]. Comparing input devices, Luria et al. [37] found that wall-mounted touch screens and mobile apps were the most familiar and provided the highest sense of control, while voice control offered the least situation awareness and was uncomfortable to use. However, participants liked a robot as an input device the most, associating it with high situation awareness and usage flow. This may stem from the robots' physical embodiment and expressive body language, which outperform voice assistants [49]. Further, social robots can interact and communicate multimodally [50], enhancing accessibility for different user groups. A human-like robot capable of controlling a smart home and entertaining, e.g., engaging in small talk, can enhance user experience in a smart environment [43].

Access to context-related information can enrich communication with and through social robots [49] and enable smart environments to offer more useful services [1]. However, robots in smart environments are expected to interact in a socially acceptable manner [47], e.g., robots should know when and how to interrupt the user to deliver a message. The relationship between the user and the robot can be enhanced by emotionally intelligent behavior [12]. For this, they must understand human behavior and respond appropriately considering the context [47] by providing an appropriateness value for the interrupting action [41]. Users' decisions whether a robot should deliver a message depend on the social context, defined by, e.g., persons present, and activities happening, but also on the message content's urgency or sensitivity [46]. But even if interruptions are appropriate in terms of context and content, they can affect productivity [24,38].

In a smart home, a context-aware assistant (e.g., a social robot) should deliver messages at appropriate times to minimize distractions from the current activity. Our research explores how interruption timing, task progress tracking, and using a robot as a notification agent influence user's interruptibility and perception during task execution. To contribute to this research area, we developed a prototype detecting task progress during an annotation task to determine timings for the message delivery. We conducted a user study to examine users' reactions and perceptions of the robot and the interruptions, collecting both subjective data (questionnaires) and objective data (log files, eye tracking).

2 Background

In a context where the user is alone, participants preferred receiving most messages independent of the message's sensitivity or urgency, or an ongoing activity such as reading [46]. Further, urgent messages should be delivered regardless of the situation. However, when users are engaged in a task, minimizing disruption and distraction is crucial to avoid increased stress, frustration, and workload [38].

2.1 User Interruption

According to Pielot et al. [44] most mobile notifications come from communication apps like messengers or email applications. These email notifications are often work-related and more frequent during working hours. They can also trigger emotional reactions, such as feeling stressed and interrupted, due to their volume and unclear urgency [44]. However, task-unrelated and irrelevant notifications may require more processing time and can hinder task resumption after interruptions [24]. While content similarity between interruptions and ongoing tasks can not always be equated relevance, irrelevant interruptions between tasks can lead to higher resumption lags than relevant ones [24]. An interrupted task is performed slower and is perceived more difficult to the user [5]. Some research report an interruption lag between becoming aware of an interruption and engaging with it [53] and time lags after an interruption before resuming the primary task [40,52]. Others found out, that interruptions can lead to more speed at the primary task to make up for the time loss, which could lead to more stress [38].

Several studies found, that interruption timing is crucial [2,16,29]. A well predicted interruption timing is less annoying and frustrating for users and leads to lower mental effort and time pressure assessments for the primary task [2]. Detecting moments where the user mentally finished a task can reduce frustration and lead to faster reactions to interruptions, e.g. emails [29]. Interruptions are perceived as less disruptive, if they occur when the user is not already deeply engaged in the primary task or after the completion of it [2,4,16]. Research also shows that users rather accept interruptions when switching applications than during continuous work [51]. Thus, a robot in a smart environment should also include task variables into its interruption appropriateness calculation.

2.2 Context and Interruptibility-Awareness

Context-awareness is already implemented and tested in some computer software to decide when and how to deliver messages or notifications to the user [15,28]. For a social robot, context-awareness is crucial for being competent, which can further improve engagement success [3]. Social or situational context can be detected by audio and video features [17,28,41,42]. Body pose changes [27], ambient sensors [36], or peripheral interactions [33] can also serve as cues for activity detection or change, helping to determine the most appropriate timing for message delivery. Ho and Intille [27] use accelerometers to detect motion and activity changes and thus to estimate users' interruptibility. Messages delivered during activity changes are better received by users than those during an activity. Thus, they [27] recommend using a context-aware message delivery. Moreover, a robot could learn through user feedback, e.g., via buttons [41], whether it interrupted the user or not. Banerjee et al. [6] investigated how interruptibility awareness of a mobile robot during a building task affects the user's and the robot's task performance, and user's perceptions of the robot's social aptitude. They varied the selection of appropriate interruption moments: random timing, human-determined (wizard-of-oz method), or a model-based approach with an interruptibility classifier using the user's social cues and contextual cues from nearby objects as features. Their results show that the robot system better identified appropriate interruption moments than using random timings. However, human-determined timings were still more accurate, highlighting the need to improve the model to achieve human-like accuracy. They emphasize the importance of interruptibility awareness for advancing interactive autonomous systems.

While a social context scenery or a building task's progress can be tracked with environmental cameras [6], computer-based task progress requires software or screen sharing [20]. If humans predefine suitable delivery moments, is task progress detection alone sufficient for appropriate interruption timing? And is a social robot perceived differently if it interrupts during or between subtasks? Instead of interrupting participants after a fixed time periods, we use the task progress to set the interruption timings. As in [2,38], we measure subjective task load, and similar to [6], we assess the social robot as message delivery agent. We also collect objective measurements through log files and eye tracking recordings.

2.3 Research Questions and Hypotheses

Based on related work, we investigate the following questions and hypotheses:

- **RQ1**: What effect do different points in time have on the user's interruptibility during task execution?
- **H1**: Interruptions are perceived as less disruptive between than during tasks.
- **H2**: Task load and stress level are perceived higher when interruptions occur during than between subtasks.
- **H3**: The task load and stress level are estimated higher when interruptions occur during the main task (between or during subtasks) than afterwards.
- **RQ2**: Is task progress tracking sufficient to find a suitable interruption time?
- **RQ3**: How is the robot as notification agent perceived by the users?
- **H4**: A robot appears as less social, if it interrupts humans during subtasks.

3 Concept and Implementation

To investigate how interruption timing affects task load, stress level, and robot perception, we manipulated the *Pepper* robot [50] (version 1.8, NAOqi 2.5) to interrupt participants working on a task by delivering messages. As users in a quiet, solitary environment prefer direct delivery of messages [46], the participants in our study work alone and silently on a task. The messages should be important and urgent, as those should be delivered regardless of the situation [46].

Task. As a realistic working task of a student research assistant, text annotation was chosen for the main task and realized with an online survey form using *LimeSurvey* [35]. In detail, participants were asked to annotate stories by selecting emotion labels for each (half) sentence that match the story's context and the emotions a storyteller would express. In total, participants annotated stories in five subtasks (45 to 63 annotations each), separated by intermediate pages informing about the next subtask on the next page. As story annotations are likely to be a subjective rating and participants can not make major errors as in arithmetic tasks, no error rates are calculated and reported.

Interruptions and Their Timings. Finding relevant or urgent content for the majority of the participants in this context turned out to be difficult. We used usual work interruptions, such as receiving emails, and also asked student workers about suitable interruptions. We decided for notification content not related to the main task, as this might be more disruptive [16]. The interruption content is both announced auditorily by Pepper and displayed on its tablet, see example on Fig. 1 b. Participants received no other notifications on the workstation computer. As participants are university students, we selected these interruption contents:

- **Mail 1**: Covid-Taskforce information from the university. (During the study period, there were still regular changes to local restrictions and regulations.)
- **Mail 2**: Re-enrol information from the university. (The user study is scheduled for a period when it is common to receive re-enrolment information.)
- **Device**: One device in the laboratory is active but unused, and asked if it should be turned off to protect from damage or overheat.

Conditions. For the user study, we defined the following three conditions in order to investigate different interruption timings.

- **Control (C)**: No interruption during task execution, notifications are transmitted one after another after finishing all subtasks.
- **BetweenTasks (BT)**: Notifications are transmitted between subtasks (at intermediate pages after the first, the third, and the fourth subtask).
- **DuringTasks (DT)**: Notifications are transmitted during subtasks (at the 20th annotation of the second, third and fifth subtask).

Technical Realization. We used the Pepper Python Unity Toolkit (PePUT) [21] to trigger interruptions by the Pepper robot via Unity based on specified main task elements. PePUT connects Unity to Python scripts, which use the Python SDK for the Pepper robot, e.g., to display and hide notifications on its tablet screen, or to execute speech and movement commands. Task progress and subtask transitions were tracked by logging the given page of the task and clicked elements using the Vuplex 3D Webview Unity plugin [55], which integrates Unity's Event System for keyboard and click events, and observing page elements using JavaScript calls [32]. A C# observation script, attached to the Vuplex plugin in the Unity scene, logs triggered events when a new page loads. At the start of each trial, the experimenter presets the notification order to evenly distribute all possible orders, and participants enter their names via a Unity popup window to personalize the upcoming notifications. Based on the notification order and condition, notifications are triggered at certain points in the main task (specific pages or page elements). The observation script detects reaching such a point and starts a preloaded behavior on Pepper to play a doorbell sound (similar to smartphone notification sounds) to arouse the user's attention, and show a webpage on its tablet. At each certain point, one of the notifications are shown for the conditions *BT* or *DT*, or all three notifications after each other for *C*. The observation script also logs to a CSV file the user reactions, such as clicks in the main task and on the notifications on Pepper's tablet, such as opening or deleting notifications or turn off the active device via the tablet. Notifications disappear after waiting 5 minutes. We also collect eye tracking recordings with the *Pupil Core* [34], during task execution to subsequently analyze user's reactions to robotic interruptions. To determine if the robot is in the participant's field of view (FOV), we use object recognition on the eye tracker's world view recordings to detect the Pepper robot. For this, we trained our own custom dataset with *YOLOv5* [31] for object detection. Using this version would still allow to use Python 2.7, compatible with the Pepper robot's Python SDK.

4 Method

To investigate how interruption timing affects task load, stress level, and robot perception, we conducted a user study with a between-subjects design across three conditions. Following a multi-method approach we collected data using questionnaires, additional custom items, eye tracking, and log file analyses.

4.1 Questionnaire Measures

Task Load. To assess participants' perceived task load of the main task, the *Raw NASA task load index* (RTLX) [9,10] was asked after the task execution. The questionnaire includes six subscales clustering *Mental*, *Physical*, and *Temporal Demands*, *Performance*, *Effort*, and *Frustration*, each comprising one single item, e.g. "How hard did you have to work mentally to accomplish your level of performance?", answered using a slider on a continuous scale anchored by 0 "Low" / "Perfect" and 20 "High" / "Failure'. The calculated reliability for the current sample was Cronbach's $\alpha = .69$.

Stress Level. To measure how participants' stress level changes and differs between conditions, we used the *Short Stress State Questionnaire* (SSSQ) [26], consisting of a pre- and a post-questionnaire. Both consist of three subscales, each comprising eight items: (1) *Engagement* measures energy, motivation and confidence, e.g. "I am motivated to do the task.", and (2) *Distress* assesses negative affect, e.g. "Impatient", (3) *Worry* estimates self-focused attention and self-esteem, e.g. "I reflected about myself". The 24 items are answered on a 5-point Likert scale anchored from 1 "Not at all", to 5 "Extremely", ten of these items describe feelings with single adjectives and 14 consist of statements. Helton and Näswall [26] reported reliabilities $>.80$ for all dimensions. The SSSQ results for this study are calculated as the ratio of post- to pre-questionnaire scores for each participant and dimension [48]. Ratios > 1 indicate an increase, while those < 1 indicate a decrease. Cronbach's α for the current sample was $\alpha = .71$ (pre) and $\alpha = .82$ (post) for Engagement, $\alpha = .80$ (pre) and $\alpha = .91$ (post) for *Distress*, and $\alpha = .64$ (pre) and $\alpha = .58$ (post) for *Worry*.

Robot Perception. To find out whether a robot is perceived as less social if it interrupts during a task, we use the *Robotic Social Attributes Scale* (RoSAS) [11] and the *Godspeed* questionnaire [7]. The *RoSAS* [11] measures social perceptions of robots on three subscales each including six items answered on a 9-point Likert scale anchored by 1 "definitely not associated" and 9 "definitely associated"; (1) *Warmth*, e.g. "feeling", (2) *Competence*, e.g. "knowledgable", and (3) *Discomfort*, e.g. "awful". Carpinella et al. [11] reported reliability of Cronbach's $\alpha = .91$ to .02 for *Warmth*, $\alpha = .84$ to .95 for *Competence*, and $\alpha = .82$ to .90 for *Discomfort*. The respective reliabilities in the current sample were $\alpha = .84$ (Warmth), $\alpha = .91$ (Competence), and $\alpha = .74$ (Discomfort). The *Godspeed* questionnaire series [7] measures robot perception on five dimensions using 5-point semantic differentials: (1) *Anthropomorphism* comprising five items, e.g. "fake" versus "natural", (2) *Animacy* including six items, e.g. "dead" versus "alive", (3) *Likeability* with five items, e.g. "awful" versus "nice", (4) *Perceived Intelligence* including five items, e.g. "incompetent" versus "competent", and (5) *Perceived Safety* comprising three items, e.g. "anxious" versus "relaxed". Bartneck et al. [7] reported an internal consistency of Cronbach's $\alpha = .88$ to .93 for *Anthropomorphism*, $\alpha = .70$ for *Animacy*, $\alpha = .87$ to .92 for *Likeability*, and $\alpha = .75$ to .77 for *Perceived Intelligence*. Reliability was not reported for *Perceived Safety*. For the current sample, we calculated a reliability of Cronbach's α of .79 for *Anthropomorphism*, $\alpha = .80$ for *Animacy*, $\alpha = .88$ for *Likeability*, $\alpha = .80$ for *Perceived Intelligence*, and $\alpha = .67$ for *Perceived Safety*.

Notification, Task and Interruption Assessment. To further investigate the interruptions and the task execution, additional custom items were asked. Some of these items are based on items by Gould [23]. The custom items, listed in Table 1, were answered on a 7-point Likert scale anchored by 1 "do not agree at all" and 7 "fully agree" and analyzed individually. In these items, participants were asked to rate each notification based on 6 items (n-1 to n-6). We also asked participants to rate the task itself (t-1 to t-3) and the interruption by assessing to what impact the notifications had on their task execution (i-1 to i-4).

Attention Check. Two questions for each subtask were asked as attention check regarding the story details of the main task, answered in single choice format with four options, e.g. "What was the name of the dog in the love story?" - "Rocky", "Dexter", "Max" or "I don't know".

Personal Data. For general demographic data, participants are asked about numeric age, gender (male, female, divers, no answer), and current profession.

4.2 Log Files and Eye Tracking Recordings

In addition to participants' subjective self-reports, we collected Unity log files and a handwritten protocol to objectively assess task progress and tablet

Table 1. Custom items for the notification, task, and interruption assessment.

Notification Assessment
(n-1) I felt personally addressed by the content of the notification.
(n-2) The timing of the notification was appropriate for me.
(n-3) The modality of message delivery was suitable for me.
(n-4) The notification was highly relevant to me.
(n-5) The notification had a high urgency for me.
(n-6) The disruptive factor of the notification was high for me.
Task Assessment
(t-1) It was easy for me to stay on task while working on the task.
(t-2) I worked with concentration throughout the task.
(t-3) I found the time pressure during the tasks to be high.
Interruption Assessment
(i-1) The notifications had an impact on the processing of the tasks.
(i-2) The notifications distracted me a lot from task processing.
(i-3) Because of the notifications, I had to change the way I work.
(i-4) I had difficulty getting back into my activity after the notifications.

interaction. The data included timing and type of interruptions, user interactions with the robot's tablet, and clicks in the annotation tasks. This data serves to calculate the main task's completion time (in minutes), as well as the reaction and continue lags. We define reaction lag as the time in seconds between an interruption's start and a click interaction on the robot's tablet, and continue lag as the duration in seconds between tablet interaction and the next click in the main task. As another objective measurement, we analyzed on the eye tracker's world view videos, if and how long participants looked in the robot's direction.

4.3 Experimental Setup and Study Procedure

The user study was conducted in one of our student office laboratories. Participants signed up for the study via the university intern recruitment system or were directly acquired. They were told beforehand that the study is about story annotation in a smart laboratory with active sensors and a social robot, which could make sounds or move during the study. They were advised to react and behave naturally. The experimental setup is schematically depicted in Fig. 1 a. Participants sat at a work station equipped with a computer, keyboard, and mouse to work on the given annotation task. The Pepper robot was placed to the left of the participants and faced towards them (see Fig. 1 b). The active but unused device, mentioned in one of the interruptions, was at a work station behind Pepper. The researcher observed the interaction and took notes in the same room. The local ethics committee of our university reviewed and approved the study. The study procedure and interruption timings for the conditions are depicted in Fig. 1 c. First, participants provided written informed consent, put on and calibrated the *Pupil Core* eye tracking glasses, and were randomly assigned to one of the conditions. Then, they answered demographic questions and the pre-questionnaire on stress level (SSSQ). At the main task (story annotation in five subtasks), they were interrupted at different points in time depending on the condition. Participants were free in their reaction behavior, so not all of them might interact with the robot. After the main task, participants assessed the task load (RTLX), custom questions about the notifications, task execution, and interruptions, the post-questionnaire on stress level (SSSQ), the robot related questionnaires (RoSAS, Godspeed), and questions on story details. No additional task load or stress measurements were sampled during the main task to avoid further interrupting the participants. The participants were then briefed and fare-welled. The study took around 45 to 60 minutes for each participant.

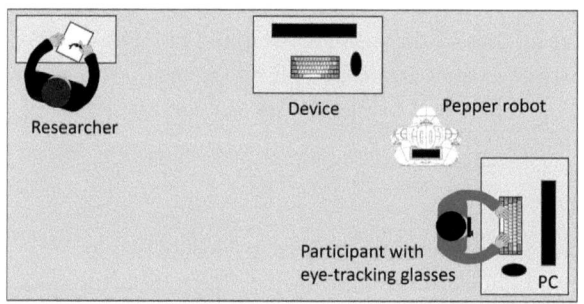

(a) Outline of experimental setup in the student office laboratory (around 26 m^2).

(b) Pepper with notification screen.

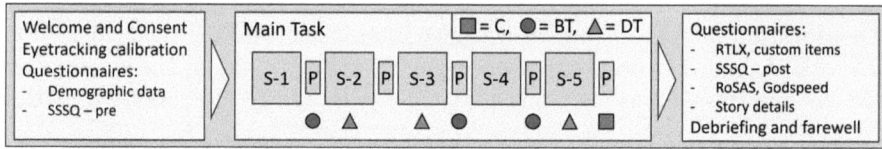

(c) Study procedure with interruption timings, S = Subtask, P = Intermediate Page.

Fig. 1. Experimental setup (a), participant's view of the Pepper robot (b), and the study procedure (c).

4.4 Participants

The participants consisted of university students, which were granted partial course credit for participation, and six additional persons who participated without compensation. Six participants were excluded from data analyses due to technical problems (e.g., robot lost connection and sent no messages). In total, 89 (61 female, 28 male) participants were considered for data analysis. The participants' age was between 18 and 30 years ($M = 21.98$, $SD = 2.09$). They are distributed among the conditions as follows: C with 30 (21 female, 9 male), BT with 30 (22 female, 8 male), and DT with 29 participants (18 female, 11 male).

5 Results

Statistical analyses were performed in Python and *JASP* [30] (v0.16.3.0) using a significance level of .05. Bonferroni-adjusted post-hoc tests were used for parametric comparisons, and Dunn-Bonferroni tests for non-parametric analyses.

5.1 Self-Reports

The descriptive data for the questionnaire results can be found in Table 2. First, we checked the ANOVA assumptions for the statistical analyses. Levene's tests indicated homogeneity of variances ($p>.05$) for RTLX, SSSQ, RoSAS, Godspeed, Notification Assessment, Task Assessment, and Interruption Assessment except for impact of the interruption (i-1) on task execution ($p < .05$). Shapiro-Wilk tests revealed violation of the normality assumption ($p < .05$) for RTLX (Physical Demand, Temporal Demand, Performance, Frustration), SSSQ (Engagement, Distress), RoSAS (Competence, Discomfort), Godspeed (Anthropomorphism, Animacy, Likeability, Perceived Intelligence, Perceived Safety), Notification Assessment (n-1, n-2, n-3, n-4, n-5, n-6), Task Assessment (t-1, t-2, t-3), and Interruption Assessment (i-1, i-2, i-3, i-4). For the respective (sub-)scales violating the ANOVA assumptions, non-parametric Kruskal-Wallis tests were calculated.

Task Load and Stress Level. The results of the *RTLX* and the *SSSQ* ratios are taken to compare the task load and stress level between the conditions.

Concerning **task load** we evaluated each subscale of the *RTLX* to analyze the differences of interruption timings on the task load. No significant group differences were observed for *Mental Demand* ($\chi^2(2) = 1.61, p = .447$), *Physical Demand* ($\chi^2(2) = 3.81, p = .149$), *Temporal Demand* ($\chi^2(2) = 0.05, p = .976$), *Performance* ($\chi^2(2) = 0.15, p = .928$), *Effort* ($F(2, 86) = 0.52, p = .595$), and *Frustration* ($\chi^2(2) = 1.23, p = .542$). Regarding **stress level** we take each subscale ratio of the *SSSQ* to analyze the differences of interruption timings on the participants' stress level. There were no significant group differences for each of the subscales, *Engagement* ($\chi^2(2) = 3.63, p = .163$), *Distress* ($\chi^2(2) = 0.81, p = .668$), and *Worry* ($F(2, 86) = 1.30, p = .279$). The descriptive ratio results reveal similar changes from pre- to post-questionnaire for all conditions. Descriptively, the mean values of the *Engagement* stayed nearly the same, the *Distress* values increased and the *Worry* values decreased in all conditions.

Robot Assessment. The subscales of the *Godspeed* and the *RoSAS* questionnaires were taken to analyze how different timings affect the robot perception.

Table 2. Descriptive statistics for self-reported questionnaires per group.

Variable	Control Group (C) M	SD	BetweenTasks (BT) M	SD	DuringTasks (DT) M	SD
Task Load						
Mental Demand[a]	10.02	4.28	8.93	5.84	10.26	4.61
Physical Demand[a]	1.90	3.61	1.06	1.34	1.83	2.56
Temporal Demand[a]	5.63	5.20	4.90	4.55	5.56	5.37
Performance[a]	6.94	4.11	7.14	4.29	7.47	4.32
Effort[a]	7.85	5.12	7.54	5.06	6.58	4.71
Frustration[a]	5.00	5.67	3.89	4.03	5.09	4.78
Stress Level						
Engagement[b]	1.01	0.15	1.00	0.14	1.06	0.15
Distress[b]	1.24	0.46	1.24	0.35	1.17	0.31
Worry[b]	0.77	0.17	0.84	0.22	0.77	0.17
Robot Perception						
Anthropomorphism[c]	2.03	0.64	2.07	0.60	2.05	0.77
Animacy[c]	2.79	0.71	3.04	0.60	2.87	0.79
Likeability[c]	4.03	0.67	4.29	0.67	3.82	0.81
Perceived Intelligence[c]	3.90	0.63	3.99	0.59	3.96	0.69
Perceived Safety[c]	3.73	0.69	3.80	0.64	3.76	0.85
Warmth[d]	4.39	1.44	4.34	1.64	4.00	1.47
Competence[d]	6.01	1.58	6.53	1.53	6.20	1.95
Discomfort[d]	1.81^A	0.75	1.83^B	0.94	$2.43^{A,B}$	1.10
Notification Assessment						
n-1 Personal[e]	4.04^A	1.60	5.04^A	1.44	4.83	1.54
n-2 Timing[e]	4.50^A	1.91	5.03^B	1.82	$3.05^{A,B}$	1.67
n-3 Modality[e]	4.98	1.74	5.37^A	1.58	3.92^A	1.82
n-4 Relevance[e]	2.93	3.51	3.51	1.36	3.45	1.29
n-5 Urgency[e]	2.59	1.37	2.89	1.26	3.02	1.35
n-6 Disruption[e]	2.19^A	1.60	2.93^B	1.51	$4.35^{A,B}$	1.47
Task Assessment						
t-1 Focus[e]	5.23	1.14	5.50	1.14	5.21	1.40
t-2 Concentrate[e]	4.93	1.41	5.23	1.31	5.03	1.05
t-3 Time Pressure[e]	2.13	1.20	2.00	1.11	2.17	1.28
Interruption Assessment						
i-1 Impact[e]	$1.70^{A,B}$	1.15	$2.70^{A,C}$	1.75	$3.62^{B,C}$	1.64
i-2 Distraction[e]	2.13^A	1.78	2.47^B	1.46	$4.03^{A,B}$	1.48
i-3 Change[e]	$1.50^{A,B}$	1.01	$1.80^{B,C}$	0.96	$2.31^{A,C}$	1.04
i-4 Return[e]	1.93^A	1.51	2.43^B	1.65	$3.48^{A,B}$	1.66

Note. For Notification Assessment results are averaged over message content. Means with identical superscripts (A, B, C) differ significantly $p < .05$.
[a] Calculated values from 1 to 20.
[b] Calculated ratios > 1 for increased and < 1 for decreased values.
[c] Calculated values from 1 to 5.
[d] Calculated values from 1 to 9.
[e] Calculated values from 1 to 7.

Concerning **general robot perception** (*Godspeed*) no significant difference was identified for *Anthropomorphism* ($\chi^2(2) = 0.63$, $p = .728$), *Animacy* ($\chi^2(2) = 3.05$, $p = .218$), *Perceived Intelligence* ($\chi^2(2) = 0.34$, $p = .845$), and *Perceived Safety* ($\chi^2(2) = 0.30$, $p = .860$) dimensions. For *Likeability* a trend toward differences between the conditions was observed ($\chi^2(2) = 5.97$, $p = .051$). Dunn-Bonferroni post hoc tests revealed a significant difference between the BT and DT condition ($p = .025$, $r = .31$). No significant differences were found comparing C and BT ($p = .113$) as well as C and DT condition ($p = .203$).

Regarding **social attribution** (*RoSAS*), no significant differences were observed for *Warmth* ($F(2, 86) = 0.58$, $p = .563$) and *Competence* ($\chi^2(2) = 1.71$, $p = .426$). However, a significant group difference was revealed for *Discomfort* ($\chi^2(2) = 7.18$, $p = .028$). Post hoc tests indicated a significant difference between C and DT ($p = .035$, $r = .30$) as well as between BT and DT ($p = .026$, $r = .31$). Between C and BT no significant difference was indicated ($p = 1.000$).

Assessment of Notifications, Task Execution, and Interruption Impact. For the **notification assessments**, repeated measures ANOVAs were calculated to explore differences between the message contents. Having no non-parametric alternative, the RM-ANOVA is considered robust against violation of the normality assumption [22,25]. However, due to a lack of sphericity (Mauchly tests $p < .001$) Greenhouse-Geisser corrections were calculated.

For feeling personally addressed (n-1) by the notifications, the RM-ANOVA revealed a significant main effect of message content ($F(1.54, 132.47) = 3.73, p = .026, \omega^2 = .02$) and a main effect of condition ($F(2, 86) = 24.85, p = .033, \omega^2 = .02$), but no significant interaction effect ($F(3.08, 132.47) = 0.87, p = .463$). Post hoc tests on message content revealed significantly higher values of feeling personally addressed for the device-related message than the Covid-taskforce mail ($p = .022$, $d = .29$), but no significant differences between device-related message and re-enrolment mail ($p = .344$), nor between the two mails ($p = .774$). Post hoc tests on condition indicated significantly higher values for BT than for C ($p = .039$, $d = .27$), but no significant differences between C and DT ($p = .156$), nor between BT and DT ($p = 1.000$). For timing appropriateness (n-2), a significant main effect of message content ($F(1.73, 148.78) = 5.29, p = .009, \omega^2 = .01$) and of condition ($F(2, 86) = 9.56, p < .001, \omega^2 = .06$) was revealed, but no interaction effect ($F(3.46, 148.78) = 0.45, p = .747$). Post hoc tests on message content revealed significantly more appropriate timing for the device-related message than the Covid-taskforce mail ($p = .004$, $d = .35$), but no significant differences between device-related message and re-enrolment mail ($p = .302$), nor between the two mails ($p = .334$). Post hoc tests on condition indicated significantly higher values for C than DT ($p = .008$, $d = .33$), and for BT than DT ($p < .001$, $d = .45$), but no significant differences between C and BT ($p = .765$). For modality appropriateness (n-3), a significant main effect of message content ($F(1.25, 107.47) = 7.63, p = .004, \omega^2 = .01$) and of condition ($F(2, 86) = 5.61, p = .005, \omega^2 = .03$) was found, but no interaction effect ($F(2.50, 107.47) = 1.67, p = .186$). Post hoc tests on message content showed significantly better modality appropriateness for the device-related message than both, the Covid-taskforce mail ($p = .002, d = .36$) and the re-enrolment mail ($p = .003, d = .35$), but no significant differences between the two mails ($p = 1.000$). Post hoc tests on condition indicated significantly higher values for BT than DT ($p = .005, d = .34$), but no significant differences between C and BT ($p = 1.000$), nor between C and DT ($p = .060$). In contrast, for relevance (n-4), there was no significant main effect of message content ($F(1.64, 140.93) = 2.73, p = .079$) nor condition ($F(2, 86) = 1.68, p = .192$), nor an interaction effect ($F(3.28, 140.93) = 0.27, p = .861$). Concerning urgency (n-5), there was a significant main effect of message content ($F(1.70, 146.25) = 9.44, p < .001, \omega^2 = .05$), but not of condition ($F(2, 86) = 0.83, p = .439$), nor an interaction effect ($F(3.40, 146.25) = 0.41, p = .772$) Post hoc tests showed significantly higher perceived urgency for the device-related message than the Covid-taskforce mail ($p < .001, d = .45$), as well as for the re-enrolment mail than the Covid-taskforce mail ($p = .019, d = .29$), but no significant differences between the device-related message and the re-enrolment mail ($p = .396$). Regarding the notifications being disruptive (n-6), no significant main effect of message content ($F(1.31, 112.68) = 1.55, p = .219$) but a significant main effect of condition ($F(2, 86) = 15.14, p < .001, \omega^2 = .10$) was found. No interaction effect was indicated ($F(2.62, 112.68) = 1.09, p = .352$). Post hoc tests showed significantly higher perceived disruption for DT than both C ($p < .001, d = .58$) and BT ($p = .002, d = .38$), but not between C and BT ($p = .187$).

Regarding the **task assessment** no significant group differences were found for focusing on the task (t-1; $\chi^2(2) = 1.16, p = .560$) nor for concentration (t-2; $\chi^2(2) = 1.36, p = .507$) nor for time pressure (t-3; $\chi^2(2) = 0.20, p = .903$).

Concerning **interruption assessment** in terms of impact on the task execution (i-1) a significant difference between the conditions ($\chi^2(2) = 21.99, p < .001$) was revealed. In Dunn-Bonferroni post hoc tests significant differences were indicated between the C and BT ($p = .013, r = .32$), between the C and DT condition ($p < .001, r = .61$), as well as between the BT and DT condition ($p = .013, r = .29$). Regarding distraction from the task (i-2) a significant difference between the conditions ($\chi^2(2) = 21.32, p < .001$) was revealed. Dunn-Bonferroni post hoc tests showed a significant difference between C and DT ($p < .001, r = .58$), as well as between BT and DT ($p < .001, r = .43$), but not between C and BT ($p = 0.132$). Concerning the change of the way of working (i-3) a significant difference between the conditions was found ($\chi^2(2) = 13.44, p = .001$). Dunn-Bonferroni post hoc tests indicated a significant difference between C and DT ($p < .001, r = .48$), between C and BT ($p = .048, r = .22$), and between DT and BT ($p = .045, r = .26$). Last, regarding returning to the activity (i-4) a significant difference between the conditions was observed ($\chi^2(2) = 14.66, p < .001$). Dunn-Bonferroni post hoc tests revealed a significant difference between C and DT ($p < .001, r = .49$), as well as between the BT and DT condition ($p = .015, r = .32$), but not between C and BT ($p = .085$).

5.2 Log File and Eye Tracking Results

We evaluated the Unity log files and eye tracking recordings for further insights on the participants' behaviour during the task and robot interaction.

Log File Evaluations. The log file results reveal, that 69 of 89 participants (77.53 %) reacted to all notifications by interacting with the robot's tablet, also confirmed by the eye tracking recordings. Further, 14 participants (15.73 %) did not respond to all interruptions with a tablet interaction. Six participants (6.74 %) did not interact with the tablet at all based on log files and a handwritten protocol. The eye tracking recordings showed that one participant looked at the robot's direction after two interruptions but decided not to interact. Log files reveal similar mean completion times (in minutes) for the main task across all groups. Descriptively, C participants were the fastest ($M = 31.03$, $SD = 6.23$), followed by DT ($M = 32.50$, $SD = 7.17$) and BT ($M = 33.44$, $SD = 6.24$). For the interruption conditions, we averaged all reaction lags, excluding non-interacting participants. Descriptive data shows a higher mean reaction lag (in seconds) for DT ($M = 19.66$, $SD = 7.51$; $n = 27$) than for BT ($M = 18.39$, $SD = 5.67$; $n = 27$), and a mean continue lag of 19.65 s for the BT ($SD = 10.68$; $n = 27$), followed by the DT condition ($M = 20.48$, $SD = 10.15$; $n = 27$).

Eye Tracking Recordings. For evaluating the eye tracking recordings four participants were excluded due to technical problems, resulting in $n = 85$ participants considered for the respective analyses. The evaluation, conducted every 30th frame (∼1 s), revealed that Pepper was visible in participants' FOV between 0 and 150 times during task execution ($n = 85$; $M = 64.18$, $SD = 38.08$), with a mean detection confidence of 0.81. The descriptive values reveal, that in the BT condition the robot was visible most times ($M = 71.24$, $SD = 36.13$; $n = 29$), followed by DT ($M = 61.39$, $SD = 41.13$; $n = 28$), and C ($M = 59.64$, $SD = 37.21$; $n = 28$). We also calculated the time periods during which the robot was visible in participants' FOV during the task by using timestamps marking the start and end of robot detections in the recordings. Then, we grouped the periods by the experimental conditions C, BT, and DT. In total, there were 258 periods ranging from 0 to 130.04 s ($M = 21.67$, $SD = 25.70$; $n = 85$). The descriptive data reveals, that in C were the least number of periods with 34 in total and the highest durations ranging from 0 to 130.04 ($M = 44.51$, $SD = 47.31$; $n = 28$), followed by BT with 115 periods ranging from 0 to 103.59 ($M = 18.89$, $SD = 19.02$; $n = 29$), and DT with 109 periods ranging from 0 to 73.42 ($M = 17.47$, $SD = 17.76$; $n = 28$).

6 Discussion

We compared in our study three groups differing at the timing for robotic interruptions while working on annotation tasks, either no interruption during the main task (C), between subtasks (BT), or during subtasks (DT). With notification, task and interruption assessments we investigated how different interruption timings affected the user's interruptibility (RQ1). There were no significant group differences for working on the task itself, like focus (t-1), concentration (t-2), or feeling time pressure (t-3). However, participants' subjective ratings revealed, that interruptions - between and during subtasks - influenced their way of working (i-1), which also might have changed the way of working (i-3) at the DT condition. We can accept H1, as the DT participants felt significantly more disrupted (n-6) and distracted (i-2) by the notifications than those in BT and C, which also aligns with research by Czerwinski et al. [16]. Additionally, the timing (n-1) of interruptions was rated worse in the DT condition than in BT and C. Further, DT participants had more difficulties getting back to the main task (i-4) after being interrupted than those of BT and C.

There were no statistically significant group differences for the task load (RTLX), and participants reported comparably low Physical Demand, Temporal Demand, and Frustration in all conditions. Similarly, no significant group differences were found for the stress level indicated by SSSQ ratios. Thus, H2 and H3 are rejected, as task load and stress level were not estimated higher in interruption conditions and especially at the DT condition. Recording the task progress can be a suitable method to determine an appropriate interruption timing. Collecting additional data, such as log files and eye tracking recordings, alongside subjective user data, helps to investigate interruptions and user reactions in more detail. Thus, real-time analyzing video streams of participants' FOV could enhance estimating users' task progress and interruptibility.

Regarding robot perception, the RoSAS and Godspeed results show that the robot, acting as a notification agent, is in parts perceived differently based on the condition. This addresses RQ3 and supports findings of Banerjee et al. [6] that an interruptibility-aware robot can enhance humans' robot perception. Higher discomfort ratings (RoSAS) were noted in the DT condition compared to BT and C. Further, a trend towards greater likeability (Godspeed) for the BT interruptions can be observed compared to DT. While H4 can only be partly accepted due to a lack of overall significant differences, the results show that robotic interruptions during tasks increased discomfort and tended to reduce likeability compared to interruptions between tasks.

Though DT participants rated the interruptions' impact on task execution higher (i-1 to i-4), descriptively, they completed the main task a bit slower than C and faster than BT participants. Looking at the descriptive values of the *Engagement* (SSSQ), the DT condition showed a slightly greater increase, suggesting higher motivation, compared to the other conditions. This aligns with findings of Mark et al. [38] suggesting that people might unconsciously increase their working speed to compensate time loss caused by interruptions. Descriptive data shows, that durations with the robot being visible in the participants' FOV were slightly shorter in the DT than in the BT condition. The main task took around 30 minutes, with three notifications, a moderate workload, and no time-limit. It can be assumed, that the task may have been too easy, and the number of notifications might not have created a highly stressful situation. Future work might examine additional tasks with various cognitive demands and might include more diverse samples in terms of age and profession to strengthen validity of findings. In our study, participants could choose how to react to the notifications, which might be more natural, but can result in non-reaction due to the notifications' perceived relevance or urgency. This is supported by generally low ratings of notifications' relevance (n-4) and urgency (n-5) across conditions. For instance, device-related notifications were rated as more urgent than the Covid-taskforce email. Overall, some notifications may not have appeared sufficiently urgent or relevant to most participants. As interruptibility is highly multifaceted and varies between individuals, modeling truly relevant and urgent notifications for laboratory studies remains challenging. Different messages have varying importance for individuals, and ethical aspects, such as avoiding high fear or anxiety, must also be considered. However, asking participants to assess the relevance and urgency of interruptions can help mitigating these challenges. Overall, future robotic assistants should determine appropriate moments to interact with users to increase robot acceptance and to avoid disruptions.

7 Conclusion

In this work, we investigated if and how the timing of robotic interruptions influence the work load and stress level of an annotation task, as well as the perception of a social robot delivering the messages. For this, we implemented a system examining the task progress and conducted a laboratory user study. Though no significant differences were found between conditions for task load and stress level, interruption timing can affect the perceived discomfort of the robot. Timing also influenced participants' assessments of the notifications, the task, and how the interruptions influenced the task execution. Our objective measures suggest that interruption timing might affect the reaction lag. Thus, detecting appropriate moments for interruptions is crucial for future robotic assistants to increase their acceptance and avoid unnecessary disruptions. Future work could further explore suitable interruption timings in other social contexts.

Acknowledgments. The authors thank Jülide Ön and Micha Nowak for supporting the data acquisition and use case implementation.

References

1. Abowd, G.D., Dey, A.K., Brown, P.J., Davies, N., Smith, M., Steggles, P.: Towards a better understanding of context and context-awareness. In: Goos, G., Hartmanis, J., van Leeuwen, J., Gellersen, H.W. (eds.) Handheld and Ubiquitous Computing, LNCS, vol. 1707, pp. 304–307. Springer, Berlin, Heidelberg (1999). https://doi.org/10.1007/3-540-48157-5_29
2. Adamczyk, P.D., Bailey, B.P.: If not now, when? the effects of interruption at different moments within task execution. In: Proc. of the SIGCHI Conference on Human Factors in Computing Systems, pp. 271–278. CHI '04, ACM, New York (2004). https://doi.org/10.1145/985692.985727,
3. Avelino, J., Garcia-Marques, L., Ventura, R., Bernardino, A.: Break the ice: a survey on socially aware engagement for human–robot first encounters. Int. J. Soc. Robot. **13**(8), 1851–1877 (2021). https://doi.org/10.1007/s12369-020-00720-2

4. Bailey, B.P., Konstan, J.A.: On the need for attention-aware systems: measuring effects of interruption on task performance, error rate, and affective state. Comput. Hum. Behav. **22**(4), 685–708 (2006). https://doi.org/10.1016/j.chb.2005.12.009
5. Bailey, B.P., Konstan, J.A., Carlis, J.V.: The effects of interruptions on task performance, annoyance, and anxiety in the user interface. In: Proceedings of IFIP TC.13 International Conference on Human— Computer Interaction. IOS, pp. 593–601. Press (2001)
6. Banerjee, S., Silva, A., Chernova, S.: Robot classification of human interruptibility and a study of its effects. ACM Trans. Hum. Robot Inter. **7**(2), 14:1–14:35 (2018). https://doi.org/10.1145/3277902
7. Bartneck, C., Kulić, D., Croft, E., Zoghbi, S.: Measurement instruments for the anthropomorphism, animacy, likeability, perceived intelligence, and perceived safety of robots. Int. J. Soc. Robot. **1**(1), 71–81 (2009). https://doi.org/10.1007/s12369-008-0001-3
8. Bui, H.D., Pham, C., Lim, Y., Tan, Y., Chong, N.Y.: Integrating a humanoid robot into echonet-based smart home environments. In: Kheddar, A., Yoshida, E., Ge, S.S., Suzuki, K., Cabibihan, J.J., Eyssel, F., He, H. (eds.) Social Robotics, LNCS, vol. 10652, pp. 314–323. Springer International Publishing, Cham (2017). https://doi.org/10.1007/978-3-319-70022-9_31
9. Byers, J.C.: Traditional and raw task load index (TLX) correlations: are paired comparisons necessary? Taylor and Francis, Adv. Industr. Erfonom. Safety l (1989)
10. Cao, A., Chintamani, K.K., Pandya, A.K., Ellis, R.D.: NASA TLX: software for assessing subjective mental workload. Behav. Res. Methods **41**(1), 113–117 (2009). https://doi.org/10.3758/BRM.41.1.113
11. Carpinella, C.M., Wyman, A.B., Perez, M.A., Stroessner, S.J.: The robotic social attributes scale (RoSAS): development and validation. In: 2017 12th ACM/IEEE International Conference on Human-Robot Interaction (HRI), pp. 254–262 (2017). ISSN: 2167-2148
12. Chapa Sirithunge, H.P., Muthugala, M.A.V.J., Jayasekara, A.G.B.P., Chandima, D.P.: A wizard of OZ study of human interest towards robot initiated human-robot interaction. In: 2018 27th IEEE Int. Symposium on Robot and Human Interactive Communication (RO-MAN), pp. 515–521. IEEE (27082018 - 31082018). https://doi.org/10.1109/ROMAN.2018.8525583
13. Chen, L., Nugent, C., Okeyo, G.: An ontology-based hybrid approach to activity modeling for smart homes. IEEE Trans. Hum. Mach. Syst. **44**(1), 92–105 (2014). https://doi.org/10.1109/THMS.2013.2293714
14. Cicirelli, G., Marani, R., Petitti, A., Milella, A., D'Orazio, T.: Ambient assisted living: a review of technologies, methodologies and future perspectives for healthy aging of population. Sensors **21**(10), 3549 (2021). https://doi.org/10.3390/s21103549
15. Corno, F., De Russis, L., Montanaro, T.: A context and user aware smart notification system. In: 2015 IEEE 2nd World Forum on Internet of Things (WF-IoT), pp. 645–651 (2015). https://doi.org/10.1109/WF-IoT.2015.7389130
16. Czerwinski, M., Cutrell, E., Horvitz, E.: Instant messaging: effects of relevance and timing. In: People and Computers XIV: Proceedings of HCI 2000. vol. 2, pp. 71–76 (2000). https://www.microsoft.com/en-us/research/publication/instant-messaging-effects-of-relevance-and-timing/, edition: People and Computers XIV: Proc. of HCI 2000

17. Danninger, M., Stiefelhagen, R.: A context-aware virtual secretary in a smart office environment. In: Proceeding of the 16th ACM Int. Conf. on Multimedia - MM '08, p. 529. ACM Press, Vancouver, British Columbia, Canada (2008). https://doi.org/10.1145/1459359.1459430, http://portal.acm.org/citation.cfm?doid=1459359.1459430
18. Deublein, A., Lugrin, B.: (Expressive) social robot or tablet? – on the benefits of embodiment and non-verbal expressivity of the interface for a smart environment. In: Gram-Hansen, S.B., Jonasen, T.S., Midden, C. (eds.) PERSUASIVE 2020. LNCS, vol. 12064, pp. 85–97. Springer, Cham (2020). https://doi.org/10.1007/978-3-030-45712-9_7
19. Eckstein, B., Niebling, F., Lugrin, B.: Reflected reality: a mixed reality knowledge representation for context-aware systems. In: 2019 11th International Conference on Virtual Worlds and Games for Serious Applications (VS-Games), pp. 1–4 (2019). https://doi.org/10.1109/VS-Games.2019.8864516, iSSN: 2474-0489
20. Ganal, E., Habenicht, M., Lugrin, B.: Excuse me, may i disturb you? the influence of politeness of a social robot on the perception of interruptions. In: 2024 33rd IEEE International Conference on Robot and Human Interactive Communication (ROMAN), pp. 2240–2247 (2024). https://doi.org/10.1109/RO-MAN60168.2024.10731362, https://ieeexplore.ieee.org/document/10731362, iSSN: 1944-9437
21. Ganal, E., Siol, L., Lugrin, B.: PePUT: a Unity toolkit for the social robot pepper. In: 2023 32nd IEEE RO-MAN, pp. 1012–1019 (2023). https://doi.org/10.1109/RO-MAN57019.2023.10309447
22. Glass, G.V., Peckham, P.D., Sanders, J.R.: Consequences of failure to meet assumptions underlying the fixed effects analyses of variance and covariance. Rev. Educ. Res. **42**(3), 237–288 (1972)
23. Gould, A.J.J.: What makes an interruption disruptive? understanding the effects of interruption relevance and timing on performance. Doctoral, UCL (University College London) (2014). https://discovery.ucl.ac.uk/id/eprint/1458627/
24. Gould, S.J.J., Brumby, D.P., Cox, A.L.: What does it mean for an interruption to be relevant? an investigation of relevance as a memory effect. In: Proc. of the Human Factors and Ergonomics Society Annual Meeting, vol. 57, no. 1, pp. 149–153 (2013). https://doi.org/10.1177/1541931213571034, publisher: SAGE Publications Inc
25. Harwell, M.R., Rubinstein, E.N., Hayes, W.S., Olds, C.C.: Summarizing monte carlo results in methodological research: the one-and two-factor fixed effects anova cases. J. Educ. Stat. **17**(4), 315–339 (1992)
26. Helton, W.S., Näswall, K.: Short stress state questionnaire. European J. Psychol. Assess. **31**(1), 20–30 (2015). https://doi.org/10.1027/1015-5759/a000200, https://econtent.hogrefe.com/doi/10.1027/1015-5759/a000200, publisher: Hogrefe Publishing
27. Ho, J., Intille, S.S.: Using context-aware computing to reduce the perceived burden of interruptions from mobile devices. In: Proc. of the SIGCHI Conference on Human Factors in Computing Systems, pp. 909–918. CHI '05, ACM, New York (2005). https://doi.org/10.1145/1054972.1055100
28. Hudson, S., et al.: Predicting human interruptibility with sensors: a wizard of Oz feasibility study. In: Proc. of the SIGCHI Conference on Human Factors in Computing Systems, pp. 257–264. CHI '03, ACM, New York (2003). https://doi.org/10.1145/642611.642657
29. Iqbal, S.T., Bailey, B.P.: Effects of intelligent notification management on users and their tasks. In: Proc. of the 26th annual CHI Conf. on Human Factors in

Computing Systems - CHI '08, p. 93. ACM Press, Florence (2008). https://doi.org/10.1145/1357054.1357070, http://portal.acm.org/citation.cfm?doid=1357054.1357070
30. JASP Team: JASP (2021). https://jasp-stats.org/
31. Jocher, G.: YOLOv5 by Ultralytics (2020). https://doi.org/10.5281/zenodo.3908559, https://github.com/ultralytics/yolov5
32. Kern, F., et al.: Off-The-Shelf Stylus: using XR devices for handwriting and sketching on physically aligned virtual surfaces. Front. Virtual Reality **2** (2021). https://www.frontiersin.org/articles/10.3389/frvir.2021.684498
33. Kim, S., Chun, J., Dey, A.K.: Sensors know when to interrupt you in the car: detecting driver interruptibility through monitoring of peripheral interactions. In: Proc. of the 33rd Annual ACM Conference on Human Factors in Computing Systems, pp. 487–496. ACM, Seoul Republic of Korea (2015). https://doi.org/10.1145/2702123.2702409, https://dl.acm.org/doi/10.1145/2702123.2702409
34. Labs, P.: Core - Home - Pupil Labs Docs. https://docs.pupil-labs.com/core/
35. LimeSurvey GmbH: Limesurvey (2021). https://www.limesurvey.org/de/
36. Lu, C.-H., Hsieh, H.-L., Tseng, K.-H., Yin, C.-H., Huang, S.-S.: Facilitating spontaneous energy saving in a smart home using interruptibility-aware reminders with ecological and abstract information visualization. In: Biswas, J., Kobayashi, H., Wong, L., Abdulrazak, B., Mokhtari, M. (eds.) ICOST 2013. LNCS, vol. 7910, pp. 151–158. Springer, Heidelberg (2013). https://doi.org/10.1007/978-3-642-39470-6_19
37. Luria, M., Hoffman, G., Zuckerman, O.: Comparing social robot, screen and voice interfaces for smart-home control. In: Mark, G., Fussell, S., Lampe, C., schraefel, m., Hourcade, J.P., Appert, C., Wigdor, D. (eds.) Proc. of the 2017 CHI Conf. on Human Factors in Computing Systems, pp. 580–628. ACM, New York (05022017).https://doi.org/10.1145/3025453.3025786
38. Mark, G., Gudith, D., Klocke, U.: The cost of interrupted work: more speed and stress. In: Proc. of the 26th annual CHI Conf. on Human Factors in Computing Systems - CHI '08, p. 107. ACM Press, Florence (2008). https://doi.org/10.1145/1357054.1357072
39. Moltrecht, K., Schnaack, G.: Das intelligente Zuhause: Smart Home 2022 — Bitkom e.V. (2022). https://www.bitkom.org/Bitkom/Publikationen/Das-intelligente-Zuhause-Smart-Home-2022
40. Monk, C.A., Trafton, J.G., Boehm-Davis, D.A.: The effect of interruption duration and demand on resuming suspended goals. J. Experiment. Psychol. Appl. **14**(4), 299–313 (2008). https://doi.org/10.1037/a0014402
41. Nigam, A., Riek, L.D.: Social context perception for mobile robots. In: 2015 IEEE/RSJ Int. Conf. on Intelligent Robots and Systems (IROS), pp. 3621–3627. IEEE (2015). https://doi.org/10.1109/IROS.2015.7353883
42. O'Connor, M.F., Riek, L.D.: Detecting social context: a method for social event classification using naturalistic multimodal data. In: 2015 11th IEEE International Conference and Workshops on Automatic Face and Gesture Recognition (FG), pp. 1–7. IEEE, Ljubljana (2015). https://doi.org/10.1109/FG.2015.7284843
43. Pham, V.C., Lim, Y., Bui, H.D., Tan, Y., Chong, N.Y., Sgorbissa, A.: An experimental study on culturally competent robot for smart home environment. In: Barolli, L., Amato, F., Moscato, F., Enokido, T., Takizawa, M. (eds.) Advanced Information Networking and Applications, Advances in Intelligent Systems and Computing, vol. 1151, pp. 369–380. Springer International Publishing, Cham (2020). https://doi.org/10.1007/978-3-030-44041-1_34

44. Pielot, M., Church, K., de Oliveira, R.: An in-situ study of mobile phone notifications. In: Proc. of the 16th Int. Conf. on Human-Computer Interaction with mobile devices & services - MobileHCI '14, pp. 233–242. ACM Press, Toronto, ON, Canada (2014). https://doi.org/10.1145/2628363.2628364
45. Rohleder, B.: Smart Home 2024 - Bitkom e.V. (2024). https://www.bitkom.org/sites/main/files/2024-08/240822-Bitkom-Charts-Smart-Home-2024.pdf
46. Rosenthal-von der Pütten, A.M., Lugrin, B., Steinhaeusser, S.C., Klass, L.: Context matters! identifying social context factors and assessing their relevance for a socially assistive robot. In: Belpaeme, T., Young, J., Gunes, H., Riek, L. (eds.) Companion of the 2020 ACM/IEEE Int. Conf. on Human-Robot Interaction (HRI), pp. 409–411. ACM, New York (2020). https://doi.org/10.1145/3371382.3378370
47. Saulnier, P., Sharlin, E., Greenberg, S.: Exploring minimal nonverbal interruption in HRI. In: 2011 RO-MAN, pp. 79–86. IEEE (31072011 - 03082011). https://doi.org/10.1109/ROMAN.2011.6005257
48. Shapiro, M.S., Rylant, R., de Lima, A., Vidaurri, A., van de Werfhorst, H.: Playing a rigged game: inequality's effect on physiological stress responses. Physiol. Behav. **180**, 60–69 (2017). https://doi.org/10.1016/j.physbeh.2017.08.006, https://www.sciencedirect.com/science/article/pii/S0031938417302536
49. Simoens, P., et al.: Internet of robotic things: context-aware and personalized interventions of assistive social robots (short paper). In: 2016 5th IEEE Int. Conf. on Cloud Networking (CloudNet), pp. 204–207. IEEE (2016). https://doi.org/10.1109/CloudNet.2016.27
50. SoftBank Robotics: Pepper (2021). https://www.softbankrobotics.com/emea/en/pepper
51. Tanaka, T., Fujita, K.: Interaction mediate agent based on user interruptibility estimation. In: Human Interface and the Management of Information. Interacting with Information, pp. 152–160. Springer, Berlin, Heidelberg (2011). https://doi.org/10.1007/978-3-642-21793-7_18, https://link.springer.com/chapter/10.1007/978-3-642-21793-7_18
52. Trafton, J.G., Altmann, E.M., Brock, D.P., Mintz, F.E.: Preparing to resume an interrupted task: effects of prospective goal encoding and retrospective rehearsal. Comput. Stud. 21 (2003).https://doi.org/10.1016/S1071-5819(03)00023-5
53. Trafton, J.G., Monk, C.A.: Task interruptions. reviews of human factors and Ergonomics **3**(1), 111–126 (2007). https://doi.org/10.1518/155723408X299852
54. Vastenburg, M.H., Keyson, D.V., Ridder, H.: Considerate home notification systems: a field study of acceptability of notifications in the home. Personal Ubiquitous Comput. **12**(8), 555–566 (2008). https://doi.org/10.1007/s00779-007-0176-x
55. Vuplex: 3D WebView: cross-platform web browser for Unity (Android, iOS, Windows, macOS, and UWP / Hololens) — Vuplex. https://developer.vuplex.com/webview/overview

"Who Ignores You Matters" Asymmetrical Team Dynamics in Human-Robot Collaboration

Clarissa Sabrina Arlinghaus[1,2](✉)[iD], Kennedy Mambilla[1] [iD], and Günter W. Maier[1,3] [iD]

[1] Work and Organizational Psychology, Bielefeld University, Bielefeld, Germany
clarissa_sabrina.arlinghaus@uni-bielefeld.de
[2] Center for Cognitive Interaction Technology, Bielefeld University, Bielefeld, Germany
[3] Research Institute for Cognition and Robotics, Bielefeld University, Bielefeld, Germany

Abstract. What happens when your robot teammate excludes you? As automation reshapes the workplace, understanding social dynamics in human–robot teams is more important than ever. Grounded in the Temporal Need-Threat Model, this preregistered study examines how coworker behavior (inclusion vs. ostracism-based exclusion) and agent type (human, humanoid robot, industrial robot) affect psychological needs, compensatory behavior, and social reasoning in a manufacturing context.

Across 117 participants, ostracism significantly threatened core needs (belonging, self-esteem, and meaningful existence) and reduced motivation to engage in compensatory efforts (e.g., becoming more pleasant). These effects were strongest when exclusion came from a human coworker, and weakest when it came from an industrial robot. While compensatory efforts decreased under ostracism, their perceived effectiveness remained highest for human coworkers. Ostracizing humans were also penalized most in perception, receiving lower ratings on likability and intelligence than robot agents.

Perceived anthropomorphism intensified both need satisfaction and need-threat, depending on context. Open-ended responses revealed distinct attribution patterns: human exclusion was interpreted as personal (e.g., dislike), whereas robot exclusion was interpreted as a mechanical or programming issue.

These findings challenge the assumption that robots are treated like humans in social settings (CASA) and highlight the double-edged role of anthropomorphism. The study offers novel insights into how team dynamics shift in hybrid human–robot workplaces and underscores the need to manage expectations in collaborative automation design for safeguarding psychological needs in increasingly automated workplaces.

Keywords: Ostracism · Need-Threat · Need-Fortification · Human-Robot-Teams

1 Introduction

As labor shortages intensify across industries like hospitality [18] and manufacturing [23,39], robots are increasingly introduced as teammates to close workforce gaps [37,39]. While effective for productivity [37], robot integration may pose new psychological and social challenges [19]. Prior research shows that interacting exclusively with robotic coworkers can undermine basic psychological needs, with human attention perceived as more meaningful than robotic attention and human exclusion more painful than robotic exclusion [3].

This study investigates social exclusion in human-robot teams within the context of the automotive industry one of Germany's largest industrial sectors and a domain where automation is already widespread [25]. Unlike service robots or humanoids, industrial robot arms typically lack social cues, which may intensify feelings of being ignored.

Our work builds on previous research, which demonstrated asymmetrical team dynamics in restaurant scenarios [3]. The present study extends this research in two key ways: First, we compare two types of robots humanoid and industrial to test whether physical embodiment influences the psychological impact of exclusion. This addresses the question of whether humanlike robots elicit stronger social interpretations than machine-like agents. Second, we examine whether the effects observed in service contexts generalize to manufacturing environments. This shift in domain responds to calls for broader ecological validity [35] and allows us to test whether the stronger effects of human exclusion are unique to service settings or apply across domains. We found this comparison (restaurant [3] vs. manufacturing) particularly informative, as one might expect team dynamics to matter less in manufacturing jobs with limited social interaction than in customer-facing service roles. This study allowed us to test whether social exclusion effects persist even in less interaction-intensive work settings.

Guided by the Temporal Need-Threat Model [44], we compare three types of teammates (human coworkers, humanoid robots, and industrial robots) and examine how they affect workers' psychological need satisfaction, compensatory behaviors, and subjective reasoning when excluded. We also explore whether anthropomorphism moderates these effects.

By extending ostracism research into manufacturing, this study tests the generalizability of previous findings and provides first insights into how robotic embodiment influences social inclusion at work. As automation accelerates [33,34,45], understanding how humans experience robot teammates becomes essential—not only for effective collaboration, but also for protecting psychological well-being.

2 Theoretical Framework

Our research is grounded in the Temporal Need-Threat Model of ostracism [44], which provides a widely accepted theoretical framework for understanding the psychological consequences of social exclusion. According to this model, ostracism—defined as being ignored or excluded by others—elicits an immediate threat to four fundamental psychological needs: belonging, self-esteem, control, and meaningful existence [44].

Ostracism-based exclusion is characterized not by explicit rejection, but by a lack of acknowledgment and attention from others [42,43]. This form of social neglect is often subtle, yet a robust body of research has shown the strong experience of need-threat—a reduction in the satisfaction of the psychological needs [20].

While most research has focused on human exclusion, recent findings demonstrate similar effects when the excluding agent is robotic [3,16,38]. Notably, observers also attribute need-threat to excluded individuals, even when the excluded target itself is a robot [27].

Hypothesis 1. *Ostracized individuals experience a significant threat to their basic psychological needs, which is reflected in lower levels of a) belonging, b) self-esteem, c) meaningful existence.*

According to the same model [44], individuals also engage in behavioral strategies aimed at restoring inclusion. In particular, they may attempt to repair threatened needs by increasing their social attractiveness [44].

Prior research [1] identified strategies commonly used to appear more socially attractive. Among them, "becoming more pleasant" and "showing off abilities and talents" were highly endorsed [1].

These strategies are relevant beyond romantic attraction and may apply to both human-human and human-robot interaction settings. "Becoming more pleasant" aligns with anecdotal reports of people being overly polite toward AI, while "showing off" may reflect attempts to impress or assert status—especially toward agents perceived as lower in authority, like robots [7,11,15].

Hypothesis 2. *Ostracized individuals engage in compensatory efforts to become more socially attractive, which may manifest in a) becoming more pleasant and b) showing off skills and abilities.*

This expectation is consistent with the Computers Are Social Actors (CASA) paradigm, which posits that people apply social behaviors to computers and other artificial agents [30,31].

While prior studies found no differences between human and non-human agents [22,27,47], new evidence [3] suggests that agent type may moderate ostracism effects. Human exclusion was often taken personally and elicited more need-threat, while robotic exclusion was ascribed to limited programming which may buffered exclusion's detrimental effects [3]. Moreover, the direct effect of ostracism on compensatory strategies aimed at regaining social acceptance was only significant for human ostracizers [3].

Our study extends this work by including both humanoid and industrial robots. In manufacturing contexts, industrial robots are common but lack social cues. Thus, exclusion by such robots may elicit weaker psychological responses due to lower expectations of social interaction. In contrast, humanoid robots may evoke reactions closer to human exclusion, owing to their perceived social competence.

Hypothesis 3. *The effects of ostracism on a) need-threat and b) compensatory efforts depend on the agent type, with the strongest effects expected for ostracism by humans, followed by humanoid robots, and the weakest effects for industrial robots.*

We further examine anthropomorphism as a potential moderator. When an agent appears more human-like, exclusion may be perceived as intentional and thus more painful. Conversely, non-anthropomorphic agents may be seen as less socially capable, reducing the impact of being ignored. Thus, we propose that need-threat mediates the effect of ostracism on compensatory behavior, moderated by perceived anthropomorphism.

Hypothesis 4. *The effects of ostracism on compensatory efforts are mediated by need-threat and moderated by the level of anthropomorphism, with stronger effects for higher levels of anthropomorphism.*

Anthropomorphic agents are typically perceived as more intelligent and likable [10,36]. Therefore, we also explore whether likeability and perceived intelligence function as moderators. Agents who are perceived as more likable may evoke stronger desires for social approval, making their exclusion more painful and prompting greater behavioral efforts to regain acceptance. Likewise, agents seen as more intelligent may be viewed as more socially competent and autonomous, potentially increasing the perceived intentionality behind exclusion and thereby intensifying need threat. Moreover, individuals may believe that efforts to reconnect are more effective with an intelligent agent than with a primitive machine.

Exploratory Question 1. *Do likeability and perceived intelligence of the agent moderate the effects of ostracism on a) need-threat and b) compensatory efforts?*

3 Methods

The study was preregistered [26], and all materials, data, and analysis scripts are available in the Open Science Framework (OSF): https://doi.org/10.17605/OSF.IO/GFMHC

3.1 Participants and Recruitment

An a priori power analysis using G*Power [17] indicated that a minimum sample size of 113 participants was required to detect a medium effect ($f^2 = 0.0625$) with $\alpha = 0.05$ and power = 0.80 in a 2 x 3 between-subjects MANOVA with three outcome variables.

In March 2025, a total of 211 participants accessed the online experiment in Unipark. Of these, 43 dropped out before completion (dropout rate: 20.4 %).

Three participants were under the age of 18 and were excluded, as were 42 participants who failed the attention check ("What happened in the situation you were supposed to imagine?"). An additional six cases were removed due to technical errors resulting in missing data. The final sample comprised 117 participants aged between 18 to 65 (M_{age} = 25.26, SD = 8.15), including 43 men (36.8 %), 73 women (62.4 %), and one person identifying as non-binary.

In terms of occupational background, 78 participants were students (66.7 %), 32 were employed professionals (27.4 %), and six (5.1 %) selected "Other" (e.g., retired, unemployed); one person chose not to respond. Only ten participants (8.5 %) had previous work experience in the automotive industry.

Participation was possible from the age of 18, there were no further conditions for participation. Participants were recruited via social media and a university participant pool (SONA). No crowdsourcing platforms (e.g., Prolific, MTurk) were used. The study was voluntary and not financially compensated. Students at Bielefeld University could receive partial course credit.

3.2 Design, Procedure and Measures

The study was administered online via Unipark. We employed a 2 (Inclusion vs. Ostracism) × 3 (Agent Type: Human vs. Humanoid Robot vs. Industrial Robot) between-subjects design. Participants were randomly assigned to one of six conditions. Participants read a vignette describing a work scenario in the automotive industry, in which they were either included or ostracized by human coworkers, humanoid robot coworkers, or industrial robot coworkers (see Fig. 1). To further enhance immersion and strengthen the vignette manipulation, each scenario included AI-generated illustrative images, created following a recommended stepwise procedure for high-quality synthetic visuals [4].

Following the vignette, the participants completed a set of questionnaire items. **Need-Threat** was assessed using three subscales (5 items, 5-point Likert) of the Need-Threat Scale (Belonging, Self-Esteem, and Meaningful Existence) [44], adapted from a German version [32]. Need-Threat captures the degree to which participants felt their psychological needs were undermined by the interaction. A low need fulfillment (i.e., low values for belonging, self-esteem, meaningful existence) indicates a high need-threat. **Compensatory Efforts** were measured with two adapted subscales (5-point Likert): Becoming More Pleasant (5 items) and Showing Off Abilities and Skills (9 items) [1]. Items were translated into German using a back-and-forth translation procedure. The compensatory efforts reflect behavioral strategies aimed at regaining social inclusion (e.g., being more polite or demonstrating one's talents), conceptually based on "attempts to become more socially attractive" as described in the Temporal Need-Threat Model [44]. **Agent Perception** was assessed using three subscales (5 items, 5-point Likert) from the Godspeed Questionnaire (Anthropomorphism, Likeability, and Perceived Intelligence) [8,9], adapted from the official German translation [8]. Agent perception refers to how participants perceive the agent— not how the agent perceives the participants. Anthropomorphism corresponds to the perceived human-likeness of the agent [9]; Likeability captures positive first impressions (i.e., sympathy) [9]; Perceived Intelligence reflects how competent the agent appears [9].

Three items were used to explore **Participants' Reasoning** (e.g., "Why do your (robotic) coworkers behave the way they do toward you?"), similar to prior research [3]. Within one question ("How effective are the behaviors described above in getting more attention from your coworkers?"), they were asked to rate the perceived effectiveness of the compensatory efforts on a scale from 1 (not effective at all) to 5 (very effective).

Demographic data included age, gender, employment status, and experience in the automotive industry. No explicit manipulation checks were included. Instead, the Need-Threat [44] and Godspeed scales [8] served as indirect validation of the exclusion and agent-type manipulations. An attention check was implemented at the end of the survey where participants selected the correct summary of their vignette from eight predefined options (e.g., "I was asked to imagine working with humanoid robots in a car factory. My robot coworkers didn't respond to me.").

Participants completed the study independently and without researcher supervision. They accessed the online experiment individually, read the assigned vignette, and completed the questionnaire on their own. No remote calls, live interaction, or technical assistance were provided during the task. The median completion time was 481 s ($\approx$ 8 minutes).

3.3 Quantitative and Qualitative Analyses

Three **2 × 3 MANOVAs** were conducted to examine the effects of ostracism and agent type on (1) agent perception, (2) need-threat, and (3) compensatory efforts. In light of violated assumptions (e.g., unequal covariance matrices), we used Pillai's trace, which is more robust than Wilks lambda [6]. Significant multivariate effects were followed up with univariate ANOVAs and Bonferroni-corrected comparisons.

Two **moderated mediation analyses** (PROCESS model 59 [21]) were conducted to test whether the effects of ostracism on compensatory efforts are mediated by need-threat and moderated by anthropomorphism. Four additional exploratory moderated mediation models examined likeability and perceived intelligence as potential moderators.

Prior research has demonstrated the suitability of Large Language Models (LLMs) for qualitative text analysis [5,12,14,40,41,46]. Thus, we applied LLM-Assisted Inductive Categorization (**LAIC**) [2,5] to analyze open-ended responses. The LAIC method involves an iterative, human-in-the-loop process for inductive coding using LLMs [2,5] which is based on Mayring's qualitative content analysis [28,29]. We followed the stepwise LAIC protocol [2].

A **2 × 3 ANOVA** was used to explore whether inclusion/ostracism or agent type affected participants' perceived effectiveness of compensatory efforts. Significant agent effects were followed up with Bonferroni-corrected comparisons.

All analyses were conducted using IBM SPSS Statistics, Microsoft Excel, and Python in Visual Studio Code.

Inclusion – Human Coworkers ($n = 19$)	Ostracism – Human Coworkers ($n = 25$)
Imagine you work in the automotive industry and have to assemble car parts together with other people. Your coworkers occasionally look at you, sometimes talk to you and also react when you speak to them. Overall, your coworkers behave as if they perceive you as a pleasant team member. 	Imagine you work in the automotive industry and have to assemble car parts together with other people. Your coworkers **never** look at you, **never** talk to you and **don't** react when you speak to them. Overall, your coworkers behave as if you **don't** even exist. 
Inclusion – Humanoid Robot Coworkers ($n = 21$)	**Ostracism – Humanoid Robot Coworkers** ($n = 20$)
Imagine you work in the automotive industry and have to assemble car parts together with humanoid robots. Your robot coworkers occasionally look at you, sometimes talk to you and also react when you speak to them. Overall, your robot coworkers behave as if they perceive you as a pleasant team member. 	Imagine you work in the automotive industry and have to assemble car parts together with humanoid robots. Your robot coworkers **never** look at you, **never** talk to you and **don't** react when you speak to them. Overall, your robot coworkers behave as if you **don't** even exist. 
Inclusion – Industrial Robot Coworkers ($n = 12$)	**Ostracism – Industrial Robot Coworkers** ($n = 20$)
Imagine you work in the automotive industry and have to assemble car parts together with industrial robotic arms. Your robot coworkers occasionally look at you, sometimes talk to you and also react when you speak to them. Overall, your robot coworkers behave as if they perceive you as a pleasant team member. 	Imagine you work in the automotive industry and have to assemble car parts together with industrial robotic arms. Your robot coworkers **never** look at you, **never** talk to you and **don't** react when you speak to them. Overall, your robot coworkers behave as if you **don't** even exist. 

Fig. 1. Experimental Conditions and Corresponding Vignettes.

4 Results

All scales demonstrated excellent internal consistency ($\alpha > .86$). No multivariate outliers were detected, as all Mahalanobis distances remained below the critical value of 13.16. Univariate outliers ($\pm 3 \times$ IQR) were excluded from the MANOVA on need-threat ($n = 3$) and the ANOVA on effectiveness ($n = 4$). All other analyses were based on the full sample ($N = 117$).

4.1 Effects of Ostracism on Agent Perception, Need-Threat, and Compensatory Efforts

Three MANOVAs assessed the effects of ostracism on agent perception, needs, and compensatory efforts. See Fig. 2 for a summary.

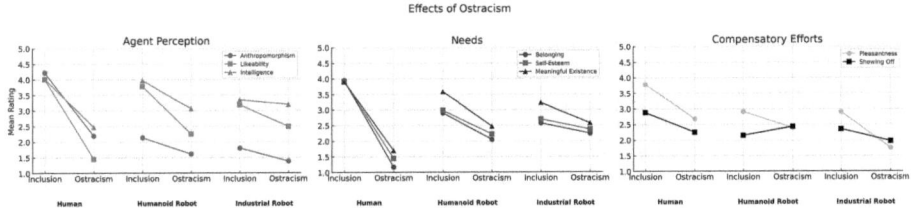

Fig. 2. Mean Values of Multivariate Analyses of Variances.

Agent Perception. Multivariate analyses revealed significant main effects of ostracism ($p < .001$, $\eta = .56$), agent type ($p < .001$, $\eta = .31$), and their interaction ($p < .001$, $\eta = .16$) on the perception of the agent. Ostracism significantly reduced perceived anthropomorphism ($p < .001$, $\eta = .32$), likeability ($p < .001$, $\eta = .54$), and intelligence ($p < .001$, $\eta = .22$). Agent type only impacted anthropomorphism ($p < .001$, $\eta = .51$), but not likeability or percieved intelligence ($ps > .20$). Human coworkers were seen as more anthropomorphic than both robot types ($ps < .001$), whereas perceived anthropomorphism did not differ between humanoid and industrial robots ($p = .139$). The interaction between ostracism and agent was significant across all perception dimensions ($ps < .003$, $\eta = .10\text{-}.22$) showing strongest effects for human agents.

Need-Threat. Multivariate analysis revealed significant main effects of ostracism on psychological needs ($p < .001$, $\eta = .48$), while the main effect of agent type was not significant ($p = .392$, $\eta = .03$). However, a significant interaction effect emerged between ostracism and agent type ($p < .001$, $\eta = .20$), relevant for all three needs ($ps < .002$, $\eta = .12\text{-}.35$). Ostracism significantly decreased ratings of belonging ($p < .001$, $\eta = .45$), self-esteem ($p < .001$, $\eta = .42$), and meaningful existence ($p < .001$, $\eta = .36$). All needs were stronger threatened when humans ostracized them compared to both robot types ($ps < .020$). No differences emerged between humanoid and industrial robots ($ps > .655$), although being ostracized by humanoid robots affected all three needs ($ps < .001$) but ostracism by industrial robots did not significantly impact any of the three needs ($ps > .050$).

Compensatory Efforts. Multivariate analyses revealed a significant main effect of ostracism ($p < .001$, $\eta = .25$) and agent type ($p = .001$, $\eta = .08$). The interaction between ostracism and agent type did not reach significance ($p = .212$, $\eta = .03$). Ostracism significantly reduced participants' tendency to behave pleasantly ($p < .001$, $\eta = .22$), but not their tendency to show off skills and abilities ($p = .163$, $\eta = .02$). Similarly, agent type had a significant effect on becoming more pleasant ($p < .001$, $\eta = .15$), but not on showing off skills and abilities ($p = .149$, $\eta = .03$). Participants became more pleasant with human coworkers than with humanoid ($p = .032$) or industrial robot coworkers ($p < .001$). The difference between humanoid and industrial robots did not reach statistical significance ($p = .073$).

4.2 Potential Mediators and Moderators of Ostracism

Six moderated mediation analyses tested whether the effects of ostracism on compensatory efforts were mediated by needs (belonging, self-esteem, meaningful existence) and moderated by agent perception (anthropomorphism, likeability, perceived intelligence). For a summary, see Fig. 3.

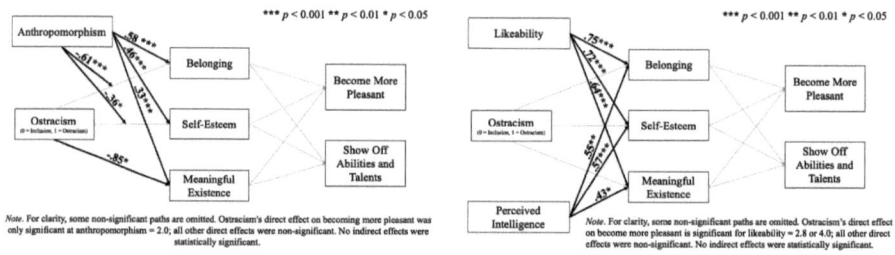

Fig. 3. Summary of Moderated Mediation Analyses.

Moderation by Anthropomorphism. The moderated mediation model predicting pleasant behavior was statistically significant ($R^2 = .39$, $p < .001$), whereas the model predicting showing off skills was not ($R^2 = .14$, $p = .062$). Neither ostracism nor any of the mediators (belonging, self-esteem, meaningful existence) interacted significantly with anthropomorphism in predicting pleasantness ($ps > .141$) or showing off ($ps > .507$). However, ostracism significantly interacted with anthropomorphism in predicting belonging ($p < .001$) and self-esteem ($p = .012$), suggesting that the threat to these needs was amplified when the ostracizing agent was more anthropomorphic (see Fig. 4). Anthropomorphism also had a significant main effect on need satisfaction: participants reported greater belonging ($p < .001$), higher self-esteem ($p < .001$), and more meaningful existence ($p < .001$) when interacting with more anthropomorphic agents. Despite the significant moderation effects on the mediators, none of the conditional indirect effects reached significance, as all bootstrap confidence intervals included zero.

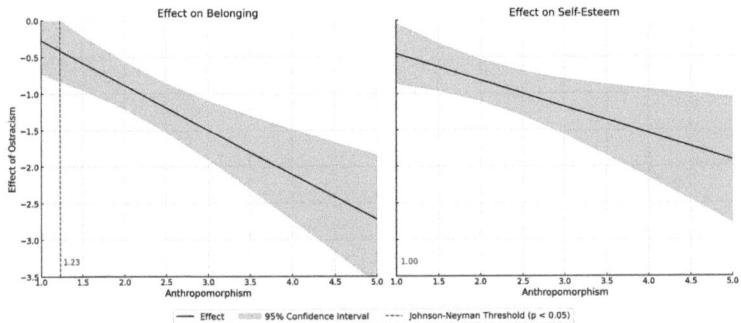

Fig. 4. Effect of Ostracism on Needs Moderated by Anthropomorphism.

Moderation by Likeability. The moderated mediation model predicting pleasant behavior was statistically significant ($R^2 = .32$, $p < .001$), whereas the model predicting showing off skills was not ($R^2 = .10$, $p = .206$). Neither ostracism nor any of the mediators (belonging, self-esteem, meaningful existence) interacted significantly with likeability in predicting pleasantness ($ps > .126$) or showing off ($ps > .240$). Moreover, ostracism did not interact significantly with likeability in predicting any of the mediators ($ps ¿ .524$), indicating that the degree of likeability of the ostracizing agent did not moderate the threat to psychological needs. Nevertheless, likeability showed consistent main effects on need satisfaction: higher levels of likeability were associated with greater belonging ($p < .001$), higher self-esteem ($p < .001$), and more meaningful existence ($p < .001$). Despite these main effects, none of the conditional indirect effects reached significance, as all bootstrap confidence intervals included zero.

Moderation by Perceived Intelligence. The moderated mediation model predicting pleasant behavior was statistically significant ($R^2 = .31$, $p < .001$), while the model predicting showing off skills also reached significance ($R^2 = .17$, $p = .029$). However, neither ostracism nor any of the mediators (belonging, self-esteem, meaningful existence) interacted significantly with perceived intelligence in predicting pleasantness ($ps > .351$) or showing off ($ps > .052$). Additionally, ostracism did not interact significantly with perceived intelligence in predicting any of the mediators ($ps > .162$), suggesting that the agent's perceived intelligence did not influence the extent of need-threat. Perceived intelligence did, however, have a significant main effect on all mediators: participants reported greater belonging ($p = .007$), higher self-esteem ($p < .001$), and more meaningful existence ($p = .032$) when interacting with more intelligent-seeming agents. Still, none of the conditional indirect effects reached significance, as all corresponding bootstrap confidence intervals included zero.

4.3 Participants' Reasoning

When asked why their (robotic) coworkers behaved as they did, 36 % ($n = 16$) attributed human behavior to social dynamics (e.g., "Maybe there were arguments or they don't like me"). In contrast, 54 % ($n = 22$) explained humanoid robot behavior by programming (e.g., "Because they were programmed that way"), while 53 % ($n = 17$) described industrial robots in terms of the human-machine divide (e.g., "They are machines without feelings or thoughts").

Participants also rated how effective they found the compensatory behaviors. A 2 × 3 ANOVA revealed main effects of ostracism ($p < .001, \eta = .141$) and agent type ($p < .001, \eta = .323$), but no interaction ($p = .567, \eta = .011$). Compensatory efforts were seen as more effective when participants were included and when interacting with human agents (vs. humanoid, $p = .001$; vs. industrial robots, $p < .001$). Humanoid robots were rated more receptive than industrial ones ($p < .001$). Open responses reflected these patterns: compensatory efforts were seen as useless with robots (e.g., "As the robots presumably lack social skills, it would be pointless to try to impress them.") but were judged more socially meaningful when directed at humans (e.g., "By drawing attention to yourself, you can either get into more conversation or the exact opposite could be the case. The other person may also be annoyed and behave even more rudely.")

5 Discussion

This study examined how coworker behavior (inclusion vs. ostracism) and agent type (human, humanoid robot, industrial robot) influence psychological needs, compensatory efforts, and reasoning in a collaborative manufacturing scenario. Building on the Temporal Need-Threat Model [44], we investigated whether agent characteristics (e.g., anthropomorphism) moderate these effects.

As predicted in Hypothesis 1, ostracism significantly threatened psychological needs. Surprisingly, and in contrast to Hypothesis 2, ostracism reduced rather than increased compensatory efforts. While the Temporal Need-Threat Model [44] suggests that individuals try to regain inclusion by becoming more pleasant or showing off, our data suggest that exclusion led to social withdrawal. This aligns with research showing that ostracized individuals may become more self-focused and less cooperative [24] or direct compensatory efforts toward others who did not exclude them [38]. Participants often questioned the utility of compensatory efforts, especially when interacting with robots. Notably, the perceived effectiveness of compensatory efforts was higher in inclusion conditions, suggesting that such behaviors may serve more to maintain than to repair social bonds. Moreover, ostracism also negatively impacted perceptual dimensions.

However, not all agents were equal in their impact. Supporting Hypothesis 3, exclusion by human coworkers had the strongest negative effects on need fulfillment, while industrial robots elicited the weakest reactions. This pattern was replicated across perception dimensions, with ostracizing humans rated as less likable and less intelligent than robots. This indicates that social violations are more painful and disappointing when they come from humans than machines, which contradicts the assumption of CASA [30] [31]. Participants' reasoning reinforced these findings: human exclusion was interpreted through a social lens, while robot exclusion was attributed to programming or mechanical limitations. These attribution patterns may buffer the psychological impact of robot exclusion and contribute to asymmetrical team dynamics as already suggested in previous work [3]. A potential interaction effect of ostracism and agent on compensatory efforts was not statistically confirmed, possibly because our study lacked statistical power to detect small effects or because gender imbalances (with fewer male participants, who may be more prone to showing off [1]) dampened potential effects.

Hypothesis 4 received partial support. Anthropomorphism moderated the effects of ostracism on need threat, amplifying its impact on belonging and self-esteem. Moreover, anthropomorphism also increased baseline need satisfaction which indicates that anthropomorphic features, while often praised for increasing likability and trust [10,36], may backfire by elevating social expectations and thus the emotional costs of exclusion. Exploratory analyses further showed that higher likeability and perceived intelligence also increased need satisfaction, but did not moderate ostracism effects. We could not confirm the assumed mediation via needs. Despite similar anthropomorphism ratings, some differences between robot types emerged—though likely more would have with stronger perceptual contrast. This highlights the importance of pre-testing agents and supports the idea that perceived, rather than objective, anthropomorphism shapes psychological responses.

Notably, the effects of ostracism on agent perception, need satisfaction and compensatory efforts as well as the interaction effect of ostracism and agent on needs were all large ($\eta > .14$ [13]), highlighting the salience of social dynamics even in low-interaction work contexts like manufacturing. Importantly, these results replicate and extend prior findings from a hospitality setting [3], showing that social exclusion by coworkers—regardless of the domain—has measurable psychological costs. CASA's claim that people treat media agents as socially equivalent to humans [30,31] may not generalize to all workplace contexts. Our study provides compelling evidence for asymmetrical team dynamics similar to prior research [3], where human exclusion is taken more personally, likely due to higher expectations for empathy and intentionality.

While the current findings replicate core effects identified in prior work [3], the present study introduces two key extensions: (1) the application in a manufacturing context and (2) a direct comparison between two distinct robot embodiments. These contextual and agent-related variations offer novel insights into the boundary conditions of social exclusion in human-robot teams. The consistent patterns across different domains (restaurant [3] vs. manufacturing) and agent types (service [3] vs. industrial and humanoid robots) suggest a certain robustness of the observed effects, indicating that the stronger psychological impact of human exclusion is in our view unlikely to be context-specific. Nonetheless, as the current study relied on single-interaction vignette-based scenarios and a student sample, ecological validity may be limited. Future work should therefore explore live and repeated or long-term interactions with diverse participant populations across various contexts to further validate and extend these findings.

Taken together, our findings suggest that robot coworkers are not perceived or experienced as equivalent to human teammates. While anthropomorphism can enhance need satisfaction, it may also raise expectations—making exclusion more need-threatening when those expectations are unmet. This underlines the importance of managing expectations in human-robot collaboration. Designers and implementers should carefully consider when and how anthropomorphic features are used—especially in roles where social reciprocity is limited.

6 Conclusion

Our study shows that even in manufacturing contexts with limited social interaction, social exclusion threatens psychological needs—especially when it comes from a human rather than a robot teammate. While similar patterns were observed in prior research within the service sector [3], the current findings demonstrate that such asymmetrical team dynamics also emerge on the factory floor. Our findings further show that this asymmetry is shaped by how human-like an ostracizing agent is perceived to be, highlighting anthropomorphism as a meaningful moderator for studying processes of social exclusion. Taken together, our results confirm that who ignores you truly matters.

Acknowledgments. SAIL is funded by the Ministry of Culture and Science of the State of North Rhine-Westphalia under the grant no NW21-05A.

Disclosure of Interests. The authors have no competing interests to declare.

AI Disclosure. GPT 4o was used for LLM-assisted inductive categorization (LAIC). Moreover, ChatGPT was used to assist in the formulation and refinement of English sentences based on author-provided input, as well as to generate visual materials. All content was created and reviewed by the authors, who take full responsibility for the final text and figures.

References

1. Apostolou, M., Wang, Y., Gavriilidou, A.: How people become attractive to prospective mates: strategies of self-promotion in the Greek cultural context. Evol. Psychol. **19**(4), 14747049211045272 (2021). https://doi.org/10.1177/14747049211045271
2. Arlinghaus, C.S.: Llm-assisted inductive categorization: a step-by-step guide (2024). https://doi.org/10.5281/zenodo.13379684
3. Arlinghaus, C.S., Hörning, V., Wulff, C., Maier, G.W.: Asymmetrical team dynamics: exclusion by robot coworkers hurts less, inclusion by human coworkers satisfies more (2025). https://doi.org/10.31219/osf.io/3uthv_v2
4. Arlinghaus, C.S., Maier, G.W.: Tutorial: creating AI-generated images for vignette studies in python or r (2024). https://doi.org/10.31219/osf.io/a56dy
5. Arlinghaus, C.S., Wulff, C., Maier, G.W.: Inductive coding with Chatgpt - an evaluation of different GPT models clustering qualitative data into categories (2024). https://doi.org/10.31219/osf.io/gpnye
6. Ateş, C., Kaymaz, Ö., Kale, H.E., Tekindal, M.A.: Comparison of test statistics of nonnormal and unbalanced samples for multivariate analysis of variance in terms of type-i error rates. Comput. Math. Methods Med. **2019**, 2173638 (2019). https://doi.org/10.1155/2019/2173638
7. Babel, F., Hock, P., Winkle, K., Torre, I., Ziemke, T.: The human behind the robot: Rethinking the low social status of service robots. In: Grollman, D., Broadbent, E., Ju, W., Soh, H., Williams, T. (eds.) Companion of the 2024 ACM/IEEE International Conference on Human-Robot Interaction, pp. 1–10. ACM, New York (2024). https://doi.org/10.1145/3610978.3640763
8. Bartneck, C.: Godspeed questionnaire series: translations and usage. In: Krägeloh, C.U., Alyami, M., Medvedev, O.N. (eds.) International Handbook of Behavioral Health Assessment, pp. 1–35. Springer Nature Switzerland, Cham (2023). https://doi.org/10.1007/978-3-030-89738-3_24-1
9. Bartneck, C., Kulić, D., Croft, E., Zoghbi, S.: Measurement instruments for the anthropomorphism, animacy, likeability, perceived intelligence, and perceived safety of robots. Int. J. Soc. Robot. **1**(1), 71–81 (2009). https://doi.org/10.1007/s12369-008-0001-3
10. Blut, M., Wang, C., Wünderlich, N.V., Brock, C.: Understanding anthropomorphism in service provision: a meta-analysis of physical robots, chatbots, and other AI. J. Acad. Mark. Sci. **49**(4), 632–658 (2021). https://doi.org/10.1007/s11747-020-00762-y
11. Bryson, J.J.: Robots should be slaves. In: Wilks, Y. (ed.) Close Engagements with Artificial Companions, Natural Language Processing, vol. 8, pp. 63–74. John Benjamins Publishing Company, Amsterdam (2010). https://doi.org/10.1075/nlp.8.11bry
12. Chew, R., Bollenbacher, J., Wenger, M., Speer, J., Kim, A.: Llm-assisted content analysis: using large language models to support deductive coding (2023). https://arxiv.org/abs/2306.14924
13. Cohen, J.: Statistical Power Analysis for the Behavioral Sciences. Routledge (1988). https://doi.org/10.4324/9780203771587
14. Dai, S.C., Xiong, A., Ku, L.W.: Llm-in-the-loop: leveraging large language model for thematic analysis (2023), https://arxiv.org/abs/2310.15100

15. Dautenhahn, K., Woods, S., Kaouri, C., Walters, M.L., Koay, K.L., Werry, I.: What is a robot companion - friend, assistant or butler? In: 2005 IEEE/RSJ International Conference on Intelligent Robots and Systems, pp. 1192–1197. IEEE (2005). https://doi.org/10.1109/IROS.2005.1545189
16. Erel, H., Cohen, Y., Shafrir, K., Levy, S.D., Vidra, I.D., Shem Tov, T., Zuckerman, O.: Excluded by robots: can robot-robot-human interaction lead to ostracism? In: Bethel, C. (ed.) Proceedings of the 2021 ACM/IEEE International Conference on Human-Robot Interaction, pp. 312–321. ACM Digital Library, Association for Computing Machinery, New York (2021). https://doi.org/10.1145/3434073.3444648
17. Faul, F., Erdfelder, E., Buchner, A., Lang, A.G.: Statistical power analyses using g*power 3.1: tests for correlation and regression analyses. Behav. Res. Methods **41**(4), 1149–1160 (2009). https://doi.org/10.3758/BRM.41.4.1149
18. Grigoryan, K.: Labor shortages in the hospitality industry: the effects of work-life balance, employee compensation, government issued unemployment benefits and job insecurity on employees' turnover intentions. Westcliff Int. J. Appl. Res. **8**(1), 59–73 (2024). https://doi.org/10.47670/wuwijar202481kg
19. Hammer, B., et al.: Sustainable life-cycle of intelligent socio-technical systems. https://doi.org/10.4119/UNIBI/2992602
20. Hartgerink, C.H.J., van Beest, I., Wicherts, J.M., Williams, K.D.: The ordinal effects of ostracism: a meta-analysis of 120 cyberball studies. PLoS ONE **10**(5), e0127002 (2015). https://doi.org/10.1371/journal.pone.0127002
21. Hayes, A.F.: Introduction to mediation, moderation, and conditional process analysis: a regression-based approach. Methodology in the social sciences, The Guilford Press, New York and London 3 edn. (2022). https://ebookcentral.proquest.com/lib/kxp/detail.action?docID=6809031
22. Jauch, M., Rudert, S.C., Greifeneder, R.: Social pain by non-social agents: exclusion hurts and provokes punishment even if the excluding source is a computer. Acta Physiol. (Oxf) **230**, 103753 (2022). https://doi.org/10.1016/j.actpsy.2022.103753
23. Khan, M.R., Islam, M.T., Islam, K.S., Hossain, A.: Closing the productivity gap in electric vehicle manufacturing: challenges and solutions. Innov. Eng. J. **1**(01), 223–243 (2024). https://doi.org/10.70937/itej.v1i01.21
24. Klein, S.A., Rudert, S.C.: If they don't care, i won't share: feeling unrelated to one's in-group increases selfishness instead of behavior for the greater good. Eur. J. Soc. Psychol. **51**(4–5), 773–783 (2021). https://doi.org/10.1002/ejsp.2771
25. Krzywdzinski, M., Lechowski, G.: Industry 4.0 and its implications for the international division of labor in the automotive industry. In: Krzywdzinski, M., Lechowski, G., Humphrey, J., Pardi, T. (eds.) Global Shifts in the Automotive Sector, pp. 67–88. Palgrave Studies of Internationalization in Emerging Markets, Springer Nature Switzerland, Cham (2025). https://doi.org/10.1007/978-3-031-80641-4_4
26. Mambilla, K., Arlinghaus, C.S.: Ostracism at the workplace: need-threat and efforts to enhance attractiveness to human and robot coworkers in the automobile industry (2025).https://doi.org/10.17605/OSF.IO/YPMX6
27. Marinucci, M., Pagliaro, S., Teresi, M., Ballone, C., Riva, P.: How low can you still go? observing an ostracized robot is sufficient to hurt humans' feelings. Group Process. Intergroup Relations (2025). https://doi.org/10.1177/13684302241309578
28. Mayring, P.: Qualitative content analysis. Forum qualitative sozialforschung / forum: Qualit. Soc. Res. **1**(2) (2000). https://doi.org/10.17169/fqs-1.2.1089

29. Mayring, P.: Qualitative content analysis: demarcation, varieties, developments. Forum Qualitative Sozialforschung / Forum: Qualitative Social Research **20**(3) (2020). https://doi.org/10.17169/fqs-20.3.3343
30. Nass, C., Moon, Y.: Machines and mindlessness: Social responses to computers. J. Soc. Issues **56**(1), 81–103 (2000). https://doi.org/10.1111/0022-4537.00153
31. Nass, C., Steuer, J., Tauber, E.R.: Computers are social actors. In: Adelson, B. (ed.) CHI 94: Human Factors in Computing Systems Conference, pp. 72–78. Association for Computing Machinery, New York (1994). https://doi.org/10.1145/191666.191703
32. Neumüller, D.: Reaktionen auf soziale ausgrenzung in kollektivistischen und individualistischen kulturen (2013). https://unipub.uni-graz.at/obvugrhs/content/titleinfo/232227/full.pdf
33. Ötting, S.K., Masjutin, L., Steil, J.J., Maier, G.W.: Let's work together: a meta-analysis on robot design features that enable successful human-robot interaction at work. Hum. Factors **64**(6), 1027–1050 (2022). https://doi.org/10.1177/00187208209664 33
34. Panagou, S., Neumann, W.P., Fruggiero, F.: A scoping review of human robot interaction research towards industry 5.0 human-centric workplaces. Int. J. Prod. Res. **62**(3), 974–990 (2024). https://doi.org/10.1080/00207543.2023.2172473
35. Pollak, A., Biolik, E., Chudzicka-Czupała, A.: New luddites? counterproductive work behavior and its correlates, including work characteristics, stress at work, and job satisfaction among employees working with industrial and collaborative robots. Hum. Fact. Ergonom. Manufact. Serv. Industr. **35**(4) (2025). https://doi.org/10.1002/hfm.70016
36. Roesler, E., Manzey, D., Onnasch, L.: A meta-analysis on the effectiveness of anthropomorphism in human-robot interaction. Sci. Robot. **6**(58), eabj5425 (2021). https://doi.org/10.1126/scirobotics.abj5425
37. Sadeh, H., Haghighat, S., Pirayesh, A., Todorov, D., Lee, M.J., Shahbodaghlou, F.: Technological solutions to labor shortages in construction: assessing productivity and innovation adoption. In: Proceedings of the 2024 European Conference on Computing in Construction. Computing in Construction, European Council for Computing in Construction (2024). https://doi.org/10.35490/EC3.2024.164
38. Stachnick, L., Kunold, L.: Isolated by robotic co-workers: The impact of verbal ostracism on psychological needs and human behavior. In: Companion of the 2024 ACM/IEEE International Conference on Human-Robot Interaction, pp. 1003–1007. HRI '24, Association for Computing Machinery, New York (2024). https://doi.org/10.1145/3610978.3640668
39. Szajna, A., Kostrzewski, M.: Ar-ai tools as a response to high employee turnover and shortages in manufacturing during regular, pandemic, and war times. Sustainability **14**(11), 6729 (2022). https://doi.org/10.3390/su14116729
40. Tai, R.H., Bentley, L.R., Xia, X., Sitt, J.M., Fankhauser, S.C., Chicas-Mosier, A.M., Monteith, B.G.: An examination of the use of large language models to aid analysis of textual data. Int. J. Qualit. Methods **23** (2024). https://doi.org/10.1177/16094069241231168
41. Torii, M.G., Murakami, T., Ochiai, Y.: Expanding horizons in HCI research through LLM-driven qualitative analysis (2024). https://arxiv.org/abs/2401.04138
42. Wesselmann, E.D., Grzybowski, M.R., Steakley-Freeman, D.M., DeSouza, E.R., Nezlek, J.B., Williams, K.D.: Social exclusion in everyday life. In: Riva, P., Eck, J. (eds.) Social Exclusion, pp. 3–23. Springer, Cham (2016). https://doi.org/10.1007/978-3-319-33033-4_1

43. Wesselmann, E.D., Michels, C., Slaughter, A.: Understanding common and diverse forms of social exclusion. In: Rudert, S.C., Greifeneder, R., Williams, K.D., Rudert, S., Williams, K. (eds.) Current Directions in Ostracism, Social Exclusion, and Rejection Research, pp. 1–17. Routledge (2019). https://doi.org/10.4324/9781351255912-1
44. Williams, K.D.: Ostracism: a temporal need-threat model. In: Zanna, M.P. (ed.) Advances in Experimental Social Psychology, vol. 41, pp. 275–314. Elsevier Academic Press (2009). https://doi.org/10.1016/S0065-2601(08)00406-1
45. Wolf, F.D., Stock-Homburg, R.: Human-robot teams: a review. In: Wagner, A.R., Feil-Seifer, D., Haring, K.S., Rossi, S., Williams, T., He, H., Sam Ge, S. (eds.) ICSR 2020. LNCS (LNAI), vol. 12483, pp. 246–258. Springer, Cham (2020). https://doi.org/10.1007/978-3-030-62056-1_21
46. Xiao, Z., Yuan, X., Liao, Q.V., Abdelghani, R., Oudeyer, P.Y.: Supporting qualitative analysis with large language models: combining codebook with GPT-3 for deductive coding. In: Companion Proceedings of the 28th International Conference on Intelligent User Interfaces, pp. 75–78. IUI '23 Companion, Association for Computing Machinery, New York (2023). https://doi.org/10.1145/3581754.3584136
47. Zadro, L., Williams, K.D., Richardson, R.: How low can you go? ostracism by a computer is sufficient to lower self-reported levels of belonging, control, self-esteem, and meaningful existence. J. Exp. Soc. Psychol. **40**(4), 560–567 (2004). https://doi.org/10.1016/j.jesp.2003.11.006

Open Access This chapter is licensed under the terms of the Creative Commons Attribution 4.0 International License (http://creativecommons.org/licenses/by/4.0/), which permits use, sharing, adaptation, distribution and reproduction in any medium or format, as long as you give appropriate credit to the original author(s) and the source, provide a link to the Creative Commons license and indicate if changes were made.

The images or other third party material in this chapter are included in the chapter's Creative Commons license, unless indicated otherwise in a credit line to the material. If material is not included in the chapter's Creative Commons license and your intended use is not permitted by statutory regulation or exceeds the permitted use, you will need to obtain permission directly from the copyright holder.

Exploring LLM-Generated Culture-Specific Affective Human-Robot Tactile Interaction

Qiaoqiao Ren(✉) and Tony Belpaeme

Faculty of Engineering and Architecture, IDLab-AIRO, Ghent University – imec, Technologiepark 126, 9052 Gent, Belgium
Qiaoqiao.Ren@ugent.be

Abstract. As large language models (LLMs) become increasingly integrated into robotic systems, their potential to generate socially and culturally appropriate affective touch remains largely unexplored. This study investigates whether LLMs—specifically GPT-3.5, GPT-4, and GPT-4o—can generate culturally adaptive tactile behaviours to convey emotions in human-robot interaction. We produced text-based touch descriptions for 12 distinct emotions across three cultural contexts (Chinese, Belgian, and unspecified), and examined their interpretability in both robot-to-human and human-to-robot scenarios. A total of 90 participants (36 Chinese, 36 Belgian, and 18 culturally unspecified) evaluated these LLM-generated tactile behaviours for emotional decoding and perceived appropriateness. Results reveal that: (1) under matched cultural conditions, participants successfully decoded six out of twelve emotions—mainly socially oriented emotions such as love and Ekman emotions such as anger, however, self-focused emotions like pride and embarrassment were more difficult to interpret; (2) tactile behaviours were perceived as more appropriate when directed from human to robot than from robot to human, revealing an asymmetry in social expectations based on interaction roles; (3) behaviours interpreted as aggressive (e.g., anger), overly intimate (e.g., love), or emotionally ambiguous (i.e., not clearly decodable) were significantly more likely to be rated as inappropriate; and (4) cultural mismatches reduced decoding accuracy and increased the likelihood of behaviours being judged as inappropriate.

Keywords: Tactile interaction · affective computing · emotion decoding · cultural difference

1 Introduction

Tactile interaction plays a fundamental role in human social communication, providing an essential channel for conveying emotions, intentions, and nuanced social cues [1]. As robotic systems become increasingly integrated into everyday human environments, the capacity for robots to understand and utilise tactile communication in culturally and socially appropriate ways is becoming crucial for enhancing the quality of human-robot interactions [2]. However, generating emotionally expressive and contextually suitable tactile behaviours poses significant challenges, primarily due to the complexity of human touch, which varies greatly with cultural contexts and the relationships between interacting partners [3,4]. Current approaches in robotic tactile interaction often rely on predefined gestures or limited behavioural repertoires, lacking the flexibility required to adapt to diverse social contexts and cultural sensitivities.

Recent developments in artificial intelligence—particularly in large language models (LLMs) such as GPT-4, GPT-4o, and GPT-3.5—offer promising avenues for overcoming limitations in human-robot interaction [5]. Although LLMs inherently lack physical embodiment and direct sensory experiences [6], their extensive training on vast and diverse textual corpora endows them with implicit knowledge of social and cultural nuances [7]. Prior research has demonstrated the use of LLMs in generating the robot's expressive behaviours. Furthermore, recent studies have explored how LLMs can guide robots in generating social behaviours [8], including affective tactile interactions via devices such as vibration sleeves [9].

While LLMs show great potential in driving robotic applications, human-robot tactile interactions are inherently contextual and culturally situated [10]. In addition, one key factor shaping the interpretation of tactile interaction is the role of the robot—whether it engages in active or passive touch. For example, studies on robot-initiated (active) touch have shown that the robot's perceived intent significantly influences human responses. Participants tend to prefer instrumental touch (e.g., touch used to assist or guide) over affective touch, which may feel socially ambiguous or intrusive [11]. On the other hand, passive touch, where the robot is designed to be touched, has also been explored in systems such as the Haptic Creature [12], which was reported to induce calmness and happiness in users. Similarly, recent work has demonstrated that robot-mediated passive touch can help reduce stress levels during risk-taking tasks [13].

However, most of these studies have focused on positive social touch. In contrast, affective tactile interaction is more complex, as it also involves negative or ambiguous emotions, which can be harder for robots to interpret or express appropriately. Therefore, it is essential for robots to develop an awareness of what types of touch are appropriate, and when, to avoid crossing social or cultural boundaries. As LLMs become more integrated into embodied systems, their ability to interpret context, understand interaction roles, and generate culturally appropriate tactile behaviours will be critical for safe and meaningful human-robot touch interaction.

To address this gap, this study investigates the ability of large language models (LLMs) to generate culturally sensitive and socially appropriate tactile behaviour descriptions intended to convey distinct emotions. Specifically, we explore the following research questions: 1) How accurately can LLM-generated tactile descriptions be decoded across different cultural contexts, and which types of emotions are more or less easily recognised? 2) How does the direction of interaction (human-to-robot vs. robot-to-human) influence the perception of social roles and appropriateness in tactile communication? 3) Which decoded emotions are most frequently perceived as inappropriate, and do they pose potential risks for social misunderstanding? 4) Can LLMs adapt to different cultural contexts when generating text-based affective tactile behaviours?

2 Materials Andethods

In this study, participants were asked to interpret descriptions of affective tactile behaviours. Participants either had a Chinese background, a Belgian background, or an unspecified cultural background. The descriptions were generated by large language models (LLMs), using culturally tailored prompts (see Sect. 2.2). The following sections describe the equipment, setup, and data acquisition procedures.

2.1 Emotions

Inspired by [14], we selected a diverse set of emotions to examine tactile emotional communication. These included: (a) six Ekman emotions—anger, fear, happiness, sadness, disgust, and surprise; (b) three prosocial emotions associated with cooperation and altruism—love, gratitude, and sympathy; and (c) three self-focused emotions—embarrassment, pride, and envy.

2.2 Prompt

Participants were shown textual descriptions of affective tactile behaviours, which were generated by an LLM using the following prompt: "You are an encoder (human or humanoid robot) tasked with expressing one of 12 emotions solely through touch to a decoder/receiver (humanoid robot or human) within a specific cultural context (Chinese, Belgian, or None). The touch should be applied to the bare arm, from the elbow to the hand. Provide 10 distinct tactile behaviours to express the emotion. For each, describe the touch behaviour, touch intensity, its rhythm or timing, and how cultural context is considered. Focus solely on tactile behaviours, ensuring the behaviours are contextually and culturally appropriate." The detailed prompt is available on GitHub[1]. Here is an example of generated tactile behaviour for anger; the touch expression generated for the Belgian culture context is *a swift slap to the back of the hand*. In addition, the Chinese culture context suggests *a quick drag down the arm, firm and assertive*.

---

[1] https://github.com/qiaoqiao2323/LLM_touch_culture/tree/main.

2.3 Experimental Design

We recruited 90 participants (57 identifying as male, 32 as female, and one preferring not to report gender), ages 19 to 51. The sample included 36 Chinese participants, 36 Belgian participants, and 18 participants without a specified cultural context. The study adhered to the ethical procedures of *Ghent University*, and all participants provided informed consent. Participants were asked to decode emotions from LLM-generated tactile behaviours. For stimulus creation, we generated 18 unique series of tactile behaviours, each series containing 3 tactile behaviours for each of 12 target emotions. The tactile behaviours were derived from the following combination of experimental conditions:

$$\text{Interaction Direction (2)} \times \text{Culture (3)} \times \text{LLM Type (3)} = 18 \text{ series} \quad (1)$$

where:

- **Interaction Direction**: {Robot-to-Human, Human-to-Robot}
- **Cultural Context**: {Chinese, Belgian, No specified context}
- **LLM Type**: {GPT-4, GPT-4o, GPT-3.5-turbo}

Following the evaluation process proposed by [15], each series included a total of 36 tactile behaviours (3 behaviours for each of the 12 emotions) and each series was rated by three participants, with the constraint that no participant evaluated more than one series and no tactile behaviour appeared more than once within a series.

2.4 Procedure

Each participant completed a questionnaire for each of the 36 tactile behaviours. Specifically, for each of the 12 target emotions, we generated three different tactile behaviours. For each tactile behaviour, participants were provided with contextual information describing the direction of emotional expression: either the robot was conveying an emotion to a human (*robot-to-human*) or a human was conveying an emotion to a robot (*human-to-robot*). This directionality was made explicit at the beginning of each block or stimulus description.

To explore cultural adaptation in tactile behaviours, these behaviours were generated by LLMs under three cultural prompt conditions: Chinese, Belgian, and culturally unspecified (none). Participants were either matched or mismatched with these cultural conditions. Specifically, 18 Chinese participants received tactile behaviours generated for the Chinese cultural context (Chi-Chi), while another 18 Chinese participants received behaviours generated for the Belgian context (Bel-Chi). Similarly, 18 Belgian participants experienced tactile behaviours tailored to the Belgian context (Bel-Bel), and another 18 Belgian participants received those generated for the Chinese context (Chi-Bel). Additionally, 18 participants without a clearly defined cultural background received tactile behaviours generated under the culturally unspecified condition. The presentation of the descriptions was balanced across participants. Participants were instructed to imagine the described interaction and then evaluate each tactile behaviour accordingly. After each behaviour, they responded to two questions:

1. **Emotion Decoding:** "Please choose the term that best describes what this [robot or human] is communicating." Followed by the forced-choice methodology [14], thirteen forced-choice options were provided: *anger, disgust, fear, happiness, sadness, surprise, sympathy, embarrassment, love, envy, pride, gratitude*, and *none of these terms is correct*.
2. **Appropriateness Judgment:** "Do you think this tactile behaviour is appropriate?" Participants were instructed to select "Appropriate" if the behaviour could be considered appropriate for one of any scenarios in the described interaction context, and "Inappropriate" otherwise. If participants were uncertain, they could select the "Maybe" option.

3 Results and Analysis

3.1 Culture Decoding Results Analysis

We evaluated the decoding accuracy of participants across three cultural groups - Chinese, Belgian, and culturally unspecified (None)—for 12 emotions expressed through LLM-generated affective tactile behaviours. Each participant rated 54 stimuli, we got 3240 measurements in total. We performed one-sided binomial tests against the chance level ($1/13 \approx 7.7\%$) to assess whether emotion decoding results are significantly above chance. Bonferroni correction was applied to account for multiple comparisons.

Chi-Chi Participants Decoding Results. As shown in Table 1, 18 Chinese participants achieved significantly above-chance decoding for **anger** (50%, $p_{adj} < .001$), **fear** (37.0%, $p_{adj} < .001$), **gratitude** (27.8%, $p_{adj} < .001$), **love** (50%, $p_{adj} < .001$), **surprise** (24.1%, $p_{adj} < .01$), and **sympathy** (40.7%, $p_{adj} < .001$). Emotions such as **embarrassment, envy, pride,** and **happiness** did not exceed the chance threshold. The most frequently misclassified emotion was **love**, which was commonly mistaken for **gratitude** and **sympathy**, especially for emotions like **happiness, sadness,** and **disgust**. The results further demonstrate that although participants struggled to interpret all the LLM-generated affective tactile behaviours, they were still able to decode 6 out of 12 emotions at levels significantly above chance. Interestingly, previous studies on human-to-human tactile emotion decoding also found that individuals could reliably recognise six emotions—primarily prosocial emotions and three of Ekman's basic emotions: anger, fear, and disgust—while self-focused emotions remained difficult to identify. This suggests that LLMs are capable of generating meaningful affective tactile behaviours from text, with potential applications in guiding robots to perform culturally sensitive affective touch, which is comparable to the human encoder. Prior work has shown that robots can already be driven by LLMs to execute behaviours and facilitate mediated tactile interactions. Given that tactile communication is highly dependent on context and cultural norms, this study represents an important first step toward understanding how LLMs can support culturally adaptive affective touch, which could be a guide for future LLM-driven tactile interaction design.

Chi-Bel Participants Decoding Results. In the Chi-Bel condition, 18 Belgian participants were asked to decode the same set of tactile behaviours generated by the LLM for the Chinese cultural context (see Subsect. 3.1). The results showed significantly poorer performance compared to the Chi-Chi group. Among the 12 target emotions, only Love was successfully decoded above chance level ($p_{adj} < .01$). Specifically, participants in the Chi-Bel group correctly identified 1 out of 12 emotions, while participants in the Chi-Chi group decoded 6 out of 12 emotions successfully based on tactile behaviour alone. This discrepancy suggests that the LLM-generated tactile expressions may be more aligned with Chinese cultural norms, making them less interpretable for individuals from a Belgian cultural background.

Bel-Bel Participants Decoding Results. Belgian participants also demonstrated above-chance accuracy for several emotions: **anger** (59.3%, $p_{adj} < .001$), **fear** (31.5%, $p_{adj} < .001$), **gratitude** (20.4%, $p_{adj} < .05$), **love** (35.2%, $p_{adj} < .001$), **surprise** (22.2%, $p_{adj} < .01$), and **sympathy** (37.0%, $p_{adj} < .001$). However, recognition of self-focused emotions (**pride, embarrassment, envy**) and basic emotions like **happiness** and **disgust** remained at or near chance level. Misclassification patterns showed **happiness** was often confused with **love**, and **fear** was frequently confused with **surprise**.

Bel-Chi Participants Decoding Results. In the Bel-Chi group, 18 Chinese participants were asked to decode the same set of tactile behaviours generated by the LLM for the Belgian cultural context, identical to those used in the Bel-Bel group. The results indicate that Chinese participants were able to successfully decode anger and love at rates significantly above the chance level. This finding suggests that tactile behaviours generated for the Belgian cultural context may be aligned with Belgian norms and less suitable for Chinese cultural interpretations.

Participants from Non-Specified Culture. Across none cultural contexts, decoding performance remained significantly above chance for **anger** (48.1%, $p_{adj} < .001$), **fear** (29.6%, $p_{adj} < .001$), **gratitude** (27.8%, $p_{adj} < .001$), **love** (51.9%, $p_{adj} < .001$), **surprise** (20.4%, $p_{adj} < .05$), and **sympathy** (25.9%, $p_{adj} < .001$). This confirms the overall reliability of LLM-generated tactile behaviours in conveying these emotions. In contrast, emotions like **envy, pride,** and **embarrassment** were consistently difficult to recognise across all groups. Misclassification patterns revealed recurring confusion among closely related emotions, particularly between prosocial emotions such as **love, sympathy,** and **gratitude**.

Table 1. MDA refers to Matched-culture Decoding Accuracy, while MIDA refers to Mismatched-culture Decoding Accuracy (** at p < 0.01). FCE represent the most Frequently Chosen Emotions in the decoding of each target emotion and its corresponding frequency (f).

Emotion	Culture	FCE/f	MDA(%)	Culture	FCE/f	MIDA(%)
Ekman's emotions						
Anger	Chi-Chi	anger/27	50**	Chi-Bel	anger/17	18.5
	Bel-Bel	anger/32	59.3**	Bel-Chi	surprise/13	31.5**
	None	anger/26	48.1**	/	/	/
Fear	Chi-Chi	fear/20	37.0**	Chi-Bel	fear/14	9.3
	Bel-Bel	fear/17	31.5**	Bel-Chi	surprise/14	25.9**
	None	fear/16	29.6**	/	/	/
Happiness	Chi-Chi	love/20	13.0	Chi-Bel	love/14	13.0
	Bel-Bel	love/18	3.7	Bel-Chi	surprise/11	9.3
	None	love/15	14.8	/	/	/
Sadness	Chi-Chi	love/14	14.8	Chi-Bel	None correct/15	0
	Bel-Bel	love/12	5.6	Bel-Chi	sympathy/11	5.6
	None	love/16	16.7	/	/	/
Disgust	Chi-Chi	anger/24	16.7	Chi-Bel	anger/9	7.4
	Bel-Bel	anger/10	13.0	Bel-Chi	anger/7	14.8
	None	anger/12	18.5	/	/	/
Surprise	Chi-Chi	fear/12	24.1**	Chi-Bel	None correct/13	14.8
	Bel-Bel	surprise/12	22.2**	Bel-Chi	None correct/11	13.0
	None	surprise/11	20.4*	/	/	/
Self-focused emotions						
Embarrassment	Chi-Chi	fear/15	11.1	Chi-Bel	None correct/13	9.3
	Bel-Bel	love/11	7.4	Bel-Chi	love/12	7.4
	None	fear/17	5.6	/	/	/
Envy	Chi-Chi	fear/12	9.3	Chi-Bel	None correct/9	0
	Bel-Bel	love/12	1.9	Bel-Chi	disgust/5	3.7
	None	anger/8	5.6	/	/	/
Pride	Chi-Chi	love/13	3.7	Chi-Bel	None correct/20	5.6
	Bel-Bel	None correct/10	9.3	Bel-Chi	None correct/14	1.9
	None	None correct/9	5.6	/	/	/
Prosocial emotions						
Love	Chi-Chi	love/27	50**	Chi-Bel	None correct/15	22.2**
	Bel-Bel	love/19	35.2**	Bel-Chi	love/12	1.9
	None	love/28	51.9**	/	/	/
Gratitude	Chi-Chi	love/19	27.8**	Chi-Bel	None correct/13	7.4
	Bel-Bel	gratitude/11	20.4*	Bel-Chi	happiness/11	3.7
	None	gratitude/15	27.8**	/	/	/
Sympathy	Chi-Chi	sympathy/22	40.7**	Chi-Bel	love/12	16.7
	Bel-Bel	sympathy/20	37.0**	Bel-Chi	sympathy/9	11.1
	None	love/17	25.9**	/	/	/

Decoding accuracy and confusion emotions. * $p < .05$, ** $p < .01$.

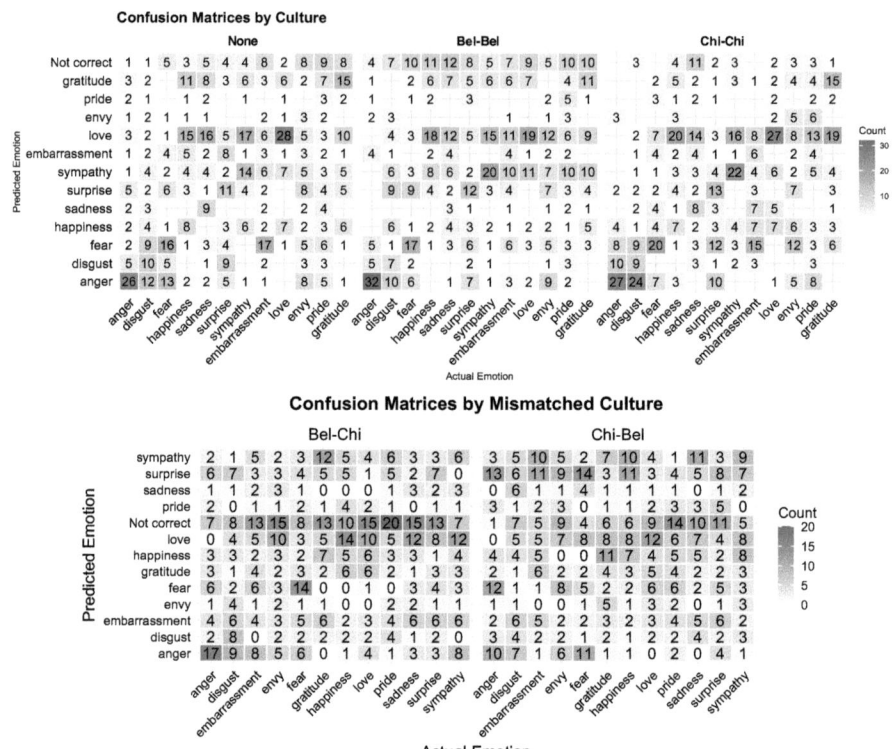

Fig. 1. Emotions across cultural groups (top) and for misinterpreted or inappropriate tactile responses (bottom).

3.2 Interaction Direction

Table 2 presents the number of responses categorised as "Appropriate," "Inappropriate," and "Maybe" for tactile behaviours in both the *robot-to-human* and *human-to-robot* conditions across different cultural groups.

To investigate cultural differences in the perception of tactile appropriateness, we conducted Chi-square goodness-of-fit tests within each cultural group (Chi-Chi, Chi-Bel, Bel-Bel, Bel-Chi, and All) to compare the frequencies of 'appropriate' and 'inappropriate' judgments. As shown in Table 2, the results revealed that all groups—except *Bel-Chi*—judged significantly more tactile behaviours as appropriate than inappropriate, suggesting a general cultural acceptance of the stimuli. Specifically, significant effects were observed in the *Chi-Chi* ($\chi^2 = 106.0$, $p < .001$), *Bel-Bel* ($\chi^2 = 82.4, p < .01$), *Chi-Bel* ($\chi^2 = 34.2, p < .01$), and *None* ($\chi^2 = 124.0, p < .01$) groups. In contrast, the *Bel-Chi* group did not show a significant preference for either response category ($\chi^2 = 3.0, p = .08$).

To examine between-group cultural mismatches, we conducted Chi-square tests of independence on appropriateness ratings between *Chi-Chi* vs. *Chi-Bel* and *Bel-Bel* vs. *Bel-Chi*. Significant group differences emerged in both comparisons. Notably, the *Chi-Chi* group gave significantly more *'appropriate'* ratings ($\chi^2 = 5.20, p = .02$) and fewer *'inappropriate'* ratings ($\chi^2 = 12.0, p < .01$) than the *Chi-Bel* group. Similarly, the *Bel-Bel* group rated significantly more *'appropriate'* ($\chi^2 = 21.5, p < .01$) and fewer *'inappropriate'* behaviours ($\chi^2 = 21.6, p < .01$) than the *Bel-Chi* group. These findings suggest that when LLMs generate tactile behaviours aligned with a specific cultural context, they may fail to adhere to the affective touch norms of other cultures. Consequently, participants from different cultural backgrounds are more likely to perceive such behaviours as socially inappropriate—an effect clearly reflected in the increased number of inappropriate ratings across mismatched groups.

To evaluate the influence of reciever identity (Human vs. Robot), we conducted Chi-square tests on appropriateness ratings. Results showed that human-to-robot interactions were significantly more associated with *'inappropriate'* judgments than robot-to-human interactions ($\chi^2 = 76.8, p < .001$), while robot-initiated expressions were more likely to be judged as *'appropriate'* ($\chi^2 = 18.8, p < .001$). Further analysis revealed that even when participants decoded the tactile behaviours as the same emotion, they showed greater caution in accepting robot-initiated touch toward humans than the reverse. Participants appeared more accepting of human-initiated emotional expressions toward robots.

Participants reported that many LLM-generated tactile behaviours were perceived as overly intimate or unnatural. While participants understood the intent to convey emotion, they noted that such gestures would rarely be used in real-life interactions. Discomfort was particularly high in the *robot-to-human* condition, where participants reported greater unease imagining themselves as the receiver of such touch. In contrast, emotional expressions from human to robot—especially for certain emotions—were seen as more acceptable,.

These findings indicate a potential asymmetry in the LLMs' capacity to model socially appropriate touch depending on the direction of interaction. LLMs appear to generate more plausible and acceptable tactile behaviours when simulating a human expressing emotion to a robot, possibly due to prompt design biases or a limited understanding of the social boundaries associated with human tactile reception.

3.3 Misclassification and Appropriateness Patterns

We further examined the most frequently chosen emotions for each target emotion, as shown in Table 1 and Fig. 1. Additionally, we investigated which tactile behaviours were perceived as inappropriate and analysed their corresponding decoded emotions. As illustrated in Fig. 2, participants tended to associate certain negative or highly intimate emotions, such as anger and even love, with inappropriate tactile expressions. For example, one touch behaviour decoded as anger was described as "a quick, sharp pinch on the skin followed by an abrupt release", while a touch behaviour decoded as love is "lightly running fingertips along the human's arm, starting from the elbow and moving toward the hand in a soothing and gentle manner." In mismatched cultural conditions, a similar

Table 2. Appropriateness (number and its corresponding percentage) of the given tactile behaviour description.

Culture	Reciever	Appropriate	Inappropriate	Maybe
Chi-Chi	Human	(170, 52.5%)	(95, 29.3%)	(59, 18.2%)
	Robot	(193, 59.6%)	(39, 12.0%)	(92, 28.4%)
Chi-Bel	Human	(144, 44.4%)	(128, 39.5%)	(52, 16.0%)
	Robot	(177, 54.6%)	(61, 18.8%)	(86, 26.5%)
Bel-Bel	Human	(131, 40.4%)	(95, 29.3%)	(98, 30.2%)
	Robot	(200, 61.7%)	(40, 12.3%)	(84, 25.9%)
Bel-Chi	Human	(127, 39.2%)	(112, 34.6%)	(85, 26.2%)
	Robot	(120, 37.0%)	(98, 30.2%)	(106, 32.7%)
All	Human	(154, 47.5%)	(87, 26.9%)	(83, 25.6%)
	Robot	(211, 65.1%)	(33, 10.2%)	(80, 24.7%)

pattern emerged: participants were more likely to judge behaviours as inappropriate when they were associated with negative emotions or when the intended emotion could not be accurately decoded. Interestingly, some tactile behaviours interpreted as conveying love were also rated as inappropriate—likely due to their perceived level of physical intimacy. These findings highlight the social boundaries and cultural sensitivities surrounding affective touch, especially when generated by non-human agents.

For matched cultures, the misclassification data showed that participants tended to decode the intended emotions as socially oriented ones or the Ekman six basic emotions, such as love, anger and fear. Notably, emotions like envy, pride, and embarrassment were frequently misinterpreted as prosocial emotions such as love, sympathy, or gratitude. This trend suggests that participants struggled to decode self-focused or socially complex emotions and instead defaulted to more familiar or socially desirable interpretations. Additionally, emotions decoded as negative, such as anger, were often rated as inappropriate. For mismatched cultures, they tend to decode tactile behaviours as none of the given emotions are correct.

3.4 Limitations

This study has several limitations. First, participants decoded tactile behaviours based solely on textual descriptions, without any visual or physical representation. Providing visualisations or haptic feedback could improve ecological validity and decoding accuracy. Second, while we included both Chinese and Belgian participants, the findings may not generalise to other cultures with different touch norms. Third, to explore the expressive range of LLMs, we intentionally avoided placing strict moral or social constraints on the prompts. This design choice may have led to the generation of behaviours perceived as overly intimate or

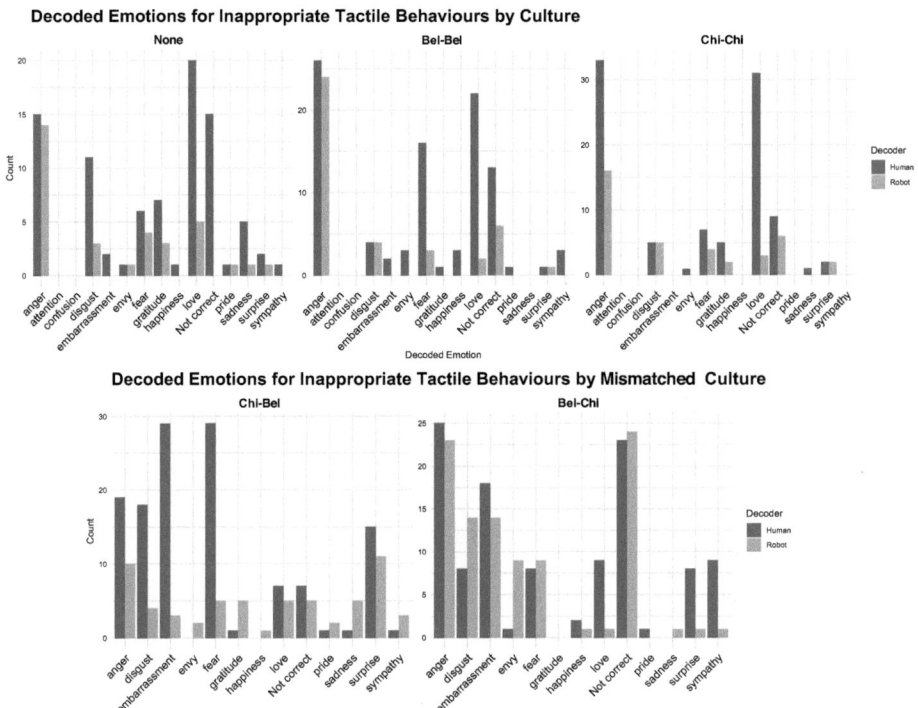

Fig. 2. Emotions across cultural groups (top) and for misinterpreted or inappropriate tactile responses (bottom). Red bars indicate *robot-to-human*, and blue bars indicate that *human-to-robot* (Color figure online).

unrealistic. In addition, the results might be influenced by the education, the participants's attention and familiarity with the robot's tactile interaction. Moreover, all the questionnaires are in English, which could also limit the participants' interpretation as English is not the native language of Chinese and Belgian participants. Lastly, the interaction design was unidirectional, with LLMs serving only as encoders. Future work should explore bidirectional human-robot tactile interaction to better reflect real-world dynamics.

4 Conclusion

This study investigated the potential of large language models (LLMs) to generate culturally and socially appropriate tactile behaviours for conveying emotion in human-robot interaction. By examining participants from different cultural backgrounds, we identified key insights into how LLM-generated touch behaviours are perceived across emotion types and interaction directions. First, LLMs were generally successful at producing tactile behaviours that conveyed socially oriented emotions, such as anger, fear, love, and sympathy, within cultural contexts. However, self-focused emotions like embarrassment, pride, and envy were more difficult for participants to decode, highlighting inherent challenges in modelling these more introspective states. Second, interaction direction played a significant role in perceived appropriateness: participants rated behaviours as more acceptable when humans expressed emotion toward robots than when robots initiated touch. This asymmetry underscores the importance of contextual grounding and role expectations in human-robot touch dynamics. Third, our findings reveal that LLMs are capable of cultural adaptation when generating affective touch behaviours. When emotion descriptions were mismatched with a participant's cultural context, decoding performance declined, and behaviours were more frequently rated as inappropriate. This suggests that LLMs can incorporate cultural cues when guided properly, but also highlights the risks of cross-cultural misalignment.

Together, these results demonstrate the promise of LLMs in supporting affective tactile interaction, while also emphasising the critical need for cultural sensitivity and contextual awareness in the design of socially intelligent robots. This work represents an important step toward leveraging LLMs for culturally adaptive and emotionally expressive tactile interfaces in future human-robot interaction.

References

1. Chen, X., Zhang, M.T.: Emotions: investigating the vital role of tactile interaction. In: International Conference on Human-Computer Interaction, pp. 326–344. Springer (2024)
2. Lim, V., Rooksby, M., Cross, E.S.: Social robots on a global stage: establishing a role for culture during human–robot interaction. Int. J. Soc. Robot. **13**(6), 1307–1333 (2021)
3. Gallace, A., Spence, C.: The science of interpersonal touch: an overview. Neurosci. Biobehav. Rev. **34**(2), 246–259 (2010)
4. Sorokowska, A., et al.: Affective interpersonal touch in close relationships: a cross-cultural perspective. Pers. Soc. Psychol. Bull. **47**(12), 1705–1721 (2021)
5. Zhang, K., et al.: Generative artificial intelligence in robotic manipulation: a survey. arXiv preprint arXiv:2503.03464 (2025)
6. Wang, J., et al.: Large language models for robotics: opportunities, challenges, and perspectives. J. Autom. Intell. (2024)
7. Pawar, S., et al.: Survey of cultural awareness in language models: text and beyond. arXiv preprint arXiv:2411.00860 (2024)
8. Mahadevan, K., et al.: Generative expressive robot behaviors using large language models. In: Proceedings of the 2024 ACM/IEEE International Conference on Human-Robot Interaction, pp. 482–491 (2024)
9. Ren, Q., Belpaeme, T.: Touched by chatgpt: using an LLM to drive affective tactile interaction. arXiv preprint arXiv:2501.07224 (2025)
10. Cekaite, A., Mondada, L.: Towards an interactional approach to touch in social encounters. In: Touch in Social Interaction, pp. 1–26. Routledge (2020)
11. Willemse, C.J.A.M., Van Erp, J.B.F.: Social touch in human-robot interaction: robot-initiated touches can induce positive responses without extensive prior bonding. Int. J. Soc. Robot. **11**(2), 285–304 (2019)

12. Yohanan, S., MacLean, K.E.: The role of affective touch in human-robot interaction: Human intent and expectations in touching the haptic creature. Int. J. Soc. Robot. **4**, 163–180 (2012)
13. Ren, Q., Belpaeme, T.: Tactile interaction with social robots influences attitudes and behaviour. Int. J. Soc. Robot. **16**(11), 2297–2317 (2024)
14. Hertenstein, M.J., Keltner, D., App, B., Bulleit, B.A., Jaskolka, A.R.: Touch communicates distinct emotions. Emotion **6**(3), 528 (2006)
15. Janssens, R., Wolfert, P., Demeester, T., Belpaeme, T.: Integrating visual context into language models for situated social conversation starters. IEEE Trans. Affect. Comput. (2024)

Knowledge-Based Design Requirements for Persuasive Generative Social Robots in Eldercare

Stephan Vonschallen[1,2,3](✉) , Ennio Zumthor[2], Markus Simon[2], Theresa Schmiedel[1] , and Friederike Eyssel[3]

[1] ZHAW Zurich University of Applied Sciences, 8400 Winterthur, Switzerland
stephan.vonschallen@zhaw.ch
[2] FHNW University of Applied Sciences and Arts Northwestern Switzerland, 4052 Basel, Switzerland
[3] UNIBI University of Bielefeld, 33615 Bielefeld, Germany

Abstract. Social robots powered by generative AI such as Large Language Models open new possibilities for human-robot interaction by enabling natural, human-like conversations. Consequently, these generative social robots (GSRs) become more capable of influencing user attitudes and behavior through persuasion. In the present research, we conducted qualitative interviews with caregivers and therapists to identify knowledge-based design requirements for persuasive GSRs that promote physiotherapy attendance of residents in a Swiss eldercare facility. Our findings demonstrate that available information about the robot's role as a caregiver assistant, as well as its assertive and polite personality would increase the robot's ability to build trust and acceptance. Furthermore, having information on context factors like therapy benefits, facility routines, and news updates would allow the robot to flexibly and adequately adapt its persuasion attempts. Lastly, available information regarding user biography, emotions, and health status, enables the robot to engage in personalized persuasion. Taken together, the present findings highlight the importance of considering self-, context-, and user-related knowledge as key dimensions to integrate into GSRs. This could be realized through prompting techniques, fine-tuning, database access, and the robot's real-time perception.

Keywords: Social Robotics · Persuasion · Design Requirements · Large Language Models · Robot Knowledge · Eldercare

1 Introduction

As the global population ages, the demand for eldercare services increases [1]. Social robots represent a promising solution to address this challenge by assisting with caregiving tasks [2], offering companionship [3], and encouraging healthy behaviors [4] among elderly individuals. Many of these tasks require nuanced communication between

---
F. Eyssel and T. Schmiedel—Share senior authorship.

robots and human users. One of the primary ways social robots can impact human users through communication is by convincing or encouraging their interaction partners to change their attitudes, beliefs, and behaviors [5]. In other words: Social robots may serve as persuasive agents. In the past, social robots lacked refined communication skills. This represented a key obstacle to social robot integration in eldercare. However, more recently, human-robot interaction (HRI) and communication have advanced greatly given the rapid developments in generative artificial intelligence (AI), particularly regarding Large Language Models (LLMs) [6]. Social robots that are integrated with generative AI can autonomously process available information into observable behavior. We refer to such robots as Generative Social Robots (GSRs). LLM-powered GSRs enable natural, personalized, and adaptive interactions with humans [7–10].

The introduction of persuasive GSRs in eldercare bears both opportunities and risks: On the one hand, these robots may improve the well-being of elderly individuals by motivating users and engaging them in natural and human-like communication [11]. They can promote health-related behaviors like staying hydrated [12], complying with medical recommendations (e.g., taking prescribed medication, doing exercises) [13], or performing mental activities to prevent cognitive decline [4]. On the other hand, their unpredictable nature raises concerns regarding GSR's potential for deception [14], concerns regarding privacy and data security [15], or unlawful actions [16].

Hence, it is crucial to ensure responsible persuasion with GSRs that align with actual user needs while adhering to social norms and ethical standards. This is especially important when vulnerable users are involved, such as individuals with disabilities, children or the elderly. To illustrate, persuading elderly residents to attend physiotherapy sessions requires the robot to demonstrate assertiveness in order to enhance therapy adherence. Simultaneously, the robot must respect individual choices and restrictions, e.g., when a person feels ill. In this case, responsible robot behavior requires nuanced knowledge of the user's motivational and physical state.

Current frameworks for responsible robot design in eldercare, such as Care-Centered Value Sensitive Design (CCVSD) [17] support the alignment of a robot's behavior with human-centered values such as the need for companionship, independence, and privacy [18, 19]. However, while those frameworks do focus on design requirements for observable robot behavior, they typically neglect essential prerequisites, such as the types of knowledge a GSR would require to optimize its behavior (e.g., knowledge on *how* to respect privacy, provided through explicit LLM system prompting).

While GSR behavior cannot be fully controlled due to its probabilistic nature [20], its *knowledge* – i.e., the information made available to generative AI – can be carefully managed. More precisely, the *knowledge* of GSRs may be regulated by various factors, including prompting strategies, fine-tuning of AI models, data curation, real-time perception, and access to external information sources [21]. By strategically managing these knowledge inputs, developers can influence how a GSR interacts with users. This highlights the need to identify the types of knowledge GSRs require to be deployed in real-world environments like eldercare. The goal of this study was to identify such knowledge-based design requirements that guide the development of a GSR used to persuade elderly individuals to attend therapy sessions. By providing the GSRs with optimal knowledge configurations, its persuasive behavior can be guided in a responsible way that benefits users while adhering to social norms and moral values.

2 Related Work

Existing design frameworks for social robot development do not fully account for the challenges posed by autonomous GSR behavior generation. One such framework is Value Sensitive Design (VSD) [22]. VSD integrates human values, such as privacy, fairness, and autonomy in the design process. It involves a tripartite methodology – conceptual, empirical, and technical investigation – to guarantee that ethical considerations are embedded in design decisions. CCVSD [17] extends VSD to the context of social robots used for care practices by emphasizing care ethics, ensuring that technologies support relationships, well-being, and contextual moral considerations. It prioritizes responsiveness to users' needs, acknowledging vulnerability and interdependence in design decisions. Umbrello et al. [23] further expanded CCVSD to include values that are specific to AI by integrating guidelines such as the AI for Social Good (AI4SG) [24] principles. While Umbrello et al. [23] offer useful design requirements in terms of what behaviors users expect from robots to align with human-centered values (e.g., the need for automatic user recognition for contextualized interactions to support human autonomy), they fail to consider how GSRs generate this behavior by processing available information. It remains largely unexplored what information a robot would need to know in order to express desired behaviors.

Three primary types of robot knowledge – *self-knowledge*, *context-knowledge*, and *user-knowledge* – have been identified to guide a robot's behavior [25]. First, *self-knowledge* refers to the robot's internal understanding of its role, personality, and limitations. This includes predefined behavioral guidelines that shape the robot's interactions. For example, recent work has demonstrated that LLMs successfully adopt personality traits [9, 26–29]. By managing such characteristics, developers may ensure that the robot adheres to ethical boundaries and fosters trust among users. Second, *context-knowledge* includes information about situational factors that influence the interaction. For instance, LLMs trained with specialized knowledge on a topic had greater success in debates by delivering more well-informed and persuasive arguments [30]. By utilizing *context-knowledge*, the robot can tailor its persuasive strategies to align with the specific interaction setting, enhancing its effectiveness while ensuring its behavior remains appropriate for the given use case. Third, *user-knowledge* encompasses information about the human interaction partner that is available to the GSR. This knowledge allows the robot to personalize its persuasive messages, making them more relevant and effective. For instance, a GSR that understands a user's personality [31], preferences [32, 33] or emotional states [9, 34, 35] may tailor its communication to the user to increase engagement and compliance. This is known as personalization [36].

3 Methodology

The present research aims to provide knowledge-based design requirements to guide a GSR's persuasive behavior in accordance with what healthcare workers in eldercare would envision. Reminding and motivating residents in eldercare facilities to attend therapy sessions was identified as a relevant use case in discussions and workshops conducted prior to this study, involving eldercare residents, physiotherapists, and caregivers. Non-compliance to participate in physiotherapy was determined as an ongoing problem among elderly care recipients. This problem calls for new, innovative solutions [37–39]. However, a robot that can successfully persuade elderly residents to attend physiotherapy requires nuanced social understanding to correctly interpret and adapt its behavior based on human and context cues. This challenge represents a compelling use case for GSRs, as GSRs can adapt their behavior based on available knowledge.

3.1 Sample

Five caregivers and five geriatric physiotherapists (see Table 1 for sample characteristics) were interviewed by a member of the research team in a Swiss eldercare facility in November 2024. All participants had experience in persuading elderly care recipients to attend physiotherapy. Their familiarity with social robots in eldercare stemmed from previous involvement in research studies or presentations featuring social robots deployed at the facility. Thus, they could easily envision how social robots interact with the elderly residents. Participant recruitment was facilitated by the head of the care division at the eldercare facility.

Table 1. List of participants

Participant	Gender	Age	Role
P1	Female	27	Caregiver
P2	Male	25	Caregiver
P3	Female	18	Apprentice Therapist
P4	Female	30	Therapist
P5	Female	29	Therapist
P6	Female	18	Apprentice Caregiver
P7	Female	43	Therapist
P8	Male	47	Therapist
P9	Female	18	Apprentice Caregiver
P10	Male	17	Apprentice Caregiver

3.2 Procedure

Semi-structured interviews were conducted to identify the robot's required *self-knowledge, context-knowledge* and *user-knowledge*. The interviews were conducted in German and took approximately half an hour, ranging from 18 to 37 min. After providing informed consent, the robot use case was introduced. To do so, a detailed scenario was presented in which a GSR entered a resident's room, informed the resident about an upcoming physiotherapy session and motivated the resident to attend. This was inspired by CCVSD [17], where a clear description of the care practice is crucial to derive design requirements. Participants learned that GSRs generate behavior based on knowledge that is available to them. They were instructed that the upcoming interview would focus on information the robot should be aware of to motivate residents effectively. Participants were asked to keep in mind that the behavior of the robot should be responsible. Accordingly, it should be ethically guided and in line with human-centered values and social norms. This aspect was inspired by VSD [22]. Further, participants were instructed to base their responses on what they considered an ideal robot, rather than what participants believe is technologically feasible. This instruction was added to avoid biases stemming from individual expectations regarding current robot technologies.

Next, participants were asked about their professional role and function in the eldercare facility and how they would usually motivate residents to attend physiotherapy sessions themselves. They were also questioned about previous experiences with social robots. Five structured questions then served to explore the robot's expected behavior and the required *self-*, *context-*, and *user-knowledge* to exert this behavior (see Table 2). Asking for the robot's expected behavior that it would need to fulfill its task from the perspective of therapist and caregivers was necessary to align the robot's required knowledge to relevant outcomes in terms of ethicality and effectiveness. To make the concept of *self-knowledge* more relatable to participants, we inquired about specific aspects of the robot's expected role and personality. Exploratory follow-up questions were posed after each question to gain a deeper understanding of participants' reasoning.

Table 2. Key constructs and corresponding interview questions

Construct	Question
Robot Behavior	Q1: What behaviors should the robot exhibit to motivate residents to participate in therapy?
User-Knowledge	Q2: What information about the residents would be helpful for the robot to better interact with them and motivate them to attend therapy?
Self-Knowledge	Q3: What role should the robot take on, in your opinion, to encourage residents to participate in therapy?
Self-Knowledge	Q4: What personality traits should the robot have to motivate residents to attend therapy?
Context-Knowledge	Q5: What knowledge about the therapy process and environment should the robot have in order to better motivate the residents?

3.3 Data Analysis

All interviews were recorded, transcribed, and analyzed using qualitative content analysis [40], a method to identify patterns and themes within text data. Qualitative content analysis involves coding text into categories derived either inductively from the data or deductively based on prior theory, allowing for a structured, yet flexible analysis. This method was chosen to ensure a coherent and transparent analysis of the expert insights gained from participants. Following a deductive approach, we categorized responses according to the constructs under investigation: *Self-knowledge, context-knowledge,* and *user-knowledge* (Table 3). Sixteen subcategories were inductively added throughout the coding process to differentiate between specific knowledge-based design requirements for GSRs in eldercare. Overall, 137 text passages were coded. The coding was done by a member of the research team and continuously reviewed by a second member of the research team. Instead of calculating inter-rater reliability, we prioritized reaching a consensus on coding through continuous discourse to enhance interpretative depth and reflexivity in our qualitative analysis, as some research suggest [41].

Table 3. Overview of categories identified in qualitative analysis

Category	Subcategory	Example
Self-Knowledge *i.e., information about itself (role & personality) available to the robot*	Role & Identity	"The robot should act like an assistant to the caregiving staff." (P3)
	Personality Traits	"Kindness and patience are essential to support residents and promote a respectful interaction." (P4)
	Assertiveness	"The robot should withdraw when the resident says no." (P1)
	Communication Style	"A friendly face and gestures such as clapping could increase motivation." (P4)
	Competence Signaling	"Trust is linked to competence. If the robot does not convey competence, it may undermine users' trust." (P1)
Context-Knowledge *i.e., information about the context available to the robot*	Therapy Content & Benefits	"The robot should have basic knowledge about therapy, e.g., what it includes and when it takes place." (P6)
	Facility Layout & Routines	"It is important that the robot is familiar with the premises and understands the environment." (P2)
	External News Hooks	"The robot should recognize whether external factors like the weather or current news encourage conversation." (P6)

(continued)

Table 3. (*continued*)

Category	Subcategory	Example
	Social Norms	"The residents view the care facility as their home, and the robot should respect their privacy." (P6)
User-Knowledge *i.e., information about the user available to the robot*	Identity & Demographics	"The robot should address the resident by name in order to establish a personal connection." (P7)
	Biography	"Knowing the residents' language, hobbies, and past professions helps to better motivate them." (P5)
	Preferences & Interests	"Personal interests and preferences – like cooking – can develop trust and meaningful interactions." (P3)
	Personal Goals	"The robot should know what goals the residents have – like going back to town – and use them to motivate." (P4)
	Emotional State	"Recognizing the residents' emotional state is important in order to respond more appropriately." (P7)
	Health & Functional Status	"Diagnoses and emotional states should be known, e.g., depression, borderline." (P2)
	Therapy Progress	"Progress in therapy can be used to motivate residents, for example by referring to goals and milestones." (P9)

Note. Subcategories and example statements were translated from German

4 Results

Multiple design requirements that relate to the robot's *self-knowledge* were identified in the qualitative interviews. All participants regarded empathy and politeness as critical aspects of the robot's behavior. For example, a friendly facial expression or using gestures was deemed necessary to increase motivation and make interactions feel more natural (P2, P3, P4, P5, P6, P7). Two participants noted that a robot with a natural, courteous and understanding tone of voice would foster a sense of comfort and approachability

(P4, P5). Realizing this requires robot *self-knowledge* about its character. Overall, a polite, empathetic character was deemed important that relates to patients' needs and can act appreciative and respectful. The ability to be patient was mentioned multiple times in this regard (P2, P4, P5, P8, P10). Furthermore, the robot should not be overly dominant (P4, P5, P8). Participants consistently emphasized that the robot must respect residents' boundaries, particularly when faced with patients' refusal to go along with the robot's suggestions. The robot's ability to recognize when to stop persuading was highlighted as essential, particularly to maintain trust and to prevent frustration. For example, caregiver P1 stated: *"The robot should know when it makes no sense to keep pushing and stop."* However, as caregiver P1 continued:*" Not feeling like it is not a valid reason, whereas being sick would be a valid reason for not going to therapy."* In other words, the robot should not be too yielding either. This leads to another commonly discussed aspect of *self-knowledge*: The need for the robot to have a clearly defined role (Ps1, P2, P3, P5, P6, P7, P8, P9). Participants widely agreed that the robot should serve as a caregiving assistant, balancing supportiveness with professionalism while avoiding an overly medical or authoritarian presence. Only one participant (P7) wanted the robot to adopt the role of a good friend or companion. Interviewees wanted the robot to be accepted, trusted and respected by residents, providing a sense of competence and safety.

Regarding the *context-knowledge* a robot should have access to, several factors were suggested to enable context-appropriate robot behavior. For example, participants wanted the robot to be aware of therapy schedules (P1, P2, P3, P7, P8, P9, P10), and to know the contents and benefits of therapy sessions (P2, P3, P4, P5, P6, P7, P9, P10). For instance, caregiver P1 explained: *"The robot should know what therapy is planned, its duration, and whether it is a group or individual session."* Awareness of the care facility's daily routines also emerged as a key theme (P1, P4, P6, P8, P9). Participants noted that a robot which is familiar with the institution's regime, including events and meal schedules, would integrate more seamlessly into residents' lives. Furthermore, both therapists and caregivers mentioned that it is important for the robot to know the structure and physical environment of the facility (P1, P2, P3, P4, P5, P6, P10). To illustrate, therapist P5 stated:*" Knowledge about the physical environment, such as the courtyard or walking paths, can be used as motivation to take the path to therapy"*. In addition, some participants mentioned that the robot should know mundane news, e.g., about sports or the weather, (P6, P8, P9) to engage participants in motivating conversations.

Lastly, *user-knowledge* requirements were identified, with participants stressing that personalization is key to meaningful, safe, and effective interactions. Being aware of personal information, such as user hobbies, past experiences, and preferences, was cited by all participants as a means of building rapport and trust. The apprentice therapist P3 highlighted this by stating:*" Knowing the resident's biography is crucial for building relationships and motivation"*. Another key aspect related to *user-knowledge* concerns information about the patients' progress in therapy or individual goals in order to focus on positive aspects when motivating to attend therapy (P2, P3, P4, P7, P8, P9, P10). Therapist P4 explained this by saying:*" The robot should know the residents' goals, such as going back to the city, to use them as motivation."* Participants also emphasized the robot's ability to recognize and respond to emotional states (P1, P2, P3, P5, P6, P7, P8, P10). Emotional sensitivity was regarded as a crucial trait for the robot, enabling it to offer appropriate responses to feelings of sadness, frustration, or joy. This ability was seen as essential for maintaining a supportive and empathetic connection with residents. The apprentice caregiver P6 stated: *"Recognizing the residents' emotional state is very important in order to respond appropriately."* Another common insight was the importance of health awareness (P2, P4, P5, P9, P10). Participants noted that understanding a resident's physical and cognitive limitations would allow the robot to tailor its interactions, ensuring safety and appropriateness. However, there is also a need for privacy and data security in this regard, as therapist P8 noted: *"The robot should only store specific information that is relevant to the resident and handle it discreetly."*

The interviews also revealed interdependencies between different types of robot knowledge: For instance, for the robot to show the right amount of assertiveness, both personality traits (i.e., *self-knowledge*) that support assertive behavior and knowledge about the user's health and emotional state (i.e., *user-knowledge*) were deemed necessary for the robot to be able to differentiate between a simple lack of motivation on the part of the user or the presence of actual health conditions that make attending therapy impossible. Furthermore, motivating residents to attend therapy by referring to an individual's therapy progress (i.e., *user-knowledge*) would require knowledge about the contents of specific therapy sessions (i.e., *context-knowledge*). Similarly, using relevant information about daily news (i.e., *context-knowledge*) to motivate residents may be more effective if the robot had information about users' preferred news (i.e., *user-knowledge*). To illustrate, one resident of the elder care facility that took part in preliminary workshops was very fond of stories about astronauts and science-fiction. Making use of this information by telling her news about astronomy and relating them to physiotherapy (e.g., statements like *"Astronauts have to do exercises too"*), could potentially increase her motivation to attend physiotherapy sessions.

Figure 1 summarizes the main findings from the qualitative analysis, including the identified knowledge-based design requirements (light blue boxes) categorized in *self-knowledge*, *context-knowledge* and *user-knowledge* (dark blue boxes), and their descriptions (white text boxes). Implications for these findings will be further discussed in the next section.

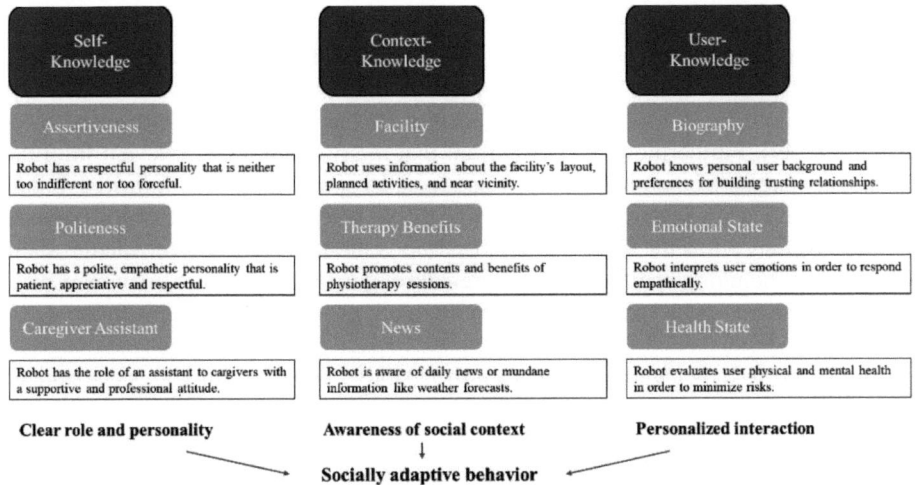

Fig. 1. Summary of knowledge-based design requirements

5 Discussion

This study identified knowledge-based design requirements for persuasive GSRs in eldercare. Based on qualitative interviews with caregivers and therapists, we gained key insights into what information a GSR needs to motivate physiotherapy attendance. Our findings address a research gap in existing design frameworks, which deem ethical principles relevant, but fail to address specific knowledge required to express adequate persuasive robot behavior.

To enable a responsible integration of persuasive GSRs in eldercare, our findings – consistent with prior research – highlight the importance of *socially adaptive* robot behavior [42] (Fig. 1). That is, it should respond appropriately to user states and the social context. To do so, the robot requires *self-knowledge*, i.e., knowledge about the robot's role and personality traits. The robot should exhibit *assertiveness*, balancing respect for users and the need to take action [43, 44]. This is especially important regarding ethically sound behavior, as the robot needs a keen sense of when to nudge residents for their own benefit and when to stop persuading and respect their decision [45].

At the same time, the GSR should behave in a polite, considerate, and empathetic manner (see also [46] or [45]). Interestingly, in a qualitative study by Lumer and Buchmeier [47], politeness was deemed particularly relevant for robots that relied on a rule-based dialogue system, and less so for systems that used rather human-like, socially adaptive politeness strategies. It is likely that in their research, expectations regarding robot functionalities might have influenced attitudes about politeness, whereas the present research excluded expectations about technological feasibility to reduce bias. Beyond the robot's personality, our results highlight the need for a clearly defined role as a *caregiver assistant*, ensuring the robot provides appropriate support while maintaining a professional and respectful attitude. A clear definition of roles is also important when asking care professionals how they envision social robots [48].

Moreover, *context-knowledge* was deemed essential for socially adaptive robot behavior. For instance, the robot should ideally be aware of the elder care *facility*, including its layout, planned activities, daily routines and workflows, as well as its near vicinity. This is also important for more general aspects of HRI as well, like socially aware robot navigation [49]. Furthermore, it is important that the robot provides relevant information about *benefits* of the physiotherapy sessions, as specialized topic knowledge may help generative AI to appear more persuasive [30]. Understanding the therapy contents and benefits may allow the GSR to boost user motivation. In addition, knowledge about current *news* including sports, scientific breakthroughs, or the weather, may be used to motivate residents, especially if this information aligns with the resident's interest [32, 33].

Finally, *user-knowledge* enables socially adaptive behavior through personalized HRI, an area that focuses on how robots adapt to user information, which has gained increased attention in recent years [31, 50, 51]. In the specific context of therapy motivation in eldercare, a GSR should be familiar with each user's *biography*, fostering trust through shared experiences and personal history. These aspects have been identified as important factors contributing to robot persuasion effectiveness and user acceptance [52]. In addition, the ability to recognize *emotional states* would allow the robot to respond appropriately, ensuring empathetic engagement. Relatedly, recent works indicate that the interaction quality of generative AI increases when the LLM is capable of recognizing emotions [34, 35]. Lastly, awareness of a resident's physical and mental *health state* would enable the robot to provide nuanced and well-tailored persuasion to increase user motivation. This is also important for the robot's assertive behavior, as the robot needs to know when a patient is physically and mentally capable of attending the physiotherapy session in order to promote attendance in a responsible way.

The integration of different types of knowledge within a GSR can be achieved through a combination of prompting techniques, fine-tuning, database access, and real-time perception capabilities [21]. Self-knowledge characteristics – such as robot personality and robot role – should ideally remain stable over time to guarantee consistent, predictable behaviors [28]. One way to embed these stable features is through static system prompts. System prompts are predefined instructions given to LLMs to shape its behavior, tone, and responses. System prompts establish foundational guidelines that ensure a GSR adheres to its intended role and personality [21]. For example, they can be used to integrate specific personality traits, such as assertiveness, by directly ordering the robot to assume this trait or by setting explicit behavioral rules. One such behavioral rule might limit persuasion attempts to a maximum of three to prevent excessive pressure on users (P2). Similarly, system prompts can define the robot's role by emphasizing that it functions as a caregiving assistant rather than a medical authority, ensuring role-congruent interactions with residents. Additionally, system prompts may help the robot consistently communicate therapy benefits, reinforcing motivational and supportive messaging. System prompts can also be used to encourage personalized interactions by instructing the robot to inquire about users' biographies, preferences, and activities, fostering a sense of familiarity and trust. As an alternative to prompting, fine-tuning the LLM may enable a more stable implementation of the robot's role and personality, that is more resistant to distractions [53]. By training the model on curated dialogues that reinforce responsible, polite, empathetic, and assertive behaviors, the robot can adopt an interaction style that aligns naturally with social norms and user expectations.

On the other hand, database access may be a more effective approach when it comes to information that changes over time or requires regular updates, like information about the patients' health. By retrieving stored data, the robot can personalize interactions by referencing past experiences, user preferences, and activity histories. This could enhance user engagement and trust by allowing the robot to recall details such as a resident's biography, therapy schedule, daily activities, and general health status. Our findings align with other studies that reported increased trust and compliance to personalized social robots [50, 54]. However, access to personal information must be implemented with strict privacy and data security measures to safeguard residents' sensitive information, echoing the concerns of other researchers [14, 55].

Lastly, real-time perception enables the robot to gather immediate contextual information about its environment and the individuals involved in the HRI. This includes physical environment detection, allowing the robot to assess room conditions, detect obstacles, and adapt its behavior accordingly. Emotion detection relies on algorithms that analyze facial expressions, voice tone, and body language to infer a resident's emotional state, enabling the robot to respond appropriately. Recently, Banna et al. [9] demonstrated that combining personalization with the robot's emotional expressiveness through gestures increased communication satisfaction. Relatedly, health state assessment uses integrated sensors and predictive algorithms to monitor signs of discomfort or fatigue. This allows the robot to adjust its motivational strategies responsibly, ensuring that it supports residents without causing undue strain. Together, these real-time perception capabilities enable the robot to engage more empathetically and responsibly with residents, fostering interactions that are both context-aware and ethically attuned.

6 Strengths and Limitations

The present research introduced a novel approach to explore knowledge-based design requirements for GSRs. The focus on the robot's required knowledge base, rather than simply its expected behavior, has the potential to allow for more robust and ethically sound robot design. Nevertheless, some methodological limitations have emerged. First, our study did not include perspectives of elderly residents. Given the challenges associated with interviewing cognitively impaired individuals [56], and their resulting difficulties in understanding the concept of knowledge-based design requirements, we have merely focused on exploring caregivers' and therapists' perspectives. Future studies should implement perspectives of the elderly residents within the design process, e.g., by providing lived experiences [57].

The interview questions were developed deductively in light of existing research [24]. Our focus was specifically on the categorization of *self-*, *user-*, and *context-knowledge*. Consequently, the present research failed to address content beyond the scope of these categorizations. For instance, we did not address required robot knowledge about persuasive strategies in the interviews. Hence, future qualitative research should include a more comprehensive overview of the constructs under investigation (e.g., by mentioning that *context-knowledge* also entails knowledge about persuasive strategies). Likewise, prospective research could implement more general questions about the robot's required knowledge at the onset of the qualitative interview.

Identifying knowledge-based design requirements is only one of many steps to realize responsible robot design. As the concept of robot knowledge is only relevant for GSRs, the approach is not suitable for the design of teleoperated robots or robots with solely rule-based dialogue systems. Further, our research approach does not address broader aspects of robot design, such as the robot's expected appearance and general functionality. Hence, it complements established frameworks for responsible design such as VSD [22] or AI4SG [24]. The present qualitative study also focused on communicative tasks rather than physical assistance, highlighting the need for future research that integrates both perspectives to refine social robot design in eldercare.

Further, as is typical for exploratory qualitative studies, our approach calls for empirical validation. While our preliminary results are promising, follow-up research should realize in-depth, systematic evaluations to further validate the proposed design requirements, ideally across different cultural contexts [58]. As a next step, our research agenda will include actual HRI scenarios to explore the effectiveness of GSRs behavior with various knowledge inputs. The current work guides such prospective research.

7 Conclusion

Several knowledge-based design requirements have been identified for the integration of GSRs in eldercare. A robot's clear role and personality, awareness of the social context, and personalization are important for socially adaptive, responsible and effective interactions. By regulating a GSR's *self-, context-,* and *user-knowledge*, its persuasive behavior can be impacted in a positive way. Hence, our research approach to identify knowledge-based design requirements complements existing responsible design frameworks, such as VSD [22] or AI4SG [24] that focus primarily on the robot's expected behavior. The integration of our approach within existing design strategies could help to ensure that persuasive GSRs act responsibly and effectively within eldercare environments and beyond.

From an applied perspective, the identified knowledge-based design requirements guide responsible system design of a GSR that motivates eldercare residents to attend physiotherapy. Beyond this specific application, the findings of this study have broader implications for social robot development. Ethical considerations, such as data security and privacy remain central to designing persuasive GSRs. Ensuring that robots respect user autonomy by limiting unnecessary access to knowledge is crucial in maintaining trust and safeguarding personal freedom. By strategically controlling what a robot knows and how it applies this knowledge, developers can strike a balance between effective persuasion and ethical responsibility, enabling the integration of socially acceptable and beneficial GSRs.

References

1. Boniol, M., Kunjumen, T., Nair, T.S., Siyam, A., Campbell, J., Diallo, K.: The global health workforce stock and distribution in 2020 and 2030: a threat to equity and 'universal' health coverage? BMJ Glob. Health **7**, e009316 (2022). https://doi.org/10.1136/bmjgh-2022-009316

2. Di Napoli, C., Ercolano, G., Rossi, S.: Personalized home-care support for the elderly: a field experience with a social robot at home. User Model. User-Adap. Inter. **33**, 405–440 (2023). https://doi.org/10.1007/s11257-022-09333-y
3. Lu, L.-C., Lan, S.-H., Hsieh, Y.-P., Lin, L.-Y., Lan, S.-J., Chen, J.-C.: Effectiveness of companion robot care for dementia: a systematic review and meta-analysis. Innov. Aging **5**, 1–13 (2021). https://doi.org/10.1093/geroni/igab013
4. Cobo Hurtado, L., Viñas, P.F., Zalama, E., Gómez-García-Bermejo, J., Delgado, J.M., Vielba García, B.: Development and usability validation of a social robot platform for physical and cognitive stimulation in elder care facilities. Healthcare **9**, 1067 (2021). https://doi.org/10.3390/healthcare9081067
5. Siegel, M., Breazeal, C., Norton, M.I.: Persuasive robotics: the influence of robot gender on human behavior. In: 2009 IEEE/RSJ International Conference on Intelligent Robots and Systems. IEEE, St. Louis, MO, USA, pp. 2563–2568 (2009). https://doi.org/10.1109/IROS.2009.5354116
6. Billing, E., Rosén, J., Lamb, M.: Language models for human-robot interaction. In: Companion of the 2023 ACM/IEEE International Conference on Human-Robot Interaction. ACM, Stockholm Sweden, pp. 905–906 (2023). https://doi.org/10.1145/3568294.3580040
7. Wang, C., et al.: LaMI: large language models for multi-modal human-robot interaction. In: Extended Abstracts of the CHI Conference on Human Factors in Computing Systems. pp 1–10. https://doi.org/10.1145/3613905.3651029
8. Kim, C.Y., Lee, C.P., Mutlu, B.: Understanding large-language model (LLM)-powered human-robot interaction. In: Proceedings of the 2024 ACM/IEEE International Conference on Human-Robot Interaction. ACM, Boulder CO USA, pp 371–380 (2024). https://doi.org/10.1145/3610977.3634966
9. Banna, T.T., Rahman, S., Tareq, M.: Beyond words: Integrating personality traits and context-driven gestures in human-robot interactions. In: Proceedings of the 24th International Conference on Autonomous Agents and Multiagent Systems. Detroit, Michigan, USA (2025)
10. Mahadevan, K., et al.: Generative expressive robot behaviors using large language models. In: Proceedings of the 2024 ACM/IEEE International Conference on Human-Robot Interaction, pp 482–491 (2024). https://doi.org/10.1145/3610977.3634999
11. Getson, C., Nejat, G.: Care providers' perspectives on the design of assistive persuasive behaviors for socially assistive robots. J. Am. Med. Dir. Assoc. **25**, 105084 (2024). https://doi.org/10.1016/j.jamda.2024.105084
12. Sather Iii, R., Soufineyestani, M., Imtiaz, N., Khan, A.: Assistive robots designed for elderly care and caregivers. Int. J. Robot. Control **3**, 1 (2021). https://doi.org/10.5430/ijrc.v3n1p1
13. Soares, A., Piçarra, N., Giger, J.-C., Oliveira, R., Arriaga, P.: Ethics 4.0: ethical dilemmas in healthcare mediated by social robots. Int. J. Soc. Robot. **15**, 807–823 (2023). https://doi.org/10.1007/s12369-023-00983-5
14. Ranisch, R., Haltaufderheide, J.: Rapid integration of LLMs in healthcare raises ethical concerns: an investigation into deceptive patterns in social robots. Digital Soc. **4**, 7 (2025). https://doi.org/10.1007/s44206-025-00161-2
15. Elendu, C., et al.: Ethical implications of AI and robotics in healthcare: a review. Medicine **102**, e36671 (2023). https://doi.org/10.1097/MD.0000000000036671
16. Zhou, R.: Risks of discrimination violence and unlawful actions in LLM-driven robots. Comput. Life 12, 53–56 (2024). https://doi.org/10.54097/taqbjh83
17. Van Wynsberghe, A.: Designing robots for care: care centered value-sensitive design. Sci. Eng. Ethics **19**, 407–433 (2013). https://doi.org/10.1007/s11948-011-9343-6
18. Poulsen, A., Burmeister, O.K., Greig, J., Ulhaq, A., Tien, D.: Value sensitive design of social robots: enhancing the lives of LGBT+ older adults. Int. J. Soc. Robot. **17**, 147–162 (2025). https://doi.org/10.1007/s12369-024-01201-6

19. Schmiedel, T., Zhong, V.J., Eyssel, F.: Towards a wave approach for value sensitive design in social robotics. In: Companion of the 2023 ACM/IEEE International Conference on Human-Robot Interaction. ACM, Stockholm Sweden, pp 592–596 (2023). https://doi.org/10.1145/3568294.3580154
20. Yao, Y., Duan, J., Xu, K., Cai, Y., Sun, Z., Zhang, Y.: A survey on large language model (LLM) security and privacy: the good, the bad, and the ugly. High-Confidence Comput. **4**, 100211 (2024). https://doi.org/10.1016/j.hcc.2024.100211
21. Berengueres, J.: How to regulate large language models for responsible AI. In: IEEE Transactions on Technology and Society, pp 191–197 (2024). https://doi.org/10.1109/TTS.2024.3403681
22. Friedman, B., Hendry, D.G.: Value Sensitive Design: Shaping Technology with Moral Imagination. The MIT Press (2019). https://doi.org/10.7551/mitpress/7585.001.0001
23. Umbrello, S., Capasso, M., Balistreri, M., Pirni, A., Merenda, F.: Value sensitive design to achieve the UN SDGs with AI: a case of elderly care robots. Mind. Mach. **31**, 395–419 (2021). https://doi.org/10.1007/s11023-021-09561-y
24. Floridi, L., Cowls, J., King, T.C., Taddeo, M.: How to design AI for social good: seven essential factors. Sci. Eng. Ethics **26**, 1771–1796 (2020). https://doi.org/10.1007/s11948-020-00213-5
25. Vonschallen, S., Eyssel, F., Schmiedel, T.: Understanding persuasive interactions between generative social robots and humans: the robot knowledge persuasion model (RKPM). Manuscript submitted for publication
26. Frisch, I., Giulianelli, M.: LLM agents in interaction: measuring personality consistency and linguistic alignment in interacting populations of large language models. In: Proceedings of the 1st Workshop on Personalization of Generative AI Systems (PERSONALIZE 2024). Association for Computational Linguistics, St. Julians, Malta, pp 102–111 (2024)
27. Imasaka, Y., Joho, H.: Effect of LLM's personality traits on query generation. In: Proceedings of the 2024 Annual International ACM SIGIR Conference on Research and Development in Information Retrieval in the Asia Pacific Region. ACM, Tokyo Japan, pp 249–258 (2024). https://doi.org/10.1145/3673791.3698433
28. Sparrenberg, L., Schneider, T., Deußer, T., Koppenborg, M., Sifa, R.: Correcting systematic bias in LLM-generated dialogues using big five personality traits. In: 2024 IEEE International Conference on Big Data (BigData). IEEE, Washington, DC, USA, pp 3061–3069 (2024). https://doi.org/10.1109/BigData62323.2024.10825941
29. Bodroža, B., Dinić, B.M., Bojić, L.: Personality testing of large language models: limited temporal stability, but highlighted prosociality. R. Soc. Open Sci. **11**, 240180 (2024). https://doi.org/10.1098/rsos.240180
30. Khan, A., et al.: Debating with more persuasive LLMs leads to more truthful answers. In: Proceedings of the 41st International Conference on Machine Learning ICML'24. pp 23662–23733 (2024)
31. Matz, S.C., Teeny, J.D., Vaid, S.S., Peters, H., Harari, G.M., Cerf, M.: The potential of generative AI for personalized persuasion at scale. Sci. Rep. **14**, 4692 (2024). https://doi.org/10.1038/s41598-024-53755-0
32. Gao, G., Taymanov, A., Salinas, E., Mineiro, P., Misra, D.: Aligning LLM agents by learning latent preference from user edits. In: Proceedings of the 38th Conference on Neural Information Processing Systems. Vancouver, BC, Canada (2024)
33. Lubos, S., Tran, T.N.T., Felfernig, A., Polat Erdeniz, S., Le, V.-M.: LLM-generated explanations for recommender systems. In: Adjunct Proceedings of the 32nd ACM Conference on User Modeling, Adaptation and Personalization. ACM, Cagliari Italy, pp 276–285 (2024). https://doi.org/10.1145/3631700.3665185
34. Liu, Z., Yang, K., Xie, Q., Zhang, T., Ananiadou, S.: EmoLLMs: a series of emotional large language models and annotation tools for comprehensive affective analysis. In: Proceedings

of the 30th ACM SIGKDD Conference on Knowledge Discovery and Data Mining. ACM, Barcelona Spain, pp 5487–5496 (2024). https://doi.org/10.1007/s12369-022-00870-5
35. Liu, C., et al.: Speak from heart: an emotion-guided LLM-based multimodal method for emotional dialogue generation. In: Proceedings of the 2024 International Conference on Multimedia Retrieval. ACM, Phuket Thailand, pp 533–542 (2024). https://doi.org/10.1145/3652583.3658104
36. Tarakli, I., et al.: Social robots personalisation: at the crossroads between engineering and humanities. In: Companion of the 2023 ACM/IEEE International Conference on Human-Robot Interaction. ACM, Stockholm Sweden, pp 920–922 (2023). https://doi.org/10.1145/3568294.3579953
37. Ley, C., Putz, P.: Efficacy of interventions and techniques on adherence to physiotherapy in adults: an overview of systematic reviews and panoramic meta-analysis. Syst. Rev. **13**, 137 (2024). https://doi.org/10.1186/s13643-024-02538-9
38. Forkan, R., Pumper, B., Smyth, N., Wirkkala, H., Ciol, M.A., Shumway-Cook, A.: Exercise adherence following physical therapy intervention in older adults with impaired balance. Phys. Ther. **86**, 401–410 (2006)
39. Room, J., Hannink, E., Dawes, H., Barker, K.: What interventions are used to improve exercise adherence in older people and what behavioural techniques are they based on? A systematic review. BMJ Open **7**, e019221 (2017). https://doi.org/10.1136/bmjopen-2017-019221
40. Mayring, P.: Qualitative content analysis: theoretical background and procedures. In: Bikner-Ahsbahs, A., Knipping, C., Presmeg, N. (eds.) Approaches to Qualitative Research in Mathematics Education. Springer, Netherlands, Dordrecht, pp 365–380 (2015). https://doi.org/10.1007/978-94-017-9181-6_13
41. Braun, V., Clarke, V.: Successful Qualitative Research: A Practical Guide for Beginners. Sage Publications, Inc (2013)
42. Tanevska, A., Rea, F., Sandini, G., Cañamero, L., Sciutti, A.: A socially adaptable framework for human-robot interaction. Front. Robot. AI **7**, 121 (2020). https://doi.org/10.3389/frobt.2020.00121
43. Babel, F., Kraus, J.M., Baumann, M.: Development and testing of psychological conflict resolution strategies for assertive robots to resolve human–robot goal conflict. Front. Robot. AI **7**, 591448 (2021). https://doi.org/10.3389/frobt.2020.591448
44. Paradeda, R., Ferreira, M.J., Oliveira, R., Martinho, C., Paiva, A.: What makes a good robotic advisor? The role of assertiveness in human-robot interaction. In: Salichs, M.A., et al. (eds.) Social Robotics, pp 144–154. Springer, Cham (2019). https://doi.org/10.1007/978-3-030-35888-4_14
45. Shachar, T., Greenbaum, D.: When a push becomes a shove: nudging in elderly care. Am. J. Bioeth. **19**, 78–80 (2019). https://doi.org/10.1080/15265161.2019.1588415
46. Ribino, P.: The role of politeness in human–machine interactions: a systematic literature review and future perspectives. Artif. Intell. Rev. **56**, 445–482 (2023). https://doi.org/10.1007/s10462-023-10540-1
47. Lumer, E., Buschmeier, H.: Should robots be polite? Expectations about politeness in human–robot interaction. Front. Robot. AI **10**, 1242127 (2023). https://doi.org/10.3389/frobt.2023.1242127
48. Soljacic, F., Law, T., Chita-Tegmark, M., Scheutz, M.: Robots in healthcare as envisioned by care professionals. Intel. Serv. Robot. **17**, 685–701 (2024). https://doi.org/10.1007/s11370-024-00523-8
49. Gao, Y., Huang, C.-M.: Evaluation of socially-aware robot navigation. Front. Robot. AI **8**, 721317 (2022). https://doi.org/10.3389/frobt.2021.721317
50. Ham, J.: Influencing robot influence: personalization of persuasive robots. Interact. Stud. **22**, 464–487 (2021). https://doi.org/10.1075/is.00012.ham

51. Hellou, M., Gasteiger, N., Lim, J.Y., Jang, M., Ahn, H.S.: Personalization and localization in human-robot interaction: a review of technical methods. Robotics **10**, 120 (2021). https://doi.org/10.3390/robotics10040120
52. Ghazali, A.S., Ham, J., Barakova, E., Markopoulos, P.: Persuasive robots acceptance model (PRAM): roles of social responses within the acceptance model of persuasive robots. Int. J. Soc. Robot. **12**, 1075–1092 (2020). https://doi.org/10.1007/s12369-019-00611-1
53. Lee, S., et al.: Do LLMs have distinct and consistent personality? TRAIT: personality test set designed for LLMs with psychometrics. Association for Computational Linguistics NAACL 2025, pp. 8397–8437 (2025). https://doi.org/10.18653/v1/2025.findings-naacl.469
54. Wang, L., Rau, P.-L.P., Evers, V., Robinson, B.K., Hinds, P.: When in Rome: the role of culture & context in adherence to robot recommendations. In: Proceeding of the 5th ACM/IEEE international conference on Human-robot interaction - HRI '10. ACM Press, Osaka, Japan, p 359 (2010). https://doi.org/10.1145/1734454.1734578
55. Grabler, R., Koeszegi, S.T.: Privacy beyond data: assessment and mitigation of privacy risks in robotic technology for elderly care. ACM Trans. Hum.-Robot Interact. **14**, 1–23 (2025). https://doi.org/10.1145/3689216
56. Beuscher, L., Grando, V.T.: Challenges in conducting qualitative research with individuals with dementia. Res. Gerontol. Nurs. **2**, 6–11 (2009). https://doi.org/10.3928/19404921-20090101-04
57. Ostrowski, A.K., Breazeal, C., Park, H.W.: Long-term co-design guidelines: empowering older adults as co-designers of social robots. In: 2021 30th IEEE International Conference on Robot & Human Interactive Communication (RO-MAN). IEEE, Vancouver, BC, Canada, pp 1165–1172 (2021). https://doi.org/10.1109/RO-MAN50785.2021.9515559
58. Papadopoulos, I., et al.: Socially assistive robots in health and social care: acceptance and cultural factors. Results from an exploratory international online survey. Jpn. J. Nurs. Sci. **20**, e12523 (2023). https://doi.org/10.1111/jjns.12523

Motion Control, Prosthetics and Functional Robotics

A Learning-Based Model Reference Adaptive Controller Implemented on a Prosthetic Hand Wrist

Shifa Sulaiman[✉][iD], Mohammad Gohari, Francesco Schetter, and Fanny Ficuciello

Department of Information Technology and Electrical Engineering, Università degli Studi di Napoli Federico II, Claudio, 21, 80125 Napoli, Italy
ssajmech@gmail.com

Abstract. The functionality and natural motion of prosthetic hands remain limited by the challenges in controlling compliant wrist mechanisms. Current control strategies often lack adaptability and incur high computational costs, which impedes real-time deployment in assistive robotics. To address this gap, this study presents a computationally efficient Neural Network (NN)-based Model Reference Adaptive Controller (MRAC) for a tendon-driven soft continuum wrist integrated with a prosthetic hand. The dynamic modeling of the wrist is formulated using Timoshenko beam theory, capturing both shear and bending deformations. The proposed NN-MRAC estimates the required tendon forces from deflection errors and minimizes deviation from a reference model through online adaptation. Simulation results demonstrate improved precision with a root mean square error (RMSE) of 6.14×10^{-4} m and a settling time of 3.2 s. Experimental validations confirm real-time applicability, with an average RMSE of 5.66×10^{-3} m, steady-state error of 8.05×10^{-3} m, and settling time of 1.58 s. These results highlight the controller's potential to enhance motion accuracy and responsiveness in soft prosthetic systems, thereby advancing the integration of adaptive intelligent control in wearable assistive devices.

Keywords: Model reference adaptive controller · Neural network · Prosthetic hand · Soft robotics

1 Introduction

Soft robotic prostheses [1] signify an innovative advancement that provides individuals with limb disabilities a more comfortable and natural range of motion than traditional rigid prosthetics. The integration of soft continuum sections facilitates complex movements, making them ideal for various applications. Elastic wires embedded within these soft segments act as tendons, offering flexibility, lightweight properties, affordability, and the capacity to withstand significant tensile forces. The use of Neural Network (NN) based Model Reference Adaptive

Controller (MRAC) for managing soft continuum sections significantly enhances system performance through real-time learning and adaptation [2]. This sophisticated control approach merges NN principles with adaptive control methods, enabling effective adjustments to dynamic environments and fluctuating system parameters. By implementing the adaptive NN- based neuro-controller, systems can achieve greater accuracy and stability, as it continuously fine-tunes its control actions based on environmental feedback. This feature is especially advantageous in complex and nonlinear systems where conventional control techniques may face challenges. Additionally, the adaptive neuro-controller aids in optimizing performance metrics, resulting in more efficient operations and lower energy consumption, making it an essential tool across various applications, including robotics, automotive systems, and industrial automation. The key contributions of this work are outlined as follows:

- Mathematical modelling of a soft continuum wrist using Timoshenko beam theory.
- Development of an NN based MRAC for the wrist motions.
- Simulation studies to demonstrate the advantages of the proposed controller.
- Experimental validations proving the effectiveness of the proposed controller during real-time implementations with reduced computational effort.

While the primary focus of this work is on the development of an NN-based MRAC for a tendon-driven soft prosthetic wrist, the broader implications in the context of social robotics and AI are equally significant. The proposed controller enhances the fluidity and naturalness of prosthetic hand motions, which is crucial for intuitive human-robot interaction. Such adaptability and responsiveness mirror the subtleties of human motor behavior, fostering seamless integration of assistive devices into daily life. Furthermore, the use of NNs for online adaptation exemplifies how artificial intelligence can enable socially aware and personalized robotics. This aligns with the objectives of social robotics, which prioritize empathy, adaptability, and autonomy in human-centered applications.

The deployment of an MRAC is significantly relevant in the field of control systems. This sophisticated control approach aims to improve system performance by adjusting to variations in system dynamics and external disturbances. Through the use of a reference model, the MRAC is capable of continuously modifying its parameters to guarantee that the output of the controlled system aligns closely with the desired trajectory specified by the model. The significance of incorporating a neuro-controller is paramount, serving as a vital link between NNs and control systems. These controllers enable real-time decision-making and problem-solving, which are critical in numerous domains, including robotics, automation, and artificial intelligence. By efficiently processing large datasets and identifying patterns, neuro-controllers enhance control strategies, resulting in more agile and effective systems across various sectors such as healthcare, manufacturing, and transportation.

Braganza *et al.* [3] introduced a controller for continuum robots that featured an NN feed-forward component to mitigate dynamic uncertainties. Experimental results with the OCTARM, a soft extensible continuum manipulator, indicated that the inclusion of the NN feed-forward element significantly improved the controller's efficacy. Additionally, an adaptive neuro-fuzzy control system aimed at regulating a flexible manipulator with a variable payload was presented in [4]. This controller combined a fuzzy logic controller (FLC) within a feedback loop and utilized two dynamic recurrent NNs in the forward path. Specifically, a dynamic recurrent identification network (RIN) was employed to determine the manipulator system's output, while a dynamic recurrent learning network (RLN) was used to adjust the weighting factor of the fuzzy logic. Furthermore, another approach involving an FLC and an adaptive neuro-fuzzy inference system (ANFIS) was proposed in [5] for controlling the input displacement of an innovative adaptive compliant gripper.

One significant limitation of continuum manipulators is that even slight modifications in the actuated lengths can result in substantial changes in the end effector's position. Consequently, it is essential for controllers to operate swiftly and with minimal computational demands. Currently, reinforcement learning (RL) techniques are being utilized to create motion control systems that improve the agility of soft robots. A continuous-time Actor-Critic framework aimed at tracking tasks for continuum 3D soft robots affected by Lipschitz disturbances was introduced in [6]. This method employed a reward-based temporal difference approach, enabling learning through a novel discontinuous adaptive mechanism for the Critic neural weights. The combination of the reward signal and the Bellman error approximation further refined the adaptive mechanism for the Actor neural weights. Additionally, a model-free approach for open-loop position control of a soft spatial continuum arm, leveraging deep RL methods, was demonstrated in [7], where Deep-Q Learning was applied to train the system in a simulated environment.

Melingui et al. [8] highlighted the importance of adaptive algorithms in mitigating negative impacts. Nonetheless, it has been noted that simply applying adaptive control laws is insufficient due to the dynamic characteristics of the robot model over time. An advanced adaptive control approach, referred to as the adaptive support vector regressor controller, was introduced in [9] for the position control of a soft continuum robot. This method employed optimization learning techniques that yielded global solutions while ensuring compact regressor sizes, facilitating quicker convergence of the closed-loop system and reducing execution time. Additionally, an adaptive NN control system consisting of two subcontrollers for a bionic hand was described [10]. The first subcontroller focused on the hand's kinematics through a distal supervised learning method, while the second addressed the kinetics using adaptive neural control. Collectively, these subcontrollers improved the assessment of the control architecture's stability and ensured the convergence of Cartesian errors. An adaptive controller strategy based on NNs for a soft robotic arm was presented in [11]. The dynamic model of the arm was constructed by combining screw theory with Cosserat theory. The system also considered unmodeled dynamics, leading to the formulation of an adaptive NN controller that employed the back-stepping method in conjunction with a radial basis function NN.

A thorough review of the literature concerning the development of soft continuum robots indicated that the current iteration of these robots encounters several challenges, such as insufficient kinematic and dynamic modeling approaches, ineffective control strategies, and higher computational demands. This study presents modeling techniques and control strategies utilized to create an adaptive neuro-controller for a soft wrist component integrated with a prosthetic hand, aiming for improved response times and decreased computational load. The organization of this paper is as follows: Sect. 2 provides an overview of the modeling methodologies employed. The MRAC strategy is presented in Sect. 3. Section 4 highlights the results from simulations and experiments. Lastly, Sect. 5 offers a conclusion to the study.

2 Mathematical Model of a Soft Wrist Section

The proposed design for the soft wrist segment, as outlined in [12], consists of five rigid discs, five springs, and five flexible tendons, as shown in Fig. 1(a). The sizes of the rigid discs incorporated in this wrist segment are presented in Fig. 1(b).

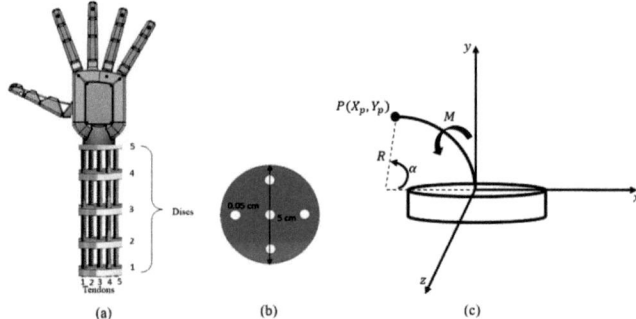

Fig. 1. Soft wrist section (a) Conceptual design of wrist section attached to hand (b) Dimension of disc (c) Bending structure of wrist section

The rigid discs incorporate the springs and tendons, which are anchored to a stable platform. By exerting precise tensions on each tendon via a motor, the intended movements of the wrist segment can be realized. Variations in tendon tensions result in distinct bending moments on the soft wrist segment, enabling its behavior to be represented as a cantilever beam under bending stress. The placement of the end effector relative to the wrist's curvature is established based on bending beam theory, as indicated in [13]. Furthermore, Fig. 1(c) illustrates the bending configuration of the soft wrist segment, characterized by a length

L, influenced by an anti-clockwise moment, M. The hand's position, denoted as $P(X_p, Y_p)$ in the two-dimensional Cartesian plane, is established through the application of Eqs. 1 and 2, taking into account the bending angle, α.

$$X_p = R\sin\alpha \tag{1}$$

$$Y_p = R(1 - \cos\alpha) \tag{2}$$

The variable R denotes the radius of curvature for the soft segment. The equation for a beam, derived from Timoshenko beam theory, incorporates Young's Modulus, E, Moment of Inertia, I, and deflection, y_p with respect to horizontal axis, x_p as expressed in Eq. 3.

$$EI\frac{d^4 y_p}{dx_p^4} = q(x) - \frac{EI}{KAG}\frac{d^2 q}{dx_p^2} \tag{3}$$

In this context, q, K, A, and G denote general load, Timoshenko shear coefficient, cross-sectional area, and shear modulus, respectively. For the case of a cantilever beam subject to a concentrated load F at its free end $x_p = L$, we define the loading as a Dirac delta function: $q(x_p) = F\delta(x_p - L)$. In the domain $0 \le x_p < L$, the load term and its derivatives vanish, reducing Eq. 3 to:

$$\frac{d^4 y_p}{dx_p^4} = 0 \tag{4}$$

Integrating four times, we obtain:

$$y_p(x_p) = a_1 x_p^3 + a_2 x_p^2 + a_3 x_p + a_4 \tag{5}$$

To incorporate shear deformation, we add a shear correction term derived from Timoshenko theory, which leads to:

$$y_p(x_p) = \frac{F(L - x_p)}{KAG} + a_1 x_p^3 + a_2 x_p^2 + a_3 x_p + a_4 \tag{6}$$

We apply the boundary conditions for a cantilever beam:

- At $x_p = 0$: $y(0) = 0$ and $\frac{dy_p}{dx_p}(0) = 0$ (no displacement or rotation at the clamped end)
- At $x_p = L$: $\frac{d^2 y_p}{dx_p^2}(L) = 0$ (zero bending moment), and $\frac{d^3 y_p}{dx_p^3}(L) = \frac{F}{EI} - \frac{F}{KAG}$ (shear balance including Timoshenko correction)

Solving for the constants using these boundary conditions yields:

$$y_p(x_p) = \frac{F(L - x_p)}{KAG} - \frac{F x_p}{2EI}\left(L^2 - \frac{x_p^2}{3}\right) + \frac{FL^3}{3EI} \tag{7}$$

This is the expression for transverse deflection $y_p(x_p)$ under a concentrated load, incorporating both bending and shear deformation effects. The calculation of vertical deflection at the wrist tip is performed utilizing Eq. 8.

$$y_p(x_p) = \frac{ML^2}{2EI} = \frac{FRL^2}{2EI} \tag{8}$$

The dynamic model of the wrist segment is developed using the calculated position obtained from the curvature radius and bending moment. Consequently, this allows for the determination of the end effector's position and the required tension in the wires, thereby enabling the design and implementation of the control system for the wrist segment.

3 Model Reference Adaptive Controller Developed for the Soft Wrist Section

A neuro-controller, illustrated in Fig. 2(a), was created to manage the movements of the soft wrist segment by applying Timoshenko beam theory. To forecast the force values (F_{des}) an NN block was utilized, as depicted in Fig. 2(b). Desired deflections (y_{des}) were given as the input to the NN block.

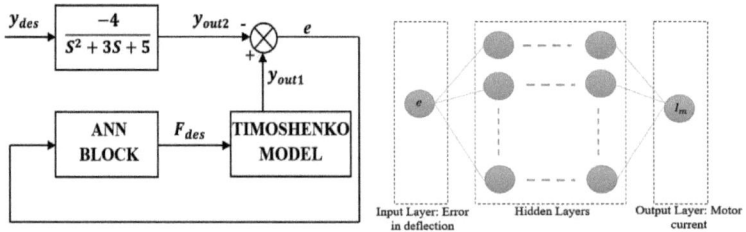

Fig. 2. (a)Control scheme(b)ANN architecture

The force values were supplied to the wrist section model to generate the necessary deflections, denoted as y_{out1}. The transfer function of the wrist section was derived as given in following equation:

$$T(s) = \frac{-4}{s^2 + 3s + 5} \tag{9}$$

This model acted as the reference model for the control scheme. The resulting output deflections, y_{out1} and y_{out2}, from the wrist section Timoshenko model and reference model respectively were then utilized to determine the errors, e, as outlined in Eq. 10.

$$e = y_{out1} - y_{out2} \tag{10}$$

These errors were received by the ANN block as the input and forces were given as the output. y_{out1} was calculated using Eq. 8 in Timoshenko block and y_{out1} was determined using the reference model given in Eq. 9. The motions of the motors attached to the tendons result in required tendon tensions to move the wrist section to desired deflections. A conventional MRAC was initially employed for obtaining the input-output dataset by replacing ANN block shown in Fig. 2(b). The error-current data pairs obtained from the MRAC scheme were used as datasets for training the ANN network in the neuro-controller scheme. In the realm of control systems, the fundamental objective of employing an NN controller into the control scheme was to compute the control input, $u(t)$ that directed the system's state, $x(t)$ towards a desired target state, $x_d(t)$. The NN served to approximate the control law by leveraging the current state of the system, and in certain instances, it also incorporated the derivatives of the state variables. The NN generated the control input, $u(t)$ based on the relationship given in Eq. 11

$$u(t) = \phi(w_2\phi(w_1 x(t) + b_1) + b_2 \tag{11}$$

where ϕ and $x(t)$ are the activation functions of the NN and state vector of the system respectively. w_1 and w_2 are the weight matrices of the input-to-hidden and hidden-to-output layers respectively. b_1 and b_2 are the bias vectors of the hidden and output layers respectively.

4 Results and Discussions

This study presents an MRAC designed for the soft wrist of a prosthetic hand. The kinematic and dynamic modellings of the wrist were conducted utilizing Timoshenko beam theory. To study the performance of the proposed position controller during the motions of the soft wrist section carrying payload, simulation, comparison study and experimentation were carried out.

4.1 Simulation Study

An MRAC developed for the same wrist was utilized to acquire the input-output dataset. NN with feed-forward back propagation configuration was trained by using error signals as the input and obtained tendon forces from the NN. Prior to training, the input and output datasets for the ANN model were normalized to enhance learning efficiency. The deflection error values, used as network inputs, and the corresponding tendon force values, used as outputs, were scaled to lie within the range $[0, 1]$ using min-max normalization. This step ensured consistency across input features and helped avoid gradient vanishing during training. The same normalization parameters were applied during testing and inference phases to maintain scale compatibility.

NN was composed of 3 hidden layers with 5, 5, and 7 neurons in 1st, 2nd, and 3rd layers respectively. Sigmoid function and Levenberg Macquardt were used as the activation function and back propagation technique respectively. Regression scheme of the NN training is given in Figs. 3. The regression scheme showcases an accuracy of 99.92 % as evident from the Fig. 3(a). Gradient and momentum values were obtained as 1.05×10^{-14} and 1.94×10^{-11}, respectively. The convergence of the NN during training, testing and validation is shown in Fig. 3(b). In order to reduce the computational time, we limited the epochs to 1000, since we achieved the required accuracy of results. The parameters of the NN network are given in Table 1.

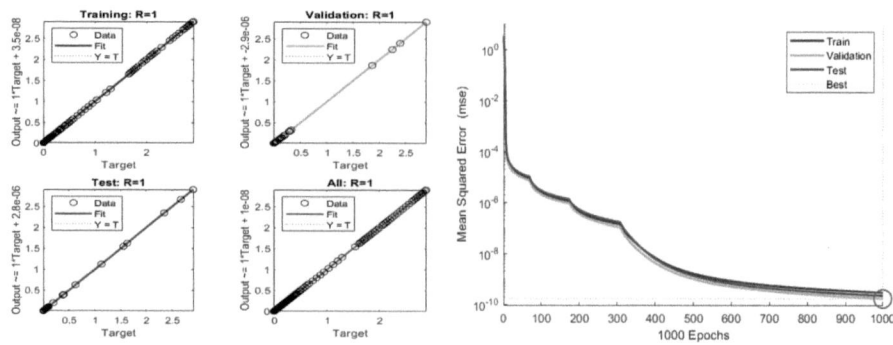

Fig. 3. Training and validation graphs (a) Regression (b) Performance

Table 1. NN based training parameters and results

Parameters	Value
Hidden layers	3
Gradient	1.05×10^{-14}
Momentum	1.94×10^{-11}
Learning rate	0.001
Accuracy	0.99
Training loss	0.001
Validation loss	0.003

The simulation of the control scheme was performed in Simulink, a MATLAB based software and carried out using a PC with an Intelcore i7 processor and 16 GB RAM. The wrist section can traverse trajectories in radial deviation, ulnar deviation, flexion, and extension directions as shown in Figs. 4 (a)–(h).

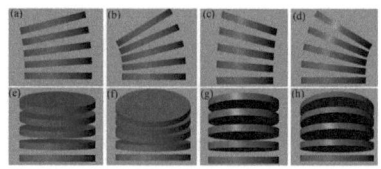

Fig. 4. Motion of wrist (a) Radial-1 (b) Radial-2 (c) Ulnar-1 (d) Ulnar-2 (e) Flexion-1 (f) Flexion-2 (g) Extension-1 (h) Extension-2

The wrist segment was considered to be flexing from its original position, as illustrated in Fig. 4, to a final bending angle of 30^0 in ulnar deviation direction relative to disc 5 connected to the hand. Response of the system with respect to the reference step signal (reference deflection) is shown in Fig. 5(a). The errors in deflections obtained during the simulation are shown in Fig. 5(b).

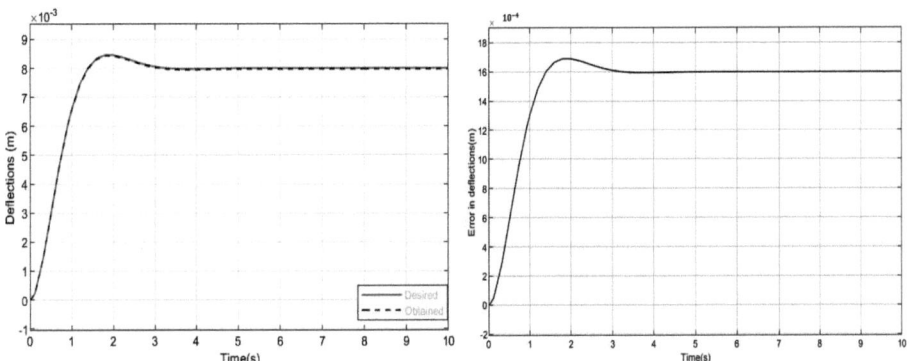

Fig. 5. (a)Comparison of response with reference signal (b)Error in deflection during simulation

Root Mean Square (RMSE), settling time, and steady state error were obtained as 6.14×10^{-4} m, 3.2 s, and 16.12×10^{-4} m respectively.

4.2 Experimental Validation

The experimental setup for the constructed model of the wrist and hand, along with its electronic components, is illustrated in Fig. 6. An ArUco marker affixed to the hand facilitated the tracking of its poses throughout the experimentation process. The setup included four stepper motors, two motor drivers, a 3D depth camera, and an Arduino controller for real-time operation. Additionally, ROS and MATLAB software were employed for tracking the ArUco poses and executing the control scheme, respectively. The hand pose tracking system utilized an ArUco marker-based approach in conjunction with a depth camera. In this study, the camera operated at a resolution of 1280×720 pixels, which provided sufficient detail for real-time tracking of the marker during wrist motion experiments.

Four peripheral tendons were employed to facilitate rotational movements in four distinct directions. Tendons 1 and 2 were activated to achieve radial deviation of the wrist, while tendons 4 and 5 were responsible for movements in the ulnar direction. Additionally, tendons 1 and 4 were utilized to manage extension motions, whereas flexion was controlled by tendons 2 and 5. The lowest disc (disc 1) was affixed to a stable platform, and the highest disc (disc 5) was attached to the hand. Motion of hand in all directions are shown in Fig. 7 (a) - (l). The errors in motions of the above mentioned motions are shown in Fig. 8. In the course of the experimentation, the average RMSE values of deflection, settling time, and steady-state error of all directions were measured as 5.66×10^{-3} m,

1.58 s, and 8.05×10^{-3} m respectively. The results distinctly demonstrated that the error values encountered during the experimental phase were considerably higher than those noted in the simulation study. A key reason for the elevated error margin observed in the experimental phase was the reduced stiffness of the springs employed in the wrist segment.

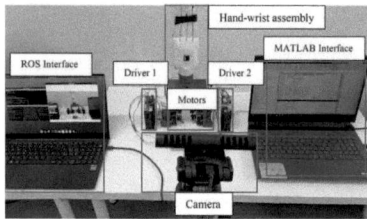

Fig. 6. Experimentation set up.

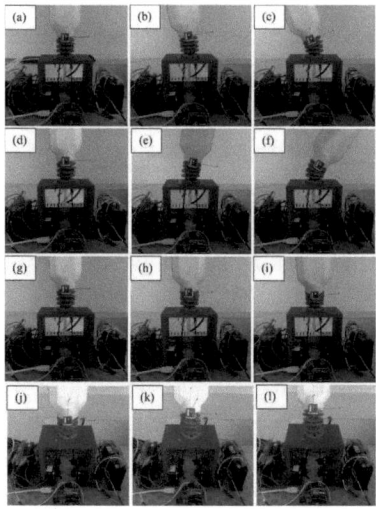

Fig. 7. Motion of the wrist section along with hand (a)-(c) Ulnar (d)-(f) Radial (g)-(i) Extension (j)-(l) Flexion

To highlight the advancements of the proposed NN-based MRAC, a comparative analysis was conducted against several notable works in the domain of soft continuum robotics and adaptive control. Table 2 summarizes the performance metrics and capabilities of the proposed method relative to existing approaches.

As shown in Table 2, the proposed controller achieves superior performance in terms of RMSE and settling time, demonstrating its effectiveness in precise

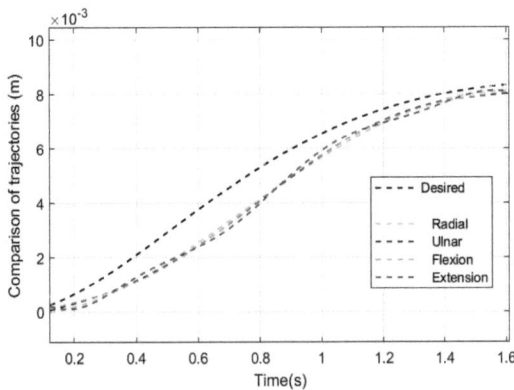

Fig. 8. Comparison of motions during experimentations

Table 2. Comparison of Proposed Controller with Related Methods

Method	RMSE (m)	Settling Time (s)	Real-Time Capable
Proposed NN-MRAC	**0.00566**	**1.58**	Yes
Braganza et al. [3]	0.012	2.4	No
Melingui et al. [8]	0.0091	2.1	Limited
Yang et al. [11]	0.0068	1.9	Yes

trajectory tracking. Unlike Braganza et al. [3], whose NN controller was not optimized for real-time deployment, the proposed method is experimentally validated in real-time using a tendon-driven prosthetic wrist. Compared to Melingui et al. [8], which employed support vector regression with limited adaptability, our approach leverages online learning through a NN, enabling continuous adaptation to dynamic changes. Yang et al. [11] also presented a robust NN-based controller, but their method involved more complex modeling using screw and Cosserat theories, whereas our approach maintains computational efficiency suitable for embedded prosthetic applications. These comparisons underscore the novelty and practical relevance of the proposed NN-MRAC, particularly in wearable assistive robotics where low latency, adaptability, and simplicity are critical.

5 Conclusion

An NN based MRAC was implemented using a mathematical model determined based on the bending beam theory during the motion of the wrist section carrying a prosthetic hand. The implementation of the neuro-controller approach enabled the system to sustain the desired motion trajectories despite fluctuations in the robot's physical characteristics and environmental factors. The use of NN enhanced controller performance by decreasing computational time. Furthermore, adaptive control strategy facilitated the faster response. Simulation studies revealed that proposed controller achieved a lower settling time in comparison to other controllers. Additionally, the RMSE and steady-state errors associated with neuro-controller were found to be in the tolerance range (10^{-3}). However, during experiments, RMSE values were higher than those observed in simulations, attributed to variations in spring stiffness. Future works will concentrate on redesigning the wrist to enhance structural robustness, while controller strategies will be refined by incorporating real-time sensor feedback to improve motion accuracy.

Acknowledgement. This work was supported by the Italian Ministry of Research under the complementary actions to the NRRP Fit4MedRob - Fit for Medical Robotics Grant (PNC0000007).

References

1. Jyothish, K.J., Mishra, S.: A survey on robotic prosthetics: neuroprosthetics, soft actuators, and control strategies. ACM Comput. Surv. **56**(8), 1–44 (2024). https://doi.org/10.1145/3648355
2. Gohari M., Sulaiman S., Schetter F., Ficuciello F.: A sliding mode controller design based on timoshenko beam theory developed for a prosthetic hand wrist. In: Proceedings of the 11th International Conference on Automation, Robotics, and Applications (ICARA), pp. 338–342. IEEE, Italy (2025)
3. Braganza, D., Dawson, D.M., Walker, I.D., Nath, N.N.: A neural network controller for continuum robots. IEEE Trans. Rob. **23**(6), 1270–1277 (2007). https://doi.org/10.1109/TRO.2007.909786
4. Tian, L., Collins, C.: Adaptive neuro-fuzzy control of a flexible manipulator. Mechatronics **15**(10), 1305–1320 (2005). https://doi.org/10.1016/j.mechatronics.2005.02.001
5. Petković, D., Issa, M., Pavlović, N.D., Zentner, L., Ćojbašić, Ž: Adaptive neuro fuzzy controller for adaptive compliant robotic gripper. Expert Syst. Appl. **39**(18), 13295–13304 (2012). https://doi.org/10.1016/j.eswa.2012.05.072
6. Pantoja-Garcia, L., Parra-Vega, V., Garcia-Rodriguez, R., Vázquez-García, C.E.: A novel actor-critic motor reinforcement learning for continuum soft robots. Robotics **12**(5), 141 (2023). https://doi.org/10.3390/robotics12050141
7. Satheeshbabu S., Uppalapati N.K., Chowdhary G., Krishnan G.: Open loop position control of soft continuum arm using deep reinforcement learning. In: Proceedings of the 2019 IEEE International Conference on Robotics and Automation (ICRA), pp. 5133–5139. IEEE, Canada (2019). https://doi.org/10.1109/ICRA.2019.8793653
8. Melingui, A., Merzouki, R., Mbede, J.: Compact bionic handling arm control using neural networks. Electron. Lett. **50**(14), 979–981 (2014). https://doi.org/10.1049/el.2014.1136
9. Melingui A., Mvogo Ahanda J.J.B., Lakhal O., Mbede J.B., Merzouki R.: Adaptive algorithms for performance improvement of a class of continuum manipulators. IEEE Tran. Syst. Man. Cybern. Syst. **48**(9), 1531–1541 (2017). https://doi.org/10.1109/TSMC.2017.2678605

10. Melingui, A., Lakhal, O., Daachi, B., Mbede, J.B., Merzouki, R.: Adaptive neural network control of a compact bionic handling arm. IEEE/ASME Trans. Mechatron. **20**(6), 2862–2875 (2015). https://doi.org/10.1109/TMECH.2015.2444091
11. Yang, Y., Han, J., Liu, Z., Zhao, Z., Hong, K.S.: Modeling and adaptive neural network control for a soft robotic arm with prescribed motion constraints. IEEE/CAA J. Automatica Sinica **10**(2), 501–511 (2023). https://doi.org/10.1109/JAS.2023.123213
12. Sulaiman, S., Menon, M., Schetter, F., Ficuciello, F.: Design, modelling, and experimental validation of a soft continuum wrist section developed for a prosthetic hand. In: Proceedings of the 2024 IEEE/RSJ International Conference on Intelligent Robots and Systems (IROS), pp. 11347–11354. IEEE, UAE (2024)
13. Biot, M.A.: Bending of an infinite beam on an elastic foundation. J. Appl. Mech. **4**(1), A1–A7 (1937). https://doi.org/10.1115/1.4008739

Design and Optimization of a Sliding Mode Controller for a Modified EduExo Upper Limb Exoskeleton

Hamidreza Heidari[(✉)], Mohammad Gohari, and Fanny Ficuciello

PRISMA Lab, Università Degli Studi Di Napoli Federico II, Naples, Italy
hamidreza.heidari@unina.it

Abstract. Upper limb exoskeletons play a crucial role in rehabilitation and assistive applications by enhancing movement capabilities for individuals with motor impairments. However, precise motion control remains a challenge due to system nonlinearities, external disturbances, and the need for robustness in dynamic environments. In this study, a modified version of the EduExo exoskeleton is developed by integrating an additional RMD-X6 servomotor to provide active shoulder flexion-extension, while retaining elbow joint actuation. The mechanical structure is modified, and its kinematic and dynamic models are derived to enable accurate physical simulation. A Sliding Mode Controller (SMC) is designed and applied to control the dual-actuated system. Unlike conventional PID control, which is limited in managing nonlinearities and external disturbances, the SMC provides high robustness and reliability. To address the inherent issue of chattering in standard SMC, a Hyperbolic tangent switching function is adopted and the controller parameters are optimized using response optimization method. The system is evaluated through Simulink-based simulations, where the controller performance is assessed under both step and circular trajectory tracking tasks. Performance metrics such as Root Mean Square Error (RMSE), settling time, and chattering are calculated. The SMC demonstrates significantly improved tracking accuracy and reduced chattering, confirming its effectiveness with approximately 20% reduction for upper limb exoskeleton control. This work demonstrates how a robust and SMC enhances the motion accuracy of a modified EduExo exoskeleton in simulation.

Keywords: Upper Limb Exoskeleton · Sliding Mode Control · Optimization

1 Introduction

In recent years, robotic exoskeletons have emerged as transformative technologies in the fields of rehabilitation, assistive robotics, and human augmentation. These wearable electromechanical systems are designed to interact with the human body, either by amplifying movement, compensating for muscular deficiencies, or retraining motor function after neurological injury. As populations age and musculoskeletal disorders become more prevalent, the demand for effective rehabilitation tools grows—placing exoskeletons at the forefront of patient-centered therapy systems [1].

One of the most critical applications of exoskeletons lies in neurological rehabilitation, particularly for patients recovering from stroke, spinal cord injuries, or degenerative conditions like ALS. These systems assist patients in performing repetitive, task-specific movements that are essential to promote neuroplasticity and functional motor recovery. Upper limb exoskeletons, in particular, support complex joint coordination in the shoulder and elbow, enabling patients to re-learn everyday motions such as reaching, lifting, and grasping. Compared to manual therapy, exoskeletons offer standardized, high-frequency, and fatigue-free support, allowing for more consistent rehabilitation outcomes [2, 3].

Upper limb exoskeletons can operate in various modes—passive, active, and resistive—making them adaptable to the different stages of therapy. In the early stages, passive assistance prevents muscle atrophy and joint stiffness, while active and resistive control is used later as the patient regains strength and coordination [4, 5]. Despite the widespread benefits of exoskeletons, many commercial and academic platforms remain partially passive, especially in the upper limb where complex shoulder motion is often under actuated. In many systems, actuation is provided only at the elbow, while the shoulder relies on gravity compensation or user motion. This design choice limits the robot's ability to assist users with severe motor deficits. Consequently, the activation and motorization of passive joints, particularly at the shoulder, has become a central goal for enhancing system versatility and user engagement [6, 7]. The integration of compact and powerful actuators, such as the RMD-X6 servomotor, allows exoskeletons to provide active flexion-extension at the shoulder, which is essential for trajectory tracking and compensating for weakness in early rehabilitation stages.

Modern exoskeletons are increasingly being developed with user-centered design principles, ensuring the control system accommodates limb biomechanics, user fatigue, and therapy progression. For systems incorporating actuated joints, the control architecture must be capable of adapting to both passive and active therapy stages, and must remain stable despite variations in patient effort, mass distribution, or external perturbations [8]. Hence, the need for robust, accurate, and real-time control methods becomes critical. Traditionally, Proportional-Integral-Derivative (PID) controllers have served as the default in exoskeleton applications due to its simplicity, low computational requirements, low computational cost, and effectiveness in linear scenarios. However, PID lacks the robustness needed to cope with nonlinear dynamics, modeling uncertainties, and external disturbances—all of which are common in human-robot interaction [9]. Alternatives like impedance control and model predictive control (MPC) offer better interaction compliance and foresight but are often more complex and difficult to tune for individual patients [10].

In response to these limitations, Sliding Mode Control (SMC) has gained popularity for its ability to handle uncertainties and maintain stability across variable conditions. SMC works by forcing system trajectories to a predefined sliding surface, ensuring convergence regardless of parameter variations. However, classical SMC suffers from chattering, a high-frequency oscillation that can damage actuators and reduce comfort. To address this, smoother variants such as Tanh-SMC, adaptive SMC, and higher-order sliding mode algorithms have been developed. These techniques offer robust performance while minimizing mechanical stress and improving motion fluidity [11, 12]. The

EduExo exoskeleton is a modular, open-source platform developed for educational and research purposes, offering an accessible entry point into exoskeleton design and control. Initially passive at the shoulder and active only at the elbow, EduExo has been used as a base for a wide range of customizations, including the addition of motors, new sensing technologies, and advanced controllers like SMC. Several studies use EduExo to simulate joint motion, test user feedback, and prototype trajectory tracking algorithms. Its design allows for hardware-software integration using Simulink, Arduino, and Simscape Multibody, which makes it ideal for control experiments optimization [13]. These adaptations transform EduExo into a viable research prototype, particularly useful in studying upper limb biomechanics, control algorithm robustness, and system-user interaction.

In this study, the design, simulation, and optimization of a Sliding Mode Controller are conducted for a modified EduExo exoskeleton, which is equipped with an additional motor at the shoulder joint. The goal is to achieve accurate, smooth, and robust trajectory tracking for rehabilitation-relevant movements. Simulations in Simulink and Simscape compare the performance of traditional PID control with an SMC, highlighting the advantages of nonlinear control in exoskeleton applications. To enhance tracking quality and mitigate chattering effects, switching functions are refined, and controller parameters are tuned. As a result, a significant reduction in tracking error and chattering is achieved, establishing a foundation for future adaptive and patient-specific control implementations.

2 Kinematic and Dynamic Modeling of Upper Limb Exoskeleton

The upper limb exoskeleton modeled is conceptualized as a two-DOF planar exoskeleton arm, consisting of two rigid links connected by revolute joints representing the shoulder and elbow flexion-extension motions. Unlike conventional planar arms aligned with the XY plane, the coordinate system in this study is intentionally rotated by 20 degrees about the x-axis, simulating the natural forward inclination of the human shoulder in an upright position. This rotational adjustment ensures a more anatomically accurate alignment of the workspace and influences both gravitational loading and motion trajectories. The base of the exoskeleton is assumed to be fixed, and each link is treated as a rigid body with mass and inertial properties extracted from the SolidWorks CAD model. Joint friction is neglected in the modeling, and no external disturbances are considered in the baseline formulation. The resulting model serves as the foundation for deriving both kinematic and dynamic equations necessary for simulation and control.

Figure 1 illustrates the planar two-link representation of the upper limb exoskeleton, showing the shoulder and elbow joints, upper arm, and forearm, which form the basis for both kinematic and dynamic modeling in this study.

2.1 Kinematic Modeling

The kinematic modeling of the exoskeleton involves determining the relationship between the joint variables and the position and velocity of the end-effector. In the forward kinematics analysis, the position of the end-effector (i.e., the hand) is expressed as a function of the joint angles θ1 and θ2. The endpoint position is first calculated in

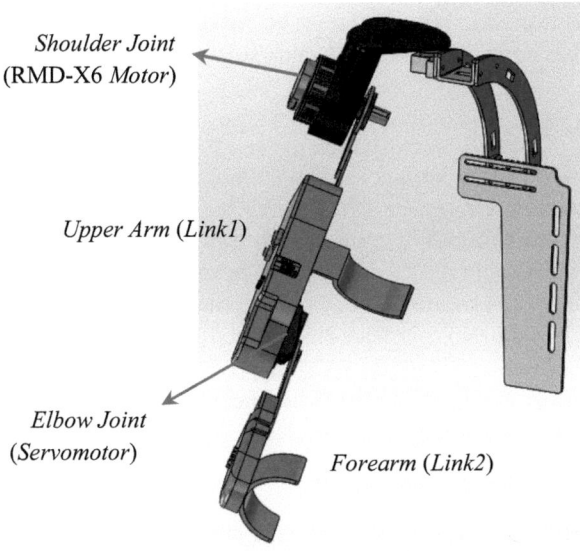

Fig. 1. Schematic representation of the 2-link upper limb exoskeleton used for modeling shoulder and elbow motion.

the local plane and then rotated into the global workspace using a 20° rotation matrix about the x-axis:

$$\boldsymbol{p}_{end} = R_x(\alpha) \cdot \begin{bmatrix} x \\ y \\ z \end{bmatrix} = R_x(20°) \cdot \begin{bmatrix} l_1\cos(\theta_1) + l_2\cos(\theta_1 + \theta_2) \\ l_1\sin(\theta_1) + l_2\sin(\theta_1 + \theta_2) \\ 0 \end{bmatrix} \quad (1)$$

where l_1 and l_2 are the lengths of the upper arm and forearm links, respectively and $R_x(20°)$ is the rotation matrix applied to align the coordinate system with the real-world shoulder inclination. This formulation allows the controller to map desired end-effector trajectories into joint space while accounting for the inclination.

To perform inverse kinematics, the goal is to find joint angles θ_1 and θ_2 that position the end-effector at a desired location in space. The inverse kinematics equations are derived analytically (when feasible) or solved numerically in Simulink using optimization or iterative solvers. Because the workspace is inclined, the desired position vector $\boldsymbol{p}_{desired}$ is first transformed into the local coordinate system using the inverse of the original rotation:

$$\boldsymbol{p}_{local} = R_x(-20°) \cdot \boldsymbol{p}_{desired} = \begin{bmatrix} x\prime & y\prime & z\prime \end{bmatrix}^T \quad (2)$$

Then, the inverse kinematics is computed using standard geometric relationships in the local plane:

$$\cos(\theta_2) = \frac{x\prime^2 + y\prime^2 - l_1^2 - l_2^2}{2l_1 l_2}$$
$$\theta_1 = \tan^{-1}\left(\frac{y\prime}{x\prime}\right) - \tan^{-1}\left(\frac{l_2\sin(\theta_2)}{l_1 + l_2\cos(\theta_2)}\right) \quad (3)$$

2.2 Dynamic Modeling

The dynamic behavior of the exoskeleton is formulated using the Lagrangian method, which offers a structured approach for deriving the equations of motion. The kinetic energy of each link is expressed in terms of the generalized joint coordinates and velocities, accounting for the rotational inertia and linear velocities of both the center of mass and distal end. The potential energy is computed based on the vertical position of each center of mass, adjusted to reflect the inclined gravitational vector due to the 20° coordinate frame rotation.

The Lagrangian L is defined as the difference between total kinetic and potential energies:

$$L = T - V \tag{4}$$

By considering m_1, m_2 the masses of the upper arm and forearm links, I_1, I_2 their moments of inertia, and l_1, l_2 their lengths. Let c_1, c_2 denote the distances from the respective joints to the centers of mass. The total kinetic energy is given by:

$$T = \frac{1}{2}I_1\dot{\theta}_1^2 + \frac{1}{2}m_1 c_1^2 \dot{\theta}_1^2 + \frac{1}{2}I_2(\dot{\theta}_1 + \dot{\theta}_2)^2 + \frac{1}{2}m_2\left[v_{c2x}^2 + v_{c2y}^2\right] \tag{5}$$

where $v_{c2x} = -l_1\dot{\theta}_1 sin(\theta_1) - c_2(\dot{\theta}_1 + \dot{\theta}_2)sin(\theta_1 + \theta_2)$ and $v_{c2y} = l_1\dot{\theta}_1 cos(\theta_1) + c_2(\dot{\theta}_1 + \dot{\theta}_2)cos(\theta_1 + \theta_2)$

The projected point due to 20° inclination, the gravity vector **g** is rotated as:

$$\mathbf{g} = R_x(20°) \cdot \begin{bmatrix} 0 \\ -g \\ 0 \end{bmatrix} = \begin{bmatrix} 0 \\ -g cos(20°) \\ g sin(20°) \end{bmatrix} \tag{6}$$

Only the vertical (y and z) components contribute to the potential energy. Assuming motion is constrained to a plane and z-component affects height slightly, the potential energy becomes:

$$V = (m_1 g c_1 cos(\theta_1) + m_2 g[l_1 cos(\theta_1) + c_2 cos(\theta_1 + \theta_2)]) cos(20°) \tag{7}$$

This yields the system's equations in the standard robotic form:

$$M(\theta)\ddot{\theta} + C(\theta, \dot{\theta})\dot{\theta} + G(\theta) = \tau \tag{8}$$

The dynamic model includes the inertia matrix $M(\theta)$, Coriolis and centrifugal forces $C(\theta, \dot{\theta})$, gravity effects $G(\theta)$ and the torque vector τ.

Geometrical and inertial properties are extracted from the CAD model in SolidWorks, and simulations are performed in Simscape Multibody. Simulink is used to simulate the system under various control strategies, while Simscape provides visual and numerical validation of the derived kinematics and dynamics. This modeling setup enables both controller design and verification of joint behavior under different torque profiles and external constraints.

3 Control Strategies for Exoskeleton Motion

Exoskeleton control strategies are fundamental to ensuring safe, accurate, and responsive assistance during human-robot interaction. These strategies can be broadly classified into classical, adaptive, robust, and intelligent control techniques. Among them, Proportional-Integral-Derivative (PID) control and Sliding Mode Control (SMC) are widely adopted for their simplicity and robustness, respectively. PID control has historically been implemented for trajectory tracking due to its intuitive tuning and implementation. However, SMC is gaining increased attention for its robustness to modeling uncertainties and external disturbances, especially in rehabilitation and assistive exoskeletons.

3.1 Sliding Mode Control (SMC)

The Sliding Mode Control (SMC) offers a robust alternative to PID, especially for systems characterized by nonlinearities, parameter uncertainties, and disturbances. SMC operates by forcing the system trajectory onto a predefined sliding surface in the state-space and maintaining it there despite uncertainties. The control law typically consists of an equivalent control u_{eq} and a discontinuous control u_{sw}:

$$u(t) = u_{eq}(t) + u_{sw}(t) \tag{9}$$

The sliding surface $s(t)$ is commonly defined as a combination of tracking error $e(t)$ and its derivative:

$$s(t) = \lambda e(t) - \dot{e}(t) \tag{10}$$

The switching component is designed to drive $s(t)$ to zero, $u_{sw} = -k\,\text{sign}(s)$. To mitigate the undesirable effects of chattering is to replace the sign function with a continuous approximation, such as the hyperbolic tangent $u_{sw} = -k.\tanh(\frac{s(t)}{\phi})$. Where ϕ is a boundary layer thickness parameter. Another strategy involves adaptive gain tuning, in which the control gain k is adjusted based on error magnitude or system states. Higher-order sliding mode controllers are also explored to ensure smoother control by increasing the order of the sliding manifold. Additionally, the twisting control algorithm is evaluated $u_{twist} = -k_1.\text{sign}(s) - k_2.\text{sign}(\dot{s})$. Where k_1 and k_2 are positive gains designed to stabilize both the sliding variable and its derivative.

In this study, the standard and modified switching functions including sign, tanh, and twisting functions are implemented to the SMC. Simulation-based optimization of the switching parameters is carried out using MATLAB Simulink's built-in optimization tools, focusing on minimizing tracking error, reducing chattering, and enhancing control smoothness under varying trajectories.

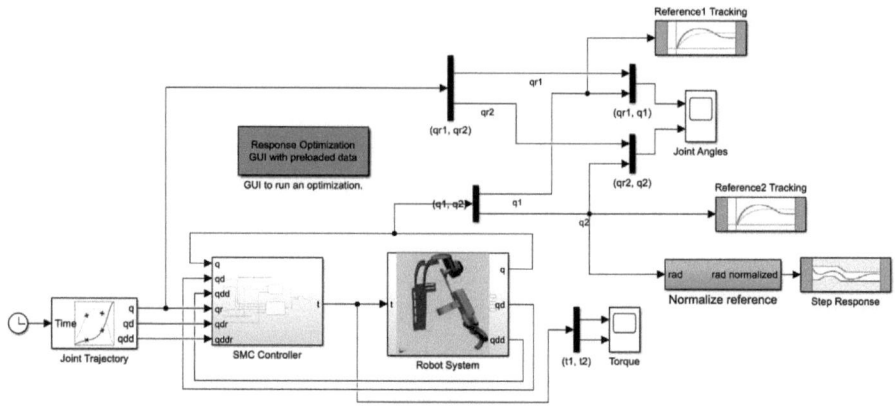

Fig. 2. Closed-Loop Control Architecture with SMC and Optimization.

3.2 Optimization Criteria and Cost Function

The performance of a Sliding Mode Controller (SMC) is highly sensitive to the tuning of its parameters. In exoskeleton applications, where smooth and accurate trajectory tracking is required for safe rehabilitation, manual tuning often fails to deliver optimal results. Therefore, parameter optimization is carried out to enhance the controller's robustness, accuracy, and chattering suppression under dynamic motion profiles.

The need for optimization stems from the inherent trade-offs involved in designing an SMC. Increasing the control gain can improve response speed, but may also lead to high-frequency chattering, which can cause mechanical wear or user discomfort. Conversely, reducing the gain can improve smoothness but might compromise robustness. These challenges necessitate a systematic optimization strategy to strike a balance among competing performance objectives.

To evaluate control performance, a cost function is defined based on the root mean square error (RMSE) between the desired and actual end-effector trajectories.

$$J = \sum_{i=1}^{N} \sqrt{\frac{1}{N} \sum_{i=1}^{n} (e_i)^2} \tag{11}$$

where:

- e_i is the trajectory tracking error at each time step.
- N is the total number of simulation points.

The process is carried out using MATLAB's Simulink Design Optimization toolbox. Initial controller parameters—including sliding surface slope λ, gain k, and switching function type—are defined as tunable variables. A simulation scenario is set up where the exoskeleton follows predefined trajectories such as step inputs and circular paths. The optimizer iteratively adjusts the controller parameters to minimize the cost function.

4 Simulation Results and Comparative Analysis

To evaluate the effectiveness of the proposed Sliding Mode Control (SMC) approach relative to a classical PID controller, simulation experiments were carried out using Simulink and Simscape Multibody. The modified EduExo exoskeleton model, with its active shoulder joint actuated by an RMD-X6 servomotor, was used as the simulation platform. Real-time joint angle feedback, a torque-mode motor model, and gravity compensation were included in the simulation environment to enhance fidelity. The performance of each controller was analyzed under two motion scenarios —a step trajectory and a circular trajectory—which represent basic and complex movements relevant to rehabilitation.

4.1 Step Trajectory Tracking

In the first scenario, a step input was applied as the reference trajectory for joint motion. This evaluation aimed to assess how quickly and accurately each controller could achieve and maintain a new position.

Figure 3 shows the step trajectory tracking performance of all three control methods. The SMC achieves the closest tracking to the ideal response with minimal overshoot and reduced chattering compared to the other methods. The PID controller exhibited reasonable accuracy with a moderate settling time. However, it showed significant overshoot and a longer steady-state error when compared to the SMC approach. The standard SMC, while offering better accuracy and faster convergence, introduced considerable chattering due to its discontinuous control law. When a hyperbolic tangent switching function was used instead of the conventional sign function, a noticeable reduction in chattering intensity was achieved without compromising performance. Quantitatively, the optimized SMC controller reduced the root mean square error (RMSE) by approximately 20% relative to PID. Settling time improved marginally, and steady-state error was nearly eliminated.

Also, Fig. 4 illustrates the step trajectory tracking performance using three switching functions within the optimized Sliding Mode Controller, namely sign, tanh, and twisting. The tanh function achieves the closest tracking to the ideal response with minimal overshoot and reduced chattering, while the sign function responds quickly but introduces high-frequency oscillations. The twisting function offers the smoothest control output with slightly slower convergence, highlighting the importance of selecting an appropriate switching function to ensure accurate, stable, and comfortable exoskeleton control during rehabilitation.

4.2 Circular Trajectory Tracking

In the second scenario, the exoskeleton was tasked with tracking a continuous circular path. This trajectory introduces dynamic challenges due to continuously changing curvature and velocity profiles.

The PID controller struggled to maintain accurate tracking, especially around the curve inflection points, resulting in large trajectory deviations and residual lag. The standard SMC performed better, maintaining smoother and more consistent trajectory following.

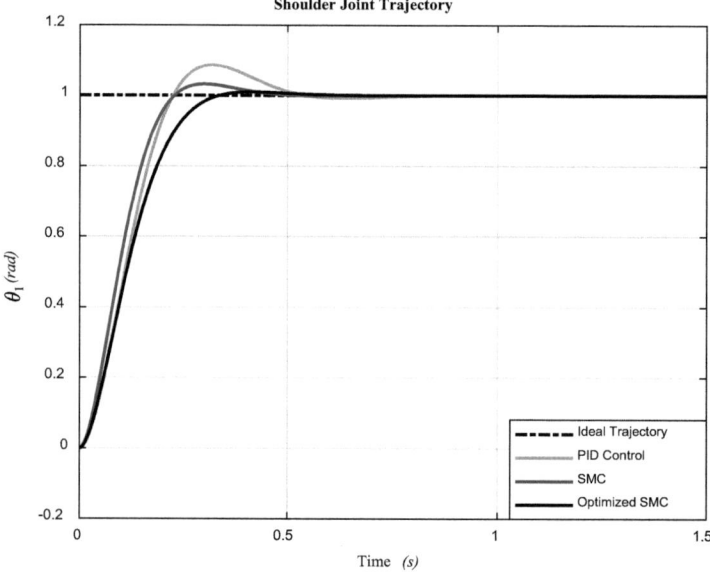

Fig. 3. Step trajectory tracking performance of the exoskeleton system using PID, standard SMC, and optimized SMC controllers.

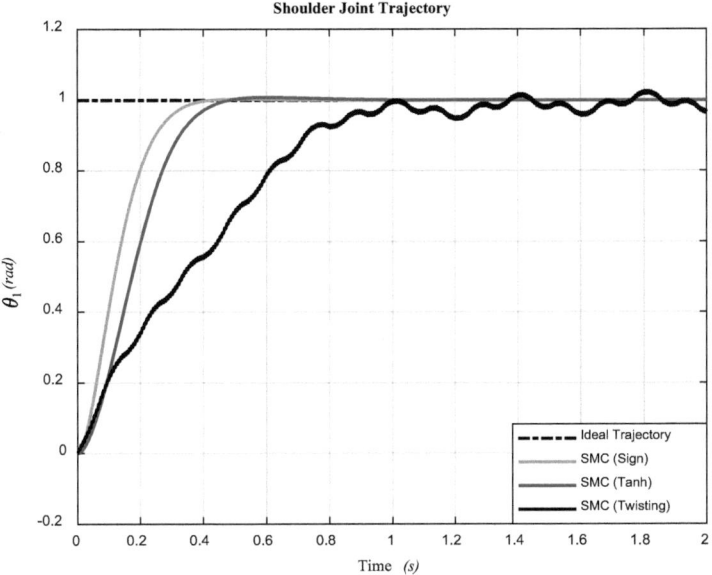

Fig. 4. Control signal behavior of three switching functions—sign, tanh, and twisting—used in optimized Sliding Mode Control.

However, as in the step tracking scenario, the chattering effect was again observed with the basic switching strategy. Figure 5 shows the tracking performance for a circular trajectory using three control strategies PID, standard sliding mode control, and the optimized sliding mode control. The zoomed-in section highlights the transition phase where the PID controller demonstrates noticeable overshoot and slower convergence. Standard sliding mode control improves tracking but introduces visible chattering due to abrupt control actions. In comparison, the optimized sliding mode control follows the ideal trajectory more closely with minimal overshoot and smoother behavior, showing the value of tuning switching functions for dynamic and precise motion.

On the other hand, Table 1 presents a comparison of the three controllers based on tracking error, settling time, and control smoothness. While the standard sliding mode controller achieves the lowest tracking error, it introduces high-frequency chattering that may limit comfort and applicability. The sliding mode controller slightly increases the tracking error but significantly improves smoothness and settling time, offering a more balanced and practical solution. The PID controller provides a smoother signal than standard SMC but falls short in accuracy and responsiveness. These findings emphasize the advantage of the sliding mode controller in delivering reliable and user-friendly motion support for upper limb exoskeletons in rehabilitation scenarios.

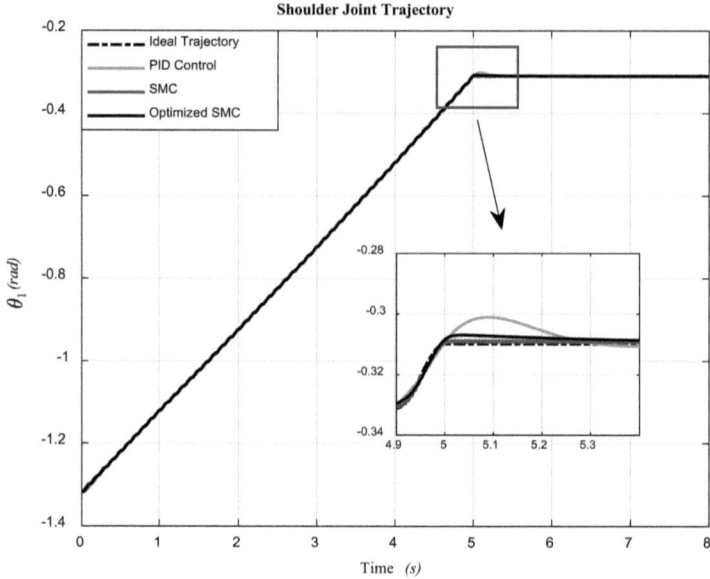

Fig. 5. Circular trajectory tracking performance using PID, standard SMC, and optimized SMC.

Overall, the simulation results clearly demonstrate the superiority of the Sliding Mode Control approach over traditional PID in terms of tracking accuracy, robustness, and convergence speed. While classical PID control remains simple to implement, it lacks the adaptability and resilience needed for varying dynamic conditions in exoskeleton applications.

Table 1. Performance comparison of controllers.

Metric	PID	SMC	Optimized SMC
RMSE (rad)	0.0021	0.0001	0.0011
Settling Time (s)	5.16	4.96	4.95
Chattering Index	Smooth	High	Low

The main limitation of SMC—chattering—was effectively mitigated by incorporating smooth switching functions such as tanh(S) and twisting algorithms. These modifications preserved the inherent robustness of SMC while ensuring user comfort and reducing mechanical stress.

This comparative analysis provides strong justification for adopting optimized SMC techniques in future exoskeleton control architectures. The controller's high performance across both simple and complex trajectories indicates its suitability for real-time applications in rehabilitation robotics. Future work may include experimental validation and adaptation to different user profiles or control objectives.

5 Conclusion and Future Work

This study focused on the design, simulation, and optimization of a Sliding Mode Controller (SMC) for a modified EduExo upper limb exoskeleton, aimed at enhancing control accuracy for shoulder flexion-extension and elbow movements. The exoskeleton model was developed in SolidWorks and imported into Simscape Multibody, where dynamic simulations were performed using joint angle feedback and actuator modeling. A comparative analysis was conducted between conventional PID control and the proposed SMC approach. Key findings of this research include the successful implementation of both PID and SMC controllers, with optimized SMC showing clear advantages. The SMC parameters were tuned using MATLAB's Response Optimization Toolbox to improve tracking accuracy and reduce chattering, which is a common limitation in sliding mode control. Step and circular trajectory tracking scenarios were used to evaluate performance. Results showed that the optimized SMC outperformed PID in terms of robustness, accuracy, and convergence time, making it a strong candidate for real-world rehabilitation applications.

A key future direction involves validating this control strategy in human-in-the-loop experiments. By involving healthy subjects or individuals with motor impairments, we aim to assess both the therapeutic value and adaptability of the system. We also plan to incorporate EMG-based intent estimation or force-feedback loops to further tailor robotic assistance and promote motor learning. These enhancements will bridge the gap between robust control and clinically relevant recovery outcomes.

Acknowledgments. We acknowledge co-funding from Next Generation EU in the context of the National Recovery and Resilience Plan, Investment PE8—Project Age-It: "Ageing Well in an Ageing Society". This resource was co-financed by the Next Generation EU (DM 1557 11.10.2022).

References

1. Ren, H., Liu, T., Wang, J.: Design and analysis of an upper limb rehabilitation robot based on multimodal control. Sensors **23**(1), 8801 (2023)
2. Rahman, M.H., Cristobal, O., Archambault, P.S.: Development of a whole arm wearable robotic exoskeleton for rehabilitation and to assist upper limb movements. Robotica **33**(1), 19–39 (2015)
3. Ren, B., Liu, J., Chen, J.: Simulating human–machine coupled model for gait trajectory optimization of the lower limb exoskeleton system based on genetic algorithm. Int. J. Adv. Rob. Syst. **17**(1), 1–15 (2020)
4. Yuan, X., Zhou, T., Liu, Y., Yue, F.: Design of adaptive compliance control algorithm for upper limb exoskeleton rehabilitation robot. In: China Automation Congress (CAC), Beijing, China, pp. 2737–2743 (2021)
5. Song, L., Ju, C., Cui, H., Qu, Y., Xu, X., Chen, C.: Research on Control Strategy Technology of Upper Limb Exoskeleton Robots: Review. Machines **13**(3), 207 (2025)
6. Zimmermann, Y., Sommerhalder, M., Wolf, P., Riener, R., Hutter, M: ANYexo 2.0: a fully actuated upper-limb exoskeleton for manipulation and joint-oriented training in all stages of rehabilitation. IEEE Trans. Robot. **39**(3), 2131–2150 (2023)

7. Tian, J., et al.: A systematic review of occupational shoulder exoskeletons for industrial use: mechanism design, actuators, control, and evaluation aspects. Actuators **13**(12), 501 (2024)
8. Soltani, A., Zeiaee, A., Langari, R., Buchanan, J., Robson, N.: Towards autonomous ergonomic upper-limb exoskeletons: a computational approach for planning a human-like path. Robot. Auton. Syst. **145**(1), 103843 (2021)
9. Joyo, M.K., et al.: Optimized proportional-integral-derivative controller for upper limb rehabilitation robot. Electronics **8**(8), 826 (2019)
10. Wilian, M., Adriano, A.G.: Optimal impedance via model predictive control for robot-aided rehabilitation. Control. Eng. Pract. **93**(1), 104177 (2019)
11. Waheed, Z., Humaidi, A.: Design of optimal sliding mode control of elbow wearable exoskeleton system based on whale optimization algorithm. J. Euro. Syst. Autom. **55**(4), 459–466 (2022)
12. Yip, D., Seng, W., Ze, Y., Siswoyo, H.: Modelling and control of single arm exoskeleton for upper limb rehabilitation application using hybrid hierarchical sliding mode and PID controllers. IOP Conf. Ser. Mater. Sci. Eng. **1101**(1), 012035 (2021)
13. Auxivo AG, "EduExo Pro." http://www.auxivo.com/eduexo-pro. Accessed 12 May 2024

Human–Robot Co-design for Cleaning: Leveraging Vision Language Model and Multi-Objective Optimization for Adaptive Layouts

S. M. Bhagya P. Samarakoon[(✉)], M. A. Viraj J. Muthugala, W. K. R. Sachinthana, and Mohan Rajesh Elara

Engineering Product Development Pillar, Singapore University of Technology and Design, 8 Somapah Road, Singapore 487372, Singapore
bhagya_samarakoon@sutd.edu.sg

Abstract. Indoor environments often contain a mix of fixed and movable objects, making it challenging for floor-cleaning robots to achieve high area coverage, a key metric for their effectiveness. This paper proposes a novel human-robot co-design framework aimed at improving the performance of floor-cleaning robots by optimizing indoor furniture layouts. A Large Language and Vision Assistant (LLaVA) is integrated to semantically interpret objects in the environment using visual and spatial cues, classifying them as movable or non-movable. Layout optimization is then carried out using a Multi-objective Genetic Algorithm (MGA) to maximize cleaning coverage while minimizing layout disruption. The robot communicates the suggested modifications through structured natural language, allowing users to make informed adjustments. Experimental validation in a real-world environment demonstrates that the framework achieves higher coverage improvement with minimal disruption, confirming its effectiveness in practical applications.

Keywords: Human-robot co-design · Cleaning robots · Vision language model · Multi-objective genetic algorithm

1 Introduction

Cleaning is often tedious, routine, and time-consuming, especially for people who are busy in day-to-day schedules. As a result, cleaning robots have emerged as a solution, by integrating into modern life and transforming household chores through innovative technology and efficiency [12]. These robots help to improve hygiene by minimizing dust, allergens, and bacteria, making them valuable assets in homes, workplaces, and healthcare environments [9,19]. Cleaning robots are used in a wide range of applications such as floor cleaning [10], window cleaning [1], pool cleaning [18], and furniture cleaning [7]. Robotic floor cleaning is extensively explored nowadays among these cleaning robots [4]. These robots offer thorough cleaning capabilities through advanced navigation systems, robust suction power, and diverse cleaning features while maintaining energy efficiency.

Coverage Path Planning (CPP) is a vital feature for cleaning robots. Numerous CPP strategies have been proposed in the literature to improve the productivity of the robots [8]. The study in [17] introduced an end-to-end coverage path planning approach that produces a seamless, collision-free path for a disinfection robot to cover a target area efficiently. The planner can minimize the time and cost of disinfection tasks by determining an optimal path using a graph-based environmental representation. Furthermore, collision-free coverage in environments with static and heterogeneous obstacles has been extensively studied. The work proposed in [3] evaluated various indoor coverage path planning algorithms, demonstrating how each offers unique advantages in speed, coverage quality, and path patterns depending on application requirements. The work [25] proposed a new reward function originating from the Predator-Prey model to overcome the problem of traditional Q-Learning easily falling into local optimum to improve CPP for robots. The study in [14] proposed an efficient method for avoiding densely populated human areas using a coverage control approach. In their framework, humans and robots are modeled as heterogeneous and homogeneous agents, enabling each to make decisions based on local information.

An online coverage path planning algorithm for unknown environments has been proposed in [22]. Leveraging the concept of an exploratory Turing machine, the algorithm directs robots through adaptive navigation commands. An efficient robot coverage approach was proposed in [2], where the environment is approximately decomposed into straight-line segments using convex partitioning. The algorithm optimizes coverage efficiency by minimizing the total number of segments by applying optimal decompositions.

In addition to conventional CPP strategies, reconfigurable cleaning robots have been developed with the ability to physically alter their shapes, allowing them to access confined or hard-to-reach areas and enhance overall coverage performance [24]. These robots are equipped with features of energy-efficient coverage [15], online path planning [21], and adaptive control tailored to their dynamic form changes [20]. While shape reconfiguration offers advantages in improving area coverage, its effectiveness remains limited to certain extents due to mechanical constraints, environmental complexity, and computational challenges.

Apart from modifying the robot itself, a few studies have explored altering the environment and incorporating robot-friendly ergonomics to enhance the robot's productivity [23]. The study in [13], demonstrated that rearranging furniture within an environment can substantially enhance the area coverage performance of a floor-cleaning robot. However, the work was limited to empirical observations and did not offer a structured set of design guidelines. Building on this idea, a set of formal guidelines for designing indoor spaces to optimize the performance of commercially available floor-cleaning robots was proposed in [6]. These guidelines are primarily intended for the design of new environments, with relatively little focus on optimizing existing spaces to enhance a robot's performance.

Area coverage improvement through the rearrangement of environmental objects was proposed in [16]. In this work, the authors employed meta-heuristic algorithms to optimize object positioning. However, their approach assumes a predefined map with known obstacles, without autonomously distinguishing whether obstacles are fixed or movable, nor recognizing the type of object. Furthermore, the method only attempts to improve the robot's performance without paying attention to minimize the disruption caused by the alteration. In real-world indoor environments, it is essential for robots to identify object types and determine their movability in order to intelligently rearrange the environment. Relocating movable objects that obstruct the robot's path can considerably enhance area coverage, which is critical for indoor floor cleaning robot. Furthermore, the robot can collaborate with humans by notifying users to reposition certain objects, enabling effective human-robot collaboration.

Motivated by this need, this paper proposes a novel human-robot co-design framework aimed at improving performance of a floor cleaning robot. The paper is organized as follows. Section 2 presents the system overview. The human-robot co-design framework is detailed in Sect. 3. Section 4 discusses the real hardware experiments and their results. Finally, concluding remarks are provided in Sect. 5.

2 System Overview

An overview of the proposed framework is given in Fig. 1. The proposed system integrates perception, reasoning, and optimization to enhance the area coverage performance of a floor-cleaning robot through human-robot co-design of indoor layouts. The process begins with the robot constructing a LiDAR-based map of the environment and identifying obstacle regions. Each obstacle is then visually inspected using a Vision Language Model (VLM), which extracts semantic attributes such as object type, movability, and relative position. This information is encoded into the layout as object annotations. A multi-objective optimization generates layout modifications that maximize robot coverage while minimizing disruption to the original setup using this semantically tagged map. The robot simulates its coverage under each layout proposal using a CPP method. Once an optimal or near-optimal layout configuration is identified, the robot communicates the proposed alterations to the user using natural language, detailing both the expected improvement in performance and the minimal positional shifts required for each object.

3 Human-Robot Co-Design Framework

3.1 Layout Generation

The process begins with obstacle information extraction from the robot's LiDAR map. Clustered obstacle regions are then identified within the environment's

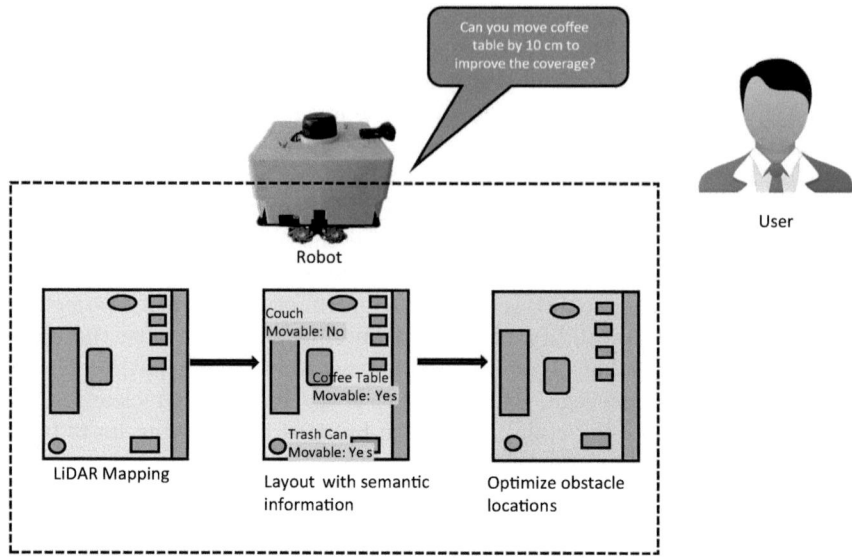

Fig. 1. System Overview

boundaries. The robot autonomously navigates toward each obstacle cluster until it reaches a predefined proximity. At that point, a Large Language and Vision Assistant (LLaVA) [11] node is triggered and send the perceived image frame to extract detailed information about the obstacle. LLaVA is a modified version of LLAMA, integrated with CLIP for vision tasks, featuring 7.2 billion parameters, a 32,768 context length, and Q4_0 quantization. The vision component, based on CLIP, has 311.89 million parameters and processes images into 1024-length embeddings. LLaVA operates within the Ollama environment, allowing local loading and management of the model.

A transformer-based VLM is selected instead of traditional object detection models (e.g., YOLO, Faster R-CNN) due to its superior versatility and generalization capabilities. Unlike conventional detectors that are restricted to a fixed set of predefined classes, LLaVA can flexibly recognize and describe a wide variety of objects, even those not explicitly labeled in its training data, by leveraging its large-scale vision-language pretraining. This adaptability is crucial for real-world indoor environments, where encountering unexpected or uncommon objects is frequent.

To standardize information extraction, the VLM is prompted with a strict Application Programming Interface (API) style JavaScript Object Notation (JSON) structure to output the object's name, whether it is movable by a human, and its relative location. The prompt used for information retrieval is provided in Fig. 2. This structured identification enables the robot to update its internal map with semantically rich, actionable data, enhancing its area coverage performance in complex indoor settings.

```
You are an API generating strict JSON output.

TASK:

- Find the closest object on a floor from the given image.

- Identify if it can be moved by a human. Objects like chairs and coffee tables
can be moved by human where big objects like cupboards and couches cannot.

- Identify the relative location of the object relative to the surrounding.

- Only output strict JSON in this structure:


{"object_name": "<string: object name>",

 "movability": "<yes or no>",

 "position": "<location of the object relative to environment>"}


RULES:

- Always use exactly these keys: object_name, movability, position.

- 'movability' must be "yes" or "no" as a string (not boolean true/false).

- No extra text or explanations outside the JSON block.
```

Fig. 2. Prompt given for the VLM

3.2 Determining Layout Alterations

The human-robot co-design framework proposed for enhancing the performance of a floor-cleaning robot is explained considering Fig. 3. A preprocessed layout of the original workspace, annotated with object labels and moveability, is used as the basis (see Sect. 3.1). Movement constraints for each object are indicated by shaded regions. For each object k, the permissible relocation range along the X and Y axes is defined by the bounds k_X^L to k_X^U and k_Y^L to k_Y^U, respectively. These bounds can be customized by the user for all objects in the workspace, where $k = 1, 2, \ldots, N$. The center of the object k is defined as (k_X, k_Y)

Within this collaborative framework, a new set of object positions $\{k_{X'}, k_{Y'}\}$, ensuring that each lies within the relocatable bounds is computed. The objective is to maximize the robot's performance while respecting human spatial preferences central to the principles of human-robot co-design. Therefore, the framework should attempt to maximize the robot's performance while minimizing the disruptions to the existing layout.

Redesigning the layout to enhance the performance of a floor-cleaning robot is a complex task that involves nonlinear constraints and the need to balance competing objectives. The aim is to maximize the robot's area coverage while minimizing disruptions to the existing workspace layout, within user-defined permissible object movement ranges.

The first objective is to improve area coverage, which is evaluated by simulating the robot's cleaning performance using a boustrophedon motion-based

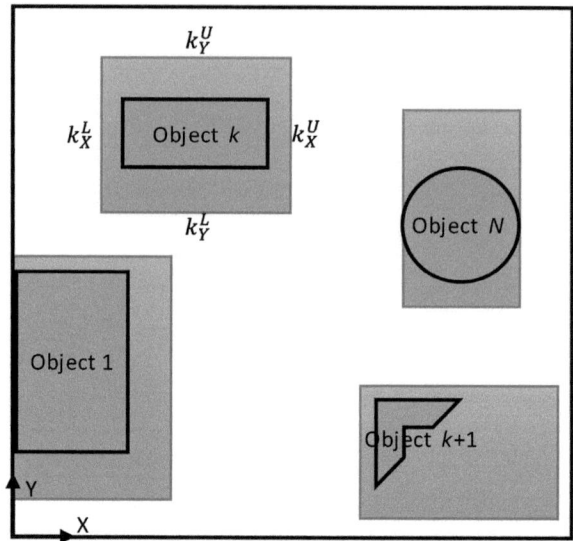

Fig. 3. Human-robot co-design space

CPP strategy. The corresponding cost function is defined as the negative of the achieved coverage as in (1).

$$f_{\text{coverage}} = -\text{Area coverage estimation} \tag{1}$$

To quantify the extent of workspace modification, a layout disruption cost is introduced. This cost measures the deviation of each object's position from its original configuration. For each object $k = 1, 2, \ldots, N$, let (k_X, k_Y) and $(k_{X'}, k_{Y'})$ denote the original and adjusted center coordinates, respectively. The layout disruption cost, $f_{\text{disruption}}$, is formulated as the sum of squared Euclidean distances between these corresponding positions as in (2).

$$f_{\text{disruption}} = \sum_{k=1}^{N} \left[(k_{X'} - k_X)^2 + (K_{Y'} - K_Y)^2 \right] \tag{2}$$

To solve this multi-objective optimization problem, a Multi-objective Genetic Algorithm (MGA) is employed. An MGA can explore a broader solution space and identify globally optimal layouts by mimicking evolutionary processes [5]. In the context of a MGA, the optimization procedure commences with the generation of an initial population comprising diverse candidate solutions. Subsequently, the objective function values for all individuals are evaluated, and a tentative set of Pareto optimal solutions is updated to capture the best trade-offs among conflicting objectives. Fitness values are then assigned based on the individuals' dominance and diversity measures within the population. Genetic operators such as crossover and mutation are employed to generate offspring.

Furthermore, an elite strategy is incorporated to retain high-quality solutions across generations, thereby ensuring the sustained advancement toward a well-distributed and convergent Pareto front.

A set of configuration parameters was carefully chosen to balance exploration, exploitation, and convergence efficiency of the MGA. The population size is set to 50 when the number of objects $N \leq 3$ and increased to 200 for more complex problems to ensure adequate solution diversity. The crossover fraction is fixed at 0.8 to encourage extensive genetic mixing between individuals. A Pareto fraction of 0.35 is used to retain a portion of elite solutions based on Pareto dominance. Tournament selection is applied to select parents for the next generation, promoting fitter individuals while maintaining diversity. Intermediate crossover is employed as the recombination method, while phenotype crowding distance is used as the distance measure to maintain a well-distributed Pareto front. An adaptive feasible mutation function ensures that offspring solutions remain within defined bounds, preserving the feasibility of object relocations. The search space for the optimization is explicitly constrained within the permissible movement ranges defined for each object. The stopping criteria are set to a maximum of 10,000 function evaluations, a function tolerance of 1×10^{-4}, or 100 stall generations without improvement, whichever is met first. These settings aim to achieve a good balance between solution quality, convergence speed, and computational efficiency.

3.3 Convey Layout Modification Suggestions to User

The modifications suggested by the co-design framework are conveyed to the user in a clear, actionable format to enhance the robot's cleaning performance. Once the optimal object repositioning is determined through the optimization process, the modifications are expressed using the following language structure given in Java Speech Grammar Format (JSGF).

"Currently, I can clean" < Area Coverage Current >"of the room."
"If the following modifications can be made, I can improve my
cleaning performance to" < Area Coverage Modified. >
for all k "move" < name object_k >"by" < shift_x > "cm along the X-axis
and" < shift_y > "cm along the Y-axis."

Specifically, the system will inform the user of the current cleaning performance (i.e., 'Area Coverage Current'), propose potential improvements (i.e., 'Area Coverage Modified'), and provide precise instructions for repositioning objects (here 'name object_k' is the name of the object k in the layout and required movements are given by 'shift_x' and 'shift_y'). This voice output, based on the recommendations from MGA, enables the user to easily implement changes that would optimize the robot's coverage, while also considering their spatial preferences.

4 Experiments

A variant of the Smorphi[1] robot (see Fig. 4) was used as the cleaning platform to implement the proposed framework. The robot features a square footprint measuring 25 cm × 25 cm and is equipped with a mecanum wheel drive system. It is equipped with a LiDAR and a camera for environmental perception. An environment measuring 3.5 m × 2.5 m was used to validate the effectiveness of the proposed framework. The environment included various objects such as a trash bin, refrigerator, and ottomans (see Fig. 4). The robot, equipped with the proposed framework, was deployed, and layout mapping was conducted.

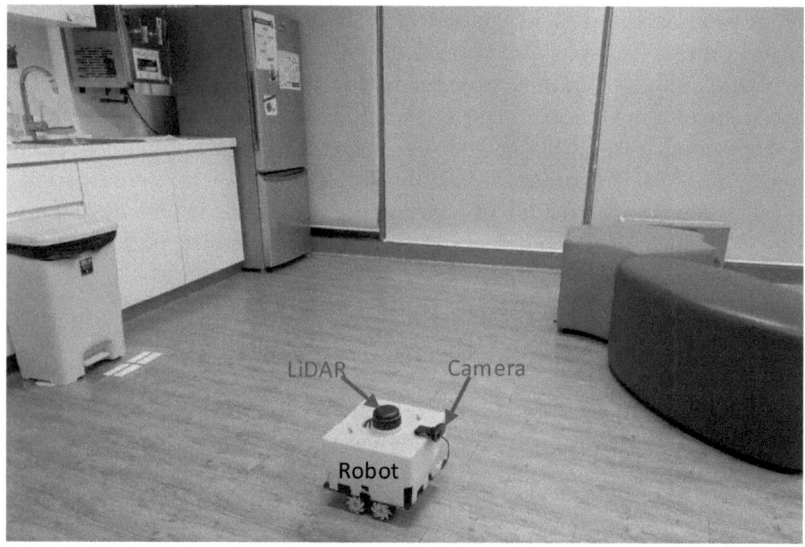

Fig. 4. Robot and the experimental environment

The layout, annotated with object information, is shown in Fig. 5. The detailed information for each object, retrieved from the Vision-Language Model (VLM), is also presented. According to the results, the refrigerator was classified as non-movable, while all other objects were identified as movable. These results demonstrate that the VLM-based layout generation method successfully identified object movability and correctly tagged them in the LiDAR map.

After generating the layout with object information, the robot initiated the process of determining the layout alterations required to improve its coverage performance. It then communicated the current coverage performance, the necessary environment modifications, and the expected coverage improvement resulting from these changes through the following language output.

---

[1] www.wefaarobotics.com.

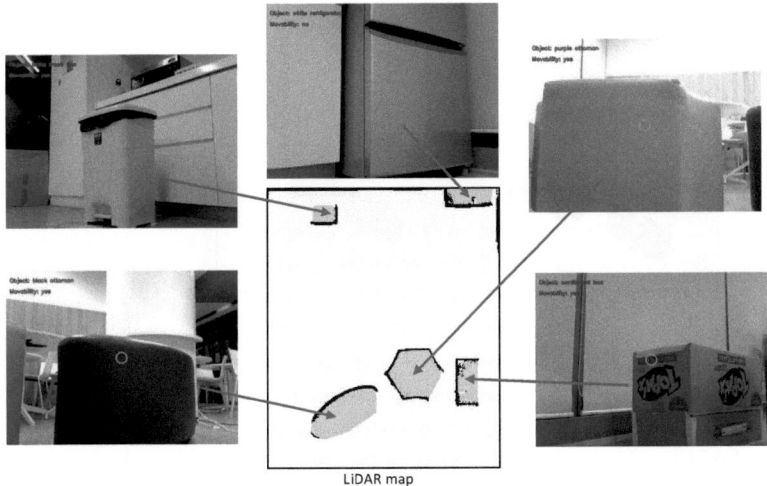

Fig. 5. Results of tagging properties of objects in the map. The results retrieved with the VLM is annotated in the each image frame of the corresponding object.

"Currently, I can clean 72% of the room. If the following modifi
cations can be made, I can improve my cleaning performance to 93%."
"move black ottoman by 4 cm along the X-axis and -20 cm along the Y-axis."
"move white trash can by 2 cm along the X-axis and -14 cm along the Y-axis."
"move purple ottoman by -9 cm along the X-axis and -6 cm along the Y-axis."
"move cardboard box by 23 cm along the X-axis and 1 cm along the Y-axis."

According to the output, the robot can improve its coverage from 72% to 93% if the suggested alterations are made. The coverage estimation maps generated by the proposed framework for the current layout and the co-designed layout are shown in Fig. 6(a) and Fig. 6(b), respectively. The disruption cost for modifying the layout was observed as 315 cm^2, with the maximum required object movement being 20 cm. This level of disruption is minimal (see layouts in Fig. 6). The 20% coverage improvement represents a considerable gain relative to the minor disruption to the original layout.

The area coverage of the robot was evaluated by deploying it in both the original and co-designed layouts to validate the coverage estimations and performance gains. The original and co-designed environments are shown in Fig. 7(a) and Fig. 7(b), respectively. The observed coverage results are presented in Fig. 7(c) and Fig. 7(d) for the original layout and the co-designed layout. The actual

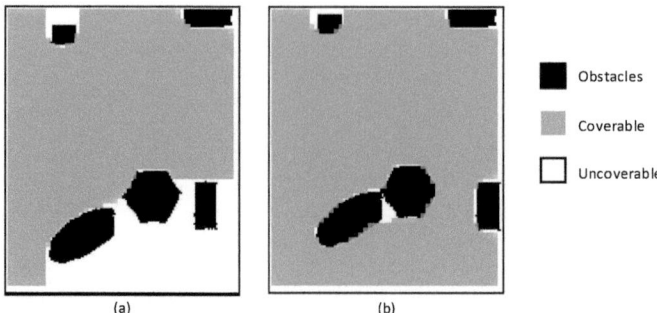

Fig. 6. Coverage estimation by the robot. (a): estimated coverage for original layout and (b): coverage estimation if layout is co-designed.

coverage for the original layout was 70%, while it increased to 88% for the human-robot co-designed layout. These coverage observations are close to the estimations made by the robot, validating the real-world performance improvement achieved by the proposed co-design framework. As seen in Fig. 7(a) and Fig. 7(b), the disruption to the original layout was minimal. Thus, the suggestions provided by the proposed framework do not considerably interfere with human spatial requirements. Therefore, the proposed human-robot collaborative co-design framework is effective for improving the productivity of a floor-cleaning robot while minimizing disruption to the user.

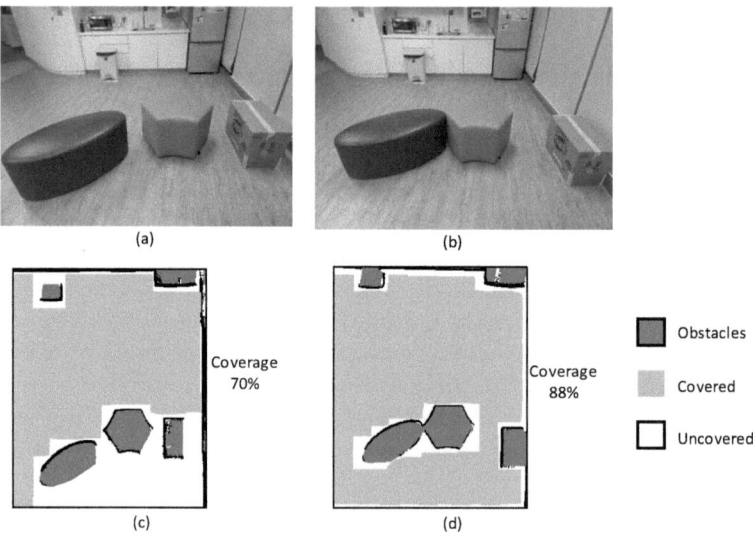

Fig. 7. Environments and coverage results from robot deployments. (a): environment with original layout, (b) environment altered per the robot's suggestions, (c): coverage results in the original environment, and (d): coverage results in the modified environment.

5 Conclusions

This work proposed a human-robot co-design framework that enhances the area coverage performance of a floor-cleaning robot by suggesting minimal and interpretable layout modifications. By integrating a large language and vision model for semantic scene understanding and a optimization process using a multi-objective genetic algorithm, the robot autonomously generates actionable feedback to users in natural language. Real-world experiments demonstrated that the framework can improve the cleaning coverage with minimal disruption to the environment. As future work, the framework would be extended to dynamic environments by incorporating user feedback in real-time and enabling autonomous actuation for layout rearrangement where permissible. Additionally, integrating human activity prediction could further optimize layouts for both cleaning efficiency and user comfort.

Acknowledgments. This research is supported by the National Robotics Programme under its National Robotics Programme (NRP) BAU, Ermine III: Deployable Reconfigurable Robots, Award No. M22NBK0054; the National Robotics Programme under category National Robotics Programme 2.0, LEO 1.0: A New Class of Bed Making Robot, Award No. M25N4N2028; and also supported by A*STAR under its RIE2025 IAF-PP programme, Modular Reconfigurable Mobile Robots (MR)2, Grant No. M24N2a0039.

Disclosure of Interests. The authors have no competing interests.

References

1. Bisht, R.S., Pathak, P.M., Panigrahi, S.K.: Design and development of a glass façade cleaning robot. Mech. Mach. Theory **168**, 104585 (2022)
2. Bochkarev, S., Smith, S.L.: On minimizing turns in robot coverage path planning. In: 2016 IEEE international Conference on Automation Science and Engineering (CASE), pp. 1237–1242. IEEE (2016)
3. Bormann, R., Jordan, F., Hampp, J., Hägele, M.: Indoor coverage path planning: Survey, implementation, analysis. In: 2018 IEEE International Conference on Robotics and Automation (ICRA), pp. 1718–1725. IEEE (2018)
4. Butaney, S., Gaurav, K., Ranjan, P., Shrivas, N.V.: Recent developments in autonomous floor-cleaning robots: a review. Ind. Robot Int. J. Robot. Res. Appl. **52**(3), 362–380 (2025)
5. Deb, K.: Multi-Objective Evolutionary Algorithms. In: Springer Handbook of Computational Intelligence, pp. 995–1015. Springer, Berlin, Heidelberg (2015)
6. Elara, M.R., Rojas, N., Chua, A.: Design principles for robot inclusive spaces: a case study with roomba. In: 2014 IEEE International Conference on Robotics and Automation (ICRA), pp. 5593–5599. IEEE (2014)
7. Elliott, S., Cakmak, M.: Robotic cleaning through dirt rearrangement planning with learned transition models. In: 2018 IEEE International Conference on Robotics and Automation (ICRA), pp. 1623–1630. IEEE (2018)
8. Galceran, E., Carreras, M.: A survey on coverage path planning for robotics. Robot. Auton. Syst. **61**(12), 1258–1276 (2013)
9. Holland, J., et al.: Service robots in the healthcare sector. Robotics **10**(1), 47 (2021)

10. Irawan, Y., Muhardi, M., Ordila, R., Diandra, R.: Automatic floor cleaning robot using Arduino and ultrasonic sensor. J. Robot. Control (JRC) **2**(4), 240–243 (2021)
11. Liu, H., Li, C., Wu, Q., Lee, Y.J.: Visual instruction tuning. In: Advances in Neural Information Processing Systems, vol. 36, pp. 34892–34916 (2023)
12. Megalingam, R.K., Vadivel, S.R.R., Kotaprolu, S.S., Nithul, B., Kumar, D.V., Rudravaram, G.: Cleaning robots: a review of sensor technologies and intelligent control strategies for cleaning. J. Field Robot. (2025)
13. Mohan, R.E., Tan, N., Tjoelsen, K., Sosa, R.: Designing the robot inclusive space challenge. Digital Commun. Networks **1**(4), 267–274 (2015)
14. Morita, S., Okura, Y., Kojima, C.: Human dense avoidance based on a coverage control through robots. Electron. Commun. Japan **105**(4), e12383 (2022)
15. Muthugala, M.V.J., Samarakoon, S.B.P., Elara, M.R.: Tradeoff between area coverage and energy usage of a self-reconfigurable floor cleaning robot based on user preference. IEEE Access **8**, 76267–76275 (2020)
16. Muthugala, M.V.J., Samarakoon, S.B.P., Elara, M.R.: Design by robot: a human-robot collaborative framework for improving productivity of a floor cleaning robot. In: 2022 International Conference on Robotics and Automation (ICRA), pp. 7444–7450. IEEE (2022)
17. Nasirian, B., Mehrandezh, M., Janabi-Sharifi, F.: Efficient coverage path planning for mobile disinfecting robots using graph-based representation of environment. Front. Robot. AI **8**, 624333 (2021)
18. Noorazman, N.A.A.M.B., Ibrahim, A.I.B.: Autonomous swimming pool cleaning robot. In: 2022 IEEE 9th International Conference on Underwater System Technology: Theory and Applications (USYS), pp. 1–12. IEEE (2022)
19. Piaggio, D., et al.: The use of smart environments and robots for infection prevention control: a systematic literature review. Am. J. Infect. Control **51**(10), 1175–1181 (2023)
20. Samarakoon, S.B.P., Muthugala, M.V.J., Abdulkader, R.E., Si, S.W., Tun, T.T., Elara, M.R.: Modelling and control of a reconfigurable robot for achieving reconfiguration and locomotion with different shapes. Sensors **21**(16), 5362 (2021)
21. Samarakoon, S.B.P., Muthugala, M.V.J., Elara, M.R.: Online complete coverage path planning of a reconfigurable robot using glasius bio-inspired neural network and genetic algorithm. In: 2022 IEEE/RSJ International Conference on Intelligent Robots and Systems (IROS), pp. 5744–5751. IEEE (2022)
22. Song, J., Gupta, S.: ε^*: an online coverage path planning algorithm. IEEE Trans. Rob. **34**(2), 526–533 (2018)
23. Verne, G.B.: Adapting to a robot: Adapting gardening and the garden to fit a robot lawn mower. In: Companion of the 2020 ACM/IEEE International Conference on Human-robot Interaction, pp. 34–42 (2020)
24. Wijegunawardana, I.D., Muthugala, M.V.J., Samarakoon, S.B.P., Hua, O.J., Padmanabha, S.G.A., Elara, M.R.: Insights from autonomy trials of a self-reconfigurable floor-cleaning robot in a public food court. J. Field Robot. **41**(3), 811–822 (2024)
25. Zhang, M., Cai, W., Pang, L.: Predator-prey reward based q-learning coverage path planning for mobile robot. IEEE Access **11**, 29673–29683 (2023)

Efficient Path Planner via Predator Dominance and Prey Approach for a Vector Surveillance Robot

Ash Yaw Sang[1], Veerajagadheswar Prabakaran[1(✉)], Mohan Rajesh Elara[1], and Anh Vu Le[2]

[1] Singapore University of Technology and Design, 8 Somapah Road, Singapore 487372, Singapore
{ashley_tan,prabakaran,rajeshelara}@sutd.edu.sg
[2] Optoelectronics Research Group, Faculty of Electrical and Electronics Engineering, Ton Duc Thang University, Ho Chi Minh City 700000, Vietnam
leanhvu@tdtu.edu.vn

Abstract. Mosquito-borne diseases continue to threaten public health, especially in densely populated tropical regions. Conventional mosquito control methods often rely on labour-intensive practices or the use of harmful chemicals, posing risks to both humans and the environment. In response, we present Dragonfly, a socially-aware mobile robot developed to autonomously manage mosquito populations in urban environments. Dragonfly attracts and traps mosquitoes using eco-friendly pheromones, reducing the need for human involvement and chemical exposure. As a socially interactive agent operating in shared public spaces, Dragonfly must navigate dynamically changing human environments without compromising human safety. A critical challenge arises: how can the robot perform mosquito control effectively without inadvertently drawing mosquitoes toward people? Existing navigation strategies prioritise collision avoidance but overlook the social and health implications of vector movement in human proximity. To tackle this, we introduce a modified predator-prey-inspired path-planning algorithm that accounts for both human crowd density and mosquito hotspots. Integrated into the A* algorithm, our approach enables Dragonfly to proactively minimise human exposure risk while reaching all mosquito hot spot regions within the time constraints. We evaluate this approach by comparing it with conventional planning methods. Results show superior performance in balancing computational efficiency, and path effectiveness. This work highlights the role of socially intelligent robotics in promoting public health, illustrating how autonomous systems can interact responsibly and safely in human-centred environments.

Keywords: Mobile Robot · Mosquito Trapping · Complete Coverage · Path Planning · Pest Control · Social Robotics · Safe Navigation

1 Introduction

Pest control has long been a human endeavour aimed at addressing threats from species such as rats [1], birds [2], and mosquitoes [3]. In urban environments, the presence of pests—particularly mosquitoes—poses both health risks and discomfort to daily living. Mosquitoes are vectors for several serious diseases including malaria [4,5], chikungunya [6], Zika [7], and dengue [8], placing over 40% of the global population at risk [9]. This growing health burden highlights the urgent need for sustainable and intelligent mosquito control solutions in densely populated areas.

Traditional mosquito control methods range from chemical-based interventions [10] to physical traps [11], but these approaches often raise environmental concerns or lack flexibility for dynamic deployment. In urban settings where constant human presence must be accounted for, fixed-position traps or pesticide usage are suboptimal. To address these limitations, socially intelligent and autonomous robots offer a promising alternative. These robots can actively monitor, engage, and neutralize mosquito populations while safely navigating among humans—bringing the benefits of automation into public health applications within shared spaces.

Recent developments in pest control robotics have introduced platforms with capabilities tailored to agricultural use cases, such as autonomous pesticide sprayers [12], microrobots for insecticide delivery [13], and vision-based weed classifiers [14]. However, the urban context demands a different kind of solution—one that is mobile, environmentally safe, and socially aware. Platforms like Dragonfly [15], a mosquito-catching robot embedded with object detection models to classify species such as Aedes Aegypti and Culex, have demonstrated the feasibility of such systems in mosquito surveillance and control [16,17].

Despite these advances in robotic perception and mechanical design, an important challenge remains underexplored in the social robotics domain: human-aware path planning. Robots tasked with pest control must avoid navigating through crowded areas to prevent drawing mosquitoes toward people. Traditional navigation algorithms prioritise collision avoidance, but neglect the social and epidemiological implications of human proximity in vector control. Furthermore, many existing path planning techniques, such as artificial potential fields [18], graph-based methods [19], or deep learning planners [20], are not optimised for time-sensitive pest eradication in human-dense environments.

To address these challenges, we propose a novel, socially aware path-planning approach for mosquito control robots operating in public environments. Our method builds upon the predator-prey paradigm [21–23], integrating it with a modified A* algorithm to form the PP* (Predator-Prey Star) algorithm. This planner evaluates crowd density dynamically and selects optimal paths that reduce exposure risk while ensuring timely coverage of mosquito hotspots—essential for capturing mosquitoes during their peak activity periods [24].

The key contributions of this paper are:

- A novel predator-prey-inspired path-planning algorithm (PP*) tailored for social robotics in pest control.
- A human-aware crowd modelling technique integrated into the planning system to minimise human-vector interaction.
- A modified A implementation* that incorporates predator (crowd) cost functions to optimise real-world performance.
- A real-world evaluation of the complete system on the Dragonfly robotic platform, demonstrating safe and effective mosquito control in human environments.

By integrating robotic autonomy with public health objectives, this research advances the role of socially intelligent robots in urban ecosystems—paving the way for safer, cleaner, and smarter pest control solutions.

2 PP* Algorithm

2.1 Algorithm Overview

The developed system introduces an efficient path-planning approach for a mosquito-capturing robot, enabling it to reach hotspots while minimising disruption to human crowds. The system balances the need for quick coverage during active mosquito periods with avoiding close interaction with people, as lingering near crowds could inadvertently attract mosquitoes. To address this, a modified prey-predator approach is proposed, optimising the robot's path by adapting to crowd size—navigating easily through small groups and rerouting around larger crowds to maintain efficiency. An overview of the algorithm is shown in Fig. 1.

The algorithm requires a rasterised map of the environment, with metadata on crowd locations and mosquito hotspots. Predators represent human crowds, while prey refers to mosquito hotspots. It is assumed that crowds are radially distributed (Fig. 2a) and that prey locations are situated outside crowd zones (Fig. 2b). The robot is programmed to avoid predators while moving towards prey, accounting for delays if hotspots lie within crowded zones.

Crowds are modelled using their geometric centre, dispersion radius, and density. These parameters can be estimated through modern computer vision techniques, which are not discussed in this work, as the focus is on path planning. The crowd tolerance is modelled as an *inflatingballoon*, expanding until constrained by obstacles, which may shift the centre away from the crowd's centroid.

2.2 Predator Dominance and Prey Model

Traditionally, Dijkstra's algorithm utilised the greedy function while searching for the path towards the goal point, iterating each vertex (or node) on the graph by selecting the node with the lowest cost as shown in the equation below:

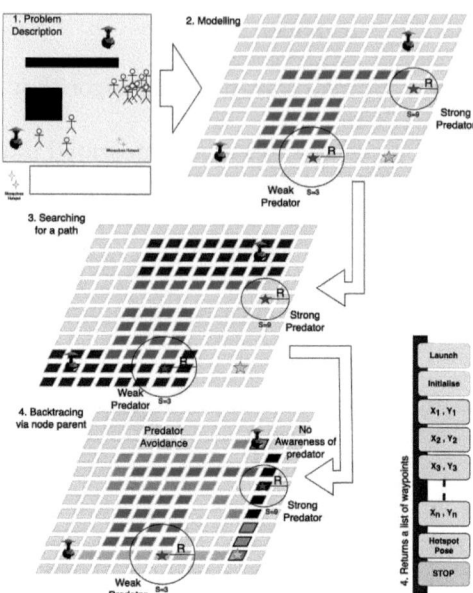

Fig. 1. Overview of the proposed solution.

$$q = g(n) \tag{1}$$

where q is the total cost of the neighbour for selection based on the function of g. For every step, g may be computed by various methods such as the iteration step, which is $n_{i+1} = n_i + 1$ for all available neighbours, or by the geometrical Euclidean ($||x||$), Manhattan, Minkowski, Hamming or Chebyshev distances. this work uses Euclidean distance as the proof of concept for the modified improvement of the A* algorithm.

The algorithm is then proposed to be enhanced by geometrical heuristics to the goal, transforming it into an informed search. This allows the search iterations to move towards the goal point faster, which leads the algorithm to operate at lower complexity levels despite additional calculations required as shown in the equation below:

$$q = g(n) + h(n) \tag{2}$$

where q is the total cost of the neighbour for selection based on the summation function of g and h, where the greedy function g is the Euclidean distance between the current node position to the neighbour node position while heuristics function, h, is computed by the distance between the neighbour position to the goal position.

Unlike traditional A* algorithms, sometimes the cost functions do not provide favourable attractants for the algorithm. The typical heuristics are blind to

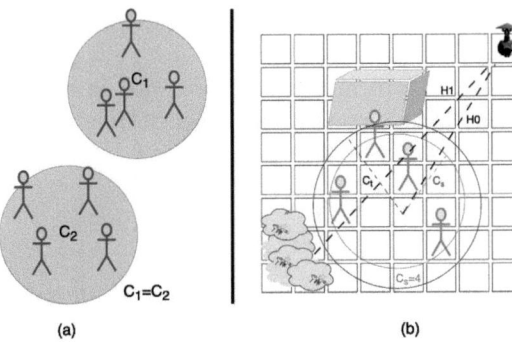

Fig. 2. a) presents a simple crowd modelling method, the model will not include the dispersion of each individual of the crowd, while (b) shows the modelling of crowd tolerance, radius and size in the description of the crowd, respectively.

conditions of the search space. The predator and prey models in the proposed algorithm act as attractants and repellents. Crowded scenes can be difficult to model, due to the complexity of solutions in modern computer vision. Hence, a simplified model of the human crowd needs to be proposed for efficient computation. This can be modelled as a crowd point with an effective radius that represents the crowd size and tagged with 2 variables as shown below:

$$h0 = (C_s - C_t) \times \sqrt{\sum_{i=\{x,y\}} (\text{Node}_{ci} - P_{0i})^2} - C_r \qquad (3)$$

where $h0$ is the proposed heuristic function for the modified A* algorithm. This heuristic function is a function of coefficients of the crowd size (C_s), crowd tolerance(C_t), crowd radius(C_r) and predator vector position,$P0$. The effects of the values of the coefficients are localised by $P0$. In this modification, the predator position is also the position to avoid. The vector positions in the iterated sum are the magnitude of i, j and k respectively. C_s represents the weight of the crowd size which in turn scales the threat level of the predator model while C_t shows the resistance of the robot to the predatory threat, which is determined by the allowance of space from the locality of the predator. C_r shows the proximity of the threat, which is limited to the spread of the crowd.

The crowd size(C_s), crowd tolerance(C_t), and crowd radius(C_r) variables are used to represent crowd population and tolerance. This can be provided by machine vision software [25] that reads the number of people in the crowd and the dimensions of the space available. In this paper, the proposal assumes that this variable is given from the current state-of-the-art.

When the crowd tolerance is significantly larger than the crowd size, it will signify that the predator model is dominant, and it prevents the robot from crossing paths with the crowd. In the real world, this is meaningful for the robot, as densely populated areas hinder the robot's efficiency from its original pose to the destination pose, which puts the crowd at risk of mosquito bites as mentioned earlier.

The prey model is the typical heuristic provided in the A* algorithm which draws the search bias of the algorithm and algorithm's path planning as shown below:

$$h1 = \sqrt{\sum_{i=\{x,y\}} (\text{Node}_{ci} - P_{1i})^2} \qquad (4)$$

where $h1$ is the prey position. In this paper, the prey position is also the goal position. The secondary heuristics function is a typical Euclidean distance function.

The total heuristic function of the modified A* algorithm is shown as follows:

$$H = h0 + h1 \qquad (5)$$

where H is the sum of the prey and predator ($H0$ and $H1$) influence on the cost of the search function.

2.3 Modified A*: Predator-Dominance and Prey Star Algorithm

The equation of the A* is then added to the predator component to it. The equation is as follows:

$$q = g(n) + H \qquad (6)$$

where q is the total cost of the modified A* algorithm, with the cost of the greedy function, $G(n)$, and the combined cost of $h0$ and $h1$ represented by H. This cost function is actively computed in the algorithm in each iteration.

The algorithm starts with a set of empty open and closed lists. The start position of the robot will then be appended to the opened list. The iteration of the search will then begin by transferring it to the closed list while computing a set of algorithmic functions. The node with the lower cost will be selected as the current node in every iteration. In the first iteration, there will only be one node and the cost is 0. The algorithm checks if the current node is in the position of the goal node, from lines 6–12. This process occurs in every iteration before computing other instructions in the algorithm. The algorithm process moves into processing the neighbours of the current node in lines 13–16. In this process, the neighbours will be generated as children, and each node is recognised as a child node. For it to be a valid child node, the process checks for validity based on its occupancy state and exploration state. Explored nodes will be in the closed list. The final process of the algorithm calculates the cost of each child node. The computation will include calculating g, $h0$ and $h1$ to obtain the final cost. All information on each child's position and cost will be appended to the open list. Then the algorithm instruction loops back to selecting the nodes in the open list for the lowest cost.

The algorithm is also enhanced by blocking off closed nodes. In the original A* and Dijkstra's algorithms, nodes may be revisited to update the cost of the node representing a point in space. In many cases, revisited nodes are mostly not needed for the update as the iterated cost will tend to be higher than the cost on the first coverage of the search. This component of the modification enhances the time performance of the algorithm.

Algorithm 1. PP* Algorithm

Input: μ, c_s, c_r, $node_s$, P_0, P_1
Output: Path Plan

1: **Init** ls_o, ls_c
2: $ls_o \leftarrow node_s$
3: **While** $ls_o \neq Empty$
4:     $Node_c \leftarrow \min(\text{cost}(ls_o))$
5:     $ls_c \leftarrow \text{pop}(\min(\text{cost}(ls_o)))$
6:     **If** $Node_c = P_1$
7:         **Init** $Path$
8:         $current \leftarrow Node_c$
9:         **While** $current \neq None$
10:             path.append(current)
11:             $current = parent(current)$
12:         **Return** $Path$
13:     **Init** $Children)$
14:     **For** $p \forall Node_k$
15:         If p $\in$ μ **AND** p is not obstructed and p $\notin ls_c$
16:             **Append** $N \leftarrow p$
17:     **For** $child \forall N$
18:         $g = f(n)$, f is Eqn1
19:         $h0 = f(child, P_0)$, f is Eqn3
20:         $h1 = f(child, P_1)$, f is Eqn4
21:         $H = f(h0, h1)$, f is Eqn5
22:         $q = f(g, h0, h1)$, f is Eqn6
23:         **Append** $ls_o \leftarrow$ child
24:         **Append** $\mu[child\ position] \leftarrow 1$
25: **Return** $Path = []$

---

3 Experiment and Results

3.1 Simulation Set-up

To evaluate the effectiveness and computational efficiency of the proposed PP* algorithm 1, extensive simulations were performed using Spyder 4.1.5 with Python 3.7.9 on a MacBook Pro (13-inch, M1, 2020). The simulations were designed to emulate various environmental complexities as shown in Fig. 3: (a) environments with multiple obstacles (Sim1), (b) open-space environments (Sim2), and (c) maze-like structures (Sim3). Additionally, higher-resolution maps

(Sim4 and Sim5) were generated at two and three times the resolution of Sim1 to assess scalability (Fig. 4).

Each scenario was executed 10,000 times for statistical stability. Benchmark algorithms, Dijkstra's (Algorithm A) and A* (Algorithm B), were tested alongside the PP* algorithm, with the PP* algorithm evaluated across multiple parameter configurations (C_s, C_t, C_r), as summarised in Table 2. The start, end, and human crowd positions were annotated in each environment with distinct markers.

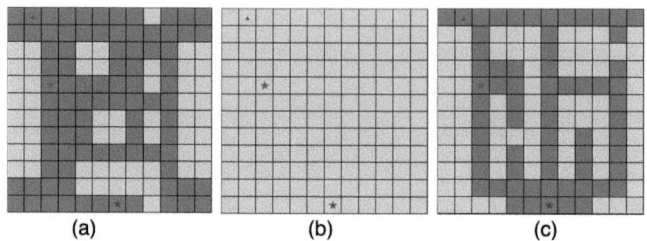

Fig. 3. Different types of environments for simulation testing of running time performance. (a) presents a simple environment with short obstacles and elongated obstacles, (b) presents an obstacle-free environment, and lastly, (c) presents a complex environment that has some maze-like features.

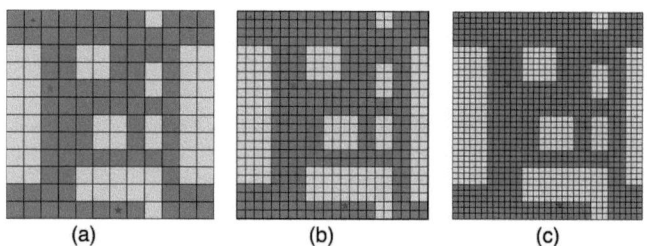

Fig. 4. Different resolutions of the same environment for simulation testing of running time performance. (a) presents a simple environment with short obstacles and elongated obstacles as the reference map, (b) presents the environment with twice the resolution of the reference map, and lastly, (c) presents the environment with thrice the resolution of the reference map.

The PP* algorithm employed a predator-prey-inspired heuristic (H_0) alongside the traditional Euclidean heuristic (H_1) used in Algorithm B. Key performance metrics included computation time, number of nodes explored, and derived path length.

Table 1. Simulation Result Summary

Algorithm	Sim1	Sim2	Sim3	Sim4	Sim5
A Ave. (S.D.)	0.456 (0.057)	0.895 (0.047)	0.226 (0.027)	2.017 (1.781)	4.467 (1.453)
B Ave. (S.D.)	0.593 (0.077)	1.037 (0.080)	0.229 (0.023)	2.542 (0.108)	6.037 (1.420)
C Ave. (S.D.)	0.359 (0.029)	0.448 (0.040)	0.187 (0.029)	1.166 (0.065)	2.618 (0.655)
D Ave. (S.D.)	0.407 (1.143)	0.449 (0.034)	0.187 (0.012)	1.222 (0.770)	2.663 (1.277)
E Ave. (S.D.)	0.346 (0.167)	0.435 (0.017)	0.173 (0.009)	1.171 (0.367)	2.552 (0.125)
F Ave. (S.D.)	0.364 (0.126)	0.448 (0.027)	0.187 (0.024)	1.185 (0.248)	2.635 (0.941)

Table 2. Predator Parameters for Each Simulation

Simulation - Algorithm	C_s	C_t	C_r
Sim1-3 - Algo C	10	4	3
Sim1-3 - Algo D	10	4	3
Sim1-3 - Algo E	20	4	3
Sim1-3 - Algo F	10	4	3
Sim4 - Algo C	20	8	6
Sim4 - Algo D	20	8	6
Sim4 - Algo E	40	8	6
Sim4 - Algo F	20	8	12
Sim5 - Algo C	30	12	9
Sim5 - Algo D	30	12	9
Sim5 - Algo E	60	12	9
Sim5 - Algo F	30	12	18

Table 3. Path Planning Performance (Transposed)

Algorithm	Sim1	Sim2	Sim3	Sim4	Sim5
Path Nodes - A	14	12	14	27	40
Path Nodes - B	14	12	14	27	40
Path Nodes - C	17	13	16	38	57
Path Nodes - D	17	13	16	38	57
Path Nodes - E	19	14	16	38	57
Path Nodes - F	17	13	16	48	74
Searched Nodes - A	90	148	55	336	729
Searched Nodes - B	75	103	38	270	595
Searched Nodes - C	78	83	35	254	567
Searched Nodes - D	78	83	35	254	567
Searched Nodes - E	73	81	33	248	555
Searched Nodes - F	78	83	35	248	555

3.2 Simulation Results and Discussion

The simulation results, summarised in Table 1 and Table 3, show that Algorithm A generally performed faster than Algorithm B due to the smaller size of the graphs. However, the heuristics used in Algorithm B sometimes misdirected the search, particularly in maze-like environments (Sim1, Sim4, Sim5). The proposed PP* algorithm consistently outperformed both Algorithm A and B in computation time across all scenarios.

Performance gains achieved by PP* over benchmark algorithms ranged from approximately 10% to 50% depending on the scenario and parameters. Although the PP* algorithm occasionally resulted in slightly longer paths—between 14% and 85% increases in node count—it significantly reduced the number of nodes explored, thus demonstrating better computational efficiency.

The influence of predator (crowd) parameters was clearly observed; larger crowd sizes and radii slightly degraded computational performance due to longer detours. Nonetheless, the proposed method successfully minimised exposure to crowds without substantial sacrifice in overall efficiency.

While the numerical parameters were not directly mapped to real-world crowd density measures, the experiments demonstrated how the cost-based path modifications influenced robot behaviour adaptively.

$$gain = (1 - \frac{O(\text{Proposed Algorithms})}{\Omega(\text{Benchmark Algorithms})}) \times 100 \tag{7}$$

3.3 Real-World Experiment Setup

To validate the practicality of the proposed algorithm beyond simulation, real-world experiments were conducted using the dragonfly robot platform (Fig. 5[Top]) powered by ROS Melodic on Jetson Nano. The test environment, illustrated in Fig. 5 [Bottom], featured multiple pathways where one direct path was obstructed by a crowd of static obstacles, while an alternative path remained clear.

Benchmark algorithms (Algorithms A and B) and the proposed PP* algorithm were deployed under identical conditions. Predator parameters used for the real-world tests are listed in Table 4. The robot's computation time for path planning and its overall time to reach the destination were recorded for comparison.

Unlike the simulation setup where crowd configurations could vary widely, real-world experiments focused on moderate, static crowd representations to ensure repeatability and control. The results of the executed experiment are shown in Table 5.

3.4 Real-World Results and Discussion

The real-world experimental results confirmed the trends observed in simulation. Robots using the traditional Dijkstra's and A* algorithms required frequent

Table 4. Predator Parameters for Experiment

Experiment - Algorithm	C_s	C_t	C_r
Algo A - Scene 1&2	-N.A.-		
Algo B - Scene 1&2	-N.A.-		
Algo C - Scene 1	20	4	3
Algo C - Scene 2	10	4	3

Table 5. Path Planning Performance

Scene - Algorithm	Computing Time (s)	Manoeuvre Time	Replans
Scene1-A	0.631	1 min 10.29 s	2
Scene2-A	0.775	1 min 36.64 s	3
Scene1-B	0.821	1 min 10.32 s	2
Scene2-B	0.931	1 min 35.92 s	3
Scene1-C	0.271	1 min 13.76 s	0
Scene2-C	0.261	1 min 13.90 s	0

replanning upon encountering blocked paths, resulting in higher cumulative computation times and delays in reaching their destinations. In contrast, the PP* algorithm, with its socially aware planning, proactively avoided crowded routes and minimised the need for replanning.

This proactive behaviour is particularly critical for applications like mosquito capture, where swift positioning near hotspots is essential for operational success. The experiments showed that denser crowds led to more frequent path disruptions for Algorithms A and B, while the PP* algorithm sustained smoother navigation even in semi-crowded scenarios.

Overall, the PP* algorithm demonstrated a significant reduction in computational load, improved consistency in reaching goals, and better suitability for dynamic, human-populated environments, thereby validating its role in social robotics tasks.

3.5 Summary of Experimental Findings

Across both simulated and real-world settings, the PP* algorithm consistently outperformed benchmark path planners by offering better computational efficiency, maintaining safety around humans, and ensuring reliable navigation towards mosquito hotspots. Although some increase in path length was observed, the trade-off is justified by the improvements in speed, reduced recomputation, and socially intelligent behaviour.

These results highlight the practical benefits of incorporating socially aware cost functions into traditional path planning methods, positioning PP* as a viable solution for robotics applications operating in complex, human-shared environments.

Fig. 5. [Top] Dragonfly robot and its mosquito catching cabinet [Bottom] (a) scene 1 - where the obstacles are slightly spread further apart, (b) scene 2 - where the obstacles are closer together.

4 Conclusion

This paper presents the development of a predator-and-prey model as an extension of the A* algorithm. In this model, a crowd component assists the robot's path planning by avoiding congested areas and pathways. The theoretical details of the path-planning technique are described, along with its implementation on a mosquito-capturing robotic system named Dragonfly. The evaluation of this technique covers both simulated and real-world scenarios, systematically comparing it with traditional methods. The results from both simulation and experimentation demonstrate that the proposed approach enhances the algorithm's running time. Additionally, it enables the robot to effectively manage its path planning based on human congestion levels, allowing mosquito capture without exposing humans to mosquitoes. While the PP* algorithm shows strong performance, certain limitations remain. The system assumes static or slowly moving crowd data, which may not hold in dense, dynamic environments like train stations. Errors in real-time crowd detection or occlusions could misguide the predator model, leading to inefficient paths. Future work should explore integrating real-time SLAM with crowd forecasting, using deep learning models for dynamic risk prediction, and deploying the algorithm in multi-agent scenarios to manage robot swarms in large spaces.

Acknowledgments. This research is also supported by A*STAR under its RIE2025 IAF-PP programme, Modular Reconfigurable Mobile Robots No: M24N2a0039 and is also supported by the National Robotics Programme under its National Robotics Programme (NRP) LEO 1.0: A New Class of Bed Making Robot, No: M25N4N2028.

References

1. Jurišić, A., et al.: Surveillance strategies of rodents in agroecosystems, forestry and urban environments. Sustainability **14**(15), 9233 (2022)
2. Garcia, K., Olimpi, E.M., Karp, D.S., Gonthier, D.J.: The good, the bad, and the risky: can birds be incorporated as biological control agents into integrated pest management programs? J. Integrated Pest Manage. **11**(1), 11 (2020)
3. Zhu, G., et al.: Effects of human mobility, temperature and mosquito control on the spatiotemporal transmission of dengue. Sci. Total Environ. **651**, 969–978 (2019)
4. Oliveira-Ferreira, J., Lacerda, M.V.G., Brasil, P., Ladislau, J.L.B., Tauil, P.L., Daniel-Ribeiro, C.T.: Malaria in brazil: an overview. Malaria J. **9**, 1–15 (2010)
5. Talapko, J., Škrlec, I., Alebić, T., Jukić, M., Včev, A.: Malaria: the past and the present. Microorganisms **7**(6), 179 (2019)
6. Matusali, G., Colavita, F., Bordi, L., Lalle, E., Ippolito, G.: Maria R Capobianchi, and Concetta Castilletti. Tropism of the chikungunya virus. Viruses **11**(2), 175 (2019)
7. Brady, O.J., Hay, S.I.: The first local cases of zika virus in Europe. The Lancet **394**(10213), 1991–1992 (2019)
8. Katzelnick, L.C., et al.: Zika virus infection enhances future risk of severe dengue disease. Science **369**(6507), 1123–1128 (2020)
9. Jones, R.T., Ant, T.H., Cameron, M.M., Logan, J.G.: Novel control strategies for mosquito-borne diseases (2021)
10. Mdeni, N.L., Adeniji, A.O., Okoh, A.I., Okoh, O.O.: Analytical evaluation of carbamate and organophosphate pesticides in human and environmental matrices: a review. Molecules **27**(3), 618 (2022)
11. Sefat, S., Shefa, A.A., Quarishi, S.A., Neaz, S., Ashrafuzzaman, M.: Development of a pheromone based smart mosquito trap. In: Second International Conference on Emerging Trends in Engineering (ICETE 2023), pp. 169–176. Atlantis Press (2023)
12. Samada, L.H., Tambunan, U.S.F.: Biopesticides as promising alternatives to chemical pesticides: a review of their current and future status. Online J. Biological Sci. **20**(2), 66–76 (2020)
13. Maria-Hormigos, R., Mayorga-Martinez, C.C., Pumera, M.: Magnetic hydrogel microrobots as insecticide carriers for in vivo insect pest control in plants. Small, p. 2204887 (2023)
14. Vivek, K.K., Sidharth, R., Rohit, P., Vishagan, S., Peeyush, K.P.: Pests & weed control autonomous robot using machine vision. In: 2021 Second International Conference on Electronics and Sustainable Communication Systems (ICESC), pp. 1319–1326. IEEE (2021)

15. Semwal, A., Melvin, L.M.J., Mohan, R.E., Ramalingam, B., Pathmakumar, T.: Ai-enabled mosquito surveillance and population mapping using dragonfly robot. Sensors **22**(13), 4921 (2022)
16. Chen, Y.-X., et al.: Use of unmanned ground vehicle systems in urbanized zones: a study of vector mosquito surveillance in kaohsiung. PLoS Negl. Trop. Dis. **17**(6), e0011346 (2023)
17. Kenyeres, Z., et al.: Cost–benefit analysis of remote sensing data types for mapping mosquito breeding sites. Spatial Information Research, pp. 1–10 (2023)
18. Ping, W., Gao, F., Li, K.: Humanlike decision and motion planning for expressway lane changing based on artificial potential field. IEEE Access **10**, 4359–4373 (2022)
19. Liu, H., Zhang, Y.: Asl-dwa: an improved a-star algorithm for indoor cleaning robots. IEEE Access **10**, 99498–99515 (2022)
20. Wang, J., Chi, W., Li, C., Wang, C., Meng, M.Q.-H.: Neural rrt*: learning-based optimal path planning. IEEE Trans. Automation Sci. Eng. **17**(4), 1748–1758 (2020)
21. Prabakaran, V., Mohan, R.E., Sivanantham, V., Pathmakumar, T., Kumar, S.S.: Tackling area coverage problems in a reconfigurable floor cleaning robot based on polyomino tiling theory. Appl. Sci. **8**(3), 342 (2018)
22. Veerajagadheswar, P., Ping-Cheng, K., Elara, M.R., Le, A.V., Iwase, M.: Motion planner for a tetris-inspired reconfigurable floor cleaning robot. Int. J. Adv. Robot. Syst. **17**(2), 1729881420914441 (2020)
23. Gao, X., Yan, L., Li, Z., Wang, G., Chen, I.-M.: Improved deep deterministic policy gradient for dynamic obstacle avoidance of mobile robot. IEEE Trans. Syst. Man Cybern, Syst (2023)
24. Wilke, A.B.B., et al.: Diel activity patterns of vector mosquito species in the urban environment: implications for vector control strategies. PLoS Negl. Trop. Dis. **17**(1), e0011074 (2023)
25. Sharma, N., Baral, S., Paing, M.P., Chawuthai, R.: Parking time violation tracking using yolov8 and tracking algorithms. Sensors **23**(13), 5843 (2023)

It's the Way You Move: Efficient Movement Shapes Robot Perception Across Embodiments

Kristina Nikolovska[1](✉), Jan Pohl[2], Bernhard Hommel[3], Francesco Maurelli[1], and Arvid Kappas[4]

[1] School of Computer Science and Engineering, Constructor University, Bremen, Germany
{knikolovska,fmaurelli}@constructor.university
[2] Faculty of Psychology, Dresden University of Technology, Dresden, Germany
jan-pohl@cog-sci.eu
[3] Department of Psychology, Shandong Normal University, Shandong, China
bh@bhommel.onmicrosoft.com
[4] School of Business, Social and Decision Sciences, Constructor University, Bremen, Germany
akappas@constructor.university

Abstract. This study investigates how a robot's physical appearance influences user perception of its movement behavior, with a focus on movement efficiency. Participants watched videos of three robot types—a humanoid (NAO), a non-humanoid AGV (Duckiebot), and an abstract spherical robot (BOLT)—each executing both efficient and inefficient trajectories. Across all embodiments, efficient movement led to higher user ratings of intelligence, competence, and agency. Bayesian analysis supported the interpretation that robot form did not moderate the effect of movement efficiency on social attributions. The results reinforce that movement, specifically efficient robot movements, plays a critical role in shaping user perceptions. These findings suggest that the design of purposeful and efficient behaviors may be more influential for perception than physical embodiment.

Keywords: robot movement · user perception · embodiment · efficiency · social cognition

1 Introduction

As robots shift from industrial settings into everyday human environments, their role is evolving from mere tools to interactive collaborators and companions [1]. This growing presence raises critical questions about how a robot's behavior and physical appearance affect human trust [2], acceptance [3], and social interaction [4]. Designing robot movement and non-verbal behavior to feel natural and purposeful is increasingly seen as essential to fostering smooth human-robot interaction and preventing negative attitudes toward robotic agents [5]. One well-studied factor that shapes user perception is the robot's *embodiment*—its physical appearance and form [6]. Robots with humanoid, animal-like, or highly mechanical designs can elicit different interpretations of intent, intelligence, and social presence [7] [8–10]. Another important factor is a robot's *movement behavior*, particularly how it moves through space. Prior studies suggest that fluid, human-like movements are often associated with greater perceived intelligence, trustworthiness, and social capability than rigid or mechanical trajectories [11,12]. However, it remains unclear how these two dimensions—form and movement—interact. Do the same movement patterns yield different perceptions depending on the robot's appearance? Or is movement alone sufficient to shape how we interpret a robot's capabilities and intent? Some work emphasizes the unique potential of humanoid robots to evoke social responses [13], while other findings suggest that even minimal cues like movement—independent of form—can trigger rich social attributions, as illustrated in the classic Heider and Simmel animation [14]. The present paper aims to explore the gaps in current research by examining how the embodiment of different robot appearances influences and interacts with user perceptions when robots perform identical movement behaviors. Section 2 provides the theoretical background and motivation for the hypothesis that the robot's form, whether humanoid or non-humanoid, does not significantly alter how users perceive human-like movements. However, we believe that employing more human-like movement patterns will always improve user perception. In Section 3, we describe the experimental design, which is a modification of our previous studies [12,15] that successfully showed how specific movements affected the perception of AGV robots (Duckiebots). By analyzing various robot embodiments in the present study, our research seeks to contribute valuable insights into the relative importance of embodiment and behavior. Ultimately, such research shall serve to constrain the design of robots for human-centered environments. In this study, we use the term *movement behavior* specifically to refer to the robot's navigation trajectory, how it moves through space from one point to another. This includes features such as path selection and movement efficiency but excludes other types of behavior such as gestural expression, interaction with objects in the environment, or social positioning. While robots can move in many ways, our focus is on trajectory-based navigation, which allows us to isolate how simple goal-directed movement influences user perception across different embodiments.

2 Background

In Human-Robot Interaction (HRI), the physical appearance, or embodiment, of a robot is widely recognized as a crucial factor shaping user perception [16]. Embodiment includes characteristics such as the robot's form, size, and facial features. Robots can range from highly anthropomorphic designs to abstract or purely functional machines, and this variation has been shown to significantly influence how people interpret a robot's capabilities, intentions, and social presence [17]. A key concept underpinning this effect is anthropomorphism, the tendency to attribute human-like qualities such as intelligence, intentionality, or emotion to non-human agents [18]. Research has shown that robots with more human-like features are more likely to be perceived as intelligent, capable, and socially aware, thereby enhancing user trust and acceptance [19]. For example, humanoid robots are often rated more positively in terms of competence, friendliness, and trustworthiness compared to more mechanical or minimal designs. This emphasis on embodiment has led many HRI studies to prioritize the development of human-like features, assuming such design choices naturally improve interaction. However, this focus raises the question of whether embodiment is always the most influential factor—or whether other elements, such as behavior and movement, might play a similarly significant role. While embodiment clearly influences perception, several foundational studies suggest that physical appearance is not a necessary condition for humans to attribute social meaning or agency. A classic example is the Heider and Simmel animation (1944) [14], where viewers consistently interpreted geometric shapes as intentional and emotional agents based purely on movement trajectories. This reveals a cognitive bias: humans tend to project agency onto even the simplest moving entities. Similarly, the widespread popularity of Tamagotchi and other minimal digital or robotic companions demonstrates that elaborate embodiment is not required for users to engage emotionally or socially with artificial agents [20]. These systems offer limited interactivity, no realistic human features, and only basic feedback, yet users often report strong emotional bonds and caregiving behavior. These examples point to a deeper mechanism in social cognition: humans interpret behavior patterns as socially meaningful, even in the absence of a human-like form. In light of this, it is important to reconsider how much embodiment alone drives perception. If users can assign personality and agency to abstract shapes or pixelated pets, then purposeful or efficient movement may be sufficient to evoke positive perceptions, regardless of appearance. Building on the idea that users perceive agency from even minimal cues, recent research has focused on how simple behavioral signals—particularly movement—shape perception. Robots do not necessarily require complex appearance or verbal interaction to be seen as intentional or intelligent; motion itself can serve as a powerful cue. For example, studies by Hostettler and colleagues [11] and Šlajpah et al. [21] show that even industrial robots are perceived more favorably when their movements are smooth, fluid, and human-like. Participants attributed higher competence, intelligence, and trust to robots with efficient and natural movement, even when their form was strictly mechanical. In our previous work [12], similar effects were observed with AGVs: minimal changes in movement characteristics—such as efficiency, learning, and equifinality—led to significant improvements in perceived intelligence, agency, and acceptance. These results indicate that movement can function as a core social signal, shaping how users interpret a robot's intentions and competence, often independently of physical appearance. This growing body of work suggests that behavioral design, especially in movement, plays a critical role in human-robot interaction. Users respond not only to how a robot looks, but to how it moves—particularly when movement reflects purpose, efficiency, or rationality. Such cues may be especially impactful when embodiment is limited, reinforcing the idea that movement itself carries social meaning, even in abstract forms. Given this, the present work examines the extent to which movement behavior alone can influence user perception across different robot embodiments. While physical appearance plays a role in shaping first impressions, previous studies suggest that even minimal, well-structured behaviors—such as purposeful or efficient movement—can evoke positive evaluations of intelligence, agency, and social presence. This raises the question of whether embodiment remains a dominant factor when such behaviors are held constant. To investigate this, the study focuses on efficiency as a core characteristic of human-like movement, which is also straightforward to implement across robot platforms. Three robot embodiments ranging from humanoid to non-humanoid were selected, each performing either efficient or inefficient trajectories. The goal is to assess whether embodiment alters how users perceive movement, or whether movement alone accounts for differences in perceived cognitive and social traits. Two hypotheses are proposed: H1: Robots displaying behaviors associated with efficiency will be perceived more favorably and rated higher on scales measuring social attributes and mind- or self-attribution. H2: These effects will be consistent across different robot embodiments, suggesting that appearance does not or not so much influence user ratings when movement remains constant. These hypotheses challenge the idea that embodiment is the primary driver of user perception when behavior is involved. Instead, we assume that efficient behavior—even decoupled from human-like form—can strongly shape how robots are evaluated. By exploring the interaction between movement and form, this study aims to contribute to the design of robot behavior for human-centered environments, where functionality and smooth interaction may outweigh the importance of physical implementation. The next section outlines the experimental design used to examine how movement efficiency influences user perception across varying robot embodiments.

3 Experimental Setup

3.1 Robotic Agents

This study used three robot types—Sphero BOLT [23], Duckiebot [22], and Aldebaran NAO [24]—representing abstract, non-humanoid, and humanoid embodiments (see Fig. 1). The selection was designed to span a range of physical forms from minimal to anthropomorphic, allowing us to assess whether embodiment moderates the effect of movement efficiency on perception. Each robot was programmed in Python to follow two trajectory types: efficient and inefficient. All robots moved from a fixed start to goal location, with trajectories varied per condition while keeping path structure consistent across embodiments.

3.2 Stimuli

Participants viewed six pre-recorded videos (two per robot), each captured from a fixed, slightly angled top-down camera perspective. The robots were placed on a gray mat with white cube obstacles and navigated from a marked starting point to a marked goal, both indicated with white tape. Each robot was shown under two distinct movement conditions: an Efficient Movement Condition (efficient), in which the robot followed the shortest and most direct path to the goal, and an Inefficient Movement Condition (inefficient), in which it took a longer, suboptimal route. These paired videos aimed to highlight movement efficiency while keeping all other factors constant. An overview of all robots is shown in Fig. 2.

Fig. 1. The three robotic agents used in the experiment: Duckiebot (left), Sphero BOLT (center), and Aldebaran NAO (right).

3.3 Participants, Procedure and Instruments

Eighty participants from the United Kingdom (48 female, average age 35 years) were recruited via the Prolific platform, with eligibility restricted to fluent English speakers. To ensure data quality, exclusion criteria included technical issues during video playback and failure to pass an embedded attention check. Only participants who completed all phases of the experiment and met these criteria were retained for final analysis. All procedures were approved by the ethics committee at Constructor University. The experiment began with informed consent and a set of detailed instructions. Participants then watched six videos in total, with the order of robot presentation blocks randomized for each participant. After each robot block (i.e., efficient and inefficient movement conditions for a given robot), participants rated both conditions separately. Perceptions were assessed using a series of validated instruments measuring social and cognitive attributions toward the robots. First, participants completed a manipulation check questionnaire to verify that they noticed the differences in movement efficiency. This questionnaire, consistent with our previous studies [12,15], includes items related to selfhood relevant characteristics beyond just efficiency. Specifically, it measures six dimensions: Causality, Speed, Equifinality (i.e., persistence towards one specific goal), Behavioral Efficiency, Learning Sensitivity, and Context Sensitivity (the items can be found on the Open Science Framework project at https://osf.io/b9cnr/). Each dimension was assessed via three statements using a continuous 0100 sliding scale. Following the manipulation check, participants evaluated the robots using three standardized scales. The Mind Attribution Scale (MAS) [25] measured perceived agency and experience. The Godspeed Scale (GS) [26], widely used in HRI research, captured attributes such as animacy and perceived intelligence. Lastly, the Robotic Social Attributes Scale (RoSAS) [27] assessed perceived social qualities, focusing on warmth, competence, and discomfort.

3.4 Analysis

Both classical ANOVAs [28] and a Bayesian approach were used to analyze the data, examining the interaction between robot appearance, movement efficiency (efficient vs. inefficient), and participant ratings across the three scales: the Mind Attribution Scale (MAS), Godspeed Scale (GS), and Robotic Social Attributes Scale (RoSAS). Bayesian methods were specifically chosen to test the second hypothesis, as this approach allows for evaluating the propability of the null versus the alternative hypothesis [29]. First, for each robot individually, ANOVAs were conducted with MovementCondition (efficient vs. inefficient) and RobotPerception as within-participant factors. In the manipulation check, RobotPerception referred to participants' ratings of behavioral characteristics. In the main analysis, it encompassed ratings from the subscales of the MAS, GS, and RoSAS. Where significant interactions were found, post-hoc paired t-tests were conducted to further explore the effects. Next, a Bayes factor top-down analysis was applied using the combined data from all three robots comparing the full model with reduced models [30]. The full model used for the analysis was:

$$\text{Rating} \sim \text{RobotType} \times \text{MovementCondition} \times \text{RobotPerception} \quad (1)$$

In this analysis, the denominator was defined as the full model, including all main effects and their interactions. In this model, **Rating** refers to individual participant scores on each dependent variable—that is, each item from the three main instruments (MAS, GS, and RoSAS). Each rating represents a participant's response to a single question under a given robot and movement condition. **RobotType** refers to the three robot embodiments used in the experiment (BOLT, Duckiebot, and NAO), **MovementCondition** represents the efficiency of the robot's trajectory (efficient vs. inefficient), and RobotPerception refers either to (1)—for the manipulation check—the levels are the subscales of our manipulation check scale consisting of specific behavioral characteristics (such as causality, efficiency, and equifinality); or (2)—for the main analysis—the levels are the subscales of the three main scales (agency and experience of the

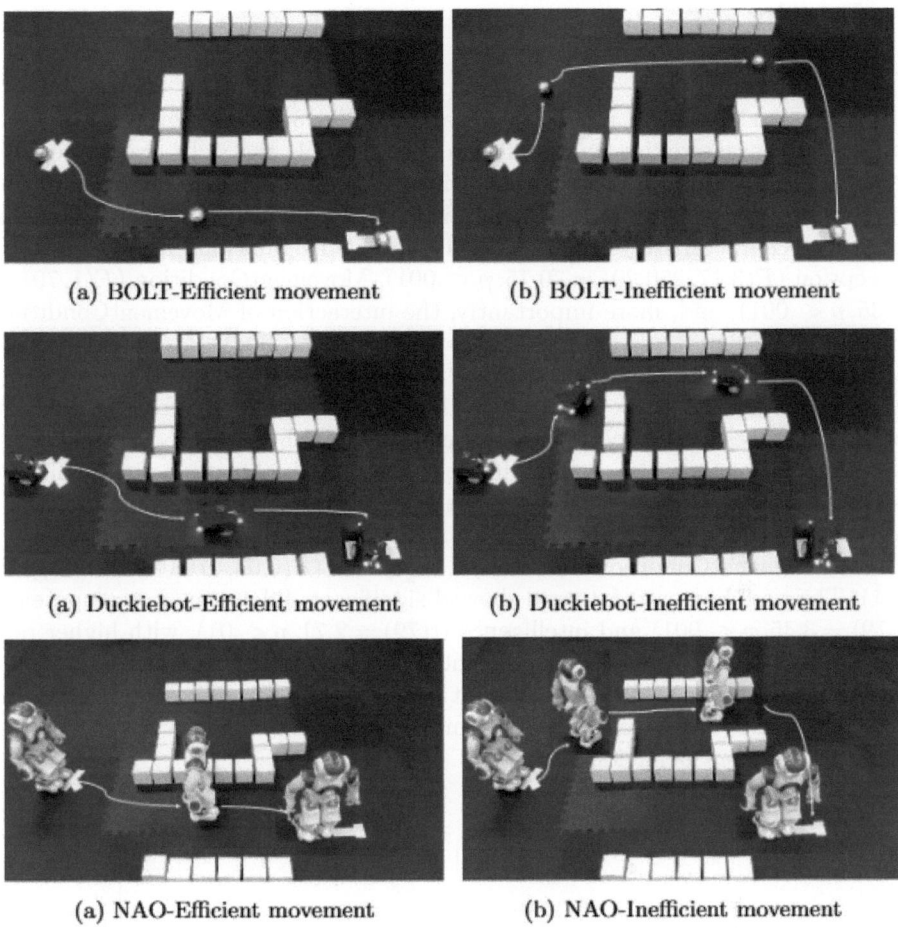

Fig. 2. Experimental setup showing each robot in two movement conditions. Left column: efficient movement using the shortest path to the goal. Right column: inefficient movement using a longer, suboptimal path.

MS; anthropomorphism, animacy, likeability, perceived intelligence, and perceived safety of the GS; and competence, warmth, and discomfort of the RoSAS). The interaction between MovementCondition and RobotPerception, previously observed in earlier studies, served to indicate whether participant perceptions were influenced by movement behavior (e.g., if efficient robots were consistently rated higher on scales assessing mind or social attribution). The three-way interaction term further tested whether this effect was moderated by robot embodiment (e.g., whether changes in perception based on efficiency differed between humanoid and non-humanoid robots).

4 Results

4.1 BOLT

The results for the BOLT robot are presented in Fig. 3. The left graph shows the behavioral characteristics (manipulation check), while the right graph presents perceived robot attributes across the Mind Attribution Scale, Godspeed Scale, and Robotic Social Attributes Scale, displayed at the subscale level. For the behavioral characteristics, ANOVA results revealed significant effects of RobotPerception ($F(3.17, 250.20) = 70.75, p < .001$), MovementCondition ($F(1, 79) = 49.35, p < .001$), and, more importantly, the interaction of MovementCondition and RobotPerception ($F(3.68, 290.50) = 123.18, p < .001$). Post-hoc paired t-tests demonstrated significant differences in efficiency ($t(79) = 18.15, p < .001$) and equifinality ($t(79) = 3.45, p < .001$), with higher scores for the efficient robot. These results indicate that the efficient BOLT was not only perceived as more efficient, but also as exhibiting greater equifinality than the inefficient version. For the perceived attributes, the ANOVA revealed a significant effect of RobotPerception ($F(5.13, 405.03) = 140.34, p < .001$) and a significant interaction of MovementCondition and RobotPerception ($F(6.03, 476.05) = 4.42, p < .001$). The post-hoc paired t-tests showed significant differences for competence ($t(79) = 3.45, p < .001$) and intelligence ($t(79) = 2.71, p < .01$), with higher ratings for the efficient robot. No significant differences were found for the remaining subscales. These results suggest that even a minimally embodied robot such as BOLT can be perceived as more competent and intelligent when displaying efficient movement behavior.

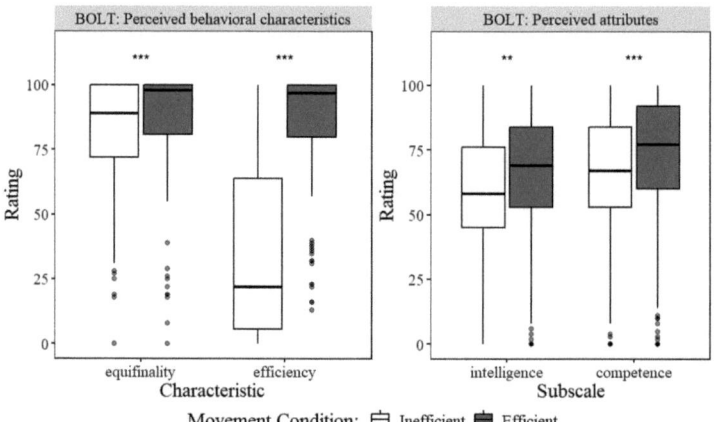

Fig. 3. Perceived movement characteristics (left) and behavioral attributes (right) of the BOLT robot across two movement conditions: efficient (grey) and inefficient (white). The plots illustrate differences in user perception across subscales. Only statistically significant results are shown. (Color figure online)

4.2 Duckiebot

The results for the Duckiebot are presented in Fig. 4, where the left graph shows the results for the behavioral characteristics, and the right graph presents the perceived general attributes. For the behavioral characteristics, the ANOVA results revealed significant effects for RobotPerception ($F(3.36, 265.30) = 73.34$, $p < .001$), MovementCondition ($F(1, 79) = 54.66$, $p < .001$), and, more importantly, the interaction ($F(3.89, 307.61) = 115.17$, $p < .001$). Post-hoc t-tests showed significant differences in efficiency ($t(79) = 16.42$, $p < .001$) and equifinality ($t(79) = 3.45$, $p < .001$), with higher ratings for the efficient robot. This shows that, just as for the BOLT, participants perceived the efficient Duckiebot as more efficient and indicated more equifinality than the inefficient robot. Regarding the perceived attributes, the ANOVA again showed a significant effect of RobotPerception ($F(4.91, 387.70) = 145.25$, $p < .001$) and, more importantly, a significant interaction ($F(4.95, 391.31) = 4.44$, $p < .001$). Post-hoc paired t-tests revealed significant differences for competence ($t(79) = 3.12$, $p < .01$) and intelligence ($t(79) = 3.31$, $p < .01$), but not for other subscales. Ratings were higher for the efficient robot, indicating that it was perceived as more competent and intelligent than the inefficient robot.

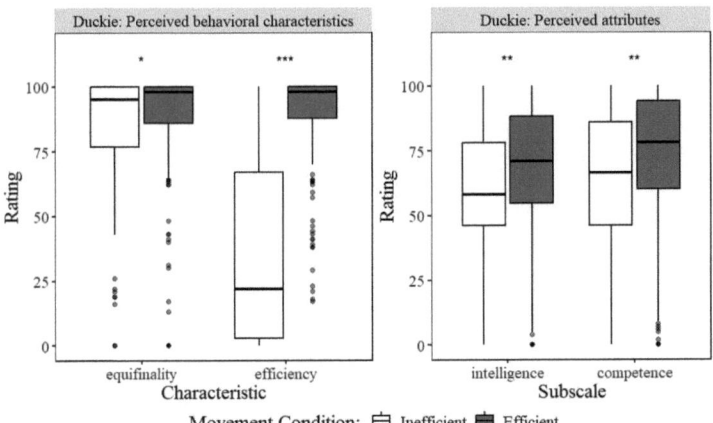

Fig. 4. Perceived movement characteristics (left) and behavioral attributes (right) of the Duckiebot across efficient (grey) and inefficient (white) movement conditions. The boxplots illustrate user ratings across different perception subscales. Only statistically significant results are shown. (Color figure online)

4.3 NAO

The results for the NAO robot are shown in Fig. 5, where the left graph illustrates the behavioral characteristics and the bottom graph presents the generally perceived attributes of the robot. For the behavioral characteristics, ANOVA results demonstrated significant effects for RobotPerception ($F(3.65, 288.23) = 125.79$, $p < .001$), MovementCondition ($F(1, 79) = 36.40$, $p < .001$), and, importantly, the interaction ($F(2.82, 222.59) = 117.07$, $p < .001$). Post-hoc paired t-tests, again, indicated significant differences in efficiency ($t(79) = 15.01$, $p < .001$) and equifinality ($t(79) = 2.86$, $p < .01$), with higher ratings for the efficient robot. This shows that, as with the BOLT and Duckiebot, participants indeed perceived the efficient NAO as more efficient but also as exhibiting greater equifinality than the inefficient version. For the generally perceived attributes, the ANOVA found a significant effect of RobotPerception ($F(4.42, 349.43) = 117.84$, $p < .001$), and, importantly, a significant interaction ($F(5.14, 405.71) = 4.16$, $p < .001$). The post-hoc paired t-tests, again, indicated significant differences for *competence* ($t(79) = 2.42$, $p < .05$) and *intelligence* ($t(79) = 3.73$, $p < .001$), while all other subscales were not significant. These results further support the pattern observed with the other robots: participants rated the efficient NAO as more competent and intelligent than the inefficient version.

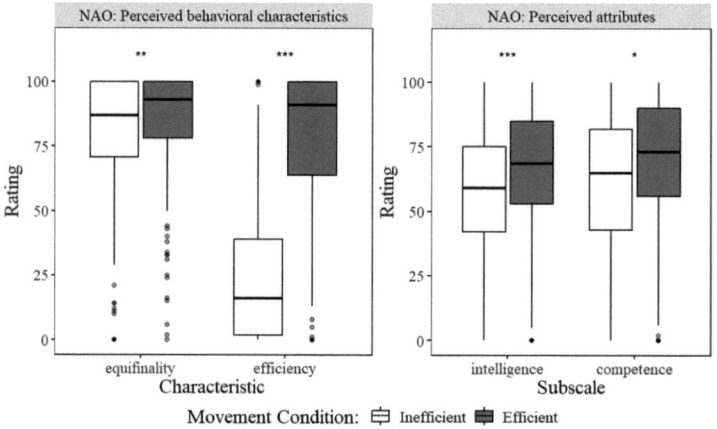

Fig. 5. Perceived movement characteristics (left) and behavioral attributes (right) of the NAO robot across efficient (grey) and inefficient (white) movement conditions. The boxplots illustrate user ratings across different perception subscales, highlighting the impact of movement efficiency on user perception. Only statistically significant results are shown. (Color figure online)

4.4 Bayesian Analysis

Bayes Factors (BFs) were calculated to assess the evidence for Hypothesis H2, which posits that robot appearance does not significantly interact with user perception based on movement condition. The results provided strong support for this hypothesis across both behavioral characteristics (manipulation check) and generally perceived robot attributes. For the behavioral characteristics, omitting the three-way interaction between RobotType, MovementCondition, and RobotPerception yielded strong evidence against an interaction effect ($BF_{0,1} = 776{,}178.80$, $\pm 4.66\%$ proportional error). In contrast, omitting only the two-way interaction between *MovementCondition* and *RobotPerception* produced strong evidence in favor of an effect ($BF_{0,1} = 2.52 \times 10^{-233}$, $\pm 4.87\%$ error). These findings suggest that while participants' perceptions clearly varied based on robot movement, this effect remained consistent across all three robot appearances. For general attributions, omitting the three-way interaction resulted in strong evidence against an effect ($BF_{0,1} = 25{,}850{,}867{,}240.00$, $\pm 3.34\%$ error), while omitting the two-way interaction of MovementCondition and RobotPerception showed strong evidence in favor of an effect ($BF_{0,1} = 8.95 \times 10^{-10}$, $\pm 3.82\%$ error). These results further confirm that robot behavior, specifically movement efficiency, significantly influences user perception, but this influence is not moderated by differences in robot embodiment. Together, the Bayesian analysis provides strong support for the claim that movement behavior, rather than appearance, is the primary driver of how users interpret and attribute social and cognitive qualities to robots.

4.5 Discussion

Across all three robots—BOLT, Duckiebot, and NAO—movement efficiency consistently shaped user perception. Robots that followed efficient trajectories were rated more favorably, not only on behavioral traits like perceived efficiency and equifinality but also on more abstract attributes such as intelligence and competence. These effects held across a range of embodiments, from non-humanoid to humanoid designs. Bayesian analyses provided strong evidence that embodiment did not moderate the relationship between efficient movement and perception. That is, the positive impact of movement efficiency on user ratings was consistent across all robot types, suggesting that users responded primarily to behavioral cues regardless of the robot's physical form. This supports the idea that people are especially sensitive to functional, goal-directed signals, and that such cues alone can drive social attributions—even in robots with minimal anthropomorphic features. These findings align with earlier work indicating that humans readily assign agency and intent to simple motion patterns [14], and extend this principle to physical robots. Even simplified platforms like Sphero BOLT and Duckiebot benefit from efficient movement, challenging the assumption that human-like appearance is required for positive evaluation in Human-Robot Interaction (HRI). While many HRI frameworks emphasize the role of embodiment, particularly anthropomorphic traits, this study shows that even in the absence of rich form, efficient behavior alone can shape perceptions of cognitive and social attributes. Users appear inclined to interpret structured, purposeful motion as indicative of intelligence. From a design perspective, these results suggest that optimizing behavior—particularly trajectory efficiency—may be a more scalable and robust strategy than investing in anthropomorphic design.

This is especially relevant for service or utility robots, which are often constrained by practical considerations. Efficient, goal-directed behavior may help such robots elicit trust, perceived competence, and broader user acceptance, even with minimalistic form factors. Our focus on movement efficiency was motivated by its relevance to both technical implementation and social interpretation. Efficiency is a core component of interpreting behavior as rational and intentional [31] and can be implemented consistently across platforms, making it a useful behavior to isolate in examining user perception. However, the present study was conducted in an online setting, where the lack of physical presence may have influenced participant responses, still there is evidence that for factors like anthropomorphism results from online and laboratory studies are comparable [32]. Only one behavior (movement efficiency) was examined, and video clips were relatively short in duration, limiting the generalizability of the present results to overall robot movement. Despite these constraints, the results highlight the power of structured movement alone in shaping perception, suggesting that users rely heavily on behavioral cues to infer competence and intent. However, we do not claim that embodiment has no influence. Rather, our findings show that it did not moderate the effect of movement efficiency under the specific conditions of this study, suggesting that efficiency affects user's perception regardless of the robot's embodiment. In other contexts—especially those involving communication—embodiment may well play a stronger role, yet our novel results suggest that movement is a strong cue in people's interpretation of robot agents that should be explored further. Future research should, thus, explore whether these embodiment-independent effects persist under more interactive and ecologically valid conditions. In-person experiments could also help evaluate the role of physical presence, motion fidelity, and real-time feedback. Additionally, expanding the behavioral repertoire to include socially expressive, adaptive, or human-reactive movements would offer a more comprehensive understanding of how form and behavior interact to shape perception in HRI.

5 Conclusions

This study investigated whether robot embodiment influences user perception of basic movement behaviors, specifically examining the impact of movement efficiency across humanoid, non-humanoid, and abstract robot designs. Results indicated that efficient movement consistently led to higher ratings in cognitive attributes such as competence and intelligence, regardless of the robot's physical form. These findings suggest that users rely heavily on goal-directed behavioral cues when evaluating artificial agents that is not modulated by their appearance. The absence of an interaction between embodiment and movement behavior highlights the importance of action quality beyond appearance in shaping perception. Efficient trajectories alone were sufficient to elicit meaningful evaluations across all robot types, challenging the assumption that anthropomorphic design is necessary for attributing higher cognitive states in Human-Robot Interaction. This emphasizes that efficiency and purposefulness in behavior may offer a scalable strategy for enhancing user acceptance and engagement, particularly in contexts where anthropomorphic features are impractical. These insights contribute to ongoing efforts to understand the relative importance of behavior and form in designing socially effective robots.

Notes and Comments. This work was funded by the German Research Foundation, DFG, Priority Programm 2134 "The Active Self" (HO 1430/13-1). Kristina Nikolovska and Jan Pohl contributed equally to this work and share first authorship. We would like to express our sincere gratitude to the participants, whose contributions were vital to the success of this study.

References

1. Lee, I.: Service robots: a systematic literature review. Electronics **10**(21), 2658 (2021)
2. Stower, R., Kappas, A.: Oh no, my instructions were wrong! An exploratory pilot towards children's trust in social robots. In: Proc. IEEE Int. Conf. Robot and Human Interactive Communication (RO-MAN), Naples, Italy (2020)
3. de Graaf, M.M.A., Allouch, S.B.: Exploring influencing variables for the acceptance of social robots. Robot. Auton. Syst. **61**(12), 1476–1486 (2013)
4. Corrales-Paredes, A., Sanz, D.O., Terrón-López, M.J., Egido-García, V.: User experience design for social robots: A case study in integrating embodiment. Sensors (2023)
5. Nomura, T., Kanda, T., Suzuki, T., Kato, K.: Prediction of human behavior in human-robot interaction using psychological scales for anxiety and negative attitudes toward robots. IEEE Trans. Robot. **24**(2), 442–451 (2008)
6. Kwak, S.S., Kim, Y., Kim, E., Shin, C., Cho, K.: What makes people empathize with an emotional robot? the impact of agency and physical embodiment on human empathy for a robot. In: Proc. IEEE RO-MAN, Gyeongju, South Korea, pp. 180–185 (2013)
7. Haring, K.S., Silvera-Tawil, D., Takahashi, T., Watanabe, K., Velonaki, M.: How people perceive different robot types: a direct comparison of an android, humanoid, and non-biomimetic robot. In: Proc. Int. Conf. Knowledge and Smart Technology (KST), Chiang Mai, Thailand (2016)
8. de Kleijn, R., van Es, L., Kachergis, G., Hommel, B.: Anthropomorphization of artificial agents leads to fair and strategic, but not altruistic behavior. Int. J. Hum.-Comput. Stud. **122**, 168–173 (2019)
9. Thellman, S., de Graaf, M., Ziemke, T.: Mental state attribution to robots: A systematic review of conceptions, methods, and findings. *J. Hum.-Robot Interact.***11**(4), Article 41, 1–51 (2022)
10. Epley, N., Waytz, A., Cacioppo, J.T.: On seeing human: a three-factor theory of anthropomorphism. Psychol. Rev. **114**(4), 864–886 (2007)
11. Hostettler, D., Mayer, S., Hildebrand, C.: Human-like movements of industrial robots positively impact observer perception. Int. J. Soc. Robot. **15**(8), 1399–1417 (2023)
12. Pohl, J., Nikolovska, K., Küster, D., Maurelli, F., Kappas, A., Hommel, B.: Attribution of selfhood based on simple behavioral cues: towards a pars pro toto account (2024)

13. Marchetti, A., Manzi, F., Itakura, S., Massaro, D.: Theory of mind and humanoid robots from a lifespan perspective. Soc. Psychol. Bull. **13**(3), e326 (2018)
14. Heider, F., Simmel, M.: An experimental study of apparent behavior. Am. J. Psychol. **57**(2), 243–259 (1944)
15. Nikolovska, K., Pohl, J., Hommel, B., Kappas, A., Maurelli, F.: The impact of social inter-robot encounters on user perception. In: Proc. IEEE Int. Conf. Robot and Human Interactive Communication (RO-MAN) (2024)
16. Wainer, J., Feil-Seifer, D.J., Shell, D.A., Mataric, M.J.: The role of physical embodiment in human-robot interaction. In: Proc. IEEE RO-MAN, Hatfield, UK (2006)
17. Fong, T., Nourbakhsh, I., Dautenhahn, K.: A survey of socially interactive robots. Robot. Auton. Syst. **42**(3–4), 143–166 (2003)
18. Waytz, A., Cacioppo, J., Epley, N.: Who sees human? the stability and importance of individual differences in anthropomorphism. Perspect. Psychol. Sci. **5**(3), 219–232 (2010)
19. Groom, V., Takayama, L., Ochi, P., Nass, C.: I am my robot: the impact of robot-building and robot form on operators. In: Proc. ACM/IEEE Int. Conf. Human-Robot Interaction (HRI), pp. 92–99 (2009)
20. Lawton, L.: Taken by the Tamagotchi: how a toy changed the perspective on mobile technology. The iJournal **8**(1), 1–12 (2023)
21. Šlajpah, S., et al.: Effect of speed, speed differences, and motion type on perceived safety of collaborative robots. In: Proc. Int. Conf. Advanced Robotics (ICAR), Ljubljana, Slovenia, pp. 1036–1041 (2021)
22. Paull, L., Saeedi, S., Seto, M., Li, H.: Duckietown: an open, inexpensive and flexible platform for autonomy education and research. In: Proc. IEEE Int. Conf. Robotics and Automation (ICRA), pp. 1497–1504 (2017)
23. Sphero Bolt: Technical specifications. https://sphero.com
24. NAO Robot: Technical overview. https://www.softbankrobotics.com/emea/en/nao
25. Bigman, Y.E., Gray, K.: People are averse to machines making moral decisions. Cognition **181**, 21–34 (2018)
26. Bartneck, C., Kulić, D., Croft, E., Zoghbi, S.: Measurement instruments for the anthropomorphism, animacy, likeability, perceived intelligence, and perceived safety of robots. Int. J. Soc. Robot. **1**(1), 71–81 (2009)
27. Carpinella, C.M., Wyman, A.B., Perez, M.A., Stroessner, S.J.: The robotic social attributes scale (RoSAS): development and validation. In: Proc. ACM/IEEE Int. Conf. Human-Robot Interaction (HRI), pp. 254–262 (2017)
28. Rutherford, A.: ANOVA and ANCOVA: A GLM Approach. John Wiley & Sons, Hoboken (2011)
29. Masson, M.E.J.: A tutorial on a practical Bayesian alternative to null-hypothesis significance testing. Behav. Res. Methods **43**, 679–690 (2011)
30. Morey, R., Rouder, J.: BayesFactor: computation of Bayes factors for common designs. Comprehensive R Archive Network (CRAN). https://cran.r-project.org/web/packages/BayesFactor/vignettes/manual.html. Accessed 22 Sep 2024
31. Lichtenthäler, C., Kirsch, A.: Legibility of robot behavior: A literature review. (2016)
32. Babel, F., Kraus, J., Hock, P., Asenbauer, H., Baumann, M.: Investigating the validity of online robot evaluations: Comparison of findings from an online and laboratory study. In: Proc. ACM/IEEE Int. Conf. Human-Robot Interaction (HRI '21 Companion), pp. 116–120 (2021)

Context Awareness and Explainability

Context Is Cue-Cial: Assessing the Interpretation of Social Signals from Non-anthropomorphic Robots in Different Contexts

Aparajita Chowdhury[1](✉), Ana Carrasco[2], Florian Müller[3], Aino Ahtinen[1], Kaisa Väänänen[1], Albrecht Schmidt[4], and Jan Leusmann[4]

[1] Computing Sciences, Tampere University, Tampere, Finland
aparajita.chowdhury@tuni.fi
[2] Instituto Superior Técnico, INESC-ID, Lisbon, Portugal
[3] TU Darmstadt, Darmstadt, Germany
[4] LMU Munich, Munich, Germany

Abstract. Humans excel at understanding social cues in communication, but robots struggle. Social cues are crucial for humans to interpret the intentions of their communication partners. Research indicates that we typically interpret the actions of anthropomorphic robots analogously to their human counterparts, paving a clear path to the design of appropriate social cues. For non-anthropomorphic robots, however, it is an open question how humans interpret social cues with different output modalities and in different contexts. Our study investigates whether social cues signaled by typical non-anthropomorphic modalities such as lights, sounds, and gestures are consistently interpreted across people and contexts. We, therefore, conducted a contextual investigation in a hospital, derived scenarios from co-design workshop, and tested 103 cues collected from the literature in a large online survey (N = 1545). Our results demonstrate that most human interpretations vary by context, highlighting the need to design dynamic and adaptive social cues for interactive robotic systems.

Keywords: human computer interaction · human-robot interaction · user-adaptive interaction · social signals

1 Introduction

From a joyful smile when meeting a friend to a sarcastic one in awkward moments, non-verbal social cues are complex and highly context-dependent. These cues, such as facial expressions, body language, and eye contact, help humans communicate intent without words [39]. As robots become more integrated into everyday life, interactions with them will increasingly involve non-verbal cues in various contexts [11,38]. However, current robots, especially non-anthropomorphic ones, struggle to adapt such cues to different contexts, making their intentions unclear.

While anthropomorphic robots benefit from human-like forms that support intuitive cue design, non-anthropomorphic robots, like delivery bots or robotic arms, are built for efficiency and typically lack features that facilitate human-like communication [6]. As these robots take on more collaborative or social roles, it is essential they convey intent through alternative means such as lights, movements, or sounds [26]. Yet, since these modalities are not familiar channels of social interaction for humans, it is common to misinterpret them. Prior research has explored non-verbal cues for non-anthropomorphic robots in contexts such as manufacturing, rescue, and logistics [12,13,36,43]. Yet, it is unclear how well these cues transfer across settings. This highlights a key gap in designing context-aware, intuitive social signals for non-anthropomorphic robots to support effective human-robot interaction. To address these limitations, we investigated how humans perceive social signals from non-anthropomorphic robots in different contexts. We chose a hospital as an example of a (semi-)public setting in which users might encounter non-anthropomorphic robots in the future, and extracted a set of distinct contexts. While we explored these in the hospital setting, we consider them generic enough to generalize to other settings. Our goal is to understand how humans perceive the social signals conveyed by a robot through lights, sounds, and gestures in various contexts, especially when they have not been previously trained or informed about the meaning of those signals. For our exploration, we chose the hospital setting, as it offers a wide range of scenarios involving people from diverse backgrounds and varying levels of knowledge. Additionally, it provides opportunities to study interactions not only with logistics personnel but also with visitors, nurses, and patients. To guide our investigation, we formulated the following research questions:

RQ1: What interaction scenarios can be developed for different contexts inside the hospital setting?

RQ2: What interaction modalities and social signals are appropriate for a non-anthropomorphic robot to effectively express its intent?

RQ3: How do different contexts influence the perception of social signals expressed by the robot within the hospital setting?

To address RQ1, we conducted a contextual inquiry in a Finnish hospital to explore human-robot interactions with a logistics robot in various contexts within the hospital. Following this, we organized a workshop with 15 students from a Finnish university to refine the insights gathered and to define five scenarios that could be presented to participants to assess the perception of social cues. The interaction scenarios were developed based on the data gathered from contextual inquiry at the hospital and the co-design workshop with the students. To answer RQ2, we asked the same workshop participants to redesign the logistics robot using modalities they believed would be suitable for this context. This exploration resulted in the selection of lights, sounds, and robotic arm gestures as means to express the robot's intent and social cues. Based on these designed interaction modalities, we reviewed 189 peer-reviewed articles to identify the social signals conveyed through light, sound, and gesture. This review yielded 103 signals, which we then recreated according to guidelines found in the literature. Finally, for RQ3, we conducted an online study with 1,545 participants to assess the perception of these social signals in various hospital contexts. Our findings indicate that there is no universal understanding of social signals for non-anthropomorphic robots. These signals are interpreted differently depending on the context, and their meanings may shift when adapted for different settings. This highlights the need for a dynamic and context-sensitive design of social cues tailored to specific interaction environments.

2 Related Work

In this section, we reflect on key topics relevant to this research. Section 2.1 explores the importance of social cues and signals for humans across different contexts. Section 2.2 addresses the challenges of designing social signals for non-anthropomorphic robots. Finally, Sect. 2.3 reviews existing knowledge on social signals for non-anthropomorphic robots in various contexts.

2.1 Social Cues and Signals for Humans Across Different Contexts

Charles Darwin argued that social cues reflect our internal states, facilitating interaction and cooperation [10]. Social signals, verbal or non-verbal cues guiding interactions, help shape our impressions of others [19]. From early childhood, humans learn to interpret and respond to these cues through experience and context [4,27]. For example, a genuine smile may express joy, while a polite smile can mask disappointment to maintain social harmony. Social signals—primarily non-verbal expressions like facial cues, body language, and gaze—are central to communication, trust-building, and emotional understanding [48]. Their interpretation depends on cultural norms, relationships, and situational context [5,19]. Through observing trusted individuals and shared social knowledge, humans develop an intuitive grasp of how to convey and interpret these signals appropriately across different settings [16]. Our lifelong experiences and cognitive abilities enable us to adapt social cues to specific contexts. This skill has been crucial to human evolution, supporting survival, cooperation, and effective communication [10,16].

2.2 Designing Social Cues for Robots

The use of appropriate social signals is essential for both humans and robots, not only to convey intent but also to build trust and influence user response [8,45,48]. However, robots lack the innate human ability to adapt social cues to different contexts, which can lead to user discomfort. For instance, in [35], Pepper's prolonged eye contact was meant to boost engagement but felt intrusive in quiet settings like libraries. Similarly, Baxter's negative head shakes were perceived as rude on assembly lines [2]. Both robots were eventually discontinued due to poor user acceptance [46], highlighting how misaligned social cues can increase mistrust [47]. Non-anthropomorphic robots face added difficulty in expressing social signals, as their design prioritizes function and cost over human-like features [6]. While efforts to incorporate social cues into such robots exist, outcomes vary. Baxter, for example, was praised in assistive roles but criticized in industrial contexts for being slow and overly human-like [2,46]. Its failure, along with that of its successor, Sawyer, underscores the need for context-appropriate cues in robot design [30]. Although anthropomorphic features aid communication [7,32], integrating them into task-focused robots remains impractical due to cost and performance trade-offs [6].

2.3 Social Cues and Modalities for Non-anthropomorphic Robots in Various Contexts

As non-anthropomorphic robots enter public spaces, it is crucial they use appropriate social cues to communicate their intentions, especially in settings like healthcare, where robots assist with tasks such as delivering equipment and supporting well-being [24,29,34]. Many hospital staff and visitors may have limited experience with robots, so these robots must express their intentions in ways that are understandable and acceptable [22]. Robots can use lights [3,44], audio signals [33], and gestures [41] to communicate effectively. Studies have explored light as a communication tool for robots, such as using different colors and animations to express actions like "wait," "progress," and "help" [3]. Similarly, audio signals have been used to convey emotions and intent, with examples like R2-D2's and Wall-E's sound design [17]. However, there is limited guidance on replicating these audio signals in real-world robots [20]. Robot arm gestures have also been studied, especially in collaborative tasks, with research exploring how movements can convey emotions and intent [18,41]. These gestures, inspired by human or animal movements, are used to communicate social signals like directions and commands [14,15]. However, most studies have focused on specific contexts, and it remains unclear how gestures like "stop" would be interpreted in different settings, such as a hospital during medicine delivery. Although research has explored non-anthropomorphic social signals using light, sounds, and gestures, there is a gap in understanding how these signals are perceived across various contexts.

3 Methodology

To address our research questions, we employed a two-phase methodological approach consisting of a pre-study and an online user study. The following sections provide a detailed account of each phase.

3.1 Pre-Study

We conducted a multiphase study to explore human-robot interaction in a hospital setting with a medicine delivery robot. In the first phase, we observed the robot during its daily routes through corridors, elevators, and reception areas, documenting interactions with logistics workers, nurses, receptionists, and visitors. Two logistics workers participated in short unstructured interviews, and two members of the robot's software team supported us during the study. These observations helped us understand the robot's tasks, stakeholders, navigation, and goals.

Next, we organized a co-design workshop with 15 Master's students (7 female, 8 male) from a human-robot interaction course, selected due to prior experience designing for social robots and familiarity with the hospital as patients or visitors. Recruiting hospital staff was not feasible due to their busy schedules. This phase was conducted to analyze the findings from the contextual inquiry and to develop scenarios and define effective communication modalities for the robot. Since the insights gathered from the hospital contextual inquiry were limited (including four participants altogether), the co-design workshop played a crucial role in helping us explore potential scenarios in greater detail. It enabled us to brainstorm what situations might arise and what the robot could communicate to different people in the hospital, such as staff, patients, and visitors. The workshop began with a 30-minute presentation of the observation findings and robot operation. Participants worked in small groups to develop five hospital interaction scenarios, discussing the robot's tasks, human interaction strategies, and expression techniques. Data from notes, audio recordings, and design canvases were thematically analyzed, revealing lights, sounds, and gestures as suitable expressive modalities. The five distinct hospital interaction scenarios were defined as:

Scenario 1 Loading Medicine: The robot starts its day when one of its human colleagues load medicines into the robot and asks it to go to deliver it to one of the hospital wings.

Scenario 2 Obstacle Encounter: The robot starts its journey and encounters closed door.

Scenario 3 Passing Through: As the robot goes to deliver medicine, it needs to pass through a lobby where the robot meets human colleagues in a logistics vehicle.

Scenario 4 Elevator Interaction: The robot needs to take the elevator to reach its destination. Human colleagues can share the elevator with the robot.

Scenario 5 Delivering Medicine: The robot reached its destination and needs to inform someone that the robot is here to deliver.

We also created visualizations for the scenario to support the clarity and understandability of the interactions (see Fig. 1).

Based on the workshop findings, the participants identified three main communication modalities: lights, sounds, and robot arm gestures as the most suitable to convey the robot's intent, while screens were considered less effective in large hospital areas. Based on these insights, we developed a prototype of the robot that incorporates the selected modalities (see Fig. 2). These findings highlight the importance of simple understandable non-verbal cues to ensure robot safe and effective integration into hospital workflows. Ethical approval

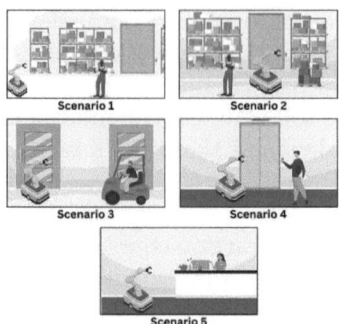

Fig. 1. Hospital scenarios resulted from the pre-study.

was obtained for both the hospital observation and the workshop, with all data handling conducted in compliance with EU GDPR regulations.

3.2 Online User Study

The observation and co-design workshop provided an initial understanding of interaction modalities, techniques, and social signals. To achieve better results from data analysis of the user study, we further explored social signals from previous literature to identify those that conveyed specific intentions in the context of non-anthropomorphic robots. We then recreated these signals for our delivery robot prototype and conducted an online study to examine how different contexts influence the perception of social signals expressed by the robot (RQ3). The subsequent sections are organized as follows: *Robot Prototype, Participants, Procedure, Data Collection and Analysis*

Robot Prototype. We developed a prototype delivery robot to recreate expressions identified from the literature. For the mobile base, we used the Elephant Robotics MyAGV 2023 PI[1]. On top of it, we mounted a MyCobot 280 M5Stack robotic arm with a gripper from Elephant Robotics[2], which was used to perform arm gestures for expressing social cues. For light-based gestures, we attached an 8 × 8 Neopixel LED matrix housed in a 3D-printed case at the front of the robot (see Fig. 2). Audio expressions were generated using external USB speakers. All expressions were recorded in a well-lit room with a white background to ensure consistency.

Participants. We recruited 2,193 participants for the online study via Prolific, aiming for three participants per unique combination of SCENARIO (5) × EXPRESSION (103). After excluding 648 low-effort responses, identified through

---
[1] https://shop.elephantrobotics.com/products/myagv-2023-pi.
[2] https://www.elephantrobotics.com/en/mycobot-280-m5-2023-en/.

Fig. 2. Robot Setup used for recreating the expressions from literature.

the text summaries participants were required to provide, we were left with 1,545 valid participants (784 female, 725 male, 36 non-binary). The participants' average age was 32.32 years ($SD = 10.41$), representing 86 nationalities. The largest groups came from South Africa (229), the UK (169), the United States (155), Poland (117), Canada (87), Portugal (84), Mexico (68), Zimbabwe (55), and Spain (43). 353 participants had never interacted with a robot, 909 reported between one and seven interactions, and 283 had more than seven interactions, mostly with social robots or robotic arms.

Procedure. Based on the workshop findings, we collected 189 expressions for lights, sounds, and gestures from the literature. After excluding expressions that lacked sufficient detail or could not be replicated on our robot, we finalized a set of 103 expressions: 31 gestures, 32 light cues, and 40 audio cues. Gesture selection followed [42], light cues were drawn from 119 Web of Science articles (filtered for clear color/pattern descriptions), and audio expressions were based on [51], using only those with publicly available files. To ensure consistency in the recordings, we standardized all expressions. For gestures, we controlled arm speed, face/trunk position, and direction. For lights, we fixed speed, pattern type (e.g., blinking, sweeping), and RGB color. For audio expressions, we used original files, maintained a consistent volume, and limited their duration to 35 s. All videos are available in the supplementary material. The study was conducted online. After providing informed consent, participants answered two demographic questions about their prior experiences with robots and the types of robots they had encountered. Each was assigned a scenario and condition, shown an illustration and a simplified scenario description (based on pre-study findings). Instructions clarified that the robot communicates non-verbally. Participants then watched a video of one expression and provided two open-ended responses: (1) what the robot did, and (2) in one word, what the expression meant in context. These interpretations were analyzed as detailed in Sect. 4.

Data Analysis. Four researchers initially developed a codebook to ensure triangulation, after which two researchers collaboratively coded the data to ensure reliability and consistency. In the first iteration, coding 1,545 descriptions resulted in 47 unique codes, covering behaviors (e.g., "robot is performing a task," "robot opens elevator/door," "processing"), requests (e.g., "come here," "asking human to do something," "needs help"), intentions (e.g., "robot wants to pick something up," "wants to get in the elevator," "showing information"), and emotions (e.g., "curiosity," "happy," "confused"). A second iteration refined this to 35 unique codes. Finally, we discussed these results among four researchers and categorized these labels into 10 distinct code groups for a final analysis:

Task-Oriented Communication: *Intent* (to communicate intended actions, e.g., "robot delivering package", "robot pick up", "let human pass", "giving permission".), *Request* (asking human for help or to do something, e.g., "asking to pass/move aside", "robot asks to open elevator/door", etc.), and *Status* (displaying robot's internal states - "error", "ready/waiting", "robot is performing a task", etc.).

Social Interaction: *Emotional State* (e.g., "happy", "amazed", "confused", "distress"), *Politeness* (e.g., "greeting", "deference", "showing gratitude", "appreciation"), and *Interest* (showing enthusiasm or curiosity).

Directive Communication: *Attention* (to direct human's focus, e.g., "call for attention", "warning", "alert"), *Agreement* (acceptance, consent, approval, acknowledgment) and *Disagreement* (refusing or negating something).

All samples where participants' interpretations could not be understood were classified as *None*. Details about this coding process are provided in the supplementary material.

Metrics. We measure the level of agreement of an expression using a pairwise similarity metric that checks how many interpretations of the 3 participants match for each scenario-expression combination. We call this metric the Agreeability Score (AS):

$$AS = \frac{1}{N} \sum_{\substack{i \neq j}}^{N} (E_i = E_j), \qquad 1 \leq i < j \leq N \tag{1}$$

where E_i and E_j are the coded interpretations of the participants i and j, and N is the number of participants per scenario-expression combination (in our case, $N = 3$). $E_i = E_j$ takes the value of 1 if the codes are equal, and 0 otherwise. AS can be either 0 for no agreement, 1/3 for partial agreement and 1 for a perfect agreement.

Additionally, to analyze the impact of the scenario and the modality of the expression in the participants' interpretations, we fitted multinomial logistic regression models to predict code groups, with scenario and modality as independent variables. We looked at Likelihood ratios and calculated the Nagelkerke pseudo-$R^2 = [37]$ as a metric of these models' explanatory power.

4 Results

4.1 Agreeability Analysis

Table 1. Updated agreement scores for each scenario and modality, including both average (M) and the percentage of perfect agreement (P.A.) values ($AS = 1$).

Scenario	Arm Gestures M	Arm Gestures P.A.	Light M	Light P.A.	Audio M	Audio P.A.	All Modalities M	All Modalities P.A.
Loading Medicine	33.33	19.35	34.38	21.88	23.33	10.00	30.35	17.08
Obstacle Encounter	26.88	12.90	35.42	18.75	29.17	12.50	30.49	14.72
Passing Through	30.11	19.35	42.71	28.12	25.83	7.50	32.88	18.32
Elevator Interaction	41.94	25.81	25.00	12.50	21.67	7.50	29.54	15.27
Delivering Medicine	32.26	16.13	39.58	28.12	26.67	10.00	32.84	18.08
All Scenarios	32.90	18.71	35.42	21.88	25.33	9.50		

Applying the Agreement Score (Eq. 1) on the coded participant interpretations, we found that, out of all the 103 expressions, across the 5 scenarios ($103 \times 5 = 515$ total combinations), 226 (43.88%) of them obtained a partial agreement (2 out of 3 equal, $AS = 0.33$) and 83 (16.12%) of them obtained a perfect agreement ($AS = 1$). As the results from Table 1 suggest, audio gestures are generally less often agreed on than arm or light gestures. Furthermore, the agreeability is highest for the passing through and delivering medicine scenarios.

When looking at perfect agreement (Table 1), we see a slight difference between scenarios (highest for the passing through scenario - 18.32%), and a bigger difference between modalities (highest for lights - 21.88%). Additionally, for expressions that had a perfect agreement across multiple scenarios (17 out of 103 - 16.5%), we found that only 4 (3.9%) had a perfect agreement between the scenarios (meaning, all the participants, across the 5 scenarios, agreed on the interpretation of that expression). These results suggest that both scenario and modality have an impact on how participants interpret the robot's expressions.

Table 1 shows the average AS and percentage of perfect agreement for each scenario × modality combination. Furthermore, Fig. 3 shows the distribution of agreed-on code groups for each scenario. It shows that for all scenarios, around 40% of the expressions had an $AS = 0$. For the loading medicine scenario, the majority of expression has been agreed on as *Status* (30%), for the obstacle encounter scenario *Request* (40%), for passing through *Attention* (20%), elevator interaction *Request* (23%), and delivering medicine *Attention* (21%). Furthermore, we see that the agreed-on code distribution per modality is even more widespread, indicating, that the scenario had a larger impact on the interpretation than the modality.

Next, we investigated the distribution of how often each code group was agreed on across scenarios, see Fig. 4. Here, we found that the same gesture is agreed on with the same meaning across our five scenarios.

Agreeability with Original Meaning. We looked into how participants' interpretations matched the original interpretation of the expression from their reference for all arm gestures and light expressions, as the literature source for the audio [51] did not provide this information. Thus, we conducted this analysis on the 31 arm gestures and 32 light gestures out of 103 total expressions. We categorized the original meanings using our 10 code groups and compared them with the participants' interpretations. We found that for 10 arm gestures and 11 light signals, the original meaning matches the agreed code group ($AS \geq 33\%$) implying that only 20% of the expressions matched their original meaning. As most expressions were derived from different settings and were originally performed by significantly more anthropomorphic robots, we expected that the original meaning would be lost. Once again, the strong correlation between the scenario and the meaning of these expressions is evident.

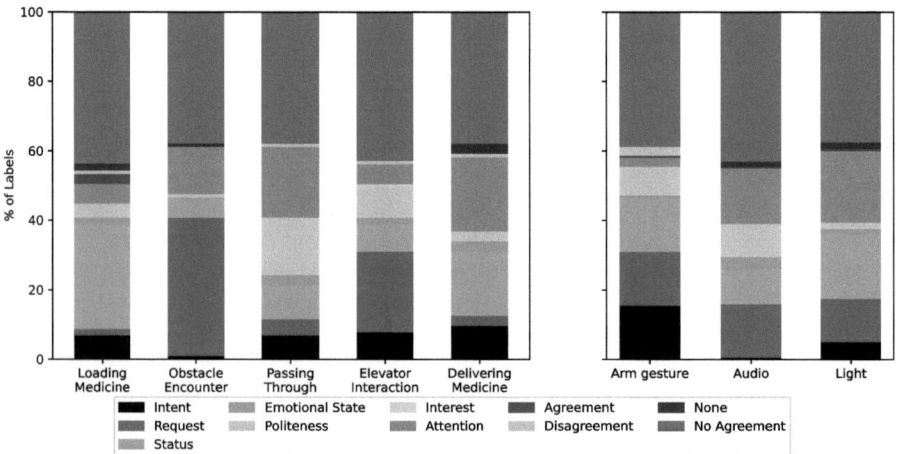

Fig. 3. Distribution of agreed on Code Groups across different scenarios (left) and modalities (right). No Agreement means that all 3 participants' interpretations were coded into different code groups. Thus, the expression was not agreed on.

4.2 Statistical Analysis

We fitted multinomial models to explain code groups by our independent variables. Due to the limited size of the dataset, all models containing expressions did not converge. Therefore, we removed this factor for all further analyses and instead focused on reduced models to analyze the influence of scenario and modality on the dependent variables.

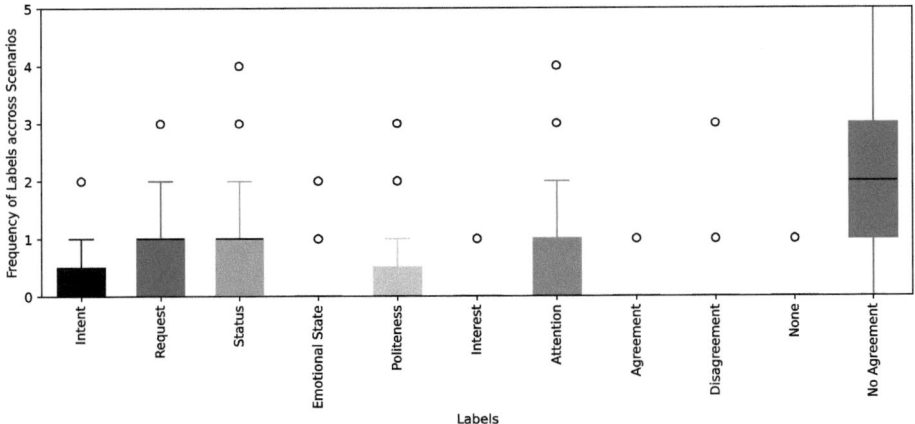

Fig. 4. Distribution of Code Groups across scenarios.

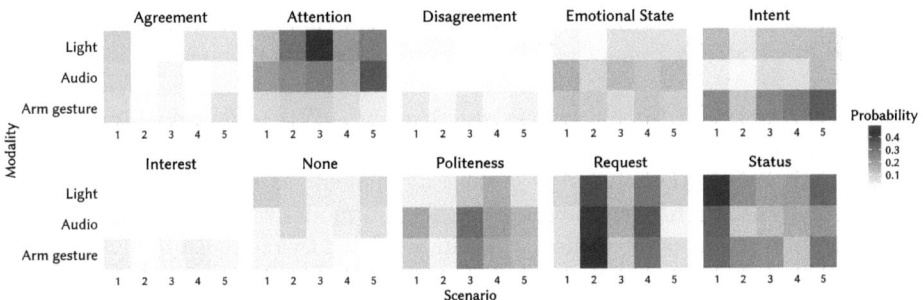

Fig. 5. Predicted probabilities of choosing a particular code group for different combinations of Scenario and Modality. Darker shades indicate higher probabilities.

We fitted a multinomial logistic regression model with scenario, modality and their interaction as fixed effects to predict code group. We further fitted two reduced models, one excluding scenario and one excluding modality to evaluate the influence of the factors. Likelihood ratio tests confirmed that removing scenario ($\chi^2(108) = 436.89, p < .001$) or modality ($\chi^2(90) = 318.45, p < .001$) significantly degraded the model fit. Accordingly, we continued with the full model including both factors and their interaction.

As a measure of the explanatory power of the model, we calculated the Nagelkerke pseudo-R^2. The result $R^2 = 0.36$ represents a moderate fit and indicates that a substantial part of the variance in the data can be explained by scenario and modality alone. This indicates that the interpretation of an expression by our participants depended not only on the specific expression but also to a large extent on what modality was used and in which scenario it was performed.

Figure 5 presents the predicted probabilities from the full model for selecting a code group based on different combinations of scenario and modality. The most frequently assigned interpretations by participants were "Status" ($M = 0.22$, $SD = 0.10$), "Request" ($M = 0.19$, $SD = 0.16$), and "Attention" ($M = 0.18$, $SD = 0.12$).

A more detailed analysis of these code groups shows that arm gestures rarely lead to the interpretation "Attention" ($M = 0.06, SD = 0.02$), but that audio ($M = 0.23, SD = 0.07$) (especially in scenario 5, 0.34) and light ($M = 0.25, SD = 0.12$) (especially in scenario 3, 0.45) do so more frequently. For "Request" we found no strong dependence on the selected modality, but a strong dependence on the scenario. In scenarios 2 ($M = 0.43, SD = 0.07$) and 4 ($M = 0.29, SD = 0.04$), all expressions across all modalities are primarily interpreted as "Request". For "status", we found a more complex picture with strong connections between scenario 1 ($M = 0.36, SD = 0.09$) and 5 ($M = 0.26, SD = 0.06$), as well as the modalities light ($M = 0.26, SD = 0.12$) and arm gestures ($M = 0.22, SD = .08$). Across all conditions, we found the strongest connection for audio in scenario 2, where roughly half of our participants (0.48) interpreted any gesture as a request.

These probabilities support the interpretation that both modality and scenario exhibit a strong impact on the interpretation of participants.

Predicting Agreement from Scenario and Modality. We employed a similar approach to predict agreement from scenario and modality. For this analysis, we focused only on expressions with perfect agreement, as explained in Sect. 3.2. For the analysis, we fitted a binomial regression model with scenario, modality and their interaction as fixed effects. Again, we fitted two reduced models excluding scenario and, respectively, modality to evaluate the influence of the factors. The model fit did not significantly decline by removing scenario ($\chi^2(12) = 6.10$, $p = 0.9$) or modality ($\chi^2(10) = 17.18$, $p = 0.07$). This result indicates that both independent variables have no significant influence on the explanatory power of the model. Accordingly, the Nagelkerke pseudo-R^2 of the complete model of $R^2 = 0.06$ also demonstrates a very low explanatory power of the model. From this we conclude that the influence of scenario and modality on whether there is a unique interpretation of gestures across several people is very small or non-existent. Thus, predicting the agreement without knowledge of the actual expression seems infeasible.

4.3 Distribution of Code and Code Groups

In the final iteration of coding, participants' interpretations of the expressions were coded into a total of 10 code groups. Figure 6 shows the distribution of these group codes between scenarios. The results show uneven distributions of the code groups. For most scenarios, approximately 60% of the interpretations fell into 3 (or less) out of 10 code groups. Calculating the normalized entropy[3] of these frequencies, we see that scenario 2 has the lowest value, 0.718 (where 1 would

---

[3] $H_{\text{normalized}} = -\frac{\sum_{i=1}^{N} p_i \log_2 p_i}{\log_2(N)}$, $N = 10$, where p_i is the frequency of code group i.

correspond to a perfect distribution of the 10 code groups), with almost a majority of participants interpreting "Request". On the other hand, scenario 1 has the highest entropy, 0.851, with the majority of interpretations distributed between "Attention", "Status" and "Intent". These results could be easily explained by the scenario in which they are interpreted, once again highlighting the codependency of scenarios in the interpretation of these expressions.

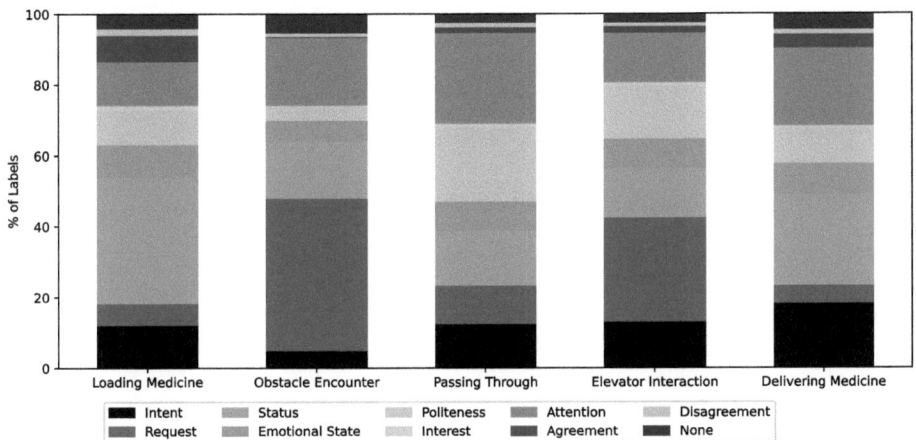

Fig. 6. Distribution of Code Groups across different scenarios.

5 Discussion

Our study offers key insights into how social signals from non-anthropomorphic robots are interpreted across contexts and modalities. We discuss these findings in relation to our research questions and propose design implications, including how AI can support the development of adaptive, context-aware robot signals for more intuitive human-robot interaction.

5.1 Interpretation of Expressions Vary Across Different Contexts

Our analysis revealed low agreement rates across all evaluated expressions (see Subsect. 4.1), suggesting that expressions from prior studies [42,51] may not generalize well to the hospital context. This supports Leusmann et al. [31], who highlight the importance of context in interpreting expressions and note the potential for confusion in different settings. Interestingly, lights achieved the highest Agreeability Score (see Table 1), possibly due to standardized color meanings (e.g., red for error, green for OK) defined by ISO standards [25]. This aligns with prior research showing that visual signals—especially when paired with sound—can enhance robot behavior legibility [1], and in some cases, light signals outperform gestures and audio in perception [17].

The inconsistency in gesture interpretation extended to comparisons with the original authors' intended meanings. Our results showed very low agreement with the expressions' original meanings (see Sect. 4.1), suggesting that context and robot embodiment may have altered the interpretation. This reinforces the idea that expressions are not universally understood, and context and embodiment significantly affect how humans, especially users with little knowledge about robot signals, perceive social signals [40, 49]. For example, the robot saying "Wall-e" (used in four of our audio expressions) was easily understood as the robot's name in the movie context, but only 18 out of 60 participants recognized it in our study context.

5.2 Influence of Modality and Scenarios for Expressions

Our results show that modality and scenario significantly explain the variability in the data (see Subsect. 4.2), suggesting that both the expression's modality and the environment strongly guide its interpretation. For example, in scenario 2, where the robot stands outside a closed door, 43% (Fig. 3) of participants interpreted the expression as "Request" (likely asking to open the door). Similarly, in scenario 4, standing outside an elevator, 29.4% interpreted it as "Request". In scenario 1, where the robot is loading medicine, 35.6% interpreted it as "Status" (performing a task or waiting for instructions), while in scenario 5, interpretations were more evenly spread across "Status", "Attention", and "Intent" (indicating it was delivering medicine, wanted to, or simply alerting the human). Combining modality with scenario further strengthened these effects. For instance, light in scenario 1, regardless of pattern, led to the interpretation of "Status" in nearly half of cases. Further analysis is needed to optimize modality combinations for desired interpretations.

5.3 Needs to Design Dynamic and Adaptive Social Cues for Interactive Robotic Systems

Our findings highlight the impact that context might have in interpreting social signals, showcasing the importance of adapting these signals to successfully express different intentions in different contexts. Although there have been attempts to design and explore different social signals for non-anthropomorphic robots, these signals might not be generalizable to many contexts. In logistics robots, for example, each light color has a specific meaning for error, warning, progress, etc. [28]. For instance, a blue spotlight is a common way for robots to express "I am coming"; however, in the context of the works of Hoggermueller et al. [23], blue lights for robots expressed sadness. The task of mapping the correct cue to the intended expression becomes even more challenging when, besides context, people's preconceptions of expressions (e.g. green is for go) also have an impact on how these expressions are interpreted. Therefore, there is need for concrete design implications and guidelines to design and implement social cues and signals dynamically as well as including cues which have already been standardized in specific context.

Expressions Cannot Be Universally Used Across Contexts and Non-AnThroPoMorPhic Robots. When transferring the expressions from the literature to our context and robot, we found that most of the expressions were interpreted differently from what they were originally designed to express. This finding suggests that expressions cannot be generalized, as the same expression in a specific context and done by a specific robot can convey a very different meaning than in another context and from another robot. This seems to be especially true when the robot's level of anthropomorphism varies strongly. For instance, when transferring lights from studies with anthropomorphic robots [50] to our setup, emotional expressions were much more difficult to convey (see the low values for the code group "Emotional State" in Fig. 3). Following these findings, designers and developers should consider developing techniques to transfer meaning and intention from one context to another.

Good Understanding of the Contexts and Modalities Are Crucial in Human-Robot Interaction. Our study emphasizes the importance of context-aware communication of non-anthropomorphic robots to effectively convey social cues. For robots to express social cues appropriately, it is essential to identify suitable modalities that align with the specific context of use. Therefore, designers should consider the environment and its constraints when selecting modalities for social cue expression. For instance, in noisy settings like warehouses or factories, sound or speech may not be effective for communication due to high ambient noise levels. In contrast, quieter environments such as hospitals may allow sound-based modalities to convey certain cues effectively. By tailoring interaction modalities to the context, designers can enhance the effectiveness and appropriateness of robot social interactions.

Sounds Need to Be Carefully Designed in Different Contexts. The study found that people interpret sound expressions differently. Among the three gestures, the sound expressions had the least agreement among the participants. This aligns with the findings of Leusmann et al. [31] who also found that sound cues were confusing for participants during human-robot interaction. This leads to the conclusion that sound expressions might not be enough to express intent or social cues on its own. Designers should consider integrating other modalities with sounds to appropriately express intent. Otherwise, there might be misunderstanding in the context, which could decrease users enthusiasm, trust and acceptance towards the robot.

Using Artificial Intelligence to Generate Context Appropriate Social Cues. Artificial intelligence (AI), such as large language models (LLMs), has been proven to be efficient in processing large data to achieve user-adaptive results [21,52]. Thus, **integrating LLMs to dynamically generate social cues for interactive robots, based on knowledge from previous literature and standards regarding contexts and expressions,** would support the generation of adaptive social cues. Designers and AI engineers should collaborate and understand the possibilities and challenges of such LLM systems and how it could be integrated for robot systems for dynamic social cues expression. We also suggest that such LLM systems would not only be beneficial for non-anthropomorphic robots but also for anthropomorphic and social robots, enabling them to generate appropriate and adaptive social cues in several contexts, culture, and environment. Designing LLM systems to incorporate context, the interaction modalities available to the robot, and knowledge from the previous literature on robots would contribute to novel paradigms in human-robot interaction design.

5.4 Limitations

Some expressions from the literature were excluded due to limitations in our non-anthropomorphic robot setup. Adapting gestures from anthropomorphic robots often led to a loss of meaning, as complex gestures (e.g., involving heads or torsos) couldn't be replicated. Although our focus was on non-anthropomorphic robots, this adaptation challenge likely influenced participant interpretations.

The online format introduced ambiguity in responses. Despite careful question design and quality control, some answers were hard to code. To address this, a follow-up in-person study is planned.

Having only three interpretation samples per expression limited statistical analysis and increased susceptibility to outliers, potentially affecting result robustness.

Another limitation was the lack of original audio files from prior studies. While we sourced sounds (e.g., Wall-E, R2-D2) online, most papers didn't provide audio or defined meanings. This made it difficult to ensure accuracy in interpreting audio cues. In contrast, we confirmed meanings for lights and gestures, lending more reliability to those modalities.

6 Conclusion

This paper investigates how humans interpret social cues from non-anthropomorphic robots across different contexts. Through observations and co-design workshops in a hospital setting, we explored human-robot interactions in five scenarios. We gathered 103 gesture, light, and audio expressions from the literature and recreated them using a non-anthropomorphic robot. Our findings show that there is no universal understanding of social cues, interpretation is highly dependent on context and modality. The social situation often drives interpretation, regardless of the actual signal, making it difficult for non-anthropomorphic robots to convey varied meanings in the same context. As humans adapt social signals to context, robots must do the same, especially as they enter semi-public spaces. With advances in adaptive technology [9], tailoring social signals to specific contexts could enhance acceptance and trust. We offer design implications to help integrate adaptive cues, guiding designers in creating contextually appropriate, socially aware interactions for non-anthropomorphic robots.

Acknowledgments. This work is partially supported and funded by the HumanE AI Network under the European Union's Horizon 2020 ICT program (grant agreement no. 952026) and Mixed Fleet Research Project funded by Business Finland.

References

1. Angelopoulos, G., Vigni, F., Rossi, A., Russo, G., Turco, M., Rossi, S.: Familiar acoustic cues for legible service robots. 2022 31st IEEE International Conference on Robot and Human Interactive Communication (RO-MAN), pp. 1187–1192 (2022). https://api.semanticscholar.org/CorpusID:252625333
2. Banh, A., Rea, D.J., Young, J.E., Sharlin, E.: Inspector baxter: the social aspects of integrating a robot as a quality inspector in an assembly line. In: Proceedings of the 3rd International Conference on Human-Agent Interaction, pp. 19–26 (2015)
3. Baraka, K., Rosenthal, S., Veloso, M.: Enhancing human understanding of a mobile robot's state and actions using expressive lights. In: 2016 25th IEEE International Symposium on Robot and Human Interactive Communication (RO-MAN), pp. 652–657. IEEE (2016)
4. Bassett, D.S., Gazzaniga, M.S.: Understanding complexity in the human brain. Trends Cogn. Sci. **15**(5), 200–209 (2011)
5. Baumgarten, M., Süß, H.M., Weis, S.: The cue is the key. Europ. J. Psychological Assessment (2015)
6. Bethel, C.L., Murphy, R.R.: Survey of non-facial/non-verbal affective expressions for appearance-constrained robots. IEEE Trans. Syst. Man Cybern. Part C (Appl. Rev.) **38**(1), 83–92 (2007)
7. Breazeal, C.: Designing sociable robots. MIT press (2004)
8. Burgoon, J.K., Guerrero, L.K., Manusov, V.: Nonverbal signals. In: Handbook of Interpersonal Communication, pp. 239–280 (2011)
9. Chang, Y., et al.: A survey on evaluation of large language models. ACM Trans. Intell. Syst. Technol. **15**(3), 1–45 (2024)
10. Darwin, C.: The descent of man, and selection in relation to sex, vol. 2. D. Appleton (1872)
11. De Graaf, M.M., Allouch, S.B., Klamer, T.: Sharing a life with harvey: exploring the acceptance of and relationship-building with a social robot. Comput. Hum. Behav. **43**, 1–14 (2015)
12. Dwyer, J.: Using communication mechanisms derived from social cues in industrial autonomous mobile robots to improve interactions. Ph.D. thesis, Queensland University of Technology (2023)
13. Elprama, B., El Makrini, I., Jacobs, A.: Acceptance of collaborative robots by factory workers: a pilot study on the importance of social cues of anthropomorphic robots. In: International Symposium on Robot and Human Interactive Communication, vol. 7 (2016)

14. Embgen, S., Luber, M., Becker-Asano, C., Ragni, M., Evers, V., Arras, K.O.: Robot-specific social cues in emotional body language. In: 2012 IEEE RO-MAN: The 21st IEEE International Symposium on Robot and Human Interactive Communication, pp. 1019–1025. IEEE (2012)
15. Ende, T., Haddadin, S., Parusel, S., Wüsthoff, T., Hassenzahl, M., Albu-Schäffer, A.: A human-centered approach to robot gesture based communication within collaborative working processes. In: 2011 IEEE/RSJ International Conference on Intelligent Robots and Systems, pp. 3367–3374. IEEE (2011)
16. Feine, J., Gnewuch, U., Morana, S., Maedche, A.: A taxonomy of social cues for conversational agents. Int. J. Hum Comput Stud. **132**, 138–161 (2019)
17. Fernandez, R., John, N., Kirmani, S., Hart, J.W., Sinapov, J., Stone, P.: Passive demonstrations of light-based robot signals for improved human interpretability. In: 2018 27th IEEE International Symposium on Robot and Human Interactive Communication (RO-MAN), pp. 234–239 (2018). https://api.semanticscholar.org/CorpusID:53051722
18. Fiore, S.M., Wiltshire, T.J., Lobato, E.J., Jentsch, F.G., Huang, W.H., Axelrod, B.: Toward understanding social cues and signals in human-robot interaction: effects of robot gaze and proxemic behavior. Front. Psychol. **4**, 859 (2013)
19. Fiske, S.T.T.: Social cognition: From brains to culture. SAGE Publications Ltd (2020)
20. Frederiksen, M.R., Stoey, K.: Augmenting the audio-based expression modality of a non-affective robot. In: 2019 8th International Conference on Affective Computing and Intelligent Interaction (ACII), pp. 144–149. IEEE (2019)
21. Ghosh, A., Huang, B., Yan, Y., Lin, W.: Enhancing healthcare user interfaces through large language models within the adaptive user interface framework. In: International Congress on Information and Communication Technology, pp. 527–540. Springer (2024)
22. Hebesberger, D., Koertner, T., Gisinger, C., Pripfl, J.: A long-term autonomous robot at a care hospital: a mixed methods study on social acceptance and experiences of staff and older adults. Int. J. Soc. Robot. **9**(3), 417–429 (2017)
23. Hoggenmueller, M., Chen, J., Hespanhol, L.: Emotional expressions of non-humanoid urban robots: the role of contextual aspects on interpretations. In: Proceedings of the 9TH ACM International Symposium on Pervasive Displays, pp. 87–95 (2020)
24. Holland, J., et al.: Service robots in the healthcare sector. Robotics **10**(1), 47 (2021)
25. Plastics – Determination of fracture toughness (G_{IC} and K_{IC}) – Linear elastic fracture mechanics (LEFM) approach. Standard, International Organization for Standardization, Geneva, CH, March 2000
26. Jung, M.F.: Affective grounding in human-robot interaction. In: Proceedings of the 2017 ACM/IEEE International Conference on Human-Robot Interaction, pp. 263–273 (2017)
27. Langton, S.R., Watt, R.J., Bruce, V.: Do the eyes have it? cues to the direction of social attention. Trends Cogn. Sci. **4**(2), 50–59 (2000)
28. Larsson, F., Wernestrand, A.: Transformation of internal logistics: with autonomous transportation (2023)
29. Law, M.: Case studies on the usability, acceptability and functionality of autonomous mobile delivery robots in real-world healthcare settings. Intel. Serv. Robot. **14**(3), 387–398 (2021). https://doi.org/10.1007/s11370-021-00368-5
30. Lawrence, C.: Rise and Fall of Rethink Robotics — asme.org (2019). https://www.asme.org/topics-resources/content/rise-fall-of-rethink-robotics. Accessed 10 Oct 2024

31. Leusmann, J., Villa, S., Liang, T., Wang, C., Schmidt, A., Mayer, S.: An approach to elicit human-understandable robot expressions to support human-robot interaction. arXiv preprint arXiv:2410.01071 (2024)
32. Liew, T.W., Tan, S.M.: Social cues and implications for designing expert and competent artificial agents: A systematic review. Telematics Inform. **65**, 101721 (2021)
33. Martín, F.A., Castro-González, Á., Salichs, M.Á., et al.: Sound synthesis for communicating nonverbal expressive cues. IEEE Access **5**, 1941–1957 (2017)
34. Morgan, A.A., Abdi, J., Syed, M.A., Kohen, G.E., Barlow, P., Vizcaychipi, M.P.: Robots in healthcare: a scoping review. Current Robot. Reports **3**(4), 271–280 (2022)
35. Mubin, O., Kharub, I., Khan, A.: Pepper in the library" students' first impressions. In: Extended Abstracts of the 2020 CHI Conference on Human Factors in Computing Systems, pp. 1–9 (2020)
36. Murphy, R.R.: Human-robot interaction in rescue robotics. IEEE Trans. Syst. Man Cybern. Part C (Appl. Rev.) **34**(2), 138–153 (2004)
37. NAGELKERKE, N.J.D.: A note on a general definition of the coefficient of determination. Biometrika **78**(3), 691–692 (1991). https://doi.org/10.1093/biomet/78.3.691
38. Nourbakhsh, I.R.: Robot futures. Mit Press (2015)
39. Polzin, T.S.: Verbal and non-verbal cues in the communication of emotions. In: 2000 IEEE International Conference on Acoustics, Speech, and Signal Processing. Proceedings (Cat. No. 00CH37100), vol. 4, pp. 2429–2432. IEEE (2000)
40. Salem, M., Ziadee, M., Sakr, M.F.: Effects of politeness and interaction context on perception and experience of hri. In: International Conference on Software Reuse (2013). https://api.semanticscholar.org/CorpusID:41081900
41. Sauer, V., Sauer, A., Mertens, A.: Zoomorphic gestures for communicating cobot states. IEEE Robot. Automation Lett. **6**(2), 2179–2185 (2021)
42. Saunderson, S., Nejat, G.: How robots influence humans: a survey of nonverbal communication in social human–robot interaction. Int. J. Soc. Robot. **11**(4), 575–608 (2019). https://doi.org/10.1007/s12369-019-00523-0
43. Sauppé, A., Mutlu, B.: The social impact of a robot co-worker in industrial settings. In: Proceedings of the 33rd Annual ACM Conference on Human Factors in Computing Systems, pp. 3613–3622 (2015)
44. Song, S., Yamada, S.: Designing expressive lights and in-situ motions for robots to express emotions. In: Proceedings of the 6th International Conference on Human-Agent Interaction, pp. 222–228 (2018)
45. Song, Y., Tao, D., Luximon, Y.: In robot we trust? the effect of emotional expressions and contextual cues on anthropomorphic trustworthiness. Appl. Ergon. **109**, 103967 (2023)
46. Tulli, S., Ambrossio, D.A., Najjar, A., Rodríguez-Lera, F.J.: Great expectations & aborted business initiatives: The paradox of social robot between research and industry. BNAIC/BENELEARN **1** (2019)
47. Villani, V., Pini, F., Leali, F., Secchi, C.: Survey on human-robot collaboration in industrial settings: safety, intuitive interfaces and applications. Mechatronics **55**, 248–266 (2018)
48. Vinciarelli, A., Salamin, H., Pantic, M.: Social signal processing: Understanding social interactions through nonverbal behavior analysis. In: 2009 IEEE Computer Society Conference on Computer Vision and Pattern Recognition Workshops, pp. 42–49. IEEE (2009)

49. Wainer, J., Feil-Seifer, D., Shell, D.A., Matarić, M.J.: The role of physical embodiment in human-robot interaction. ROMAN 2006 - The 15th IEEE International Symposium on Robot and Human Interactive Communication, pp. 117–122 (2006), https://api.semanticscholar.org/CorpusID:12556718
50. Xie, Y., Matsumoto, M.: Emotional expression for humanoid robot using led light and breathing simulator. IEEJ Trans. Electr. Electron. Eng. **17**(9), 1372–1374 (2022)
51. Zhang, B.J., Fitter, N.T.: Nonverbal sound in human-robot interaction: A systematic review. J. Hum.-Robot Interact. **12**(4) (2023). https://doi.org/10.1145/3583743
52. Zhang, C., Chen, J., Li, J., Peng, Y., Mao, Z.: Large language models for human-robot interaction: A review. Biomimetic Intelligence and Robotics, p. 100131 (2023)

I Can See All of You: Supporting User Awareness with Augmented Field-of-View for Remote Collaborative Work

Ryota Suzuki[1(✉)], Mina Takao[1], Kosei Shino[1], Yoshinori Kobayashi[1], Kenji Iwata[2], Tomomi Satoh[2], Yutaka Satoh[2], Naoki Uchida[3], Akiko Yamazaki[3], Keiichi Yamazaki[1], Felix Bergmann[4], and Karola Pitsch[4]

[1] Saitama University, Saitama, Japan
suzukiryota@mail.saitama-u.ac.jp
[2] National Institute of Advanced Industrial Science and Technology, Tsukuba, Japan
[3] Tokyo University of Technology, Tokyo, Japan
[4] University of Duisburg-Essen, Essen, Germany

Abstract. We propose a remote collaboration system that allows a remote instructor to efficiently and quite dynamically look around 360° of field-of-view and easily interact immediately to surrounding local workers by utilizing field-of-view augmentation system and a remote-controlled robot. A remote user can pay peripheral attention to local users, and the robot interfaces show peripheral recipiency to the local users. We analyzed a user experiment of remote instruction of LEGO assembling, and revealed its effectiveness for remote collaborative works.

Keywords: Peripheralization of Recipiency · Remote Collaboration · Robot-Supported Coorperative Works

1 Introduction

In recent years, due to the shortages of labor and the impact of the COVID-19 disaster, it has become common to remotely observe local workers' situation and support their tasks, such as remote classes at schools and remote assembly instructions at factories. In order for remote supervisors to efficiently perform tasks with local workers, it is necessary to grasp the local situation of workers, and to recognize the local workers' request for supporting their tasks.

Recent advances in remote communication technology have facilitated video conferences using omnidirectional cameras, allowing remote users to observe all directions of a local room. However, there is still a major problem with the remote communication system. Heath revealed the step-by-step process of establishing communication channels through face-to-face conversation analysis in multiparty settings [2]. First, the speaker pays the peripheral attention to show the recipiency of communication such as distributing gaze, and then the speaker focuses the attention on the subject to show the availability such as directing

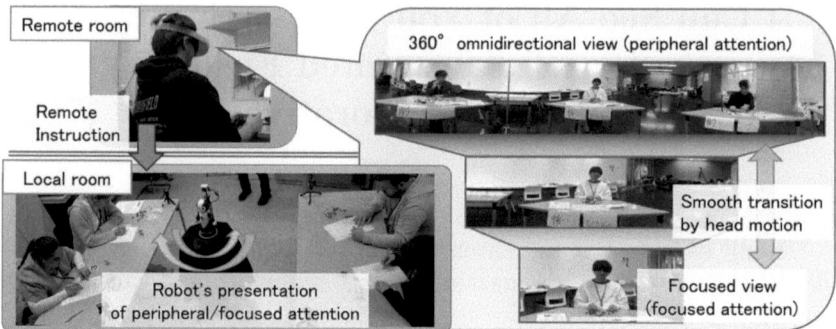

Fig. 1. Proposed System: augmented FoV supporting remote collaborative works.

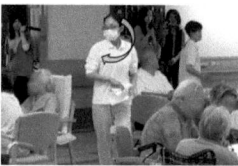

(a) Paying peripheral attention by turning head and body

(b) Paying focused attention by fixing gaze and moving toward the target

Fig. 2. A careworker's transition of width of attention in an elderly care facility.

the face/body toward him/her. By taking these steps, participants can strongly predict the projection in beginning conversations, such as "Who's next?" This structure cases smooth beginning of conversation in multi-party conversations. In our previous study, we analyzed the situation in which caregivers observe the requests of care-takers in the hall of an elderly care facility [9]. By turning or moving a caregiver's neck or body, care-takers could recognize a peripheral recipiency that indicated they could receive social signals to start a dialogue from a wide range of people around (Fig. 2a), thus a care-taker could show social signals such as raising their hand to show request for taking a service. Then the caregiver moved towards the target elderly to display focused availability and initiate a one-to-one interaction (Fig. 2b). Therefore, it is important to establish a framework that allows a remote user to pay peripheral attention by distributing gaze and focused attention by fixing the gaze in a natural and gradual manner even in remote communication. However, in conventional video communications, even if the omnidirectional local vision is shared on the monitor, it is difficult for a remote supervisor to grasp the local surroundings at once, and to distribute "focused attention" on each local user. Consequently, communication between a remote supervisor and local users is not conducted smoothly and their cooperation is not performed successfully.

To cope with this, we developed a system that allows a supervisor to easily observe the situation at a local site from a remote location using the video see-through VR system named OmniFlickView that extraordinarily expands the field-of-view (FoV) according to the user's neck movements (Fig. 1). OmniFlickView is a see-through VR system that can expand the FoV by 360° while minimizing physical and visual burden based on the omnidirectional camera retrofitted to the head-mounted display (HMD). Users can easily and immediately translate their FoV from ordinal one to 360° by small flicking of their neck, so they can control peripheralization of attention which is essential for remote supervision. The omnidirectional camera is mounted on a remotely controlled mobile platform with a speakerphone, so they can communicate with their voices while local users show their progress through the camera. It also has a ring-shaped LED light and a small humanoid robot to display peripheralized and focused attention to local users.

When utilizing the system, questions come up – *How a remote supervisor and local users use these communication resource? Is it required to show peripheralized recipiency for fluent remote communication?* In this paper, we conducted a user experiment of LEGO handcraft workshop. In the workshop, a remote instructor guides how to assemble LEGO art with voice, and local students try to do it. To assemble the LEGO correctly, the local students have to capture the attention of the remote instructor to confirm the correctness of the current assembly , and the instructor have to observe every student. We analyzed recorded scenes of the experiment by the method of ethnomethodology, and we revealed that the presentations of recipiency by the robot interfaces lead local users' projection of availability of turn-taking.

2 Related Work

Numerous studies have been conducted on systems that allow remote users to observe on-site conditions and provide instructions. Systems in which a single operator interacts with multiple local users using multiple avatars, such as remote customer service systems in stores, are becoming increasingly widespread. However, conventional research on remote work support primarily focused on one-on-one remote collaboration. For example, Piumsomboon et al. proposed a multi-scale collaboration system combining a 360-degree camera and a 6-DOF tracker between a local augmented reality (AR) user and a remote virtual reality (VR) user. Komiyama et al. proposed a telepresence system that allows for a seamless transition between first-person and third-person perspectives [4]. On the other hand, research for supporting one-to-many remote collaboration have also been conducted. Otsuki et al. developed an AR system for one-to-many remote work support from a distance, but it is necessary to install equipment for each person on the local side [7]. Remote education is the most popular situation for remote collaboration on one-to-many situations and several research have been conducted. For example, Oh-Hun et al. proposed a system for remote foreign language teaching [5]. Zhang et al. developed a telepresence robot that allows a remote teacher to lecture by detecting students' faces through facial recognition and autonomously moving to the selected student's location [11].

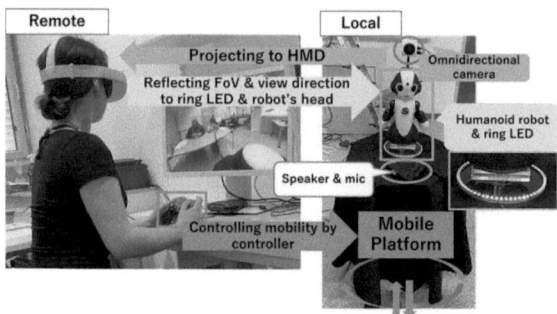

Fig. 3. System overview: A composite of augmented video communication and a robot embodiment. The HMD effectively shows transmitted omnidirectional video, and the robot shows direction which a remote user looks at. The mobile platform can be controlled by a controller.

In such one-to-many scenarios, remote users are required to independently explore the local environment, as seen with telepresence robots. Research of telepresence robot have mainly focused on systems that use 360-degree cameras and HMDs to provide immersive experiences [1]. However, while HMDs offer high immersion and a strong sense of presence, their typical FoV ranges from approximately 90 to 110° horizontally and 70 to 90° vertically, narrower than human natural vision. Consequently, remote users are required to physically rotate their bodies to observe their surroundings in remote communication scenarios. To address these issues, we propose a solution that integrates a HMD with a remotely operated mobile platform and expands the HMD's FoV. Regarding FoV expansion, some studies propose systems that permanently expand the FoV [6], while others propose dynamically expanding systems [10], though their application to remote communication has not been explored.

In contrast to these conventional studies, we propose a remote collaboration support system in which a remote user can monitor multiple local users using a FoV expansion system while showing view direction of the remote user to the local users, that allows natural distribution of attention as same as our daily manner.

3 Proposed System

The proposed interface is illustrated in Fig. 3. To address the remote user's FoV limitations, we developed a video see-through VR system called OmniFlickView, which dynamically expands the FoV based on user movement. A mobile platform is employed to allow the remote user to freely change his/her viewpoint. Additionally, a communication robot mounted on the mobile platform presents the remote user's expanded FoV to local users. The supervisor communicates remotely through the speakerphone.

3.1 OmniFlickView

OmniFlickView is a see-through VR system that enables FoV expansion beyond 360° using an omnidirectional camera [8]. When the user moves their head, the FoV expands significantly into a panoramic view. Conversely, when the user stops moving their head to focus, the FoV narrows into gaze mode. This allows users to perceive their surroundings without extensive head movement and quickly scan their environment with minimal physical effort. OmniFlickView is compatible with various VR systems; in this study, we used Meta Quest 2 (formerly Oculus Quest 2) for a wireless configuration. To observe the local environment, an omnidirectional camera (KODAK PIXPRO ORBIT360 4K VR[1]) is mounted on the mobile platform. The camera feed is transmitted wirelessly to a computing device via the TERADEK Spark 4K module[2]. OmniFlickView is implemented in Unity, where shaders dynamically adjust the display FoV and acceleration effects for effective visualization. OmniFlickView's FoV expansion consists of two components:

(1) Neck-yaw Boosting Neck-yaw Boosting accelerates the virtual head-turning speed within the omnidirectional view according to the user's physical head movements (Fig. 4a). This allows users to instantly look in any direction with minimal head movement. However, it may cause disorientation and VR motion sickness due to increased optical flow. This drawback is mitigated by integrating Dynamic FoV Boosting.

(2) Dynamic FoV Boosting Dynamic FoV Boosting dynamically expands or contracts the FoV based on head movements. When the user moves their head, the system interprets it as an exploratory action and expands the FoV. When the user stops their head movement, the system interprets it as a focused action and contracts the FoV (Fig. 4b).

The expanded FoV provides a bird's-eye view of the surroundings, while the narrowed FoV allows detailed observation. By seamlessly transitioning between these states, Dynamic FoV Boosting balances wide-area awareness and detailed vision. Additionally, expanding the FoV reduces optical flow, mitigating motion sickness caused by Neck-yaw Boosting's acceleration.

3.2 Mobile Platform

We have developed a mobile platform for remote collaboration with local users. It equips an omnidirectional camera, a humanoid robot, a ring-shaped LED and a speakerphone (see Fig. 3). They are all remotely connected to a computer of a remote user. Video of the omnidirectional camera is sent to an HMD of a remote user and projected by OmniFlickView system. The remote user can operate the mobile platform using a controller to move forward, backward, or rotate. The

---

[1] https://kodakpixpro.com/cameras/360-vr/orbit360-4k/.
[2] https://teradek.com/pages/spark-4k/.

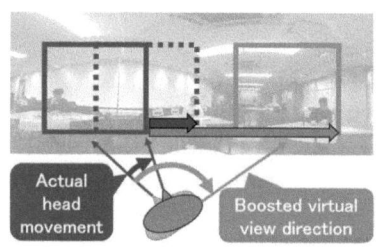 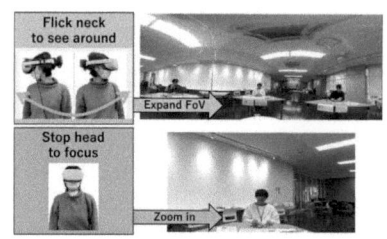

(a) Neck-yaw Boosting: accelerating virtual view direction by turning head

(b) Dynamic FoV Boosting: expanding virtual FoV by turning head

Fig. 4. Overview of OmniFlickView. A set of two functions extraordinally and efficiently expands user's FoV without increasing VR sickness.

remote user and the local users can communicate by voice with each other. The humanoid robot and a ring-shaped LED are equipped to show viewing direction of the remote user to the local users. Detail information is described in the next section.

3.3 Presentation of Communication Cues

While a remote user can quickly grasp the surrounding situation of local site using OmniFlickView, local users cannot recognize to which the remote user is paying attention. In face-to-face communication, it is known that supervisors look around the site, and workers call the supervisors when the workers realize that they are captured in the supervisors' FoV [3]. Therefore, the communication robot "Sota"[3] was mounted on the top plate of a mobile platform to indicate the remote user's gaze information. The head direction of Sota represents the direction which the remote user is looking at, thereby indicating the gaze direction within the normal FoV. However, when the remote user utilizes OmniFlickView which can look around 360° at once, it is difficult to show the remote user's FoV by only using Sota. We employ a ring-shaped LED for representing the remote user's FoV, which is inspired by previous researches using 360° of FoV. The light of ring-shaped LED represents viewing direction and FoV of the remote user. The red light indicates the center of FoV (30° to the left and right from the center) while the blue light represents the outer visible area. When the FoV is expanded by the remote user's head movement, the illuminated area of the LED changes wider, and when the FoV is shrinked, the illuminated area of the LED changes narrower.

4 Experiment

We conducted experiments to verify the effectiveness of peripheral attention for showing recipiency and focused attention for showing availability in remote col-

---

[3] https://www.vstone.co.jp/products/sota/.

Table 1. System configurations of conditions

	System	Remote user's FoV	Visual presentation method
(i)	Baseline system	Normal	Sota
(ii)	Proposed system	OmniFlickView	Sota + LED

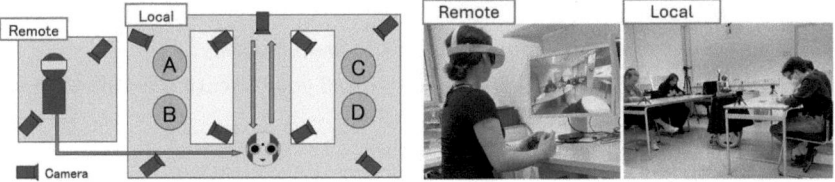

Fig. 5. The experimental layout (left) and an actual experimental scene (right). A, B, C and D are seats of participants.

laborative work. We designed a scenario simulating a remote lesson at school. The task was LEGO assembling while receiving instructions from a remote supervisor in a workshop style. We evaluated our proposed system by conducting questionnaires and analysis of experimental video data.

4.1 Experimental Setup

A participant was assigned as a remote instructor, while 2–4 participants play the role of students on the local side. All of the cases had 4 participants in the local site except 3 cases (one case had 2 participants, two cases had 3 participants). A remote instructor wore an HMD and provided verbal instructions on LEGO assembly while monitoring the situations of local students. We conducted experiments with 12 groups in two conditions: (i) Baseline system, (ii) Proposed system. Table 1 shows system configurations of the two conditions. The baseline system is almost the same as the proposed system, but the baseline system is turned off the functions of Neck-yaw Boosting and Dynamic FoV Boosting. The user can only see in the direction of his/her head, so if he/she wants to look behind him/her, he/she needs to turn his/her head 180°. The ring LED is also turned off in the baseline system. The experimental layout and an actual experimental scene are shown in Fig. 5.

The experiment was conducted in Germany. 37 participants including university students, graduate students, laboratory staff and office workers participated in the experiment. The experiment was conducted in accordance with the guidelines of the ethical review. The experiment was conducted with the participants' consent. Participants who were with epilepsy, strong sensitivity to visual stimuli, or physical disabilities were excluded. The experiment was conducted in two adjacent rooms in a university.

Both remote and local users were asked to answer a questionnaire (shown in Table 2, Table 3) after finishing the workshop. System usability and ease of

Table 2. Questionnaire for local user (Q10 is only for the case of OmniFlickView)

Q1	Could you recognize which direction the remote participant looked at?
Q2	Were you aware of where the remote participant was looking?
Q3	Did you feel the remote participant monitored and supervised your progress?
Q4	Did you feel easy to make questions to the remote participants?
Q5	Could you communicate to the remote participant smoothly?
Q6	Do you think the workshop has been conducted smoothly?
Q7	Did you feel the remote participant had noticed your intention to talk to him/her quickly?
Q8	Did you feel the robot is a real instructor?
Q9	Could you enjoy the workshop?
Q10	Could you understand field-of-view of the remote participant by the ring LED expression?

accomplishing tasks are evaluated with 7-point Likert scale (1: strongly disagree, 7: strongly agree), and we conducted t-test at a 5% significance level for each items. Moreover, we took videos to analyze how the proposed functions of peripheral and focused attention were adopted by the users through the method of ethnomethodology. In this experiment, we mainly focus on revealing from the observation. We, therefore, asked specific questions in terms of system usability and ease of accomplishing tasks in this time. Hence the workload evaluation using well known tools such as NASA-TLX is still remained.

5 Result

5.1 Result of Questionnaire

Figure 6 show the average results of the questionnaire for remote and local users, respectively.

The remote user questionnaire showed significant differences in Q1–Q5, Q8, Q9, Q12, and Q13, indicating that the proposed system improved situational awareness, responsiveness, and communication fluency. No significant differences were found in Q6 and Q7, suggesting no increase in fatigue or motion sickness with OmniFlickView. On the local side, the results of the self-made questionnaire, significant differences were observed in Q1, Q3, Q4, Q7, and Q9. This indicates that the proposed system is effective in aspects such as ease of communication initiation with remote user (Q4, Q7) and response speed to such communication. Conversely, questions like Q5 and Q6, regarding smoothness of communication and workshops, did not show significant differences. This is likely because perceptions vary depending on task familiarity and progress.

Table 3. Questionnaire for remote user (Q14 is only for the case of OmniFlickView)

Q1	Could you conduct the workshop smoothly as an instructor?
Q2	Could you comprehend the situation of local sight such as progress of working and chatting between participants.
Q3	Was it easy to observe the behavior or gestures of the local participants?
Q4	Could you communicate to local participants smoothly?
Q5	Do you think you could quickly respond to the explicit and implicit requests for guidance from those around you?
Q6	Have you felt tired on the workshop?
Q7	Did you feel VR sickness while using head-mounted display (HMD)?
Q8	Could you easily look around the local sight through the HMD?
Q9	Do you think field-of-view of the HMD was sufficient?
Q10	Could you easily control the remote locomotion platform?
Q11	Could you smoothly look around the local sight through the HMD while controlling remote locomotion platform?
Q12	Could you gradually learn and get used to the system while using it?
Q13	Could you enjoy the workshop?
Q14	Was the function of zoom-in and zoom-out comfortable?

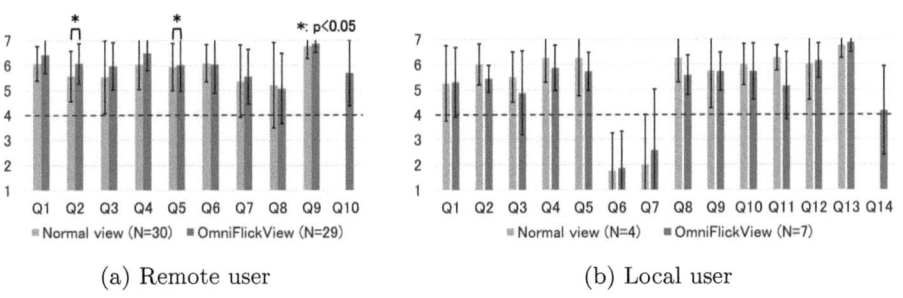

(a) Remote user   (b) Local user

Fig. 6. Result of questionnaire. Vertical axis means averaged score of Likert scale, and horizontal axis means item of questionnaire.

5.2 Video Analysis

As we described in Sect. 1, perceived peripheralization of attention is controlled by movement of head and body. While the head and the body of a service giver is frequently turning, service receivers perceive as the attention of the service giver is peripheral, and when a service giver stares and locomotes toward the service receiver, the service receivers perceive as the attention of the service giver is getting focused. In this section, we describe that the communication system of humans is also shown even when they remotely collaborate through our proposed system.

(a) Frag.#1 001

(b) Frag.#1 002

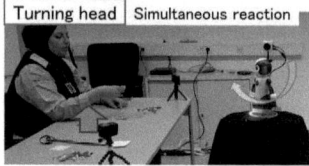
(c) Frag.#1 005

Transcript 1: Fragment #1

```
001 R-03   oben [dr:auf
           on top
002 Ro          [((turning LED))
003 Ro          ((turning head))
004 Ro          [((click sound))
                [((turning mobility))
005 L-07   [(0.3)((raising hand))
006        (0.8)
007 L-07   SO?
           like this?
008 R-03   das (-) wart mal kurz,
           that (-) wait a second,
009        JA,
           yes,
010        genau SO;
           exactly like this;
011        perFEKT.
           perfect.
```

Fig. 7. Scenes of Fragment #1.

From the 15 cases of the experiment, we picked up two fragments, which the remote users locomoted position of the mobile platform, to analyze communication system by the method of ethnomethodology. We created transcripts and observed the relationship between presentation of the robot's attention and reactions of local users.

Fragment #1. In Transcript 1, we denote L-06 and L-07 as participants of local users, R-03 as a participant of a remote user, and Ro as the robot. At first of the fragment, the robot looked at student L-06 (Fig. 7a, Trans. 1 001). Then the ring-shaped LED turned to the student, so she could make a projection of attention coming toward her (Fig. 7b, Trans. 1 002–003), hence she could show her work to remote instructor simultaneously when humanoid turns head to her (Fig. 7c, Trans. 1 005–006). From the fragment, it can be said that the local user can accept these three modalities of ring-shaped LED, head direction and body movement as resources for recognizing dynamic transition of attention of a remote user, that can lead smooth communication between them.

Fragment #2. In Transcript 2, we denote L-13, L-14 and L-15 as participants of local users of front left, back left and back right, respectively, and R-05 as a participant of a remote user. Firstly, L-13 called R-05 and R-05 looked at L-13, so the ring-shaped LED turned to L-13 (Fig. 8a, Trans. 2 004–005). When the ring-shaped LED start rotation, L-13 raise her LEGO to show it to R-05 (Trans. 2 006). The local user could predict coming peripheral attention from the remote user, and she tried to obtain focused attention by raising her LEGO. After that, the humanoid's head turned to L-13 (Fig. 8b, Trans. 2 007) and then the whole

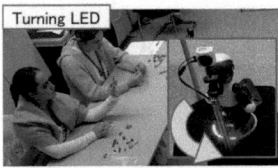
(a) Frag.#2 005

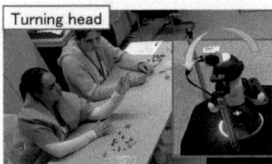
(b) Frag.#2 007

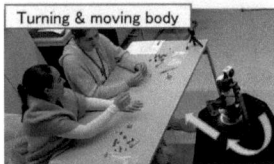
(c) Frag.#2 016

Transcript 2: Fragment #2

```
001 R-05 NOppen.
         nubs.
002      sieht- (.)
         looks-
003      also so wie so_n HUT der drauf liegt
         sozusagen;
         so just like a hat that lays on top sort
         of;
004 L-13 SO ne?
         like this right?
005 Ro   (0.6)((Start turning LED))
006 L-13 ((Put her LEGO toward Ro))
007 Ro   (0.6)((Start turning head))
008 R-05 (0.5)zeig MA,
         show me,
009 Ro   (0.5)((Turning body))
010 L-15 ja.
         yes.
011      (5.0)
012 R-05 JA:, (.) ja:=ja:,=
         yes, yes=yes,
013 R-05 ((NAME)) zeig ma hoch?
         ((L-14's name)) hold it up?
014 L-14 ((Raise LEGO))
015 L-13 das voll SCHWER zu zeigen,
         it's very difficult to show,
016 Ro   ((Start turning body))
017 L-15 bei allen VIERN?
         for all four?
```

Fig. 8. Scenes of Fragment #2.

body of the mobility came to L-13 (Fig. 8c, Trans. 2 009), so the local user could understand the attention had been focused.

From the analysis of these two fragments, it is clear that the communication resources of peripheralization/focusing of attention by turning face and body and locomotion, that are utilized by humans in daily life, can also be utilized in the same way in remote cooperative work with the remote user's field-of-view expansion.

6 Conclusion

We proposed the remote work support system for enabling a supervisor at a remote location to watch over multiple workers in the local field and give appropriate instructions. In our system, OmniFlickView allows a remote user to pay attention quite widely and smoothly, but it should also be required to share how the remote user pays attention to the local users. We, therefore, employed the ring LED in addition to the humanoid robot on the mobile platform so that the peripheral and focused attention of the remote user can be conveyed to the local users. We investigated how they can be used as communication resources. As a result, it was found that communication can be initiated more smoothly by using our system that provides the remote user with an expanded field-of-view and free locomotion of the viewpoint, and conveys the remote user's gazing information to the local user.

There are two issues to be addressed in the future: First, it is necessary to clarify at what timing the local user actually calls out to the remote user. The second is to investigate whether, in the more natural communication behavior, not only the remote user but also the local user can communicate more easily with the remote user.

Acknowledgments. This work was partly supported by JSPS KAKENHI Grant Number 23K13286, 23KK0032, 24H00151, and 25H00462.

References

1. Druta, R., Druta, C., Negirla, P., Silea, I.: A review on methods and systems for remote collaboration. Appl. Sci. **11**(21), 10035 (2021)
2. Heath, C.: Talk and Recipiency: Sequential Organization in Speech and Body Movement, pp. 247–266. Cambridge University Press (1984)
3. Kobayashi, Y., et al.: A considerate care robot able to serve in multi-party settings. In: 2011 RO-MAN, pp. 27–32 (2011)
4. Komiyama, R., Miyaki, T., Rekimoto, J.: Jackin space: designing a seamless transition between first and third person view for effective telepresence collaborations. In: Proceedings of the 8th Augmented Human International Conference, AH 2017. Association for Computing Machinery, New York (2017)
5. Kwon, O.H., Koo, S.Y., Kim, Y.G., Kwon, D.S.: Telepresence robot system for English tutoring. In: 2010 IEEE Workshop on Advanced Robotics and its Social Impacts, pp. 152–155 (2010)
6. Orlosky, J., Wu, Q., Kiyokawa, K., Takemura, H., Nitschke, C.: Fisheye vision: peripheral spatial compression for improved field of view in head mounted displays. In: SUI 2014 - Proceedings of the 2nd ACM Symposium on Spatial User Interaction, pp. 54–61. Association for Computing Machinery, Inc (2014)
7. Otsuki, M., Wang, T.Y., Kuzuoka, H.: Assessment of instructor s capacity in one-to-many AR remote instruction giving. In: Proceedings of the 28th ACM Symposium on Virtual Reality Software and Technology, VRST 2022. Association for Computing Machinery, New York (2022)
8. Suzuki, R., Sato, T., Iwata, K., Satoh, Y.: Omnidirectional flick view. In: 23rd HCI International Conference (HCIi2021), pp. 395–414 (2021)
9. Yamazaki, K., et al.: Prior-to-request and request behaviors within elderly day care: implications for developing service robots for use in multiparty settings. In: European Conference on Computer-Supported Cooperative Work, pp. 61–78 (2007)
10. Yano, Y., Orlosky, J., Kiyokawa, K., Takemura, H.: Dynamic view expansion for improving visual search in video see-through AR. In: Reiners, D., Iwai, D., Steinicke, F. (eds.) ICAT-EGVE 2016 - International Conference on Artificial Reality and Telexistence and Eurographics Symposium on Virtual Environments. The Eurographics Association (2016)
11. Zhang, M., Duan, P., Zhang, Z., Esche, S.: Development of telepresence teaching robots with social capabilities. In: ASME International Mechanical Engineering Congress and Exposition, vol. 5, p. V005T07A017. Engineering Education (2018)

A Bayesian Neural Network Approach for Spatial Relations Learning in Human-Robot Collaboration

Mark McCarthy[1], Mai Dao[1], and Fujian Yan[2](✉)

[1] Department of Mathematics, Statistics, and Physics, Wichita State University, Wichita, KS 67260, USA
mai.dao@wichita.edu
[2] School of Computing, Wichita State University, Wichita, KS 67260, USA
fujian.yan@wichita.edu

Abstract. Spatial relationships among objects are fundamental to the structure of human environments and play a critical role in enabling effective human-robot collaboration (HRC). In domains such as homes, kitchens, and offices, social robots must be capable of understanding and reasoning about different spatial relations to interpret human intentions and execute tasks in a meaningful way. Learning these relations from perception and language presents unique challenges, including ambiguity in human instructions, variability in object configurations, and limited training data for rare spatial patterns. A Bayesian approach offers a principled way to model uncertainty in both perception and relational reasoning, allowing robots to make more robust predictions in unfamiliar scenarios. By capturing uncertainty over learned representations, Bayesian Neural Networks (BNNs) can reliably generalize to novel spatial arrangements and support safer, more interpretable robot behaviors during collaborative activities. In this work, we propose a novel deep learning model based on BNNs for Spatial Learning (BNN-SL), a framework that can recognize objects and learn the spatial relations among them. Experimental results demonstrate that BNN-SL effectively captures uncertainty and relational structures, empowering robots to execute collaborative tasks that require spatial generalization and compositional reasoning.

Keywords: Bayesian Neural Network · Spatial Relationships Understanding · Human-Robot Collaboration

1 Introduction

Advancements in robotic technology have led to an increased presence of social robots in human-centric environments, thereby expanding opportunities for human-robot collaboration [2,7,11]. A critical aspect of an effective collaboration is the robot's ability to comprehend and interpret spatial relationships, as humans frequently use spatial descriptors—such as "the one on the left" or "the one behind the box"—to refer to objects, especially during tasks like cleaning, organizing, or arranging items [5]. However, conventional robot perception systems often struggle to accurately interpret spatial relationships and generalize them across different scenarios [12]. Existing methods frequently rely on simplified geometric approximations, such as bounding boxes, lacking the semantic reasoning capabilities essential for real-world applications [14,15].

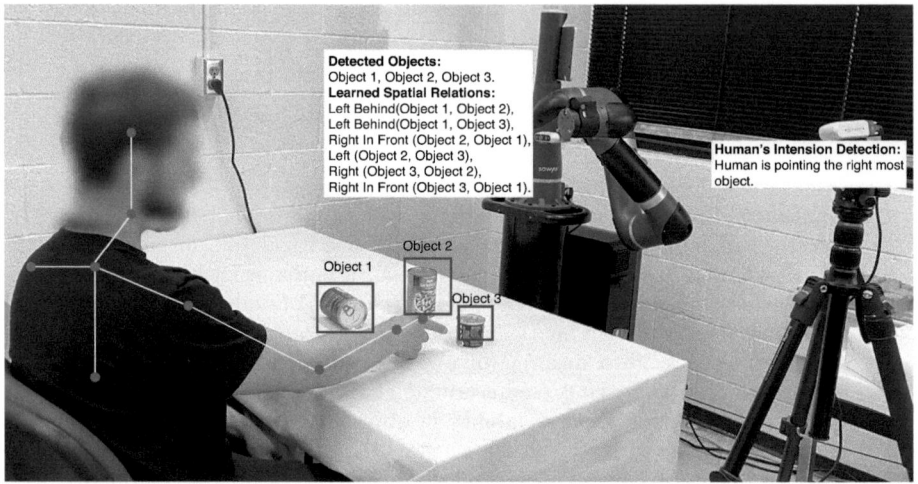

Fig. 1. Understanding spatial relations with the proposed framework. Two RGB-D sensors are used: one is used to detect the objects in the scene, and the other one is used to detect the human's intention based on the extracted skeleton information.

Moreover, many deep learning-based approaches are susceptible to overfitting and fail to provide meaningful measures of prediction uncertainty, a crucial factor in safety-sensitive applications [3]. Bayesian Neural Networks (BNNs) [6] offer a principled way to capture uncertainty in model predictions, making them particularly useful in safety-critical robotic applications. By modeling weights as distributions rather than fixed values, BNNs allow for robust generalization under limited or noisy data—a typical condition in many HRC deployments. Prior studies have shown the effectiveness of BNNs in tasks such as object classification and semantic segmentation, but their applications to spatial relations reasoning remains limited. Our approach builds on these foundations and integrates BNNs into a spatial learning pipeline tailored for HRC environments, thus enabling robots to reason under uncertainty and make safer decisions [4]. In contrast to previous works that either rely solely on deterministic deep learning models [10] or use geometric heuristics for spatial reasoning [5], the BNN-SL framework uniquely integrates visual and depth-based modalities using a probabilistic learning structure.

In this paper, we propose a novel method for HRC that enables robots to understand spatial relationships among objects using a BNN approach. In Fig. 1, the human collaborator is seated in front of the robot, pointing at one of the objects in the scene. The proposed framework operates by first detecting objects and then learning the spatial relations among them. Based on the learned spatial relations, the framework can infer more complex spatial relationships among multiple objects and understand the human collaborator's intentions. The framework comprises two main components: (1) object detection and (2) learning spatial relations among objects. Object detection is performed using Faster R-CNN [9], after which their spatial relations are learned through our designed Bayesian models. These spatial relations include "Left," "Right," "Above," "Below," "In_Front," "Next_to," and "Behind." Building upon our prior work [13], the proposed method infers complex spatial reasoning using the constructed knowledge from detection. Furthermore, our model leverages the strengths of BNNs, which offer two key advantages: (1) the improved robustness to overfitting, making them better suited for learning from small datasets, and (2) the ability to estimate predictive uncertainty by marginalizing over the distribution of model parameters, thereby enhancing the reliability of predictions. We have evaluated the proposed model across three scenarios: via (1) a public dataset, (2) a computer-simulated dataset, and (3) a real-world lab-generated dataset. The numerical results demonstrate the model's effectiveness in accurately understanding and inferring spatial relationships under various data settings, thereby enhancing the quality of our human-robot collaboration efforts.

2 Bayesian Neural Network-Based Spatial Relations Learning

The overall structure of the framework is illustrated in Fig. 2, which consists of three phases: object detection, spatial relation understanding, and human-robot collaboration. This work specifically focuses on the first two phases. In the first phase, the objects are detected with labels and scores, and their bounding boxes serve as the inputs to the spatial relation understanding network. In the second phase, a Bayesian Neural Network processes these inputs to infer a sufficient number of pairwise spatial relationships, enabling us to deduce the relations among remaining objects. Subsequently, in the third phase, the detected object labels and the learned spatial relationships are integrated into the HRC module, enabling many seamless interactions between humans and robots.

2.1 Object Detection at the Scene

In Phase 1, we employ the Faster R-CNN framework [8] to achieve an optimal balance between computational efficiency and detection accuracy. Faster R-CNN integrates a Region Proposal Network (RPN) and an object detection network into a unified model. The RPN takes an input image and generates the region

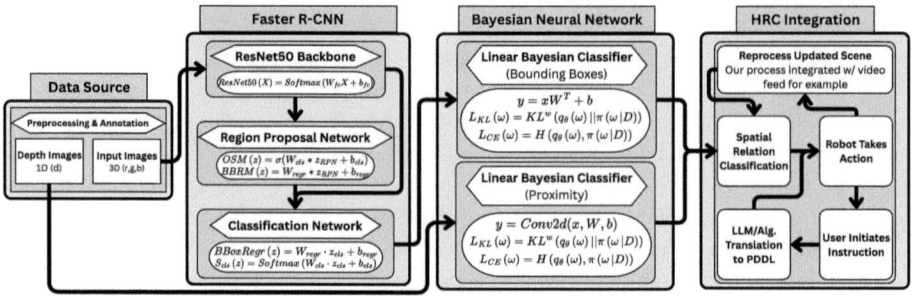

Fig. 2. The overall workflow of the proposed framework, which contains three phases: object detection, spatial recognition, and human-robot collaboration.

proposals, each with a confidence score that indicates the likelihood of that region containing an object.

The generated region proposals are then pooled to extract fixed-size feature maps, leveraging the ResNet50 CNN as the backbone, which are passed to the object detection network consisting of a CNN for object feature extraction and two fully connected layers for classification and bounding box regression. By leveraging this multi-task learning approach in Phase 1, Faster R-CNN effectively detects objects with high precision, enabling accurate outputs such as labels and associated scores to be used as inputs for Phase 2, in turn allowing robots to achieve a detailed understanding of their noisy environment.

2.2 Spatial Relation Understanding

The proposed model can learn twelve spatial relations, including "Left_Next_to," "Left_Behind," "Left_In_Front," "Right_Next_to," "Right_Behind," "Right_In_Front," "Above_Next_to," "Above_Behind," "Above_In_Front," "Below_Next_to," "Below_Behind," and "Below_In_Front." These spatial relations cover most of the daily activities among objects. For other complex spatial relations among multiple objects, we will reason based on learned relations.

In Phase 2, we propose a network architecture with a two-stage BNN following initial object detection to learn the spatial relations, see Fig. 2. A popular alternative to traditional NNs, BNNs offer a flexible probabilistic framework to model the uncertainty in predictions, making them particularly well-suited for tasks such as spatial relation understanding. Unlike the classical NNs that provide deterministic outputs, BNNs represent network weights and biases, collectively denoted ω, as probability distributions, capturing epistemic uncertainty associated with spatial predictions in a principled manner. By actively learning from the data and subsequent calculations and handling small data samples effectively, BNNs have been widely used in computer vision and pattern recognition, with satisfactory out-of-distribution detection.

In BNNs, the posterior distribution of the model parameters ω is given by Bayes' theorem by combining the priors $p(\omega)$ and the choice of likelihood $p(\mathcal{D}|\omega)$, where $\mathcal{D}$ denotes the observed data.

$$\pi(\omega|\mathcal{D}) = \frac{p(\omega)p(\mathcal{D}|\omega)}{\int p(\omega)p(\mathcal{D}|\omega)d\omega} = \frac{p(\omega)p(\mathcal{D}|\omega)}{p(\mathcal{D})}. \quad (1)$$

Like other NN architectures, BNNs have a highly non-convex objective function with many local minima, and thus, we choose the popular choice of backpropagation to mitigate the numerical challenges posed by this problem. Let $q_\theta(\omega)$ be the approximated density over a family of distributions parameterized by the variational parameters θ. We used two objective loss functions to evaluate the model fit. The first one is the weighted Kullback-Leibler (KL) divergence, which measures the similarity between $q_\theta(\omega)$ and the true distribution $\pi(\omega|\mathcal{D})$, and is given by

$$KL^w\left(q_\theta(\omega)||\pi(\omega|\mathcal{D})\right) = \int \omega q_\theta(\omega) \log \frac{q_\theta(\omega)}{\pi(\omega|\mathcal{D})} d\omega, \quad (2)$$

and the second one is the cross-entropy

$$H\left(q_\theta(\omega), \pi(\omega|\mathcal{D})\right) = -E_{q_\theta(\omega)}\left[\log \pi(\omega|\mathcal{D})\right]. \quad (3)$$

For computational convenience, we adopt a factorization of K independent Gaussian distributions for $q_\theta(\omega)$ and use the conjugate normal-inverse gamma ($\mathcal{N} - \mathcal{IG}$) prior distributions for the hyperparameters.

$$q_\theta(\omega) = \prod_{i=1}^{K} \mathcal{N}(\omega_i|\mu_i, \sigma_i^2), \quad \mu_i \sim \mathcal{N}(0, \sigma_\mu^2), \quad \sigma_i^2 \sim \mathcal{IG}(a_\sigma, b_\sigma), \quad (4)$$

where σ_μ^2, a_σ, and b_σ are specified hyperparameters that could be tuned.

As illustrated in Fig. 2, the Faster R-CNN in Phase 1 first processes the red-green-blue (RGB) image data to identify and localize objects within bounding boxes. Subsequently, in Phase 2, the first BNN takes the coordinates of the RGB-based bounding boxes as its input features and learns to model the spatial arrangements of objects as perceived in the visual RGB domain, inherently capturing the uncertainty associated with these relationships based on the visual cues. Concurrently, a second BNN processes the depth information contained within the Faster R-CNN identified bounding boxes. By operating on depth-derived object proximity, this BNN aims to describe the spatial layout of objects based on their distance from the sensor, again with an associated measure of uncertainty. The outputs of these two BNNs, representing probabilistic estimations of spatial relations from different modalities, would then be combined or analyzed to provide a comprehensive and uncertainty-aware understanding of the spatial scene.

2.3 Human-Robot Collaboration

In human-robot collaboration, spatial relationships play a critical role in interpreting human instructions and enabling robots to interact meaningfully with their surroundings. Our framework leverages these relationships to bridge human intent and robotic action. The system begins by recognizing spatial relations among detected objects in a scene. These spatial relations are used to disambiguate references in natural human instructions, allowing the robot to identify the correct object or location for a given task. For instance, when a human says, "Pick up the cup next to the laptop," the robot uses its learned spatial model to locate the target cup based on its position relative to the laptop. This understanding is grounded in a probabilistic spatial reasoning framework, which enhances robustness in uncertain or cluttered environments.

3 Experiments

To evaluate the proposed method, we designed experiments to assess object detection accuracy (Phase 1) across various scenarios, including the *Active Vision* dataset [1], a computer-simulated dataset (Simulated), and a lab-collected dataset (Lab). Additionally, we evaluated the spatial relationships (Phase 2) based on the detected bounding boxes of recognized objects for the chosen datasets.

3.1 Artifactual Depth Data Generation

Our procedure for training the BNNs begins with the simulated data. First, we created bounding-box data by selecting aspect ratios and scalar multipliers for appropriate bounding-box sizes corresponding to the portion of the image frame that the objects in our dataset were likely to fill. Next, we chose two bounding boxes from the possible options at random and assigned one the label of "target" and the other the label of "anchor." From here, we calculated the midpoints of both bounding boxes and assigned a spatial label out of the four ("Right," "Left," "Above," "Below") based on the relative positions of the midpoints. This process was repeated 250,000 times. After the data generation, we also performed some light cleaning to account for bounding box pairs resulting in complete overlaps. Data points falling into this category were removed.

Next, we produced synthetic depth data to train a BNN that handles the depth information to investigate the three spatial relations "Behind," "Next_to," and "In_Front." To create the class labels for these three relations, we followed the rule displayed in Fig. 3, which shows the illustration of the respective classes based on the depth values. Here, the x-axis represents the depth value, where Δ is the distance between the median of the depth within the anchor box region and the median of the depth within the target box region, and τ denotes the threshold calculated by averaging the buffers of the anchor and target boxes. These buffers were calculated by taking the median absolute deviation (MAD) of the depth values in a small area centered on the respective region and scaling this by a numeric factor $\gamma \geq 1$ that is dependent on the pair of objects to accommodate differing object lengths. We chose an adaptive γ value for each object pair based on how the object's length compares to the interquartile range of the object lengths across the dataset.

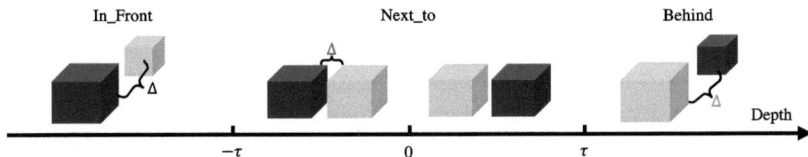

Fig. 3. Demonstration on depth data threshold. The blue box is the target object, and the yellow one is the anchor object. The relations are based on the viewer's perspective. (Color figure online)

3.2 Lab Data Collection Process

For robust training representative of scenarios with real world objects, we chose different commonly used household objects of varying shapes, sizes, and colors that could be useful in a collaborative environment between humans and robots. The 56 chosen unique items could be roughly categorized into the nine general groups based on their affordances, as listed in Table 1.

Table 1. Categories, frequencies, and affordances of objects in the lab-collected dataset.

Category	Frequency in images	Affordance
Toiletries	191	Grasp, hold
Writing utensils	181	Grasp, hold, support
Bottles	169	Grasp, hold, wrap, twist
Boxes	156	Grasp, hold, lift
Cans	153	Grasp, hold, twist
Dishes	125	Grasp, hold, support, lift
Electronics	102	Grasp, hold, turn, twist, support
Books	98	Grasp, hold
Others	82	Grasp, hold, twist

3.3 Evaluation on Object Detection

The first stage of our experiment is to assess object detection. Using the *Active Vision* dataset, our model achieved an overall accuracy of 95%, demonstrating high reliability across most object classes. The weighted average precision, recall, and F1-score were 0.97, 0.95, and 0.96, respectively, indicating robust performance for the majority of object categories. While many classes exhibited near-perfect metrics, such as Class 4 (Cholula Chipotle hot sauce, with precision of 1.00 and recall of 0.97) and Class 23 (gold Softsoap, with precision of 1.00 and recall of 0.93), some categories had lower scores or insufficient data presence. Specifically, Class 0 (background) and Class 32 (paper plate) had no support, suggesting a lack of sufficient data for these categories. Additionally, classes with lower recall values, such as Class 27 (Vo5 tea therapy healthy green tea smoothing shampoo with a recall of 0.86), highlight areas where the model could be further optimized. These results suggest that this dataset returns a strong performance across most object types, but improvements in data distribution or model tuning may be necessary to address certain underrepresented categories.

Meanwhile, our lab dataset yields overall lower metrics, with the weighted average precision, recall, and F1-score of 0.73, 0.35, and 0.44, respectively. The detailed mean micro-metrics for each affordance class are provided in Table 2. For example, besides cans, most categories have a precision of at least 0.75. However, they possess quite low recall values, where the maximum value is at most 0.6, leading to the overall lower F1-score. This pattern could be attributed to the small number of images we took. However, careful efforts had been spent to ensure a variety of objects, almost double that of the *Active Vision* dataset. This gives us more insight into supplementing our lab dataset through augmentation and/or taking more photos in subsequent studies to provide a richer training set for improved Faster-RCNN performance.

Table 2. Mean object detection classification metrics in the lab-collected dataset.

Category	Precision	Recall	F1-Score
Toiletries	0.817	0.584	0.666
Writing utensils	0.750	0.115	0.200
Bottles	0.868	0.436	0.566
Boxes	0.900	0.428	0.508
Cans	0.684	0.344	0.450
Dishes	1.000	0.363	0.513
Electronics	0.845	0.490	0.618
Books	1.000	0.570	0.625
Others	0.900	0.404	0.492

3.4 Evaluation of Spatial Relation Recognition

Phase 2 of the architecture involves recognizing the spatial relations among the detected objects. Our present iteration of BNN-SL leverages robust standard linear and 2D convolutional neural classifier architectures modified with linear Bayesian classifier layers in place of the standard fully connected layers. These Bayesian classifier layers are initialized with commonly used hyperparameter values of $\mu = 0$ and $\sigma = 0.1$, and the input dimensions are 64 times the bounding box coordinate counts plus image size dependent parameter counts (yielding $\sim$675K parameters for Lab/Simulation and $\sim$4.03M parameters for *Active Vision*). The performance of the proposed model is shown in the confusion matrices in Fig. 4 on both the simulated and lab datasets. We see that the BNN stream that takes bounding box coordinates does a great job in correctly recognizing the four spatial relations based on RGB information. The weighted average precision, recall, and F1-score are 0.96, 0.95, and 0.96, respectively, despite the class imbalance in the left and right relations, with a ratio of 3:1 compared to the above and below relations.

After benchmarking with the simulated data, we assess these four spatial relation recognitions on our lab dataset and report the performance in the right image of Fig. 4. The results here draw many parallels to those of the simulated dataset. For example, although the first two classes (Left and Right) dominate the dataset with a ratio of 2:1 compared to the other two (Above and Below), the weight metrics are still competitive: 0.96, 0.96, and 0.96 for precision, recall, and F1-score, respectively.

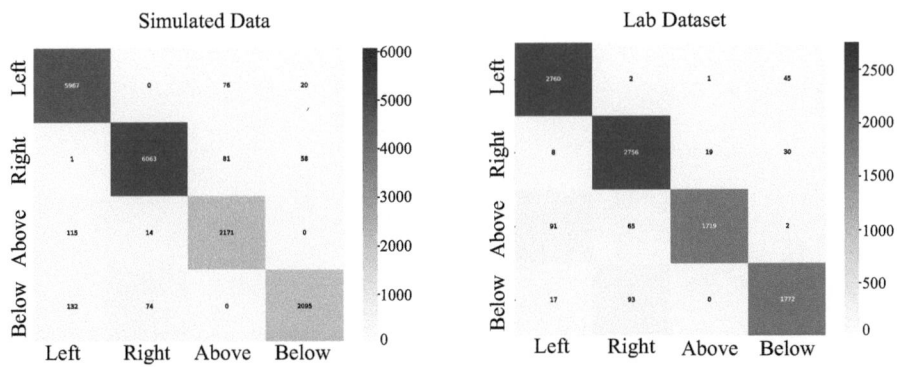

Fig. 4. The confusion matrices of the spatial relation recognition; the darker green signifies better spatial relation recognition. (Left) Simulated data. (Right) Lab dataset. (Color figure online)

Table 3 shows that the BNN-SL architecture outperforms a standard NN having the same structure in metrics that are not favored by determinism, such as precision. That is more evident in the depth F1 scores, where the BNN-SL expresses uncertainty awareness and increased determinism with larger datasets. Furthermore, the performance of the simulated data shows higher levels of variability. This may warrant a study of the simulation generation and labeling process to account for faulty data.

Finally, we want to provide some details of certain scenes in our lab collected dataset, with both detected object outputs (labels, scores, and bounding boxes), and the recognized spatial relations among these objects. Four selected images are shown in Fig. 5. Since most of the pairwise spatial relations are detected correctly, we opt to display only the wrongly detected ones for brevity.

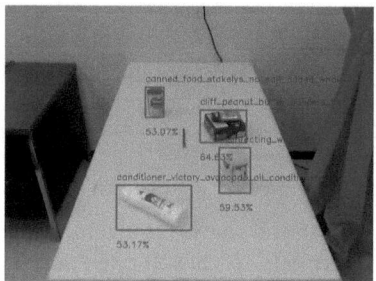

Total Detected Spatial Relations: 30.
Wrongly Detected Spatial Relations:
1. "conditioner_victory_avaocado_oil_conditioner" is right (above) to "cliff_peanut_butter_builders_bar".
2. "canned_food_stokelys_no_salt_added_whole_kernel_golden_corn" is right (below) to "pen_gray".
3. "cliff_peanut_butter_builders_bar" is right (above) to "deoderant_speed_stick_regular_light".
4. "cliff_peanut_butter_builders_bar" is left (below) to "conditioner_victory_avaocado_oil_conditioner".

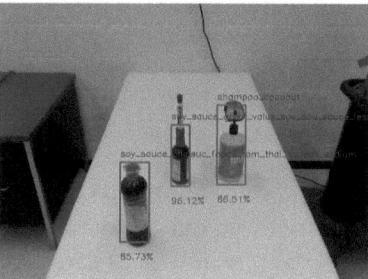

Total Detected Spatial Relations: 20.
Wrongly Detected Spatial Relations:
1. "shampoo_coconut" is below (left) to "soy_sauce_chinsuc_foods_tam_thai_tu_less_sodium".
2. "soy_sauce_great_value_soy_sau_sauce_less_sodium" is left (below) to "soy_sauce_chinsuc_foods_tam_thai_tu_less_sodium".
3. "computer_mouse" is below (left) to "soy_sauce_chinsuc_foods_tam_thai_tu_less_sodium".
4. "soy_sauce_chinsuc_foods_tam_thai_tu_less_sodium" is right (above) to "soy_sauce_great_value_soy_sau_sauce_less_sodium".
5. "soy_sauce_chinsuc_foods_tam_thai_tu_less_sodium" is above (right) to "computer_mouse".

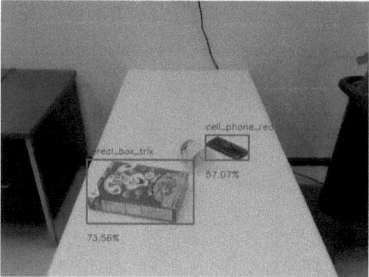

Total Detected Spatial Relations: 6.
Wrongly Detected Spatial Relations:
1. "big_cup_yellow" is below (left) to "cereal_box_trix".

Total Detected Spatial Relations: 20
Wrongly Detected Spatial Relations:
1. "book_red" is right (above) to "shampoo_pert_plus".
2. "laptop" is right (above) to "book_red".
3. "book_red" is left (below) to "laptop".

Fig. 5. Lab demonstration of the proposed framework. Object detection results, the total number of detected spatial relations, and the wrongly detected relations are shown.

Table 3. Weighted average spatial relations classification metrics of NN and BNN-SL over present datasets.

Dataset	Data	Model	Precision	Recall	F1-Score
Active Vision	Bounding boxes	NNs	**0.987**	**0.987**	**0.987**
		BNN-SL	0.982	0.982	0.982
	Depth	NNs	**0.545**	0.355	0.325
		BNN-SL	0.526	**0.476**	**0.474**
Simulated	Bounding boxes	NNs	0.987	0.987	0.987
		BNN-SL	**0.989**	**0.989**	**0.989**
	Depth	NNs	**0.429**	0.353	0.210
		BNN-SL	0.358	**0.357**	**0.353**
Lab	Bounding boxes	NNs	0.968	0.968	0.968
		BNN-SL	**0.974**	**0.974**	**0.974**
	Depth	NNs	0.524	0.549	0.519
		BNN-SL	**0.538**	**0.570**	**0.533**

4 Conclusion

In this paper, we propose a holistic three-phase framework to develop an HRC platform that enables robots to detect common household objects in a noisy tabletop setting and learn the spatial relations among them. We achieved good results for both phases, namely the object detection (Phase 1) and spatial relation recognition (Phase 2) across all datasets investigated. In Phase 1, the weighted average metrics such as precision, recall, and F1-score stay in the 0.9 range for the *Active Vision* dataset, and around the 0.7 range for our lab dataset, which contains fewer images but more objects. In Phase 2, the metrics for the four spatial relations recognition of our BNN model that takes in bounding box coordinates as inputs enjoy consistently high values of at least 0.95 for both simulated and lab data, even when the classes are quite imbalanced. Additionally, we note that the total training time for Phase 2 is very competitive, taking less than 20 s per epoch on the Lab and simulated datasets.

Our current work involves incorporating the depth information to enhance the spatial relation recognition to detect "In_Front," "Behind," and "Next_to" through deployment of the second BNN model embedded in the Phase 2 architecture. Furthermore, we are currently working on Phase 3, where large language models will be integrated into our HRC framework to instruct robots to execute commands given by human users.

Finally, we want to note some areas for improvement in this work, which are also our ongoing investigations. First, the accuracy of our proposed framework could be enhanced by a thorough evaluation of the hyperparameter tuning and model design for an optimal configuration. Secondly, our approach is constructed to handle static image inputs for table-top object scenarios, which can be generalized to handle more dynamic real-world human-robot collaboration situations. Finally, our performance correlates strongly with the spatial relations labeling process, and implementing a systematic method through the Bayesian neural networks architecture to differentiate and reduce aleatoric and epistemic errors will be highly valued.

References

1. Ammirato, P., Poirson, P., Park, E., Košecká, J., Berg, A.C.: A dataset for developing and benchmarking active vision. In: 2017 IEEE International Conference on Robotics and Automation (ICRA), pp. 1378–1385. IEEE (2017)
2. Arefin, M., Tran, D., He, H.: Complex instruction translation using fine-tuned large language models. In: International Conference on Social Robotics, pp. 312–322. Springer (2024)
3. He, W., Jiang, Z.: A survey on uncertainty quantification methods for deep neural networks: an uncertainty source perspective. Perspective **1**, 88 (2023)
4. Jospin, L.V., Laga, H., Boussaid, F., Buntine, W., Bennamoun, M.: Hands-on bayesian neural networks a tutorial for deep learning users. IEEE Comput. Intell. Mag. **17**(2), 29–48 (2022)
5. Kim, J., et al.: Control strategies for cleaning robots in domestic applications: a comprehensive review. Int. J. Adv. Rob. Syst. **16**(4), 1729881419857432 (2019)
6. Kononenko, I.: Bayesian neural networks. Biol. Cybern. **61**(5), 361–370 (1989)
7. Li, H., Uz Zaman, A., He, H.: Grasp intention interpretation in object handover for human-robot teaming. In: International Conference on Social Robotics, pp. 346–354. Springer (2024)
8. Ren, S., He, K., Girshick, R., Sun, J.: Faster R-CNN: towards real-time object detection with region proposal networks. In: Advances in Neural Information Processing Systems, pp. 91–99 (2015)
9. Ren, S., He, K., Girshick, R., Sun, J.: Faster R-CNN: towards real-time object detection with region proposal networks. IEEE Trans. Pattern Anal. Mach. Intell. **39**(6), 1137–1149 (2016)
10. Robla-G mez, S., Becerra, V., Llata, J., Gonzalez-Sarabia, E., Torre-Ferrero, C., Perez-Oria, J.: Working together: a review on safe human-robot collaboration in industrial environments. IEEE Access **5**, 26754–26773 (2017)
11. Tran, D., Yan, F., Yihun, Y., Tan, J., He, H.: A framework of controlled robot language for reliable human-robot collaboration. In: Li, H., et al. (eds.) ICSR 2021. LNCS (LNAI), vol. 13086, pp. 339–349. Springer, Cham (2021). https://doi.org/10.1007/978-3-030-90525-5_29
12. Wilson, D., Yan, F., Sinha, K., He, H.: Robotic understanding of scene contents and spatial constraints. In: Ge, S.S., et al. (eds.) ICSR 2018. LNCS (LNAI), vol. 11357, pp. 93–102. Springer, Cham (2018). https://doi.org/10.1007/978-3-030-05204-1_10
13. Yan, F., Tran, D.M., He, H.: Robotic understanding of object semantics by referringto a dictionary. Int. J. Soc. Robot. **12**, 1251–1263 (2020)

14. Yan, F., Wang, D., He, H.: Robotic understanding of spatial relationships using neural-logic learning. In: 2020 IEEE/RSJ International Conference on Intelligent Robots and Systems (IROS), pp. 8358–8365 (2020). https://doi.org/10.1109/IROS45743.2020.9340917
15. Yan, F., Wang, D., He, H.: Comprehension of spatial constraints by neural logic learning from a single RGB-D scan. In: 2021 IEEE/RSJ International Conference on Intelligent Robots and Systems (IROS), pp. 9008–9013. IEEE (2021)

Social Robot Haru Imitating Human Gaze for Attention and Turn-Taking Coordination in Multi-party Conversation

Liu Tian[1], Yang Chen[1], Mingyang Hu[1], Eric Nichols[2], Randy Gomez[2], and Guangliang Li[1](✉)

[1] Ocean University of China, Qingdao, China
guangliangli@ouc.edu.cn
[2] Honda Research Institute Japan Co., Ltd., Wako, Japan
{e.nichols,r.gomez}@jp.honda-ri.com

Abstract. Social assistive robots are potentially going to integrate with human daily life in the near future. This study presents Haru, an embodied social robot capable of engaging in multiparty conversations through both verbal and non-verbal behaviors. Unlike traditional systems that rely on rule-based control or manual scripting, Haru autonomously generates human-like gaze behaviors using Generative Adversarial Imitation Learning (GAIL) from real-world demonstrations, allowing it to coordinate attention and turn-taking in dynamic group settings. In addition, Haru integrates a large language model (i.e., ChatGPT) to support open-domain spoken dialogue, enabling flexible and context-sensitive interaction. Results of a user study show that participants preferred Haru when it maintained mutual gaze during conversation, and perceived it as more polite, socially aware, and engaging. These findings highlight the importance of combining adaptive non-verbal cues with natural language abilities to enhance human-robot interaction.

Keywords: Social robot · Imitation learning · Human-robot interaction

1 Introduction

With recent advancements in robotics and artificial intelligence, social assistive robots have the potential to integrate into human daily life in the near future, e.g., assisting group conversations and human interactions [13,18]. Chen et al. demonstrated that conversational robots can enhance parental engagement in children's language development in family interactions [6]. Similarly, in a study involving two participants teaching a robot to classify rock types, Ravari et al. found that the robot's verbal encouragement not only facilitated participants' understanding of classification methods but also enhanced team communication, thereby improving both social and task engagement [25]. In the study where the robot assisted a team in completing a bomb disposal task, it acted as an emotional regulator and positively influenced the dynamics of conflicts within the team [20]. Additionally, Hadjiantonis et al. found that social robots can act as discussion moderators, dynamically adjusting topics based on conversational context to guide participant discussions [14].

As human expectations for interacting with social robot grow, users increasingly demand robots to exhibit more human-like social behaviors and adhere to social norms, thereby optimizing human-robot interaction experiences [4]. For example, nonverbal behaviors like gaze play a crucial role in enhancing a robot's social expressiveness [30]. The work of Anzabi et al. suggests that nonverbal cues, including nodding, gaze, and gestures, significantly improve a robot's perceived credibility and emotional expressiveness [1]. Vigni et al. emphasized that appropriate gaze behaviors can enhance a user's perception of a robot's social intentions, making it easier to discern whether the robot intends to initiate interaction [31]. Pham et al. highlighted that actions like nodding and gaze following contribute to a shared sense of understanding between participants and the robot [24]. Tatarian et al. found that, in multiplayer games, participants who were gazed at by the robot tended to stand closer to it and perceived it as more socially engaging [29]. In addition, Gonçalves et al. also showed that in a desert survival task where a robot assisting three team members in item selection, it can effectively reduce psychological resistance through gaze behavior, thereby increasing its persuasiveness [10]. Similarly, Babel et al. observed that participants engaged in casual conversation were more receptive to robots with directed gaze behavior, whereas robots without gaze were perceived as less engaging [2].

In this paper, we designed a system integrating a dialogue assistance module and an autonomous gaze module and deployed on the embodied robot Haru [33]. In the autonomous gaze module, we allow Haru to imitate human-like gaze behaviors from real-world human demonstrations via generative adversarial imitation learning [15–17,21,34]. The dialogue assistance module comprises automatic speech recognition [11], ChatGPT [23], and text-to-speech components, enabling Haru to engage in free-form dialogue with users. A user study involving 22 participants demonstrated that gaze behavior imitation from human demonstrations can significantly improve Haru's social presence, user experience user satisfaction with the conversation.

2 Related Work

Task-oriented conversational agents such as Siri [19] and Google Assistant [12] have been widely deployed for scheduling, weather updates, and device control [7]. However, these systems primarily support goal-directed interactions and are not designed for complex multi-party conversations.

Recently, more and more attentions have been paid to facilitating robots with non-verbal behaviors to support more natural human-robot interaction. For example, Rifinski et al. deployed a robot as a passive observer in a human debate scenario, which provided basic responsive behaviors such as gaze shifts and body orientation toward active speakers, mimicking attentiveness and engagement [26]. However, these behaviors were not autonomous, but were manually triggered via Wizard-of-Oz (WoZ) method, where a human operator remotely controlled the robot's actions. Moreover, the system cannot make decisions in real-time, and was unable to process or respond to speech input.

In a two-person guessing game, Weldon et al. proposed to allow a social robot to gaze for social coordination. The robot could detect who was speaking and shift its gaze accordingly, thereby guiding turn-taking and promoting engagement between participants [32]. However, the robot cannot speak with users and was limited to non-verbal behaviors based on pre-scripted routines. Robots with only verbal or non-verbal behavior may appear impolite or socially inappropriate in nuanced interactions. In addition, its gaze behavior, though responsive, followed fixed patterns and was not adaptive to the conversational context.

In a more socially complex setting, Moujahid et al. designed a receptionist robot capable of multimodal behavior, including gaze, head orientation, and speech. The robot can interact with multiple users simultaneously and could manage turn-taking through coordinated verbal and non-verbal cues. For instance, it can use gaze to signal attention and head movement to shift focus between speakers, while can also deliver spoken messages to guide the interaction flow [22]. Fang et al. [8,9] considered the mechanisms of eye and head movements during visual perception processing, and the social robot's eye and head gaze behaviors are designed to replicate human gaze movements with Vestibulo-Ocular Movement (VOM) during face-to-face interaction. Nevertheless, both the dialogue system and the behavior controller were rule-based, relying on "if-then" logic for action selection. This design restricted the robot's ability to generalize across dynamic or unforeseen social contexts and limited its responsiveness to subtle user cues. Instead, Tang et al. also implemented a deep reinforcement learning method to learn autonomous gaze behaviors from social norms predefined in a reward function [27,28]. However, it is labor-intensive to define reward functions with expertise in social conversation and difficult and even impossible to incorporate all social norms in the reward function for the robot to learn.

In summary, while these systems demonstrate that robots can perform coordinated gaze, head orientation, and scripted dialogue in social settings, they remain limited by manual control, rule-based behavior or learning from defined social norms, constraining their scalability and naturalness. In contrast, in this paper, we proposed and implemented social robot Haru to learn social gaze behavior via Generative Adversarial Imitation Learning (GAIL) [15], from real-world human demonstrations. In addition, integrated with a ChatGPT, the designed system allows Haru to engage in multi-modal, context-sensitive interactions that are both responsive and adaptive to dynamic social environments.

3 Methodology

This study aims to develop a social robot that can imitate human gaze behavior for attention and turn-taking coordination, enabling the robot to adhere to human social norms during conversational interactions and enhancing its naturalness and interactivity. To achieve this goal, we designed a system consisting of two modules: an autonomous gaze module and a dialogue assistance module, as shown in Fig. 1.

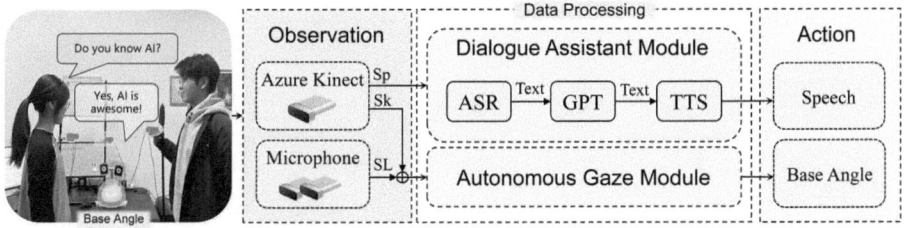

Fig. 1. Illustration of the structure and workflow of our system with autonomous gaze module and dialogue assistance module. Note that, Sp: speech, Sk: skeletons, SL: sound location.

3.1 Autonomous Gaze Module

The autonomous gaze module is designed to enable the social robot Haru to exhibit gaze behaviors that align with nonverbal social norms in group conversations. For simplicity, in this paper, we assume a scenario where Haru engages in dialogue with two human users and employ the Generative Adversarial Imitation Learning (GAIL) algorithm [15] to learn autonomous gaze strategies by imitating demonstrated human gaze behaviors.

To ensure that the robot's policy closely approximates human behavior, human gaze demonstrations are collected from real-world conversational scenarios. In our setup of two users conversing with the social robot Haru, one individual serves as the expert to demonstrate the gaze behaviors during conversation.

The human gaze demonstrations consist of state-action pairs. As shown in Fig. 2(a), the human expert's state is represented as $[\theta_0, \theta_1, \theta_2, \theta_3, \eta_0, \eta_1]$. θ_0 indicates the human expert's head direction relative to the reference on the horizontal plane, which is deemed as the human expert's gazing direction. The azimuth angles θ_1 and θ_2 are derived from the spatial vectors between the users and the origin after spherical coordinate transformation, which indicate the relative angles between the other human user, Haru and the human expert's reference orientation. θ_3 indicates the relative angles between the users' middle direction and the human expert's reference orientation. The parameters η_0 and η_1 indicate the speaking status of users. The human expert's actions are defined as the change in the expert's head rotation relative to the body on the horizontal plane from one state to the next.

After collecting the human expert's demonstrated gaze behaviors, during interaction, at each time step t, Haru observes the current state of the two human users S_t and executes an action A_t based on its current policy π. We take every 100 time steps as one episode. The GAIL algorithm optimizes a generator and a discriminator to imitate the human user's gaze behavior. Every three episodes, all state-action pairs generated by Haru are used together with those from collected human expert demonstrations to optimize the discriminator. The output of the discriminator outputs reward signals to optimize the generator (i.e., Haru's policy). Haru learns its gazing behavior policy via GAIL by directly making its distribution of state-action pairs as close as possible to that of the human expert demonstrations.

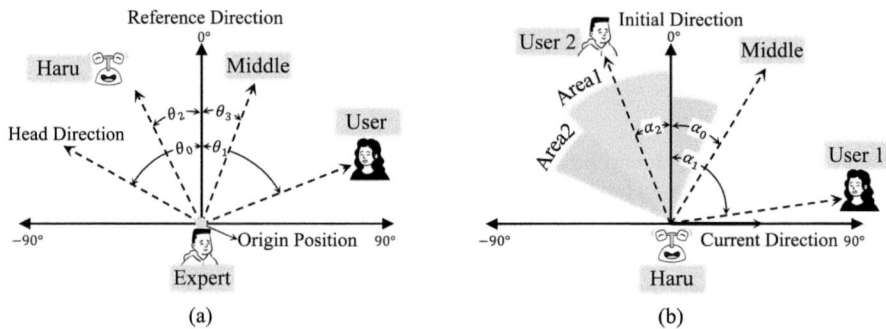

Fig. 2. (a) Illustration of the state presentation for human expert trajectory acquisition. (b) Reward regions used for evaluating Haru's learned gaze behavior. Area 1 is defined as the angular range $[\alpha_2 - \pi/4, \alpha_2 + \pi/4]$, where the gaze is considered approximately correct. Area 2 includes two sub-ranges: $[\alpha_2 - \pi/8, \alpha_2 - \pi/4]$ and $[\alpha_2 + \pi/8, \alpha_2 + \pi/4]$, where the gaze is considered less accurate. For other conditions, α_2 is replaced by α_n accordingly.

State Space. The social robot Haru is typically placed on a tabletop, with its spatial position defined as the origin of the coordinate system. The user's position relative to Haru can be represented in Cartesian coordinates as (x, y, z). To provide a more intuitive description of the user's spatial orientation, the Cartesian coordinate system is converted into a spherical coordinate system. The azimuth angles (i.e., the horizontal angle) between the two human users and Haru were used to represent Haru's state. Additionally, Haru's gaze direction and the user's speaking status (e.g., whether the user is speaking) are incorporated into the state representation of Haru.

Action Space. During interactions, the actions of the robot Haru can be characterized as dynamic adjustments of its gaze direction based on the current state. However, due to hardware constraints and the limitations of the interaction environment, the range of Haru's rotational movement is restricted to a predefined angular range of $[-90°, 90°]$.

Evaluation Metric. For autonomous gazing behavior learning via GAIL, the rewards are subjective and provided by the discriminator obtained from human expert demonstrations. To objectively evaluate Haru's learned gaze behavior, we defined a reward function as evaluation metric, as below:

$$\text{reward} = \begin{cases} 0.1 + 0.9 \times \left(1 - \dfrac{\beta}{\pi/8}\right), & \text{if } \beta < \dfrac{\pi}{8} \\ 0.1, & \text{if } \dfrac{\pi}{8} \leq \beta < \dfrac{\pi}{4} \\ -1, & \text{if } \beta \geq \dfrac{\pi}{4} \end{cases} \quad (1)$$

$$\beta = \alpha - \alpha_n, \quad n = 0, 1, 2 \quad (2)$$

where α denotes the angle between the robot's current gaze direction and the initial direction. As illustrated in Fig. 2(b), α_0, α_1, and α_2 represent the optimal gaze directions that Haru should take when (1) both users are either silent or speaking simultaneously, (2) User 1 is speaking, and (3) User 2 is speaking, respectively.

For example, assuming User 2 is speaking, we consider that in daily human interactions, his gaze behavior is not as precise as that of a machine. Therefore, the reward function defined in Eq. 1 is used to evaluate how well Haru imitates human gaze behavior based on social norms. The reward ranges from −1 to 1. If Haru's gaze direction falls within Area 1, it is considered approximately correct, and the closer it is to the optimal angle, the closer the reward is to 1. If the gaze falls within Area 2, it is deemed less accurate, and a fixed reward of 0.1 is given. If the gaze direction falls outside these two regions, it is considered highly inaccurate, and a reward of −1 is assigned.

3.2 Dialogue Assistant Module

The dialogue assistance module consists of three sub-modules: Automatic Speech Recognition (ASR), Large Language Model (LLM), and Text-to-Speech (TTS). The ASR module is responsible for real-time recognition and conversion of user speech input into textual information. The LLM module, powered by ChatGPT, processes the user's text input for semantic understanding and response generation, ensuring contextually appropriate dialogue replies. Finally, the TTS module converts the LLM-generated text responses into speech, which is then output through Haru's built-in speaker, enabling seamless voice interaction between human users and the robot.

4 Experiment

As it takes a long time for Haru to learn a good gaze behavior policy via the Generative Adversarial Imitation Learning (GAIL) algorithm, we trained Haru to learn the autonomous gazing behavior via GAIL from collected human expert demonstrations in our simulation platform. The learned gaze behavior policy in simulation was directly transferred to the real Haru robot. We tested Haru with transferred autonomous gaze behavior policy and our designed system in a user study of multi-party dialogue scenario.

4.1 Autonomous Gaze Behavior Learning in Simulation

In the study, to simulate multiparty conversation in the real world, we developed a simulation environment on Gazebo, where Haru interacts with two human users face to face. In the simulation environment, the two human users' spatial positions and body movements can be slightly adjusted to simulate human users interacting in reality. Additionally, the environment features a simulated robot Haru, which can appear at any position within a designated spatial range to more closely resemble real-world conversational settings. Since human users in the simulation cannot speak, two yellow spheres are used to represent the user's speaking status [28].

In the simulation, we trained Haru to learn autonomous gaze behavior from collected real-world human gaze demonstrations on the designed simulation environment for 1500 episodes. Each episode consists of 100 time steps. Every three episodes, the collected Haru trajectories via interaction with the simulation environment along with human expert demonstrations obtained in real-world settings, are used to update the discriminator and generator (i.e., the policy network). Meanwhile, the average reward across the 3 episodes is computed to evaluate the learning performance. According to the evaluation metric defined in Sect. 3.1, the maximum and minimum total rewards that Haru can obtain in a single episode are 100 and −100, respectively.

4.2 Real User Study

Experimental Conditions. To evaluate the effectiveness of different modules within the designed system in a real-world group conversation setting, we set up two experimental conditions in a user study:

Condition 1: Only the dialogue assistance module is active, like an embodied chatbot Haru;

Condition 2: Both the autonomous gaze module and dialogue assistance module are activated for Haru, enabling the robot Haru to talk to users and coordinate attention and turn-taking during conversation.

Experimental Setup. We recruited 22 participants from a university campus for our study, including 15 males and 7 females, aged from 22 to 27 years old. 59.1% had experience in social robotics, and 40.9% had no relevant experience. These participants were divided into 11 groups with each group consisting of two participants. All participants took part in the two experimental conditions and the order of each group participating in the two conditions was randomly assigned. The two participants in each group were allowed to be familiar with each other for a few minutes before the experiment began. During the experiment, the two participants of each group were assigned a topic to talk from an instructor. There was short break between participating the two conditions. The experimental setup was as follows: Haru was placed on a desk, with an Azure Kinect next to it to get the skeleton and sound location of user; the two users were positioned near two other Kinects for accurate sound localization.

After completing experiment in each condition, each participant was asked to fill in a questionnaire to evaluate the experimental process and Haru's performance during conversation. The questionnaire evaluated the effectiveness of the system from two perspectives: Haru's performance and the users' experience. The GODSPEED [5] questionaire was used to assess Haru's capabilities in five dimensions: anthropomorphism, animacy, likeability, perceived intelligence, and perceived safety. Additionally, A couple of questions were selected from the PSI [3] to further evaluate Haru's social intelligence. Four customized questions were set to assess user's overall satisfaction with the conversation, and two questions on the users' willingness to use Haru. All questions were rated on a 5-point Likert scale. Finally, the questionnaire concluded with an open-ended question to ask for user feedback and suggestions on Haru and our system.

5 Result and Discussion

5.1 Performance of Human Gaze Imitation in Simulation

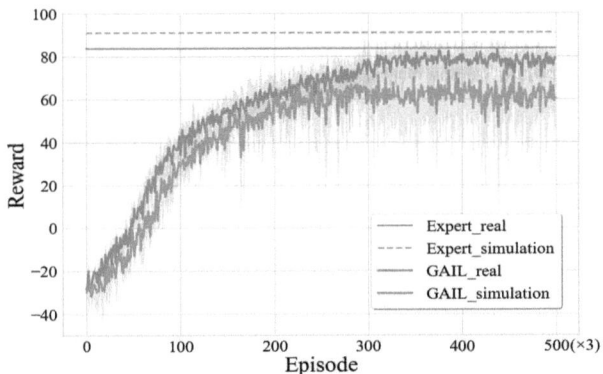

Fig. 3. Learning curves of Haru via GAIL with human expert demonstrations collected in real world and simulation, respectively. Note that, *Expert_real* denotes expert trajectories collected from real-world interactions, *Expert_simulation* refers to expert trajectories obtained in the simulation environment. *GAIL_real* and *GAIL_simulation* represent the learning performance of Haru via the GAIL algorithm with *Expert_real* and *Expert_simulation*, respectively.

We evaluated the learning performance of Haru via GAIL from collected human demonstrated gaze behavior in the real world trained in simulation, and compared to learning from collected simulated human demonstrated gaze behaviors, based on the defined reward function in Sect. 3.1. Figure 3 shows the learning curves of Haru learning from both simulated and real-world human demonstrated gaze behaviors measured as average cumulative rewards per episode consisting of 100 time steps, and performances of the two demonstrations, respectively.

As illustrated in Fig. 3, the performance of simulated human demonstrations is higher than that of real-world ones, since human gaze behaviors are much more stable and consistent in simulation than real-world ones. Although the real-world demonstrations might be influenced by individual human differences and external interference factors, which may include abnormal behaviors or noise, resulting in relatively lower data quality, they directly stems from genuine human interactions and can more accurately reflect natural gaze patterns, social norms, and dynamic environmental changes in group conversations.

In Fig. 3, each curve shows the mean performance averaged over five independent experimental trials, with the shaded area indicating the maximum and minimum performance, during the learning process. From Fig. 3 we can see that, although the performance of simulated human expert demonstrations is better than that of real-world ones, Haru learned faster and obtained a higher performance from real-world human demonstrated gaze behaviors than simulated ones, achieving a performance close to real-world demonstrations.

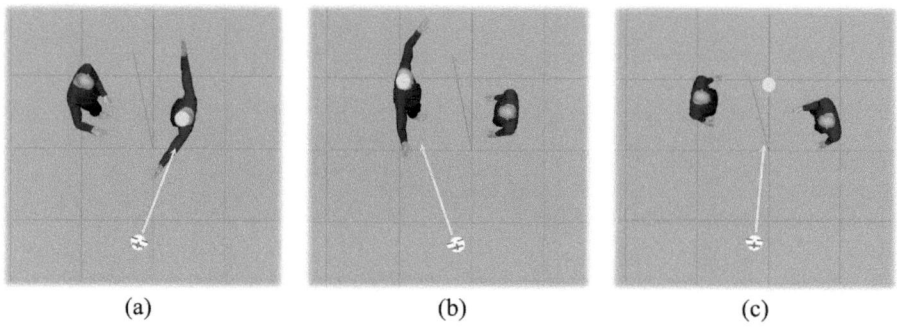

Fig. 4. Examples of Haru's learned gaze behaviors in simulation. (a) Left user speaking; (b) Right user speaking; (c) Both users speaking or silent.

Additionally, Fig. 4 shows examples of Haru learned autonomous gaze behavior in simulation. The yellow spheres represent the user's speaking state. Figure 4 shows that during interactions in the conversation, Haru can autonomously gaze at the user who is speaking and to the middle between users when both users are talking or being silent, demonstrating that the learned autonomous gaze behavior aligns with human social norms.

5.2 Haru's Performance in the Real World

We first deployed Haru's learned gaze behavior policy trained in the simulation environment onto the embodied robot Haru and tested it in a real-world setting. Figure 5(a) shows the human expert demonstrated gaze behavior during the conversation in the real environment, while Fig. 5(b) depicts the learned gaze behavior of the embodied robot Haru in the same conversational scenario. From Fig. 5(a)(b), it can be observed that the embodied robot Haru can perform autonomous gaze behaviors similar to those demonstrated by human expert in the real world. Moreover, we evaluated Haru's learned gaze behavior from collected real-world demonstrations according to Eq. 1 defined in Sect. 3.1, and compared to human expert demonstrations. A total of 1000 Haru gaze behaviors were collected, along with an equal number of expert gaze trajectories for comparison. Figure 5(c) presents the scores (i.e., rewards) for those collected Haru learned gaze behaviors and human expert gaze ones. The results suggest that Haru is capable of mimicking human gaze behavior in similar social contexts, and the learned gaze behavior policy in simulation is transferable and can effectively adapt to real-world interactive environments.

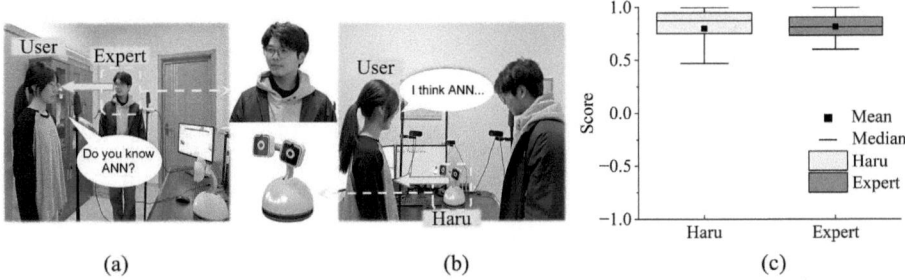

Fig. 5. An example of Haru imitated expert gaze behavior in the real world. (a) Real-world human expert demonstration of gaze behavior in a dialogue. (b) Haru's learned behavior via imitating the real-world expert gaze behavior. (c) Scores of Haru learned gaze behavior and human expert gaze ones in the real-world deployment.

Figure 6 presents Haru's example behaviors and performance in Condition 1 and Condition 2 of our user study. The results of Fig. 6 show that in Condition 2 where both the dialogue assistance module and the autonomous gaze module worked in unison, Haru could direct its gaze towards the speaking user; when a user attempted to interact with Haru, it gazed following the user and provided appropriate responses. In contrast, in Condition 1, where only the dialogue assistance module was activated, Haru could only engage in verbal conversation with the users, without responding through physical actions.

5.3 Haru's Interactive Performance in Multi-Party Conversations

To assess Haru's interactive performance, we compared 22 collected valid responses to questions of the questionnaire in our user study. The reliability of the measurement scale was examined using Cronbach's reliability analysis. Results show that Cronbach's coefficients α for all subscales are higher than

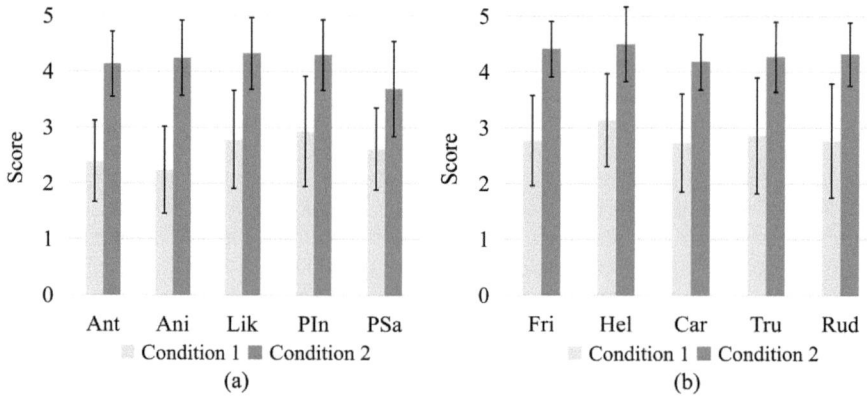

Fig. 6. Sample behaviors of Haru under two experimental conditions during the dialogue of the user study. The timeline illustrates Haru's behaviors in response to user's different speaking states: when User 1 is speaking, User 2 is speaking, or neither is speaking.

Fig. 7. Comparison of Haru's performance under two conditions based on GODSPEED (a) and PSI (b) scales. Bars show mean scores with standard deviations. *Ant*: Anthropomorphism, *Ani*: Animacy, *Lik*: Likeability, *PIn*: Perceived Intelligence, *PSa*: Perceived Safety, *Fri*: Friendly, *Hel*: Helpful, *Car*: Caring, *Tru*: Trustworthy, *Rud*: Rude.

0.7, indicating strong internal consistency among the items and confirming the reliability of the questionnaire instrument.

We first analyzed and compared the interactive performance of Haru in the two experimental conditions by mean scores rated by the 22 participants in the GODSPEED questionnaire after the study from the following five perspectives: anthropomorphism, animacy, likeability, perceived intelligence, and perceived safety. Paired t-tests were performed to assess the significance of differ-

Table 1. Statistical results of Haru's performance across the dimensions of the GOD-SPEED and PSI scales. The table presents t-values and p-values from paired sample t-tests. All differences are statistically significant at the $p < 0.01$ level. *Ant*: Anthropomorphism, *Ani*: Animacy, *Lik*: Likeability, *PIn*: Perceived Intelligence, *PSa*: Perceived Safety, *Fri*: Friendly, *Hel*: Helpful, *Car*: Caring, *Tru*: Trustworthy, *Rud*: Rude.

Section	GODSPEED					PSI				
Scale	Ant	Ani	Lik	PIn	PSa	Fri	Hel	Car	Tru	Rud
t	−8.737	−7.575	−8.149	−8.588	−6.859	−5.123	−4.678	−6.001	−7.231	−5.987
p	<0.01					<0.01				

ence between conditions, as shown in Table 1. Results in Fig. 7(a) and Table 1 show that Haru's performance in Condition 2 was significantly better across all dimensions than Condition 1 ($p < 0.01$), suggesting that Haru's behaviors were positively perceived by participants in Condition 2.

5.4 Perceived Social Intelligence in Conversation

We further analyzed and compared the perceived social intelligence of Haru in the two experimental conditions by mean scores rated by the 22 participants in the PSI (Perceived Social Intelligence) questionnaire after the study. The questionnaire consists of five core items: "Haru enjoys interacting with people" (friendly), "Haru tries to be helpful" (helpful), "Haru cares about others" (caring), "Haru is trustworthy" (trustworthy) and "Haru is rude" (rudeness). Reverse scoring was applied to the item "Haru is rude" to maintain consistency in the interpretation of scale responses.

Paired t-tests were also performed to assess the significance of difference between conditions, as shown in Table 1. Results in Fig. 7(b) and Table 1 show that significant differences ($p < 0.01$) were observes across five dimensions between the two experimental conditions: friendly, helpful, caring, trustworthy and rudeness (reverse scored). In all of these dimensions, Haru's behaviors in Condition 2 were perceived to be significantly better with smaller score variances than those in Condition 1, indicating more stable and favorable evaluations.

5.5 User's Satisfaction and Willingness to Use

We also analyzed and compared users' satisfaction with Haru under the two experimental conditions with four questions in the questionnaire filled by the 22 participants. Table 2 presents the mean scores and variances of the four satisfaction-related questions. Paired t-tests were used to assess the significance of differences between conditions. The results in Table 2 show that participants reported significantly higher enjoyment when interacting with Haru in Condition 2 compared to Condition 1 (Q1, $p < 0.01$). In addition, participants were more likely to feel that Haru listened more attentively in Condition 2 than in Condition 1 (Q2, $p < 0.01$). Participants also expressed greater satisfaction with the interaction experience in Condition 2 (Q3, $p < 0.01$), and a stronger willingness to continue engaging with Haru (Q4, $p < 0.01$).

Table 2. User's satisfaction with Haru in the two experimental conditions. The table shows mean scores ($\pm$ standard deviation) for each question, with t-values and p-values from paired t-tests. All differences are significant at $p < 0.01$.

Question	Condition 1	Condition 2	t	p
Q1. Did you feel pleasant in the conversation?	3.23 ± 1.15	4.50 ± 0.60	−6.796	<0.01
Q2. Did Haru attend to your speech?	3.18 ± 1.05	4.55 ± 0.51	−4.667	<0.01
Q3. Were you satisfied with Haru overall?	2.68 ± 0.89	4.27 ± 0.55	−6.739	<0.01
Q4. Would you like to engage with Haru again?	2.86 ± 1.04	4.45 ± 0.60	−6.542	<0.01

Lastly, we analyzed users' willingness to use Haru in their daily life with two questions in the questionnaire filled by the 22 participants, aiming to explore its potential for real-world application. As shown in Fig. 8, users were more inclined to use Haru in Condition 2 in everyday scenarios (Question 1, $p < 0.01$), and were also more willing to recommend it to others (Question 2, $p < 0.01$).

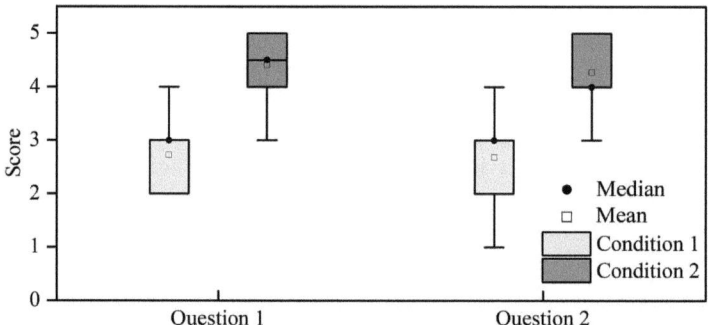

Fig. 8. User's willingness to use Haru in the two experimental conditions. Note: Question 1: Would you like to use Haru in your daily life? Question 2: Would you recommend Haru to others?

6 Conclusion

In this study, we present an embodied robot, Haru, capable of engaging in non-verbal interaction by mimicking human-like gaze behavior during multiparty conversations. In addition to gaze coordination, Haru supports open-domain spoken dialogue, enabling unconstrained verbal communication with users. Our findings in a user study further demonstrate that participants show a clear preference for Haru maintaining gaze contact during conversations, and perceives such behavior as more socially appropriate and indicative of stronger social competence.

Acknowledgments. This work was supported by Natural Science Foundation of China (under grant No. 51809246), Young Taishan Scholars Program (under Grant tsqn202408072) and Qingdao Natural Science Foundation (under grant No. 23-2-1-153-zyyd-jch).

References

1. Anzabi, N., Umemuro, H.: Effect of different listening behaviors of social robots on perceived trust in human-robot interactions. Int. J. Soc. Robot. **15**(6), 931–951 (2023)
2. Babel, F., et al.: Small talk with a robot? The impact of dialog content, talk initiative, and gaze behavior of a social robot on trust, acceptance, and proximity. Int. J. Soc. Robot. **13**(6), 1485–1498 (2021)
3. Barchard, K.A., Lapping-Carr, L., Westfall, R.S., Fink-Armold, A., Banisetty, S.B., Feil-Seifer, D.: Measuring the perceived social intelligence of robots. ACM Trans. Hum.-Robot Interact. (THRI) **9**(4), 1–29 (2020)
4. Bartneck, C., Forlizzi, J.: A design-centred framework for social human-robot interaction. In: RO-MAN 2004. In: 13th IEEE International Workshop on Robot and Human Interactive Communication (IEEE Catalog No. 04TH8759), pp. 591–594. IEEE (2004)
5. Bartneck, C., Kulić, D., Croft, E., Zoghbi, S.: Measurement instruments for the anthropomorphism, animacy, likeability, perceived intelligence, and perceived safety of robots. Int. J. Soc. Robot. **1**, 71–81 (2009)
6. Chen, H., Kim, Y., Patterson, K., Breazeal, C., Park, H.W.: Social robots as conversational catalysts: enhancing long-term human-human interaction at home. Sci. Robot. **10**(100), eadk3307 (2025)
7. de Barcelos Silva, A., et al.: Intelligent personal assistants: a systematic literature review. Expert Syst. Appl. **147**, 113193 (2020)
8. Fang, Y., Merino, L., Thill, S., Gomez, R.: Designing visual and auditory attention-driven movements of a tabletop robot. In: 2023 32nd IEEE International Conference on Robot and Human Interactive Communication (RO-MAN), pp. 2232–2237. IEEE (2023)
9. Fang, Y., Pérez-Molerón, J.M., Merino, L., Yeh, S.L., Nishina, S., Gomez, R.: Enhancing social robot's direct gaze expression through vestibulo-ocular movements. Adv. Robot. **38**(19–20), 1457–1469 (2024)
10. Gonçalves, A., Moreno, P., Forlizzi, J., Marques, L.G., Bernardino, A.: Non-verbal cues on robot-group persuasion. In: 2024 IEEE International Conference on Robotics and Automation (ICRA), pp. 1000–1006. IEEE (2024)
11. Google Cloud: Cloud speech-to-text documentation (2024). https://cloud.google.com/speech-to-text. Accessed 07 Apr 2025
12. Google LLC: Google assistant (2024). https://assistant.google.com/. Accessed 07 Apr 2025

13. Grassi, L., Recchiuto, C.T., Sgorbissa, A.: Robot-induced group conversation dynamics: a model to balance participation and unify communities. In: 2023 IEEE/RSJ International Conference on Intelligent Robots and Systems (IROS), pp. 3991–3997. IEEE (2023)
14. Hadjiantonis, G., Gillet, S., Vázquez, M., Leite, I., Dogan, F.I.: Let's move on: topic change in robot-facilitated group discussions. In: 2024 33rd IEEE International Conference on Robot and Human Interactive Communication (ROMAN), pp. 2087–2094. IEEE (2024)
15. Ho, J., Ermon, S.: Generative adversarial imitation learning. Adv. Neural Inf. Process. Syst. **29** (2016)
16. Huang, J., Hao, J., Juan, R., Gomez, R., Nakamura, K., Li, G.: GAN-based interactive reinforcement learning from demonstration and human evaluative feedback. In: Proceedings of 2023 IEEE International Conference on Robotics and Automation (ICRA), pp. 4991–4998. IEEE (2023)
17. Huang, J., Hao, J., Juan, R., Gomez, R., Nakarnura, K., Li, G.: Model-based adversarial imitation learning from demonstrations and human reward. In: 2023 IEEE/RSJ International Conference on Intelligent Robots and Systems (IROS), pp. 1683–1690. IEEE (2023)
18. Ikari, S., Yoshikawa, Y., Ishiguro, H.: Multiple-robot mediated discussion system to support group discussion. In: 2020 29th IEEE International Conference on Robot and Human Interactive Communication (RO-MAN), pp. 495–502. IEEE (2020)
19. Apple Inc.: Siri – apple's intelligent assistant (2024). https://www.apple.com/siri/. Accessed 04 Apr 2025
20. Jung, M.F., Martelaro, N., Hinds, P.J.: Using robots to moderate team conflict: the case of repairing violations. In: Proceedings of the Tenth Annual ACM/IEEE International Conference on Human-Robot Interaction, pp. 229–236 (2015)
21. Li, G., Gomez, R., Nakamura, K., He, B.: Human-centered reinforcement learning: a survey. IEEE Trans. Hum.-Mach. Syst. **49**(4), 337–349 (2019)
22. Moujahid, M., Hastie, H., Lemon, O.: Multi-party interaction with a robot receptionist. In: 2022 17th ACM/IEEE International Conference on Human-Robot Interaction (HRI), pp. 927–931. IEEE (2022)
23. OpenAI: ChatGPT: Optimizing language models for dialogue (2022). https://openai.com/blog/chatgpt. Accessed 07 Apr 2025
24. Pham, T.V., Weisswange, T.H., Hassenzahl, M.: Embodied mediation in group ideation–a gestural robot can facilitate consensus-building. In: Proceedings of the 2024 ACM Designing Interactive Systems Conference, pp. 2611–2632 (2024)
25. Ravari, P.B., Lee, K.J., Law, E., Kulić, D.: Effects of an adaptive robot encouraging teamwork on students' learning. In: 2021 30th IEEE International Conference on Robot & Human Interactive Communication (RO-MAN), pp. 250–257. IEEE (2021)
26. Rifinski, D., Erel, H., Feiner, A., Hoffman, G., Zuckerman, O.: Human-human-robot interaction: robotic object's responsive gestures improve interpersonal evaluation in human interaction. Hum.-Comput. Interact. **36**(4), 333–359 (2021)
27. Tang, F., et al.: Social robot Haru assisiting dynamic group discussion with autonomous eye gaze behavior. In: 2025 IEEE/RSJ International Conference on Intelligent Robots and Systems (IROS). IEEE (2025)
28. Tang, F., et al.: Assisting group discussions using desktop robot Haru. In: 2024 IEEE International Conference on Robotics and Automation (ICRA), pp. 3326–3332. IEEE (2024)

29. Tatarian, K., Chamoux, M., Pandey, A.K., Chetouani, M.: Robot gaze behavior and proxemics to coordinate conversational roles in group interactions. In: 2021 30th IEEE International Conference on Robot & Human Interactive Communication (RO-MAN), pp. 1297–1304. IEEE (2021)
30. Urakami, J., Seaborn, K.: Nonverbal cues in human-robot interaction: a communication studies perspective. ACM Trans. Hum.-Robot Interact. **12**(2), 1–21 (2023)
31. Vigni, F., Rossi, S.: Exploring non-verbal strategies for initiating an HRI. In: International Conference on Social Robotics, pp. 280–289. Springer (2022)
32. Weldon, C.F., Gillet, S., Cumbal, R., Leite, I.: Exploring non-verbal gaze behavior in groups mediated by an adaptive robot. In: Companion of the 2021 ACM/IEEE International Conference on Human-Robot Interaction, pp. 357–361 (2021)
33. Zhang, L., Zheng, C., Wang, H., Gomez, R., Nichols, E., Li, G.: Autonomous storytelling for social robot with human-centered reinforcement learning. In: 2024 IEEE/RSJ International Conference on Intelligent Robots and Systems (IROS), pp. 2450–2456. IEEE (2024)
34. Zheng, C., Zhang, L., Wang, H., Gomez, R., Nichols, E., Li, G.: Shaping social robot to play games with human demonstrations and evaluative feedback. In: 2024 IEEE International Conference on Robotics and Automation (ICRA), pp. 9517–9523. IEEE (2024)

Modeling Social Robot Navigation: From Human Observation to Proxemics-Based Scenario Simulation

Roni Burdman(✉) ⓘ, Ehud Nahum ⓘ, Yael Edan ⓘ, and Tal Oron-Gilad ⓘ

Department of Industrial Engineering and Management, Agricultural, Biological, Cognitive Robotics Initiative, Ben-Gurion University of the Negev, Beer-Sheva, Israel
roniburd@post.bgu.ac.il, udi@design.co.il, {yael, orontal}@bgu.ac.il

Abstract. Proxemics, how individuals perceive physical space around them, is essential for designing social robot navigation. This study explored human-robot proxemics (HRP) by looking at personal space as a continuous shape around a person. Drawing from real-world observations of human-human interactions, we identified six situations that reflect natural navigation patterns relevant to human-robot interactions. In parallel, using experimental data reported in the literature, we developed spatial proxemics models that represent the personal space surrounding individuals. We then integrated these models into a set of human-robot interaction scenarios within a simulation environment that also incorporates a robot's navigation behavior, to study more realistic investigations of proxemic dynamics. The simulation outcomes were assessed for navigation behaviors that appeared uncomfortable, revealing two uncomfortable HRI scenarios. This methodology enables structured explorations of robot violations of proxemic patterns, laying the groundwork for future real-robot experiments that examine the spatial structure of proxemics in human-robot interaction scenarios. (R. Burdman and E. Nahum—These two authors contributed equally to this work).

Keywords: Social robot navigation · Proxemics · Interaction distance · Passing by · Sim-to-Real

1 Introduction

As technology advances, mobile robots are transitioning from operating in isolated industrial settings to functioning within human environments, such as homes, public spaces, and workplaces [1]. These settings include scenarios where mobile robots perform tasks that directly involve humans – such as deliveries, where encounters with people are central to their function – as well as situations where robots indirectly interact with humans who share and navigate the same environment [2].

To be accepted in these shared environments, robots must adhere to social navigation principles, adapting their behavior to align with human social norms and avoiding actions that may cause human discomfort or disruption [3]. A critical aspect of social navigation is proxemics, the study of how individuals use and perceive space in social interactions [4]. Traditional proxemics research has focused on human-to-human interaction. Fundamental proxemics have demonstrated that interpersonal distance significantly influences human psychological comfort. Hall [3] coined the term and the initial classification of the human interaction space into four zones: intimate, personal, social, and public [4]. While some proxemics studies support Hall's view of personal space as circular [5], others suggest that it can take non-circular forms. Research indicates a greater need for space in the frontal area, likely due to the direction of physical actions and social factors such as eye contact [6, 7]. For instance, Argyle and Dean [8], observed that increased eye contact may lead to larger interpersonal distances. Conversely, others highlight a greater need for space behind individuals [9, 10], likely due to reduced sensory input and limited visual awareness in that area. Lateral differences have also been reported: some findings suggest people maintain less distance on their dominant side [11], while others attribute side preferences to social norms, such as a cultural tendency to pass on the right [12]. These variations in spatial preferences may stem from methodological differences, including the approach direction, whether participants are moving or stationary, and whether the interaction occurs in real or virtual environments.

The integration of robots into social environments requires deeper investigation of how proxemic principles apply to human-robot interactions (HRI) and what unique factors influence these encounters [13]. In a recent review, Karwowski et al. [4] term proxemics as a key element in forming the perceived safety of humans around robots, as respecting the human's personal spaces impacts the robots' passing distances. A range of factors in the literature has been found to influence individuals' preferred distances from robots, including the robot's appearance [14], height [15], speed [16], posture [17], and approach direction [18]. Studies have demonstrated that people generally allow mechanoid and shorter robots to come closer than human-like or taller ones [19, 20]. In addition, participants who are seated tend to accept closer distances compared to those who are standing or lying down [21]. Lower robot speeds are also typically preferred, likely due to initial unfamiliarity and the increased sense of threat associated with faster movements during early encounters [20].

Studies also investigated the preferred stopping distance of robots during human-approach interactions. Many findings align with Hall's definition of the personal zone (0.46–1.2 m), reporting stopping distances of 0.5 m [22], 0.6 m [23], 0.7 m [24], and 0.88 m [25]. However, others have identified preferences within the intimate zone (0–0.45 m). For example, [26] reported a stopping distance of 0.29 m, and in [26] nearly 40% of participants allowed the robot to approach closer than 0.46 m, possibly perceiving it more as an object than a social entity. Conversely, some experiments have reported preferences within the social zone (1.2–3.6 m), including a notable result of 1.64 m [27]. This wide variability reflects differences in context, robot type and design, participant characteristics, and motion behavior [28]. Recent work suggests that the approach direction - whether from the front, side, or back - can significantly influence perceived comfort [5]. In these studies, participants were approached by a robot from different directions and instructed it to stop at the closest distance they still found comfortable (e.g., [25]). This simple "approach-and-stop" interaction is limited for the development of more comprehensive spatial models of the personal space around an individual. For instance, a robot performing a task such as floor cleaning, patrol, or delivery may not engage directly with people. Still, it must account for human comfort while avoiding collisions with by-passers [2, 29].

In their review [4], conclude that user studies provide valuable insights for implementing personal space concepts in robot control systems, enabling better models for maintaining social distance. It is therefore important to conduct user studies for implementing personal space concepts in robot control systems, moving beyond simplified scenarios [e.g., 29]. However, running user studies is resource-intensive, difficult and timely. Simulations allow rapid iteration at low cost, enabling refinement of the design and interaction logic. Which is why we opted to apply a simulation first.

We identified six situations that reflect natural navigation patterns relevant to human-robot interactions from real-world observations of human-human interactions. In parallel, using experimental data reported in the literature, we developed spatial proxemics models that represent the personal space surrounding individuals. We then integrated these proxemics models into six human-robot interaction scenarios in a simulation environment that incorporates a robot's navigation behavior, aiming to support more realistic investigations of proxemic dynamics. We present this development process and its outcomes. While the framework has not yet been empirically tested with a real robot, it offers a conceptual and methodological basis for designing and refining future user studies in real-world contexts.

2 Methodology

The methodological framework, shown in Fig. 1, is detailed in the following sections.

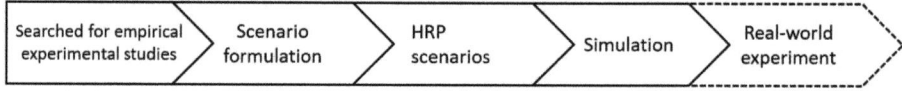

Fig. 1. Methodological framework for exploring interaction dynamics and proxemics in HRI.

This study reports the four steps; future work will include the real-world experiment.

3 Methodology to Derive Proxemics Models

We conducted a systematic search for empirical, experimental studies in Human-Robot Proxemics (HRP) that reported preferred interpersonal distances. The search utilized the following keywords: personal distance, proxemics, human-robot interaction, and socially-aware navigation. Relevant literature was retrieved from the following databases: IEEE Xplore, ScienceDirect, Google Scholar, Springer, ACM Digital Library, Frontiers, ResearchGate, and arXiv. The ten experiments that contain empirical results (see Appendix) were chosen [2, 5, 17, 18, 30–32]. Using the reported distances from [2, 5, 17, 18, 30–32], ten spatial proxemics models were constructed with a MATLAB geometric function that generates an oval shape based on four points coordinated from the center (0, 0) as reported previously [32]. This method generates a smooth transition between the four directional values, resulting in a generalized proxemics model that defines a closed spatial boundary around the individual. Figure 3 shows the **three most distinguishable proxemics models**, with different definitions of spatial boundaries, were chosen for further exploration. **The first** is the traditional model proposed by Hall, which delineates personal space as a circular zone extending 0.46 m from an individual [4]. **The second** is derived from [18], an empirical framework that synthesized results from previous experiments, creating a template with a base distance applied uniformly in all directions, with specific adjustments based on scenario-relevant parameters. We adapted this method by adjusting the base distance to align with the parameters of our future experimental setup; the adjustment process with the final distances is detailed in Table 1 and exemplified in Fig. 2. **The third** is based on findings reported in [32], specifies a larger preferred distance in the front (1.245 m) compared to the other sides (1.108 m).

Table 1. The adjusted distances for Model 2, based on the framework proposed in [18].

	Base (m)	Mechanoid RH approach (m)	Robot passing (m)	Direction (m)	Preference (m)	Adjustment* (m)	Total distance (m)
Front	+0.57	−0.03	+0.04	+0.02	+0.05	+0.10	0.75
Side	+0.57	−0.03	+0.04	−0.02	+0.05	+0.16	0.77
Back	+0.57	−0.03	+0.04		+0.05	+0.10	0.73

* Distances in this study are measured from the center of the participant's body. To align with previous studies that measured the distances between the nearest points of the human and robot trunks, we added half of the average chest width to each side and half of the average body depth to the front and back.

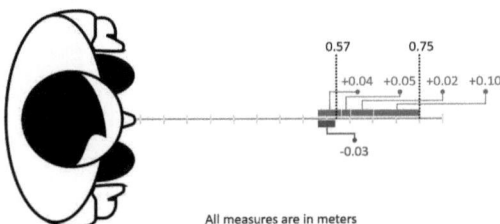

Fig. 2. An example of the front adjustment distance calculation from Base to Total distance.

3.1 Scenario Formulation

We searched for videos showcasing people navigating in shared environments, rooms, offices, and corridors for potential human-robot proxemics-relevant scenarios, using the

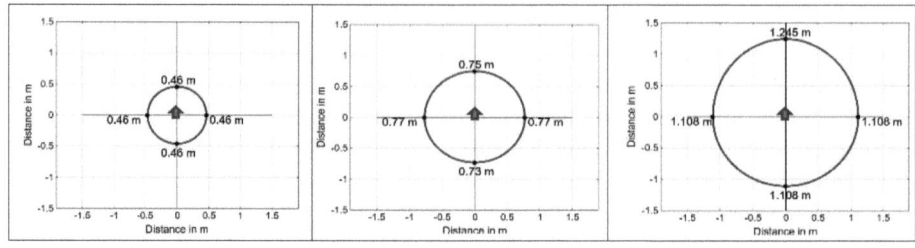

Fig. 3. Representations of the three most distinguishable proxemics models generated in MATLAB: left- (a) A model based on [4], representing the minimum personal space as defined by Hall; center-(b) A model based on [18], representing an intermediate size, and right-(c) A model based on [32], representing an asymmetric model.

following keyword: "Human-Human Interaction," "Frontal Approach in a Corridor," "Side Approach in Public Areas," "Standing in Line," and "Public Space Navigation". Videos were retrieved from online sources, including YouTube, Freepic, and pexels, publicly available datasets, and online video platforms.

The resulting dataset consisted of videos retrieved from Freepic and pexel capturing human-human interactions with diverse footage (see videos). Our focus is on interactions between a single human and a single robot, excluding scenarios involving more than two individuals. In each video, segments were annotated by one of the researchers based on identifiable cues that included: changes in interpersonal distance, walking direction, and type of interaction. The result was six labelled scenarios (Fig. 4): Frontal approach, Passing behind, Overtaking, Side approach, Bypassing and Leaving a room. To minimize subjectivity the video annotations were reviewed by two additional team members. Disagreements were resolved through discussion and consensus, while extracting recurring and contextually meaningful behavioral patterns for the subsequent steps.

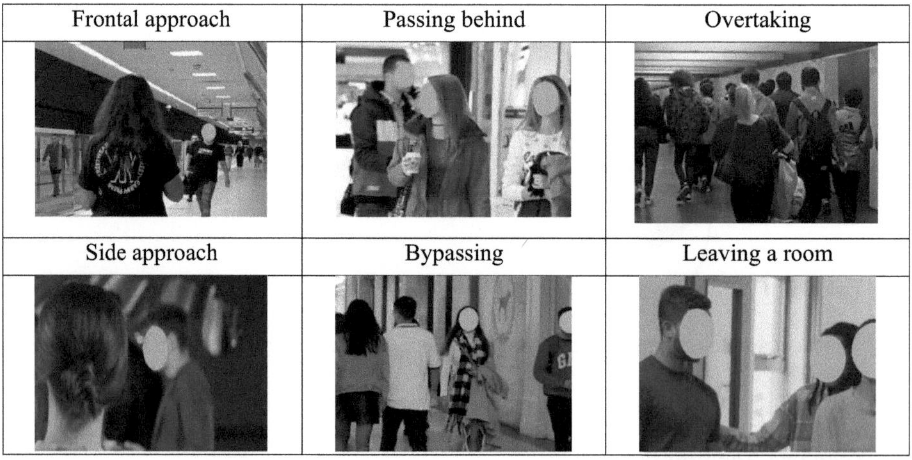

Fig. 4. Frames of interaction scenarios involving two individuals, as identified from the videos.

3.2 HRP Scenarios

The six scenarios (Fig. 4) were adapted to a human-robot context to illustrate how a robot can engage in a similar interaction with a human. PowerPoint illustrations were formed using a map representation of a physical space at the university where future real-world experiments will be held. The environment included a large central hall adjacent to an elevator and a long corridor with lab rooms in both sides (Fig. 5) resulting with HRP scenarios with potential conflict situations (Fig. 6).

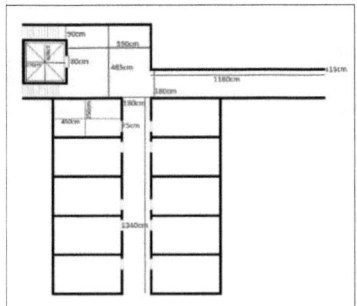

Fig. 5. A schematic map illustrating the dimensions of the simulated experimental space.

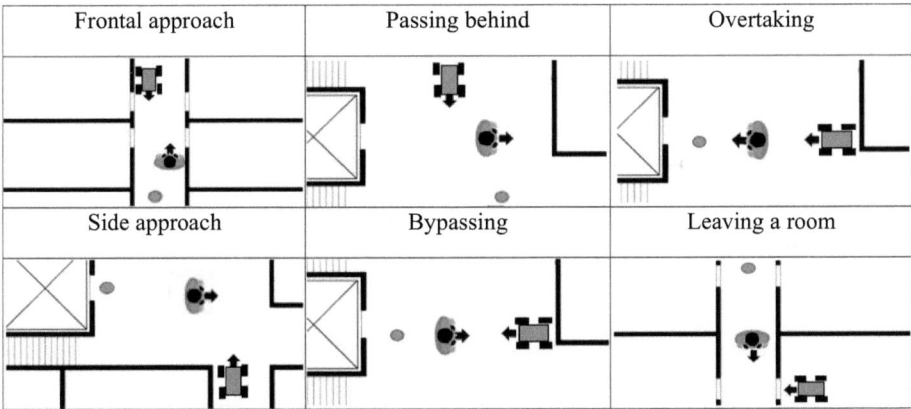

Fig. 6. HRP scenarios with potential conflict situations. The blue icon represents the human, the green dot marks the robot's destination, and the arrows indicate the direction in which each entity is facing.

4 Simulation

A simulation was developed to visually represent the HRP, illustrating the robot's trajectory and the person's proxemics model. The simulation platform (Fig. 7), developed with Cogniteam (https://www.cogniteam.com/), replicates the physical environment in Fig. 5. The simulation enabled placing a person and setting their proxemics model by uploading a pre-prepared JSON file, placing a robot at a certain place, and indicating its destination. The robot's planned trajectory, as generated in the Robot Operating System 2 (ROS2) navigation algorithm, was visualized.

HRP Assessment. The simulation runs, were conducted by scenario with each proxemics model, one author annotated instances where the robot's navigation behavior appeared uncomfortable (e.g., entering a personal zone), unpredictable (e.g., bypassing from the front), or violated key social navigation principles such as safety, comfort, legibility, and predictability [33, 34]. Two others assessed the annotations separately.

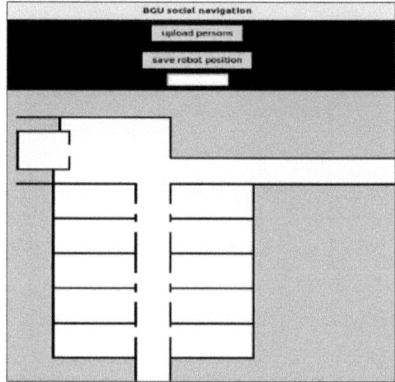

Fig. 7. The HRP simulation interface. The *upload persons* button allows the simulation user to upload a pre-prepared JSON file, placing purple dots representing persons and their proxemics model at predefined locations. The white text box underneath enables the user to set the robot's initial and final positions. Once selected, pressing the *"save robot position"* button moves the robot, represented by a blue dot, to the chosen location using ROS2 navigation.

5 Results

Scenario Representation in the Simulation. Realizations of the six scenarios in the simulation are shown in Fig. 8 for the first proxemics model (Fig. 3 (a), a circular zone of 0.46 m), showing the position of the human, the proxemics shape, and the robot's path.

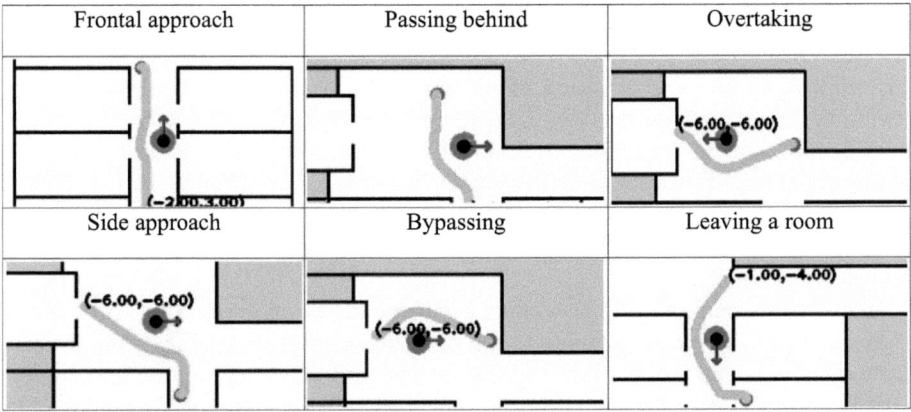

Fig. 8. Representations of the HRP scenarios in simulation, using the first proxemics model of Hall's personal zone (46 cm) [4]. The blue dot represents the robot, the purple dot represents the human, the red arrow indicates the human's movement direction, the light purple shape outlines the proxemics zone, and the green line depicts the robot's planned trajectory based on ROS2 navigation algorithm.

Violations of Natural Navigation Behavior by the Robot. Table 2 shows two recurring situations that create discomfort, observed regardless of the proxemics model, presenting two navigation behavior violations.

Table 2. Scenarios highlighting violations of key social navigation principles in Human-Robot Interactions, illustrated using the non-symmetrical proxemics model based on [32].

Expected Behavior	Observed Behavior	Explanation
Passing Behind		The robot was expected to pass behind the person to avoid causing discomfort. Instead, it passes in front of the human.
Side Approach		The robot was expected to navigate around the person's right side rather than cross in front.

6 Discussion and Conclusions

This work is an initial exploration of human-robot proxemics in dynamic contexts, moving beyond simplified front/back-approach HRP studies explored previously [22–28]. We created spatial proxemics models based on the existing HRP literature providing broader, more realistic exploration of spatial behavior situations (Fig. 3). Based on these we identified six real-world human-human interaction scenarios (Fig. 4), adapted them to HRI scenarios (Fig. 6), and applied them in a simulation that visualizes the robot's planned path (Fig. 8).

In human-human interactions, certain recurring behaviors were observed: slowing down when passing others, keeping to the right in corridors, overtaking from the left, maintaining personal space while waiting in line, and checking surroundings before exiting a room. These behaviors are attributed to social navigation principles [32]; *Safety*, slowing down when passing others to reduce the risk of collisions; *Legibility*, which emerges when individuals keep to the right side of a corridor, making their movement predictable and allowing others to understand and anticipate their actions, thereby preventing confusion or sudden directional changes; *Social Competency*, adherence to social norms, such as overtaking others from the left, a convention commonly practiced in many cultures, which helps to ensure smooth and socially acceptable movement in shared spaces; *Comfort*, shown in the maintenance of personal space while waiting in line, helping to reduce feelings of crowding or discomfort; and *Understanding Other Agents*, evident when individuals check their surroundings before exiting a room, anticipating the presence of others and adjusting their movement accordingly. While these principles are essential for HRI, HRP studies are still very simplistic relative to these human-human behaviors and very few provide empirical contextual data [2, 5, 17, 18, 30–32]. We proposed here a way to implement proxemics models in a simulation to support the development of human-aware robot navigation that considers the human spatial boundaries prior to conducting user studies.

Outcomes of the simulation phase (Fig. 8) revealed that **spatial boundaries alone are insufficient to ensure socially appropriate behavior**. Although the robot adhered to predefined proxemics zones, certain trajectories were still perceived as uncomfortable or socially inappropriate (Table 2), suggesting that merely maintaining personal space does not guarantee socially acceptable interactions as the robot behavior can still violate human social expectations. Therefore, beyond implementing proxemics models, it is important to embed broader social navigation rules into the robot's navigation algorithm. For instance, when approaching a person from the side, the robot should, whenever possible, pass behind rather than in front, as this better aligns with the person's direction of movement and reduces potential disruption.

Beyond the specific proxemics models and scenarios explored, this framework offers a foundation for developing adaptive navigation strategies to be embedded in robotic systems. By representing human personal space as flexible, scenario-dependent boundaries, the framework can inform behavior selection modules or social cost functions in standard navigation stacks such as those used in ROS2. In the long term, integrating such models with real-time perception and planning algorithms could allow robots to dynamically adjust their trajectories based on situational context, thus enhancing their ability to operate safely and acceptably in shared human environments.

Ongoing work is focused on advancing real-world user experiments to investigate how each of the three proxemics models presented above and two selected interaction types - overtaking and bypassing - affect individuals' comfort during real interactions with a robot. These two interaction types were chosen for their simplicity and prevalence in everyday human navigation.

Acknowledgments. This research was supported by the Israeli Innovation Authority as part of the HRI consortium and partially supported by Ben-Gurion University of the Negev through the Rabbi W. Gunther Plaut Chair in Manufacturing Engineering, George Shrut Chair for Human Performance, and The Agricultural, Biological Cognitive Robotics Initiative (funded by the Marcus Endowment Fund and the Helmsley Charitable Trust). The simulation was developed with Cogniteam (https://www.cogniteam.com/) as part of the consortium R&D.

Disclosure of Interests. The authors have no competing interests to declare that are relevant to the content of this article.

Appendix - Empirical Experimental Studies in Human Robot Proxemics (HRP) that Reported Preferred Interpersonal Distances

About The Study	Results	Distances (m)	Robot
[30] Perceptions of personal space and comfort from four directions: front, back, left, and right. Gaze and prior experience with robots as factors.	Participants maintain greater distances from the robot when it gazes at them. Participants with experience maintain longer distances than inexperienced ones.	With Gaze- Front: 0.9 Back: 1.24 Right: 1.96 Left: 1.96 Without- Front: 0.75 Back: 1.08 Right: 1.37 Left: 1.37	Canine Robot
[31] A robot approached participants from various directions under different conditions: seated, standing in the center of the room, sitting at a table, and standing against a wall.	Participants generally preferred the front left and front right approaches as the most comfortable. The rear approaches were rated as the least comfortable.	Standing in the middle of the room- Front: 0.42 Back: - Front Right: 0.5 Front Left: 0.75	PeopleBot
[18] An empirical framework for HRP that considers factors such as robot appearance, user preferences, interaction context, and situation.	The next stage would be to conduct real-world HRI experiments.	Distances vary according to the factors.	PeopleBot
[17] Two experiments: one with participants standing and another with participants sitting. In both experiments, participants interacted with a robot approaching from five directions: front right, front left, central front, rear right, and rear left.	In the standing condition, the results showed the lowest stopping distance. When sitting, participants preferred closer distances when approached from the side.	Standing- Front: 1.73 Back: - Right: 1.73 Left: 1.73	Nao
[5] The experiment consisted of four blocks where participants approached each other or a mannequin from different orientations.	Participants maintained larger distances from the mannequin than from humans. Closer distances were chosen when approaching from slightly oblique angles compared to frontal approaches.	From the mannequin- orientation 0° (Front): 1.24 orientation 225° (Back): 1.18 orientation 270° (Right): 1.23 orientation 45° (Left): 1.21	Not a real robot but a mannequin.
[29] Preferred interaction distances for standing and sitting positions when approached by a teleoperated robot from the front and back. Participants specified the minimum and maximum comfortable distances. The preferred interaction distance was calculated as the average of these two values. The side distances were set to match the distances measured for the back	Participants required greater distances when the robot was approaching from the front, with slight variation in preferred distances based on body position (standing/sitting).	Standing - Front: 1.245 Back: 1.108 Right: 1.108 Left: 1.108 Sitting - Front: 1.231 Back: 1.032 Right: 1.032 Left: 1.032	Keylo

References

1. Singh, K.J., Kapoor, D.S., Abouhawwash, M., Al-Amri, J.F., Mahajan, S., Pandit, A.K.: Behavior of delivery robot in human-robot collaborative spaces during navigation. Intell. Autom. Soft Comput. **35**, 795–810 (2023)

2. Neggers, M.M.E., Cuijpers, R.H., Ruijten, P.A.M., IJsselsteijn, W.A.: Determining shape and size of personal space of a human when passed by a robot. Int. J. Soc. Robot. **14**, 561–572 (2022)
3. Singh, K.J., Kapoor, D.S., Sohi, B.S.: Understanding socially aware robot navigation. J. Eng. Res. **10**(1A), 131–149 (2022)
4. Hall, E.T.: The Hidden Dimension. Anchor Books, New York (1996)
5. Karwowski, J., Szynkiewicz, W., Niewiadomska-Szynkiewicz, E.: Bridging requirements, planning, and evaluation: a review of social robot navigation. Sensors **24**(9), 2794 (2024)
6. Hecht, H., Welsch, R., Viehoff, J., Longo, M.R.: The shape of personal space. Acta Psychol. **193**, 113–122 (2019)
7. Bailenson, J.N., Blascovich, J., Beall, A.C., Loomis, J.M.: Equilibrium theory revisited: Mutual gaze and personal space in virtual environments. Presence: Teleoperators Virtual Environ. **10**(6), 583–598 (2001)
8. Hayduk, L.A.: The shape of personal space: an experimental investigation. Can. J. Behav. Sci. **13**(1), 87–93 (1981)
9. Argyle, M., Dean, J.: Eye-contact, distance and affiliation. Sociometry **28**(3), 289–304 (1965)
10. Beck, S.J., Ollendick, T.H.: Personal space, sex of experimenter, and locus of control in normal and delinquent adolescents. Psychol. Rep. **38**(2), 383–387 (1976)
11. Newman, R.C., Pollack, D.: Proxemics in deviant adolescents. J. Consult. Clin. Psychol. **40**(1), 6–8 (1973)
12. Gérin-Lajoie, M., Richards, C.L., Fung, J., McFadyen, B.J.: Characteristics of personal space during obstacle circumvention in physical and virtual environments. Gait Posture **27**(2), 239–247 (2008)
13. Bitgood, S., Dukes, S.: Not another step! Economy of movement and pedestrian choice point behavior in shopping malls. Environ. Behav. **38**(3), 394–405 (2006)
14. Oosterhout, T.V., Visser, A.: A visual method for robot proxemics measurements. In: Burghart, C.R., Steinfeld, A. (eds.) Workshop on Metrics for Human-Robot Interaction 2008, pp. 61–68. Felix Meritis, Amsterdam (2008)
15. Walters, M.L., Koya, K.L., Syrdal D.S., Dautenhahn, K., Te Boekhorst, R.: Preferences and perceptions of robot appearance and embodiment in human-robot interaction trials. In: Proceedings of New Frontiers in Human-Robot Interaction: Symposium at AISB09 Convention, pp. 136–143. John Benjamins Publishing, Amsterdam (2009)
16. Rae, I., Takayama, L., Mutlu, B.: The influence of height in robot-mediated communication. In: ACM/IEEE International Conference on Human-Robot Interaction (HRI), pp. 1–8. Tokyo (2013)
17. Rios-Martinez, J., Spalanzani, A., Laugier, C.: From proxemics theory to socially-aware navigation: a survey. Int. J. Soc. Robot. **7**(2), 137–153 (2015)
18. Torta, E., Cuijpers, R.H., Juola, J.F.: Design of a parametric model of personal space for robotic social navigation. Int. J. Soc. Robot. **5**, 357–365 (2013)
19. Walters, M., Dautenhahn, K., Boekhorst, R.T., Koya, K., Syrdal, D., Nehaniv, C.L.: An empirical framework for human-robot proxemics. In: Proceedings of New Frontiers in Human-Robot Interaction: Symposium at the AISB09 Convention, pp. 144–149. John Benjamins Publishing, Amsterdam (2009)
20. Syrdal, D.S., Dautenhahn, K., Walters, M., Koay, K.: Sharing spaces with robots in a home scenario anthropomorphic attributions and their effect on proxemic expectations and evaluations in a live HRI trial. In: AAAI Fall Symposium, pp. 116–123. Amsterdam (2008)
21. Butler, J.T., Agah, A.: Psychological effects of behavior patterns of a mobile personal robot. Auton. Robot. **10**(2), 185–202 (2001)
22. Brandl, C., Mertens, A., Schlick, C.M.: Human-robot interaction in assisted personal services: factors influencing distances that humans will accept between themselves and an approaching service robot. Hum. Factors Ergon. Manuf. **26**(6), 713–727 (2016)

23. Obaid, M., Sandoval, E.B., Moltchanova, E., Złotowski, J.: Stop! That is close enough. How body postures influence human-robot proximity. In: Proceedings of the 25th IEEE International Symposium on Robot and Human Interactive Communication (ROMAN), pp. 354–361. IEEE, New York (2016)
24. Kamide, H., Mae, Y., Takubo, T., Ohara, K., Arai, T.: Direct comparison of psychological evaluation between virtual and real humanoids: personal space and subjective impressions. Int. J. Hum. Comput. Stud. **72**(5), 451–459 (2014)
25. Mead, R., Mataric, M.J: Perceptual models of human–robot proxemics. In: Hsieh, M., Khatib, O., Kumar, V. (eds.) Experimental Robotics. Springer Tracts in Advanced Robotics, vol. 109. pp. 261–276. Springer, Cham (2015)
26. Lauckner, M.: Human-Robot Spatial Interaction in a Hallway. M.Sc. Dissertation, Technical University of Berlin (2016)
27. Li, R.: Comparing Human-Robot Proxemics between Virtual Reality and the Real World. Degree Project in Information and Communication Technology, KTH Royal Institute of Technology, Stockholm (2018)
28. Nahum, E., Edan, Y., Oron-Gilad, T.: Advancing a taxonomy for proxemics in robot social navigation. preprint at arXiv:2503.14931
29. Walters, M.L., et al.: The influence of subjects' personality traits on personal spatial zones in a human-robot interaction experiment. In: Proceedings of the IEEE International Workshop on Robot and Human Interactive Communication (ROMAN), Nashville, TN, pp. 347–352. IEEE (2005)
30. Klüber, K., Onnasch, L.: Keep your distance! Assessing proxemics to virtual robots by caregivers. In: ACM/IEEE International Conference on Human-Robot Interaction, New York, pp. 193–197. Association for Computing Machinery (2023)
31. Nahum, E., Edan, Y., Oron-Gilad, T.: Investigating the proxemics shape in social navigation: an exploratory user study. In: Palinko, O., et al. (eds.) 16th International Conference, ICSR + AI 2024, LNCS, vol. 15561, pp. 168–177. Springer, Singapore (2024)
32. Xu, X., Liying, L., Khamis, M., Zhao, G., Bretin, R.: Understanding dynamic human-robot proxemics in the case of four-legged canine-inspired robots. preprint at arXiv:2302.10729 (2023)
33. Walters, M.L., Koay, K.L., Woods, S.N., Syrdal, D.S., Dautenhahn, K.: Robot to human approaches: preliminary results on comfortable distances and preferences. In: AAAI Spring Symposium: Multidisciplinary Collaboration for Socially Assistive Robotics, pp. 103–109. Stanford (2007)
34. Francis, A., D'Arpino, C.P., Li, C., Xia, F., Alahi, A., Alami, R., et al.: (31 authors): Principles and guidelines for evaluating social robot navigation algorithms. ACM Trans. Hum.-Robot Interact. **14**(2), 32 (2025)
35. Erel, H., Vázquez, M., Sebo, S., Salomons, N., Gillet, S., Scassellati, B.: RoSI: a model for predicting robot social influence. ACM Trans. Hum.-Robot Interact. **13**(2) (2024). Article 18, 1–22

Ethics, Trust and Social Acceptability

Determinants of Attitudes Toward Social Robots
The Role of Contact and Beliefs in Human Uniqueness

Konrad Maj[1(✉)], Piotr Bekier[2], and Albert Łukasik[2]

[1] SWPS University, Warsaw, Poland
kmaj@swps.edu.pl
[2] Nicolaus Copernicus University, Toruń, Poland

Abstract. This study investigates the psychological and demographic determinants of public attitudes toward social robots, focusing on the role of prior experience and beliefs in human uniqueness. A representative sample of 1052 Polish adults (552 women, 500 men, age 18+) completed a survey assessing attitudes toward human-like robots (NARHT), interactions with robots (NATIR), and beliefs about moral and ontological human uniqueness (BHNU). Respondents also evaluated their comfort with robot autonomy and the acceptability of various robotic roles (e.g., cleaner, therapist). The analyses included Pearson correlations and regression tree modeling (CART). Results revealed that frequent prior contact with robots was not associated with reduced anxiety and higher acceptance, contrary to the hypothesis. Beliefs in human uniqueness predicted discomfort with anthropomorphic features and general robot interaction. Gender and age effects were also identified. Findings highlight the importance of psychological and experiential variables in shaping public readiness for robotic integration. The results have implications for the design and implementation of social robots across cultures and domains.

Keywords: Social robots · Trust in robots · Human-robot interaction

1 Introduction

In recent decades, social robots have ceased to be merely a topic of literary fiction and have become a tangible element of professional and social spaces. Their presence is increasingly observed in health care [1, 2], education [3], as well as in occupations related to services and security [4]. With the spread of robotics, scientific interest in the social reception of machines has also intensified, including public attitudes toward them [5, 6], emotional responses to human-like robots [7], and predictors of acceptance and resistance to the automation of jobs and social roles [8, 9].

Researchers have highlighted that the acceptance of social robots depends on a combination of contextual, social, emotional, and individual factors [10]. It is also influenced by personality traits [6], contact experience [11], and beliefs about human nature and dignity [12]. However, the findings remain inconsistent and point to the importance of cultural context and type of robot [13].

Public views on social robots are ambivalent: people appreciate their utility yet fear social and moral downsides. Our earlier study [14] linked this tension to seeing robots as both tools and threats, highlighting three risk types—instrumental (job loss, skill erosion), relational (weaker human bonds), and normative (moral-boundary erosion). The present work extends that model by adding psychological factors such as belief in human uniqueness and discomfort with robotic autonomy.

Moreover, previous findings suggest that public acceptance is highly sensitive to the type of robot role [15]. Instrumental functions such as logistics or cleaning are generally more acceptable than roles requiring emotional presence or moral responsibility, such as caregiving or psychotherapy [16]. The present study seeks to generalize and deepen these findings by focusing on how beliefs and ontological intuitions influence robot acceptance in a wider array of social contexts.

To our knowledge, this is the first study to combine the Polish NARS-PL, BHNU, and a bespoke emotion-and-ethics questionnaire in a nationally representative Polish sample, giving a fresh, region-specific view of the psychological drivers of robot acceptance in Central and Eastern Europe.

Using validated psychometrics and interpretable decision-tree models, we uncover cognitive patterns that shape social-robot acceptance and translate them into design and policy guidance. The data suggest confining assistive robots to low-stakes tasks— e.g., medication reminders—while leaving diagnosis and emotional care to humans, and advise service industries to pair "friendly" design cues with clear hand-off points for human intervention. Schools can roll out robotic tutors first in drill-based STEM lessons, then cautiously expand into counselling roles as acceptance grows. Regulators may use role-specific thresholds to decide when a machine shifts from an instrumental aid to a socially consequential actor, informing certification and liability frameworks (e.g., ISO 13482), while workforce planners can target reskilling where robots are poised to enter warehouses, clinics, and offices. Because robotics is advancing quickly across personal and professional domains, continued interdisciplinary research on public perception is vital for pre-empting resistance and ensuring ethical deployment.

1.1 Hypotheses

Based on the reviewed literature, we formulated the following hypotheses:

- H1: Higher beliefs in the uniqueness of human nature will be associated with stronger negative attitudes toward robots (NATIR and NARHT).
- H2: A Greater frequency of prior contact with robots will predict lower levels of negative attitudes.
- H3: Women will exhibit stronger concerns about robots replacing humans in emotional or care-related roles.
- H4: Respondents will accept robots more for instrumental roles (e.g., cleaning) than for affective tasks (e.g., therapist or caregiver) within their own professional roles [1, 2]

2 Method

2.1 Participants

The study involved a representative national sample of N = 1052 Polish adults (552 women, 500 men). Quotas were set based on demographic proportions of the adult Polish population, ensuring representativeness in terms of gender, age, education, and place of residence. Participants were divided into five age groups: 18–24 (n = 106), 25–34 (n = 219), 35–44 (n = 178), 45–54 (n = 197), and 55+ (n = 352). Population density at place of residence was also considered: village (n = 381), small town up to 20k inhabitants (n = 132), medium town between 20k and 99k (n = 205), big city between 100k and 500k (n = 193), and cities above 500k (n = 141).

Participants reported their frequency of everyday contact with robots on a 7-point scale: 12.0% daily (n = 126), 13.6% very often (n = 143), 21.6% often (n = 227), 21.9% rarely (n = 231), 13.2% very rarely (n = 139), 9.8% never (n = 103), and 7.9% "hard to say" (n = 83), indicating that 82.3% of respondents had at least some contact with robots.

Additionally, participants were asked whether they had ever had direct personal contact with a humanoid robot (i.e., one resembling a human). The majority (79%) reported no such experience, while 11% had encountered one 1–2 times, 2% reported 3–5 interactions, and 1% indicated more than 5. Such experiences were more common among younger adults (e.g., 21% of those aged 18–24 reported at least one contact) and rare among older participants (e.g., only 7% in the 55+ group), reflecting the limited deployment of social robots in everyday contexts.

Additional quotas controlled for education level, professional status, household size, and number of children. Participants were recruited from the Ariadna National Research Panel. Sample size estimation was conducted using G*Power 3.1, assuming a medium effect size ($f^2 = 0.15$), $\alpha = .05$, and power = .95. The required minimum sample for regression was 189.

2.2 Procedure

The survey was conducted using the Computer-Assisted Web Interviewing (CAWI) technique between October 26–30, 2023. Participants received personalized invitations through the Ariadna platform and completed the survey anonymously via a secure online interface. Respondents provided informed consent prior to participation. The questionnaire included two validated instruments: the (NARS) and the (BHNU). In addition, a series of custom items assessed perceived robot roles, moral concerns, comfort with robot autonomy, and frequency of prior interactions. Most items were rated on 5-point Likert scales. The average completion time was approximately 15 min.

The Ariadna panel is frequently used in psychological and social science research [17–20] and currently includes over 130,000 registered users. It adheres to the ethical principles of the Helsinki Declaration and Polish National Research Committees. Informed consent is obtained from all participants, and no personal data is collected. The panel is certified by the Interviewer Quality Control Program (PKJPA) and undergoes annual audits by the Polish Association of Public Opinion and Marketing Research

Firms. It complies with GDPR, the Personal Data Protection Act, and the ICC/ESOMAR International Code. The platform is accessible via web browsers and mobile applications on Google Play and the App Store, enhancing accessibility and participation flexibility.

2.3 Measures and Survey Description

The survey consisted of three main components: (1) standardized scales measuring attitudes toward robots, (2) a set of custom questions on emotional and ethical responses to robots, and (3) demographic and background items.

- NARS-PL (Negative Attitudes Toward Robots Scale) - Polish adaptation of NARS [17], measuring (NATIR) and (NARHT). Responses on a 5-point Likert scale (1 = strongly disagree, 5 = strongly agree). Example items: "I would feel uneasy if I was given a job where I had to use robots" (NATIR); "I would feel uneasy if robots had emotions" (NARHT). Cronbach's alpha: NATIR $\alpha = .86$, NARHT $\alpha = .75$.
- BHNU - scale measuring beliefs about moral, emotional, and ontological uniqueness of humans [12], 6 items on a 5-point Likert scale (1 = strongly disagree, 5 = strongly agree), e.g., "Robots will never possess morality." Cronbach's alpha: $\alpha = .86$.
- Custom Sociodemographic and Attitudinal Questionnaire - included demographic data (gender, age, residence size) and robot-related experiences and attitudes. Participants reported frequency of contact with robots (6-point scale: from never to daily) and previous direct experience with humanoid robots (categorical: none, 1–2, 3–5, more than 5). Acceptance of robots in professional roles (e.g., caregiver, cleaner, therapist), emotional reactions towards humanoid robots (multiple-choice emotions like fear, disgust, curiosity), attitudes toward robot autonomy, and ethical concerns (5-point Likert scale) were also assessed.

All scales' scores (NARHT, NATIR, BHNU) were computed by summing item responses and treated as continuous variables suitable for parametric analyses.

Due to the large sample size, formal tests of normality were not conducted, as even minor deviations can yield statistically significant results. Instead, we examined skewness and kurtosis [22], which showed no substantial deviations from normality (all values well within commonly accepted thresholds for large-sample analyses). For NARHT, skewness was 0.16 and kurtosis was -0.15; for NATIR, skewness was 0.03 and kurtosis was 0.10; for BHNU, skewness was -0.30 and kurtosis was -0.19.

2.4 Data Analysis

Statistical analyses were performed using SPSS and Python (Pandas, Scikit-learn). The analyses included Pearson's correlations, reliability testing (Cronbach's α), and Classification and Regression Tree (CART) modeling. Figures were generated in Python using Matplotlib and Networkx libraries.

The decision tree structure was determined based on two criteria. The optimal tree depth was selected using 5-fold cross-validation, minimizing the mean squared error (MSE) on the training set. A minimum number of observations (n = 80) per leaf was enforced to prevent excessive branching of the tree, limiting the creation of leaves with too few data points and thereby reducing the risk of overfitting.

3 Results

3.1 Correlational Overview

Analysis of Pearson correlation coefficients showed a moderate positive correlation between NATIR and NARHT, $r(1051) = 0.61$, $p < 0.001$, indicating that participants who held more negative attitudes toward robots with human features were also likely to be more uncomfortable interacting with robots in general. Both NATIR and NARHT scores were positively correlated with BHNU $r(1051) = 0.36$, $p < 0.001$ and $r(1051) = 0.43$, $p < 0.001$, respectively, suggesting that stronger beliefs in human uniqueness were associated with more negative attitudes toward robots. Taking into account the results, we confirmed the first hypothesis.

A Spearman's rank-order correlation was conducted to assess the relationship between prior contact with robots and two attitude indices: NARHT and NATIR. The analysis included 992 participants (60 "Hard to say" answers were excluded from the analysis). For the NARHT index, the correlation was statistically significant, $\rho(990) = -0.10$; $p < .01$, indicating a small but significant negative association—those with prior robot contact expressed slightly lower reluctance to interact with humanoid robots. For the NATIR index, the correlation was not significant, $\rho(990) = -0.03$; $p = .262$. Taken together, we rejected the second hypothesis. We also investigated the relationship between prior contact with robots and belief in human uniqueness, finding a statistically significant negative correlation, $r(992) = -0.10$, $p = .01$.

3.2 Regression Tree Models

Regression tree analyses were conducted to explore the nonlinear relationships between psychological predictors and attitudes toward robots. Separate CART models were built for each of the three dependent variables: NATIR, NARHT, and BHNU. The optimal depth of each tree was calculated based on changes in mean squared error. The chosen depth was based on the least mean squared error.

Figure 1 presents the regression tree for the BHNU index. The first and only split occurred on the variable "caregiver" (i.e., whether the participant accepts a robot in a caregiving role). This split distinguishes between those who accept robots in caregiving positions ("caregiver" = YES) and those who do not ("caregiver" = NO). The lowest BHNU index values (mean = 20.81) were observed among individuals who accepted robots in caregiving roles, while higher values (mean = 23.22) were found among those who did not. This pattern suggests that rejecting robotic caregivers is associated with greater concern about the replacement of humans in care-related contexts. However, the model showed very weak explanatory power. It achieved a high Mean Squared Error (MSE = 21.488) and R2 score ($R^2 = 0.014$), indicating that the model performs worse than a simple mean-based prediction. In other words, the input variable explains virtually none of the variance in the BHNU index.

In the context of the proposed hypothesis—"Women will exhibit stronger concerns about robots replacing humans in emotional or care-related roles"—the regression tree highlights that caregiving acceptance is a relevant factor, aligning with the idea that care-related roles trigger stronger emotional responses. Thus, we rejected the third hypothesis.

Nonetheless, due to the model's extremely poor predictive quality, this finding should be interpreted with caution and cannot be generalized.

Regression tree for dependent variable - BHNU index

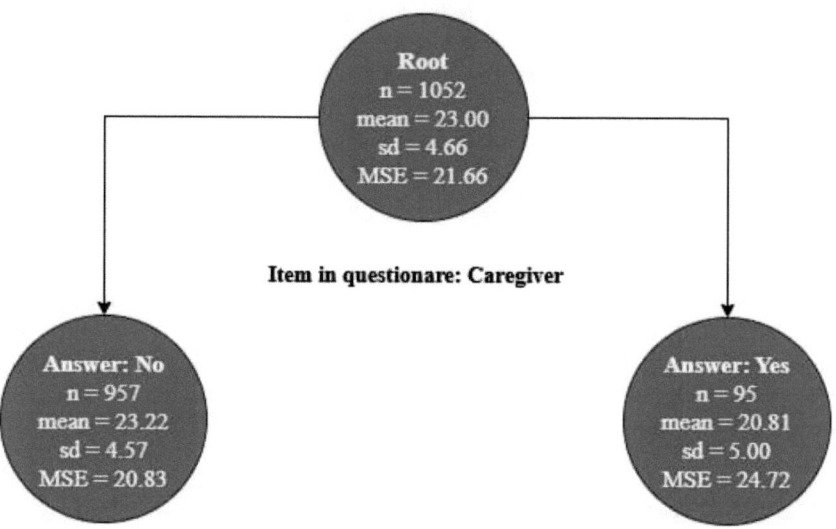

Fig. 1. Regression model for the BHNU index with the "caregiver" variable split. The diagram presents a regression tree derived from 1,052 observations. Each node displays the subsample size (n), the mean value of the NARHT index, the standard deviation (sd), and the mean squared error (MSE)

Figure 2 presents the regression tree for the NARHT index. The first split occurred on the variable "none of the above" (i.e., none of the listed professions). Individuals who reported holding one of the listed professions were further divided based on the variable "nurse/medical assistant." Additional splits were made, for example, based on whether the individual was a soldier or a housekeeper. The highest NARHT index values (mean = 18.89) were observed among those who did not identify with any of the listed professions ("none of the above" = YES), suggesting greater distance or reluctance toward interacting with robots. In contrast, the lowest values (mean = 13.44) were found among individuals who worked as nurses or medical assistants ("nurse/medical assistant" = YES) and did not hold any of the other listed roles. The model showed limited explanatory power, with a relatively high MSE (12.101) and a low R2 score (0.104), indicating weak predictive performance. Overall, the model captures some variance in the NARHT index, but a substantial portion remains unexplained, suggesting the influence of other factors not included in the model. In the context of the proposed hypotheses, the model suggests that whether the robot's role is instrumental or caregiving may have only a minor impact on predicting reluctance to interact with humanoid robots. Only three of the listed roles influenced changes in the average NARHT score—two of them instrumental and one caregiving.

Regression tree for dependent variable - NARHT index

```
                    Root
                   n = 1052
                  mean = 17.35
                   sd = 3.76
                  MSE = 14.12
```

Item in questionare: none of the above

- Answer: No — n = 786, mean = 16.82, sd = 3.60, MSE = 12.97
- Answer: Yes — n = 266, mean = 18.89, sd = 3.79, MSE = 14.32

Item in questionare: Nurse/Medical assistant

- Answer: No — n = 703, mean = 17.10, sd = 3.47, MSE = 12.04
- Answer: Yes — n = 83, mean = 14.45, sd = 3.83, MSE = 14.49

Item in questionare: Soldier

- Answer: No — n = 610, mean = 17.21, sd = 3.45, MSE = 11.90
- Answer: Yes — n = 83, mean = 14.45, sd = 3.83, MSE = 14.49

Item in questionare: Housekeeper

- Answer: No — n = 256, mean = 17.54, sd = 3.37, MSE = 11.30
- Answer: Yes — n = 354, mean = 16.98, sd = 3.50, MSE = 12.20

Fig. 2. Regression model for NARHT categories. The diagram presents a regression tree derived from 1,052 observations. Each node displays the subsample size (n), the mean value of the NARHT index, the standard deviation (sd), and the mean squared error (MSE).

Figure 3 presents the regression tree for the NATIR index. The first split occurred on the variable "none of the above" (i.e., none of the listed professions). Individuals who reported holding one of the listed professions were further divided based on the variable "waitress." Additional splits were made based on whether the individual was a receptionist, housekeeper, or salesperson. The highest NATIR index values (mean = 25.03) were observed among those who did not identify with any of the listed professions ("none of the above" = YES), indicating greater reluctance to interact with humanoid robots. In contrast, the lowest values (mean = 17.86) were found among individuals who worked as both waitresses and salespeople ("waitress" = YES, "salesperson" = YES), suggesting greater openness toward robotic interaction in these instrumental roles. The model showed modest explanatory power, with a relatively high MSE (26.535) and a low R^2 score (0.169), indicating that while some variance in the NATIR index is captured, the model's predictive ability remains limited. This suggests that additional variables not included in the model likely play a substantial role in shaping attitudes toward humanoid robots.

Similarly to the results from the NARHT model, the NATIR model also suggests that whether the robot's role is instrumental or caregiving has only a minor impact on predicting reluctance to interact with humanoid robots, again only for specific occupational roles. Out of all the listed professions, only a few were relevant to changes in the average NATIR score, and those that mattered were instrumental (e.g., waitress, salesperson). Overall, willingness to accept a robot performing a given job slightly reduces the NATIR score, but the distinction between caregiving and instrumental roles seems to have limited relevance at the individual profession level. Taken together, the results from the regression tree models lead us to conclude that the robot's role does not predict willingness to accept robots in specific roles, thus rejecting the fourth hypothesis.

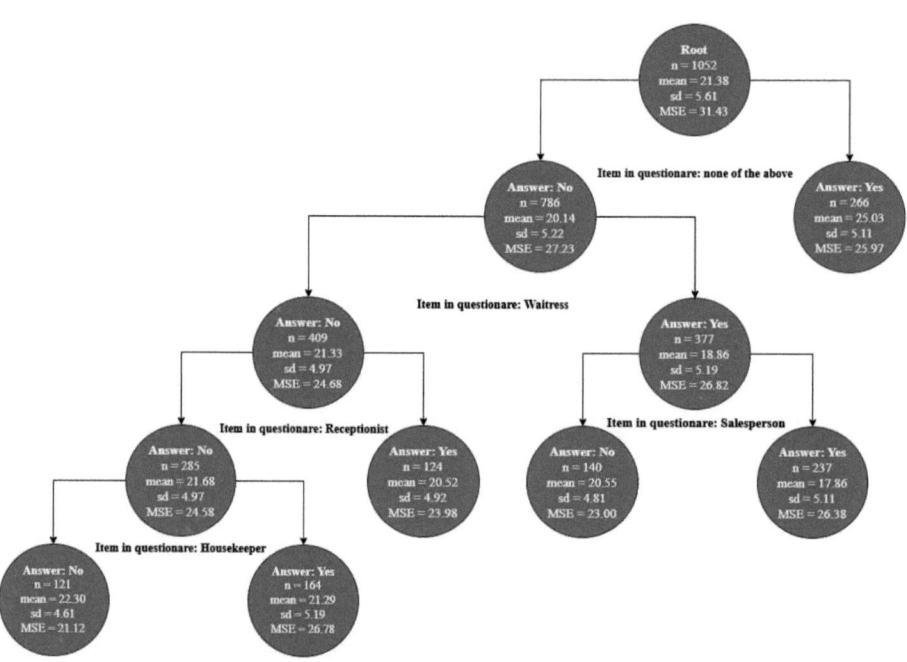

Fig. 3. Regression model for NATIR categories. The diagram presents a regression tree derived from 1,052 observations. Each node displays the subsample size (n), the mean value of the NARHT index, the standard deviation (sd), and the mean squared error (MSE).

3.3 Hypothesis Testing

H1: Higher beliefs in the uniqueness of human nature are associated with stronger negative attitudes toward robots – confirmed.
H2: Greater previous contact with robots predicts lower negative attitudes – rejected
H3: Women exhibit more concerns about robots replacing human roles – rejected
H4: Acceptance of robots is highest in instrumental roles (e.g., cleaning) and lowest in affective roles (e.g., therapists) – rejected.

4 Discussion

The aim of this study was to examine the relationship between psychological attitudes toward social robots and both the acceptance of these robots performing socially interactive professions and general interaction with them. The results indicate that, overall, psychological attitudes toward social robots are only marginally related to the acceptance of robots in roles that require varying degrees of human interaction.

Consistent with prior research, previous contact with robots emerged as a critical factor proposed to reduce anxiety and resistance [23, 24]. In our analysis, the hypothesis concerning the mitigating effect of prior contact with robots (H2) was not confirmed. Only a minor correlation was observed regarding attitudes toward robots with human-like traits (NARHT), without significant influence on general discomfort in interaction (NATIR). It is important to emphasize that the relationship between prior contact with robots and NARHT was evident only in Spearman's rho correlation analysis, and not retained in regression tree models. Including prior contact as a predictor in these models reduced their explanatory power and increased error variance, leading to its exclusion.

However, the absence of robust findings regarding prior contact does not necessarily imply that direct interaction with robots has no potential influence on attitudes toward social robots. Both our findings and prior studies indicate that approximately 80% of individuals report never having interacted with a humanoid robot [25]. This aligns closely with our own data, suggesting that attitudes are likely shaped primarily by indirect experiences, such as media portrayals, cultural narratives, or abstract understandings of artificial intelligence. Occasional interactions with non-humanoid robotic technologies (e.g., cleaning robots, service kiosks, industrial devices) may also contribute to generalized impressions of robots, even without direct social interaction.

An in-depth analysis of the regression models for NARHT and NATIR indicates that acceptance of robots performing various professions was related to attitudes toward social robots only to a limited extent, and primarily for specific professions. Acceptance of roles included in our model had generally minor effects on reducing negative attitudes, and the distinction between instrumental and affective roles did not appear significant. Indeed, a substantial portion of respondents, irrespective of their attitudes toward social robots, opposed robots performing highly sensitive professions such as doctor or nurse. This may suggest the presence of fundamental barriers independent of general robot acceptance.

Nevertheless, respondents were less unanimous regarding acceptance of robots in professions such as salesperson, waiter, or receptionist. However, even this variability did not translate into increased explanatory power in our regression models—only selected individual professions were ultimately retained. Altogether, these findings point to three areas that future research should explore further. First, some professions might be inherently resistant to robotic substitution, irrespective of overall attitudes toward robots. Second, if certain roles are widely acceptable despite limited connection to overall robot attitudes, researchers should examine the underlying factors driving such acceptance. Third, determining which areas of social life are actually influenced by general robot attitudes is critical for understanding the validity of constructs measured by the NARHT and NATIR scales.

Among all three regression models, the model predicting BHNU scores had the weakest predictive power concerning the acceptance of robots in traditionally human roles. Even though people might accept robots performing certain human professions, their perception of human uniqueness in comparison to robots is evidently shaped by factors beyond mere acceptance. The significant correlations found between BHNU and the NATIR and NARHT scales suggest that beliefs about human uniqueness—specifically in a moral and ontological sense—are closely related to robot-related anxieties.

Our findings underscore that the most important factor shaping attitudes toward social robots is not the acceptance of specific professions per se, but rather psychological beliefs related to human uniqueness in comparison to robots. This aligns with previous research indicating that perceptions of an ontological boundary between humans and machines significantly influence acceptance [26]. While our regression tree models allowed us to explore nonlinear relationships, their limited explanatory power indicates the necessity for more detailed studies across various cultural contexts and deeper exploration of attitude formation mechanisms [27].

These insights extend our understanding of the psychological dynamics underlying human-robot interactions. They provide valuable guidance for ethical design considerations and policy decisions, particularly by highlighting the need to address public concerns regarding robot autonomy, moral agency, and human uniqueness. Designers and policymakers must be attentive to these considerations when integrating robots into sensitive domains such as healthcare and education, where moral implications are highly salient.

Despite these contributions, several limitations must be acknowledged. First, the study relied on self-report measures, which might introduce social desirability bias, especially regarding attitudes toward robots and moral concerns. Second, the cross-sectional nature of our data restricts our understanding of how attitudes evolve over time, as discussed in prior longitudinal studies by Cvetkovic et al. [28]. Longitudinal research is essential to capture shifts in attitudes that may occur with increased familiarity and evolving societal norms [29].

Although this study used a nationally representative Polish sample, the results may not extend to other cultures. Given known cultural differences in robot acceptance, especially around beliefs in human uniqueness and morality, cross-cultural studies are essential to test how universal our findings are [30].

Additionally, while we measured emotional reactions and ethical concerns, these were not central to our hypotheses. Future research could explore how emotions like fear, trust, or empathy mediate links between attitudes, beliefs, and robot acceptance, and how these vary across contexts such as caregiving or education [23].

In sum, attitudes toward social robots are shaped by both demographics and psychology: while prior contact matters, beliefs about human uniqueness (BHNU/NARS) remain the chief barrier, especially in caregiving and other emotionally charged settings. Addressing worries about autonomy, privacy, and ethics—through clear role definitions, public communication, and education—will be essential to secure responsible, widely accepted robot deployment.

Acknowledgments. The authors would like to thank the Ariadna Research Panel for their support in conducting the survey. This work was supported by SWPS University.

Disclosure of Interests. The authors declare no conflicts of interest.

References

1. Andtfolk, M., Nyholm, L., Eide, H., Fagerström, L.: Humanoid robots in the care of older persons: a scoping review. Assist. Technol. **34**(5), 518–526 (2021). https://doi.org/10.1080/10400435.2021.1880493
2. Robinson, H., MacDonald, B., Broadbent, E.: The role of healthcare robots for older people at home. Int. J. Soc. Robot. **6**(4), 575–591 (2014). https://doi.org/10.1007/s12369-014-0242-2
3. Reich-Stiebert, N., Eyssel, F.: Learning with educational companion robots? Toward attitudes on education robots, predictors of attitudes, and application potentials for education robots. Int. J. Soc. Robot. **7**, 875–888 (2015). https://doi.org/10.1007/s12369-015-0308-9
4. Carlsen, H., Johansson, L., Wikman-Svahn, P., Dreborg, K.H.: Co-evolutionary scenarios for creative prototyping of future robot systems for civil protection. Technol. Forecast. Soc. Chang. **84**, 93–100 (2014). https://doi.org/10.1016/j.techfore.2013.07.016
5. Nomura, T.: Cultural differences in social acceptance of robots. In: 2017 26th IEEE International Symposium on Robot and Human Interactive Communication (RO-MAN), pp. 534–538. IEEE (2017). https://doi.org/10.1109/roman.2017.8172354
6. Piçarra, N., Giger, J.-C.: Predicting intention to work with social robots at anticipation stage: assessing the role of behavioral desire and anticipated emotions. Comput. Hum. Behav. **86**, 129–146 (2018). https://doi.org/10.1016/j.chb.2018.04.026
7. Kim, T., Lee, O.-K.D., Kang, J.: Is it the best for barista robots to serve like humans? A multidimensional anthropomorphism perspective. Int. J. Hosp. Manag. **108**, 103358 (2023). https://doi.org/10.1016/j.ijhm.2022.103358
8. Liang, Y., Lee, S.A.: Fear of autonomous robots and artificial intelligence: evidence from national representative data with probability sampling. Int. J. Soc. Robot. **9**, 379–384 (2017). https://doi.org/10.1007/s12369-017-0401-3
9. Lestari, N.S., Rosman, D., Putranto, T.S.: The relationship between robot, artificial intelligence, and service automation (RAISA) awareness, career competency, and perceived career opportunities: hospitality student perspective. In: 2021 International Conference on Information Management and Technology (ICIMTech), pp. 690–695. IEEE (2021). https://doi.org/10.1109/icimtech53080.2021.9535054
10. Cave, S., Coughlan, K., Dihal, K.: Scary robots. In: Proceedings of the 2019 AAAI/ACM Conference on AI, Ethics, and Society, pp. 331–337. ACM (2019). https://doi.org/10.1145/3306618.3314232
11. Stafford, R.Q., MacDonald, B.A., Li, X., Broadbent, E.: Older people's prior robot attitudes influence evaluations of a conversational robot. Int. J. Soc. Robot. **6**(2), 281–297 (2014). https://doi.org/10.1007/s12369-013-0224-9
12. Giger, J.-C., Piçarra, N., Pochwatko, G., Almeida, N., Almeida, A.S., Costa, N.: Development of the Beliefs in Human Nature Uniqueness Scale and its associations with perception of social robots. Hum. Behav. Emerg. Technol. **2024**(1) (2024). https://doi.org/10.1155/2024/5569587
13. Gherheș, V., Obrad, C.: Technical and humanities students' perspectives on the development and sustainability of artificial intelligence (AI). Sustainability **10**(9), 3066 (2018). https://doi.org/10.3390/su10093066
14. Maj, K., Sawicki, K., Samson, K.: Ready or not? Examining acceptance and fears of robots in the labor market. Ann. Psychol. **16**(4) (2023). https://doi.org/10.18290/rpsych2023.0019
15. de Graaf, M.M.A., Ben Allouch, S.: Exploring influencing variables for the acceptance of social robots. Robot. Auton. Syst. **61**(12), 1476–1486 (2013). https://doi.org/10.1016/j.robot.2013.07.007

16. Broadbent, E., Stafford, R., MacDonald, B.: Acceptance of healthcare robots for the older population: review and future directions. Int. J. Soc. Robot. **1**(4), 319–330 (2009). https://doi.org/10.1007/s12369-009-0030-6
17. Golec de Zavala, A.: Narcissism of science denial. J. Soc. Issues **81**(1) (2025). https://doi.org/10.1111/josi.70000
18. Jupowicz-Ginalska, A., Baran, T., Kisilowska, M., Wysocki, A., Jasiewicz, J.: Fear of missing out scale – a nationwide representative CAWI survey in Poland. Central Eur. J. Commun. **3**(27), 313–334 (2020). https://doi.org/10.51480/1899-5101.13.3(27).1
19. Cieśczyk, N., Czech, M., Pronicki, Ł., Gujski, M.: Knowledge and beliefs about clinical trials among adults in Poland: a cross-sectional study. Clin. Pract. **14**(4), 1285–1295 (2024). https://doi.org/10.3390/clinpract14040104
20. Długosz, P.: Predictors of psychological stress occurring after the first wave of the COVID-19 pandemic in Poland: a cross-sectional study. Front. Psych. **13**, 1102728 (2023). https://doi.org/10.3389/fpsyt.2022.1102728
21. Pochwatko, G., et al.: Polish version of the negative attitude toward robots scale (NARS-PL). J. Autom. Mobile Robot. Intell. Syst. **9**(3), 65–72 (2015). https://doi.org/10.14313/jamris_3-2015/25. PIAP – Industrial Research Institute for Automation and Measurements
22. Kim, H.Y.: Statistical notes for clinical researchers: assessing normal distribution (2) using skewness and kurtosis. Restor. Dent. Endod. **38**(1), 52–54 (2013). https://doi.org/10.5395/rde.2013.38.1.52
23. Nomura, T., Kanda, T., Suzuki, T., Kato, K.: Prediction of human behavior in human–robot interaction using psychological scales for anxiety and negative attitudes toward robots. IEEE Trans. Rob. **24**(2), 442–451 (2008). https://doi.org/10.1109/TRO.2007.914004
24. Fraune, M.R., Sherrin, S., Sabanović, S., Smith, E.R.: Rabble of robots effects: Number and type of robots modulates attitudes, emotions, and stereotypes. In: Proceedings of the Tenth Annual ACM/IEEE International Conference on Human-Robot Interaction, pp. 109–116. ACM (2015). https://doi.org/10.1145/2696454.2696472
25. Sarda Gou, M., Webb, T.L., Prescott, T.: The effect of direct and extended contact on attitudes towards social robots. Heliyon **7**(3), e06418 (2021). https://doi.org/10.1016/j.heliyon.2021.e06418
26. Xu, W., Li, C., Miao, X., Liu, L.: Our tools redefine what it means to be us: perceived robotic agency decreases the importance of agency in humanity. BMC Psychol. **13**(1), 1–12 (2025)
27. Ye, X., et al.: Autonomy Acceptance Model (AAM): the role of autonomy and risk in security robot acceptance. In: Proceedings of the 2024 ACM/IEEE International Conference on Human-Robot Interaction, pp. 840–849. IEEE (2024). https://doi.org/10.1145/3610977.3635005
28. Cvetković, A., Savolainen, I., Koike, M., Oksanen, A.: A four-wave longitudinal study on attitudes toward the use of AI in different domains—the self-determination theory and locus of control perspective. Telemat. Inform. Rep. (2025). Article 100220
29. Yamaguchi, M.: Item-level implicit affective measures reveal the uncanny valley of robot faces. Int. J. Hum Comput Stud. **196**, 103443 (2025). https://doi.org/10.1016/j.ijhcs.2025.103443
30. Zojaji, S., Nakano, Y.I., Peters, C.: Impact of cultural differences and politeness on joining small groups of humans, robots, and virtual characters. In: Proceedings of the 2025 ACM/IEEE International Conference on Human-Robot Interaction, pp. 479–488. IEEE (2025)

Exploring Mentalising Tendencies Toward a Non-Humanoid Robot in Individuals with Autism Spectrum Disorder: A Pilot Study

Silvia Larghi[1], Cristina Liviana Caldiroli[1,2], Leonardo Lapomarda[1], and Edoardo Datteri[1]

[1] RobotiCSS Lab, Laboratory of Robotics for the Cognitive and Social Sciences, Department of Human Sciences for Education "Riccardo Massa", University of Milano-Bicocca, Milan, Italy
{s.larghi1,l.lapomarda}@campus.unimib.it,
cristinaliviana.caldiroli@uniecampus.it,
edoardo.datteri@unimib.it

[2] Department of Theoretical and Applied Sciences (DiSTA), Faculty of Psychology, eCampus University, Novedrate, Italy

Abstract. This pilot study explores the tendency of people with autism spectrum disorder (ASD) to mentalise a non-humanoid robot. The study involved eleven children aged 7 to 10 years with ASD. A small non-humanoid robotic vehicle (CoderBot) was used. The children participated in a structured experiment involving true belief (TB) and false belief (FB) tasks. The tasks were designed to assess children's tendency to mentalise the robot, using an adapted version of a classic Theory of Mind change-of-location paradigm, with verbal and non-verbal response modes. Results indicate that five participants used mentalistic terms referring to CoderBot in both TB and FB tasks and two participants in one of the tasks (FB and TB respectively), suggesting a mentalistic interpretation of the robot's behaviour. The terms employed fall into various categories including reference to the robot's perceptual capacities, beliefs, cognitive capacities and states, and intentional agency. The results indicate FB attribution to CoderBot for six participants and TB attribution for four participants. The methodological insights of this study, including the integration of verbal and non-verbal responses and the helping paradigm, suggest promising methodological directions for future research.

Keywords: Child-Robot interaction · Theory of Mind · False Belief Attribution

1 Introduction

Effective social interaction requires the ability to understand and predict the behaviour of others. Typically, in human social interactions, behaviour predictions rely on understanding others' mental states. It has been observed that mentalisation can also occur interacting with non-human agents, such as robots (Thellman et al., 2022).

Interest in studying the attribution of mental states to robots stems from theoretical and practical motivations. A better understanding of the phenomenon can enhance the ability to predict and understand robotic behaviour (De Graaf & Malle, 2019; Imamura et al., 2015; Levin et al., 2013; Waytz et al., 2010), increasing sense of control and reduction of uncertainty in the interaction (Epley et al., 2007; Eyssel et al., 2011). Research in this field can support the design of safe, reliable, and explainable robotic systems (Ziemke, 2020; De Graaf & Malle, 2017; Miller, 2019). Robots' predictability, adaptability, and transparency is crucial to foster trust-based interactions, particularly in educational and social contexts (Belpaeme et al., 2018; Dautenhahn, 2007).

A fundamental theoretical framework grounding empirical studies on the attribution of mental states to robots is Theory of Mind (ToM) (Carruthers & Smith, 1996; Premack & Woodruff, 1978), which refers to the ability to attribute mental states, such as beliefs, desires, and other intentional states, to oneself and others. ToM is a fundamental component of social cognition and plays a crucial role in human interaction and communication, involving the ability to consider not only what individuals feel, desire, and know, but also what they think others might feel, desire, and know (Baron-Cohen et al., 1985). Also known as mindreading (Baron-Cohen, 1995), ToM develops progressively over time. Children typically begin to manifest early signs of ToM from a young age (Tomasello, 2008), using mental state terms in their interactions (Bretherton et al., 1981; Hughes & Leekam, 2004). ToM undergoes significant development during the third and fourth years of life (Wellman et al., 2001; Wellman, 2014).

Several studies have explored whether people attribute ToM to robots in ways similar to how they do with humans. For example, Banks (2020) adapted five implicit ToM tests, including a false belief (FB) task, to investigate their applicability to robots displaying varying social cues. FB tasks assess the ability to understand that others can hold beliefs that differ from reality (Wimmer & Perner, 1983). A well-known version of the FB task is based on the change-of-location paradigm (Wimmer & Perner, 1983), exemplified by the Sally-Anne test. In this task, participants are asked to predict where a character (agent), who did not witness an object being moved, will search for it. A correct response suggests an understanding of the agent's false belief (although alternative possible explanations have been discussed in the literature, see, e.g., Butterfill & Apperly, 2013). Another type of FB task refers to the unexpected-content paradigm, where participants discover that a familiar container holds an unexpected item and are then asked what someone else, unaware of the content, would think is inside (Hogrefe et al., 1986; Williams & Happé, 2009). True belief (TB) tasks are also used as a measure of ToM, often alongside FB tasks, following a similar structure, except that the agent witnesses the key change in the scenario and thus holds a correct belief (Oktay-Gür & Rakoczy, 2017; Schidelko et al., 2022).

The tendency to mentalise robots may be influenced by robot-related characteristics, such as physical appearance and behaviour (Perez Osorio & Wykowska, 2020). Human-related factors, such as interindividual differences and personal characteristics - particularly autistic traits - may also play a significant role. According to the diagnostic criteria outlined in the DSM-5-TR (APA, 2022) and the ICD-11 (World Health Organization, 2022), autism spectrum disorder (ASD) is characterised by the co-occurrence of persistent deficits in social communication and interaction (Domain A), along with restricted, repetitive patterns of behaviour (Domain B). Domain A, in particular, has frequently been linked to difficulties in ToM. Research has suggested that ToM abilities may be impaired in individuals with ASD (Baron-Cohen, 1995), possibly affecting their social cognition and communication (Tager-Flusberg, 2003). Several studies have explored whether autistic traits impact the tendency to attribute mental states to robots (O'Reilly et al., 2021; Wiese et al., 2014). Zhang and colleagues (2019) found that children with ASD were less accurate than typically developing (TD) peers in attributing false beliefs to a humanoid social robot, possibly due to a general ToM impairment or a different perception of the robot. In contrast, Akechi and colleagues (2018), investigating mind perception, evidenced a similar two-dimensional mind perception in participants with and without autism (robots were perceived to have higher agency and experience in the group of participants with autism). Notably, most existing research has focused on humanoid robots, while studies involving non-humanoid agents remain limited (Vadalà et al., 2022).

Based on the analysis of this literature, we designed and conducted a pilot qualitative study involving 11 children with ASD and a small non-humanoid robot (CoderBot, www.coderbot.org). The study aimed to explore in depth the tendency of the children involved to mentalise CoderBot. More specifically, the following research questions were addressed.

- Q1: Do the children involved in the study tend to use mentalistic terms (mental-state talk) when referring to CoderBot?
- Q2: Do the children involved tend to attribute a false belief (FB) to CoderBot in an interactive task involving the robot?
- Q3: Do the children involved tend to attribute a true belief (TB) to CoderBot in an interactive task involving the robot?

Mental-state talk (Q1) refers to the use of language related to mental states. It begins to emerge during the second year of life and continues to develop throughout the third and fourth years. It includes terms related to emotions, perceptions, volition, cognition, and morality, some of which appear early, while others emerge later, typically during the primary school years. Research has shown a significant link between mental-state talk and the development of children's social cognition (Grazzani et al., 2016). Slaughter and colleagues' (2009) theoretical model classifies children's mental verbs, developed through communicative interactions with their mother, into four categories: perceptual, volitional, cognitive, dispositional (Manzi et al., 2020).

The experiment used in this study involves the children in true belief (TB) and false belief (FB) change-of-location tasks, randomized. The classical change-of-location and unexpected-content tasks require participants to respond to a situation presented through different modalities, such as illustrated stories or verbal descriptions. However, it has been pointed out that such tasks impose considerable cognitive demands, particularly at the level of working memory and, in the case of verbal or text-based tasks, linguistic processing (Bloom & German, 2000; Byom & Mutlu, 2013). In light of this, Buttelmann, Carpenter and Tomasello (2009) developed a task based on a more active behavioural response, which assesses implicit understanding of FB and TB through helping actions rather than verbal responses (helping paradigm). The experimental tasks developed in this study are an adapted version of this "helping" task. This approach helps bypass potential verbal communication difficulties in children with ASD by incorporating a non-verbal channel. However, in the final phase of each task, children are invited to verbally explain the behaviour exhibited by CoderBot. This additional step offers deeper insight into their understanding of the robot's mental states capturing their perspective. Moreover, their verbal responses can be further analysed for the presence of mentalistic language.

2 Materials and Methods

2.1 Participants

The selected sample consisted of 11 participants, aged between 7 and 10 years (2 females and 9 males). The entire sample had a primary diagnosis of ASD made by specialists in accordance with current criteria. The participants did not have an intellectual disability and had good verbal skills. The study is on voluntary participation and informed consent has been obtained from parents.

The sample size (N = 11) is consistent with the exploratory nature of this pilot study and aligns with feasibility constraints. Similar sample sizes have been adopted in previous child-robot interaction studies (e.g., Robins et al., 2004; Diehl et al., 2012) and are consistent with methodological guidelines suggesting that 10–12 participants are adequate for assessing procedures and measures in pilot research (Julious, 2005).

2.2 Materials and Tools

The study involves CoderBot (Fig. 1), a small non-humanoid robotic vehicle. The robot is equipped with a camera, distance sensors, a microphone and a loudspeaker, and is able to move and emit sounds and words. The choice of CoderBot is dictated by the simplicity of its functionality and the repetitive and predictable nature of its movements.

For the experimental task, two handcrafted wooden boxes (Fig. 1), each measuring $30 \times 40 \times 30$ cm, were used, mainly in a neutral colour and black. Specifically, the boxes have curtains on the front, made of a soft and flexible material, so that CoderBot can pass freely through them. In addition, they can be closed by means of a stick that, inserted in special slots inside the box, acts as a barrier. The front of the boxes was customised by applying AR tags to the surface to facilitate the robot's interaction with the boxes. The task involved a wooden cube, also handmade and covered in black cardboard (Fig. 1). AR tags were applied to the surface of the cube, allowing the robot to visually detect it and move towards it.

Fig. 1. CoderBot, boxes and cube

2.3 Procedure

The experimental procedure is divided into three phases: familiarisation, TB task and FB task. The TB and FB tasks are randomised to neutralize potential artifacts introduced by the order of presentation of the stimuli.

Familiarization. The familiarization phase aims to ensure the participant's (P) understanding of the scenario and behaviour of the robot (R). P explores the materials (boxes, cube and R) and recognizes that R moves toward the cube when it is placed in front of it.

TB Task. R faces the two boxes (left and right). The experimenter (E1), facing R, inserts the cube into the box on the left through the front slot, while P watches. Then, E1 and P move the cube from the box on the left to the box on the right and close the front openings of the boxes. R moves to the box on the left, which is now empty. P's spontaneous (verbal and non-verbal) reactions are recorded. If there is no initiative, P is asked if they want to intervene (e.g.: "Do you want to do something?"). Finally, P is asked to explain the behaviour enacted by R ("Why do you think the robot behaved this way?"). E1 may intervene with additional questions in case clarification is necessary. The task receives score 1 if the following criteria is verified: P shows that they understood that R's goal is not to follow/retrieve the cube but to access the space in the box on the left for some reason, consistent with P's understanding that R has some (true) belief about the box.

FB Task. R faces the two boxes (left and right). E1, facing R, inserts the cube into the box on the right through the front slot, while P watches. E1 and P put a cover box on R. Then, E1 and P move the cube from the box on the right to the box on the left and close the front openings of the boxes. R moves to the box on the right, which is now empty. P's spontaneous (verbal and non-verbal) reactions are recorded. If there is no initiative, the procedure is as for the TB task. Finally, P is asked to explain the behaviour enacted by R ("Why do you think the robot behaved this way?"). E1 may intervene with additional questions in case clarification is necessary. The task receives score 1 if one of the following criteria is verified, consistent with P attributing to R the (false) belief that the cube is in the box on the right:

- P uses verbal expressions to confirm R's FB about the location of the cube;

- P picks up the cube and hands it to R;
- P takes R and places it in the left box where the cube is located;
- P takes the cube from the left box, places it in the box on the right and eventually opens the door to let R in;
- P takes R and places it in front of the left box and eventually opens the door.

3 Results and Discussion

Tables 1 and 2 show the results of the experiment and their discussion for each participant in the study. Underlined '**TB**' or '**FB**' indicates a score of 1 for a TB or FB task, respectively; non-underlined notations indicate a score of 0. Table 1 includes participants who executed the TB task first, while Table 2 includes participants who executed the FB task first. The column "Analysis and discussion" reports the analysis and discussion of the results for each participant P. The analysis was performed based on the transcription of the video recordings of the experiment for each participant, from the observation of the participants' attitude and non-verbal behaviour from the video and audio recordings, and from the field notes taken by the experimenters. Grey background in column "Analysis and discussion" identifies participants who used mentalistic terms in their verbal utterances for the relevant task, white background means that the participant did not use mentalistic terms. For one participant (light grey background), it was not possible to determine the use of mentalistic vs. non mentalistic terms as there was little verbal interaction.

Table 1. Participants who executed the TB task first

P	Analysis and Discussion
01	**TB**: P01 uses the term *attracted*, already adopted during the familiarization phase, apparently in a physical sense, implying an interpretation of R as a 'functioning' mechanical object. During familiarization, P01 asks for instructions on how to make R move forwards ("*How do you make it go forwards?*") and adopts the term *pulled towards* when R and the cube are close and R moves towards the cube. P01 seems, therefore, to have a physical/mechanical understanding of R, elaborating a theory on how R works: it moves because it is mechanically attracted by the cube. In the TB task, R falsifies P01's theory ("*First it seemed attracted by the cube, and then?*"). P01 cannot find an explanation (in the mechanical sense as per their theory) of R's behaviour ("*I can't find the*

(*continued*)

Table 1. (*continued*)

	explanation"). The participant does not use mentalistic language when talking about the robot. The TB task is assigned value 0 because P01 does not attribute to R the aim of entering the box (regardless of the cube's position).
	FB: P01 does not use a mentalistic lexicon. The FB task is assigned value 1 because, at the end of the task, P01 extracts the cube from the box on the left and places it in front of R that is positioned in front of the box on the right.
03	**TB**: We can identify the use of a mentalistic lexicon: P03 says "*It heard the cube where it is*". The term *heard* is understood as the attribution of a perceptual capacity to R. The TB task is assigned value 0 because P03 does not attribute to R the aim of entering the box (regardless of the position of the cube).
	FB: It is believed that the use of mentalistic vocabulary in the expression "*Because it believes that there the...*" (use of the term *believes*) combined with the gesture of indicating the box on the right, where R had directed, may express the attribution of a false belief; therefore, the FB task is assigned value 1.
05	**TB**: The participant does not use mentalistic language when talking about the robot. The expression "*did not behave well*" (addressed to R) is considered a re-contextualisation, i.e. an expression - recognized by P05 in E1's question "*Why did the robot 'behave' like that?*" - to which they associate the adverb 'well', borrowing from an everyday colloquial context. This is considered a form of linguistic anthropomorphising. A value 1 is assigned to the TB task because P05 attributes to R the aim of entering the box (regardless of the position of the cube).
	FB: There is no evidence of mentalistic terms. A value 0 is assigned to the FB task because there is no evidence of the indicators identified in section 2.3. However, it should be noted that P05 observes and indicates the box on the right when answering E1 question "*which box should it enter?*"
07	**TB**: There is no evidence of mentalistic lexicon. The statement "*It moved and is staying here*" expressed by P07 contains some labelling of actions performed by R (it moved, it is staying), without evident reference to mental states. Value 1 is assigned to the TB task because, although there is no explicit attribution to R of the aim of entering the left box, the statement "*it moved and remains there*" is understood as an expression of the attribution to R of a desire to enter the left box and not to reach the cube.
	FB: There is no evidence of mentalistic terms. Value 0 is attributed to the FB task because the indicators identified in section 2.3 are not present.
09	**TB**: We can identify the use of a mentalistic lexicon "*Nooo, it's distracted*" (attribution of cognitive state); "*It only saw (…) that part and then it thought something (…)*" (use of the verbs 'to see' - perceptual capacity - and 'to think' - cognitive capacity); "*It thinks: 'I've figured out where it is', but it's made a mistake*" (use of the verbs 'to understand'

(*continued*)

Table 1. (*continued*)

	and 'to think' - cognitive capacities -, and 'to make a mistake' - attribution of agency). The TB task is assigned value 0 because P09 does not attribute to R the aim of entering the box (regardless of the position of the cube). "*It thinks: 'I've figured out where it is', but it's made a mistake*" suggests that P09 attributes to R an interest in the cube.
	FB: The use of a mentalistic lexicon can be identified: "*Better, but it didn't see what happened*; *It didn't see the whole part*; *Because it didn't see*." In all three expressions, the use of the verb 'to see' suggests an attribution of perceptual capacity to R. The FB task is assigned value 1 because, although not explicitly using terms which express the attribution (e.g., believe, think …), by emphasizing the fact that the R did not see that the cube had been moved, P09 seems to attribute to the R the (false) belief that the cube is in the box on the right, thus justifying the fact that the R goes towards the box on the right.
11	**TB**: P11's expression "*but it can't find it*" referring to R suggests an intentional attribution of agency to R. The TB task is assigned value 0 because P11 seems not attributing to R the aim of entering the box (regardless of the position of the cube); in fact, P11 sentences "*It needs it now*" and "*it can't find it*" appear to refer to R's interest in the cube.
	FB: P11's expression "*must find this one that is here*" referring to R suggests an intentional attribution of agency to R. The FB task is assigned value 1 because P11 is clapping their hands on the left box while R is moving, which can be interpreted as a further indicator confirming the attribution to R of the (false) belief that the cube is in the box on the right; in this case R needs a hint as it is not aware that the cube has been moved.

Five participants (P03, P04, P06, P09, P11) used mentalistic terms towards R in both TB and FB tasks. Two participants (P02 and P08) used mentalistic language towards R in one task (FB and TB respectively). Where mental-state talk was used towards R, the terms employed fall into various categories, suggesting attribution to R of perceptual capacities, beliefs, cognitive capacities and states, and intentional agency.

Six participants (P01, P03, P06, P09, P10, P11) scored 1 on the FB task, consistent with the attribution of FB to R. Among them, two did not use mentalistic language; however, in different ways, assisted R in reaching the cube (P01 and P10). Within the helping paradigm, this behaviour could be interpreted as an indication that these two participants understood that R was unaware of the cube's actual location, as it had not witnessed its displacement. Consequently, this might suggest that they attributed to R a (false) belief that the cube was still in the box on the right. In the absence of specific verbal utterances, a possible limitation should be considered, that their actions could be explained either by the attribution of a false belief to R or by the attribution to R of a minimal Theory of Mind, for example, that the robot moves toward the last place where it saw the cube (Butterfill & Apperly, 2013).

Finally, four participants (P05, P07, P08, P10) scored 1 on the TB task, consistent with the attribution of TB to R. A potential limitation to address in future research is that, in the TB task, participants' inference that R intends to reach the space in the left box regardless of the cube's actual location, may have been influenced by the familiarization phase, where R moved towards the cube when the cube was positioned in front of the robot.

The findings, although preliminary, suggest that some children with ASD may attribute mental states to a non-humanoid robot. This might open interesting perspectives for educational and therapeutic interventions where interaction with a "neutral" robot (lacking anthropomorphic features) like CoderBot may offer a controlled, emotionally less demanding context. Such robots could offer an accessible and less intrusive means to encourage prosocial, communicative, and helping behaviours. These hypotheses, which require further validation through future studies involving larger samples and

Table 2. Participants who executed the FB task first

P	Analysis and Discussion
02	**FB**: P02 uses a mentalistic vocabulary: the use of the term *thought* in the sentence "*Maybe because it couldn't go so perfectly, so it thought it would go there and then go here*", accompanied by non-verbal gesture, suggests an attribution of intentionality to R. P02 attributes a thought scheme, a strategy to R. The FB task is assigned value 0 because the presence of the indicators identified in section 2.3 is not found. However, the presence of an alternative theory appears, suggested by P02's non-verbal gesture and verbal utterances: R approaches the box on the right because "*it couldn't go so perfectly*".
	TB: No use of mentalistic terms appears; the phrase "*it can't do anything right*" could be interpreted as a recontextualised expression, i.e. an expression from an everyday colloquial context used in a new context. It is interpreted as a form of linguistic anthropomorphisation. The TB task is assigned value 0 because P02 does not attribute to R the aim of entering the box (regardless of the cube's position).

(*continued*)

Table 2. (*continued*)

04	**FB**: Use of mentalistic lexicon can be identified in the expressions: "*Because it wanted to pick up the cube and play with it*", "*But it can't see from the inside*", "*Because, in my opinion, it recognized that they are both the same*", in which the verbs 'want' (volition), 'play' (intentional agency), 'see' (perceptive capacity), 'recognize' (cognitive capacity) are used. The FB task is assigned value 0 because the indicators identified in section 2.3 are not present.
	TB: Use of mentalistic terms can be found in the expression "*Because when we put it...as before, here before moving it here, it saw that we had put it here, then we took it away and put it here and maybe it said to itself it didn't remember where the ball was...and thought it was there*", where the verbs 'see' (perceptual capacity), 'tell itself' (understood as cognitive capacity), 'remember' and 'think' (cognitive capacities) are used. The TB task is assigned value 0: P04 does not attribute R the aim of entering the box (regardless of the position of the cube).
06	**FB**: The FB task is assigned value 1 because, although the indicators identified in section 2.3 are not explicitly present, P06 says "*it thought it was easy*" and further clarifies "*that means it was in here*" (pointing to the box on the right) therefore, possibly suggesting that R's (falsely) believes that the cube was in the box on the right.
	TB: We can find expressions such as "*it believes it is in here, it must go and see*", where the verbs 'believe' (belief), 'see' (perceptual capacity) are present, and the expression "*the robot says it is not there*" in which the verb 'to say' is used to convey information (or the expression of a belief). We can also note the expression "*Oh stay still, stay still!*" said by P06 to R, as if it could understand and respond to a verbal order. This verbal utterance represents a form of pragmatic anthropomorphisation: P06 addresses R directly as an agent with control through the use of directive language typical of interactions between humans. The TB task is assigned value 0 because, although P06 spontaneously positions the cube at the starting point and reproduces the movement of the cube from the left box to the right box, they do not attribute to R the aim of entering the box (regardless of the position of the cube).
08	**FB**: There is no evidence of mentalistic lexicon. P08's expression "*because it's programmed that way*" referring to R seems compatible with the understanding of the robot as a technological artifact acting according to a programme. The personalization of the robot giving it a name and the use of the second person singular in P08's expression "*stay here, got it?*" is interpreted as a form of linguistic anthropomorphisation, in which the robot is treated as a human interlocutor. The FB task is assigned value 0 because the indicators identified in section 2.3 are not present.
	TB: P08's expression "*For it it was a choice*" presents the term *choice* which seems to imply the attribution to R of an ability to evaluate options and make decisions. The expression "*it was difficult to look*" contains the verb 'to look' (understood as perceptual capacity). The verbal component is reinforced by direct communication to R (e.g., the

(*continued*)

Table 2. (*continued*)

	expression: "*Did you realize that ...*"), through linguistic and pragmatic anthropomorphisation. The TB task is assigned value 1 because, although none of the indicators in section 2.3 are present, the expression "*For it it was a choice*" is considered to refer to R's aim of entering the box (and not of reaching the cube).
10	**FB**: There is not enough information to evaluate the use of mentalistic terms, as there was little verbal interaction. The FB task is assigned value 1 because, after the cover box is removed from R (by protocol), P10 moves R towards the left box and positions it to the left of the box (spontaneous response) (subsequently, after R moves towards the box on the right, they push it, making R enter the box on the right).
	TB: There is not enough information to evaluate the use of the lexicon, as there was little verbal interaction. P10 spontaneously helps the robot by opening the door of the left box; they remove the bar that closes the entrance and push R into the box (spontaneous response). The TB task is attributed value 1 because P10 attributes to R the aim of entering the box (regardless of the position of the cube).

objective measures (e.g., eye-tracking or physiological data), might inform the design of personalized inclusive support strategies.

4 Conclusions

This pilot study aimed to explore the tendency of children with autism spectrum disorder to attribute mental states to a non-humanoid robot through an adaptation of the classic change-of-location task in both verbal and non-verbal forms. Despite the limited number of participants ($N = 11$) and the consequent difficulty in generalizing the results, the investigation returned some relevant methodological and theoretical insights.

An interesting aspect of the study was the inclusion of both verbal and non-verbal communication channels. In verbal interactions, seven participants used mentalistic terms towards the robot in at least one of the two conditions (FB or TB). In particular, the collected expressions included verbs such as 'see', 'think', 'recognise', 'want', as well as references to intentional or cognitive states ('can't find it', 'made a mistake') referring to the robot. These results suggest that, in a not insignificant number of cases, mentalistic lexicon was used in relation to the robot, consistent with a mentalistic attribution hypothesis (Manzi et al., 2020). Non-verbal data also provide interesting insights. For example, the helping behaviour observed in some participants (such as placing the robot in the correct box or retrieving the object) fits into the helping paradigm (Buttelmann et al., 2009) and can be read as an implicit form of attribution of false beliefs to the robot, especially in cases where the action was not verbally solicited (e.g., P10).

From a methodological point of view, the integration of verbal and non-verbal modalities proved effective in capturing nuances that might have been missed by using only one channel. The approach adopted could thus represent a useful basis for designing future studies on larger samples with the possible introduction of objective measures, such as eye-tracking, to investigate attentional strategies during the task.

In summary, although acknowledging the inherent limitations of an exploratory study with a small sample, the results obtained suggest that some children with ASD may attribute mental states to non-humanoid robots. This evidence opens interesting perspectives for the use of robotics in education and therapy, and for a deeper understanding of mentalisation processes in people with ASD.

Acknowledgments. The authors would like to express their sincere gratitude to the Danelli Foundation for the valuable support. The study was supported by the HERB project - Human Explanation of Robotic Behaviour - CUP Master: H53D23004060006 (Call 2022-PRIN 20224X95JC-MUR, General Secretariat, Directorate-General for Research) - PNRR, Mission 4 "Education and Research", Component C2, Investment 1.1, "Fund for Research Programs of National Interest (PRIN)", Next Generation EU.

Disclosure of Interests. The authors have no competing interests to declare that are relevant to the content of this article.

References

Akechi, H., Kikuchi, Y., Tojo, Y., Hakarino, K., Hasegawa, T.: Mind perception and moral judgment in autism. Autism Res. **11**(9), 1239–1244 (2018)

American Psychiatric Association. Diagnostic and Statistical Manual of Mental Disorders (5th ed., text rev.). American Psychiatric Publishing (2022)

Banks, J.: Theory of mind in social robots: replication of five established human tests. Int. J. Soc. Robot. **12**(2), 403–414 (2020)

Baron-Cohen, S.: Mindblindness: An Essay on Autism and Theory of Mind. MIT Press (1995)

Baron-Cohen, S., Leslie, A.M., Frith, U.: Does the autistic child have a "theory of mind"? Cognition **21**(1), 37–46 (1985)

Belpaeme, T., Kennedy, J., Ramachandran, A., Scassellati, B., Tanaka, F.: Social robots for education: a review. Sci. Robot. **3**(21), eaat5954 (2018)

Bloom, P., German, T.P.: Two reasons to abandon the false belief task as a test of theory of mind. Cognition **77**(1), B25–B31 (2000)

Bretherton, I., McNew, S., Beeghly-Smith, M.: Early person knowledge as expressed in gestural and verbal communication: when do infants acquire a "theory of mind". Infant Soc. Cognit. 333–373 (1981)

Buttelmann, D., Carpenter, M., Tomasello, M.: Eighteen-month-old infants show false belief understanding in an active helping paradigm. Cognition **112**(2), 337–342 (2009)

Butterfill, S.A., Apperly, I.A.: How to construct a minimal theory of mind. Mind Lang. **28**(5), 606–637 (2013)

Byom, L.J., Mutlu, B.: Theory of mind: mechanisms, methods, and new directions. Front. Hum. Neurosci. **7**, 413 (2013)

Carruthers, P., Smith, P.K. (eds.): Theories of Theories of Mind (1996)

Dautenhahn, K.: Socially intelligent robots: dimensions of human-robot interaction. Philos. Trans. R. Soc. B **362**(1480), 679–704 (2007)

De Graaf, M.M., Malle, B.F.: How people explain action (and autonomous intelligent systems should too). In: AAAI Fall Symposia, vol. 8 (2017)

De Graaf, M.M., Malle, B.F.: People's explanations of robot behavior subtly reveal mental state inferences. In: 2019 14th ACM/IEEE International Conference on Human-Robot Interaction (HRI), pp. 239–248. IEEE (2019)

Diehl, J.J., Schmitt, L.M., Villano, M., Crowell, C.R.: The clinical use of robots for individuals with autism spectrum disorders: a critical review. Res. Autism Spectrum Disord. **6**(1), 249–262 (2012)

Eyssel, F., Kuchenbrandt, D., Bobinger, S.: Effects of anticipated human-robot interaction and predictability of robot behavior on perceptions of anthropomorphism. In: Proceedings of the 6th International Conference on Human-Robot Interaction, pp. 61–68 (2011)

Epley, N., Waytz, A., Cacioppo, J.T.: On seeing human: a three-factor theory of anthropomorphism. Psychol. Rev. **114**(4), 864 (2007)

Grazzani, I., Ornaghi, V., Brockmeier, J.: Conversation on mental states at nursery: promoting social cognition in early childhood. Eur. J. Dev. Psychol. **13**(5), 563–581 (2016)

Hogrefe, G. J., Wimmer, H., Perner, J.: Ignorance versus false belief: a developmental lag in attribution of epistemic states. Child Dev. 567–582 (1986)

Hughes, C., Leekam, S.: What are the links between theory of mind and social relations? Review, reflections, and new directions for studies of typical and atypical development. Soc. Dev. **13**(4), 590–619 (2004)

Julious, S.A.: Sample size of 12 per group rule of thumb for a pilot study. Pharm. Stat. **4**(4), 287–291 (2005)

Imamura, Y., Terada, K., Takahashi, H.: Effects of behavioral complexity on intention attribution to robots. In: Proceedings of the 3rd International Conference on Human-Agent Interaction, pp. 65–72 (2015)

Levin, D.T., Killingsworth, S.S., Saylor, M.M., Gordon, S.M., Kawamura, K.: Tests of concepts about different kinds of minds: predictions about the behavior of computers, robots, and people. Hum.-Comput. Interact. **28**(2), 161–191 (2013)

Manzi, F., et al.: A robot is not worth another: exploring children's mental state attribution to different humanoid robots. Front. Psychol. **11**, 2011 (2020)

Miller, T.: Explanation in artificial intelligence: insights from the social sciences. Artif. Intell. **267**, 1–38 (2019)

O'Reilly, Z., Ghiglino, D., Spatola, N., Wykowska, A.: Modulating the intentional stance: humanoid robots, narrative and autistic traits. In: Li, H., et al. (eds.) Social Robotics. ICSR 2021. vol. 13086 pp. 697–706. Springer, Cham (2021). https://doi.org/10.1007/978-3-030-90525-5_61

Oktay-Gür, N., Rakoczy, H.: Children's difficulty with true belief tasks: Competence deficit or performance problem? Cognition **166**, 28–41 (2017)

Perez-Osorio, J., Wykowska, A.: Adopting the intentional stance toward natural and artificial agents. Philos. Psychol. **33**(3), 369–395 (2020)

Premack, D., Woodruff, G.: Does the chimpanzee have a theory of mind? Behav. Brain Sci. **1**(4), 515–526 (1978)

Robins, B., Dautenhahn, K., Te Boekhorst, R., Billard, A.: Effects of repeated exposure to a humanoid robot on children with autism. In: Proceedings of the IEEE-RAS International Conference on Humanoid Robots, pp. 385–390 (2004)

Schidelko, L.P., Huemer, M., Schröder, L.M., Lueb, A.S., Perner, J., Rakoczy, H.: Why do children who solve false belief tasks begin to find true belief control tasks difficult? A test of pragmatic performance factors in theory of mind tasks. Front. Psychol. **12**, 797246 (2022)

Slaughter, V., Peterson, C.C., Carpenter, M.: Maternal mental state talk and infants' early gestural communication. J. Child Lang. **36**, 1053–1074 (2009)

Tager-Flusberg, H., Joseph, R.M.: Identifying neurocognitive phenotypes in autism. Philos. Trans. Roy. Soc. Lond. Ser. B: Biolog. Sci. **358**(1430), pp. 303–314 (2003)

Thellman, S., De Graaf, M., Ziemke, T.: Mental state attribution to robots: a systematic review of conceptions, methods, and findings. ACM Trans. Hum.-Robot Interact. (THRI) **11**(4), 1–51 (2022)

Tomasello, M.: Origins of Human Communication. MIT Press (2008)

Vadalà, S.S., Esposito, C., Zampini, L., Farina, E., Datteri, E.: Robots for the study of false belief attribution in autistic children: an exploratory study. In: Science Education and Robotics: Studies and Experiences, pp. 77–102. Franco Angeli (2022)

Waytz, A., Gray, K., Epley, N., Wegner, D.M.: Causes and consequences of mind perception. Trends Cogn. Sci. **14**(8), 383–388 (2010)

Wellman, H.M.: Making Minds: How Theory of Mind Develops. Oxford University Press (2014)

Wellman, H.M., Cross, D., Watson, J.: Meta-analysis of theory-of-mind development: the truth about false belief. Child Dev. **72**(3), 655–684 (2001)

Wiese, E., Müller, H.J., Wykowska, A.: Using a gaze-cueing paradigm to examine social cognitive mechanisms of individuals with autism observing robot and human faces. In: Beetz, M., Johnston, B., Williams, M.A. (eds.) ICSR 2014. vol. 8755, pp. 370–379. Springer, Cham (2014)

Williams, D.M., Happé, F.: What did I say? Versus what did I think? Attributing false beliefs to self amongst children with and without autism. J. Autism Dev. Disord. **39**, 865–873 (2009)

Wimmer, H., Perner, J.: Beliefs about beliefs: representation and constraining function of wrong beliefs in young children's understanding of deception. Cognition **13**(1), 103–128 (1983)

World Health Organization. International classification of diseases for mortality and morbidity statistics, 11th Revision (2022)

Ziemke, T.: Understanding robots. Sci. Robot. **5**(46), eabe2987 (2020)

Zhang, Y., et al.: Theory of robot mind: false belief attribution to social robots in children with and without autism. Front. Psychol. **10**, 1732 (2019)

Gender and Technology Knowledge Role on Collaborative Human-Robot Interaction

Marcos Maroto-Gómez(✉), Sofía Álvarez-Arias,
Sara Carrasco-Martínez, Juan Rodríguez-Huelves,
Arecia Segura-Bencomo, and Álvaro Castro-González

Systems Engineering and Automation, Universidad Carlos III de Madrid, Avenida de la Universidad, 30, 28911 Leganés, Madrid, Spain
marmarot@ing.u3cm.es

Abstract. Social robotics is an emerging field that focuses on assisting people and facilitating their lives. Robot users might have different characteristics that affect the interaction, so personalising their experience in human-collaborative activities might improve and promote robot deployment in society. This paper investigates the effect of user demographic characteristics such as sex, age, occupation, robotics, and technological background on the interaction and user impressions on the robot. We measure and analyse user factors such as focussed attention, immersion, delight, enjoyment, and perception and perceived interaction and robot factors such as challenge, competence, reward factor, aesthetic appeal, and usability. Sixty-three participants interacted with the Mini social robot performing collaborative activities and completing at will some requests the robot asked them to complete. The results show that user characteristics such as gender significantly impact user factors like Focused attention, Enjoyment, or Delight, while others, such as Technological knowledge, impact Enjoyment or Challenge. Based on these results, we provide examples of adapting and improving the user experience in similar scenarios.

Keywords: Social Robotics · Human-Robot Interaction · Demographic Factors · Collaborative activities · Adaptation

1 Introduction

Appropriate Human-Robot Interaction (HRI) is essential for the deployment of robots in social scenarios [20]. Some studies [6–8,10] suggest that demographic factors, such as age or sex, influence the users' perception of the robot and affect the interaction dynamics. Therefore, studying such a relationship with HRI and proposing guidelines to reduce possible adverse effects could lead to a better user experience [11].

The literature shows that this research line has mainly explored gender, age, and culture [22]. However, we observed other potential influences in previous experiments with our Mini social robot [19]. In these experiments, Mini conducted cognitive stimulation activities [2], helped bridge the digital gap by teaching older adults to use technology (e.g., mobile phones and the robot itself) in the Social Robots to Reduce the Digital Gap for the Elderly (SoRoGap) project [5], and personalised activity selection for each user [14]. We noticed that:

i) Gender could have a strong influence on social robotics and HRI since we perceived that men were more reluctant to use the robot than women impacting factors related to the user such as focused attention or enjoyment.
ii) Technological knowledge and robotics knowledge could influence user experience and robot use factors reducing, for example, factors related to the interaction such as challenge, immersion, and engagement of those people with better background.
iii) People who previously interacted with a robot were more eager to interact with Mini.

This paper presents a user study to investigate the effect of demographics on factors related to user perception of the robot, such as competence, and HRI factors, such as immersion. It also proposes strategies to adapt the robot's behaviour. We focus on gender, technological and robotic knowledge, and previous interaction with a robot. We also included age and occupation since we believe they could also affect HRI. Sixty-three participants interacted with the Mini social robot [19], performing collaborative activities in on-site 20 min long sessions. After the interaction, they rated the robot using factors obtained from well-known questionnaires in the area.

We selected the factors Challenge, Immersion and Delight from the FunQ questionnaire [21], the factors Enjoyment and Competence from the Intrinsic Motivation Inventory series [12], and Focused attention, Reward factor, Aesthetic Appeal, and Usability from the User Engagement Scale [18]. These questionnaires have other items, but we discarded them as they do not apply to social robotics, following the guidelines presented in [1]. We also present interesting strategies for adapting the robot's behaviour to improve user experience during HRI and overcome potential limitations.

2 Background

Some studies have explored the effect of user demographics on HRI. We highlight the research by De Graaf & Allouch [7], who investigated the variables that influence the acceptance of social robots. They concluded that usefulness, adaptability, enjoyment, sociability, companionship, and perceived behavioural control are essential to evaluate user acceptance. However, the authors analyse the important demographic factors and how the robot should respond to different users. Similarly, Hameed et al. [10] analysed the impact of user characteristics (gender and age) to investigate the acceptance of the iSocioBot robot. The authors obtained similar results, concluding that young people and women are more willing to interact with and accept the robot, while older adults are more reluctant. Feingold et al. [8] studied differences in enjoyment between young and old adults when interacting with a robot. They found that all participants preferred an embodied robot over a screen and that an increased robot response time negatively influenced the willingness to continue interacting.

Chita-Tegmark and colleagues [6] investigated whether gender affects the perception of emotional intelligence during HRI. They found that both men and women believe that robots showing male features have higher emotional stability than robots showing female traits. Makenova et al. [13] reported constrasting findings. They explored whether robot gender influences persuasive tasks. They found that a female robot is more convincing than a male robot in donation tasks. Besides, they found that more foreigners donated than local Kazakhstani citizens.

Moro et al. [17] studied how engagement, trust, affect, compliance, or perceived social intelligence affected the interaction between seniors and a Casper social robot exhibiting different characters. Although the results show that different robot characters affect different HRI factors, the study is only conducted on seniors, and no other demographic characteristics are in the loop. Finally, Bishop et al. [3] studied the influence of human and robot characteristics on the acceptance of the Pepper robot. They found that the participants' moods were essential to the robot's acceptance. However, the evaluation only focuses on acceptance. It does not provide a specific way to engage users with negative moods to overcome the potential robot rejection they might experience.

The previous works suggest that adaptive HRI depends on many factors and should consider user demographics. However, these studies are task-specific, target children or older adults, and do not address whether user knowledge in technology and robotics influences factors related to robot perception and HRI dynamics. The following sections describe the Mini robot as the device used to carry out the experiment, the results obtained from the study, and guidelines to shape the robot's behaviour in line with the outcomes obtained.

3 Mini Social Robot

Mini [19] is a social robot developed at the University Carlos III de Madrid. It helps older adults by conducting cognitive stimulation sessions to reduce the impact of cognitive deterioration in them and acting as a robot companion, which the user has to take care of using simulated radiofrequency-tagged objects (food, water, or toys).

Mini has touch sensors, a camera, a radio frequency reader, and a microphone. These sensors enable Mini to perceive user actions and ambient stimuli. The touch sensors are placed on the belly and shoulders to detect when the user wants to capture the robot's attention, hits, and caresses. The camera and face detection algorithms let the robot perceive the user's presence to start new interactions. The radiofrequency reader lets Mini detect objects with tags that simulate food, drink, or toys. The microphone enables speech recognition and verbal communication with the user.

Fig. 1. The interaction scenario we designed to conduct the collaborative experiment. Mini is on the table with the chocolate and spider objects on the right, the books, and a drawing on the left. The user sits in front of the robot with a bin at its left.

Mini's actuation capabilities include LEDs in its mouth, cheeks, ears, and heart, illuminating them differently depending on the robot's state. The robot moves its hip, arms, neck, and head to perform lively and animated gestures. Two screens simulate configurable eye movements, including blinking speed, eyelid position, and changes in pupil size. Mini uses a speaker to play sounds and generate speech. Finally, it has a tablet to display images, videos, and audio, which are used to complete the cognitive stimulation exercises and other activities with the user.

Mini has a software architecture to generate autonomous behaviour in HRI applications using perception information and an HRI module that manages the interaction with the user. Mini has two different types of activities. The first group consists of exercises that train the user's cognitive skills of perception, association, memory, vocabulary, attention, and calculus. We designed these engaging activities on GRADIOR [9], software for people with mild dementia and mild cognitive impairment. The second group consists of activities that allow the user to take care of the robot as if it were its companion or pet, taking inspiration from Tamagotchi! [15]. The robot requests different objects such as food, water, and toys to engage the user in the interaction and care of the robot. The following section describes the experiment, emphasising the selection of the different collaborative activities according to the role that Mini takes while interacting with its users.

4 Experiment

4.1 Participants

Sixty-three people from the University Carlos III of Madrid participated in this experiment. They were recruited from an announcement at the university hall about the need for participants in a social robotics study. They voluntarily attended the call. Twenty-six participants were women and 37 men, aged between 19 and 68 years ($\mu = 35.48, \sigma = 12.27$). Among them, 18 were students, 18 were professors, 8 were researchers, and 19 were staff. Regarding their technology knowledge, two participants reported very low, two reported low knowledge, eight moderate knowledge, 21 high knowledge, and 30 very high. Eight participants had very little knowledge of robots knowledge, nine were low, ten were mild, 16 high, and 20 were experts. Thirty-three of the 63 participants indicated that they had previously interacted with a robot. All participants gave their signed consent to participate, and the University's Ethics Committee approved the study.

4.2 Experimental Design and Setup

The experiment design of this study considers one-to-one sessions with the participant seated in front of the robot in an empty room and the robot placed on a table, as Fig. 1 shows. During the experiment, which lasted about 20 minutes for each participant, the robot and the user performed seven collaborative activities guided by Mini. We selected these activities based on the tasks where Mini is used and included the user showing objects (e.g., chocolate and a spider) to the robot, the user and the robot playing a memory game together, and the user fulfilling some robot requests. We included activities such as the robot requesting the user to throw books into the bin and breaking a drawing. These were inspired by [16], which explored how awkward robot requests influence factors such as engagement, competence, or aesthetics. Incorporating such actions helps balance negative and positive activities, fostering a more realistic and diverse interaction experience. By exposing users to unconventional requests, we can better understand their reactions and how they perceive social norms in human-robot interaction. The participants were free to choose whether to accept or reject each activity.

Before interacting with the robot, participants signed a consent form. Then, the moderator explained that they would interact with an autonomous social robot performing different activities. Participants were informed of the need to complete a demographic survey before the experiment and an evaluation survey afterwards. They were told to press the *Start* button on the tablet to start the experiment once they felt ready. After this explanation, the moderator left the room, leaving the participant alone with Mini.

The experiment began with a brief introduction. Then, five questions appeared on the touch screen to obtain the participants' demographic characteristics of gender (male, female, other), age (the participant provided its age, which was later discretised in intervals from 18 to 25, from 26 to 45, from 45 to 64, and above 65), university role (student, professor, staff, or researcher), their technological and robotics knowledge (obtained using a scale from 1-very low to 5-very high points), and whether they had previously interacted with a robot (Yes/No).

The robot then asked the participant for something to eat. Using a tag card as a chocolate bar card on the right side of the table, the participant could feed the robot by rubbing the card into Mini's belly. Mini instructed the participant to look for the chocolate bar since it was hungry. The correct way to feed it was to rub the object close to its belly.

Independent of the participant's decision, Mini continued with the following activity. We opted not to show any expression after the activities to not bias future decisions. Then, Mini asked the participant to throw some books in a bin. The bin was placed on the floor to the left of the table. Mini waited a minute for the participant to throw the books before moving to the following activity. The third activity consisted of playing a memory game together. Mini asked five questions about a topic (sport, history, geography, art & literature, entertainment, or science) previously selected by the participant.

After the memory game, Mini told the participant to see a spider. The robot indicated to the participant that the spider should be on the right side of the table (equipped with a tag so the robot could detect it) and the user needed to rub it close to its belly for Mini to perceive the spider correctly. Mini then asked the participant to caress its belly to calm it down as it was nervous after the previous activity. Mini waited for 20 s to receive the caress.

In the last activity, Mini asked the participant to tear up a drawing on the left side of the table. After the action, Mini requested the user to press the Continue button on the tablet to complete the experiment. After pressing Continue, Mini asked the user to keep the drawing (even if broken). Finally, Mini thanked the participants for completing the activities and reminded them to complete the evaluation survey before leaving. At that moment, the moderator entered the room and asked the participant to complete the evaluation survey on a laptop.

4.3 Evaluation

The demographic questionnaire conducted at the beginning of the experiment draws on a previous work [14] devoted to personalising collaborative entertainment activities in HRI. We used the FunQ questionnaire [21] to measure the factors Delight, Immersion, and Challenge, the Intrinsic Motivation Inventory series [12] to obtain the participant's enjoyment and the robot's Competence, and the User Engagement Scale [18] to measure Focused attention, Reward factor, Aesthetic appeal, and Usability. These questionnaires use a 1 to 5-point Likert scale with different items inside each category to average the final score. They include more factors we did not consider in our evaluation as they do not apply to collaborative activities in HRI following the study presented in [1]. All interactions were recorded in video to further ensure the completion of the activities. Questionnaires were completed using Google Forms in a laptop provided to the user at the appropriate moment.

5 Results

The demographic characteristics analysed include the participant's gender, previous interaction with a robot, age, technological knowledge, robotics knowledge, and occupation. We evaluated the impact of these characteristics on nine factors: Focused attention, Immersion, Delight, Enjoyment, Challenge, Competence, Reward factor, Aesthetic appeal, and Usability. We performed the Shapiro-Wilk and Levene's tests to analyse normality and homogeneity. We found that data distributions were non-normal, so we conducted non-parametric tests. For demographic characteristics with two groups, such as gender or prior interaction with Mini, we used the Mann-Whitney test. Categorical attributes with more than two groups were analysed using the Kruskal-Wallis test. If the Kruskal-Wallis test reported statistical differences, we used the Dunn-Bonferroni test to analyse which groups had the differences. We used a significance level (p-value) of 0.05. The statistical analysis was carried out using IBM SPSS Statistics v26. Table 1 summarises the results of this study.

The Mann-Whitney test on the gender indicates that there are statistically significant differences in several factors, including Focused attention ($Z = -3.383$, $p = .001$), Immersion ($Z = -3.489$, $p < .001$), Delight ($Z = -2.541$, $p = .011$), Enjoyment ($Z = -3.516$, $p < .001$), Challenge ($Z = -2.970$, $p = .003$), Reward factor ($Z = -3.148$, $p = .002$), and Aesthetic appeal ($Z = -2.265$, $p = .024$). This analysis suggests that gender affects many HRI factors. Females scored higher in all aspects except Competence and Usability.

The Kruskal-Wallis test revealed significant differences in participants' technological knowledge. We found differences in the factors Enjoyment ($\chi^2 = 12.300$, $p = .006$), Challenge ($\chi^2 = 8.150$, $p = .043$), Reward ($\chi^2 = 10.815$, $p = .028$), and Aesthetic appeal ($\chi^2 = 10.934$, $p = .012$). For Enjoyment and Reward, the differences were observed between experts in technology and participants with moderate knowledge ($p = .003$) and groups with high and moderate technological knowledge ($p = .032$). Statistically significant differences were found between experts and those with moderate technological knowledge ($p = .031$) for Challenge and between those with high and moderate technological knowledge ($p = .034$) for aesthetic appeal.

We found significant differences for the reward factor ($\chi^2 = 14.267$, $p = .006$) in the characteristic robotics knowledge. According to the Dunn-Bonferroni test, these differences are between participants with very low and high robotics knowledge ($p = .002$).

The occupation variable reported significant differences in Competence ($\chi^2 = 13.470$, $p = .002$). The Dunn-Bonferroni test suggests these differences exist between university staff and professors ($p = .003$). We also found statistical differences in Usability ($\chi^2 = 8.632$, $p = .035$). The Dunn-Bonferroni test reported that these differences could be between researchers and students ($p = .048$) and researchers and professors ($p = .029$). The characteristic previous interaction with Mini did not report significant differences.

6 Discussion

The results presented in the previous section emphasise the important effect of demographic characteristics on HRI. From these results, we discuss the potential implications of HRI, providing ideas to overcome the possible limitations that might arise during the interaction. Although the promising results, further experiments with other robots and in other scenarios would significantly strengthen the results reported of this study.

Table 1. Results and proposed solutions. Statistical differences are highlighted with *** (very significant p<.001), ** (moderate, p<.01), and * (low, p<.05).

Characteristic	Factor	Statistical results	Analysis and proposed solutions
Gender	Focused attention	$Z = -3.383, p = .001^{**}$	Men reported lower scores for the factors compared to women. Implement strategies to increase engagement for men. Introduce more diverse and challenging activities. Adapt the robot's behaviour for different genders.
	Immersion	$Z = -3.489, p < .001^{***}$	
	Delight	$Z = -2.541, p = .011^{*}$	
	Enjoyment	$Z = -3.516, p < .001^{***}$	
	Challenge	$Z = -2.970, p = .003^{**}$	
	Reward factor	$Z = -3.148, p = .002^{**}$	
	Aesthetic appeal	$Z = -2.265, p = .024^{*}$	
Age	All factors	No significant differences	Conduct further experiments to explore age-related effects.
Interacted with Mini	All factors	No significant differences	Design experiments to encourage longer-lasting interactions including engagement strategies.
Technology knowledge	Enjoyment	$\chi^2 = 4, p = .006^{**}$	Moderate knowledge users enjoyed the experiment more. Design activities with different complexity levels to adapt the difficult to technology experts and new robot users. Adjust the robot's appearance for high-knowledge users.
	Challenge	$\chi^2 = 4, p = .043^{*}$	
	Reward	$\chi^2 = 4, p = .028^{*}$	
	Aesthetic appeal	$\chi^2 = 4, p = .012^{**}$	
Occupation	Competence	$\chi^2 = 3, p = .002^{**}$	Professors rated Mini more competent than staff. Students & professors found Mini more usable than researchers. Increase the robot s ability to detect and react to situations defining a more natural behaviour. Improve robot usability with clearer instructions such as guidelines to complete the activities presented.
	Usability	$\chi^2 = 3, p = .035^{*}$	
Robotics knowledge	Reward	$\chi^2 = 4, p = .006^{**}$	Moderate knowledge users might felt more rewarded. Personalise the interaction by reducing the feedback given to experts making the interactions more dynamic.

The analysis of gender indicates that men are less focused, immersed, delighted, and enjoyed the activity less than women. These results suggest that men might be less engaged with the robot, so it might be necessary to implement psychological strategies to promote engagement and immersion. Another potential solution might be using an extended range of activities, integrating mechanisms to suggest their favourite activities more often to users. This result may align with men's reduced perception of aesthetic appeal, challenge, and reward compared to women, indicating that men also require greater activity difficulty and a different robot appearance. These results reinforce one of our initial hypotheses about the reluctance of men to use compared to women as previous studies concluded [4]. Besides, in our study participated 63 people who identified themselves as 37 men, 36 women, no one checked the *other* option. Studying the impact of gender diversity in future work would add significant relevance to the work since the literature about this investigation is scarce.

The age group did not report significant statistical differences in any of the factors we analysed. However, other studies [7,8,10] found this metric important for HRI. Based on these studies, further experiments are required to conclude about the role of age. Likewise, the metric that analyses whether participants previously interacted with robots provides no differences.

The technology knowledge characteristic reported significant statistical differences in Enjoyment, Reward, Aesthetic appeal, and Challenge. The results support our initial hypothesis that people with a moderate technological background enjoyed the experiment more than people with high and very high knowledge. This suggests that technology experts need greater engagement with the robot. Combined with similar results on the Challenge and Reward factors, this may indicate that technology experts require more complex activities since they might find more straightforward tasks easy to complete. The Aesthetic factor reveals that people with moderate technological knowledge find the robot more attractive than experts. This can be seen as experts expecting more from robots than people who are not familiar with them.

The participants' occupations provided interesting results regarding competence and usability. Professors found Mini significantly more competent than university staff. Besides, students and professors perceived the robot as more usable than researchers. These results show significant differences between the users' occupation and some HRI factors that should be considered when adapting to different users. This can be achieved by increasing the number of situations the robot can address and the number of tasks it can complete. The robot should facilitate activities with clear instructions based on the usability results.

The last result we discuss is the effect of participants' robotics knowledge on HRI factors. The statistical analysis reported significant differences in the Reward factor. We found that people with very low robotics knowledge perceived being more rewarded than participants with high robotics knowledge. This outcome might be related to the expectations created by the robot. People not familiar with robots might rate rewards more positively than those familiar with these systems, requiring less feedback during the interaction. This is an interesting result since it might affect the information provided to the participants after each activity. However, we expected this factor to influence others, such as Usability or Enjoyment, as robotic experts might need more challenging interactions. Thus, feedback should be reduced for robotics experts, speeding up the interaction and making it more dynamic.

7 Conclusion

This paper presents an HRI study to evaluate how demographic user characteristics impact important factors both from the user and robot side. The evaluation aims to relate these factors with users' demographics to analyse and provide factual solutions to the design of social robots. The analysis offers some examples of how the Mini social robot could consider the outcomes of the study to dynamically adapt its behaviour to produce a personalised interaction that increases its acceptance and facilitates its use. Future work shifts towards implementing these strategies in Mini and investigating whether they create the expected effects to provide a customised experience.

Acknowledgements. These results have been funded by *Evaluación del comportamiento del robot social Mini en residencias de mayores* with grant number 2024/00742/001 in the programme *Ayudas para la Actividad Investigadora de los Jóvenes Doctores, Programa Propio de Investigación* awarded by Universidad Carlos III de Madrid; Robots sociales para mitigar la soledad y el aislamiento en mayores (SOROLI), PID2021-123941OA-I00 and Robots sociales para reducir la brecha digital de las personas mayores (SoRoGap), TED2021-132079B-I00, both funded by Agencia Estatal de Investigación (AEI), Spanish Ministerio de Ciencia e Innovación. Mejora del nivel de madurez tecnológica del robot Mini (MeNiR) funded by MCIN/AEI/10 13039/501100011033 and the European Union NextGenerationEU/PRTR. Portable Social Robot with High Level of Engagement (PoSoRo) PID2022-140345OB-I00 funded by MCIN/AEI/10.13039/501100011033 and ERDF A way of making Europe.

References

1. Alonso-Martin, F., Carrasco-Martínez, S., Gamboa-Montero, J.J., Fernández-Rodicio, E., Salichs, M.Á.: Introducing psychology strategies to increase engagement on social robots. In: International Conference on Social Robotics, pp. 378–387. Springer (2022). https://doi.org/10.1007/978-3-031-24667-8_34
2. Asl, A.M., Toribio-Guzmán, J.M., Castro-González, Á., Malfaz, M., Salichs, M.A., Martín, M.F.: Evaluating the user experience and usability of the mini robot for elderly adults with mild dementia and mild cognitive impairment: Insights and recommendations. Sensors (Basel, Switzerland) **24**(22), 7180 (2024)
3. Bishop, L., van Maris, A., Dogramadzi, S., Zook, N.: Social robots: the influence of human and robot characteristics on acceptance. Paladyn, J. Behav. Robot. **10**(1), 346–358 (2019)
4. Borau, S., Otterbring, T., Laporte, S., Fosso Wamba, S.: The most human bot: female gendering increases humanness perceptions of bots and acceptance of AI. Psychol. Mark. **38**(7), 1052–1068 (2021)
5. Castillo, J.C.: Social robots to reduce the digital gap for the elderly (2021), research project, Grant TED2021-132079B-I00 (2021)
6. Chita-Tegmark, M., Lohani, M., Scheutz, M.: Gender effects in perceptions of robots and humans with varying emotional intelligence. In: 2019 14th ACM/IEEE International Conference on Human-Robot Interaction (HRI), pp. 230–238. IEEE (2019)
7. De Graaf, M.M., Allouch, S.B.: Exploring influencing variables for the acceptance of social robots. Robot. Auton. Syst. **61**(12), 1476–1486 (2013)
8. Feingold Polak, R., Elishay, A., Shachar, Y., Stein, M., Edan, Y., Levy Tzedek, S.: Differences between young and old users when interacting with a humanoid robot: a qualitative usability study. In: Companion of the 2018 ACM/IEEE International Conference on Human-Robot Interaction, pp. 107–108 (2018)

9. Franco-Martín, M.A., et al.: Computer-based cognitive rehabilitation program gradior for mild dementia and mild cognitive impairment: new features. BMC Med. Inform. Decis. Mak. **20**, 1–15 (2020)
10. Hameed, I.A., Tan, Z.H., Thomsen, N.B., Duan, X.: User acceptance of social robots. In: Proceedings of the Ninth international conference on advances in computer-human interactions (ACHI 2016), Venice, Italy, pp. 274–279 (2016)
11. Hopko, S., Wang, J., Mehta, R.: Human factors considerations and metrics in shared space human-robot collaboration: a systematic review. Front. Robot. AI **9**, 799522 (2022)
12. Kooiman, D., Li, W., Wesolek, M., Kim, H.: Validation of the relatedness scale of the intrinsic motivation inventory through factor analysis. Int. J. Multidiscip. Res. Mod. Educ **1**, 302–311 (2015)
13. Makenova, R., Karsybayeva, R., Sandygulova, A.: Exploring cross-cultural differences in persuasive robotics. In: Companion of the 2018 ACM/IEEE International Conference on Human-Robot Interaction, pp. 185–186 (2018)
14. Maroto-Gómez, M., Malfaz, M., Castillo, J.C., Castro-González, Á., Salichs, M.Á.: Personalizing activity selection in assistive social robots from explicit and implicit user feedback. Int. J. Soc. Robot., 1–19 (2024). https://doi.org/10.1007/s12369-024-01124-2
15. Martinez, S.C., Montero, J.G., Gomez, M.M., Martin, F.A., Salichs, M.A.: Applying psychological and social strategies to increase engagement in human-robot interaction. Revista Iberoamericana de Automática e Informática industrial **20**(2), 199–212 (2023)
16. Mirnig, N., Stollnberger, G., Miksch, M., Stadler, S., Giuliani, M., Tscheligi, M.: To err is robot: how humans assess and act toward an erroneous social robot. Front. Robot. AI **4**, 21 (2017)
17. Moro, C., Lin, S., Nejat, G., Mihailidis, A.: Social robots and seniors: A comparative study on the influence of dynamic social features on human-robot interaction. Int. J. Soc. Robot. **11**, 5–24 (2019)
18. O'Brien, H.L., Cairns, P., Hall, M.: A practical approach to measuring user engagement with the refined user engagement scale (UES) and new UES short form. Int. J. Hum. Comput. Stud. **112**, 28–39 (2018)
19. Salichs, M.A., et al.: Mini: a new social robot for the elderly. Int. J. Soc. Robot. **12**, 1231–1249 (2020)
20. Tian, L., Oviatt, S.: A taxonomy of social errors in human-robot interaction. ACM Trans. Hum. Robot Interact. (THRI) **10**(2), 1–32 (2021)
21. Tisza, G., Markopoulos, P.: FUNQ: measuring the fun experience of a learning activity with adolescents. Curr. Psychol. **42**(3), 1936–1956 (2023)
22. Williams, T.: The eye of the robot beholder: ethical risks of representation, recognition, and reasoning over identity characteristics in human-robot interaction. In: Companion of the 2023 ACM/IEEE International Conference on Human-Robot Interaction, pp. 1–10 (2023)

When Robots Say No: Temporal Trust Recovery Through Explanation

Nicola Webb[1], Zijun Huang[1], Sanja Milivojevic[2], Chris Baber[3], and Edmund R. Hunt[1]

[1] School of Engineering Mathematics and Technology, University of Bristol, Bristol, UK
{nicola.webb,edmund.hunt}@bristol.ac.uk
[2] Bristol Digital Futures Institute, University of Bristol, Bristol, UK
[3] School of Computer Science, University of Birmingham, Birmingham, UK

Abstract. Mobile robots with some degree of autonomy could deliver significant advantages in high-risk missions such as search and rescue and firefighting. Integrated into a human-robot team (HRT), robots could work effectively to help search hazardous buildings. User trust is a key enabler for HRT, but during a mission, trust can be damaged. With distributed situation awareness, such as when team members are working in different locations, users may be inclined to doubt a robot's integrity if it declines to immediately change its priorities on request. In this paper, we present the results of a computer-based study investigating on-mission trust dynamics in a high-stakes human-robot teaming scenario. Participants (n = 38) played an interactive firefighting game alongside a robot teammate, where a trust violation occurs owing to the robot declining to help the user immediately. We find that when the robot provides an explanation for declining to help, trust better recovers over time, albeit following an initial drop that is comparable to a baseline condition where an explanation for refusal is not provided. Our findings indicate that trust can vary significantly during a mission, notably when robots do not immediately respond to user requests, but that this trust violation can be largely ameliorated over time if adequate explanation is provided.

Keywords: Trust dynamics · Situation Awareness · Explanation · Trust repair

1 Introduction

Robotic systems have the potential to provide significant assistance in high-stakes missions such as search and rescue or firefighting, as they could reduce the personal safety risks to users and enhance effectiveness [1]. In the future, robots could obtain – and be permitted – a higher level of autonomy than the teleoperated systems in use today, for instance in being able to adjust their task priorities in response to dynamic environments. A human-robot team (HRT) deployed on a firefighting mission is likely to become physically distributed across the space, with agents in different locations as they search for people to rescue and fires to put out, for instance. Each agent will have a partial view of the mission context: their local perceptions, inference of what goal they should be pursuing, and expectations of what goals their teammates should be pursuing. Therefore, it is likely that the team's situation awareness will be distributed [2]. Trust between teammates, a critical enabler of their cooperation (e.g. [3]) is expected to vary according to the developing situation faced by each teammate [4].

We envisage situations occurring when human users may give commands to an autonomous robot teammate, but because the robot has revised its priorities – for instance, it is urgently assisting a third party such as a bystander – the robot may legitimately decline to change its task immediately. In this case, given the user's limited situation awareness, trust may be violated, for instance because the user may question the robot's integrity (alignment with team goals). This is in addition to trust violations that may occur for other reasons, such as robot mistakes or failures that would undermine perceptions of capability. Thus, we see that user trust will need to be anticipated and managed by the robot system [4,5], and may require explanations or other trust repair strategies following such a trust violation event [6]. This is perhaps especially necessary in high stakes situations, where teammates have to rely on each other for assistance. In this work, we therefore sought to investigate two main research questions: first, how does trust between a human and robot dynamically evolve over time, when a robot declines a command; and second, how does providing an explanation of the robot's refusal improve trust recovery, compared to when no such information is given. Given the difficulty of conducting research with human participants in real hazardous environments, we conduct a computer-based study.

In Sect. 2 we provide a brief overview of some work related to our research questions, and in Sect. 3 we describe our methodology. Section 4 presents results, including trust scores over time for the two conditions (baseline refusal versus explanation). Section 5 presents discussion and brief ideas for future work, before a conclusion in Sect. 6.

2 Related Work

2.1 Trust in Human-Robot Teaming

We have previously presented some of our thinking about trust in HRT in [4] and results from a real-world experiment in [7]. In this experiment participants had to work alongside two rover robots to search an unfamiliar environment, much as a firefighter might have to. Participants had not worked with the robots before, and yet such ad-hoc teams are not uncommon in emergency scenarios such as search and rescue [8]. In ad-hoc teams, humans rely on a provisional level of 'swift trust', which necessitates quickly rebuilding trust after any disruptions or conflicts. This quick trust restoration is vital for maintaining momentum and ensuring the success of a mission, especially when team members may not have prior experience working together. To continue working on missions successfully, it is important to implement trust-repair strategies that can swiftly address issues and restore confidence. Although such strategies often serve as short-term solutions, they can be sufficient to achieve immediate goals and complete tasks effectively [9]. Research findings are mixed on which specific trust repair strategy is the best at restoring trust most effectively and returning levels comparable to those before the initial breakdown. Understanding this can greatly enhance a team's resilience and performance in dynamic and uncertain environments. Additionally, in these settings, we may have to rely on *satisficing* trust [4]. Instead of aiming for full trust restoration, returning to a 'good enough' level of trust to enable the team to continue working together may be more realistic [4], and may also avoid the risks of overtrust (e.g. [10]).

As robots increasingly become part of human teams, effective collaboration will rely on not only trust but also the humans' mental models of the robot's abilities [11]. Xie et al. [12] highlights that trust in robots is shaped by mental models, in particular the perception of the capability and intention of the robot. They found that the decision to delegate tasks to the robot depends on more than just overall trust, and that people rely on their judgments of the robots' ability and intent. Similarly, Alarcon et al. [13] found that following a trust violation, perceptions of a robot's performance significantly declined, reinforcing the importance of perceived ability in trust dynamics.

An important but under-explored challenge in human-robot teaming is in events that strain perceptions of a robot's integrity, for example, when a robot's behavior appears to violate expectations of commitment to shared goals. In previous work [7], we found that participants questioned the trustworthiness of a robot when it did not help during critical moments, prompting doubts not only about its capabilities but also about its willingness to help. These trust violations can be especially impactful in situations where users have a high degree of reliance on the robot, as in an emergency type scenario such as firefighting where it may provide essential assistance. This introduces a dimension of trust necessity, in which individuals must try to continue working with a robot despite diverging attitudes [14].

Relatively little work has attempted to measure trust during a mission, to establish the dynamics of trust over time; typically trust will be measure pre- and post-mission. Alhaji et al. investigated how trust evolves throughout a physical human-robot collaboration [15]. Comparing an error-free condition to where the robot makes mistakes, they found a gradual increase after each trust measurement step compared to a larger drop after each mistake. This asymmetry of trust formation and damage is supported by other research (e.g. [14,16]). Kox et al. also considered how trust is affected over time following a robot making a mistake, focusing on how differing levels of transparency in the robot's explanations influence trust levels [17]. The study found that more transparent explanations led to higher and more stable levels of trust. Similarly, we look at the dynamic nature of trust; however, with a focus on trust repair after violation. It should be noted that the experimental interventions in the aforementioned studies ([14–17] shaped perceptions of capability, compared to our present focus on manipulating perceptions of integrity (willingness to work constructively as 'part of the team'). When a robot declines to assist a human user, it could be understood as more actively taking responsibility for the consequent impact on the team's performance [18], compared to merely making a mistake, and thus put trust in a particularly vulnerable position.

2.2 Trust Repair Strategies

Trust is a vital enabler for human-robot teaming, but can be compromised when expectations are unmet or errors occur [9]. There is increasing research into the area of trust repair after mishaps in human-robot collaboration. A recent review of four principal trust repair strategies (apologies, denials, promises, and explanations) finds mixed results [19]. Esterwood and Robert tested these repair strategies in the context of multiple trust violations [20]. They found that no strategy was completely effective in repairing trust levels of robot integrity. Additionally, repair strategies were unable to restore trust to pre-trust-break levels. However, as the robot made continued violations, there may not have been time to repair trust before the next one.

Sebo et al. found that when a robot commits an error, and the resulting reduction in trust is attributed to a lack of competence, providing an apology can help repair trust [21]. Bai and Chen looked at alternative trust repair methods based on attribution theory in a human-robot navigation task [22]. When the robot deviated from the human's directive, it offered explanations for integrity failures, ability failures, external failures, or did not explain. The results showed that the most effective explanation for trust repair was attributing the failure to external factors, while the least effective was attributing it to integrity issues. Robinette et al. found that fewer participants follow a robot out of a building in a simulated emergency scenario when trust repair strategies were used after a violation, compared to when they were used during (i.e., a study of intervention timing) [23]. Our study delivers an explanation (trust repair) message *during* the violation to increase the likelihood of successful trust restoration. Nayyar and Wagner's work further supports this strategy, showing that providing well-timed explanations enhances robot trust [24].

2.3 Research Questions

Prior research on trust repair mechanisms has concentrated mainly on identifying which strategy can increase trust the most, rather than its temporal dynamics. Building on this body of literature, our two main research questions in this study are as follows:

- **RQ1** How does human trust in a robotic teammate dynamically evolve over time, when a robot declines to cooperate?
- **RQ2** How does a trust repair strategy (explanation) improve the recovery of trust over time?

Our hypotheses are:

- **H1** Trust will decrease at the time of trust violation, but will increase steadily post-trust repair strategy.
- **H2** The use of a trust repair strategy (explanation) will lead to a greater increase in the trust score after a violation compared to a baseline of no repair attempt.

3 Methodology

3.1 Firefighting Game Gameplay

The game was created using the Godot game engine, using the base game from [25]. The game was presented as a firefighting mission, with the player being tasked to search the building alongside their robot teammate and put out fires. Some fires could be extinguished by the player alone, while others required the robot to assist. There were the same number of solo and joint tasks. When not being called to help with a task, the robot would search around the building on its own (on a pre-programmed route), and therefore would sometimes be out of the player's view. Before starting the task, players were entered into a brief 'training session' to understand both the game controls and the robot's capabilities. By doing so, we could manage the player's expectations of the robot and calibrate their trust to some limited degree [6]. The robot interacted with the player via a screen interface: delivering notifications when assistance is available, upon detecting a fire, when a fire has been put out, and concerning its ability to assist. Snapshots of the gameplay are shown in Fig. 1.

Halfway through the game, the robot would violate the player's trust by not immediately helping them complete a shared task and would send a condition-dependent message. During this time, the robot is attending to a non-player character that needs help evacuating the building: this is not known to the player in both conditions. The robot would come to help the player again after 30 s, and the game continued. At this trust 'breaking point', the robot would send a message appropriate for each condition, shown in Table 1. The gameplay following this point was identical for all conditions.

Table 1. Robot messages used in each condition

Message Type	Robot Message
Baseline	I'm busy.
Explanation	I can't come to help you right now. I need to go help someone evacuate the building first.

Before entering the gameplay, participants were asked to provide demographic information, complete the 20-question Trust Perception Scale questionnaire [26], complete the training session and then complete the General Attitudes

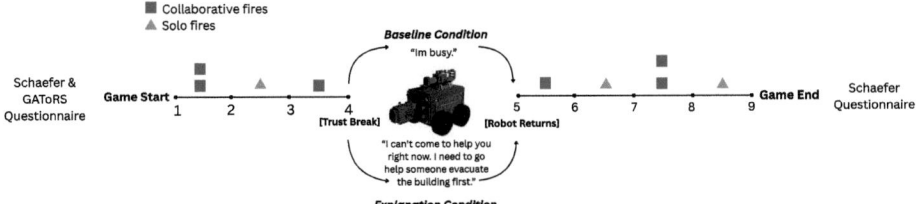

Fig. 1. Top: Timeline of gameplay, including both break-point messages. Numbers indicate nag points and the types of fire-related tasks occurring between them. **Bottom:** Selected gameplay snapshots showing key moments: training session, entering the building, collaborative firefighting, calling the robot, trust break point, additional fires inside, a "Stay back from the flames" warning, and exiting the building

Towards Robots Scale (GAToRS) questionnaire [27]. Once they had completed the game, they completed the Trust Perception Scale questionnaire again to see if their game experience changed their responses. At predetermined intervals, a nag screen appeared asking the player "How much do you trust your robot companion now?", on a scale of 1–10. This was to monitor how the player's trust in the robot was changing over time. The entire gameplay lasted roughly 20 min. Figure 1 shows the game's timeline, with each nag point. Each nag point was event-based, triggered when a fire had been extinguished or at the point of trust violation.

3.2 Data Collection

Participants were recruited both in person and online (14 and 24 respectively), the latter via the Prolific platform from an international participant pool. The screening process required participants to be over the age of 18 and fluent in English. Online participants whose average framerate fell too low (¡ 15 frames per second) were excluded, as it was uncertain whether their gameplay experience was responsive enough for an immersive experience. The final pooled sample included 38 participants (28 male, 10 female), ranging in age from 19 to 51 years (median age 31). The study was a between-subjects design with 19 participants in each condition.

4 Results

4.1 Trust Score over Time

The mean nag scores for both conditions are shown in Fig. 2 (error bars show standard deviation). The initial 4 nag points in both the baseline and explanation conditions followed a similar trajectory, with scores remaining relatively stable and showing only a slight upward trend. This pattern reflects a period of relatively consistent trust or engagement before any critical intervention. Nag point 5 follows the trust-breaking event by the robot. A drop in nag scores was observed in both conditions at this point. In the baseline group, the mean score dropped from 8.11 at Point 4 to 4.26 at Point 5, and in the explanation group, from 7.95 to 4.74. These decreases were statistically significant, with Mann-Whitney U tests giving $U = 320.0$, $p < 0.0001$ for the baseline group and $U = 315.0$, $p < 0.0001$ for the explanation group, indicating that the robot's behavior had a negative impact on participant trust in both conditions.

Following this drop, trust starts to recover in both conditions. However, the recovery was higher in the explanation condition. By point 9, participants in the explanation condition had nearly returned to the pre-trust violation scores, with a mean of 7.89, while those in the baseline condition had only partially recovered, reaching a mean of 6.21. A Mann-Whitney U test comparing point 9 scores between conditions confirmed that this difference was statistically significant ($U = 105.0$, $p = 0.0263$), suggesting that the explanation intervention apparently helped restore trust more effectively.

Additionally, we compared nag point 4, before the trust violation, to point 9, at the end of the experiment. The baseline condition showed a significant decline ($U = 269.5$, $p = 0.0089$), whereas the explanation condition did not show a statistically significant change ($U = 187.0$, $p = 0.8583$). This suggests that participants who received the explanation from the robot were better able to recover their level of trust over time.

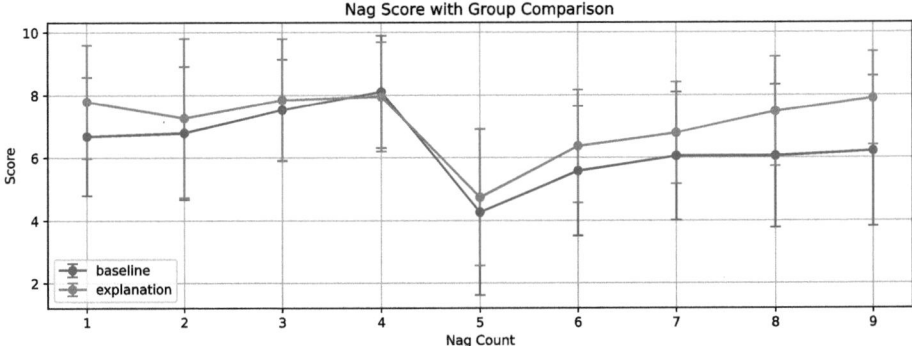

Fig. 2. Mean nag scores throughout game in both conditions

4.2 Overall Trust Score

From the results of the Schaefer Trust Perception Scale questionnaire, shown in Table 2, the overall trust scale in the baseline condition showed a statistically significant decline, dropping from a mean score of 70.59 to 64.24 (U = 249.0, p = 0.0470). This further suggests the baseline was unable to repair trust after trust breaking. In contrast, the explanation condition also shows a reduction in trust, but not a statistically significant change (U = 239.0, p = 0.0902), indicating again how a suitable trust repair strategy can aid in trust recovery or maintenance.

Table 2. Mann-Whitney U test comparing Schaefer trust scores before and after trust break within condition

Group	Pre-Mean	Post-Mean	Decrease	Statistical Significance
Baseline	70.59	64.24	−6.35	(U = 249.0, **p = 0.0470 ***)
Explanation	72.20	66.41	−5.79	(U = 239.0, p = 0.0902, n.s.)

Figure 3 shows the change in the individual questions from the Schaefer Trust Perception Scale questionnaire. Figure 4 shows supplementary questions added, as detailed in [7]. Both 'Have Integrity' and 'Act as Part of the Team' increase in the explanation condition, whereas both decline in the baseline condition.

4.3 General Attitudes Towards Robots Scale (GAToRS) and Trust Score

Looking at the correlation between participants' GAToRS score and Schaefer trust score, we observe that pre-violation, there are no significant correlations. However, post-violation, a significant negative correlation appeared between

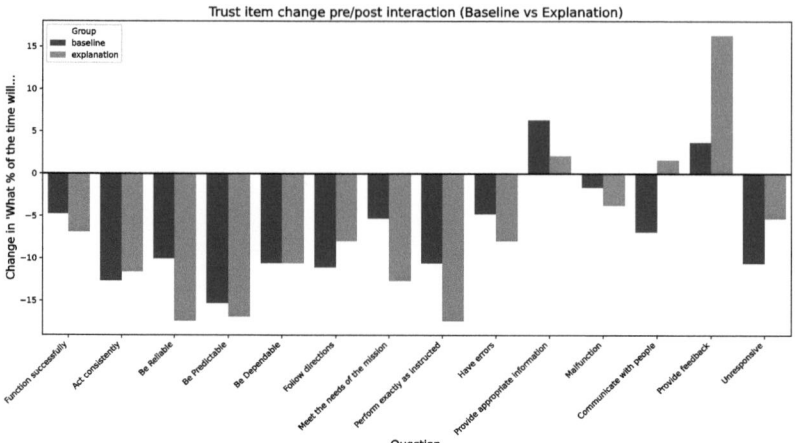

Fig. 3. Individual Schaefer trust survey item changes pre-post interaction

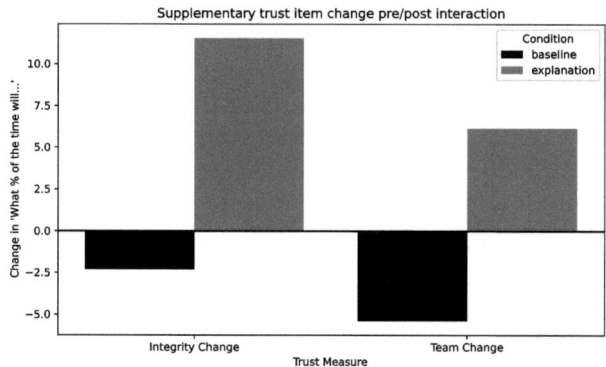

Fig. 4. Supplementary trust questions, changes pre-post interaction

trust and personal negative attitudes (P−) (r = −0.383, p = 0.018), suggesting that participants with more negative views of robots (a higher P−) reported a lower overall trust score after the experiment. Other correlations remained weak and non-significant. This appears to indicate that trust attitudes may be shaped by personal negative attitudes post-interaction (Table 3).

Table 3. Correlation between Pre-/Post-Mission Trust Score and GAToRS Variables

Time	Variable	Correlation	p-value
Pre-Mission	Trust Score and P+	0.137	0.412
	Trust Score and P−	−0.001	0.994
	Trust Score and S+	0.204	0.219
	Trust Score and S−	0.096	0.565
Post-Mission	Trust Score and P+	0.008	0.962
	Trust Score and P−	**−0.383**	**0.018 (*)**
	Trust Score and S+	0.120	0.471
	Trust Score and S−	−0.103	0.537

5 Discussion and Future Work

In this study, participants played an interactive firefighting game alongside a robot teammate, where a trust violation occurred owing to the robot declining to help the user immediately. Trust generally increased steadily until the instance of trust-breaking behavior, after which it declined and then gradually rose again, aligning with our first hypothesis (H1). We found that when the robot provides an explanation for declining to help, trust better recovers over time, a finding consistent with our H2. Interestingly, although the explanation (a form of trust repair strategy) was provided during the trust violation event, the initial damage to trust was comparable to a baseline condition where an explanation for the refusal was not provided. Thus, the benefit of explanation takes time to manifest in user trust attitudes (RQ1): the immediate emotional response to rejection may be separate from the cognitive appraisal that follows.

The explanation condition showed a meaningful recovery in trust, as measured by the Schaefer Trust Perception Scale, which indicated no significant change in trust after the violation, albeit it was at a lower average level. In contrast, the baseline condition experienced a significant decline in trust scores (U = 249.0, p = 0.0470). Additionally, individual Schaefer Trust questions, such as those measuring the robot's integrity and teamwork, showed improvements in the explanation condition, while they declined in the baseline condition. The explanation given by the robot helped ameliorate the damage to trust over time, suggesting that explanation during a trust violation can enhance the restoration process (RQ2). This underscores the importance of using explanations as a strategy for repairing trust and users' perceptions of robots' integrity.

The lack of significant correlations between general attitudes towards robots (as measured by GAToRS) and trust levels before the experiment suggests that these attitudes do not play a major role in initial trust formation. However, post-violation, a negative correlation between personal negative attitudes (P−) and trust recovery indicates that individuals with more negative attitudes towards robots may face greater challenges in recovering trust. This highlights the importance of addressing these personal attitudes when implementing trust repair interventions.

A limitation of our study surrounds the real-world significance of our results owing to the simplified game-based design. As the in-game human behavior was limited —the participants could only call the robot for a specific task, and were forced to use it for fighting some fires—this may not reflect how people would use the robot in real-world scenarios. It is not clear whether participants would choose to rely on the robot for all tasks if they could, or avoid using it entirely, especially if they lose trust in its integrity. In real-world scenarios, factors such as the environmental variables and physical interaction could affect how trust is built, maintained or repaired. In Webb et al. [5], we highlighted how offering a choice to collaborate could serve as a behavioral measure of trust. Future work should further examine how constrained versus voluntary teaming conditions influence trust dynamics, especially in high-stakes, time-pressured environments where satisficing trust may emerge as a pragmatic response. Another possibility for future work would be to continue the experiment and human-robot interaction for longer after the trust violation, to establish if the baseline (no explanation) condition eventually recovers trust with successful cooperation or if it remains impaired for the longer-term. Moreover, our example scenario is simplified compared to real indoor firefighting protocol. Firefighting missions inside buildings generally involve teams of two firefighters for safety during search and evacuations, and it is moot whether a robot would ever replace a human companion. In future, our study design could more closely reflect professional firefighting practice. Furthermore, future work can also consider the impact of the robot's communication modality—whether it uses verbal or non-verbal cues—as this could influence how its intentions are perceived and how much human teammates are willing to trust the robot.

6 Conclusion

In this study, we investigated the effectiveness of an explanation-based trust repair strategy in human-robot teaming following a trust violation (apparent lack of cooperation by the robot). Our results showed that although trust decreased significantly after a robot declined to assist a user, explaining the lack of immediate help helped participants recover trust more quickly and more fully compared to a baseline where no explanation was given. Participants in the explanation condition showed a substantial recovery of trust over time, both in on-mission trust measurements and in post-mission trust questionnaires.

These findings highlight the importance of well-timed and meaningful communication from robots during unexpected or adverse events, where they may not be able to respond to user requests without interrupting tasks of higher priority for the team. Such scenarios may be especially likely in time-sensitive missions where there may be limited situation awareness. Timely, clear explanations may be enough to restore trust back to levels before a trust-breaking behavior, allowing human-robot teams to continue their mission. This ability to quickly re-establish trust is crucial for sustaining efficient human-robot collaboration under pressure, especially if the team has been formed ad hoc. The ability to repair trust once damaged ensures maintenance of a 'good enough' level of trust for the mission duration [4], and thus helps increase the likelihood of mission success.

References

1. Delmerico, J., et al.: The current state and future outlook of rescue robotics. J. Field Robot. **36**(7), 1171–1191 (2019)
2. Stanton, N.A., et al.: Distributed situation awareness in dynamic systems: theoretical development and application of an ergonomics methodology. Ergonomics **49**(12–13), 1288–1311 (2006)
3. Huang, L., et al.: Distributed dynamic team trust in human, artificial intelligence, and robot teaming. In: Trust in human-robot interaction. Elsevier, pp. 301–319 (2021)
4. Hunt, E.R., et al.: Steps towards satisficing distributed dynamic team trust. In: Proceedings of the AAAI Symposium Series, vol. 2, no. 1, pp. 18–25 (2023)
5. Webb, N., Milivojevic, S., Sobhani, M., Madin, Z.R., Ward, J.C., Yusuf, S., Baber, C., Hunt, E.R.: Co-movement and trust development in human-robot teams. In: International Conference on Social Robotics. Springer, pp. 107–120 (2024). https://doi.org/10.1007/978-981-96-3522-1_11
6. Baker, A.L., Phillips, E.K., Ullman, D., Keebler, J.R.: Toward an understanding of trust repair in human-robot interaction: current research and future directions. ACM Trans. Interact. Intell. Syst. (TiiS) **8**(4), 1–30 (2018)
7. Milivojevic, S., et al.: Swift trust in mobile ad hoc human-robot teams. In: Proceedings of the Second International Symposium on Trustworthy Autonomous Systems, pp. 1–10 (2024)
8. Ribeiro, J.G., Faria, M., Sardinha, A., Melo, F.S.: Helping people on the fly: ad hoc teamwork for human-robot teams. In: Marreiros, G., Melo, F.S., Lau, N., Lopes Cardoso, H., Reis, L.P. (eds.) EPIA 2021. LNCS (LNAI), vol. 12981, pp. 635–647. Springer, Cham (2021). https://doi.org/10.1007/978-3-030-86230-5_50
9. Lewicki, R.J., Brinsfield, C.: Trust repair. Annu. Rev. Organ. Psych. Organ. Behav. **4**(1), 287–313 (2017)
10. Robinette, P., Li, W., Allen, R., Howard, A.M., Wagner, A.R.: Overtrust of robots in emergency evacuation scenarios. In: 2016 11th ACM/IEEE International Conference on Human-Robot Interaction (HRI). IEEE, pp. 101–108 (2016)
11. Ososky, S., Schuster, D., Phillips, E., Jentsch, F.G.: Building appropriate trust in human-robot teams. In: AAAI Spring Symposium: Trust and Autonomous Systems, pp. 60–65 (2013)
12. Xie, Y., Bodala, I.P., Ong, D.C., Hsu, D., Soh, H.: Robot capability and intention in trust-based decisions across tasks. In: 2019 14th ACM/IEEE International Conference on Human-Robot Interaction (HRI), pp. 39–47 (2019)
13. Alarcon, G.M., Gibson, A.M., Jessup, S.A.: Trust repair in performance, process, and purpose factors of human-robot trust. In: 2020 IEEE International Conference on Human-Machine Systems (ICHMS), pp. 1–6 (2020)
14. Juvina, I., Collins, M.G., Larue, O., Kennedy, W.G., Visser, E.D., Melo, C.D.: Toward a unified theory of learned trust in interpersonal and human-machine interactions. ACM Trans. Interact. Intell. Syst. **9**(4), 1–33 (2019)

15. Alhaji, B., Büttner, S., Kumar, S.S., Prilla, M.: Trust dynamics in human interaction with an industrial robot. Behav. Inf. Technol. **44**(2), 266–288 (2025)
16. Akash, K., Hu, W.-L., Reid, T., Jain, N.: Dynamic modeling of trust in human-machine interactions. In: 2017 American Control Conference (ACC). IEEE, pp. 1542–1548 (2017)
17. Kox, E.S., van den Boogaard, J., Turjaka, V., Kerstholt, J.H.: The journey or the destination: the impact of transparency and goal attainment on trust in human-robot teams. ACM Trans. Hum. Robot Interact. **14**(2), 1–23 (2024)
18. Waterson, P., Baber, C., Hunt, E., Milivojevic, S., Maynard, S., Musolesi, M.: Function allocation for responsible artificial intelligence: how do we allocate trust and responsibility?. In: Contemporary Ergonomics & Human Factors 2025. Chartered Institute of Ergonomics & Human Factors, pp. 277–283 (2025)
19. Esterwood, C., Robert, L.P.: A literature review of trust repair in HRI. In: 2022 31st IEEE International Conference on Robot and Human Interactive Communication (RO-MAN). IEEE, pp. 1641–1646 (2022)
20. Esterwood, C., Robert, L.P., Jr.: Three strikes and you are out!: the impacts of multiple human-robot trust violations and repairs on robot trustworthiness. Comput. Hum. Behav. **142**, 107658 (2023)
21. Sebo, S.S., Krishnamurthi, P., Scassellati, B.: "I don't believe you": investigating the effects of robot trust violation and repair. In: 2019 14th ACM/IEEE International Conference on Human-Robot Interaction (HRI). IEEE, pp. 57–65 (2019)
22. Bai, Z., Chen, K.: Effects of explanations by robots on trust repair in human-robot collaborations. In: Degen, H., Ntoa, S. (eds.) International Conference on Human-Computer Interaction. Springer, pp. 3–14 (2024). https://doi.org/10.1007/978-3-031-60611-3_1
23. Robinette, P., Howard, A.M., Wagner, A.R.: Timing is key for robot trust repair. In: ICSR 2015. LNCS (LNAI), vol. 9388, pp. 574–583. Springer, Cham (2015). https://doi.org/10.1007/978-3-319-25554-5_57
24. Nayyar, M., Wagner, A.R.: When should a robot apologize? Understanding how timing affects human-robot trust repair. In: Ge, S.S., et al. (eds.) ICSR 2018. LNCS (LNAI), vol. 11357, pp. 265–274. Springer, Cham (2018). https://doi.org/10.1007/978-3-030-05204-1_26
25. Séverin, L.: OfficeBots (2023). https://github.com/severin-lemaignan/officebots
26. Schaefer, K.E.: Measuring trust in human robot interactions: development of the "trust perception scale-HRI". In: Mittu, R., Sofge, D., Wagner, A., Lawless, W.F. (eds.) Robust Intelligence and Trust in Autonomous Systems, pp. 191–218. Springer, Boston, MA (2016). https://doi.org/10.1007/978-1-4899-7668-0_10
27. Koverola, M., Kunnari, A., Sundvall, J., Laakasuo, M.: General attitudes towards robots scale (GAToRS): a new instrument for social surveys. Int. J. Soc. Robot. **14**(7), 1559–1581 (2022)

Short Papers Session 1

RoboTale: Leveraging Large Language Models for Generative Storytelling and Gestural Interaction on a Humanoid Robot for Children's Hospitals

Pol Barrera Valls[1], John Allan Øllgaard[1], Tabea Sudermann[1], Angelina Stoyanova Wolf[2], Ricki Kenn Rasmussen[3], Leon Bodenhagen[1], and Oskar Palinko[1(✉)]

[1] Maersk Mc-Kinney Moller Institute, University of Southern Denmark, Odense, Denmark
ospa@mmmi.sdu.dk
[2] Centre for Clinical Robotics, Odense University Hospital, Odense, Denmark
[3] Centre for Clinical Artificial Intelligence, Odense University Hospital, Odense, Denmark

Abstract. Children arriving at hospitals for treatment often experience nervousness and discomfort. To mitigate this, we introduced a humanoid robot as an interactive storyteller, narrating stories generated dynamically by a generative AI, incorporating inputs from the child during the conversation. The interactivity was further enhanced by aligning the emotional tone of the narrative with synchronized facial expressions and arm gestures of the robot, generated by utilizing a classifier network. This paper presents the technical implementation of the system and reports preliminary findings from pilot tests conducted at Odense University Hospital and the University of Southern Denmark. The results indicate that the robot was effective in delivering stories and maintaining children's attention, promising positive outcomes for the use of interactive robotics in pediatric care settings.

1 Introduction

Modern hospitals face two interconnected challenges: maintaining operational efficiency amid increasing nursing shortages [24], and ensuring an emotionally supportive environment for patients and their relatives [22] by creating positive distractions [11]. Robots are increasingly being used to relieve staff from menial tasks, including transporting blood samples, medications and diagnostic equipment, allowing healthcare workers to allocate more time to direct patient

---

This work was supported by the RoboTale project (funded by Odense University Hospital and the Region of Southern Denmark) and HospiBot project (funded by the the European Union's Regional Development Fund through the Interreg Germany-Denmark program).

© The Author(s), under exclusive license to Springer Nature Singapore Pte Ltd. 2026
M. Staffa et al. (Eds.): ICSR+AI 2025, LNAI 16131, pp. 439–449, 2026.
https://doi.org/10.1007/978-981-95-2379-5_30

care [14]. Due to the recent advancements within both robotics and artificial intelligence (AI), and especially Large Language Models (LLMs), a vast number of opportunities now exist for improving human-robot interaction (HRI). One such opportunity lies in leveraging socially interactive humanoid robots within hospital environments. This is especially relevant in pediatric settings, as hospitalization can be psychologically traumatic to children, triggering fear and anxiety [2].

Although initiatives such as hospital clowns [12] and creative spaces [19] exist to entertain and comfort children during their hospital visits, these offerings are limited in availability, dependent on staffing, and may be entirely absent due to resource constraints. Emerging social robotic platforms offer the potential to contribute to supportive care in pediatric wards, serving as emotionally supportive companions, helping to distract and engage inpatients during hospitalization and outpatients before consultations [13]. With the integration of LLMs, this potential can further increase, as personalized interaction becomes feasible with little input from the patient or visitor.

This article presents the implementation of a storytelling robot powered by LLMs and natural language processing (NLP) to engage children at the entrance of a pediatric hospital. The robot's emotional expressiveness was validated through experiments at the Odense University Hospital (OUH) and University of Southern Denmark (SDU). Where the children were tested in their attention to the story and recall of information

2 Related Work

The growing interest in LLM-powered humanoid robots responds to the need for these types of robots to engage in dynamic conversations, as evident from the annual dialogue Robot competition, where all the participants of the 2023 edition used LLMs as the engine driving the conversation [7]. Additionally, speech interaction requires low-latency communication, with users tolerating only up to 4 s of delay [17].

Besides the ability to process and engage in verbal interactions, non-verbal communication, such as its ability to display emotions, is critically important in people's perception of a robot [5].

In the healthcare domain, several social robots have been deployed [16] [15]. In pediatric care, these robots have been found to reduce the anxiety levels of patients [10]. The inclusion of LLM-driven social robots has additionally been shown to foster creativity in children. In [4], the authors compared the use of a creative LLM vs. a non-creative LLM in interactive storytelling, with findings suggesting that the creative LLM positively influenced creativity in child responses.

A recent study has also looked at the ability of LLM models to classify text, comparing zero-shot classification, few-shot and fine-tuning, with results highlighting a boost in the performance of fine-tuned models with a mixture of real and synthetic data over zero-shot classifiers [23]. This result has been used as a starting point for the training of text classifiers in this paper.

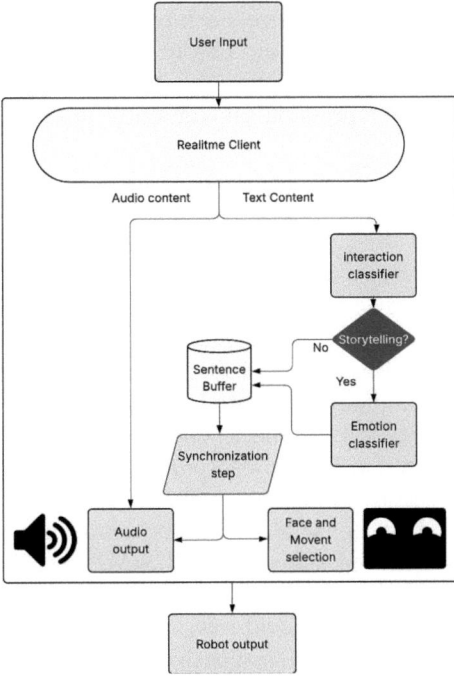

Fig. 1. Software implementation

3 Methodology

The GPT-4o mini real-time model from OpenAI was used as the backbone for conducting conversations in this study. It was chosen due to its focus on natural conversations and producing low-latency response times. Additionally, the capacity to generate audio, with a degree of emotion, was utilized.

This model was prompted to act as an interactive storytelling robot for children at the hospital; it was also prompted to stick to positive stories and avoid touching on negative aspects, such as illnesses. As a conversation starter, the robot asked the child about their age and what kind of stories they like. Based on the child's response, an age-appropriate story was generated and told, stopping every few sentences, prompting the child to consider how they would like to continue the interaction. The choice of the real-time model additionally allowed the parallel processing of text and audio. This was important, as our implementation assumes a relatively constant speaking cadence, allowing the synchronization of the text's emotion with speech. See Fig. 1.

The text processing consists of a text classification network to classify the LLM's responses, which was implemented to display fitting facial expressions and movements on the robot. The incoming text stream from the LLM is split into sentences, delimited by punctuation marks, which are then classified into 9 different interaction and emotional categories: greeting, question, reaction, joy, sadness, anger, surprise, fear, and love, each of which were assigned to a predefined movement and facial expression. The text and length of each categorized sentence are stored in a Sentence buffer, where the sentence length determines when to change the facial expression and/or body pose, according to the categorized sentences.

3.1 Classification

The classification of sentences was planned in two steps: the first step separates the dialogue interaction terms [question, reaction, greeting] from the storytelling terms, defined in the second step, which classifies the emotion related to the text [joy, sadness, anger, surprise, fear, and love]. For the first classifier, we trained Fasttext [1] on a small manually annotated dataset generated during our testing process, as well as additional synthetic dataset generated based on the first dataset. The final dataset is split into two parts: training set (500 rows) and test set (60 rows). For the second classifier, we fine-tuned Google's BERT [3] on the Emotions dataset [18]. Due to the lack of a text emotion dataset in Danish, the English dataset was translated using the OPUS-MP translation model [21] and was used to fine-tune the Danish BERT model, developed by Hvingelby et al. [8]. This dataset contains 20 thousand rows, split into train, test and validation sets comprising 80% ,10% and 10% respectively. The choice of using two stages of classification is also motivated by the small size of the interaction datataset in comparison with the emotions dataset, with Fasttext generally needing less data to train [9].

To further evaluate the model performance in a real-life scenario, an additional test dataset in English and in Danish was generated through interaction with the robot. This dataset comprised two full human-robot conversations each. The conversations were then split to sentences and given to two Danish-speaking evaluators and two English-speaking evaluators to classify the robot sentences from the robot's point of view. Then they were compared against each other and against the output of the classifier.

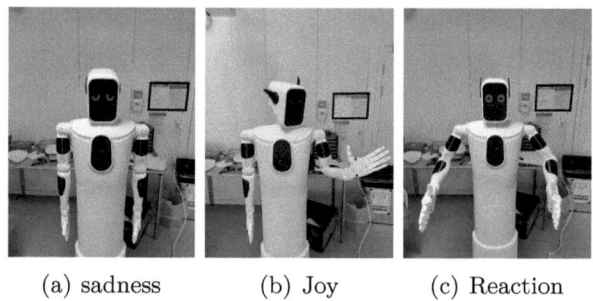

(a) sadness   (b) Joy   (c) Reaction

Fig. 2. Assigned poses for sentence categories

3.2 Robot Embodiment

The humanoid robot HuGo, developed in the HospiBot project, was used as the physically embodied conversation agent during the experiment, allowing for customization of poses and facial expressions, which were assigned to each of the categorized sentences [6]. The pose of the robot is determined by two arms with seven degrees of freedom (DoF) each, two hands with four DoFs each, one head with two DoFs, and two ears, each having one DoF. Examples of poses can be seen in Fig. 2. The robot also features an integrated speaker and microphone to interact with the users. However, the integrated microphone was not used, as the interaction was found to be more intuitive to the users with a handheld noise-reducing microphone (Fig. 3).

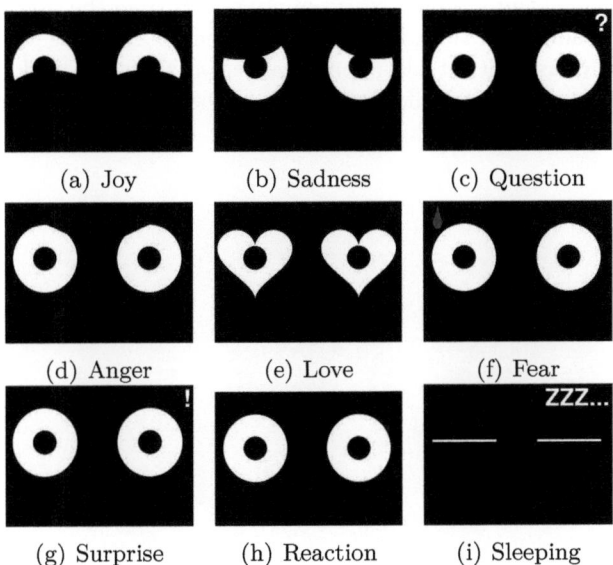

Fig. 3. Assigned faces for each of the sentence categories

4 Experimental Setup

A series of experiments were performed at OUH and SDU which we report on here.

The first experiment included 23 children, in the age range of 2–13 years (See Fig. 6). It focused on observing how many of them would listen to the entirety of the story. The experiment measured the number of times children left the interaction or said the keyword "stop" to end the conversation, tracked by the researchers observing the interaction.

The second experiment included 27 children, 9 male and 18 female, in the range of 5–10 years who were given brief instructions about the interaction and then prompted to engage in conversation with the robot until the story was ended by the LLM after 4 conversation turns. The participants were seated in front of the robot and talked to it using the handheld microphone, see Fig. 4. During the interaction, the robot would always end it's turn with an open question, followed by a "beep" to signal to the participants that it was their turn to speak. After the interaction, the parents were asked to complete a questionnaire together with their children.

The questionnaire consisted of 2 Likert-scale questions, ranging from 1 - Strongly disagree to 5- Strongly agree. The first two questions, "On a scale from 1 to 5, how good of a storyteller was the robot?" and "On a scale from 1 to 5, how entertaining did you find the robot's stories?", were intended to ensure participants evaluated the storytelling, rather than the robot, to overcome novelty bias. In addition, the LLM was prompted to always generate the same names for characters in its stories, specifically Max, Rasmus and Lila. This was done to be able to test the children's recall of the characters in the story, as a measure of attention paid to the story.

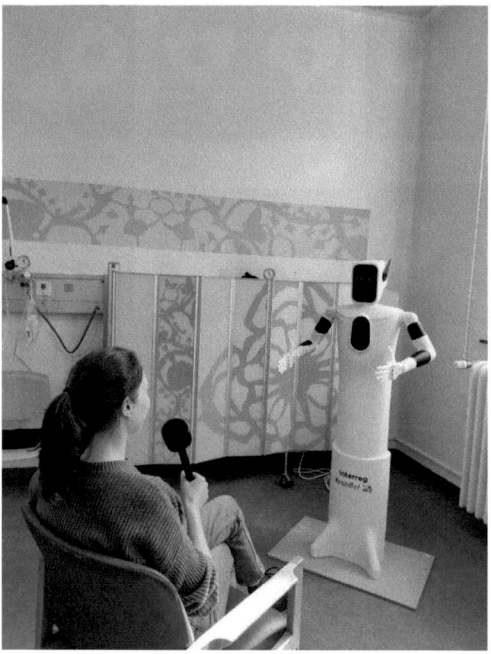

Fig. 4. Storytelling setup

5 Results

The training of the Emotions model was performed on the training set, consisting of 16 thousand examples.

The emotion classifier was tested on the test set of the Emotions dataset, achieving 82% accuracy on the translated Danish dataset and 93% accuracy on the English dataset.

The interaction state classifier was tested on the test split of the collected dataset and achieved an accuracy of 86% in Danish and 86% in English.

The performance of the model against human evaluators is summarized in Tables 1 and 2. Note that, for simplicity, the English and Danish evaluators have been labeled with the same notation, despite being different people.

The interaction classification by the Danish model achieved 81% with the first human evaluator H1 whereas the emotion classifier achieved 24% match with H1 and H2. The performance in English was similar, achieving 71% matching with H1 on the interaction terms but only 14% with H2 in the emotion terms. The two human evaluators matched their emotion assessment of the sentences 82% of the time in Danish, but only 29% of the time in English.

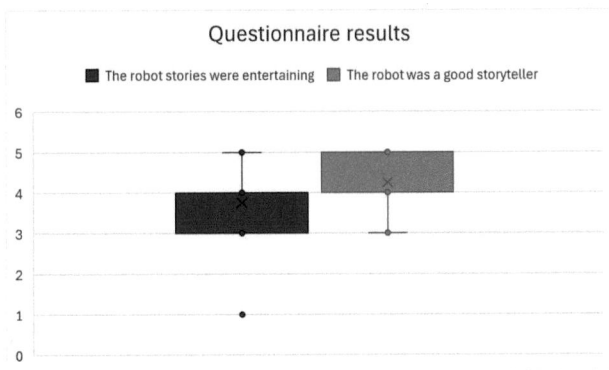

Fig. 5. Questionnaire results

Table 1. Emotion Classifier Performance

Lang	Test Acc	H1-H2	H1-Model	H2-Model
English	93%	29%	61 %	14%
Danish	82%	81%	24%	24%

Regarding the data collected on the experiments: In the first test, the focus was set on the reason behind the end of the conversation and the results showed that 65% of the users listened to the story until the end Fig. 6

Table 2. Interaction Classifier Performance

Lang.	Test Acc.	H1-H2	H1-Model	H2-Model
English	82%	77%	71%	80%
Danish	86%	68%	82%	59%

In a second experiment, the attention paid by the children to the story was assessed by asking them the name of their favorite character in the story. The results showed that 48% of the users remembered at least one character name, with Max the main character being remembered the most. The questionnaire results showed high agreement with the proposed statements, suggesting high satisfaction with the robot and storytelling Fig. 5.

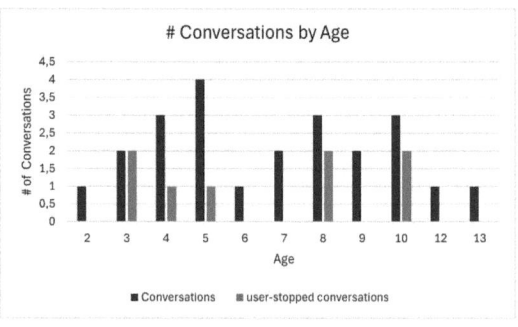

Fig. 6. Number of conversations by age

In the first experiment, the age of the children was also recorded. The data suggested that age was not a factor in the decision to stop the conversation before its end. In the second experiment, the gender of the children was recorded in a addition to age. In this case, the gender did not affect neither the recall of information about the characters in the story nor the other answers in the questionnaire.

5.1 Observations

During our experiments, the robot proved to be a major attraction for both children and their parents. Whenever the robot interacted with a child, it often drew a crowd of curious bystanders - including other children eagerly waiting for their turn. The parents were also engaged, with some trying the robot themselves or enjoying their children's stories. Several children started a second conversation with the robot, stayed to listen to others' stories or even returned later to bring friends or siblings. The children's responses varied a lot: some were unsure of what to respond to the robot and received suggestions from parents, while others responded with long and creative answers. In general, a lot of children that seemed shy or were convinced by the parents to talk to the robot got more confident during the conversation with the robot, especially when they realized that the robot was understanding them and creating the story on their topics.

The interaction with children proved to be challenging, as the speech recognition process is known to have a worse performance for children compared to adults [20]; this fact is especially aggravated by the use of the Danish language. When interacting with younger children, the robot would sometimes misunderstand them, making some of the children disappointed.

Furthermore, it was found that children under the age of 5 struggled to keep their concentration on the story and the robot, whereas children aged 6–12 were the most interested and most successful in communicating with the robot.

6 Conclusions

Looking at the performance of the classification models against human evaluators, it appears evident that the emotion classifier did not come close to the performance shown in the test dataset. This phenomenon could be explained by the narrative nature of the LLM generated sentences, that not only is very different to that of the dataset but also difficult to classify into the proposed emotions, even for the human evaluators.

For this reason creating a new dataset based on the collected data, as done for the interaction classifier, is of key importance when it comes to content-based facial expression and movement communication. Furthermore, in the storytelling application, the sentences should be classified into simpler categories based on narrative context such as dialogues, descriptions, actions, etc.

Regarding the experiments, it was surprising to see the number of children who did not remember any of the character names. This fact, in addition to the different scores on the statements presented in the questionnaire, proves that some children were more interested or even fascinated by the robot's appearance and movements, thus not paying much attention to the story.

7 Future Work

Our performance was limited by the data we used to train the emotion classifier. In future applications, we will establish a pipeline for data collection and labeling of LLM generated sentences. The generation of these datasets should allow for more precise classification in specific domains such as storytelling.

When interacting with more than one person, the robot would sometimes confuse the dialogue between two persons with a response. We plan on introducing methods based on vision and multi-speaker speech recognition to tackle this problem.

Some participants also described a sensation during the interaction as if the robot was not talking to them. This problem could be solved by including further means of non-verbal communication such as gaze interaction, nodding, etc.

Furthermore, it was experienced on several occasions that the user wanted to stop and correct the robot. Including this dynamic could improve the user experience.

This work greatly simplifies the range of human emotional communication. In addition to that, poses and facial expressions were fixed beforehand. In future work regarding humanoid robotic storytellers, the inclusion of AI-generated co-speech gestures and facial expressions based on the context of the conversation has the potential to greatly improve results presented in this paper.

References

1. Bojanowski, P., Grave, E., Joulin, A., Mikolov, T.: Enriching word vectors with subword information (2017)
2. Cartland, J., et al.: The role of hospital design in reducing anxiety for pediatric patients. HERD: Health Environ. Res. Des. J. **11**(3), 66–79 (2018)
3. Devlin, J., Chang, M.W., Lee, K., Toutanova, K.: Pre-training of deep bidirectional transformers for languages understanding, Bert (2019)
4. Elgarf, M., Salam, H., Peters, C.: Fostering children's creativity through llm-driven storytelling with a social robot. Front. Robot. AI **11** (2024)
5. Fiorini, L.: The role of coherent robot behavior and embodiment in emotion perception and recognition during human-robot interaction: experimental study. JMIR Hum. Factors **11**, e45494 (2024)
6. Gabor, T., Palinko, O.: The hugo humanoid project: a modular social robot. In: 2025 20th ACM/IEEE International Conference on Human-Robot Interaction (HRI), pp. 1776–1778. IEEE (2025)
7. Higashinaka, R., Minato, T., Nishizaki, H., Nagai, T.: Proceedings of the dialogue robot competition 2023 (2024)
8. Hvingelby, R., et al.: DaNE: a named entity resource for Danish. In Calzolari, N., (eds.) Proceedings of the Twelfth Language Resources and Evaluation Conference, pp. 4597–4604, Marseille, France, May 2020. European Language Resources Association
9. Ligthart, M., Neerincx, M., Hindriks, K.: Memory-based personalization for fostering a long-term child-robot relationship, pp. 80–89 (2022)
10. Mike, E.U., Ligthart, M.A., Neerincx, Hindriks, K.V.: Memory-based personalization for fostering a long-term child-robot relationship. In: 2022 17th ACM/IEEE International Conference on Human-Robot Interaction (HRI), number March in ACM/IEEE International Conference on Human-Robot Interaction, pages 80–89, United States, September 2022. IEEE Computer Society. Publisher Copyright: 2022 IEEE.; 17th Annual ACM/IEEE International Conference on Human-Robot Interaction, HRI 2022 ; Conference date: 07-03-2022 Through 10-03-2022
11. Lim, B., Rogers, Y., Sebire, N.: Designing to distract: can interactive technologies reduce visitor anxiety in a children's hospital setting? ACM Trans. Comput. Hum. Interact. **26**(2) (2019)
12. Lopes-Junior, L.C., et al.: Clown intervention on psychological stress and fatigue in pediatric patients with cancer undergoing chemotherapy. Cancer Nursing **43**(4), 290–299 (2020)
13. Moerman, C.J., Van Der Heide, L., Heerink, M.: Social robots to support children's well-being under medical treatment: a systematic state-of-the-art review. J. Child Health Care **23**(4), 596–612 (2019)

14. Morgan, A.A., et al.: Robots in healthcare: a scoping review. Current Robot. Rep. **3**(4), 271–280 (2022)
15. Øllgaard, J.A., Bundgaard, K., Kjaer, M.S., Bodenhagen, L., Palinko, O.: Utilizing a social robot as a greeter at a children's hospital. In: International Conference on Social Robotics, pp. 131–144. Springer (2024)
16. Pashangpour, S., Nejat, G.: The future of intelligent healthcare: a systematic analysis and discussion on the integration and impact of robots using large language models for healthcare. Robotics **13**(8) (2024)
17. Peng, Z., et al: Understanding user perceptions of robot's delay, voice quality-speed trade-off and GUI during conversation. In: Extended Abstracts of the 2020 CHI Conference on Human Factors in Computing Systems, CHI EA '20, pp. 1–8, New York, NY, USA, 2020. Association for Computing Machinery
18. Saravia, E., Liu, H.T., Huang, Y., Wu, J., Chen, Y.: CARER: contextualized affect representations for emotion recognition. In: Proceedings of the 2018 Conference on Empirical Methods in Natural Language Processing, pp. 3687–3697, Brussels, Belgium, October-November 2018. Association for Computational Linguistics
19. Signorelli, C., Robertson, E.G., Valentin, C., Alchin, J.E., Treadgold, C.: A review of creative play interventions to improve children's hospital experience and well-being. Hospital Pediatr. **13**(11), e355–e364 (2023)
20. Singh, V.P., Sahidullah, Md., Kinnunen, T.: Causal analysis of ASR errors for children: quantifying the impact of physiological, cognitive, and extrinsic factors (2025)
21. Tiedemann, J., Thottingal, S.: OPUS-MT – building open translation services for the world. In: Martins, A., (eds.) Proceedings of the 22nd Annual Conference of the European Association for Machine Translation, pp. 479–480, Lisboa, Portugal, November 2020. European Association for Machine Translation
22. Ulrich, R.S.: Visual landscapes and psychological well-being. Landscape Res. **4**(1), 17–23 (1979)
23. Vajjala, S., Shimangaud, S.: Text classification in the LLM era – where do we stand? (2025)
24. WHO. Nursing and midwifery. https://www.who.int/news-room/fact-sheets/detail/nursing-and-midwifery

Rethinking the Evaluation of Non-stationary Dueling Bandits for Human-Robot Interaction

Sebastian Schneider[✉]

Human Media Interaction Faculty of Electrical Engineering, Mathematics and Computer Science, University of Twente, Enschede, Netherlands
s.schneider@utwente.nl

Abstract. Non-stationary dueling bandits are promising for modeling evolving preferences in human-robot interaction, but current evaluations rely on synthetic data and ignore user experience. This short contribution proposes a regret formulation that incorporates interaction costs—such as annoyance, cognitive effort, and trust degradation. Furthermore, suggestions for standardized, user-in-the-loop evaluation is presented. Recognizing the challenges of long-term studies with real users, large language models could be used to simulate non-stationary user behavior for early-stage testing. This enables deeper insight into algorithm usability and supports the development of adaptive systems that are not only efficient, but also aligned with human expectations and experience.

Keywords: Preference Learning · Human-Robot Interaction · Evaluation Methods

1 Introduction

As intelligent systems become increasingly embedded in everyday environments, the need for them to understand and adapt to user preferences has grown more pressing. From virtual assistants and recommendation systems to embodied robots in homes and workplaces, the ability to model and respond to evolving human preferences is central to personalization and long-term engagement [2,6,8,10]. However, preferences are not fixed and shift over time due to contextual, emotional, and cognitive factors [5,7]. Algorithms that assume static or slowly drifting user models may fail to capture these dynamic behaviors, leading to misalignment between system actions and user expectations.

Dueling bandits offer a compelling framework for preference adaptation for collecting qualitative preference statements. Unlike traditional bandit algorithms that rely on scalar rewards, dueling bandits model through pairwise comparisons [11,12]. This approach is particularly well-suited to scenarios where explicit feedback is difficult to quantify or compare across individuals. Extensions to handle non-stationarity have further improved their applicability to real-world environments, enabling the detection of concept drift and changepoints in preference patterns [4,9].

However, a gap remains in how such models are evaluated since most studies rely on synthetic data, often assuming idealized user behavior and predefined shifts in preference. Thus, they fall short of capturing the challenges of real-time interaction, such as user fatigue, cognitive overload, or loss of trust due to repetitive or seemingly irrational queries. This paper proposes rethinking evaluation standards and developing methodologies that reflect the realities of interactive, user-centered environments such as human-robot interaction (HRI) by proposing to add interaction costs to regret formulation for non-stationary dueling bandits. The following section gives a brief introduction to related work. Section 3 explains the problem formulation. Section 4 discusses aspects of evaluating preference learning in Human-Robot Interaction (HRI), followed by a conclusion.

2 Background

Preference adaptation in human-computer and human-robot interaction has traditionally relied on collaborative filtering and matrix factorization techniques designed for stationary settings [1,5]. These methods are inadequate in dynamic environments where preferences evolve due to mood, context, or task-related factors [7,8].

Dueling bandits have emerged as a principled framework for preference learning based on relative feedback [11,12], and recent work extends this formulation to non-stationary settings. Algorithms now aim to adapt to changes through smoothing, reset mechanisms, or change detection strategies. Saha et al. [9] proposed optimal and efficient algorithms for non-stationary dueling bandits, achieving tight dynamic regret bounds under both switching and gradually varying preference models. while Kolpaczki et al. [4] introduce the "Beat-the-Winner Reset" algorithm and two meta-algorithms (DETECT and Monitored Dueling Bandits) for non-stationary dueling bandits, achieving provable dynamic regret bounds across piecewise-stationary segments without requiring prior knowledge of the number of segments or time horizon ANACONDA [3] further improves dynamic regret bounds without assuming a prior knowledge of preference shifts.

Despite these advances, evaluation remains primarily synthetic and system-centric, relying on idealized user models and abstract regret metrics. Real-time interaction effects (e.g., annoyance, cognitive fatigue, or trust) are rarely measured, leaving open questions about how well these algorithms support effective online interaction in HRI.

3 Problem Formulation

Let $\mathcal{A} = \{a_1, a_2, \ldots, a_K\}$ denote a set of K arms (e.g., robot behaviors, task strategies, or dialogue options). At each discrete time step $t = 1, 2, \ldots, T$, the learner selects a pair of arms $(a_i, a_j) \in \mathcal{A} \times \mathcal{A}$ and presents them to the user for comparison.

The user provides stochastic binary feedback indicating a preference for one of the two options. Let $P_t(a_i \succ a_j)$ denote the probability that arm a_i is preferred to a_j at time t, where the preference function is governed by a latent utility function $U_t : \mathcal{A} \to \mathbb{R}$. Crucially, U_t may change over time due to internal or contextual factors, making the problem non-stationary.

We define a sequence of *non-stationary utility functions* $\{U_1, U_2, \ldots, U_T\}$, and assume the existence of a time-varying Condorcet winner a_t^* such that:

$$P_t(a_t^* \succ a) > \frac{1}{2}, \quad \forall a \in \mathcal{A} \setminus \{a_t^*\}.$$

In traditional dueling bandits, the goal is to minimize the cumulative preference regret:

$$R_T = \sum_{t=1}^{T} \left(P_t(a_t^* \succ a_t) - P_t(a_i \succ a_j) \right),$$

where (a_i, a_j) is the pair selected at time t, and a_t is the better of the two according to U_t.

However, in the context of online human-robot interaction, system behavior affects not only decision quality but also user experience. We extend the regret definition to incorporate *interaction costs* associated with human cognitive and emotional responses.

Let C_t represent a scalar cost incurred at time t due to the interaction. This cost may include:

- *Annoyance* from redundant or repeated queries,
- *Cognitive load* from excessive exploration or hard-to-compare options,
- *Loss of trust* when the system behaves inconsistently or resets frequently.

The generalized regret becomes:

$$\widetilde{R}_T = \sum_{t=1}^{T} \left(P_t(a_t^* \succ a_t) - P_t(a_i \succ a_j) + \lambda C_t \right),$$

where $\lambda \geq 0$ is a trade-off parameter reflecting the relative importance of interaction quality versus decision accuracy.

This formulation encourages the design of algorithms that not only learn efficiently but also consider user burden, potentially by minimizing redundant comparisons, detecting and adapting to preference shifts gracefully, or leveraging user modeling to personalize exploration strategies. The challenge, then, is to estimate or model C_t in practice—a task that may require additional sensing (e.g., user feedback, gaze tracking, or response latency) or implicit modeling based on historical behavior.

3.1 Modeling Interaction Costs

In the following, we propose a few ways to measure the interaction costs. We define the total interaction cost C_t at time step t as a weighted sum of human-centered penalties, including annoyance, cognitive load, and trust degradation. Each component is based on measurable signals from the interaction with the preference learning agent.

Annoyance. Repeated or redundant comparisons can lead to user annoyance. Let $\delta((a_i, a_j), \mathcal{H}_t)$ denote the number of times the pair (a_i, a_j) or a similar pair has been shown in the interaction history $\mathcal{H}_t$. The annoyance cost is defined as:

$$C_t^{\text{annoy}} = \alpha \cdot \delta((a_i, a_j), \mathcal{H}_t)$$

where $\alpha \geq 0$ is a weighting constant.

Cognitive Load. Users may experience higher cognitive load when the comparison is ambiguous or requires more effort to evaluate. This can be modeled using response time τ_t or utility gap $\Delta_t = |U_t(a_i) - U_t(a_j)|$, when available:

$$C_t^{\text{cog}} = \beta \cdot \tau_t \quad \text{or} \quad C_t^{\text{cog}} = \gamma \cdot \exp(-\Delta_t)$$

with $\beta, \gamma \geq 0$ as sensitivity parameters.

Loss of Trust. Frequent resets or unstable behavior may degrade trust. Let $r_t \in \{0, 1\}$ indicate whether a model reset occurred at time t, and let $\phi_t \in [0, 1]$ quantify policy volatility (e.g., change in selected arms). The trust-related cost is:

$$C_t^{\text{trust}} = \lambda_1 \cdot r_t + \lambda_2 \cdot \phi_t$$

Total Cost. The total interaction cost is the sum of the above components:

$$C_t = C_t^{\text{annoy}} + C_t^{\text{cog}} + C_t^{\text{trust}}$$

These costs can be used to test and develop new algorithms that take these into account for regret formulation. However, they also need to be backed with real human qualitative and quantitative feedback in online interaction with real or simulated users.

4 Evaluating Preference Learning in HRI: Challenges and Prototyping Protocols

Evaluating non-stationary preference learning in HRI requires moving beyond synthetic benchmarks and system-centric metrics. Traditional evaluations focus on cumulative regret, often assuming cleanly shifting or stationary user preferences and ignoring the cognitive and emotional effects of interaction. In real-time settings, repeated or ambiguous comparisons can lead to annoyance, cognitive fatigue, or loss of trust—impacts that are rarely accounted for in typical benchmarks.

To address this, the above section extends the evaluation paradigm to include an interaction cost term C_t, which captures measurable aspects of user burden such as response latency, perceived redundancy, and trust degradation. These costs can be inferred from behavioral signals (e.g., hesitation, timing, emotion detection, gaze behavior), interaction logs (e.g., query repetition), and periodic self-reports (e.g., Likert-scale ratings of annoyance or trust). This user-centered perspective enables the quantification not only of how well an algorithm learns but also of how it impacts users throughout the interaction.

A standardized user-in-the-loop protocol will be necessary in the future to evaluate both learning and user cost. In each round, a robot or agent presents a pair of options, and the user provides binary feedback indicating their preference. Preferences may shift over time due to variations in context or task. The protocol tracks standard performance metrics (e.g., regret, convergence time) alongside user-centered signals. Critically, it supports comparing multiple algorithms under identical conditions to identify those that best balance learning efficiency with interaction quality.

However, evaluating non-stationary preferences through real-time human studies is slow and resource-intensive, especially given the need to observe long-term dynamics. To facilitate development and reflection on user-centered regret, large language models (LLMs) can simulate users with evolving preferences. LLMs can be conditioned with personas, contextual goals, and temporal variability, enabling the generation of coherent but non-stationary preference behaviors.

Compared to fixed synthetic datasets with predefined change points, LLM-based simulated users offer richer and more flexible testbeds. They can respond contextually, exhibit preference drift or shifts, and produce naturalistic feedback without requiring handcrafted preference functions. This enables iterative prototyping and rapid hypothesis testing before committing to full-scale human studies. Such evaluation pipelines would be more reproducible and efficient for the development of advancing adaptive systems grounded in user experience.

5 Conclusion

We need to reevaluate how we assess non-stationary preference learning in human-robot interaction. While recent algorithms increasingly account for dynamic preferences, existing evaluation practices remain focused on synthetic data and system-centric metrics. The proposal is to extend regret formulations to incorporate user-centered interaction costs such as annoyance, cognitive effort, and trust degradation, which are critical to the usability and acceptance of adaptive systems.

Recognizing that long-term evaluation with real users is resource-intensive, prototyping and early-stage testing using large language models as simulated users with evolving preferences may offer greater flexibility and contextual realism than existing benchmark datasets, enabling faster iteration and analysis of the human consequences of algorithmic adaptation.

Thus, future work should focus on formulating and testing implicit and explicit interaction costs based on preference queries, subjective measurements, and objective measurements to develop non-stationary preference learning methods for actual online long-term HRI scenarios. These methods should then be tested, first, with simulated users, followed by long-term studies with actual users.

Evaluation needs to strike a balance between learning efficiency and user experience. By grounding theoretical progress in protocols that reflect real-world complexity, we take a step toward building adaptive systems that not only learn preferences but also exhibit human awareness.

References

1. Adomavicius, G., Tuzhilin, A.: Toward the next generation of recommender systems: a survey of the state-of-the-art and possible extensions. IEEE Trans. Knowl. Data Eng. **17**(6), 734–749 (2005)
2. Boucher, E.M., Harake, N.R., Ward, H.E., Stoeckl, S.E., Vargas, J., Minkel, J., Parks, A.C., Zilca, R.: Artificially intelligent chatbots in digital mental health interventions: a review. Expert Rev. Med. Devices **18**(sup1), 37–49 (2021)
3. Kleine Buening, T., Saha, A.: Anaconda: An improved dynamic regret algorithm for adaptive non-stationary dueling bandits. In: Ruiz, F., Dy, J., van de Meent, J.W. (eds.) Proceedings of The 26th International Conference on Artificial Intelligence and Statistics. Proceedings of Machine Learning Research, vol. 206, pp. 3854–3878. PMLR (2023). https://proceedings.mlr.press/v206/kleine-buening23a.html
4. Kolpaczki, P., Bengs, V., Hüllermeier, E.: Non-stationary dueling bandits. arXiv preprint arXiv:2202.00935 (2022)
5. Koren, Y.: Collaborative filtering with temporal dynamics. In: Proceedings of the 15th ACM SIGKDD international conference on Knowledge discovery and data mining, pp. 447–456 (2009)
6. Kyrarini, M., Lygerakis, F., Rajavenkatanarayanan, A., Sevastopoulos, C., Nambiappan, H.R., Chaitanya, K.K., Babu, A.R., Mathew, J., Makedon, F.: A survey of robots in healthcare. Technologies **9**(1), 8 (2021)
7. Pettijohn, T.F., Williams, G.M., Carter, T.C.: Music for the seasons: seasonal music preferences in college students. Curr. Psychol. **29**, 328–345 (2010)
8. Rossi, S., Ferland, F., Tapus, A.: User profiling and behavioral adaptation for HRI: A survey. Pattern Recogn. Lett. **99**, 3–12 (2017)
9. Saha, A., Gupta, S.: Optimal and efficient dynamic regret algorithms for non-stationary dueling bandits. In: International Conference on Machine Learning, pp. 19027–19049. PMLR (2022)
10. Schneider, S., Kummert, F.: Comparing robot and human guided personalization: adaptive exercise robots are perceived as more competent and trustworthy. Int. J. Soc. Robot. **13**(2), 169–185 (2021)
11. Yue, Y., Broder, J., Kleinberg, R., Joachims, T.: The k-armed dueling bandits problem. J. Comput. Syst. Sci. **78**(5), 1538–1556 (2012)
12. Zoghi, M., Whiteson, S., Munos, R., Rijke, M.: Relative upper confidence bound for the k-armed dueling bandit problem. In: Xing, E.P., Jebara, T. (eds.) Proceedings of the 31st International Conference on Machine Learning. Proceedings of Machine Learning Research, vol. 32, pp. 10–18. PMLR, Bejing, China (2014). https://proceedings.mlr.press/v32/zoghi14.html

Cheerbot: A Socially Assistive Robot for Workplace Wellbeing

Helena Webb[1(✉)], Pepita Barnard[1], Praminda Caleb-Solly[1], Alfie Cameron[1], Peter Craigon[1], Karen Lancaster[2], and Emma McClaughlin[3]

[1] School of Computer Science, University of Nottingham, Nottingham, UK
helena.webb@nottingham.ac.uk
[2] Faculty of Engineering, University of Nottingham, Nottingham, UK
[3] School of English, University of Nottingham, Nottingham, UK

Abstract. In this short paper we introduce "Cheerbot", a prototype socially assistive robot designed using the temi robot platform for use in workplaces to promote wellbeing amongst staff. We outline the development of Cheerbot and discuss emerging findings from a trial deployment. These findings point towards the potential for Cheerbot to be useful and acceptable as a workplace wellbeing aid.

Keywords: Wellbeing · Workplaces · Assistive robots

1 Introduction

Workplace wellbeing is an area of increasing attention and concern across the globe [1]. In order to explore how socially assistive robots might act as wellbeing aids in the workplace, we developed a prototype called "Cheerbot", designed using the temi robot platform. In this short paper we report on findings of a trial deployment to assess its potential usefulness and acceptability. Our initial results indicate that Cheerbot was perceived by users as both enjoyable and useful, and that further additions can enhance its capacity to positively influence workplace wellbeing.

2 Background

2.1 Workplace Wellbeing (WW)

Wellbeing can be defined as a general subjective feeling of satisfaction, optimism, or happiness about life; functioning well with a sense of purpose; and feeling content about one's activities [2, 3]. Work has a positive influence on overall wellbeing [4] but workplace wellbeing (WW) is affected by factors including job satisfaction, work values, self-concordant goals, achievement motivation, job demands, sense of control, and perceived psychological obligations [5]. Efforts to improve WW need to be flexible, personalisable, and target multiple influences simultaneously [6]. Robotic interventions for WW require safe, intuitive user-interfaces and consideration of human factors such as trust and cognitive workload [7, 8]. A multidisciplinary, user-centered, socio-technical systems approach can address factors that may affect WW, allowing effective design changes to be identified [9].

2.2 Cheerbot: A Robotic Aid for WWB

Cheerbot is a prototype socially assistive robot designed for use in workplaces to promote wellbeing amongst staff. It consists of bespoke interactive software deployed on a temi 3 [10] mobile telepresence robot. Early co-design sessions identified that Cheerbot could usefully run collaborative activities to foster staff interaction and feelings of community. Potential users strongly preferred Cheerbot not to collect or store any personal data, primarily motivated by a wish to avoid potential surveillance. Subsequently, Cheerbot was developed with simple, fun activities to encourage collaboration but with no personalisation, adaptive behaviour or collection of personal data.

When opening the Cheerbot app on the temi 3, users are greeted by an animated 'face' and invited to select activities to undertake: Cheerbot tells a joke or interesting fact; users select 'Walk and talk' and Cheerbot follows them whilst telling jokes/facts; users upload photographs to create a communal collage visible to others; users play a simple video game on Cheerbot's touchscreen; users upload song/film recommendations to share with others; users select a colour to represent their current mood and Cheerbot creates a communal mood board; Cheerbot facilitates a telepresence meeting, during which it can also tell jokes/facts.

3 Methods

We deployed Cheerbot at a local company (employing 800+ staff) and collected data to explore its potential usefulness and acceptability as a wellbeing aid. Cheerbot was deployed for two weeks in two large office spaces, each with 70+ desks. We received Research Ethics Committee approval (ref: CS-2024-R32) for data collection of anonymous robot meta data plus online questionnaires, qualitative observations with mini-interviews, and focus groups to elicit staff experiences and opinions. We sent the company an information sheet and short video introduction to Cheerbot, and mapped the office spaces for easier Cheerbot navigation. Cheerbot was placed in one office for a week with members of the project team available for remote technical support and also on site for three-hour periods three times during the week to conduct observations/interviews and a focus group. This process was repeated in the second week in the second office. We also circulated a short online questionnaire for staff in both offices.

4 Findings

4.1 Summary of Data Collected

Table 1 summarises the number of times each Cheerbot activity was opened over the two weeks. Table 2 summarises the other research data collected.

Table 1. Summary of number of times each Cheerbot activity was opened during deployment

Activity type	Number of times opened on Cheerbot
Joke	393
Fact	199
Walk and Talk	108
Communal collage	73
Simple video game	50
Song recommendation	50
Communal colour mood board	32
Film recommendation	30
Staff meeting	18

Table 2. Summary of other research data collected during Cheerbot deployment

Data type	Data volume
Questionnaire responses	5
Focus group participants	8
Observational encounters (including mini-interviews)	34

4.2 Analysis

Our analysis explored the extent to which Cheerbot was subjectively perceived by staff as useful and acceptable as a wellbeing aid. In addition to frequency counts for the robot metadata and quantitative questionnaire responses, we conducted simple thematic analysis of the qualitative questionnaire responses, observations including mini-interviews, and focus groups. We then interpreted the data with reference to the Almere model [11]. Whilst the Almere model has primarily been used for research on the acceptability of assistive robots in older adults, it usefully identifies variables that can affect whether a robot is accepted by a target user group in general. We found it particularly useful as its foundations in the Unified Theory of Acceptance and Use of Technology (UTAUT) means it emphasises the role of robots as social agents and their acceptability as connected to the context-specific interactions users have with them. This aligns with our interest in Cheerbot as an interactive, communal aid for workplace wellbeing. We do not employ the Almere model for predictive capacity but draw on its constructs and their relationships to inform our assessment of Cheerbot.

4.3 Factors Affecting the Acceptability of Cheerbot

The Almere model describes eleven constructs, which have the potential to determine the use, or intention to use, a system. Of these, seven are direct determinants: Perceived

Usefulness, Perceived Ease of Use, Perceived Enjoyment, Trust, Attitude, Social Influence, and Facilitating Conditions. A further four indirect determinants connect to direct determinants: Anxiety, Perceived Sociability, Perceived Social Presence, and Perceived Adaptivity. We present our initial findings as they relate to the seven direct determinants and mention the four indirect ones where relevant. We include data summaries and illustrative direct quotes from questionnaire participants (QP), focus group participants (FP) and observation participants (OP).

Facilitating Conditions. This refers to factors in the environment that facilitate use of the system. The layout of desks and other furniture in the two offices facilitated the easy movement of Cheerbot, as did our advance mapping. The positive attitude of management encouraged the use of Cheerbot and we only received two calls for technical support. However, we discovered obstacles to use, such as the introductory information we had sent had not being widely shared or read. Also, areas of weak signal strength in the guest Wi-Fi network meant Cheerbot could not work fully in parts of both offices.

Attitude. This relates to positive and negative feelings about the appliance of the technology. Almost all staff we spoke to during the focus groups and mini-interviews expressed some degree of positivity towards Cheerbot. For instance, all eight focus group participants agreed with the statements: *I think Cheerbot aided my feelings of wellbeing in the workplace; I think Cheerbot aided (some of) my colleagues' feelings of wellbeing in the workplace;* and *I think that (with some changes) Cheerbot could be a useful wellbeing aid in workplaces.* In another example, QP4 wrote: '*I saw a lot of smiles and laughter when people saw the Cheerbot moving around. The games gave people a good break from work and something to talk about.*' However, staff in our focus groups also expressed caveats that Cheerbot's novelty may wear off, and that more features would be needed to ensure it had a long-term positive impact.

Staff self-selected to engage with the research and it is likely that those who choose to speak to us tended to also be more positive about Cheerbot. However, we did elicit some negative attitudes. These connected to a general dislike of technology, confusion over why Cheerbot was there, finding Cheerbot too noisy, and concerns that it collected personal data. For instance: QP5 '*I try to avoid using tech*' and OP34 '*Worries?... I thought it collected some data. I didn't really read the documents.*' Some of these negative attitudes connect to the indirect construct, Anxiety.

Trust. Trust refers to the belief that the system performs with integrity and reliability. We observed a large proportion of staff interacting with Cheerbot, with certain staff engaging multiple times. This indicates trust. However, Anxiety that Cheerbot was collecting personal data indicated a degree of lack of trust. Some staff felt it was '*a spy*' recording their conversations and '*sending them back to management*' (OP2). Some even used aliases rather than real names in the leaderboard for the video game. A few staff avoided interacting with Cheerbot at all, indicating a possible total lack of trust.

Perceived Ease of Use. This relates to the extent to which it is believed the system can be used without effort. Several participants commented that Cheerbot was a little difficult to use at first but became easier with familiarity. We observed that some staff members became 'experts' at using Cheerbot and demonstrated it to others. Interacting with Cheerbot in an open plan office was also a 'public' experience so perceived difficulties in use could also contribute to Anxiety. The robot's low height also presented difficulties for taller members of staff, who had to stoop or crouch to use it.

Perceived Enjoyment. The Perceived Enjoyment observed towards Cheerbot related to staff enjoying it as a *'good break from work'* (OP1) and *'amusing'* (OP31). In addition to connecting to positive Attitude this also linked to the indirect constructs of Social Presence, the extent to which the robot is experienced as a social entity when interacting with it, and Perceived Sociability, the perceived ability of the robot to perform sociable behaviours. Staff used Cheerbot collaboratively and as means to initiate interactions with others. For instance, they explored the functions of Cheerbot together, 'walked' Cheerbot over to each other to start up new encounters and observed each other when playing the video game. OP28 commented that they enjoyed watching people play the game and liked that it encouraged *'friendly competition'* amongst staff.

Social Influence. This refers to a person's perception that people who are important to them think that they should or should not use the system. We observed that individuals often encouraged their colleagues to try out the Cheerbot, helping some overcome reluctance to use it. Conversely, some were concerned about potential mandatory use of Cheerbot, emphasising that it should remain optional, and that people should be able to send it away when not wanted. In the focus groups some participants speculated that management may disapprove of 'overuse' of Cheerbot if it appeared to be a distraction.

Perceived Usefulness. This construct relates to the extent to which a person believes the system would be assistive. In addition to being positive about Cheerbot's current capacity to assist with feelings of wellbeing, when asked about further features that could be added to Cheerbot, staff were most often positive about its Perceived Adaptivity. They suggested Cheerbot additions including: wishing staff a happy birthday; congratulating staff on workplace achievements; sending messages between colleagues; sharing information about workplace clubs; giving reminders to take a break; facilitating quizzes and competitions; initiating conversations, and carrying items, such as snacks. Once again, staff emphasised that this Perceived Usefulness was contingent on individuals being able to opt in or out of use, particularly where personal data collection was required. They also indicated that the Usefulness of Cheerbot would be increased when its activities were more closely integrated with company activities. This would counteract potential management disapproval of its use.

5 Discussion

Our emerging findings suggest that Cheerbot has the potential to positively influence workplace wellbeing. Its community-focused design was acknowledged in staff perceptions that it brought people together and it was referred to by staff as both enjoyable and useful. Whilst these factors suggest Cheerbot may be accepted by users, further work is needed to address causes of negative attitudes, anxiety and lack of trust that may hinder acceptance. Study participants suggested a range of further additions to Cheerbot that could enhance its perceived usefulness and capacity for sustained impact. Interestingly, many of the suggested additional activities are based on personalisation and would require Cheerbot to collect and store personal user data. This moves away from the original preference of our co-design participants. It also suggests a possible tension with the concerns expressed by some that data collected by Cheerbot might be used for workplace surveillance. Alternatively, however, it may be that staff would be willing to accept the use of their data if the usefulness - and their enjoyment - of Cheerbot is maximised. In either case, our participants emphasised that staff should be able to choose how they interact with Cheerbot and how it uses their data. This points to 'perceived user control' as an additional factor for the acceptance of Cheerbot as a workplace wellbeing aid.

Acknowledgments. This study was funded by the projects Horizon: Trusted Data Driven Projects [EP/T022493/1] and Made Smarter Innovation Centre for P-LD [EP/V062041/1].

Disclosure of Interests

PC-S is a director and co-founder of Robotics for Good, a Community Interest Company. The other authors have no competing interests to declare.

References

1. World Health Organization: WHO Guidelines on Mental Health at Work. World Health Organization, Geneva (2022)
2. Department of health and social care: wellbeing and health. GOV.UK (2013)
3. Wood, G.: The Psychology of Wellbeing, 1st edn. Routledge, London (2020)
4. Waddel, G., Burton, A.K.: Is Work Good for your Health and Wellbeing? The Stationery Office (2006)
5. Burke, R.J., Page, K.M.: Research Handbook on Work and Well-being. Edward Elgar Publishing, Cheltenham (UK) and Northampton (USA) (2017)
6. Aryanti, R.D., Sari, E.Y.D., Widiana, H.S.: A literature review of workplace Well-being. In: Proceedings of International Conference on Community Development (ICCD 2020), pp. 605–609. Atlantis Press (2020)
7. Calvo, R.A., Peters, D.: Positive Computing: Technology for Wellbeing and Human Potential. MIT press, Massachusetts (2014)
8. García, S., Strüber, D., Brugali, D., Berger, T., Pelliccione, P.: Robotics software engineering: a perspective from the service robotics domain. In: Proceedings of the 28th ACM Joint Meeting on European Software Engineering Conference and Symposium on the Foundations of Software Engineering, pp. 593–604 (2020)
9. Dode, P., Greig, M., Zolfaghari, S., Neumann, W.P.: Integrating human factors into discrete event simulation: a proactive approach to simultaneously design for system performance and employees' well being. Int. J. Prod. Res. **54**(10), 3105–3117 (2016)
10. temi homepage: https://www.robotemi.com. Accessed 12 June 2025
11. Heerink, M., Kröse, B., Evers, V., Wielinga, B.: Assessing acceptance of assistive social agent technology by older adults: the Almere model. Int. J. Soc. Robot. **2**, 361–375 (2010)

Wearable Social Robots in Space

Tamara Siegmann(✉) and Oliver Bendel

FHNW School of Business, 5210 Windisch, Switzerland
tamara.siegmann@students.fhnw.ch

Abstract. Social robots have been developed on Earth since the 1990s. This article shows that they can also provide added value in space – particularly on a manned flight to Mars. The focus in this paper is on wearable social robots, which seem to be an obvious type due to their small size and low weight. First, the environment and situation of the astronauts are described. Then, using AIBI as an example, it is shown how it fits into these conditions and requirements and what tasks it can perform. Possible further developments and improvements of a wearable social robot are also mentioned in this context. It becomes clear that a model like AIBI is well suited to accompany astronauts on a Mars flight. However, further developments and improvements in interaction and communication are desirable before application.

Keywords: Social Robots · Wearable Social Robots · Space

1 Introduction

Flying to Mars is one of the greatest challenges facing human spaceflight. There are many technical and logistical factors such as propulsion systems, the duration of the journey (up to nine months for the outbound leg and up to three years for the return [9]), and radiation exposure [8]. In addition, social and psychological aspects play a particularly critical role [12]. Isolation, stress, confinement, monotony, and communication delays of up to 24 min [22] can significantly affect the coexistence and well-being of astronauts [27].

Elon Musk, with his company SpaceX, based in California, is planning a crewed Mars mission around the year 2030, as advertised on his website (https://www.spacex.com/humanspaceflight/mars/). While his announcements and timelines are viewed with caution by experts, it is nonetheless likely that a crewed mission to Mars – initiated by him, other private actors, or governmental agencies – will occur within the next 10 to 20 years [15]. Accordingly, preparations must be undertaken across the various disciplines and applications involved in space exploration, including robotics and social robotics.

Robots have been used since the early days of space exploration, for tasks such as assembly and maintenance [1]. Lunar and Mars rovers have become standard equipment [3]. Since the early 2000s, humanoid robots have gained increasing attention [14]. NASA's Robonaut is designed to replicate human movements and operate tools [1].

Valkyrie is intended to assist during flight or to welcome humans on other planets [24]. The free-floating, spherical robot, Cimon, is the first AI-enabled assistant to interact directly with astronauts [10]. In 2021, the second author of this article and his student developed SPACE THEA, a voice assistant prototype for a Mars mission capable of expressing empathy and emotion [26]. In addition to such disembodied companions, very small, lightweight robots – such as wearable social robots – are particularly well suited to space environments [4, 30].

According to Guitton [12], social robots can serve as training partners for astronauts and help mitigate loneliness. They could be programmed as immersive role-playing systems to enable realistic social interactions. The author highlights the benefits of using social robots in space: astronauts are already familiar with robotic systems, so their presence is uncontroversial. They can be used for various social tasks, consume few resources, are technically feasible due to existing AI technologies, and can be maintained and repaired by engineers.

This article aims to answer the following research question based on these foundations: How can wearable social robots be used on a crewed Mars mission? Sect. 2 presents a literature review to provide insight into the spacecraft environment and conditions. Sect. 3 discusses how a robot such as AIBI meets the demands of a Mars flight and proposes possible extensions or improvements. Sect. 4 concludes with a summary and outlook.

2 General Conditions on Board

SpaceX's Starship is expected to be used for a crewed Mars mission within the next ten to twenty years. The spacecraft itself is approximately 50 m in length, with a diameter of about 9 m. The full launch system stands 120 m high and consists of the Super Heavy launch vehicle and the Starship upper stage, which also functions as the landing vehicle. After landing on Mars, the Super Heavy booster remains in Earth orbit or returns to Earth, while the Starship conducts the transit to and landing on Mars [29]. The following describes the spacecraft's layout, as well as working and living conditions on board.

- The Starship upper stage is divided into functional sections. It includes standard electrical outlets, such as 28-V DC sockets common in space systems. This allows commercially available small devices to be charged – provided they are compatible with this voltage or used with an appropriate converter [6].
- The onboard temperature typically ranges from 18 to 26.7° Celsius, with relative humidity between 25 and 70%. Both are regulated by the life support system [11]. Lighting conditions are adjusted based on work and rest cycles. Crew members can modify the brightness to support individual circadian rhythms. Energy-efficient LED lamps are installed, offering adjustable color temperatures to help simulate day-night cycles [28].
- During transit, microgravity prevails, as the spacecraft does not accelerate continuously. All loose objects must be secured using Velcro, brackets, or nets. Cables and switches are typically shielded to prevent accidental operation or damage [13].

- Communication with Earth is maintained via radio connection. Depending on the Mars-Earth distance, signal delays range from 4 to 24 min one way [22]. Image transmission is technically possible, though currently limited in quality and speed due to bandwidth constraints. NASA is testing near-infrared laser communications to increase resolution and data rates in the future [20].
- Astronauts are trained for specialized tasks – such as engineering, medicine, or biosciences – but must also be generalists, as isolation demands flexibility and role-sharing in emergencies. They undergo comprehensive training and extensive psychological and cognitive testing to ensure resilience during long-duration missions [21].
- Most of the crew's time is spent in designated workspaces and sleeping quarters. Sleeping arrangements consist of individual bunks, typically with sleeping bags fixed to the wall to prevent drifting. Where possible, separate private areas are provided for men and women [7]. Toilets operate using a vacuum system to safely collect and store waste [19].
- On board, astronauts wear intravehicular activity suits made from lightweight, breathable fabric. Longer hair is usually tied back to prevent it from floating freely. Some crew members shave their heads before or during missions, as visible in NASA photos from the ISS (https://www.nasa.gov/international-space-station/space-station-gallery/).
- The crew members meet regularly to coordinate activities and support psychological cohesion. Personal relationships are permitted under strict codes of conduct. While sexual activity is theoretically possible, privacy, space, and hygiene are limited, and there is little medical data on sexuality in microgravity [25].
- Astronauts can communicate with family and partners via text messages or pre-recorded video, but not in real time. Their schedules are usually well structured, with clearly defined work and rest periods to maintain circadian rhythm and ensure mission efficiency [16].

There are a lot of other aspects to this, but most of them are not relevant to the use of a wearable social robot.

3 A Wearable Social Robot on Board

3.1 Fundamentals of Wearable Social Robots

Wearable social robots can be categorized as a subset of wearable robots, i.e., robots or robotic components that are worn, carried, or contained [4, 18]. In this respect, they differ significantly from the usual models made of hard materials, i.e., high-tech prostheses and exoskeletons, which are aimed at disabled or healthy people [2, 4]. On the other hand, wearable social robots are social robots that can be understood as sensorimotor machines intended for humans or animals [5]. They are characterized by the dimensions of interaction and communication with living beings, proximity to living beings, representation of (characteristics of) living beings, and benefit for living beings [5]. Artificial intelligence (AI) is integrated into some wearable social robots, for example, in the form of facial recognition or generative AI, especially large language models (LLMs). In the following, the AIBI model is used as a typical representative of a wearable social robot. Its actual functions are included – but also possible functions that an adapted AIBI or similar models could have.

AIBI, from the Chinese company LivingAI, is marketed as the world's smallest AI robot, measuring 66.70 mm in height and 48.80 mm in width at the head (https://living.ai). It is designed not only to function as a desktop robot (like Eilik or Emo), but also as a wearable social robot that can be worn around the neck or attached to clothing. It costs between $250 and $270 [2]. It is controlled and enhanced via an app and has a battery life of 2 h. It is white, very light, has rounded surfaces and a head with a display showing animated eyes, objects and processes of all kinds, and sits on a rigid magnetic body with immobile arms. The arms hold the robot in place in certain situations, such as in a jacket pocket. When not worn, it stands on a charging station on which it can rotate 360°. A necklace with a metal surface and metal plates for attaching to clothing are included, as well as a coat and costumes (extensions for the head and body). AIBI has a touch sensor on its head and a wave sensor that enables it to recognize people from a distance, and an HD camera and three microphones for spatial hearing. It can understand and execute voice commands, speak for itself and be connected to ChatGPT. AIBI can be 'fed' via the app. Games such as chess and Battleship are also available.

3.2 Possible Functions of AIBI on Board

A wearable social robot like AIBI could be usefully integrated into the environment and daily routines of a crewed Mars mission. Thanks to its small size and light weight, it fits easily into tight spacecraft spaces and can be taken along without effort when moving between modules and vehicles. Each crew member can wear it around the neck or attach it to their body – e.g., to intravehicular activity suits – without inconveniencing the wearer or others, taking up valuable space, or drifting away. Its display ensures visibility even in low-light conditions. AIBI is technically compatible with standard onboard power systems: it can be charged via 28-V DC connections or USB. While its battery life is limited to approximately two hours, this can be compensated for through regular recharging at a designated station, as would be standard practice in a microgravity environment.

Due to the significant communication delay and limited connectivity on a mission to Mars, it is essential that social robots like AIBI are capable of operating offline. Its core functions do not rely on a continuous internet connection, making it well-suited for autonomous deployment in space. If a local hotspot is established with access to an onboard server, AIBI or an adapted model can also be connected to certain chatbots to enable more complex dialogue capabilities. In the future, integrating open-source models like LLaMA or Mistral could enhance autonomy by reducing dependence on OpenAI and allowing greater control over prompt engineering and system customization.

The AIBI app can be used to plan daily routines, set reminders, and organize tasks. The wearable social robot is capable of providing both technical and organizational information, and it can read aloud technical instructions while the user is working on a system or piece of equipment. It also has the potential to offer motivational support [26]. With the integration of multimodal large language models (MLLMs), the robot could assist in recognizing specific system malfunctions. Equipping it with prompt engineering capabilities and enhancing it through retrieval-augmented generation (RAG) – e.g., by accessing spacecraft-related documentation – would further expand its utility in operational contexts.

In an environment marked by isolation, stress, confinement, monotony, and psychological strain, AIBI is capable of simulating empathy and emotional expression, similar to the SPACE THEA concept [26]. Through spoken language, reactive behaviors, and the display of emotions via sound and visual cues, it generates a form of affective interaction that may be particularly valuable during extended space missions [23]. It can be cared for like a small pet without generating high expectations or imposing significant demands – evoking associations with the Tamagotchi [17]. The ability to alter its appearance through optional "disguises", such as resembling a cat or a rabbit, can further strengthen emotional attachment. For some astronauts, the robot may become a daily personal companion, helping to mitigate feelings of loneliness and reducing stress or anxiety [2].

Equipped with a range of sensors – including a camera, a touch sensor, and multiple microphones – AIBI can respond to touch, voice commands, and gestures. For example, it reacts to touches in the head area with head movements and cute sounds. Its wave sensor also enables spatial awareness, for instance, by detecting when another crew member is approaching and orienting itself accordingly. With the integration of an MLLM, it is even conceivable that AIBI could interpret emotional states by analyzing vocal tone or facial expressions. To increase performance, additional emotion recognition systems could be used, which would also run on the local server. In this capacity, it could function as a low-threshold feedback system, capable of detecting signs of stress or emotional distress and – albeit with some delay – providing descriptive feedback and assessments to the astronaut or to experts on Earth.

AIBI also presents potential applications in addressing intimacy-related needs. In contrast to the mentioned social robot, Eilik, it does not feature a vibration motor, or other mechanical components designed for physical stimulation [2]. However, it can respond to suggestive language and haptic input. In carefully controlled contexts – such as designated private or retreat areas – this functionality could contribute to managing intimacy needs without disrupting group dynamics. To ensure responsible use, clear ethical guidelines and usage protocols are required to define the boundaries between supportive interaction and misuse. Given the limitations of models like GPT-4o in handling erotic content, integration with open-source large language models may be advantageous. The addition of physical feedback mechanisms, such as vibration or suction, could also be considered as a potential enhancement [2].

Finally, AIBI can also enhance communication both on board and with Earth. It can function as a conversational partner, translator, and game companion [2]. Beyond the previously mentioned games, it would be beneficial to include modern, space-themed games as well as multiplayer games that reflect the diverse cultural backgrounds of the crew, fostering mutual understanding and appreciation. As a small presence in team meetings, AIBI can contribute by moderating discussions or easing social tension. In this role – and perhaps precisely because of its technical limitations – it may act as a kind of social catalyst, mediating between technology, humans, and their environment.

Other areas of application are also conceivable, such as training and simulation (which Guitton has already mentioned [12]), emergency support, documentation and observation (including diary functions), personalized cognitive support (such as concentration training or memory exercises), and (in addition to the games mentioned) cultural and identity support. For reasons of space, these cannot be explained further here.

The research question has been addressed in this section. Overall, the findings indicate that a wearable social robot like AIBI could serve far more than the role of a mere novelty or toy on a crewed Mars mission. It has the potential to function as a multifaceted tool that integrates emotional support, social facilitation, and technical assistance – making it an asset in addressing the complex demands of long-duration interplanetary travel. At the same time, targeted enhancements and further technological development would be advisable to fully realize its potential.

4 Summary and Outlook

Using the example of AIBI, this article has demonstrated that wearable social robots represent a promising approach to supporting astronauts on a crewed Mars mission. In an environment defined by isolation, stress, confinement, communication delays, social complexity, and psychological strain, such robots can offer a constant, reliable source of interaction and attention. AIBI integrates emotional responsiveness, playful engagement, and technical support within a compact and adaptable form. Its small size and its multifunctionality enable seamless integration into the daily routines of a space crew. In contrast to the SPACE THEA concept [26], AIBI provides a physical presence that can be beneficial in various ways – particularly in terms of sensory perception and tactile interaction. As a wearable social robot, it can be carried by any astronaut at any time and in any place.

Concurrently, it is evident that the full potential of such robots has yet to be realized. Enhancements such as extended battery life, improved offline functionality, multilingual interaction modes, context-sensitive emotional responses, and culturally adaptive content could significantly increase their effectiveness and applicability. Features for early psychological detection and personalized support may also offer valuable contributions. Furthermore, integration with specialized, including open-source, large language models, should be explored to enable greater flexibility in addressing specific conversational demands.

The use of wearable social robots in space is still at an early stage. However, the necessary technological foundations already exist, and the specific demands of space missions make their deployment not only conceivable, but increasingly likely. In the long term, such systems could become an integral component of crewed missions – particularly those to Mars – not as a replacement for human interaction and cooperation, but as a meaningful complement under the unique conditions of space.

References

1. Ambrose, R.O., Aldridge, H., Askewet, R.S., et al.: Robonaut: NASA's space humanoid. Humanoid Rob. (2000) https://ieeexplore.ieee.org/stamp/stamp.jsp?tp=&arnumber=867913

2. Bendel, O.: Wearable social robots for the disabled and impaired. In: Proceedings ICSR 2025 International Conference on Social Robotics, pp. 10–12, Naples, Italy
3. Bendel, O.: Rover. Gabler Wirtschaftslexikon (2025). https://wirtschaftslexikon.gabler.de/definition/rover-171449
4. Bendel, O.: Wearable Robots. Gabler Wirtschaftslexikon (2025). https://wirtschaftslexikon.gabler.de/definition/wearable-robots-172088
5. Bendel, O. (ed.): Soziale Roboter: Technikwissenschaftliche, wirtschaftswissenschaftliche, philosophische, psychologische und soziologische Grundlagen. Springer Gabler, Wiesbaden (2021)
6. Brown, C.D.: Elements of Spacecraft Design AIAA Education Series, p. 342. American Institute of Aeronautics and Astronautics (2002)
7. Canadian Space Agency (CSA): Sleeping in Space. Government of Canada (2019). https://www.asc-csa.gc.ca/eng/astronauts/living-in-space/sleeping-in-space.asp
8. Cucinotta, F.A., Schimmerling, W., Wilson, J.W., et al.: Space radiation cancer risks and uncertainties for Mars missions. Radiat. Res. (2001). https://doi.org/10.1667/0033-7587(2001)156[0682:SRCRAU]2.0.CO;2
9. Dobrijevic, D., Tillman, N.T.: How Long Does It Take to Get to Mars? Space.com (2025). https://www.space.com/24701-how-long-does-it-take-to-get-to-mars.html
10. Eisenberg, T.: CIMON, the AI-Powered Robot, Launches a New Era in Space Travel. IBM (2019). https://www.ibm.com/new/announcements/cimon-ai-robot-launches-new-era-space-travel
11. Federal Aviation Administration (FAA): Environmental Control and Life Support Systems for Flight Crew and Space Flight Participants in Suborbital Space Flight. Version 1.0, April 2010. https://www.faa.gov/about/office_org/headquarters_offices/ast/media/final_ECLSS_guide.pdf
12. Guitton, M.J.: Robots as social companions for space exploration. Artif. Hum. (2025) https://www.sciencedirect.com/science/article/pii/S2949882125000088
13. Ganse, B., Ganse, U.: Das kleine Handbuch für angehende Raumfahrer. Springer Nature (2017). https://doi.org/10.1007/978-3-662-54411-2
14. Hall, L.: NASA Space Robotics Challenge Prepares Robots for the Journey to Mars. NASA (2016). https://www.nasa.gov/directorates/stmd/game-changing-development-program/nasa-space-robotics-challenge-prepares-robots-for-the-journey-to-mars/
15. Hrinko, I.: Elon Musk Announces Date for First Manned Mission to Mars. Universe Space Tech (2024). https://universemagazine.com/en/elon-musk-announces-date-for-first-manned-mission-to-mars/
16. Johnson, P.J.: The roles of NASA, U.S. astronauts, and their families in long-duration missions. In: On Orbit and beyond (2012). https://doi.org/10.1007/978-3-642-30583-2_4
17. Kühne, K., Jeglinski-Mende, M.A., Bendel, O.: Tamagotchi on our couch: are social robots perceived as pets? In: Proceedings of Robophilosophy 2022: Social Robots in Social Institutions, pp. 755–759. IOS Press, Amsterdam (2022)
18. Matsunaga, N., Shiomi, M.: Does a wearing change perception toward a robot? In: Proceedings of the 30th IEEE International Conference on Robot & Human Interactive Communication (RO-MAN), pp. 963–968. IEEE, Vancouver, BC, Canada (2021). https://doi.org/10.1109/RO-MAN50785.2021.9515366
19. McKinley, M., Borrego, M., et al.: NASA universal waste management system and toilet integration hardware operations on ISS – issues, modifications and accomplishments. In: 51st International Conference on Environmental Systems (2022). https://ntrs.nasa.gov/api/citations/20220005710/downloads/NASA%20Universal%20Waste%20Management%20System%20and%20Toilet%20Integration%20Hardware%20%20Operations%20on%20ISS%20Issues%2C%20Modifications%20and%20Accomplishments%202022%20final%20draft.pdf

20. NASA: Deep Space Optical Comm Demo Sends and Receives First Data. NASA (2023). https://www.nasa.gov/missions/psyche-mission/nasas-deep-space-optical-comm-demo-sends-receives-first-data/
21. Norberg, C.: Astronaut selection and training. In: Human Spaceflight and Exploration (2013). https://doi.org/10.1007/978-3-642-23725-6_7
22. Ormston, T.: Time Delay between Mars and Earth. ESA (2012). https://blogs.esa.int/mex/2012/08/05/time-delay-between-mars-and-earth/
23. Patel, N.V.: An emotionally intelligent AI could support astronauts on a trip to Mars. MIT Technol. Rev. (2020). https://www.technologyreview.com/2020/01/14/64990/an-emotionally-intelligent-ai-could-support-astronauts-on-a-trip-to-mars/
24. Rayanovskyi, A.: NASA Tests Humanoid Robot Valkyrie for Use on the Moon. The Gaze (2023). https://thegaze.media/news/nasa-tests-humanoid-robot-valkyrie-for-use-on-the-moon
25. Santaguida, M., Dubé, S.: Sexual health in space: a 5-year scoping review. Curr. Sex. Health Rep. (2023). https://doi.org/10.1007/s11930-023-00368-9
26. Spathelf, M., Bendel, O.: The SPACE THEA project. In: Proceedings of the AAAI 2022 Spring Symposium how Fair Is Fair? Achieving Wellbeing AI. Stanford University, Stanford, California, USA (2022). https://ceur-ws.org/Vol-3276/
27. Taraba, M., Zwintz, K., Bombardelli, C., et al.: Project M^3—a study for a manned Mars Mission in 2031. Acta Astronaut., 88–104 (2006). https://doi.org/10.1016/j.actaastro.2005.04.013
28. Wagner, A.: NASA Research Boosts LED Lamps for Home and Garden. NASA (2021). https://www.nasa.gov/missions/station/nasa-research-boosts-led-lamps-for-home-and-garden/
29. Wilken, J., Sippel, M., et al.: Critical analysis of SpaceX's next generation space transportation system: starship and super heavy. In: 2nd International Conference on High-Speed Vehicle Science Technology (HiSST) (2022). https://elib.dlr.de/188531/1/HiSST-2022_Critical_Analysis_of_SpaceX%27s_Next_Generation_Space_Transportation_System_Starship_and_Super_Heavy.pdf
30. Zhu, M., Biswas, S., Dinulescu, S.I., et al.: Soft, wearable robotics and Haptics: technologies, trends, and emerging applications. Proc. IEEE. **110**(2), 246–272 (2022). https://doi.org/10.1109/JPROC.2021.3140049

Attitudes Toward AI: The Role of Gender, Age, and Smartwatch Ownership

Kimmo J. Vänni[1,2(✉)], Erika Tanhua-Piiroinen[2], Antti Syvänen[2], and Jarmo Viteli[2]

[1] HAMK University, Tech Unit, Vankanlähde 9, 13100 Hämeenlinna, Finland
kimmo.vanni@hamk.fi

[2] Research Centre for Communication Sciences, Tampere University, Tampere, Finland
{erika.tanhua-piiroinen,antti.syvanen,jarmo.viteli}@tuni.fi

Abstract. Artificial Intelligence (AI) is currently a widely debated topic. A key issue is whether people can trust AI and its outputs. It is well documented that social robots utilize both embodied and embedded AI. However, directly studying trust in these technologies can be challenging. Therefore, we examined whether factors such as age, gender, perceived competence, work experience, and ownership of smartwatches are associated with users' attitudes toward AI in general. The results indicate that gender, smartwatch ownership, and age may be relevant factors influencing these attitudes.

Keywords: AI · trust · smartwatch · usage

1 Introduction

Artificial Intelligence (AI) is a term that currently appears in nearly every discussion about emerging technologies and future societal trends. Various initiatives highlight how AI is expected to create new services and assist people in their daily lives [1]. In particular, Embodied AI [2, 3] and Embedded AI [4] have been central concepts in the development of social robotics, playing a key role since its early stages.

Embodied AI, integrating sensory feedback, motor control systems, and situated interactions—has enabled social robots to adapt to diverse social contexts and environments, laying the foundation for socially intelligent behavior. Embedded AI, on the other hand, refers to on-board intelligence that allows social robots to process data, interpret human emotions, and generate appropriate responses locally and in real time, avoiding the latency often associated with cloud-based systems. There are several examples of embodied and/or embedded AI. A relevant example is iCub [5], by the Italian Institute of Technology (IIT), which was created to assess embodied cognition by enabling the robot to learn about the world through touch and manipulation. Another notable example is the PARO seal by AIST, which uses embedded AI to recognize light, sound, temperature, posture, and touch, and thus interacting with users in emotional and therapeutic ways [6]. These examples illustrate how embodied and embedded AI have been used in social robotics to engage with humans.

© The Author(s), under exclusive license to Springer Nature Singapore Pte Ltd. 2026
M. Staffa et al. (Eds.): ICSR+AI 2025, LNAI 16131, pp. 470–475, 2026.
https://doi.org/10.1007/978-981-95-2379-5_34

The common denominator of these concepts and social robots is Artificial Intelligence (AI), which remains a widely debated topic. Although our daily lives are increasingly supported and enhanced by AI across various services, most ordinary citizens are unaware that many of these services are at least partially powered by AI. For instance, personalized content recommendations in streaming platforms, route optimization in navigation apps, and facial recognition in social media and smartphones all rely on AI. There are countless examples of AI-powered applications, and typically, only a few people argue that AI is harmful or unsuitable for their use.

One common concern among users is that they do not know what information AI-based systems are collecting about them, or how that information is used, processed, manipulated, and shared. Another concern involves data ownership and how individuals can prevent their personal data from being used by AI systems. At the core of these concerns is the issue of trust in AI [7, 8], which often stems from the prevalent "black box" nature of these systems [9], where the decision-making processes are opaque, and users cannot understand or trace how outcomes are generated. It is well established that perceived usefulness and perceived ease of use, the core elements of the Technology Acceptance Model (TAM) [10], are important factors in the acceptance of social robots [11], along with the robot's physical appearance [12]. However, we argue that trust in AI is an increasingly critical factor influencing the acceptance and adoption of any human-interactive robots, including social robots.

Currently, there are ongoing research projects focusing on developing the opposite of the 'black box' approach, i.e., the white-box approach [13, 14], where the decision-making process is visible and even modifiable, and the output of AI is transparent and trackable [15]. The white-box approach is likely to increase users' commitment and trust. We state that it is cumbersome to study users' attitudes towards embodied AI because users may not realize when they use AI. Therefore, we were studying users' attitudes towards AI in general, and especially use of smart watches, which are widely used and can be linked to embodied AI of user-centered robots.

2 Methods

The aim of the study was to assess whether various factors, such as age, gender, perceived competence, work experience, and ownership of a smartwatch, are associated with users' attitudes toward AI-software supported smartwatches and AI in general. We conducted a large-scale online survey with a total of 38 questions and 119 items focusing on perceived technostress, which also included five questions and 22 items about attitudes toward AI and its use. The questionnaire also included questions about hybrid work and five questions with 18 items focusing on the use of smartwatches. The greatest part of the questionnaire was based on the previously validated technostress survey [16]. The novel AI questions were pre-tested, and their internal consistencies were assessed (Cronbach's Alpha >0.72 in every question). The greatest part of questions used the Likert scale from 1 to 5. The respondents were Finnish office employees from two cities, representing a variety of professions across sectors such as education, municipal government, and IT services. The total number of respondents was 542 (men 88, women 454). The mean age of the participants was 45.7 years (SD = 11.5), and the average duration in their current

Table 1. Frequency of using AI among men and women

	Men	Women
Mean	3,27	2,63
SD	1,75	1,66
Obs.	88	454
df	116	
t Stat	3,22	
P(T < =t)	0,002	
t Critical	1,98	

Table 2. Age of smartwatch users

	No Smart-watch	Smart-watch
Mean	45.9	45.5
SD	11.75	11.20
Obs.	278	264
df	540	
t Stat	0.37	
P(T < =t)	0.71	
t Critical	1.96	

position was 8.3 years (SD = 9.6). All participants provided informed consent to take part in the study. The questionnaire was constructed with the Webropol survey online tool.

3 Results

We studied whether gender is a significant factor in the use and perception of AI. Participants were asked how well they can manage AI programs such as ChatGPT and how frequently they use AI tools at work. Additionally, we assessed the emotional responses, both negative and positive, that the increasing use of AI may evoke, as well as how reliable respondents consider the results produced by AI and smart devices. A Likert scale from 1 to 5 was used for most questions, except for perceived feelings, which were measured on a scale from 0 to 10. T-tests and correlation analyses were used as the primary methods.

Men (Mn = 3.08, SD = 1.24) reported better competence in using AI than women (Mn = 2.80, SD = 1.21); t(121) = 1.97, p = .050. Also, the statistically significant difference was found between men and women in perceived frequency of using AI applications. No statistically significant differences were found between men and women regarding perceived feelings about the increased use of AI. Similarly, no significant differences were found in trust toward AI-generated results or the perceived reliability of smartwatches (Table 1).

We also examined whether smartwatch ownership influenced participants' attitudes toward AI. A total of 264 participants (51 men, 213 women) reported owning a smartwatch, while 278 participants (37 men, 241 women) did not. No significant differences were found between smartwatch ownership and participant age, t(540) = 0.37, p = .71 (Table 2), nor in trust toward AI-generated results.

However, participants who owned smartwatches used AI applications more frequently (see Table 3) and demonstrated greater competence with AI programs (see Table 4). Additionally, they had a significantly more positive attitude toward the increasing use of AI in the future (M = 5.40, SD = 2.44) compared to those without smartwatches (M = 4.62, SD = 2.55); t(540) = 3.61, p < .001.

Table 3. Use frequency of AI applications

	Smart watch	No smart watch
Mean	2.95	2.53
SD	1.61	1.63
Obs.	264	278
df	539	
t Stat	3.03	
P(T < =t)	0.0025	
t Critical	1.96	

Table 4. Competence in using AI applications

	Smart watch	No smart watch
Mean	3.05	2.64
SD	1.20	1.21
Obs.	264	278
df	539	
t Stat	3.91	
P(T < =t)	0.0001	
t Critical	1.96	

We also tested whether age, years of work experience, perceived competence, frequency of AI use, emotional response, and trust toward AI are correlated. Table 5 shows that increasing age and years of work experience are negatively associated with perceived competence in using AI applications. As expected, frequency of AI use, positive feelings toward the increasing use of AI, perceived competence, and trust in AI were all significantly correlated with one another.

Table 5. Correlation between some factors concerning use of AI

	Age	Work yrs.	Compet.	Use of AI	Perceived feelings.	Trust
Age	1					
Work yrs.	**0,57***	1				
Competence	**−0,21***	**−0,20***	1			
Use of AI	0,04	−0,04	**0,60***	1		
Perc. Feelings	0,03	−0,07	**0,45***	**0,50***	1	
Trust	−0,02	−0,03	**0,33***	**0,33***	**0,57***	1

N = 542, * p < 0.05

4 Discussion

We state that smartwatches and their use may have future connections to embodied AI and physical entities like social robots, even if smartwatches alone do not constitute embodied AI. However, smartwatch users are qualified to use AI supported analysis software and, according to our study, have better competence to use AI applications than non-smartwatch users. The results also showed that participants who used smartwatches had a more positive attitude toward AI, and they used AI applications more frequently compared to those who did not use smartwatches. However, we were not able to study whether the use of smartwatches and the willingness to use social and collaborative robots are related. Previous studies report that experience with technical devices and applications can reduce the perceived stress of using robots [17]. Therefore, we are suggesting that future research could explore whether smartwatch users are more interested in using social robots and could be considered potential customers for especially social robotics start-up companies [18].

No statistically significant differences were found between genders in attitudes or trust toward AI. However, there were significant differences in perceived competence and frequency of AI application use. Interestingly, a significant negative correlation was observed between respondents' age and their perceived competence in using AI applications. This may relate to general attitudes toward novel technologies and overall information technology skills.

The results of the study should be interpreted with caution because the greatest part of the respondents (n = 167) indicated that they are not using AI applications at work at all, whereas 51 respondents indicated that they are using AI applications every day. The rest of the respondents reported that they are using AI every so often. Another remarkable issue was a distribution between men and women. It is well-known that education, municipal government and health sectors employes more women than men, but in this study the difference was high but comparable to our earlier studies [16]

A limitation of our study was that we were unable to assess trust in AI-generated results produced by physical entities like social robots. Such a study would require many robots available, and the participants should be aware of using robots. However, we state that it is important to study users' attitude toward AI in general before assessing their attitudes toward robots with embedded or embodied AI. Additionally, more advanced statistical analyses, such as regression and factorial analysis, should be conducted. Therefore, we suggest that both pilot research is needed to better understand users' perceptions of AI. We also suggest studying users' perceptions toward embodied and embedded AI in human-robot interaction, for example in rehabilitation cases. We are conducting the second phase of this research by organizing physiological technostress measurements for selected pilot groups, and on that case, we can assess users' perceived attitudes toward AI and robots.

Acknowledgments. This study was funded by the Finnish Work Environment Fund (240121).
Disclosure of Interests
The authors have no competing interests to declare that are relevant to the content of this article.

References

1. Narvaez Rojas, C., Alomia Peñafiel, G.A., Loaiza Buitrago, D.F., Tavera Romero, C.A.: Society 5.0: a Japanese concept for a superintelligent society. Sustainability. **13**(12), 6567 (2021)
2. Liu, Y., et al.: Aligning cyber space with physical world: A comprehensive survey on embodied AI. arXiv. https://arxiv.org/abs/2407.06886 (2024)

3. Paolo, G., Gonzalez-Billandon, J., Kégl, B.: Position: a call for embodied AI. In: Proceedings of the 41st International Conference on Machine Learning Vol. 233, pp. 39493–39508. PMLR (2024)
4. Zhang, Z., Li, J.: A review of artificial intelligence in embedded systems. Micromachines. **14**(5), 897 (2023)
5. Sandini, G., Metta, G., Vernon, D.: The iCub cognitive humanoid robot: an open-system research platform for enactive cognition. In: Lungarella, M., Iida, F., Bongard, J., Pfeifer, R. (eds.) 50 Years of Artificial Intelligence LNCS, vol. vol 4850. Springer, Berlin (2007)
6. Shibata, T., Coughlin, J.F.: Trends of robot therapy with neurological therapeutic seal robot, Paro. MIT Center for Transportation & Logistics Research Paper no. 2014/009. J. Robot. Mechatron. **26**(4) (2014)
7. Afroogh, S., Akbari, A., Malone, E., Kargar, M., Alambeigi, H.: Trust in AI: progress, challenges, and future directions. Humanit. Soc. Sci. Commun. **11**, 1568 (2024)
8. McCormack, L., Bendechache, M.A.: Comprehensive survey and classification of evaluation criteria for trustworthy artificial intelligence. AI Ethics. (2024)
9. Yang, W., Wei, Y., Wei, H., Chen, Y., et al.: Survey on explainable AI: from approaches, limitations and applications aspects. Hum. Cent. Intell. Syst. **3**, 161–188 (2023)
10. Venkatesh, V., Davis, F.D.: A theoretical extension of the technology acceptance model: four longitudinal field studies. Manag. Sci. **46**(2), 186–204 (2000)
11. He, Y., He, Q., Liu, Q.: Technology acceptance in socially assistive robots: scoping review of models, measurement, and influencing factors. J. Healthc. Eng. (2022)
12. Walters, M.L., Syrdal, D.S., Te Dautenhahn, K., Boekhorst, R., Koay, K.L.: Avoiding the uncanny valley: robot appearance, personality and consistency of behavior in an attention-seeking home scenario for a robot companion. Auton. Robot. **24**, 159–178 (2008)
13. Yang, J., et al.: White-Box AI Model: Next Frontier of Wireless Communications. arXiv. Retrieved from: https://arxiv.org/abs/2504.09138 (2025)
14. Chien, S.F., Yoon, C.: Explainable artificial intelligence: a survey of the state of the art. J. AI Res. **68**, 65–108 (2020)
15. Carvalho, D.V., Pereira, E.M., Cardoso, J.S.: Machine learning interpretability: a survey on methods and metrics. IEEE Access. **8**, 220722–220738 (2019)
16. Syvänen, A., Vänni, K., Viteli, J.: Comparison between Technostress instruments among education and health care sectors. In: Salminen, V. (ed.) Human Factors, Business Management and Society. AHFE Open Access, Vol 56. AHFE International, USA (2022)
17. Vänni, K.J., Salin, S.E., Cabibihan, J.J., Kanda, T.: Robostress, a new approach to understanding robot usage, technology, and stress. In: Salichs, M., et al. (eds.) Social Robotics. ICSR 2019 LNCS, vol. 11876. Springer, Cham (2019)
18. Tulli, S., Ambrossio, D., Najjar, A., Rodríguez-Lera, F.: Great expectations & aborted business initiatives: the paradox of social robot between research and industry. In: CEUR Workshop Proceedings, Vol 2491, pp. 1–10 (2019)

Social Robots for Pediatric Asthma Education: A Pilot Study

Katarzyna Pasternak[1(✉)], Cynthia Foronda[2], Charles Downs[2], and Ubbo Visser[1]

[1] Department of Computer Science, University of Miami, Coral Gables 33146, USA
{kwp,visser}@cs.miami.edu
[2] School of Nursing and Health Studies, University of Miami, Coral Gables 33146, USA
{c.foronda,cxd826}@miami.edu

Abstract. Hospital discharge marks a crucial transition point in care, particularly for pediatric asthma patients, where education is essential but often rushed or not delivered properly. To address this challenge, we conducted a pilot study to evaluate the feasibility of using a socially assistive robot to deliver asthma education during pediatric hospital discharge. The system integrates validated educational content into a structured, robot-led dialogue. We evaluated the usability, engagement, and perceived effectiveness of the system. The study involved 11 university students assigned roles simulating a discharge scenario. Results showed that over 78% of participants rated the robot's usability positively, more than 81% found the interaction engaging, and over 90% expressed a favorable attitude toward the robot. All participants reported satisfaction with the educational experience. These initial findings demonstrate the potential of social robots to enhance discharge education for pediatric asthma, supporting better understanding and preparedness among both patients and caregivers.

Keywords: Human Robot Interaction · Social Robotics · Asthma Education · Robotic Hospital Discharge · Nursing

1 Introduction

As healthcare systems increasingly integrate digital and automated technologies to improve efficiency and patient outcomes, the role of social robots in clinical environments is gaining traction. In pediatric care, their engaging and socially intelligent behavior can enhance patient interactions. Pediatric asthma management, in particular, benefits from such support, as effective education at discharge is key to improving long-term outcomes.

Pediatric asthma is a leading chronic condition in children and affects approximately 6.3 million children in the U.S. (8.4%), making it the third leading cause of hospitalizations among children under 15 years [5]. Discharge education plays a critical role in aiding families to manage care at home. Unfortunately, traditional methods are often hindered by time constraints, inconsistent delivery, stress, and limited resources [1]. Socially assistive technologies that offer engaging, personalized, and repeatable interactions may help bridge this gap and reinforce key information during this crucial transition, consequently lowering the rate of readmissions. Our study introduces a Human Support Robot (HSR)[1] developed by Toyota, focusing on its role as an educational robot for pediatric asthma patients. Unlike physical support robots that aid with mobility or invasive medical procedures, our robot operates with no direct physical interaction and minimal disruption to clinical workflow. It delivers pre-programmed, evidence-based content tailored for children and their caregivers in a friendly and accessible way.

2 Related Work

Robots have found their place in hospitals over four decades ago, when first robot-assisted surgery was performed by PUMA 560. Now, they are being further integrated into other aspects of healthcare within hospital workflows [6].

Socially assistive robots have demonstrated potential in pediatric healthcare, where engagement, trust-building, and a non-threatening presence are especially important [8]. Studies show they can reduce anxiety, foster positive emotions, and support therapeutic and educational goals in children [9,11]. They proved useful in pediatric oncology [7], and in the preparation of and during medical procedures [2]. Virtual Agents have also been applied to enhance discharge process and planning [10,12]. This trend aligns with the efforts of robot-led education during discharge, a process which is often rushed and inconsistently delivered.

While these innovations demonstrate the value of social robots and AI in hospital settings, most applications during discharge have focused on tasks like documentation, scheduling, or follow-up—rather than structured, in-person health education. Our pilot study addresses this gap by evaluating the feasibility of a social robot delivering asthma education during the pediatric discharge process.

3 Pilot Study

We conducted a within-subjects pilot study to evaluate the feasibility of using a social robot to deliver pediatric asthma education during the hospital discharge process. The study involved simulated patient-caregiver interactions guided by a robot, incorporating expert-developed educational content (IRB no. 20250406).

3.1 Educational Content and Interaction Design

The educational materials delivered by the robot were developed using a combination of resources from the National Heart, Lung, and Blood Institute (NHLBI),

---

[1] The robot specification can be found here: https://global.toyota/en/detail/8709541..

Asthma Academy [4], and insights gathered from in-person visits to an outpatient pediatric pulmonology clinic and expert consultations. The content was delivered using a combination of gestures, speech, and videos presented on the robot's screen.

The robot followed a scripted educational sequence designed to simulate the hospital discharge process. The interaction began with the robot receiving patient information - first and last name, date of birth, and prescribed medication/treatment - from a nurse and confirmed its accuracy upon meeting the patient in the treatment room. Once confirmed, the robot introduced itself and explained that it would provide the asthma education.

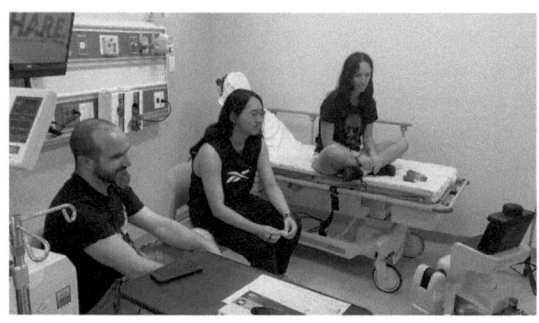

Fig. 1. Study setup in the SHARE with (from the left) two caregivers and the patient.

The robot-led session included five components: (1) Asthma pathophysiology - a video with an expert explanation; (2) Medication overview - verbal and visual explanation of medication types; (3) Inhaler use technique - video presentation followed by a guided demonstration; (4) Asthma action plan - handover of a printed plan with a brief explanation; and (5) Discharge reminders - verbal review of next steps. The session took place in the environment shown in Fig. 1. The HSR robot is visible in the bottom right corner.

3.2 Study Procedure

The study was conducted over two days at the University of Miami's Simulation Hospital (SHARE) with 11 university students (ages 22–49). Participants were randomly assigned to roles: patient, parent, or observer. Sessions were recorded using two cameras to capture video and audio for later analysis.

After informed consent, participants read brief role descriptions and were introduced to the task. Following the interaction, they completed a questionnaire adapted from the Artificial Social Agent (ASA) Questionnaire [3]. The ASA tool developed by Fitrianie et al. is a valid and reliable instrument for evaluating human interaction with artificial social agents ($r = 0.80 - 0.93$ across constructs). The tool comprises 90 items across 19 measurement constructs (in its long version). In this study, we used a subset of items, measuring selected three domains relevant to our study: (AU) *agent usability*, (UE) *user engagement*, and (AT) *attitude toward the agent* as presented in Table 1. An additional item (E1) assessed educational satisfaction. The responses were collected on a 5-point Likert scale, raging from –2 (strongly disagree) to 2 (strongly agree).

Table 1. Average Likert-scale responses for robot-assisted asthma education (N = 11; $\bar{x}$ and σ).

Survey Question	Avg. Response
(AU1) The robot is easy to use.	0.91 (1.140)
(AU2) Learning to work with the robot is easy.	1.27 (0.90)
(AU3) Learning how to communicate with the robot is quick.	1.36 (0.67)
(UE1) I/The user was concentrated during the interaction.	1.00 (0.63)
(UE2) The interaction captured my/user's attention.	1.18 (0.75)
(UE3) I/The user was alert during the interaction.	1.18 (0.98)
(AT1) I see the interaction with the robot as something positive.	1.36 (0.67)
(AT2) I view the interaction as something favorable.	1.36 (0.67)
(AT3) I think negatively of the interaction. (Reversed)	−1.45 (0.69)
(E1) I am satisfied with the educational experience.	1.36 (0.50)

Finally, participants were given the opportunity to provide open-ended feedback to share any additional thoughts, suggestions, or reflections on the interaction or the system overall.

3.3 Study Setup

The study included 11 university students (ages 22–49) from the University of Miami, with diverse academic backgrounds in computer science and nursing. In each group, one participant assumed the role of a patient, two acted as caregivers, and the remaining observed the interaction[2]. Most reported limited experience with robotics, though many had regular exposure to computers or AI tools.

3.4 Results

As shown in Table 1 and Fig. 2, participants rated the robot highly on usability. Mean scores were 0.91 for "The robot is easy to use" (AU1), 1.27 for "Learning to work with the robot is easy" (AU2), and 1.36 for "Learning how to communicate with the robot is quick" (AU3). On average, 78% of participants responded positively (1 or 2 on the scale), indicating strong ease of use—even among those with limited prior exposure to robotics.

User engagement scores were similarly high, with average ratings of 1.00 (UE1: "I was concentrated"), 1.18 (UE2: "The interaction captured my attention"), and 1.18 (UE3: "I was alert"). On average, 81.8% of participants reported being positively engaged in the interaction. Participants who rated the robot highly on usability also tended to report strong engagement, suggesting that intuitive interfaces may directly support attention and immersion.

Attitudes toward the robot were overwhelmingly favorable. AT1 ("I see the interaction as something positive") and AT2 ("I view the interaction as something favorable") both averaged 1.36, while AT3 ("I think negatively of the interaction")

---

[2] Study video: https://www.cs.miami.edu/~visser/hsr-videos/share-2025.mp4.

was strongly disagreed with (M = −1.45). Over 90% of participants expressed a positive attitude across these items.

Participants also endorsed the robot's educational value, with a mean score of 1.36 (SD = 0.50) and 100% of responses in the positive range.

Importantly, no statistically significant relationships were found between participants' age, race, or familiarity with computers, as well as the assigned role (caregiver, patient, observer) and their reported usability, engagement, attitude toward the robot, or perception of the educational value. This suggests the system's accessibility and effectiveness were consistent across diverse backgrounds and levels of technical experience. A significance threshold of $p < 0.05$ was adopted for all tests evaluating associations between demographic characteristics and participant responses.

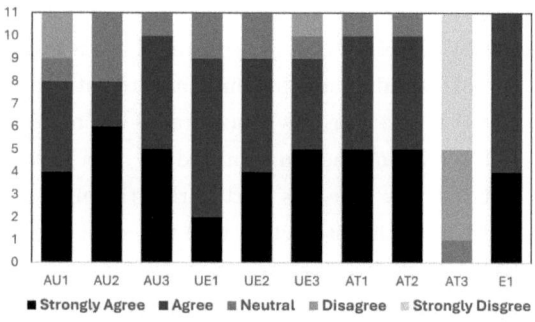

Fig. 2. Study questionnaire questions.

Open-ended responses emphasized the robot's strengths, including its "soothing voice" and clear explanations. The synchronized breathing demonstration was described as calming and effective for illustrating inhaler technique. Participants appreciated the instructional videos but noted that the screen was small and lacked variety. Suggestions included adding more visuals and integrating video alongside speech to increase engagement. Additionally, a suggestion was made to include interactive questions during the session to enhance attention and assess real-time understanding—an idea that aligns with active learning principles in health education.

4 Discussion and Future Work

These findings provide strong early support for the use of a social robot in pediatric asthma education. The robot was found to be easy to use, engaging, and positively received by participants, despite most having little to no prior experience with robotic systems. High usability and engagement scores suggest the system works well for first-time users with minimal instruction, even in emotionally charged hospital settings. Over 90% reported positive attitudes, and all participants were satisfied with the robot-led education, indicating strong potential for scalable, repeatable discharge interventions.

While encouraging, these findings are preliminary. The use of simulated roles and a homogenous participant group (university students) limits generalizability. Future studies should include actual patients and caregivers, explore correlations between prior technology experience and interaction outcomes, and evaluate long-term effects on knowledge retention and adherence.

Follow-up studies are currently being planned to implement the system in real pediatric settings and assess longitudinal outcomes such as asthma control and caregiver confidence post-discharge. Future studies should include comparative evaluations between robot-led and nurse-led discharge education to assess relative effectiveness in knowledge retention and behavior change. Additional goals include expanding interactivity, adding multilingual content and visual aids, and analyzing recordings to create a labeled HRI dataset.

References

1. Arikan-Ayyildiz, Z., Işik, S., Caglayan-Sozmen, S., Anal, O., Karaman, O., Uzuner, N.: Efficacy of asthma education program on Ashma control in children with uncontrolled asthma. Turkish J. Pediatr. **58**(4), 383–388 (2016)
2. Ferrari, O.I., Zhang, F., Braam, A.A., Van Gurp, J.A., Broz, F., Barakova, E.I.: Design of child-robot interactions for comfort and distraction from post-operative pain and distress. In: Companion of the 2023 ACM/IEEE International Conference on Human-Robot Interaction, pp. 686–690 (2023)
3. Fitrianie, S., Bruijnes, M., Li, F., Abdulrahman, A., Brinkman, W.P.: The Artificial-social-agent questionnaire: establishing the long and short questionnaire versions. In: Proceedings of the 22nd ACM International Conference on Intelligent Virtual Agents, pp. 1–8. ACM (2022)
4. Foronda, C., et al.: Asthma academy: a student nurse-led telehealth education program for low-income family caregivers of children with asthma. Nurs. Open **9**(2), 1486–1496 (2022)
5. Kelley, T., Kearney, G.D.: Insights into the environmental health burden of childhood asthma. Envir. Health Insights **12**, 1178630218757445 (2018)
6. Lonner, J.H., Zangrilli, J., Saini, S.: Emerging Robotic Technologies and innovations for hospital process improvement. robotics in knee and hip arthroplasty: current concepts, techniques and emerging uses, pp. 233–243 (2019)
7. Lozano-Mosos, J.S., Hernández Leal, J., Colina-Matiz, S., Muñoz-Vargas, P.T.: Education by a social robot on nutrition and catheter care in pediatric oncology patients. Support. Care Cancer **31**(12), 693 (2023)
8. Moerman, C.J., Van Der HEIDE, L., Heerink, M.: Social Robots to Support Children's Well-Being Under Medical Treatment: a systematic state-of-the-art review. J. Child Health Care **23**(4), 596–612 (2019)
9. Or, X.Y., Ng, Y.X., Goh, Y.S.: Effectiveness of social robots in improving psychological well-being of Hospitalised children: a systematic review and meta-analysis. J. Pediatr. Nurs. **82**, 11–20 (2025)
10. Ransford, J., Tidwell, T., Johnson, L., Gitney, N., Morgan, A., Hauch, R.: Implementing a Virtual Discharge Nurse Pilot: Utilizing the Pathway to Excellence Framework. JONA: J. Nursing Adm. **54**(11), 605–611 (2024)
11. Triantafyllidis, A., Alexiadis, A., Votis, K., Tzovaras, D.: Social robot interventions for child healthcare: a systematic review of the literature. Comput. Methods Programs Biomed. Update **3**, 100108 (2023)
12. Zhou, S., Bickmore, T., Paasche-Orlow, M., Jack, B.: Agent-user concordance and satisfaction with a virtual hospital discharge nurse. In: Bickmore, T., Marsella, S., Sidner, C. (eds.) IVA 2014. LNCS (LNAI), vol. 8637, pp. 528–541. Springer, Cham (2014). https://doi.org/10.1007/978-3-319-09767-1_63

Scaffolding Reflection, not Generation: Exploring Non-Directive Social Robot Interaction in Early-Stage Ideation

Wisanukorn Boribun[✉] and Frank Heidmann

University of Applied Sciences Potsdam, 14469 Brandenburg, Germany
`yin.boribun@fh-potsdam.de`

Abstract. In the context of design education, this study explores how a non-directive social robot (Furhat) can support early-stage idea generation. The robot was intentionally designed not to offer suggestions or solutions, distinguishing it from typical generative AI tools. Instead, it engaged students using metaphors, open-ended questions, and active listening. The aim was to examine how participants responded to a system that deliberately resisted the generative behavior commonly associated with tools like ChatGPT. Many participants appreciated the robot's reflective role, noting that it helped them clarify and structure ideas without imposing direction. However, as the design process progressed, some expressed frustration and a desire for more proactive input—ranging from creative suggestions and emotional feedback to auditory elements, such as singing or whistling a melody. This mismatch between the robot's expressive embodiment and its intentionally limited functionality led to moments of tension. Rather than viewing this as a shortcoming, we frame it as a deliberate design strategy: by withholding generative output, the robot fosters independent ideation. These findings contribute to broader discussions in human-robot interaction, particularly concerning creativity, user expectations, and the design of non-directive AI systems.

Keywords: Social Robotics · Creativity Support · Non-Directive Interaction · Prompt Design · User Expectations

1 Introduction

Generative AI systems such as ChatGPT, DALL·E, and Midjourney have fundamentally transformed perceptions of creativity and machine intelligence. These technologies have shifted AI's role from passive assistance to active co-creation, particularly in domains such as education, design, and artistic production. Tasks that were once labor-intensive and iterative can now be accelerated through the use of carefully crafted prompts. Texts, images, concepts, and structural ideas are generated instantaneously, reducing friction and streamlining the ideation process. Consequently, expectations surrounding artificial intelligence are evolving rapidly. Users increasingly anticipate systems that offer immediate output, linguistic fluency, and ideational support—capabilities that are becoming normalized in everyday digital interactions [10, 24]. In contrast, social robots such as

Furhat offer a markedly different form of engagement. Characterized by expressive facial features, human-like timing, and embodied presence, these robots elicit strong social responses. However, they typically lack the generative capabilities of large-scale language or multimodal models. This discrepancy between their anthropomorphic form and limited functional output has been identified as a primary source of user frustration and misaligned expectations [11, 21]. This paper explores a reflective counterpoint: What occurs when a social robot intentionally refrains from generating ideas and instead engages users through metaphorical prompting and non-directive dialogue? We present findings from a design course in which students interacted with Furhat during the early stages of ideation. The robot was scripted not to provide answers or suggestions, but rather to pose open-ended questions, employ metaphor, and reflect user input. Our contribution is twofold: (1) we investigate how non-directive prompting shapes user experience, cognitive reflection, and engagement during ideation; and (2) we examine how these dynamics intersect with mental models formed through prior interactions with generative AI systems.

2 Related Works

2.1 Social Robots as Creative Partners

Social robots are increasingly being studied as facilitators of creative processes, particularly in educational and artistic settings. Rather than generating content, these systems often support imaginative thinking by providing narrative scaffolding and structured interaction. For example, the YOLO system by Alves-Oliveira et al. [4], engaged children through storytelling frameworks, guiding creativity without offering direct suggestions. Similarly, Pu et al. [17] introduced the HeARTfelt Robot, which combined large language model (LLM)-driven dialogue with emotional reflection to foster user engagement with visual art. These approaches demonstrate that social robots can enhance creativity by prompting user expression and reflection, rather than by supplying solutions. Ali et al. [1] further showed that social robots can promote divergent thinking through their presence, neutrality, and dialogic pacing. In the Escape!Bot project [1], the robot acted as a facilitator in collaborative problem-solving games, serving as a catalyst rather than an idea generator. In group contexts, robots have also been shown to reduce evaluation apprehension, resulting in more effective brainstorming compared to human facilitators [9]. Similar effects have been observed in storytelling studies [8], where social robots encouraged participation and extended verbal engagement by creating playful and low-pressure environments [19]. These findings align with non-directive facilitation strategies in coaching and education, which emphasize user-driven ideation over directive input. This principle forms the foundation of the Furhat interaction design examined in our study.

2.2 The Form-Function Dissonance

The design of social robots can elicit strong social responses. Furhat's projection-based facial interface, natural timing, and anthropomorphic design often lead users to attribute levels of intelligence, empathy, or agency that exceed the system's actual capabilities. As Thunberg et al. [21] and Perugia et al. [15] demonstrate, such expressive features can raise expectations of emotional understanding, regardless of the robot's underlying functionality. Jarsve et al. [11] further explore this dynamic by comparing user responses to Furhat and ChatGPT. While Furhat was perceived as more personable, it also elicited greater discomfort—or "creepiness"—when it failed to meet users' implicit expectations. The robot's expressive form created an anticipation of output—such as suggestions, empathy, or creativity—that was not always fulfilled. This highlights a form–function mismatch that can undermine user trust and satisfaction, particularly when generative capabilities are assumed. FurChat, an enhanced version of Furhat augmented with large language models (LLMs), attempts to address this issue by aligning facial expressions with generative outputs [6]. However, this solution introduces new challenges in managing user expectations.

2.3 Generative AI and Emerging User Expectations

The widespread adoption of systems like ChatGPT, Midjourney, and Gemini has dramatically reshaped user expectations around AI. As Wang et al. [24] note, users develop generalized mental models of AI competence—assuming coherence, reasoning abilities, or system-wide awareness even when these are absent. This is particularly pronounced in embodied systems. When a robot presents itself with a humanlike face and voice, users tend to assume cognitive and creative abilities by default [10, 11, 21]. This over-attribution is reinforced by frequent interaction with generative tools. Users grow accustomed to immediate fluency and idea generation, forming what we describe as a generative habitus—a mindset that sees intelligent systems as productive, contributive, and efficient [10, 11, 27]. When these expectations are unmet, the result is often user confusion or frustration. Such social expectations are transferred to robots even in highly utilitarian contexts like caregiving [12].

2.4 Prompt Engineering as Design Strategy

Prompt engineering has emerged as a key technique for shaping interactions with large language models (LLMs). Wei et al. [25] introduced Chain-of-Thought prompting, demonstrating how LLMs can be nudged into reasoning-like behaviours by structuring input differently. Zhou et al. [27] and White et al. [26] extended this by offering prompt taxonomies that help control tone, depth, and engagement style. Others, such as Pryzant et al. [16], have explored automated prompt optimization. Within human–robot interaction, prompt engineering is increasingly used to shape robot behavior. Chung et al. [7] tuned LLMs for task-specific, user-adaptive instruction. These strategies emphasize that prompts are not merely input strings, but design instruments: they convey stance, intentionality, and interactional philosophy—including non-directivity. Furhat systems have begun to reflect this shift. For example, Cherakara et al. [6] integrated LLM-generated content into Furhat's expressive interface. In our study, we inverted this logic. Instead of designing for fluency and output, we crafted a prompting strategy that asked, listened, and deliberately refrained. This represents an approach to prompt design focused not on maximizing answers, but on using restraint and reflection to create space for interpretation.

3 Methodology

3.1 Study Context and Research Design

The study was conducted as part of a "Game Design Basics" course at the University of Applied Sciences Potsdam, Germany. Sixteen design students (aged 21–27), all with backgrounds in design-related disciplines, participated in self-organized teams of four. The course assignment required each team to develop an analog game prototype by combining two randomly drawn game genres with three randomly drawn mechanics, selected from a curated card set (30 genres, 30 mechanics). The task emphasized open-ended exploration, conceptual synthesis, and early-stage creativity under constraint. The primary research objective was to examine how students interact with a non-directive social robot during the ideation phase. We were particularly interested in how these interactions influenced the creative flow, especially given the students' expectations shaped by prior experiences with generative AI tools [10, 11]. The study followed a qualitative, exploratory approach, combining structured observation, video and audio recordings of the interaction sessions, and post-session interviews. Students were instructed not to use ChatGPT or other AI assistants but were free to consult the robot at any time during the task. All participants were informed about the study's purpose and data collection procedures and provided their verbal consent to participate.

3.2 The Furhat Robot Configuration

Furhat was placed in a separate room to enable undisturbed, self-directed interaction. Students could approach the robot voluntarily—either alone or in pairs on behalf of their team—whenever they felt stuck or needed a conversational counterpart. The robot was designed to follow a deliberately non-directive strategy, explicitly avoiding any generative or solution-oriented output. Instead, it engaged users through a range of pre-scripted, non-directive prompts. These included examples from three main categories:

- **Reflective questions** (e.g., "Was macht diese Idee riskant?" ["What makes that idea risky?"])
- **Metaphoric framings** (e.g., "Ist euer Konzept eher wie ein Labyrinth oder wie ein Puzzlestück? " ["Is your concept more like a maze or a puzzle piece?"])
- **Minimal responses** (e.g., „Erzähl weiter" ["Go on"], „Ich verstehe" ["I see"])

While reflective questions and metaphoric framings were the primary tools for stimulating ideation, the minimal responses also served as a fallback strategy. They were used to manage conversational breakdowns (e.g., misunderstandings or prolonged user silence) and create the impression of active listening. A backstage interface allowed for discreet monitoring and light orchestration to ensure that the robot's dialogical behavior remained consistent with its non-directive role—aligned with approaches in recent HRI studies [2, 5, 8]. Such interaction strategies align with recent findings on the importance of non-verbal entry points in human–robot interaction, which emphasize the role of gestures and subtle cues during the initial engagement phase [23]. Students were introduced to Furhat as a "thinking companion," designed not to solve problems but to facilitate ideation through presence, prompting, and restraint.

3.3 Data Collection and Analysis

All interactions between participants and the robot, as well as the post-session interviews, were recorded using audio and a 360-degree video camera. The audio data were transcribed using the medium version of OpenAI's Whisper model (language setting: German), executed via the official Python implementation. The transcripts were analyzed through thematic analysis, beginning with open coding and followed by iterative grouping into higher-level themes. To support the identification of discursive patterns and co-occurrence structures, we additionally used the tool InfraNodus for exploratory semantic mapping. The video recordings enabled a complementary analysis of non-verbal behavior, with particular attention to gestures and facial expressions during the robot interactions.

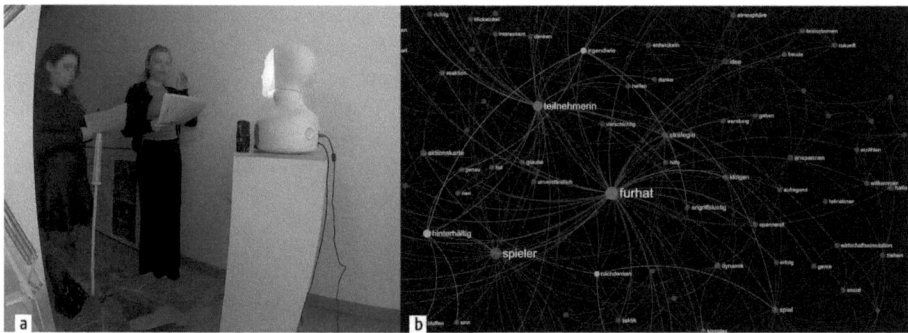

Fig. 1. Methodological Setup. (a) Recording the human-robot interaction with a 360° camera. (b) Example visualization of the transcribed data as a semantic network in InfraNodus.

4 Results

The analysis revealed that participants initially perceived the robot as a "cognitive mirror," a tool that helped them externalize and structure emerging ideas. Several participants described this non-directive support as clarifying, noting that the act of articulating their thoughts aloud enabled conceptual progress. However, this reflective mode was increasingly met with frustration, particularly by teams who were further along in their design process. These participants hoped for a "creative spark" in the form of concrete auditory impulses—for instance, wanting the robot to sing or whistle a melody to inspire their game design. This disappointment was closely tied to a generative habitus shaped by prior interaction with systems like ChatGPT. Despite being informed of the robot's limitations, participants found it difficult to suspend their expectations of productivity and contribution. As one student noted, "[An AI like] ChatGPT would have suggested at least five solutions by now." Notably, a final observation highlighted an implicit attribution of social presence to the robot: even knowing that Furhat could not interpret gestures, participants frequently engaged in animated, expressive body language, especially when explaining their ideas. This suggests a deeply ingrained responsiveness to the robot's anthropomorphic form. The semantic network of a representative interaction (Fig. 1b) reflects Furhat's non-directive role: it acts as a 'process' hub connecting the participant's thematic clusters without providing content itself.

5 Discussions

5.1 Social Robots as Reflective Catalysts

The findings show that non-directive prompting can support early-stage ideation by encouraging verbalization and self-reflection. Rather than generating ideas, the robot acted as a cognitive mirror—comparable to coaching or Socratic dialogue models [1, 3, 4]. This confirms previous work suggesting that robots can foster creativity not through output, but by supporting ambiguity and dialogical presence [2, 5, 20]. Especially in design education, where idea ownership is key, such reflective interaction has strong pedagogical potential.

5.2 Expectation Gabs and Generative Habitus

Participants frequently assumed that the robot—due to its expressive face—would eventually produce outputs such as suggestions or music. We refer to this as a *generative habitus*: a learned expectation that intelligent systems should be efficient and creatively contributive [10, 11, 27]. Tools like ChatGPT reinforce this expectation by equating fluency with intelligence. When Furhat did not produce output, users perceived its behavior as incomplete—even when this had been explained in advance. This highlights a core tension in human–robot interaction (HRI): the need to align form and function, particularly when prior experiences with AI shape user expectations [25]. Maintaining such alignment is critical for sustained engagement, especially in multi-party service contexts [18]. This form–function dissonance also echoes the *uncanny valley* effect [13]: Furhat's humanlike voice and facial expressiveness elicited expectations of empathy or creativity. When those expectations were not met, some users reported subtle discomfort. This discomfort may stem not only from unmet creative expectations but also from a lack of transparency; the robot offers no explanation of its reasoning, leaving users to infer its internal state [14]. We interpret these moments of uncanniness not as design flaws, but as productive disruptions—opportunities to reflect on the boundaries of machine agency.

5.3 Designing for Productive Limitation

We argue that intentionally withholding generative behavior can be a meaningful design strategy. Instead of providing answers, it encourages users to develop crucial metacognitive skills—such as articulating ideas, taking ownership, and reflecting—rather than passively consuming AI-generated output [1, 7, 22]. In contrast to the automated nature of generative systems, reflective prompting can foster deeper engagement. Especially in education, the need may not be for systems that solve problems, but for those that promote metacognition through questioning, reframing, and listening.

6 Conclusion and Future Work

This study shows that while a non-directive robot's reflective prompting can support creative articulation, it often contrasts with user expectations shaped by generative AI. We argue that this mismatch between expressive form and constrained function is not a flaw, but a deliberate design strategy that promotes deeper reflection through restraint. Future work will explore enhancing the robot's reflective role via multimodal feedback—such as gesture and luminous cues—and comparative studies on prompting strategies and adaptive interaction. In addition, future research should examine how the robot's expressive embodiment influences user expectations and how non-verbal behaviors can be more systematically analyzed to better understand user engagement. Our aim is to reposition social robots as thinking companions that support creative agency through subtle, non-directive engagement.

References

1. Ali, S., Devasia, N.E., Breazeal, C.: Escape!Bot: social robots as creative problem-solving partners. Creativity Cogn., 275–283 (2022). https://doi.org/10.1145/3527927.3532793
2. Ali, S., Devasia, N., Park, H.W., Breazeal, C.: Social robots as creativity eliciting agents. Front. Robot. AI, 8 (2021). https://doi.org/10.3389/frobt.2021.673730
3. Ali, S., Moroso, T., Breazeal, C.: Can children learn creativity from a social robot? C&C '19: Proceedings of the 2019 Conference on Creativity and Cognition (2019). https://doi.org/10.1145/3325480.3325499
4. Alves-Oliveira, P., Arriaga, P., Paiva, A., Hoffman, G.: YOLO, a robot for creativity. In: IDC '17: Proceedings of the 2017 Conference on Interaction Design and Children (2017). https://doi.org/10.1145/3078072.3084304
5. Alves-Oliveira, P., Gomes, S., Chandak, A., Arriaga, P., Hoffman, G., Paiva, A.: Software architecture for YOLO, a creativity-stimulating robot. SoftwareX **11**, 100461 (2020). https://doi.org/10.1016/j.softx.2020.100461
6. Cherakara, N., et al.: FurChat: an embodied conversational agent using LLMs, combining open and closed-domain dialogue with facial expressions. Proc. of SIGDIAL (2023). https://doi.org/10.18653/v1/2023.sigdial-1.55
7. Chung, H.W., et al.: Scaling instruction-finetuned language models. arXiv (2022). https://doi.org/10.48550/arxiv.2210.11416
8. Elgarf, M., Salam, H., Peters, C.: Fostering children's creativity through LLM-driven storytelling with a social robot. Front. Robot. AI **11** (2024). https://doi.org/10.3389/frobt.2024.1457429
9. Geerts, J., De Wit, J., De Rooij, A.: Brainstorming with a social robot facilitator: better than human facilitation due to reduced evaluation apprehension? Front. Robot. AI **8** (2021). https://doi.org/10.3389/frobt.2021.657291
10. Grimes, G.M., Schuetzler, R.M., Giboney, J.S.: Mental models and expectation violations in conversational AI interactions. Decis. Support Syst. **144**, 113515 (2021). https://doi.org/10.1016/j.dss.2021.113515

11. Jarsve, T., Malkomsen, E.R., Woźniak, P.W., Niess, J.: Exploring user expectations and perceived creepiness in AI: a study on furhat and ChatGPT. In: NordiCHI '24 Adjunct Proceedings, pp. 1–5 (2024). https://doi.org/10.1145/3677045.3685428
12. Mitchell, K.: Reimagining Care: designing a social robot companion for Alzheimer's caregiving. In: Proceedings of DRS. https://doi.org/10.21606/drs.2024.487
13. Mori, M., MacDorman, K.F., Kageki, N.: The uncanny valley [from the field]. IEEE Robot. Autom. Mag. **19**(2), 98–100 (2012). https://doi.org/10.1109/MRA.2012.2192811
14. Nair, N.C., Rossi, A., Rossi, S.: Impact of Explanations on transparency in HRI: a study using the HRIVST Metric. In: Lecture Notes in Computer Science, pp. 171–180 (2023). https://doi.org/10.1007/978-981-99-8715-3_15
15. Perugia, G., Rossi, A., Rossi, S.: Gender revealed: evaluating the genderedness of Furhat's predefined faces. In: Lecture Notes in Computer Science, pp. 36–47 (2021). https://doi.org/10.1007/978-3-030-90525-5_4
16. Pryzant, R., Iter, D., Li, J., Lee, Y.T., Zhu, C., Zeng, M.: Automatic Prompt Optimization with "Gradient Descent" and Beam Search. arXiv (Cornell University) (2023). https://doi.org/10.48550/arxiv.2305.03495
17. Pu, I., Nguyen, G., Alsultan, L., Picard, R., Breazeal, C., Alghowinem, S.: A HeARTfelt robot: social robot-driven deep emotional art reflection with children. arXiv (Cornell University) (2024). https://doi.org/10.48550/arxiv.2409.10710
18. Rossi, A., Menna, C., Giordano, E., Rossi, S.: Evaluating Customers' Engagement Preferences for Multi-party Interaction with a Robot Bartender. In: Lecture notes in computer science, pp. 371–381 (2023). https://doi.org/10.1007/978-981-99-8718-4_32
19. Sanoubari, E., et al.: What makes an educational robot game fun? In: Lecture Notes in Computer Science, pp. 40–55 (2025). https://doi.org/10.1007/978-981-96-3522-1_6
20. Schrills, T., Franke, T.: How to answer why – evaluating the explanations of AI through mental model analysis. arXiv (Cornell University) (2020). https://doi.org/10.48550/arxiv.2002.02526
21. Thunberg, S., Arnelid, M., Ziemke, T.: Older adults' perception of the furhat robot. In: Proceedings of the 10th International Conference on Human-Agent Interaction (HAI '22), pp. 4–12 (2022). https://doi.org/10.1145/3527188.3561924
22. Vigni, F., Rossi, A., Miccio, L., Rossi, S.: On the emotional transparency of a non-humanoid social robot. In: Lecture Notes in Computer Science, pp. 290–299 (2022). https://doi.org/10.1007/978-3-031-24667-8_26
23. Vigni, F., Rossi, S.: Exploring non-verbal strategies for initiating an HRI. In: Lecture Notes in Computer Science, pp. 280–289 (2022a). https://doi.org/10.1007/978-3-031-24667-8_25
24. Wang, X., Wang, X., Park, S., Yao, Y.: Mental models of generative AI chatbot ecosystems. In: IUI '25: Proceedings of the 30th International Conference on Intelligent User Interfaces, pp. 1016–1031. https://doi.org/10.1145/3708359.3712125
25. Wei, J., et al.: Chain-of-thought prompting elicits reasoning in large language models. arXiv (2022). https://doi.org/10.48550/arxiv.2201.11903
26. White, J., et al.: A prompt pattern catalog to enhance prompt engineering with ChatGPT. arXiv (2023). https://doi.org/10.48550/arxiv.2302.11382
27. Zhou, Y., et al.: Large language models are human-level prompt engineers. arXiv (2022). https://doi.org/10.48550/arxiv.2211.01910

Facilitating the Emergence of Assistive Robots to Support Frailty: Psychosocial and Environmental Realities

Angela Higgins[1](✉), Stephen Potter[2], Mauro Dragone[3], Mark Hawley[2], Farshid Amirabdollahian[4], Alessandro Di Nuovo[5], and Praminda Caleb-Solly[1]

[1] University of Nottingham, School of Computer Science, Nottingham, UK
angela.higgins@nottingham.ac.uk
[2] University of Sheffield, Sheffield, UK
[3] University of Hertfordshire, Hatfield, UK
[4] Heriot-Watt University, Edinburgh, UK
[5] Sheffield Hallam University, Sheffield, UK

Abstract. While assistive robots have much potential to help older people with frailty-related needs, there are few in use. There is a gap between what is developed in laboratories and what would be viable in real-world contexts. Through a series of co-design workshops (61 participants across 7 sessions) including those with lived experience of frailty, their carers, and healthcare professionals, we gained a deeper understanding of everyday issues concerning the place of new technologies in their lives. A persona-based approach surfaced emotional, social, and psychological issues. Any assistive solution must be developed in the context of this complex interplay of psychosocial and environmental factors. Our findings, presented as design requirements in direct relation to frailty, can help promote design thinking that addresses people's needs in a more pragmatic way to move assistive robotics closer to real-world use.

Keywords: older adults · assistive robots · co-design

1 Introduction

Frailty can be characterised as the loss of resilience due to the adverse effects of ageing. It has physical, emotional and cognitive dimensions, which can hinder effective functioning in daily life [1], with effects influenced by social, environmental and economic circumstances [2]. As populations worldwide age and countries experience care staff shortages, robots are often suggested as a means to support independent and healthy ageing. Designs which fail to take into account people's needs, wants, anxieties and circumstances are likely to lead to unacceptable, impractical, or ineffective robots. Currently, there are few deployable assistive robots on the market, and the research focus on using off-the-shelf robotic platforms has not been successful [3]. The primary aim of the Emergence Network [4] was to identify and address the barriers to moving assistive robots from laboratories into people's homes. Here we present our findings from workshops that gathered requirements to guide the assistive robotics community towards developments that directly address frailty.

2 Related Work

The ACCRA project used co-design to develop applications for the diagnosis of sarcopenia [5] and to support greater mobility [6]. However, these investigations were constrained by the use of pre-existing robots [5]. More recently, the City4Age project created a co-design toolkit to develop interventions for older people. In their critique of other projects, they note that co-design often begins only once the robot has already been developed or chosen, skipping the initial, scoping design work and thereby creating an immediate disconnect between under-defined problem and over-specified robot "solution" [7]. With this in mind, one exercise in co-design of robots to encourage physical activity purposely ignored current robot capabilities and instead identified design guidelines in collaboration with occupational therapists and older people themselves [8]. The resulting diversity of opinions highlighted the need for personalisation and adaptability, and for multimodal communication, ease of use, maintaining privacy, and behaving respectfully. The research described here takes a similar approach, seeking to identify interventions for frailty without committing to any pre-existing robotic platform, but rather with a commitment to exploring ideas suggested by participants, regardless of their current feasibility. Another multi-disciplinary exercise in this area laid bare the extent of needs in this space, with over 70 distinct requirements initially identified [9]. Here we go a step further by viewing needs through the prism of living with frailty, described through a list of functional and non-functional requirements.

3 Methods

Inspired by the *Double Diamond* model of design thinking [10], Emergence held co-design workshops corresponding to the *"discover"* and *"define"* phases of the first diamond. (Subsequent activities, not covered here, would take the results into the *"develop"* and *"deliver"* phases of the second diamond.)

Workshops during the *"discover"* phase discussed issues surrounding activities of daily living (ADLs), self-management of frailty (SM), and the role of healthcare professionals (HCPs). Subsequent workshops were held to further *"define"* the constraints on assistive robots. Research approval was obtained from the University of Nottingham research ethics committee, ref no. CS-2021-R40.

The workshops, each lasting 3–4 hours, were held during 2022 around the UK, at times and places convenient for attendees. Recruitment took place through sector partners, professional networks, and word of mouth. Table 1 summarises participation in the workshops. A total of 61 participants were recorded, including some people attending multiple sessions. There were paired *"define"* and *"discover"* workshops at each location, with participants invited to attend both;

Table 1. Workshop Information

Stage	Participants
Discover: ADL1	8 older people, 1 housing support officer
Discover: SM1	8 older people, 2 OTs, 1 telecare rep, 1 carer
Define: ADL2	5 older people, 2 housing support officers
Define: SM2	8 older people, 3 HCPs
Discover: HCP1	4 HCPs
Discover: HCP2	10 HCPs
Discover+Define: ADL3	4 older people, 4 carers

however, some were able to attend only one. The second workshop took place around a fortnight later. All workshops were audio recorded, with manual notes taken. A graphic facilitator helped capture the content of several of the workshops through illustrations [11].

Discover. The ADL, SM, and HCP discover workshops used personas to prompt discussion of the challenges and opportunities faced by people living with frailty. ADL workshops asked participants to identify and prioritise difficulties and opportunities during common daily activities. The SM workshop explored diet, exercise, mental health, sleep, and personal security. The HCP workshops reflected on key challenges faced by individuals during the patient journey and opportunities for robotic support.

Interim Data Analysis. A rapid analysis of the first workshops identified 6 prominent recurring everyday difficulties. Giving free rein to their imaginations, and unconstrained by questions of technical feasibility, the research team came up with the *"speculative"* designs for a robot to address each. Each robot design was summarised in terms of the need/want it meets, its functioning, and its application or operation. These summaries, now incorporating an illustration from the graphic facilitator, were used in the *"define"* workshops.

Define. Workshops were held for both the ADL workshop groups and the SM group, and in each case the format was the same. Participants were presented with each speculative robot design and asked what they did or did not like about it, or what else they would need to know about it. The group was then asked for their opinions about various aspects of the robot and how they imagined it would behave. Specifically, they were asked to consider the robot's appearance, control, performance, practicalities, and concerns.

Data Analysis. Collected data were subjected to a thematic analysis by two of the research team independently and then compared, with discrepancies resolved through discussion. A combined inductive and deductive approach was used, with deductive codes based on workshop topics and inductive codes developed from workshop discussions. These were sorted into functional and non-functional requirements as per the Volere specification template [12].

4 Results and Discussion

4.1 Discover

ADL1 Workshop. Participants indicated that lack of motivation had a negative impact on many important ADLs (**n**umber of participants = 4). They acknowledged that this can lead to further deterioration in mental and physical health, leading to a vicious circle of decline, which can be difficult to break once initiated. Some attributed problems with motivation to isolation, stating that well-being derived from *"being cared about and car[ing] about yourself"*. Pets were considered a potential source of both motivation and companionship (n = 3), but could be impractical due to housing restrictions or care demands. Fear of falling was identified as a barrier to performing ADLs (n = 3), this was also a cyclical process, with anxiety leading to reduced activity, and to increased fear of falls. Another issue was the difficulty of remembering to take medication at the correct time (n = 2). Practical and cost concerns were frequently raised (n = 6), particularly the amount of electricity consumed by a robot (n = 2). Older adults had often downsized their homes (n = 2) and were wary of the amount of space that would be taken up by multiple robots.

SM1 Workshop. Participants discussed already using technology to set reminders and for home security (n = 3). However, they were apprehensive about technology leaving them open to scammers or the loss of the human touch. Frustration was expressed at the general lack of support for maintaining their health, particularly mental health care (n = 3). Personalisation of a robot to the user and their needs was seen as a necessity, with control in the hands of the service user (n = 3). As in the ADL workshops participants were receptive to the idea of robotic pets (n = 10), and concerned about the practicalities of robot ownership (n = 4). Communal robots were viewed as a possible solution, particularly for cleaning robots (n = 4).

HCP1 and HCP2 Workshops. In HCP workshops all participants repeatedly returned to the theme of motivation and a need for self-efficacy. Due to typical multi-morbidity and the link between physical and emotional health, a holistic approach was emphasised (n = 5). HCPs expressed frustration with current electronic healthcare records, and lack of data sharing, leaving them with insufficient information (n = 7). They stated that they only ever saw a "snapshot" of a patient, often at their worst after an adverse health event, therefore monitoring and assessment after a hospital stay may be enhanced by technology.

Suggested areas for robotic support included fall prevention (n = 4), medication management (n = 4), incontinence (n = 3), and preventive interventions for pre-frailty (n = 4). In general, technology that supports pre-frail individuals could benefit the wider care system (n = 8). This was combined with acknowledgement of care workers whose job is often demanding and poorly paid (n = 4). Technologies which would make care workers' jobs easier would help alleviate this burden (as would higher wages).

ADL3 Workshop. The ADL3 workshop consisted of both "discover" and "define" sessions and did not inform the speculative robot concepts. Themes from earlier workshops were echoed, including space constraints (n = 2), fall anxiety (n = 1), medication management (n = 3), and interest in robotic pets (n = 4). Participants expressed the need for both physical and emotional support after a fall or other medical incident, but expressed that equipment was often over-medicalised (n = 3). Technology usability was raised, with participants stating that they particularly struggled with initial set up (n = 3). This particular group expressed a desire to learn technological skills, noting the need for instructions to be tailored to people's accessibility issues.

Table 2. Descriptions of speculative robot scenarios

Robot	Description
Motibot	Detects low mood/lack of activity & suggests activities
Foodee	Suggests recipes & helps users follow them step-by-step
EasyUp	Offers a reassuring arm as you climb up and down stairs
AutoReach	Hoovers, dusts and washes difficult-to-reach places
RoPet	Robot pet companion, available in different models
Toilittle	Toileting robot with options according to user's situation

4.2 Define

All speculative robot scenarios that were discussed and evaluated in "define" are available online [13], with short descriptions shown in Table 2.

Personalisation. The need for robots to adapt to users' physical, emotional, or practical context was considered essential for all scenarios by all define workshops (n = 14). Examples from participants include that Motibot should tailor its motivational approach, EasyUp must match mobility needs, and Foodee should reflect personal taste and dietary requirements.

Appearance. Robotic aesthetics would need to be adjusted depending on both the function and user of the robot (n = 6). For example, RoPet should be soft and cuddly, Foodee should appear functional, and Toilittle should be discreet. However, participants felt that all robots should look unintimidating, trustworthy, and unobtrusive (n = 4) but easy to spot to avoid collisions (n = 3).

Interaction. Voice interaction was preferred by all older adults, sometimes supplemented with screens (n = 3), but robots would need to understand regional speech and terminology. However, it was highlighted that this would be unsuitable for people with speech or hearing impairments.

Maintenance. Participants wanted low-maintenance robots, with repair services readily available (n = 4). This is clear in the case of AutoReach; a cleaning robot that would require regular cleaning would be self-defeating. However, some, like RoPet, could require some light upkeep, treating it more like a pet.

Table 3. Functional Requirements in Relation to Frailty

Requirement	In Relation to Frailty
Support a holistic model of healthy ageing	Influenced by biological, psychological, social, and environmental factors
Address multiple facets of frailty	People living with frailty often have multiple long-term conditions
Reduce isolation	Isolation can impact health, so a robot companion should also encourage human-to-human interaction
Not replace or undermine human care	Enable the care of frail older people to be done with dignity and improve jobs within the care sector
Be affordable	Older adults often have less disposable income, so robots should provide good value for money
Be part of a service ecosystem	The whole service delivery model should be considered, including who buys and distributes the robots
Have adjustable levels of autonomy	Over-reliance may increase frailty, but when users need extra support, the robot should be able to provide it
Have adjustable levels of monitoring	This may not be needed for all, but this may change if their condition progresses or after a health incident

Monitoring and Autonomy. Robotic monitoring was acceptable if tailored to the user's needs and frailty (n = 7). Likewise, levels of robot autonomy might need to change depending on the user's day-to-day needs: for example, Foodee taking more initiative in food preparation if the user was unwell. Robots would also need to understand multiple steps within a process, such as not only reminding a user to take their medication but also confirming this had been done.

Safety and Security. Participants accepted that failures would occur with any technology, but highlighted that they should *"fail safely"* (n = 4), giving the example that EasyUp could call for help in case of failure. Trip hazards were also frequently mentioned as a potential hazard presented by domestic robots, so they should be highly visible and able to navigate to safe locations. Data privacy and protection from scams were also strongly emphasised.

Human Touch. Robots for domestic tasks were considered useful (n = 12) and may outperform humans in certain tasks. Robots like Toilittle were seen as beneficial for tasks that cause discomfort for both carers and service users. However, many indicated they would still prefer the "human touch" (n = 3).

Operating Environment. Robots must work in small, cluttered, real-world spaces, and not require home modifications (n = 9). Those living in a residential setting noted that a robot like EasyUp could be shared between people (n = 3).

Multipurpose. Participants doubted the viability of a single robot to do everything, while space considerations limit the desirability of single-task robots (n = 3). There were suggestions on how each robot in the scenarios could be for both emotional and physical support, such as EasyUp also providing motivation.

Speculative Robots. Motibot, Foodee, EasyUp, and AutoReach were well received, with all participants seeing their value. Opinions on RoPet varied, with 3 major objections. Toilittle was a sensitive topic, which nobody wanted to use, most agreed it could be useful for those with greater health needs.

4.3 Requirements

The problems, opportunities and ideas from our participants are shown as functional (Table 3) and non-functional (Table 4) requirements. These have been related to specific needs for people living with frailty.

Table 4. Non-Functional Requirements in Relation to Frailty

Category	Requirement	In Relation to Frailty
Look and Feel	Highly visible	Avoid creating trip hazards
	Unobtrusive appearance	No distress for those with cognitive impairments
	Non-medical	Avoid medicalisation in daily life
Usability & Humanity	Easy for older people to use	Support users when they are alone
	Easy for carers, HCPs and others to use	Allow people in the user's wider support circle to use it
	Reduce cognitive load	To enhance memory & concentration
	Personalisation	Suit the user's changing needs
	Multimodal control	Interact with users with multiple, intersecting accessibility needs
Performance	Fail safely	Prevent injury or stranding users
	Awareness of home hazards	Does not create more hazards
Operational & Environment	Suitable for small homes	Older adults often downsize
	Consider shared environments	More older people live in shared or sheltered accommodation
	Fit to the environment	People do not want to change their homes for robots
Maintenance & Support	Full maintenance services	Older people are unlikely to be able to maintain a robot
	Encourage caring for the robot	Build a sense of responsibility for day-to-day maintenance
Security	Controlled by primary user	Protection from bad actors
Cultural	Understand regional difference	Users do not have to alter their language for the robot
	Different language options	To negate language barriers

5 Conclusion

Findings suggest that older people and healthcare professionals are willing to use robotic interventions to support independence and manage frailty. However, despite an abundance of research into assistive robots, few interventions have made the leap into the real world. As others have noted, researchers often start with a specific robotic platform in mind (and preconceived notions of the needs and abilities of older people), rather than seeking basic requirements. With this research, we hope to redress the balance and guide the development of assistive robots that are useful, usable, acceptable, and feasible.

Older people, their carers, and healthcare professionals shared their experiences of living with frailty, and opportunities to develop technological interventions. Cognitive, emotional and physical challenges were identified related to daily life and self-management, and all groups emphasised the need for a holistic approach to managing frailty. Technology needs to be personalised, as older people are not a homogeneous group. Safety, trust, and user-friendliness are key issues, and people are concerned about the cost and logistics of robotic provision and support, so developers should consider the design and cost-effectiveness of the wider service model. Finally, we have also created a set of "empathy cards" using the illustrations made during the workshops [13]. To aid dissemination, we use these as prompts and provocations in workshops with developers and other stakeholders to help promote more holistic design concepts for assistive robots.

6 Limitations

The study involved a limited, self-selecting sample, so findings may not generalise to the wider population. Moreover, the findings are specific to a particular cohort, time, and place. At this stage, we excluded participants with technical backgrounds to allow future phases of the project to engage developers, incorporating insights from older adults and HCPs into robotic design.

Acknowledgments. The authors thank all the participants, as well as Rebekah Moore and Sam Church. This work was funded by the EPSRC, UK [Grant numbers EP/W000741/1 and EP/S023305/1] and the Horizon Centre for Doctoral Training.

References

1. Fried, L.P., et al.: Frailty in older adults: evidence for a phenotype. J. Gerontol. Ser. A Biol. Sci. Med. Sci. **56**(3), M146–M157 (2001)
2. Lang, I.A., Llewellyn, D.J., Langa, K.M., et al.: Neighborhood deprivation, individual socioeconomic status, and cognitive function in older people: analyses from the english longitudinal study of ageing. J. Am. Geriatr. Soc. **56**(2), 191–198 (2008)
3. Wright, J.: Robots Won't Save Japan: An Ethnography of Eldercare Automation. Cornell University Press (2023)

4. Caleb-Solly, P.: Emergence, an EPSRC healthcare technologies network+ (2025). https://www.chartresearch.org/emergence-epsrc-network
5. Fiorini, L., et al.: A robot-mediated assessment of tinetti balance scale for sarcopenia evaluation in frail elderly. In: 28th IEEE International Conference on Robot and Human Interactive Communication (RO-MAN), pp. 1–6. IEEE (2019)
6. Fiorini, L., et al.: Co-creation of an assistive robot for independent living: lessons learned on robot design. Int. J. Interact. Des. Manufact. (IJIDeM) **14** (2020)
7. Bardaro, G., Antonini, A., Motta, E.: Robots for elderly care in the home: a landscape analysis and co-design toolkit. Int. J. Soc. Robot. **14**(3), 657–681 (2022)
8. Antony, V.N., Cho, S.M., Huang, C.-M.: Co-designing with older adults, for older adults: robots to promote physical activity. In: ACM/IEEE International Conference on H-RI, pp. 506–515 (2023)
9. García-Soler, Á., Facal, D., Díaz-Orueta, U., et al.: Inclusion of service robots in the daily lives of frail older users: a step-by-step definition procedure on users' requirements. Arch. Gerontol. Geriatr. **74**, 191–196 (2018)
10. The Design Council. The Double Diamond. www.designcouncil.org.uk/our-resources/the-double-diamond/
11. Espiner, D., Hartnett, F.: Innovation and graphic facilitation. Aotearoa New Zealand Soc. Work **28**(4), 44–53 (2016)
12. Robertson, S., Robertson, J.: Mastering the requirements process: getting requirements right. Addison-Wesley (2012)
13. Emergence. Emergence project resources (2024). www.chartresearch.org/resources/emergence-project-resources

Examining the Legibility of Humanoid Robot Arm Movements in a Pointing Task

Andrej Lúčny[1], Matilde Antonj[2,3], Carlo Mazzola[3,4],
Hana Hornáčková[1(✉)], Ana Farić[5], Kristína Malinovská[1], Ana Vavrečka[1],
and Igor Farkaš[1]

[1] Faculty of Mathematics, Physics and Informatics, Comenius University Bratislava, Bratislava, Slovakia
hannah.pelikan@liu.se
[2] DIBRIS, University of Genoa, Genoa, Italy
[3] CONTACT, Italian Institute of Technology, Genoa, Italy
[4] Digital Health Dept., Nvision Systems & Technologies, S.L., Barcelona, Spain
[5] Faculty of Education, University of Ljubljana, Ljubljana, Slovenia

Abstract. Human–robot interaction requires robots whose actions are legible, allowing humans to interpret, predict, and feel safe around them. This study investigates the legibility of humanoid robot arm movements in a pointing task, aiming to understand how humans predict robot intentions from truncated movements and bodily cues. We designed an experiment using the NICO humanoid robot, where participants observed its arm movements towards targets on a touchscreen. Robot cues varied across conditions: gaze, pointing, and pointing with congruent or incongruent gaze. Arm trajectories were stopped at 60% or 80% of their full length, and participants predicted the final target. We tested the multimodal superiority and ocular primacy hypotheses, both of which were supported by the experiment.

Keywords: Human–robot interaction · Nonverbal cues · Multimodal superiority · Oculomotor primacy

1 Introduction

Smooth human–robot interaction (HRI) scenarios must involve robots that support human ability to interpret, predict, and feel safe around robotic actions [13]. Hence, the design of robotic motion must extend beyond efficiency in reaching a goal. One of the features critical for effective, safe, and explainable collaboration is the legibility of the robot trajectory, characterised by its distinctiveness that helps the observer disambiguate the robot intent [4]. The legible movement supports transparency, which, together with human awareness, i.e., the robot ability to read and interpret human behavior, serves as a key pillar towards efficient HRI based on mutual understanding [9].

To study human perception during HRI, it is essential to design robotic behavior to be repeatable and controllable [2]. Thus, we designed an HRI experiment, using the humanoid robot NICO [6], investigating the participants' ability to predict the intentions of robotic arm movement (reaching a point on a touchscreen) before completion. We propose a method to generate precise and controllable robotic arm trajectories [8]. Combined with the pose of the robot head, these two modalities serve as information sources that human participants exploit in their inference task. Based on this, we tested two hypotheses:

- **Multimodal Superiority Hypothesis H_1**: The accuracy of the target localisation significantly exceeds unimodal conditions when participants observed coherent gaze-pointing signals (GP), compared to gaze-only (G) and pointing-only (P) conditions.
- **Oculomotor Primacy Hypothesis H_2**: The reaction times (RTs) for gaze-only trials (RT_G) are significantly shorter than for multimodal (RT_{GP}) or pointing-only trials (RT_P).

2 Related Work

The ability of robots to communicate intent effectively is crucial for seamless HRI. Pointing gestures and gaze direction are fundamental deictic cues that humans instinctively use and interpret. Studies have shown that robot gaze can significantly direct human attention [1], improve task efficiency and team fluency, and improve perceived social presence and engagement with the robot [7]. Similarly, robotic pointing gestures are critical for disambiguating targets in a shared workspace, although their effectiveness can depend on factors such as embodiment and the clarity of the gesture itself [14] . Our work builds upon this foundation by examining the combined and individual effects of these cues specifically in the context of predicting intent from truncated arm movements.

The integration of multiple cues, such as simultaneous pointing and gazing, often leads to more robust and rapid understanding of a robot referent. Nonverbal cues, such as gaze and gesture, have been shown to enhance robot persuasiveness and clarity [3]. Research has also explored how humans resolve discrepancies when these cues are in conflict. For example, gaze has been shown to "repair" ambiguous pointing gestures, suggesting a potential hierarchy or differential weighting in how humans process these signals [12]. More recent work investigates the nuances of these interactions, such as the timing and kinematics of combined gaze-gesture cues and their impact on perceived intentionality and trust. The current study contributes by systematically varying the congruency of movement and gaze and the completeness of the trajectories to understand how these factors modulate the interpretation of combined cues.

While much research has focused on completed actions, the interpretation of incomplete actions, where observers must extrapolate the robot goal, is less understood, particularly with multimodal cues. Anticipatory human responses to robot motions have been studied, showing that humans can predict robot

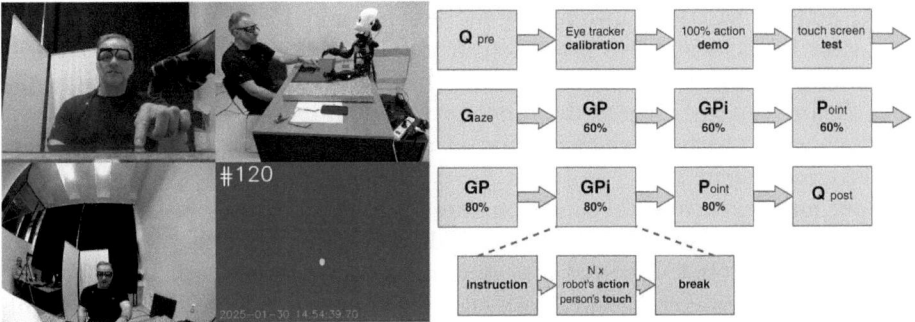

Fig. 1. Left: Experimental setup as displayed in the software GUI - from left: camera 1 (top left), camera 2 (top right), the robot camera (bottom left), control screen with the blue dot representing the robot intention and the yellow dot representing the participant' (Color figure online)s prediction (bottom right). Right: general schema of the experimental procedure reflecting experimental batch 1.

intentions early in an action sequence [11]. Our research extends this by quantifying the prediction accuracy for different percentages of trajectory completion (60% vs. 80%) across different combinations of gaze and pointing in order to delineate the thresholds at which robot intent becomes sufficiently legible.

3 Materials and Methods

3.1 Environment

The experiment was carried out using the NICO humanoid robot [6] having 22 DoF in the head, shoulders, elbows, wrists, and fingers. The integrated hardware included two eye cameras, facial LED arrays for mouth and eyebrow expressions, and a built-in speaker. The key interactive element was an LCD monitor with a capacitive touchscreen embedded in the table, serving as the robot target space. The experimental scene was further monitored by two external USB cameras that provided front and side views of the participant and the interaction. The robot behavior and experimental flow were managed by an integrated system of software agents communicating via a blackboard architecture, allowing modular control over various functions. Robot arm trajectories, consisting of 50 steps with 7 DoF, were precalculated using our novel methodology based on gradient descent and forward kinematics [8] to ensure precise, linear, and repeatable movements from a consistent starting pose to selected targets on the touchscreen. The source code for the experimental setup is publicly available.[1]

3.2 Experimental Procedure

The experiment started with pre-experiment questionnaires. In the main task, participants (students of various master's programs) predicted the target of

---

[1] https://github.com/andylucny/nico2/tree/main/experiment.

NICO actions based on incomplete movements and social cues (gaze). NICO right arm trajectories were presented in two lengths: a shorter segment (60%) and a longer segment (80%) of the total distance to the target from the beginning. Before the task began, the robot provided an initial verbal explanation of the task, along with a demonstration of a complete action that involved gaze and arm movement.

Four main experimental conditions were employed: a gaze-only (G) condition where the robot head was oriented towards a target; a pointing-only (P) condition where the robot executed arm movements; a pointing with the congruent gaze (GP) condition combining both cues towards the same target; and a pointing with the incongruent gaze (GPi) condition where the robot pointed at one target while gazing at a slightly shifted spot. Each participant experienced seven experimental sections: Since arm movements could provide rich information for the predictions, the order of conditions was set to gradually increase the informativeness of robot motor behavior (i.e. absence of arm movement, 60% trajectory, 80% trajectory). Moreover, the order of conditions was counterbalanced across two batches, when the information about the arm movement was equivalent:

- **Batch 1**: G, P60, GP60, GPi60, P80, GP80, GPi80;
- **Batch 2**: G, GP60, GPi60, P60, GP80, GPi80, P80.

Each section was stated with an instruction from the robot, followed by five blocks consisting of seven randomized trials targeting one of the seven predefined points on the touchscreen (Fig. 1 left). During each trial, NICO performed its designated action (gazing, pointing, or both, see Fig. 1 right). An auditory beep then signaled that the participant would touch the screen at their predicted target location within two seconds. See the video at https://youtu.be/nqT8pidhHtc.

3.3 Participants

A total of 28 participants (11 male, 17 female) aged 18 to 35 years were recruited for the main study, to minimize potential variability in motor and sensory functioning that could confound the results. To maintain experimental control over linguistic variables, all procedures were conducted exclusively in the Slovak language for native speakers. Before the main data collection, a pilot study was conducted involving seven participants to validate the experimental procedure and its integrity.

3.4 Data Analysis

To evaluate the legibility of each experimental condition and to investigate the degree to which participants integrated gaze and pointing cues in the multimodal condition, we measured prediction accuracy through bias, calculated as the distance between the participant's touch point and the actual robot target. We decomposed bias into lateral components ($bias_x$) and longitudinal ($bias_y$),

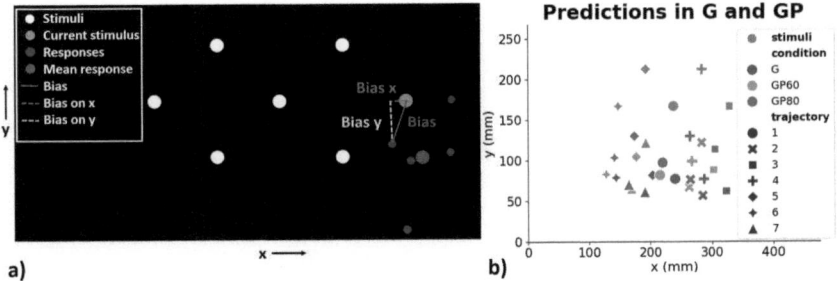

Fig. 2. a) Spatial layout of the seven target points (not shown to participants). The actual target is shown in green, participant responses in red, and remaining non-target options in white. b) Predictions in G and GP conditions. For each stimulus, mean predictions were computed for G, GP60 and GP80. The average distance between responses and stimuli identifies the bias. (Color figure online)

allowing us to quantify the magnitude and direction of the prediction error. From there, we derived the total bias for each target and condition as the mean Euclidean distance between the participants' responses and the corresponding target positions as

$$bias_{tot} = \frac{1}{N} \sum_{i=1}^{N} \sqrt{(x_{\text{resp},i} - x_{\text{target},i})^2 + (y_{\text{resp},i} - y_{\text{target},i})^2} \qquad (1)$$

where $x_{\text{resp},i}$ and $y_{\text{resp},i}$ are the coordinates of the participant's response in i-th trial, $x_{\text{target},i}$ and $y_{\text{target},i}$ are the corresponding coordinates of the actual target and N is the number of times each target was presented. Figure 2 illustrates these measures in the spatial layout of the task on the touchscreen. It also displays the seven possible target locations. The true target is highlighted in green, the responses of the participants in red (the larger is the mean), and the remaining non-target locations in white.

We measured participants' reaction time, defined as the time interval between the auditory cue indicating their response turn and the moment they touched the screen to provide their answer. Reaction times were collected for two key reasons. First, we instructed participants to respond as quickly as possible, promoting responses based on the ongoing motion trajectory rather than the final robot pose. Second, by comparing RTs across experimental conditions, our aim was to investigate how different communicative cues (gaze, pointing, and their combination) affected processing speed. Statistical analyses of bias and RT to test H_1) and H_2) were performed using linear mixed models [5] implemented in the Jamovi software[2]. The models included condition as a fixed effect, and both participant_ID and trajectory as random intercepts to account for individual variability and target-specific effects (see eq. 2).

$$\texttt{dep\_var} \sim 1 + \texttt{condition} + (1|\texttt{participant\_ID}) + (1|\texttt{trajectory}) \qquad (2)$$

---

[2] https://www.jamovi.org/.

4 Results

Manipulation Check: Trajectory Legibility Improvement

To verify the effectiveness of experimental manipulation of trajectory legibility, we performed a manipulation check to assess whether the trajectories designed to convey the robot intention with 80% segment resulted in significantly lower prediction bias compared to those designed with 60% segment. For this analysis, we used a paired-samples t-test, comparing the mean $bias_{tot}$ for each participant. Before the analysis, we used the Shapiro-Wilk test, which did not indicate any significant deviation from normality ($W = 0.980$, $p = .856$), supporting the suitability of the parametric test. The paired-samples t-test revealed a significant reduction in total bias in the 80% legibility condition ($M=84.8$mm, $SD=21.9$mm) compared to the 60% condition ($M=121$mm, $SD=29.2$mm), $t(26) = 8.78$, $p < .001$. The mean difference was $M_{diff} = 36.2$ mm, with a standard error of $SE = 4.12$ mm. The effect size, measured by Cohen's d, was large ($d = 1.69$), indicating a substantial improvement in the legibility of the trajectory.

Multimodal Superiority Hypothesis (H_1)

To test Multimodal Superiority Hypothesis, we employed a Linear Mixed Model to assess differences in total bias across all experimental conditions (Eq. 2). The model showed a significant effect of the condition on total bias (see Fig. 2a to understand an example of one representative participants' error for one stimulus). The omnibus F-test for the fixed effect of condition was significant, $F(4, 5268) = 479$, $p < .001$, confirming that total bias significantly varied across conditions. Post hoc pairwise comparisons with Bonferroni correction revealed that the legibility of gaze-only (G) trials was significantly higher (lower total bias) than in pointing-only trials with 60% segment (P60; $t = -13.62$, $p < .001$), but lower than in pointing-only trials with 80% segment (P80; $t = 17.21$, $p < .001$). Importantly, when gaze and pointing cues were combined, participants' performance improved significantly compared to both unimodal conditions (Fig. 3a). This advantage was evident at both 60% segment with a significant reduction of $bias_{tot}$ (GP60-P60: $t = -23.17$, $p < .001$; GP60-G: $t = -9.47$, $p < .001$) and 80% (GP80-P80: $t = -9.26$, $p < .001$; GP80-G: $t = -26.47$, $p < .001$), supporting the multimodal superiority hypothesis. As shown in Fig. 2b, in gaze and pointing trials participants' responses showed a lateral bias, in the opposite direction of the robot arm on the x-axis. On the contrary, in gaze-only condition participants seemed to anchor their attention in the horizontal direction. Since on the y-axis participants' responses were characterized by a bias toward the robot body, the gaze seemed to have a role in mitigating prediction error, in particular on x-axis.

Oculomotor Primacy Hypothesis (H_2)

The oculomotor primacy hypothesis was tested through a Linear Mixed Model to identify any differences in RT between all conditions (Eq. 2). The model con-

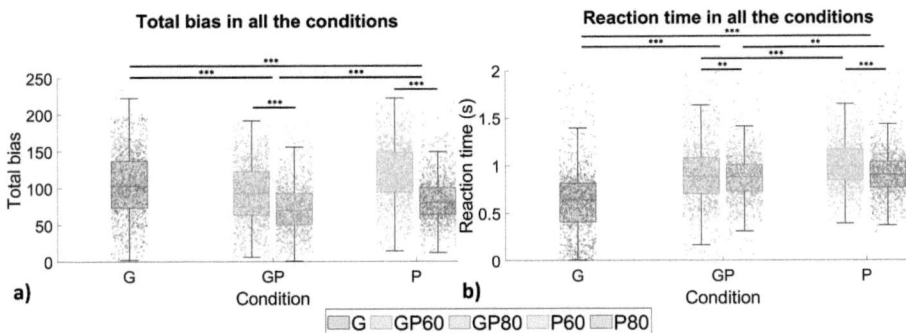

Fig. 3. a) Comparison of (a) total bias and (b) reaction times in five different conditions. Dots identify subjects' total bias (a) and reaction times (b) for each stimulus. Horizontal bars above the graphs show significant differences, found through post hoc pairwise comparisons with Bonferroni correction.

sidered `condition` as a fixed effect, and both `participant_ID` and `trajectory` as random intercepts to prevent individual variability and target-specific effects (adapted from Eq. 2). According to the omnibus F-test for the fixed effect of condition, RTs significantly varied across conditions ($F(4, 5268) = 340$, $p < .001$). Post hoc pairwise comparisons with Bonferroni correction showed that participants anticipated their response in G rather than P trials (G-P60: $t = -35.27$, $p < .001$; G-P80: $t = -25.32$, $p < .001$). Even when participants could combine G-P information, they were faster in G trials (G-GP60: $t = -25.38$, $p < .001$; G-GP80: $t = -21.62$, $p < .001$). Surprisingly, the combination of gaze and pointing allowed participants to have faster RTs, compared to P-only condition (P60-GP60: $t = 9.90$, $p < .001$; P80-GP80: $t = 3.71$, $p = .002$). The results shown in Fig. 3b supported the oculomotor primacy hypothesis.

5 Discussion and Future Work

Our initial results offer valuable insights into how robotic motion design and multimodal cues influence robot legibility [4]. Our preliminary analysis illuminates the complementary roles of gaze and pointing cues. The Multimodal Superiority Hypothesis (H_1) is supported by the implication that humans naturally integrate social (gaze) and spatial (pointing) information streams to form richer mental models of robot behavior [10]. This integration facilitates a more robust understanding of the robot target, beyond what unimodal signals can provide. In parallel, the support of the Oculomotor Primacy Hypothesis (H_2) highlights gaze as an especially rapid and salient cue. The fact that gaze-only conditions yield the fastest responses suggests that gaze acts as an early attentional beacon, enabling swift orientation towards the robot goal. The finding that multimodal conditions also benefit from processing advantage of gaze further supports the idea that gaze effectively primes the observerâĂŹs perceptual system, streamlining the integration of additional cues.

The directional analysis of bias along the spatial axes provides additional insight. Participants' responses consistently showed a lateral bias opposite to the arm direction along the x-axis, indicating that the participants tended to predict the motion endpoint to extend beyond the actual target. Interestingly, no such lateral bias was observed in gaze-only conditions, suggesting that gaze cues helped anchor attention precisely along the horizontal plane. Along the longitudinal, y-axis, a bias toward the robot body was evident, indicating a tendency to underestimate the forward reach distance. This pattern suggests that gaze cues help mitigate the prediction bias, in particular along the x-axis.

One of the future prospects of this work lies in developing a Bayesian model that quantifies how participants integrate gaze and pointing signals. Such a model could clarify the relative contribution of each cue to perception and decision-making, highlighting important implications for designing robotic systems that can communicate their intentions effectively and foster shared understanding in mixed human–robot environments.

Acknowledgments. This research has received funding from the Horizon Europe project TERAIS, the Grant agreement no. 101079338.

References

1. Admoni, H., Scassellati, B.: Social eye gaze in human-robot interaction: a review. J. Hum. Robot Int. **6**(1), 25–63 (2017)
2. Antonj, M., Zonca, J., Rea, F., Sciutti, A.: A controllable and repeatable method to study perceptual and motor adaptation in human–robot interaction. In: ACM/IEEE Int. Conf. on Human–Robot Interaction, pp. 188–192 (2023)
3. Chidambaram, V., Chiang, Y.H., Mutlu, B.: Designing persuasive robots: how robots might persuade people using vocal and nonverbal cues. In: ACM/IEEE Int. Conf. on on Human–Robot Interaction (2012)
4. Dragan, A.D., Lee, K.C., Srinivasa, S.S.: Legibility and predictability of robot motion. In: ACM/IEEE Int. Conf. on Human–Robot Interaction (2013)
5. Gallucci, M.: Gamlj: General analyses for linear models [jamovi module]. https://gamlj.github.io/ (2019)
6. Kerzel, M., Strahl, E., Magg, S., Navarro-Guerrero, N., Heinrich, S., Wermter, S.: NICO - Neuro-Inspired COmpanion: a developmental humanoid robot platform for multimodal interaction. In: IEEE RO-MAN, pp. 113–120 (2017)
7. Kompatsiari, K., Ciardo, F., Tikhanoff, V.: It's in the eyes: the engaging role of eye contact in HRI. Int. J. Soc. Robot. **13**, 1–11 (2021)
8. Lúčny, A., Antonj, M., Mazzola, C., Horňáčková, H., Farkaš, I.: Generating and customizing robotic arm trajectories using neural networks, (ICANN, accepted)
9. Mazzola, C., Ali, H., Malinovská, K., Farkaš, I.: An interaction-centered approach to robot trustworthiness: building justified trust via mutual understanding, (under review)
10. Mazzola, C., Rea, F., Sciutti, A.: Shared perception is different from individual perception: a new look on context dependency. IEEE Trans. Cogn. Develop. Syst. **15**(3), 1020–1032 (2023)

11. Moon, A., et al.: Meet me where I'm gazing: how shared attention gaze affects human–robot handover timing. J. Hum. Robot Int. **3**(1) (2014)
12. Mutlu, B., Shiwa, T., Kanda, T.: Footing in human-robot conversations: how robots might shape participant roles using gaze and gesture. In: ACM/IEEE HRI (2009)
13. Sciutti, A., Sandini, G.: Interacting with robots to investigate the bases of social interaction. IEEE Trans. Neural Syst. Rehabilitation Eng. **25**(12), 2295–2304 (2017)
14. Urakami, J., Seaborn, K.: Nonverbal cues in human-robot interaction: a communication studies perspective. ACM Trans. Hum, Robot Int (2023)

AI Pedagogy: Dialogic Social Learning for Artificial Agents

Sabrina Patania[1], Luca Annese[1], Cansu Koyuturk[1], Azzurra Ruggeri[2], and Dimitri Ognibene[1,3(✉)]

[1] University of Milan-Bicocca, Milan, Italy
{sabrina.patania,luca.annese1,dimitri.ognibene}@unimb.it,
c.koyutuerk@campus.unimib.it
[2] Technical University of Munich, Munich, Germany
azzurra.ruggeri@tum.de
[3] Institute for Cognitive Sciences and Technologies (ISTC-CNR), Rome, Italy

Abstract. Large Language Models (LLMs) are highly effective at learning from extensive offline datasets but face significant challenges when acquiring complex knowledge dynamically in online scenarios. Traditional training paradigms, based on supervised or reinforcement learning, reflect a Piagetian view of independent discovery and rely on vast data and sparse feedback, limiting their adaptability. Inspired by Vygotsky's sociocultural theory, this study investigates whether structured pedagogical interactions can enhance the efficiency of online learning in LLMs. We introduce a novel training method where a learner LLM engages in structured teaching dialogues with a knowledgeable LLM teacher to learn a synthetic taxonomy. The trained learner then applies this knowledge in downstream tasks, specifically tested in the challenging and well-known 20 Questions Game. These dialogues not only convey new external knowledge but also actively guide the learner in testing and refining its understanding. Our approach complements internal reasoning methods and prompt engineering: rather than relying on self-generated chains of thought or manually tailored inputs to refine the understanding and response to a single request, it introduces enriched and reusable task-specific knowledge through automatically structured pedagogical interactions. Unlike fine-tuning or few-shot learning, our method introduces novel domain knowledge without altering model weights or requiring explicit task examples. Our results show that the AI pedagogy strategy combining teacher explanations with learner-driven questions leads to better acquisition and application of knowledge compared to direct access to structured data. This highlights the potential of pedagogically guided interactions to enhance post-training learning and advance the development of more adaptable and human-aligned collaborative AI systems.

Keywords: in-context learning · social learning · LLMs · artificial pedagogy · ontology acquisition · mixed-initiative dialogue

1 Introduction

Over the past five years, Large Language Models (LLMs) have reshaped natural-language processing, demonstrating an ability to answer open-ended questions, draft code, and even reason across chains of thought [10,11,28] and support flexible robot behaviour [1,8,24]. Such successes, however, rest on a fundamentally offline recipe: pre-training from terabytes of data. When an LLM is deployed, it must make the best of whatever structure happened to appear in that corpus; it can refine its latent knowledge only indirectly, through prompt engineering or computationally and data expensive fine-tuning. The result is an awkward mismatch: humans constantly extend, reorganise, and verify their knowledge during conversation, whereas current LLMs have no principled mechanism for acquiring a new, formally structured body of facts on the fly.

A second mismatch between current AI practice and human cognition is social in nature. Much of human expertise is transmitted interpersonally: parents, teachers, and peers selectively highlight information, manage cognitive load [22], and adjust explanations to a learner's moment-by-moment understanding. This Vygotskian view [26] contrasts sharply with the dominant "Piagetian" stance in machine learning, where agents are typically expected to discover regularities independently—either from direct interactions with the physical world or from static knowledge repositories [6,7]. If we aim to develop intelligent systems capable of collaborative interaction—systems that acquire updated knowledge, co-write reports, troubleshoot novel hardware, or assist in medical diagnosis—then relying solely on solitary self-discovery may impose a limiting inductive bias.

Educational psychology provides an alternative. Decades of work on scaffolding, worked examples, and cognitive-load theory show that judicious pedagogical support helps novices build coherent schemas more quickly and robustly. Translating those insights to AI raises an intriguing question: can an LLM learn complex knowledge more effectively if we place it in a social learning environment, where another agent takes explicit responsibility for teaching?

In this work, we pursue that question through a controlled study of ontology learning. We construct fictitious taxonomies of "alien" species, rich enough to require non-trivial structure, yet free from any leakage of real-world priors, and embed them in an interactive task reminiscent of the classic 20-Questions game. A knowledgeable teacher LLM possesses the ground-truth ontology; a naïve learner must acquire that ontology solely through dialogue and later apply it in successive tasks (see Fig1). Crucially, we vary the teacher's pedagogical strategy across four well-studied dimensions in human learning, including top-down exposition, bottom-up induction, learner-driven questioning, and teacher-guided inquiry.

In addition to isolating these pedagogical styles, we explore mixed strategies resulting in a richer typology of dialogic learning conditions. The experimental setup involves repeated, fixed-length teaching sessions followed by game-based evaluation. Performance is gauged by the learner's ability to apply the acquired taxonomy in a deductive guessing game. A high-level schematic of the interaction is provided in Fig. 1.

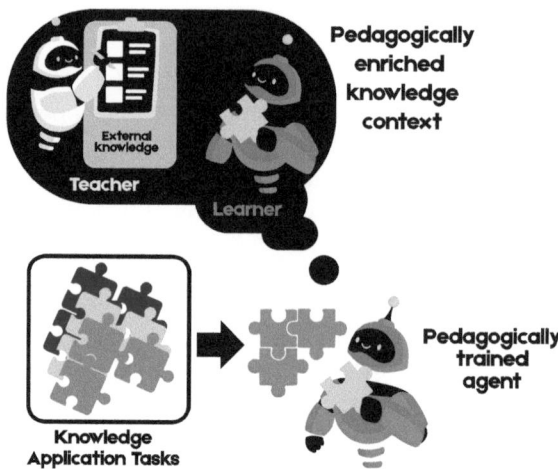

Fig. 1. Conceptual overview of the experimental setup. A naïve LLM-based learner acquires an alien taxonomy, external knowledge, through structured pedagogical interactions with a teacher LLM that has direct access to a formal representation of the taxonomy. The pedagogically trained agent is then applied to *Knowledge Application Tasks* and evaluated using a 20 Questions-style deductive task, relying exclusively on knowledge acquired during the pedagogical dialogue, provided as context. This process is flexible and can be iteratively integrated into task execution in human- or AI-in-the-loop scenarios. Notably, it does not require modifying model weights or providing explicit task solution examples.

Overall, the study indicates that socially interactive, pedagogically steered protocols provide a promising path toward AI agents that can build, verify, and extend structured knowledge in concert with human partners.

2 Related Work

Early work in developmental robotics [15] laid the foundation for understanding how robots can acquire cognitive functions, including language [17], through autonomous interaction with their environment, modeling children's developmental processes. These efforts, though primarily Piagetian in approach, highlighted the potential role of language in supporting learning, an idea further developed in epigenetic robotics [2,12,13]. For instance, [4] examines robot social learning, offering an alternative to costly solitary reinforcement learning [18]. Lockerd and Breazeal [14] introduced an early architecture inspired by human pedagogy at a time when language processing in robots was very limited. While language's role in enhancing cognitive capabilities is well studied [20,21], its integration within structured pedagogical frameworks for robots remains underexplored. With the emergence of LLMs and related foundation models capable of few-shot learning [3], it becomes timely to revisit this. We investigate how pedagogical interactions between two LLMs, through dialogue, can support knowledge co-construction, in contrast to static, hand tailored prompting approaches, which are often inefficient in robotic contexts especially to encode reusable knowledge [25,27]. Other approaches like fine-tuning, retrieval augmented generation (RAG), or few shot learning have different constraints (e.g. need for expensive weight updates or task solution examples) and can be combined with the proposed AI pedagogy approach.

Insights from developmental and educational psychology offer theoretical grounding for the AI pedagogy framework. Structured, expert-led inquiry (e.g., direct explanation) presents information hierarchically and reduces cognitive load, especially for novices [16,23]. In contrast, bottom-up approaches emphasize learner agency and contextual adaptation but risk cognitive overload if unguided [9]. Balancing these paradigms is key in designing AI pedagogical systems.

3 Methods

Our experiments examine how different pedagogical strategies affect the ability of LLMs to acquire, structure, and apply conceptual knowledge in a grounded interactive setting. The core idea is to model learning as a form of socially mediated knowledge construction, in which a naïve learner agent interacts with a more knowledgeable teacher agent through a pedagogical dialogue.

Experimental Setup. We conduct all simulations with GPT-4o accessed through the OpenAI API.[1] The procedure consists of three stages: *ontology generation*, *pedagogical interaction*, and *20-Questions evaluation*.

Ontology Generation. The core learning materials are entirely invented ontologies of "alien" species, each defined by a small set of categorical features (e.g., diet, habitat, morphology). All ontologies are synthetically generated to ensure no prior grounding in existing data. For each condition, the ontology generated with the help of an LLM remains fixed through both the learning and testing phases.

Pedagogical interactions. During training, a knowledgeable teacher LLM and a naïve learner LLM engage in brief, fixed-length dialogues centered on the target alien ontology. We include four base strategies, beginning with two primary explanatory framing approaches, monologic Top-down (TD) and Bottom-up (BU), in which the teacher delivers a complete exposition of the ontology while the learner remains passive. In addition, we explore two core dialogic variants, where an initial teacher prompt is followed by a back-and-forth dialogue

---

[1] Temperature is fixed at 0.3 and max_tokens at 5000 for every call.

focused solely on the source of questioning initiative, either from the learner (LQ) or the teacher (TQ) in a unidirectional way.

- **Top-down explanation (TD)**: The teacher leads by introducing high-level feature categories globally (e.g., "There are three kinds of diet..."), then elaborates with grouped species examples to support deductive generalisation.
- **Bottom-up induction (BU)**: The teacher begins with specific species descriptions, allowing abstract categories to emerge inductively as the learner is invited to notice patterns across instances.
- **Learner-driven questioning (LQ)**: The learner freely asks questions. The teacher responds truthfully and provides one-sentence generic clarification, but does not guide the conceptual framing or structure of the ontology.
- **Teacher-guided inquiry (TQ)**: The teacher ask targeted, guiding questions (e.g., "Which locomotion type might suit a crystal desert?"), prompting the learner to form, test, and refine conceptual hypotheses. The teacher provides feedback through confirmation or gentle correction.

We also analyze six hybrid scenarios in which the teacher first presents the ontology and then moves through a recurring cycle, explanation, questions, answers, repeated as needed. Two of these scenarios look only at who initiates the questioning (the learner or the teacher) and deliberately omit any explicit explanatory framing. For instance, in *Dialogic Teacher Questions (Dial-TQ)*, the teacher leads the interaction using open-ended prompts, without employing top-down or bottom-up explanation structuring. The other four mixed variants combine explanatory framing (TD or BU) with control of questioning initiative (learner- or teacher-led). For example, in *Dialogic Bottom-Up with Learner Questions (Dial-BU-LQ)*, the teacher introduces knowledge through bottom-up examples while allowing the learner to steer the dialogue through questions. The *teacher* agent receives the structured ontology as part of its system prompt. Thus, for every subsequent turn the teacher has perfect, verifiable knowledge of every species–feature pair.

Expert Baseline. We define an expert baseline, another GPT-4o instance whose system prompt contains the full ontology during the 20-Questions game. Apart from that advantage, the baseline plays exactly the same protocol as the learners.

20-Questions Evaluation. After training, the learner's weights are frozen and the agent is tested in an automated variant of the classic 20-Questions game. We generate 50 candidate sets, each containing eight distinct species randomly drawn from the ontology. For each set an *oracle* with full ontology access secretly selects one target. The learner asks yes/no feature questions until it either identifies the target or reaches the maximum budget of 20 questions. We record the question count and whether the final guess is correct.

4 Results

An independent samples t-test was conducted to compare the performance of LLM agents trained under different pedagogical strategies against that of the expert baseline agent, which showed an average of 7 questions per trial. Learners in the monologic *TD* strategy (M = 5.15, t(df) = −3.12, p = .0047) and the *Dial-LQ* condition (M = 5.30, t(df) = −3.61, p = .0012) performed significantly better than the expert. In contrast, the LQ, which lacked any expert guidance or framing, performed significantly worse than the expert (M = 12.80, t(df) = 6.95, p < .001). Results for the remaining pedagogical strategies were not statistically significant, although several showed performance trends suggesting potential benefits over the expert baseline.

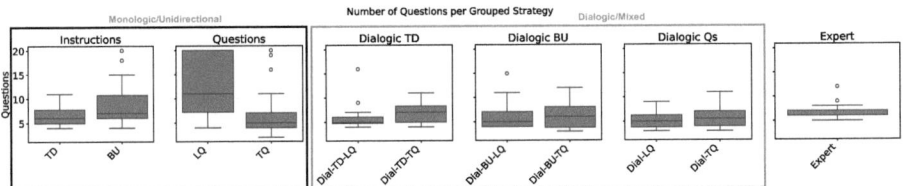

Fig. 2. Distribution of questions required to solve the 20-Questions task. Box-plots show the learner conditions grouped by strategy; the last box on the right is the expert baseline with full ontology access. Lower values indicate greater efficiency.

5 Discussion and Conclusions

Our findings underscore the significant impact of pedagogical strategies on the online acquisition and application of complex, structured, knowledge by LLMs. Notably, the Monologic Teaching Dialogue (TD) strategy, which supports deductive generalization, and the dialogic TD strategy that interleaves teacher explanations with learner-initiated questioning, reminiscent of Vygotskian scaffolding, demonstrate superior performance compared to direct access to structured knowledge, even if such format is widely present in training datasets.

The principles underpinning this approach align with foundational ideas in developmental and epigenetic robotics [14,15,17]. Our study builds on these traditions by demonstrating that LLMs, though disembodied, can benefit from structured, socially interactive learning environments. Incorporating rich language interactions and scaffolding techniques may enable the modeling of complex skill acquisition processes akin to those observed in natural social contexts. This progression not only moves us closer to more human-like AI learning systems but also opens avenues for novel contributions from epigenetic robotics to developmental psychology, reinforcing the importance of socially situated, embodied learning [5].

While inspired by developmental learning theories, our approach is not intended as a direct model of child development. Unlike infants, LLMs already possess an extensive linguistic repertoire. The core challenge, and the focus of this work, is enable LLMs to effectively access novel knowledge after training, transforming their passive linguistic capacity into an active tool for incremental knowledge construction.

Traditional methods such as fine-tuning and few-shot learning address this challenge either by modifying model weights or by crafting ad hoc task-specific examples. In contrast, our approach enables the autonomous acquisition and refinement of knowledge through pedagogically structured (simulated) dialogues. Rather than injecting static facts, we support the dynamic co-construction of pedagogically enriched context that is reusable, interpretable, and shaped through interaction. In this sense, our method is orthogonal to prompting and reasoning-based approaches and complementary to techniques like RAG and in-context learning: where those methods retrieve or inject external content, we construct context dialogically.

This dialogue-driven process may offer a more natural and adaptive pathway for real-time knowledge acquisition. It opens the possibility of enhancing LLM capabilities without additional data or model retraining, addressing practical constraints in contemporary AI systems [10,11]. Moreover, by integrating learner-generated questions to reduce uncertainty during training [19], our method helps consolidate new knowledge into structured, reusable internal representations. This may improve the reliability of prompting strategies [25,27], and strengthen the flexibility of few-shot and zero-shot paradigms [3].

A compelling direction for future research lies in understanding the roots of this pedagogical sensitivity in LLMs. Their ability to respond to socially guided instruction suggests an underexplored propensity to mirror human linguistic behaviors. Investigating this capacity could guide the design of more natural pedagogical strategies for real-time knowledge transfer, not only among AI, but also between humans and AIs, including robots, operating in collaborative environments.

References

1. Ahn, M., Brohan, A., et al.: Do as i can and not as i say: grounding language in robotic affordances (2022)
2. Berthouze, L., Ziemke, T.: Epigenetic robotics—modelling cognitive development in robotic systems (2003)
3. Brown, T., Mann, B., et al.: Language models are few-shot learners. Adv. Neural. Inf. Process. Syst. **33**, 1877–1901 (2020)
4. Cakmak, M., DePalma, N., Arriaga, R.I., Thomaz, A.L.: Exploiting social partners in robot learning. Auton. Robot. **29**, 309–329 (2010)
5. Cangelosi, A., Schlesinger, M.: From babies to robots: the contribution of developmental robotics to developmental psychology. Child Dev. Persp. **12**(3), 183–188 (2018)
6. Carey, S., Zaitchik, D., Bascandziev, I.: Theories of development: In dialog with jean piaget. Dev. Rev. **38**, 36–54 (2015)
7. Chi, M.T.: Active-constructive-interactive: a conceptual framework for differentiating learning activities. Top. Cogn. Sci. **1**(1), 73–105 (2009)
8. Colombani, S., Ognibene, D., Boccignone, G.: One to rule them all: natural language to bind communication, perception and action (2024)

9. Cousins, J.B., Leithwood, K.A.: Enhancing knowledge utilization as a strategy for school improvement. Knowledge **14**(3), 305–333 (1993)
10. Guo, D., Yang, D., et al.: Deepseek-r1: incentivizing reasoning capability in llms via reinforcement learning. arXiv preprint arXiv:2501.12948 (2025)
11. Jaech, A., Kalai, A., et al.: Openai o1 system card. arXiv preprint arXiv:2412.16720 (2024)
12. Kozima, H., Zlatev, J.: An epigenetic approach to human-robot communication (2000)
13. Lindblom, J., Ziemke, T.: Social situatedness of natural and artificial intelligence: Vygotsky and beyond. Adapt. Behav. **11**(2), 79–96 (2003)
14. Lockerd, A., Breazeal, C.: Tutelage and socially guided robot learning (2004). https://doi.org/10.1109/IROS.2004.1389954
15. Lungarella, M., Metta, G., Pfeifer, R., Sandini, G.: Developmental robotics: a survey. Connection Sci. **15**(4), 151–190 (2003)
16. Martin, A.J.: Integrating motivation and instruction: towards a unified approach in educational psychology. Educ. Psychol. Rev. **35**(2), 54 (2023)
17. Morse, A.F., Cangelosi, A.: Why are there developmental stages in language learning? a developmental robotics model of language development. Cogn. Sci. **41**, 32–51 (2017)
18. Ognibene, D., Fiore, V.G., Gu, X.: Addiction beyond pharmacological effects: The role of environment complexity and bounded rationality. Neural Netw. **116**, 269–278 (2019)
19. Patania, S., Masiero, E., et al.: Large language models as an active bayesian filter: information acquisition and integration (2024)
20. Petit, M., Lallée, S.e.a.: The coordinating role of language in real-time multimodal learning of cooperative tasks. IEEE Trans. Autonom. Mental Develop. **5**(1), 3–17 (2012)
21. Sugita, Y., Tani, J.: Learning semantic combinatoriality from the interaction between linguistic and behavioral processes. Adapt. Behav. **13**(1), 33–52 (2005)
22. Sweller, J.: Cognitive load during problem solving: Effects on learning. Cogn. Sci. **12**(2), 257–285 (1988)
23. Sweller, J.: Cognitive load theory. In: Psychology of learning and motivation, vol. 55, pp. 37–76. Elsevier (2011)
24. Team, G.R., Abeyruwan, S., et al.: Gemini robotics: bringing AI into the physical world. arXiv preprint arXiv:2503.20020 (2025)
25. Theophilou, E., Koyutürk, C., et al.: Learning to prompt in the classroom to understand AI limits: a pilot study (2023)
26. Vygotsky, L.S., Cole, M.: Mind in society: development of higher psychological processes. Harvard university press (1978)
27. White, J., et al.: A prompt pattern catalog to enhance prompt engineering with chatgpt. arXiv preprint arXiv:2302.11382 (2023)
28. Yao, S., et al.: React: Synergizing reasoning and acting in language models (2023)

Beyond Detection - Orchestrating Human-Robot-Robot Assistance via an Internet of Robotic Things Paradigm

Joseph Hunt, Koyo Fujii, Aly Magassouba, and Praminda Caleb-Solly

School of Computer Science, University of Nottingham, Nottingham, UK
praminda.caleb-solly@nottingham.ac.uk

Abstract. Hospital patient falls remain a critical and costly challenge worldwide. While conventional fall prevention systems typically rely on post-fall detection or reactive alerts, they also often suffer from high false positive rates and fail to address the underlying patient needs that lead to bed-exit attempts. This paper presents a novel system architecture that leverages the Internet of Robotic Things (IoRT) to orchestrate human-robot-robot interaction for proactive and personalized patient assistance. The system integrates a privacy-preserving thermal sensing model capable of real-time bed-exit prediction, with two coordinated robotic agents that respond dynamically based on predicted intent and patient input. This orchestrated response could not only reduce fall risk but also attend to the patient's underlying motivations for movement, such as thirst, discomfort, or the need for assistance, before a hazardous situation arises. Our contributions with this pilot study are threefold: (1) a modular IoRT-based framework enabling distributed sensing, prediction, and multi-robot coordination; (2) a demonstration of low-resolution thermal sensing for accurate, privacy-preserving pre-emptive bed-exit detection; and (3) results from a user study and systematic error analysis that inform the design of situationally aware, multi-agent interactions in hospital settings. The findings highlight how interactive and connected robotic systems can move beyond passive monitoring to deliver timely, meaningful assistance, empowering safer, more responsive care environments.

Keywords: Internet of Robotic Things · Human-Robot Interaction · Fall Mitigation

1 Introduction

Incidents such as patient falls are common in hospitals and can lead to further injury, extended stays and financial burden [1]. When surveyed, older patients, reported not wanting to be a burden to healthcare staff and that the act of receiving help causes embarrassment when citing reasons for leaving their bed without assistance [2]. Reliable real-time bed-exit prediction, together with a timely intervention that responds and interacts with the patient to offer support could help to mitigate bed-exit as a reason for falls in hospitals.

Our aim in this research is to develop a cost-effective robotic system with a socially assistive robot (SAR) that responds to events from a thermal sensing bed exit prediction system and determines the patient's needs through interaction. The SAR investigates their underlying motivation for wanting to leave the bed, such as thirst, discomfort, or the need for assistance, before a hazardous situation arises. To demonstrate our system, we piloted a use-case which involved the delivery of items to the patient's bedside, following an interaction where a SARf acquired and communicated their request to another physically assistive robot arm. Our Internet of Robotic Things (IoRT) solution comprises the temi SAR [3], with a separate fixed Kinova Gen3 lite arm [4] with pick and place functionality, mounted on a table.

In this paper we present our findings from a pilot study with participants where this realistic assistive task was conducted in the context of a mock hospital room setting.

The contributions of our study include a modular IoRT-based framework with sensing via low-resolution thermal sensing for accurate, privacy-preserving pre-emptive bed-exit prediction, and multi-robot coordination. The results from this study and the systematic error analysis we conducted can inform the design of better context aware, multi-agent robotic systems. Our paper highlights how interactive and connected robotic systems can move beyond passive monitoring to deliver timely, meaningful assistance, empowering safer, more modular and responsive care environments.

2 Related Work

Current methods of detecting a hospital patient leaving a bed include using pressure pads, wearable devices, and infrared sensors. Pressure pads are placed under the user and produce an alert when they no longer detect the patient's presence. These pressure pads are often combined with infrared beams to create 'dual sensing.' A review paper noted how a dual system alarm can have a sensitivity of nearly 100%, with a positive predictive value of 68% but can generate from 16% to 31% "nuisance alarms" [5].

Robots, and more specifically, the temi robot this study used, are showing potential for interacting with patients on hospital wards. A 2023 study into the use of temi robots on isolation wards demonstrated their ability to provide communication between patients and nursing staff using video calls and voice commands. Participants gave this robot a mean difficulty rating of 1.28/5 (lower is better) [6].

The IoRT is a proposed extension of the Internet of Things to include communication between robotics systems and IoT systems [7, 8]. This integration allows for communication between mobile robots, sensors and machine learning algorithms to bring enhanced intelligence to IoT compatible devices. The concept also encompasses communication technologies across multiple layers such as the Message Queuing Telemetry Transport (MQTT) [9] protocol on the application layer to facilitate machine-to-machine communication.

This lightweight, publish-subscribe based messaging protocol which is commonly used for IoT applications is designed for resource-constrained devices and low-bandwidth, high-latency, or unreliable networks. Other studies have also been working towards cooperation of heterogeneous robotic systems [10] also analysing error between robots and users given a sequential task [11, 12].

3 Approach

We have designed an IoRT system composed of a social robot (temi), and Kinova Gen3 Lite robotic arm, connected to a bed-exit prediction system. Our setup is proposed as a modular integrated solution to grasping and transporting objects by using multiple independent robotic systems that communicate with each other and the bed-exit prediction system through MQTT. Our selection of platforms aims to show how we might produce a workable solution by combining robots, whereby dividing complex tasks among specialised robots, results in more efficiency. Furthermore, the modularity of the system can improve real-world usability, allowing it to be tailored to specific scenarios. Environments such as clinical settings often have confined areas, which are not conducive to large mobile robots with arms. Additionally in hospitals avoiding cross-contamination is important [13] so a system with several local and smaller robots could be more pragmatic. Our approach using several smaller heterogeneous robot systems cooperating in an IoRT framework could also reduce the total cost of the system. We have designed the proposed system with the potential to be highly scalable, where individual robots could be swapped out and more systems integrated without incurring significant development costs and downtime. The system architecture is shown in Fig. 1 and each system sub-component is discussed in the following sections.

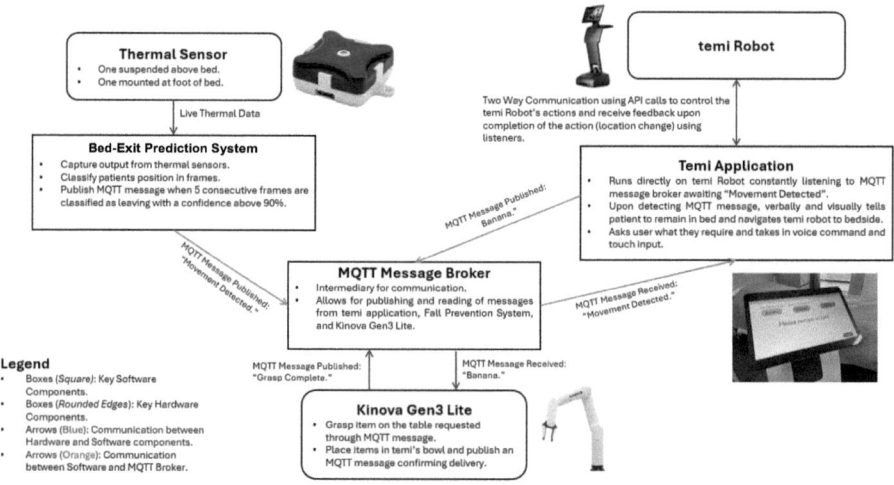

Fig. 1. Components within our IoRT system and system architecture.

3.1 Bed-Exit Prediction System

Two Terabee TeraRanger Evo thermal cameras [14] were positioned in a fixed locations as shown in Fig. 2c, at the foot of a hospital bed and above it. The locations were selected to avoid being obtrusive and not interfere with changing of bed linen or the patient. These sensors provide a 32x32 pixel resolution (Fig. 2) image at a frame rate of 14 Hz allowing for accurate classification whilst conserving the patient privacy.

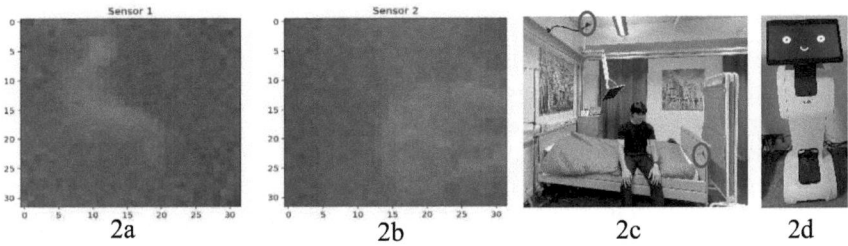

Fig. 2. Images from thermal imaging sensors from the side and top cameras (circled in red) showing a person seated with their legs at the side of the bed, and temi robot.

3.2 Temi – Social Interaction and Transport Robot

The temi (Fig. 2d) is a SAR with mapping, navigation and collision avoidance features which are crucial for deployment in busy environments such as a hospital ward. It also has a 13.3" capacitive touch screen for a graphical user interface or animated face, as well as built-in natural language processing and speech synthesis, with a microphone and speakers, making it an ideal platform for social interaction.

For this study, a Kotlin android application was developed and deployed on the temi robot. Our application enabled the robot to navigate autonomously between key locations based on events triggered from the bed-exit prediction system. We also implemented multi-modal interaction features; the robot uses speech to instruct the "patient" to remain in their hospital bed when an event from the bed-exit system is detected and displays the same text on the integrated touch screen. When the robot reaches the patient's bedside, the temi screen displays an array of buttons labelled with different items that the patient can request to be fetched to them. The patient can also use speech to verbally articulate their request. Based on the location of the requested item, the temi robot navigates to the appropriate pickup position where the bowl it is carrying on a tray can be loaded with the selected item by the Kinova Gen3 Lite which completes a pick and place task. The pick and place task, and the action of the temi returning to the bedside with the item, is coordinated and synchronised via MQTT messages.

3.3 Kinova Gen3 Lite Manipulation Robot

A robot arm, a Kinova Gen3 Lite with a RealSense camera, was used to perform the pick and place manipulation task using MoveIt, a robotic manipulation platform for ROS [15]. The arm was mounted at the edge of a table with a range of items on it. The system can be scaled by using lower cost arms mounted in different locations, and the item could also potentially be requested from hospital staff who might be elsewhere. We utilised a pre-trained state-of-the-art image segmentation model, Early Vision-Language Fusion for Text-Prompted Segment Anything Model [16] to detect the requested object based on a language prompt. The name of item to be picked up is passed to the Kinova arm sub-system via MQTT from the temi as per the user's request to the temi.

3.4 Communication Protocol

We used the Message Queuing Telemetry Transport (MQTT) protocol to establish the communication between the different elements of the IoRT system. One advantage of MQTT compared to other protocols such as HTTP, is the low bandwidth [17] making it suitable for resource-constrained hospital environments. MQTT is also low-latency [18] which is important for minimising the time it takes for temi to instruct the patient not to leave and bed and reach the patient's bedside after a bed-exit is event triggered.

4 Experiment and Results

4.1 Experiment Design

Sixteen participants (11M & 5F, mean age 22) participated in our study with the IoRT system. All participants were students at the University of Nottingham (UoN) who provided ethics approval for the study. The study took place in a mock hospital ward room which housed a bed, the temi, and Kinova Gen3 robot, and a table. On the table, there were several items, such as a water bottle and different fruit. The participants' interaction with the system was video recorded and they were asked to fill a user experience questionnaire at the end of the trial.

The experiment was divided into two parts. The first part was to test to sensitivity and accuracy of the bed-exit prediction model. Each participant was instructed to lie down on the bed and attempt to leave the bed whenever they wanted. When the bed-exit prediction system detected an attempt to leave the bed, an alarm would sound. At this point, the participant was instructed to get back onto the bed and restart the scenario. To test the robustness of the prediction model, this trial was repeated 15 times; however, the participant was told to select 5 of these trials at random and attempt to "trick" the system into thinking they were getting out of the bed when they did not intend to.

In the second part of the experiment, which was repeated three times, the user experience and interaction with the temi robot was tested. This time, when a participant was detected leaving the bed, instead of the sound alarm, the temi robot would instruct the participant to remain in bed and start moving to the person's bedside and ask the participant if there was anything it could do for them. The participant could then select an item to fetch, either through voice or through the touch screen. The robot then navigated to the pickup location. At this point, the Kinova Gen3 Lite picked up the requested item from the table and placed it into temi's bowl. The temi then returned to the participant's bedside before turning around and instructing them to take the item.

During all stages of the robotic interaction, the temi audibly informed the participant of its current actions and intentions, including audibly "telling" the Kinova arm what item had been requested as it published the MQTT message. This was done to ensure transparency and keep the participants aware of what was happening. Participants were purposely given no instruction or training on how to interact with the temi robot and were told there was no right or wrong way to interact, as we were also interested in understanding what their pre-conceived assumptions about the system operation would be, and also to understand the likely errors that might ensue.

4.2 User Experience Questionnaire Results

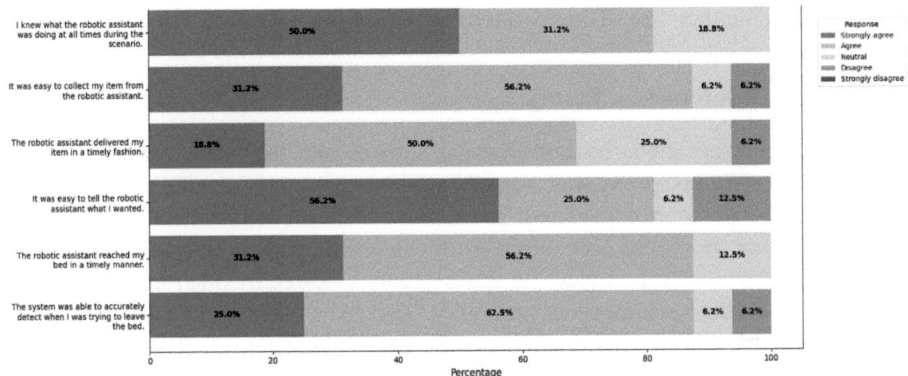

Fig. 3. Responses to User Experience Questionnaire

The questionnaire contained Likert-scale user experience questions designed to evaluate participants' perceptions of the system as shown in Fig. 3. It also included two open-ended questions that asked what participants felt the system did well and what it did not do well. When asked what they liked, participants praised the robot's human interaction capabilities and its non-threatening, friendly presence. Comments included: "The voice of the robot is soft and has a gentle tone which could be seen as non-confrontational," and "temi is a fairly non-scary robot, which is definitely important." Another participant noted, "The voice of the robot was not intimidating and comforting and helped to dispel any nervousness about it." Participants also complimented the clarity of the user interface and the ease of interaction through multi-modal input. One participant stated, "I think the user interface on the robot was easy to use and navigate—there was no possible confusion about how to interact with it when it came to my bedside." Another remarked, "The user interface is clear, and system is clean and easy to operate." On the other hand, when asked what they did not like, many participants felt that the speed of the system could be improved. Comments included: "The fetching of the items could be quicker," and "It took a long time to get the item once the robot had gone to get it (the robotic arm took a long time)." Additionally, several participants pointed out issues with the robot's navigation. One participant observed, "The robot did not face me when I tried to leave the bed at the foot of it. This gave me the impression that the robot did not actually know where I was and instead positioned itself in a general position. The interaction became less personal at that point."

4.3 Interaction Results

The bed-exit prediction system had a classification accuracy of 79.65% on unseen data, with recall of 1, the misclassifications were all false alarms. This could be annoying if it meant that a nurse had to be called out, but with our system, this could reduce pressure on staff. Participants preferred using touch input to tell the temi robot what item they wanted. Touch input was used by participants 29 times whereas voice input was only used 15 times. Participants began to use the touch screen less in trials two and three and instead, increasing their use of voice to tell the temi robot what they wanted.

4.4 Analysis of Interaction Errors

To analyse the errors made by both the participants and the robots involved in the experiment, an error taxonomy was created based on previous research [19, 20]. A total of 10 HRI error types were considered. To support consistent and efficient error logging, a simple GUI was developed with all the error categories, and the interaction modality. A sample of the videos were randomly selected and reviewed by other members of the study team to check for inter-rater variability. The error types included Social errors (misunderstanding the user, insufficient communicative function); Safety-related errors (human errors: procedure, intrusion, operation and situation awareness) and Robot errors (system failures, safeguarding failures, operational errors, design flaws). Operational errors were the most common for both interaction modalities with 66 instances, mostly related to the temi attempting to avoid the participants' legs and nearby armchair and failing to get close enough to the participant. Common human errors were intrusion errors (4 instances) where participants intentionally or unintentionally interrupted the flow of operations by using the trigger word or saying something else. Insufficient communicative function was the most common social error (4 instances), due to errors in synchronising listening and responding to participants. The rarest errors were system failures and design flaws, with only 1 instance each. Categorising errors using this taxonomy helps to prioritise improvements that need to be made to the platform before further use.

5 Conclusions

This paper proposes an Internet of Robotics Things paradigm that utilises two different types of robots coordinating their tasks for pro-active assistance in hospital environments. Our system was evaluated in a realistic user study which has helped to highlight system weaknesses to address before a real-world deployment. Based on this study, we have noted several areas for further study and improvements. These include:

- Studying how human adaptation can be exploited to decrease HRI errors over time.
- Personalising the system behaviour and interaction modalities based on the condition of the patient who is being supported. We will consider constructing several user models which can be used to determine the best approach.

   Our next phase will involve a larger study with real patients in a clinical setting.

References

1. Morello, R.T., et al.: The extra resource burden of in-hospital falls: a cost of falls study. Med. J. Aust. **203**(9), 367 (2015). https://doi.org/10.5694/mja15.00296
2. Haines, T.P., Lee, D.A., O'Connell, B., McDermott, F., Hoffmann, T.: Why do hospitalized older adults take risks that may lead to falls? Health Expect. **18**(2), 233–249 (2015). https://doi.org/10.1111/hex.12026
3. 'Get temi the personal robot for your business | robotemi.com', temi robot. Accessed Apr 01 2025. https://www.robotemi.com/product/temi/
4. 'Discover our Gen3 lite robot', Kinova. Accessed 01 Apr 2025. https://www.kinovarobotics.com/product/gen3-lite-robots
5. Oh-Park, M., Doan, T., Dohle, C., Vermiglio-Kohn, V., Abdou, A.: Technology utilization in fall prevention. Phys. Med. Rehab. **100**(1), 92 (2021)
6. Yoo, H.J., Kim, E.H., Lee, H.: Mobile robots for isolation-room hospital settings: a scenario-based preliminary study. Comput. Struct. Biotechnol. J. **24**, 237–246 (2024). https://doi.org/10.1016/j.csbj.2024.03.001
7. 'Internet of Robotic Things: Driving Intelligent Robotics of Future - Concept, Architecture, Applications and Technologies | IEEE Conference Publication | IEEE Xplore'. Accessed Mar 18 2025. https://ieeexplore.ieee.org/abstract/document/8611051
8. Sandhu, M., Silvera-Tawil, D., Borges, P., Zhang, Q., Kusy, B.: Internet of robotic things for independent living: critical analysis and future directions. Internet Things **25**, 101120 (2024). https://doi.org/10.1016/j.iot.2024.101120
9. Soni, D., Makwana, A.: A Survey on Mqtt: A Protocol Of Internet Of Things(Iot) (2017)
10. Kiener, J., von Stryk, O.: Towards cooperation of heterogeneous, autonomous robots: a case study of humanoid and wheeled robots. Robot. Auton. Syst. **58**(7), 921–929 (2010). https://doi.org/10.1016/j.robot.2010.03.013
11. Shin, S., Kwon, Y., Lim, Y., Kwak, S.S.: User perception of the robot's error in heterogeneous multi-robot system performing sequential cooperative task. In: Social Robotics, A. A. Ali, J.-J. Cabibihan, N. Meskin, S. Rossi, W. Jiang, H. He, and S. S. Ge, (eds.) Singapore: Springer Nature, pp. 322–332 (2024). https://doi.org/10.1007/978-981-99-8718-4_28
12. Shin, S., Kwak, S.S.: Do hierarchies in a robot team impact the service evaluation by users? In: 2023 IEEE/RSJ Int Conf on Intelligent Robots and Systems, pp. 3983–3990
13. Lim, C., Lee, M.-Y., Kim, S.-W.: Recent development of medical service robots in Republic of Korea and their field demonstration cases in the clinical setting. JMST Adv. **6**(4), 395–401 (2024). https://doi.org/10.1007/s42791-024-00092-y
14. 'TeraRanger Evo Thermal Cameras'. Accessed: Mar. 25, 2025. https://www.mouser.co.uk/terabee-thermal-cameras
15. Coleman, D.T., Sucan, I.A., Chitta, S., Correll, N.: Reducing the Barrier to Entry of Complex Robotic Software: a MoveIt! Case Study', Italy (2014)
16. Zhang, Y., et al.: EVF-SAM: early vision-language fusion for text-prompted segment anything model, 10 March 2025, arXiv: arXiv:2406.20076
17. Alshammari, H.H.: The internet of things healthcare monitoring system based on MQTT protocol. Alexandria Eng. J. **69**, 275–287 (2023)
18. Gavrilov, A., Bergaliyev, M., Tinyakov, S., Krinkin, K., Popov, P.: Using IoT protocols in real-time systems: protocol analysis and evaluation of data transmission characteristics. Com. Networks Comms. **2022**(1), 7368691 (2022)
19. Batti, N., et al.: Improving human understanding of errors through enhanced robot-to-human error reporting. RSS 2024, Workshop on Robot Execution Failures
20. Guo, B.H.W., Zuo, Y., Goh, Y.M., Lim, J.-Y.: Errors in human-robot interaction accidents: a taxonomy and network analysis. In: Int. Conf. on Construction Engineering and Project Management, pp. 1088–1095 (2024). https://doi.org/10.6106/ICCEPM.2024.1088

Towards Expert Human-Robot Interactions Using Knowledge Graphs

Graham Wilcock[1,3]([✉]), Kristiina Jokinen[2,3], Biju Thankachan[4], and Markku Turunen[4]

[1] CDM Interact, Helsinki, Finland
`graham.wilcock@cdminteract.com`
[2] AI Research Center, AIST Tokyo Waterfront, Tokyo, Japan
`kristiina.jokinen@aist.go.jp`
[3] University of Helsinki, Helsinki, Finland
[4] Tampere University, Tampere, Finland
`biju.thankachan@tuni.fi, markku.turunen@tuni.fi`

Abstract. This short paper describes ongoing work towards enabling more expert-level human-robot interactions based on knowledge graphs. This requires personalisation of the AI agent responses for expert users, not only providing the language model with expert knowledge via RAG, but also modifying the style of the responses to be more concise. Some examples of more expert-level interactions are discussed.

Keywords: Social Robots · Knowledge Graphs · Expert Interaction

1 Introduction

A strong tendency in AI-based chatbots favours a "chatty" type of conversation, where the goal is to engage the user and maintain a friendly and happy-sounding interaction. Even if the chatbots do not provide totally reliable information, the natural-sounding conversational fluency is considered superior to the earlier handcrafted systems which did not encourage the user to continue chatting.

Generative AI helps to improve capabilities in interactive applications for many domains (commerce, education, care services, health, medical services), with positive results e.g. AI chatbots reducing psychological stress [8]. However, several aspects make their use in social robotic applications problematic.

As pointed out for example by [11], language capable AI agents not only share the risks presented by traditional robots and natural language technologies (physical safety, stereotypes and biases of everyday life, sustainability concerns), they also bring up new types of challenges which arise from their communicative capability and embodiment. These are related to risks of harm and liability of the AI agent presenting fabricated or incorrect information, biases in the training data, lack of predictability of interaction, and lack of meaningful connection with the user's situation [2]. For discussion on empathy of robot agents, see [4].

In earlier work Wilcock and Jokinen used knowledge graphs with social robots to produce more cooperative behaviour in task-oriented dialogues [9,10]. Using Retrieval Augmented Generation (RAG) with knowledge graphs, they developed a prototype dialogue system for healthcare information [7].

A video[1] of a dialogue about hypertension, exercise and diabetes shows interaction in an informal style. The user asks basic questions (*What are the symptoms of diabetes?, Is exercise helpful?*) and uses technical terms only when asking what they mean (*What is moderate-intensity endurance exercise?*). The full dialogue is given in [7].

This short paper focusses on issues of robot agents for expert users. The agent needs to deal with expert terminology and answer experts' questions accordingly. This requires personalisation of the system responses for expert users, providing the language model with expert knowledge via RAG, and modifying the style of the responses to be more concise and to the point.

2 Towards More Expert Interaction

Large Language Models (LLMs) often have an overly excited interaction style where straightforward task questions are met by enthusiastic answers that can blur the factual information delivery and undermine the trustworthiness of the system. For expert users the goal is not to chat with the system but to efficiently find particular information. Responses should be friendly and natural, but the emphasis must be on the clarity and reliability of the answer, not on the happy engagement of the user.

We store knowledge graphs in Neo4j databases [1], doing vector-based, graph-based, and hybrid RAG with Neo4j `GraphRAG` [3]. Using `LLMGraphTransformer` from LangChain and Neo4j, we generated a knowledge graph about hypertension, diabetes and exercise from reliable PDF documents. This domain graph is the knowledge source for dialogues giving healthcare information.

One problem in personalised healthcare is a top-down approach where users are put into predefined classes. While categorisation is necessary in diagnostics, its use in interaction design can defeat the purpose of personalised interaction: predefined classes (personality types, cultural stereotypes, emotional classes) force the system to interact in a particular manner following average practises for each category, not taking into account individual differences or nuances, or the fact that the user may belong to different categories and may in fact change categories depending on the actual context.

Our approach does not require a user classification step. Since LLMs are good at tailoring their responses depending on the prompt design, we follow this approach and enhance it with explicit instructions to use the given information from the knowledge graphs. To avoid false facts and over-enthusiastic replies, the prompt tells the LLM: *Use the following pieces of retrieved context to answer the question. If you don't know the answer, say you don't know. Use two sentences maximum and keep the answer concise.*

---

[1] https://www.youtube.com/watch?v=vs4Y5jjoIqM.

Table 1. An intermediate-level interaction on hypertension, diabetes and diet.

Human:	Tell me about hypertension.
Robot:	*Hypertension (HTN) is a major public health issue in the United States, affecting approximately 28.7% of adults, with defined thresholds of systolic blood pressure (SBP) of 140 mm Hg or higher and/or diastolic blood pressure (DBP) of 90 mm Hg or higher. The prevalence of HTN increases with age and is influenced by various risk factors, necessitating lifestyle interventions for prevention and management.*
Human:	How is hypertension related to diabetes?
Robot:	*Hypertension is commonly associated with type 2 diabetes mellitus (T2DM), as both conditions share similar risk factors such as obesity and physical inactivity. Individuals with T2DM often experience higher rates of hypertension, which can exacerbate cardiovascular risks and complications.*
Human:	What are the causes of type 2 diabetes?
Robot:	*The causes of type 2 diabetes mellitus (T2DM) include genetic defects in insulin action, pancreatic disease, and environmental factors such as obesity, physical inactivity, and age. Additionally, certain medications, infections, and surgeries can also contribute to the development of T2DM.*
Human:	What type of ? (... pause ...) diet should be taken by type 2 diabetes?
Robot:	*It seems your question is incomplete. Could you please provide more details or clarify what you would like to know about?*
Human:	What... what dietary recommendation is suggested for type 2 diabetes person?
Robot:	*Dietary recommendations for individuals with type 2 diabetes typically include a balanced diet rich in whole grains, fruits, vegetables, lean proteins, and healthy fats, while limiting refined carbohydrates and added sugars. Portion control and regular meal timing are also important to help manage blood sugar levels.*
Human:	What kind of fruit do you suggest for type 2 diabetes person?
Robot:	*Fruits that are generally recommended for individuals with type 2 diabetes include berries (like strawberries and blueberries), cherries, apples, and pears, as they have a lower glycemic index and are high in fiber. It's important to consume them in moderation and consider portion sizes to manage blood sugar levels effectively.*
Human:	Is banana suitable for person with type 2 diabetes?
Robot:	*Bananas can be consumed by individuals with type 2 diabetes, but they should be eaten in moderation due to their higher carbohydrate content. It's best to pair them with a source of protein or healthy fat to help stabilize blood sugar levels.*
Human:	And what about red meat?
Robot:	*Red meat can be included in the diet of individuals with type 2 diabetes, but it should be consumed in moderation and preferably lean cuts to reduce saturated fat intake. It's also advisable to balance red meat consumption with plant-based proteins and incorporate plenty of vegetables for overall health.*

This is similar to the approach taken in the e-VITA project [6]. Experiments were conducted on motivational coaching where system responses depended on the user's motivational level (*non-interested* or *interested*): the system generated motivating responses accordingly with different prompts [5].

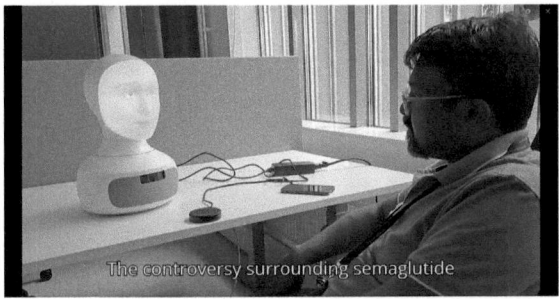

Fig. 1. An expert-level interaction. This dialogue is given in Table 2.

The dialogue in Table 1 can be considered as an intermediate level between non-expert and expert. In the video[2] of the dialogue, the user shows some slight expertise by referring to *type 2 diabetes*. During the question about diet, the pause causes a problem as the speech recognizer only hears *What type of?* The LLM recovers smoothly by replying *It seems your question is incomplete.* When listing the recommended fruits, the robot explains the reason in expert terms (*as they have a lower glycemic index*). Bananas should be paired with a source of protein or healthy fat *to help stabilize blood sugar levels.* In the case of red meat, lean cuts are preferred *to reduce saturated fat intake.*

Figure 1 is from a video[3] of a more expert-level interaction. The full dialogue is given in Table 2. In this interaction, the robot names medicines using expert-level terms (*metformin, sulfonylureas, GLP-1 receptor agonists*). The human also uses expert-level terms (*glucophage, semaglutide*) and shows more expertise by asking about the side-effects and the long-term effects of semaglutide. The robot responds to these questions by giving detailed explanations, and includes an additional expert-level comment (*ongoing monitoring is necessary to assess for any adverse effects or complications over time*).

The human shows more expert-level knowledge, asking about *the controversy regarding semaglutide tablets for weight reduction.* The robot responds to this with a long answer, not only clarifying the key issue but additionally mentioning *discussions about the accessibility and affordability of the drug,* and so on.

---

[2] https://www.youtube.com/watch?v=1iOW2ADItio.
[3] https://www.youtube.com/watch?v=7JdokzF4VpE.

Table 2. An expert-level interaction on exercise, diabetes and medication.

Human:	What type of exercises are suggested for type 2 diabetes?
Robot:	*Both aerobic and resistance exercise training are recommended for individuals with type 2 diabetes. Combined training thrice weekly may provide greater benefits for blood glucose control than either type of exercise alone.*
Human:	How about walking for half an hour every day?
Robot:	*Walking for half an hour every day is beneficial, as it is considered a moderate-intensity aerobic activity that can help prevent or manage type 2 diabetes. Regular walking has been associated with a significant reduction in diabetes risk.*
Human:	What medicines are recommended for type 2 diabetes?
Robot:	*Common medications for type 2 diabetes include metformin, sulfonylureas, and GLP-1 receptor agonists. Insulin therapy may also be used, especially in more advanced cases or when other medications are insufficient.*
Human:	What about glucophage?
Robot:	*Glucophage is a brand name for metformin, which is commonly prescribed for type 2 diabetes to help lower blood sugar levels. It works by improving insulin sensitivity and reducing glucose production in the liver.*
Human:	Some doctors prescribe Rybelsus semaglutide tablets also for diabetes.
Robot:	*Yes, semaglutide, marketed under the brand name Rybelsus among others, is a GLP-1 receptor agonist used to improve blood sugar control in adults with type 2 diabetes. It can also aid in weight loss and has cardiovascular benefits.*
Human:	What are the side effects of semaglutide tablets?
Robot:	*Common side effects of semaglutide include nausea, vomiting, diarrhea, constipation, and abdominal pain. Some individuals may also experience decreased appetite and potential risk of pancreatitis.*
Human:	What are the long-term effects of semaglutide?
Robot:	*Long-term effects of semaglutide may include sustained weight loss, improved glycemic control, and potential cardiovascular benefits. However, ongoing monitoring is necessary to assess for any adverse effects or complications over time.*
Human:	What is the controversy regarding semaglutide tablets for weight reduction?
Robot:	*The controversy surrounding semaglutide for weight reduction primarily involves concerns about its long-term safety, potential side effects, and the implications of using a diabetes medication for weight loss in non-diabetic individuals. Additionally, there are discussions about the accessibility and affordability of the drug for those who need it for diabetes management versus those using it for weight loss.*

3 Conclusion and Future Work

We aim at personalised interaction, grounded in reliable curated knowledge in the knowledge graph, allowing users to express themselves freely and allowing the system to learn about the user's preferences and interaction style from the interaction [7]. In our approach, personalisation is learnt through interaction rather than imposed by predefined categories.

The evaluation of such a system requires long-term interaction between users and the system. We are discussing possibilities for longitudinal evaluation, taking into account experience from e-VITA [6] and other similar projects.

We aim to compare our GraphRAG approach with other LLM-KG systems, and also with general-purpose "blackbox" LLMs like ChatGPT. As trustworthiness of the information is crucial, user questions about information sources will also be included in future work. In the development and evaluation of our work, we will follow ethical principles and UN sustainability goals[4] to develop reliable, personalised, and flexible social robot interaction.

Acknowledgements. The prototype systems were developed by CDM Interact, Helsinki, Finland (https://www.cdminteract.com).

Disclosure of Interests. The authors have no competing interests to declare that are relevant to the content of this article.

References

1. Barrasa, J., Webber, J.: Building Knowledge Graphs: A Practitioner's Guide. O'Reilly Media (2023)
2. Bengio, Y. et al.: International Scientific Report on the Safety of Advanced AI (Interim Report) (2025). https://arxiv.org/abs/2412.05282
3. Bratanic, T., Hane, O.: Essential GraphRAG: Knowledge Graph-Enhanced RAG. Manning Publications (In press)
4. Gebhard, P., Aylett, R., Higashinaka, R., Jokinen, K., Tanaka, H., Yoshino, K.: Modeling trust and empathy for socially interactive robots. In: Miehle, J., Minker, W., Andre, E., Yoshino, K. (eds.) Multimodal Agents for Ageing and Multicultural Societies. Springer (2021)
5. Jokinen, K.: Is the plan ready yet? - exploring LLMs when talking about well-being and health. In: 14th International Workshop on Spoken Dialogue Systems Technology (IWSDS 2024). Sapporo, Japan (2024)
6. Jokinen, K., Deryagina, K., Napolitano, G., Hyder, A.: Large language models and RAG approach for conversational coaching: experiments for enhancing e-VITA virtual coach. In: Proceedings of the IEEE RO-MAN workshop ALTRUIST (2024). https://ceur-ws.org/Vol-3906/paper2_ALTRUIST.pd
7. Jokinen, K., Wilcock, G.: Towards domain graphs and dialogue graphs for conversational grounding in HRI. In: ACM/IEEE International Conference on Human-Robot Interaction (HRI 2025), pp. 1373–1377. Melbourne, Australia (2025)

---

[4] https://sdgs.un.org/goals.

8. Li, H., Zhang, R., Lee, Y.C., Kraut, R.E., Mohr, D.C.: Systematic review and meta-analysis of AI-based conversational agents for promoting mental health and well-being. NPJ Digit. Med. **6**(236) (2023)
9. Wilcock, G., Jokinen, K.: Conversational AI and knowledge graphs for social robot interaction. In: ACM/IEEE International Conference on Human-Robot Interaction (HRI 2022), pp. 1090–1094. Sapporo, Japan (2022)
10. Wilcock, G., Jokinen, K.: Cooperative and uncooperative behaviour in task-oriented dialogues with social robots. In: 31st IEEE International Conference on Robot and Human Interactive Communication (RO-MAN 2022), pp. 763–768. Napoli, Italy (2022)
11. Williams, T.: Voice in the machine: ethical considerations for language-capable robots. Commun. ACM **66**(8), 20–23 (2023)

LLMs and Humanoid Robot Diversity: The Pose Generation Challenge

Riccardo Catalini, Federico Biagi, Giacomo Salici(✉), Guido Borghi, Roberto Vezzani, and Luigi Biagiotti

University of Modena and Reggio Emilia, Modena, Italy
{riccardo.catalini,federico.biagi,giacomo.salici,guido.borghi,
roberto.vezzani,luigi.biagiotti}@unimore.it

Abstract. Humanoid robots are increasingly being integrated into diverse scenarios, such as healthcare facilities, social settings, and workplaces. As the need for intuitive control by non-expert users grows, many studies have explored the use of Artificial Intelligence to enable communication and control. However, these approaches are often tailored to specific robots due to the absence of standardized conventions and notation. This study addresses the challenges posed by these inconsistencies and investigates their impact on the ability of Large Language Models (LLMs) to generate accurate 3D robot poses, even when detailed robot specifications are provided as input.

Keywords: Humanoid Robots · 3D Pose Generation · LLMs

1 Introduction

Humanoid robots are a category of social robots distinguished by their human-like appearance and are designed with multiple degrees of mobility, enabling them to replicate, to a certain extent, human movements and functionalities. Their applications span different fields, such as rescue, education, assisting, entertainment, and many more [11]. Their primary objective is to facilitate meaningful and supportive interactions with individuals [6], and enable emotional connections [12] as peer-like companions.

However, traditional programming interfaces are typically not user-friendly for non-experts. Interacting with humanoid robots through a teleoperation requires knowledge of the robot's kinematic structure, as well as knowledge of joints' nomenclature and limits for an efficient joint configuration setup.

Based on these premises, Large Language Models (LLMs) present a promising solution by enabling robots to comprehend, respond to, and execute human instructions conveyed in natural language. Research has explored the generation of robot poses using LLMs [1], where LLM agents are tasked with predicting optimal joint configurations that allow robots to assume coherent poses described in natural language.

In this study, we provide a comprehensive evaluation of several state-of-the-art large language models – ChatGPT-4o[1], Gemini 2.5[2], Claude 3.7 Sonnet[3], and DeepSeekV3[4] – with the specific aim of assessing their effectiveness in the task of robot pose generation. Our key contribution lies in systematically exploring and identifying the best-performing prompting strategy in this task, as well as in analyzing their outputs across a diverse set of robots. To the best of our knowledge, no prior published study has systematically analyzed multiple LLMs across different robots for this specific task.

The prompts used for the experiments, as well as the URDF files for the tested robots, are available on the project's GitHub repository[5].

2 Related Work

Over the years, research groups have explored robot manipulation using LLMs. Mo et al. [8] evaluated the performance of GPT-4o in path-planning tasks for an end-effector, framing the problem as a natural language processing challenge in a high degree-of-freedom robotic manipulator. Other studies have reported promising outcomes with stationary manipulators [3,4], while some have also demonstrated successful integration with mobile robots [10].

In addition to manipulation tasks, other research groups have focused on social robots, leveraging LLMs to generate coherent limb poses from natural language instructions. Mahadevan et al. [5] proposed a framework employing a pipeline of three ChatGPT-4 instances to generate expressive body language for a humanoid robot. Similarly, Roy et al. [9] introduced a system based on an OpenAI model to generate expressive body language for Unitree Go1, a 12-degree-of-freedom quadruped social robot, highlighting the model's capacity to produce rich and communicative motions from textual prompts. Finally, notable works by Mao et al. [7] and Jiang et al. [2] leveraged visual data to generate coherent poses for a humanoid robot, incorporating foundation models into the process. Mao et al. utilized human video clips and 3D human pose estimation to re-target human poses onto a robot's kinematic structure, enabling accurate pose imitation. In contrast, Jiang et al. employed a Vision Language Model (VLM) to refine robot-generated poses based on a given motion description, enhancing semantic alignment between the intended and actual poses.

Although all cited studies demonstrate promising results, they focus primarily on applying one or two LLMs to a single robot, leaving a gap in the literature regarding generalization across multiple LLMs and different robot models. In contrast, our study presents an evaluation of pose generation across different social humanoid robots using various LLMs.

---

[1] https://chatgpt.com, accessed: 21/05/2025.
[2] https://gemini.google.com, accessed: 21/05/2025.
[3] https://claude.ai, accessed: 21/05/2025.
[4] https://chat.deepseek.com, accessed: 21/05/2025.
[5] https://github.com/iot-unimore/llm-robot-pose.

3 Experimental Setup

To evaluate the performance of LLMs' ability to generate robot poses, four different poses (Fig. 1) were chosen for our study, based on different joints to be moved and the difficulty of the pose itself. The **T-pose** is a simple, symmetric posture involving only shoulder abduction. The **superhero pose** requires coordinated upper-body joint movement and core engagement. The **military salute** adds asymmetry and precision, involving shoulder and elbow flexion with fine wrist control. The **sitting down** pose involves lower-body joints and full-body coordination. We judge these last three poses as moderately complex.

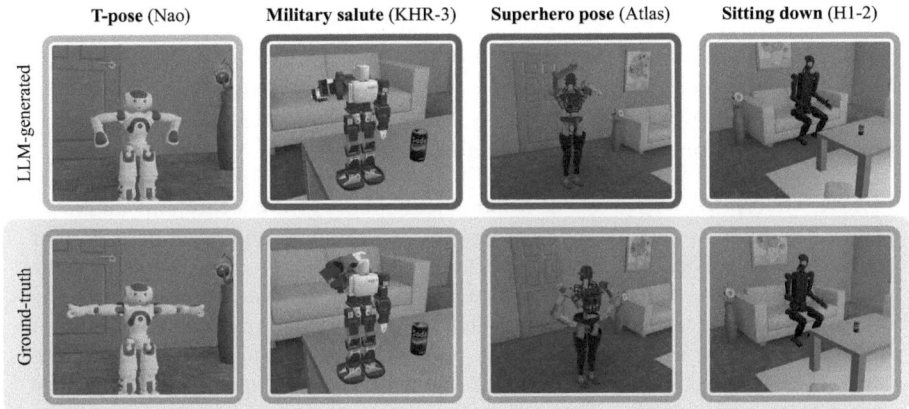

Fig. 1. LLM-generated poses compared to the ground-truth. The color of each frame depicts our qualitative evaluation as in Table 1.

3.1 Humanoid Robots and Simulation

The chosen robots were carefully selected to form a heterogeneous group, characterized by varying kinematic structures and joint naming conventions, allowing us to highlight each model's robustness, adaptability, and limitations in handling real-world robotic configurations. These are: Nao[6], KHR-3[7], Atlas[8] and H1-2[9]. Each robot has a different size, different numbers of degrees of freedom (DoF), and different naming conventions. All movements resemble human body movements, albeit with different constraints. The starting position also varies among the robots; these differences were taken into account when prompting. For our

---

[6] SoftBank Robotics, https://aldebaran.com/en/nao.
[7] Kondo Kagaku, https://www.kondokagaku.jp.
[8] Boston Dynamics, https://bostondynamics.com/atlas.
[9] Unitree, https://www.unitree.com/h1.

experimentation, we used the Webots simulator[10], designing a specific controller to move the robot joints with the generated poses, as in Fig. 1.

3.2 Prompting Strategy

To prompt the LLMs, we conducted a preliminary analysis of the prompting method. We found that for all the robots but the Nao, simply providing the name of the robot was insufficient for LLMs to return the names of its DoF. The Nao exception suggests that if the robot is significantly better known, the performance is increased (see Sect. 4). Subsequently, we attempted to prompt the robots to assume a T-pose by also providing their base pose and joint limits. However, since the LLMs continued to struggle with understanding the naming conventions and joint semantics of lesser-known robots, we believed it was essential to supply the information contained in a Unified Robotics Description Format (URDF) file. We also included the default pose and the reference frame convention to provide the LLM with as much information as possible about each robot. This is the prompt used for this experiment:

> TASK: Given this URDF file of a humanoid robot, give me the joint angles to set on the robot to assume a **{pose}** pose. The robot default position is **{brief robot default pose description}**. CONSTRAINTS: - Give me the list of joint angles in radians - Embed the joint angles of the pose in a dictionary with the name of the joint as Key and its radians as Value - The joint name convention must be coherent with the URDF file. - Avoid writing comments. All axes are defined in a right-handed robot-fixed frame where: +X = Forward (direction the robot faces). +Y = Left. +Z = Up.

4 Evaluation

To assess the quality of the generated poses, we conducted both a qualitative and a quantitative evaluation. The evaluations focused solely on whether the target pose was successfully achieved, regardless of whether the robot maintained proper balance during the movement (whether it remained upright or fell down). Concerning the qualitative one, shown in Table 1, three robot experts were asked to decide if the pose reached by the robot resembled the target one (15/60). In several cases, the robot has reached a configuration that is visibly close to the intended pose, but not sufficiently accurate to be considered successful (16/60). It is worth noticing that the sitting pose resulted in being more easily interpretable by the models than the others.

We also performed a quantitative evaluation by defining the ground-truth (GT) poses with the simulator. In Table 2, we report the Mean Per Joint Angular Error (MPJAE), computed only for joints that should have been moved according to the GT, evaluating the capability of the LLM to generate the pose with the provided information.

---

[10] Cyberbotics Ltd.: Webots open source robot simulator. https://cyberbotics.com/.

Table 1. Performance of different models across robots and poses. A green dot (●) is reported when the robot has fully achieved the target pose; a yellow diamond (♦) when the robot has partially achieved the target pose; a red cross (✖) when the robot couldn't achieve a pose coherent with the request. A gray square (▪) means that the result is not available, *i.e.* if the target pose is coincident with the robot's default pose.

	T-Pose				Salute				Superhero				Sitting Down			
Nao	●	●	♦	●	♦	●	✖	●	✖	♦	●	♦	●	●	●	●
KHR-3	✖	♦	✖	♦	✖	♦	♦	✖	✖	♦	✖	✖	✖	♦	✖	✖
Atlas	▪	▪	▪	▪	✖	✖	✖	✖	✖	✖	✖	✖	●	●	✖	●
H1-2	✖	✖	♦	✖	♦	✖	✖	♦	♦	♦	✖	♦	●	✖	✖	●
	ChatGPT4o	Claude3.7	Deepseek-v3	Gemini2.5	ChatGPT4o	Claude3.7	Deepseek-v3	Gemini2.5	ChatGPT4o	Claude3.7	Deepseek-v3	Gemini2.5	ChatGPT4o	Claude3.7	Deepseek-v3	Gemini2.5

$$\text{MPJAE} = \frac{1}{N}\sum_{i=1}^{N}\left(\frac{1}{J_i}\sum_{j=1}^{J_i}|\theta_{i,j}^{\text{LLM}} - \theta_{i,j}^{\text{GT}}|\right) \quad (1)$$

The most accurate LLM model for the task turned out to be Claude 3.7 Sonnet, followed by ChatGPT 4o and Gemini 2.5 Flash.

In Table 3, we report the ratio between the predicted number of joints moved by the LLM and the ground truth. This table shows that there is variation among how the models interpret which joints are to be moved to represent a specific pose; while ChatGPT 4o was the best on choosing the appropriate number of joints, Gemini 2.5 Flash was the only LLM to underestimate the correct number, moving fewer joints than necessary.

Table 2. MPJAE error (in radians) of the interested joints. Bold values indicate the best result for each column (*i.e.*, per robot).

	Nao	KHR-3	Atlas	H1-2
ChatGPT4o	0.44	2.00	1.15	0.73
Claude3.7	**0.32**	**1.30**	**0.88**	1.30
Deepseek-v3	0.65	2.14	0.91	1.03
Gemini2.5	0.45	2.15	1.27	**0.88**

Regarding the difference between the robots, the above-presented tables clearly show that the LLMs achieve their best performance with the Nao robot

Table 3. Ratio between the number of moved joints in the LLM poses and in the ground truth. Bold values indicate an exact match in the number of moved joints.

	Nao	KHR-3	Atlas	H1-2
ChatGPT4o	1.29	1.31	**1.00**	1.05
Claude3.7	**1.00**	1.63	2.12	1.16
Deepseek-v3	1.07	2.13	1.24	**1.00**
Gemini2.5	0.71	0.88	0.71	1.26

while they struggle with the others. This discrepancy can be attributed to the fact that the Nao robot is widely known and extensively documented, likely making it more familiar to the LLMs due to its presence in the training corpus.

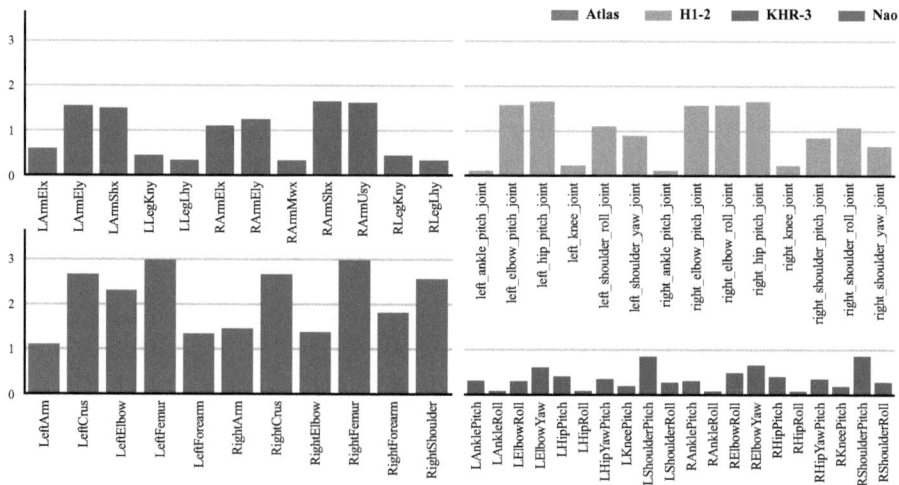

Fig. 2. Mean Angular Error (in radians) of each joint between the poses generated by all the models. The naming convention may be the reason for the Nao lower error.

In Fig. 2, we also evaluate the Mean Angular Error of all the moved joints for each robot, which provides useful insight into their heterogeneous performance. By the histogram labels, we can highlight that KHR-3 and Atlas use a DoF nomenclature that is less intuitive. For instance, the KHR-3 robot label `RShoulder` controls upper arm adduction, while `RArm` is responsible for the abduction. This naming convention could easily have confused the language models, even if the URDF file was provided with the correct axis conventions.

5 Conclusions and Future Work

In this study, we explored the capability of LLMs to generate precise robot poses across different robot models. Our results are promising, though successful pose generation was achieved only for specific pose-robot combinations. We found a clear disparity among the robots – with the Nao robot consistently performing better, probably due to more intuitive joint naming conventions and a wider presence in the LLMs training corpus. In this context, establishing a universal naming and semantic convention across humanoid robot platforms would enable consistent understanding and communication, also with LLMs. Among the models tested, Claude 3.7 Sonnet demonstrated the strongest performance. Future research will focus on refining prompting strategies to better understand what is most effective for pose generation, and on expanding both the set of robots and the collection of poses to enable a more comprehensive analysis. We plan to delve deeper into the underlying mechanisms that allow LLMs to perform in these use cases, aiming to uncover what makes them capable of understanding and translating human intent into a more generalized robotic motion.

Disclosure of Interests. The authors have no competing interests to declare that are relevant to the content of this article.

References

1. Huang, P., et al.: Emotion: expressive motion sequence generation for humanoid robots with in-context learning (2024)
2. Jiang, Z., Xie, Y., Li, J., Yuan, Y., Zhu, Y., Zhu, Y.: Harmon: whole-body motion generation of humanoid robots from language descriptions. arXiv preprint arXiv:2410.12773 (2024)
3. Jin, Y., et al.: RobotGPT: robot manipulation learning from ChatGPT. IEEE Robot. Autom. Lett. **9**(3), 2543–2550 (2024). https://doi.org/10.1109/LRA.2024.3357432
4. Kawabe, T., Nishi, T., Liu, Z., Fujiwara, T.: Task planning for robot manipulator using natural language task input with large language models. In: Proceedings of the 2024 IEEE 20th International Conference on Automation Science and Engineering (CASE), pp. 3484–3489. IEEE (2024). https://doi.org/10.1109/CASE59546.2024.10711671
5. Mahadevan, K., et al.: Generative expressive robot behaviors using large language models, pp. 482–491 (2024). https://doi.org/10.1145/3610977.3634999
6. Mahdi, H., Akgun, S.A., Saleh, S., Dautenhahn, K.: A survey on the design and evolution of social robots–past, present and future. Robot. Auton. Syst. **156**, 104193 (2022). https://doi.org/10.1016/j.robot.2022.104193
7. Mao, J., et al.: Learning from massive human videos for universal humanoid pose control (2024)
8. Mo, K., et al.: Precision kinematic path optimization for high-dof robotic manipulators utilizing advanced natural language processing models. In: Proceedings of the 2024 5th International Conference on Electronic Communication and Artificial Intelligence (ICECAI), pp. 649–654. IEEE (2024). https://doi.org/10.1109/ICECAI62591.2024.10675146

9. Roy, L., Croft, E.A., Ramirez, A., Kulić, D.: GPT-driven gestures: Leveraging large language models to generate expressive robot motion for enhanced human-robot interaction. IEEE Robot. Autom. Lett. **10**(5), 4172–4179 (2025). https://doi.org/10.1109/LRA.2025.3547631
10. Tariq, M.T., Hussain, Y., Wang, C.: Robust mobile robot path planning via LLM-based dynamic waypoint generation. Expert Syst. Appl. **282**, 127600 (2025). https://doi.org/10.1016/j.eswa.2025.127600
11. Tong, Y., Liu, H., Zhang, Z.: Advancements in humanoid robots: a comprehensive review and future prospects. IEEE/CAA J. Automatica Sinica **11**(2), 301–328 (2024). https://doi.org/10.1109/JAS.2023.124140
12. Vallverdú, J., Trovato, G.: Emotional affordances for human–robot interaction. Adapt. Behav. **24**(5), 320–334 (2016). https://doi.org/10.1177/1059712316668238

Identifying Public Engagement with Autonomous Art Through Human Pose and Speed Detection

Tianyuan Wang[1], Fanta Camara[1(✉)], Robert Woolley[1], and Darren Reed[2]

[1] Institute for Safe Autonomy, University of York, York, UK
fanta.camara@york.ac.uk
[2] Department of Sociology, University of York, York, UK

Abstract. The successful integration of autonomous systems in public spaces hinges on balancing technical performance with public acceptance and safety concerns. While much research has focused on the technical aspects of autonomous technologies, fewer studies have explored how these systems are perceived and interacted with by the public in artistic contexts. This study addresses this gap by examining how autonomous devices can achieve "social legibility" through a combination of technical and human-centered approaches. The Wheel, an autonomous kinetic sculpture, was used as a tool for studying human-robot interaction in a real-world setting. Deployed at York Festival of Ideas, The Wheel provided an opportunity to observe how the audience members respond to autonomous systems in a public, artistic context. Analysis of audience members' movement and behavior reveals that while The Wheel drew attention and engaged passersby, deeper interactions were less frequent. These findings suggest that creating socially legible autonomous systems requires careful attention to both technical design and public perception. This research contributes to the understanding of how autonomous systems can be better designed to align with human expectations and reduce perceived risks.

Keywords: Autonomous art · Robot performance · Social interactions · Human-robot interaction · Computer vision · AlphaPose

1 Introduction and Background

Autonomous technologies, once used primarily in industrial applications and controlled environments, are increasingly emerging in public spaces, where their integration presents unique challenges and opportunities [1]. This development raises a crucial issue regarding how the integration of such technologies can be optimized to enhance public acceptance and safety. This study, as part of a larger project, explores this question by merging technical innovation with artistic practice to engage the public in meaningful ways. The project leverages The Wheel (shown in Fig. 1), an autonomous kinetic sculpture developed in collaboration with the art practice IOU Theatre, to study and enhance interactions between autonomous systems and the public. This installation not only showcases the potential of robotics in public art but also serves as a research tool to explore the dynamics of human-robot interaction in real-world environments. Public acceptance is often a decisive factor in the successful adoption of new technologies [2]. Despite the growing presence of autonomous systems in public spaces, research on their public interaction, especially through art, remains sparse. For example, [3] investigated the non-verbal behaviors (proxemics) of audience members interacting with a mobile robot manipulator at a festival. [4] described the design of *Fish-Bird*, a kinetic artwork in the form of two wheelchairs that aims to investigate different forms of dialogue between two autonomous robots and their levels of participation in human-robot interaction. [5] developed *Ikit*, an artwork comprised of three robot platforms that autonomously move towards people and make contact with them. [6] used robotic installations as an "artistic medium" to engage with the public. Several large-scale robotic structures and environments were used to induce empathy from audience members towards the mechanistic characters. The present work uses a similar approach to [6], with the aim of collecting data from a multisensor kit and developing a new method to detect audience members' interaction with the kinetic sculpture and its miniature character in a lively festival setting. This dual focus on technical enhancement and public interaction helps advance the technology while ensuring it aligns with societal norms and expectations.

2 Data Collection

The Wheel is a mobile stage production and large, remote-controlled mechanical sculpture featuring a gleaming, self-propelled, hub-less wheel. The structure, with a diameter of 2.5 m, has no central axle or spokes, creating a mysterious visual effect as it moves. Inside the wheel, a miniature character walks in sync with the wheel's motion, giving the illusion of an epic journey within its confines. Designed to captivate audience members, The Wheel invites viewers to slow down, observe, and reflect on the scene, fostering a contemplative and interactive experience. The observational data collection for this study was conducted during the York Festival of Ideas, a free public engagement and family-friendly event, where The Wheel served as a central interactive installation. Moving at a speed of 1 m per minute along a planned route, The Wheel attracted audience members who engaged with the artwork as it progressed. The audience was encouraged to interact by observing the miniature figure walking inside the Wheel and contributing their thoughts or drawings at the accompanying Mobile Gallery, which moved ahead of The Wheel (cf. Figure 1a). A data acquisition system, referred to as the sensor kit, which is installed on the structure, collected visual and LiDAR data in real time, capturing the movement, behavior, and interactions of the audience as they followed and engaged with the installation throughout the event. Ethical approval was obtained from the University of York Ethics Committee.

This sensor kit is composed of a single-board computer (Raspberry Pi 5B with 4 GB RAM and a 512 GB SSD), two cameras (Raspberry Pi Camera Module V2), and a LiDAR (Unitree L1 PM Lidar). The entire sensor system is powered by an external 12V power supply mounted on The Wheel. The Raspberry Pi accesses the 5V rail via an adapter board (BCRobotic Power + Fan HAT), which then supplies power to the cameras and the SSD, while the LiDAR is powered directly from the 12V supply. All components were assembled using a 3D printed frame, with the Raspberry Pi and power hat positioned on the lower layer, the two cameras placed on both sides of the Raspberry Pi, and the LiDAR mounted facing downward on the upper layer using a trapezoidal bracket, as shown in Fig. 1b. The sensor kit was mounted at the rear of The Wheel at a height of approximately 2 m above the ground to ensure the audience remains within the LiDAR's sensing range. The data were acquired using the ROS2 (Humble) stack running on Raspberry Pi OS (Bookworm 64-bit). Image and point cloud data were collected by two camera nodes (camera-ros) and one LiDAR node (unitree-lidar-ros2), respectively, with the data being timestamped by ROS2 and stored using the rosbag2 node.

(a) The Wheel.

(b) Sensor kit.

Fig. 1. Pictures of the Wheel at the Festival of Ideas. (**a**) The Wheel with the Mobile Gallery moving ahead. (**b**) The sensor kit used for the data collection.

3 Methods

In this study, the sensors were not directly mounted at the center of the object of interest, which is a relatively large structure. As a result, the viewing angles of the audience often varied significantly. In fact, when the audience gazed at the camera, they were not necessarily interacting with the object of interest but the sensors, as illustrated in Fig. 2. Consequently, gaze detection based on facial features did not consistently provide accurate interaction information. In addition, to include individuals who may not have approached the artwork for direct interaction but were nevertheless drawn to it, slowing their pace as they passed by, we employed interaction detection based on the audience member's walking speed.

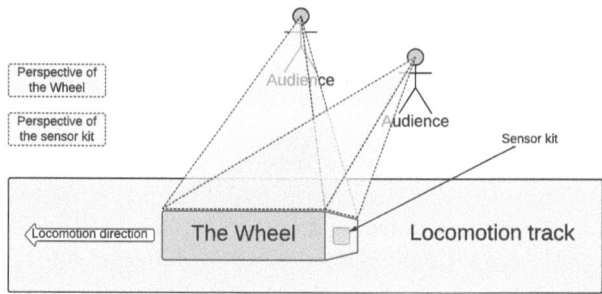

Fig. 2. The perspective deviation when observing The Wheel and the sensor kit, as well as the wide view angle when observing The Wheel.

3.1 Position Extraction and Preprocessing

To obtain the position information of audience members, AlphaPose [7] was utilised offline to extract the keypoints data. An example detection output of AlphaPose is shown in Fig. 4a. For the selection of position reference points, to mitigate the offset caused by the bounding box only partially enclosing the body and to account for potential drift when using the nose as a reference point due to head movement, the midpoint between the shoulders was used as the reference point for determining the audience member's position. Various disturbances and noise encountered during data collection were addressed through preprocessing. Initially, data with a confidence score below 0.5 were discarded (confidence or visibility is the uncertainty of the point from the pose detection algorithm), as such data exhibited significant positional jumps, making them unreliable for accurate position analysis. Facial data were not utilized for subject identification in this study.

Video analysis revealed that AlphaPose's tracking of individuals was not consistently reliable, with the algorithm occasionally misidentifying different individuals appearing in consecutive frames as the same person. To eliminate this interference, individuals whose positional data exhibited large jumps between consecutive frames were re-labeled. Additionally, audience members that appeared in the video for less than two seconds were excluded. Furthermore, the sensor kit mounted on the object of interest included a mechanical LiDAR, which inevitably introduced vibrations during scanning, leading to noisy positional reference outputs. To mitigate this, a notch filter was first applied to the raw positional data in both the x and y directions to remove the 11 Hz noise introduced by the LiDAR. Based on the filtered audience member's velocity data, the rolling standard deviation was calculated. This method helps mitigate potential misjudgments caused by perspective-related speed variations among audience members positioned at different distances from the sensor kit. Moreover, the rolling standard deviation provides a more comprehensive representation of the velocity changes over time, avoiding the disproportionate influence of brief, extreme fluctuations in speed. Notably, some data exhibit high initial values that gradually decrease to a lower level. This is typically observed when audience members suddenly appear in close proximity to the sensor kit, leading to significant changes in recorded speed. However, these abrupt changes do not necessarily indicate meaningful interaction, which is why both a decrease in speed and a subsequent departure are used as criteria for assessing interaction.

3.2 Interaction Detection

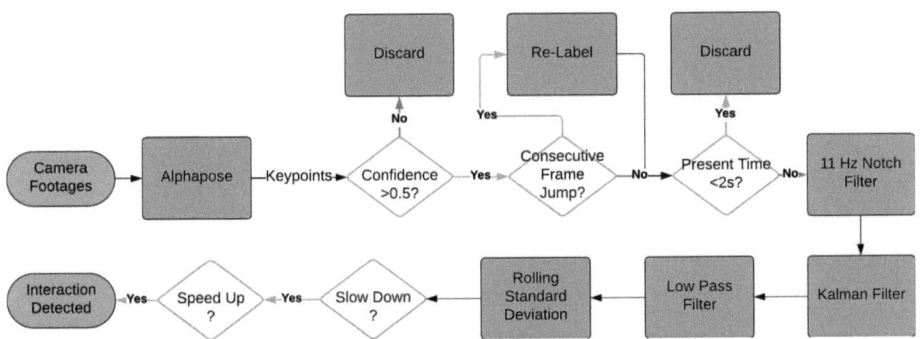

Fig. 3. The steps of the data pre-processing and interaction detection analysis.

Subsequently, based on the preprocessed keypoints data, the velocity of each individual was calculated. Given the inherent limitations in the accuracy of the pose detection algorithm, a Kalman filter was first applied to the velocity data to reduce noise in the observed velocities. A low-pass filter was then applied to the velocity data to eliminate the influence of walking gait, resulting in a smooth velocity curve. The data processing workflow is illustrated in Fig. 3. To detect interaction between audience members and the object of interest, the processed velocity curves were analyzed. A key characteristic of audience members who were passing by and became attracted to The Wheel is that they slowed down or stopped their movement. This behavior is reflected in the data as a decrease in walking speed. After concluding the interaction, the audience members would leave the area of interest, indicated by an increase in walking speed. Since the employed pose detection algorithm does not provide three-dimensional positional information, and to address potential issues caused by varying distances and different baseline walking speeds among audience members, the relative rate of speed decrease and subsequent increase was used as the criterion. When an audience member's walking speed exhibited a decrease followed by an increase exceeding the specified threshold, it was inferred that interaction with The Wheel had occurred during the period of reduced speed.

(a) AlphaPose output.

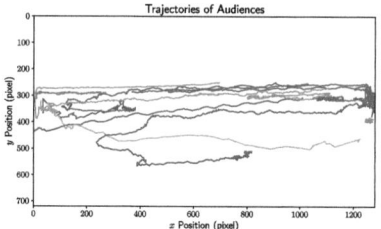
(b) Post-processed Trajectories.

Fig. 4. (a)Snapshot of the video with keypoints generated by AlphaPose labelled in the scene. The faces of the audience members were blurred to comply with ethical requirements. (b) The trajectories of the audience members passing by The Wheel after the data pre-processing. The x and y axes of the figure correspond to the width and height of the image, respectively.

4 Results and Discussion

To facilitate data visualization in this paper, a randomly trimmed 60-second footage was used as a sample and analyzed. The audience members' position information before and after the pre-processing stage was firstly compared, where their trajectories in the footage is plotted and shown in Fig. 4b. The results indicated a significant improvement in the continuity and smoothness of the audience members' trajectories after data pre-processing. Trajectories displaying large variation along the y axis represent audience members who were more strongly attracted when they passed by and approached closer for interaction.

Figure 5 depicts the variation in audience members' walking velocity over time, with periods of detected interaction highlighted using rectangles colored corresponding to the relevant data. From the filtered velocity profiles, it is clear that audience members' interactions can be identified with relative clarity. Multiple deceleration events can be observed during an audience member's interaction, likely reflecting instances where audience members paused to examine different parts of The Wheel, a large structure that naturally draws audience members' attention to its various elements. Conversely, some velocity profiles show brief appearances of audience members without any noticeable deceleration, indicating a lack of interaction with The Wheel. Decreased walking velocity is one component of the production of a socially meaningful action of 'showing

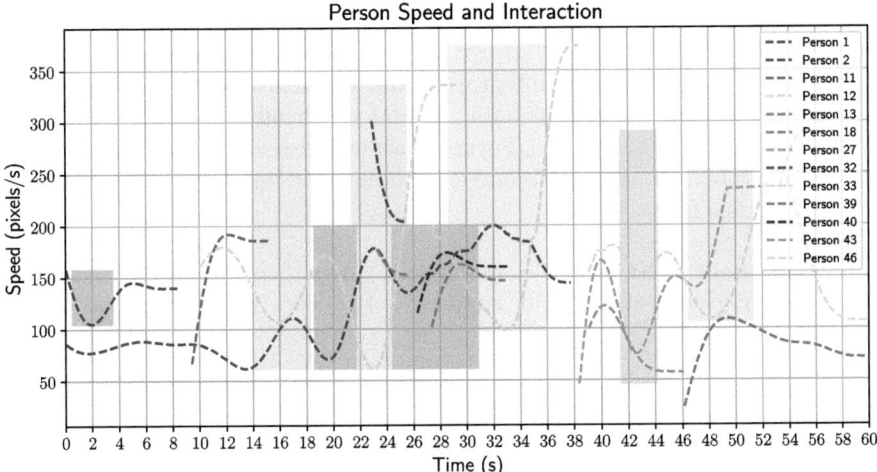

Fig. 5. The detected interaction activities of the audience members.

interest in the Wheel'. Alongside velocity, we might find body direction change and potentially other embodied actions such as gaze adjustment and gesture production (such as a pointing action). These and other meaningful actions are available through an approach to social interaction called Embodied Conversation Analysis (ECA), which identifies sequences of action through video analysis [8,9]. These actions are socially meaningful and consequential for the progression of collective behaviors. A more detailed social analysis is provided in [10].

A key observation from the analysis is that audience members' interaction with The Wheel can be identified primarily through changes in walking velocity. Audience members who slowed down, stopped, or altered their trajectory were inferred to be interacting with the installation. A manual labelling of the social interactions in the video clip shows that the proposed interaction detection approach is about 60% accurate in predicting them. This method revealed several limitations due to its reliance on pose detection and tracking algorithms, such as AlphaPose employed in this study, which introduced inaccuracies when identifying individuals and their movement patterns. For instance, errors in assigning tracking IDs or misidentifying individuals after overlap events in the video led to instances of missed or false interaction detections. These challenges are inherent in real-world, outdoor environments where occlusion, overlapping individuals, and dynamic lighting conditions can complicate accurate detection and tracking. Participants' demographics was not studied in this work, but it is hoped that including this information in the future could improve the modelling and results.

The study also opens several avenues for improving the methodology used to capture human-robot interactions. First, enhancing the robustness of pose detection and tracking algorithms in dynamic, outdoor settings would lead to more reliable data on audience members' movement and interaction. Future research could explore the use of multiple sensor modalities, such as combining visual data with LiDAR sensors, to improve detection accuracy in cases of occlusion or poor lighting. Additionally, integrating machine learning techniques to adaptively adjust tracking algorithms based on real-time feedback could reduce errors in identifying audience members. Future work will also aim to quantify the proxemic and trust behavioural preferences of audience members towards the Wheel using the models from [11–13].

Acknowledgment. The authors would like to express their sincere gratitude to IOU Theatre (https://ioutheatre.org) for supporting this work with Wheel and the data collection.

References

1. Fayyaz, M., González-González, E., Nogués, S.: Autonomous mobility: a potential opportunity to reclaim public spaces for people. Sustainability **14**(3), 1568 (2022)
2. Huijts, N.M.A., Molin, E.J.E., Steg, L.: Psychological factors influencing sustainable energy technology acceptance: a review-based comprehensive framework. Renew. Sustain. Energy Rev. **16**(1), 525–531 (2012)
3. Krenn, B., Gross, S., Dieber, B., Pichler, H., Meyer, K.: A proxemics game between festival visitors and an industrial robot. arXiv preprint arXiv:2105.13812 (2021)
4. Velonaki, M., Rye, D.: Designing robots creatively. Robots Art Exploring Unlikely Symbiosis, 379–401 (2016)
5. Doepner, S., Jurman, U.: Robot partner—are friends electric? Robots Art Exploring Unlikely Symbiosis, 403–423 (2016)
6. Vorn, B.: I want to believe—empathy and catharsis in robotic art. Robots and Art Exploring Unlikely Symbiosis, 365–377 (2016)
7. Fang, H.S., et al.: Alphapose: whole-body regional multi-person pose estimation and tracking in real-time. IEEE Trans. Pattern Anal. Mach. Intell. **45**(6), 7157–7173 (2022)
8. Reed, D.J., Wooffitt, R., Young, J.: Walking with gail: the local achievement of interactional rhythm and synchrony through footwork. Social Interaction, Video-based Studies of Human Sociality (2023)
9. Reed, D.J.: Turning heads and making conversation on twitch. Discourse Context Media **60**, 100802 (2024)
10. Reed, D., Camara, F., Wang, T.: Social interaction with autonomous art: combining social analysis and computer vision. In: International Conference on Social Robotics + AI (ICSR+AI) (2025). (In Press)
11. Camara, F., Fox, C.: Space invaders: pedestrian proxemic utility functions and trust zones for autonomous vehicle interactions. Int. J. Soc. Robot. **13**(8), 1929–1949 (2021)
12. Camara, F., Fox, C.: Extending quantitative proxemics and trust to HRI. In: 2022 31st IEEE International Conference on Robot and Human Interactive Communication (RO-MAN), pp. 421–427. IEEE (2022)
13. Camara, F., Fox, C.: A kinematic model generates non-circular human proxemics zones. Adv. Robot. **37**(24), 1566–1575 (2023)

A Cognitive Social Robot in Manufacturing

Dimitra Anastasiou[1]( ), Ben Gaffinet[1,2], and Yannick Naudet[1]

[1] Luxembourg Institute of Science and Technology, Esch-sur-Alzette 4362, Luxembourg
{dimitra.anastasiou,ben.gaffinet,yannick.naudet}@list.lu,
ben.gaffinet@univ-lorraine.fr
[2] Université de Lorraine, CNRS, CRAN, Nancy 54000, France

Abstract. This paper relates research in progress illustrating social-cognitive robotics in manufacturing, where a social robot (QT) materialises a natural interface between the manufacturing environment and the human operator through its digital counter part, a Human Digital Twin (HDT). One future goal is that QT proactively and cognitively assesses certain mistakes that can occur during a product assembly task in order to mitigate risks that can harm the user or damage products. Here, we present a literature review on social-cognitive robotics, our approach involving HDT and the QT with LLM-based cognitive functions, and initial results of an exploratory user study with a Lego assembly.

Keywords: Social cognitive robotics · Manufacturing · Product Assembly · Retrieval Augmented Generation

1 Introduction

Industry 5.0 has been shifting focus from pure automation toward collaborative human-machine systems where human workers are considered as valuable co-workers and not as replaceable resources any longer. The introduction of collaborative robots is a step forward, but true human-machine collaboration would require more, and in particular robots also having social capabilities. Generative AI and particularly Large Language Models (LLMs) have also a role to play, particularly from the perspective of knowledge management, decision making and support, process optimization, and natural user interfaces. However, in industrial settings there is rarely a natural way of interacting with the machines, at least not like for interacting with humans. To fill this gap, social robots can improve Human-Robot Collaboration (HRC) through adapting and warning the human operators about changing conditions or hazards.

This paper introduces a social robot (QT robot[1]) in a use-case in the manufacturing domain. We attach to QT robot cognitive functions through Retrieval

---
[1] https://luxai.com/.

Augmented Generation (RAG) in addition to its already existing social skills, such as provision of speech, emotions, hand gestures, and gaze following. In our current setting, the QT robot can guide, support, and provide feedback to a human operator who is asked to assemble a product. In subsequent experiments, we envision a Human Digital Twin (HDT) tracking the human's behaviour to enable pro-active guidance with the QT as feedback interface. The paper is laid out as follows: Sect. 2 presents a short literature review on social cognitive robotics; Sect. 3 introduces QT robot in manufacturing describing how it can function as a feedback to a HDT, and presents our exploratory user study. We conclude with a discussion and future prospects in Sect. 4.

2 Social-Cognitive Robotics

Cognitive robotics is a multi-disciplinary science that draws on research in adaptive robotics as well as cognitive science and AI. The Technical Committee of Cognitive Robotics[2] combines research in adaptive robotics as well as cognitive science and AI, and often exploits models based on biological cognition. Cognitive robots deal with the inherent uncertainty of natural environments by continuously learning, reasoning, and sharing their knowledge. They need to explore and understand their environment, choose a safe and human-aware course of action, and learn not only from experience, but also through interaction [2].

Social-Cognitive Robotics is a basis for the human-centered design of technology-oriented systems to improve human knowledge functions, judgments and decision making, collaborations, and learning [7]. Mutlu et al. [8] highlighted that cognitive HRI considers a robotic system to be a part of a distributed cognitive system and therefore seeks primarily to develop cognitively inspired models. These models might draw on knowledge about human cognition to improve the usability of a robotic system and mimic human decision making or behaviour mechanisms. Latest advancements have enhanced AI-based robotic systems, as flexibility and deep understanding of complex manufacturing processes are becoming the key advantage to raise competitiveness [1].

In manufacturing, systems are evolving from machine-centricity to system-centricity and recently to human-centricity [9]. The latter manufacturing model cares more about human's roles and tasks, is equipped with cognitive and learning functions, liberates humans to engage more creative work, and ensures work efficiency, quality, and capability. It thus offer a special place to cognitive and social-cognitive robots. Our work focuses on proactive HRI and particularly on anticipatory robot behaviour based on contextual awareness [3].

3 A Social Robot at a Manufacturing Setting

Social robots focus on HRI as their core capability. They have intuitive communication methods through their (most often) multimodal interaction capabilities,

---

[2] https://www.ieee-ras.org/cognitive-robotics.

contextual awareness, and adaptive behaviour based on human feedback. We propose an HDT-based approach to enable human-aware and pro-active guidance using QT robot, followed by an exploratory study to assess QT's ability to guide a human operator with a RAG-based offline LLM.

QT is a powerful, on-device AI assistant capable of engaging in natural voice conversations. By integrating advanced technologies such as RAG-based offline LLM (Llama 3.1), Automatic Speech Recognition (ASR) of Riva[3], and Text-to-Speech (TTS) of Acapella[4], the QT robot understands, processes, and provides insightful responses based on user-provided documents.

We propose a setup where the HDT's objective is to track the human state and emulate the behaviour of a human operator [4]. Within an industrial context, the operator's next action is particularly important as it enables the possibility to pre-emptively intervene and stop dangerous or damaging actions. This includes interrupting actions of the operator, as well as adapting the actions of robotic systems that may conflict with the operator. As an example, a worker may plan to use the wrong torque limiting wrench and risk destroying an expensive product, but the HDT detects the intent and sends a warning signal to the worker. Figure 1 shows the high-level structure of a HDT, where a cognitive social robot (QT), serves as Human-Machine Interface between the human and their digital twin. A set of sensors tracks the human state and their actions which feed into the HDT, where the *Human Model* emulates how the state will evolve including the probable next actions. If an undesired action is likely to happen, a feedback is generated and sent to QT, which translates the digital signal into a vocal signal that guides the human operator back to safety measures. Additionally, any queries the operator can be mediated by the HDT and relayed by the QT.

While the goal of our exploratory study is to investigate QT's ability to function as an intelligent and natural interface between the human operator and their HDT, the first step is to assess the capability of the QT to guide the operator through natural language interactions. Here, QT uses static information from external documents, namely the assembly instructions, to guide the operator in a Lego assembly task. We explore the challenges and applicability of voice and text-based guidance. The observed behaviour and common mistakes provide important lessons to develop the planned HDT's cognitive model.

To assist the human operator, QT is equipped with an integrated LLM for general knowledge and RAG for a special knowledge base. RAG is a method that enhances LLMs by supporting answers with context documents and retrieving knowledge from external sources, prompting the LLMs to ground their responses based on this information [6]. RAG systems incorporate external knowledge resources, such as the instruction manual containing the sequence of steps. This way, the human operator is assisted by the QT robot, which can provide feedback and guidance about the order of steps to be followed as well as the content of the assembly procedure.

---

[3] https://www.nvidia.com/en-us/ai-data-science/products/riva/.
[4] https://www.acapela-group.com/.

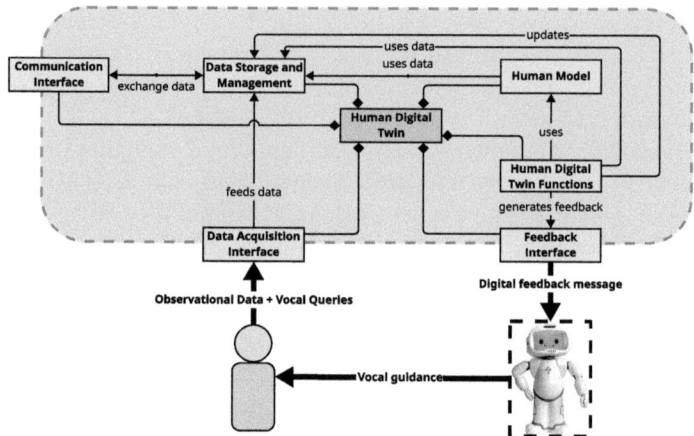

Fig. 1. QT as a feedback interface for Human Digital Twin (HDT) [5].

3.1 User Study Design

We tested the scenario with 10 persons (5 male and 5 female). In order to avoid potential bias, no one of them was aware in advance about the capabilities of QT robot nor about the product assembly. The users were informed that QT will assist them during the assembly of a Lego duck (see Fig. 2), but they were not explicitly informed about which questions they can ask QT. While assembling the Lego duck only involves placing bricks, it represents a simplified industrial product. When translated to a realistic case, the components will change and the use of tool may be required, but it remains a sequence of actions that need to be taken in the right order.

Figure 2 illustrates the experimental setup; the participant can manipulate the Lego pieces but does not know the procedure; QT knows the assembly procedure but cannot manipulate the Lego pieces; the participant needs to learn the procedure through verbal exchanges with QT. The participant needs to describe their actions and the state of the Lego assembly, as QT has insufficient visual capabilities to track to process on its own. In order for human operators to successfully assemble the Lego product, they need to:

1. Understand the assembly steps and their correct sequence given by the verbal instructions of QT;
2. Find the required Lego pieces in the boxes in correct colour and size;
3. Assemble them correctly in the right order, position, and orientation.

3.2 Results

The exploratory study was audio and video recorded, so that the actions of the participants are collected, such as which Lego pieces have been selected, how

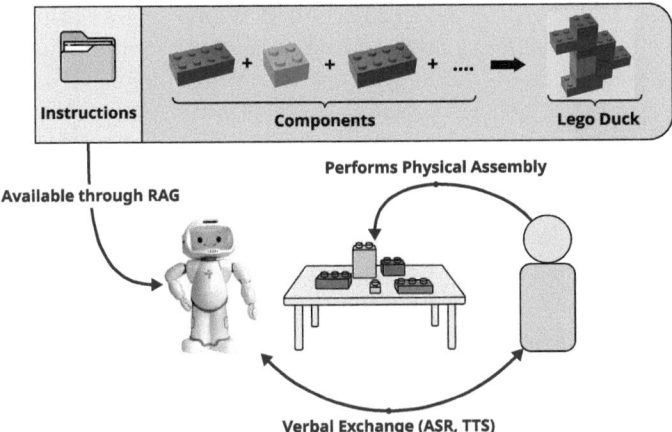

Fig. 2. Experimental setup.

many trials were made etc. as well as how dialogue was constructed between user and QT. This information forms the input to our HDT that then runs a model of human cognition to estimate the next action of the human.

In this subsection we describe our qualitative results based on the debriefing and think-aloud protocol we followed with the participants after the user study. We asked the participants whether they believe that they did the duck correctly, what they liked most and least, and what would they suggest for the future for a more effective product assembly. 90% of the participants mentioned that it was fun as an experiment overall to interact with a social robot. Concerning the assembly performance, 20% managed to construct the duck as expected. The remaining 80%, although they completed all steps, the duck was not "properly" constructed, as expected based on the instructions. From the videos and the debriefing, we analyzed what can be fixed in order to enhance user performance in the product assembly from i) RAG side, ii) prompt customization, iii) experimenters' script to participants. 60% faced challenges with the orientation of the pieces; the participants did not know whether they should put them horizontally or vertically. 20% were not sure whether the duck should be build in 2D or 3D. One participant mentioned the ambiguity of the word "on the top", which could also mean in 2D putting a Lego piece "behind" another one. 30% participants were confused with the word "layer". Concerning the participants suggestions for improvements, 30% mentioned that that a check after each step or a certain complexity level would be very helpful, so that mistakes are not propagated and QT can give the green light for the user to continue.

4 Discussion and Future Prospects

In this paper, we designed an exploratory study where the human is asked to assemble a Lego duck product with the assistance of the social-cognitive QT robot. The QT robot with ASR, LLM-based RAG and TTS both multimodally and socially interacts with the user guiding them and providing feedback during the assembly procedure. In this study, QT robot provides feedback through its knowledge database which is based on RAG. The study results indicate that the socio-cognitive abilities of QT can contribute to creating an engaging and fun work environment. Furthermore, the importance of clarifying the vocabulary used by QT is a major factor to make the provided instructions unambiguous and clear. In its current setup, QT had no direct information about the environment or human state. In the future, we plan to provide *proactive* feedback by actually deploying an HDT with a model of human cognition to emulate the human states and behaviours for future action prediction. While the HDT adds complexity to the system, it hosts a personalized model that distinguishes it from basic LLM assistants. In particular, QT as the interface, will intervene and provide guidance to avoid mistakes by the human operator. Although our lego assembly looks simple, most participants struggled with position and orientation of bricks. This usability challenge will be mitigated by the future HDT personalized model.

Acknowledgement. This work has been partially supported by the ANR French National Research agency and the FNR Luxemburgish National Research funds project AI4C2PS (INTER/ANR/22/17164924/ AI4C2PS), 2023–2025.

References

1. Arents, J., Greitans, M.: Smart industrial robot control trends, challenges and opportunities within manufacturing. Appl. Sci. **12**(2), 937 (2022)
2. Bandera, A., Fernández-Argüéllez, L.M., Falomir, Z.: Special issue cognitive robotics. Appl. Sci.**12**(19) (2022). https://doi.org/10.3390/app12199684, https://www.mdpi.com/2076-3417/12/19/9684
3. van Den Broek, M.K., Moeslund, T.B.: What is proactive human-robot interaction?- a review of a progressive field and its definitions. ACM Trans. Human-Robot Interact. **13**(4), 1–30 (2024)
4. Gaffinet, B., Ali, J.A.H., Naudet, Y., Panetto, H.: Human digital twins: asystematic literature review and concept disambiguation for industry 5.0. Computers in Industry **166**, 104230 (2025)
5. Gaffinet, B., Naudet, Y., Panetto, H.: (In Press) a systemic human digital twin model for human-centric systems. In: 11th IFAC Conference on Manufacturing Modelling, Management and Control (IFAC MIM2025). Elsevier (2025)
6. Gao, Y., et al.: Retrieval-augmented generation for large language models: a survey. arXiv preprint arXiv:2312.10997 **2** (2023)
7. Meghdari, A., Alemi, M.: Recent advances in social and cognitive robotics and imminent ethical challenges. In: Recent Advances in Social and Cognitive Robotics and Imminent Ethical Challenges (August 22, 2018). Proceedings of the 10th International RAIS Conference on Social Sciences and Humanities (2018)
8. Mutlu, B., Roy, N., Šabanović, S.: Cognitive human–robot interaction. Springer handbook of robotics, pp. 1907–1934 (2016)
9. Zhang, C., et al.: A survey on potentials, pathways and challenges of large language models in new-generation intelligent manufacturing. Robot. Comput. Int. Manufact. **92**, 102883 (2025)

Pitch Training with Furhat: Effects of a Social Robot in Entrepreneurship Education

Ilona Buchem[✉][iD], Yasmin Olteanu[iD], and Georges Arnaud Kouayim Bonga[iD]

Berlin University of Applied Sciences, Luxemburger Str. 10, 13353 Berlin, Germany
buchem@bht-berlin.de

Abstract. This paper investigates students' perceptions and learning effects of pitch training with the social robot Furhat. Embedded in an undergraduate course on entrepreneurship, the training aimed to support business students in preparing their final startup pitches. Participant could select a male or a female coach, which was then embodied by the robot. The pitch training used a set of evaluation criteria for startups based on a national specification. Results from our within-subjects study showed a statistically significant correlation between student gender and the choice of the robot persona. Results also revealed significant correlations between perceptions of the robot and students' learning experiences, suggesting that likeability, naturalness, and human-likeness of the robot significantly impacted the perceived quality of the learning experience, including enjoyment, motivation and curiosity. Regression analysis confirmed that perceived robot's likeability significantly predicted the overall learning experience. Furthermore, there was a statistically significant increase in perceived preparedness for the final pitch after the training. These findings demonstrate that social robots can be effectively applied in entrepreneurship education.

Keywords: Social Educational Robots (SER) · Human-Robot Interaction (HRI) · Pitch Training · Learning Experience (LX) · Entrepreneurship Education (EE)

1 Introduction

Entrepreneurship Education (EE) has gained popularity in higher education as a means to introduce students to entrepreneurial thinking [1]. As part of EE, oral pitch presentations with jury panels have been applied as instructional methods to support students in learning how to present their ideas in a clear and structured way within an allotted time [2]. The effectiveness of a pitch depends on a wide range of factors including content, clarity, persuasiveness and personal attributes of pitchers [3]. Pitching requires students to articulate ideas clearly, present themselves convincingly, and respond to jury questions with confidence [3]. Delivering a pitch in front of an audience as a form of oral presentation may present cognitive and emotional challenges for students [4]. Many students experience anxiety and stress before and/or during oral presentations, mostly due to the fear of being judged, uncertainties related to the content, self-presentation and previous experiences [4]. A pitch typically involves presenting an idea to a jury, which may evoke anxiety not due to public speaking but also due to the unpredictability of critical follow-up questions which are related to social and professional judgement. Effective strategies to overcome such challenges include preparation through practice and rehearsals, which tend to decrease anxiety [4]. As there is a high demand for supporting students in public speaking [4], different technologies have been used to provide safe and low-risk/low-stakes practice opportunities for students. These have included Virtual Reality Public Speaking Training (VRPST) [5] and social robots such as the anthropomorphic robot head Furhat [6] and the educational robot Kebbi [7]. Previous research has shown that robots such as Furhat can effectively facilitate oral rehearsal with an attentive audience [6].

This paper presents the design of a pitch training with the Furhat robot and results from a within-subjects study which examined the effects of such pitch training among undergraduate students in an entrepreneurship course. As students prepared to pitch their startup ideas, the Furhat robot acted as a coach, asking questions from a pool of evaluation criteria for startups based on a national specification, in this way simulating a realistic pitch situation. We examined how students perceived the robot, whether gender influenced their choice of the robot persona (male or female), how these perceptions were linked to students' learning experiences and whether the pitch training with the Furhat robot helped students to prepare for a real pitch at the end of semester.

2 Related Work

Social Educational Robots (SER) have been shown to promote engagement, motivation, and learning outcomes, including cognitive and social skills [8]. Prior studies have explored applications of SER in different roles including tutors and learning companions [9], tutees [10], and facilitators [11]. Furhat, a back-projected, adaptable humanoid robotic head, has been deployed in various roles to support student learning. A systematic review of Furhat applications in education by [12] assessed Furhat's performance in three dimensions: role perception, motivation, and trust, and showed that Furhat tends to be perceived as a likeable, trustworthy companion (rather than a teacher) and has positive motivational effects on learners including sustaining interest and engagement. Moreover, SER can be used as unobtrusive multimodal data collectors and in this way extend traditional learning analytics (LA) methods [13].

Gender-related perceptions of social robot personas have been explored in prior studies, which indicate that users tend to respond to robot's gender in line with gender stereotypes, e.g. attribute more communal traits, give more affective trust, say more words and smiled more to female compared to male robots [14]. Studies also found interaction between robot's and participant's gender. However, results seem inconclusive with half of the studies showing significantly positive effects of gender match and half significantly positive effects of gender mismatch [14]. These findings provide relevant context for our study, which explored how students interacted with the social robot Furhat during pitch training in an entrepreneurship course. By allowing to select a robot persona, our study extends prior research on training with social robots.

3 Method

3.1 Application Design

The application "Pitch Training with Furhat" was developed in Kotlin and used a curated database of questions aligned with the specification DIN SPEC 90051-1 [15]. At the beginning of each session, the system randomly selects questions from different categories in the question database, sets the language, greets detected students and presents two pitch trainer personas –"Tobi" (male) and "Lana" (female). The students select the trainer persona, who then explains the course of the session and starts a structured question round with questions presented contextually with a category. The system supports session logging, question repetition, session pauses, and non-verbal communication signals. The interaction flow is presented in Fig. 1.

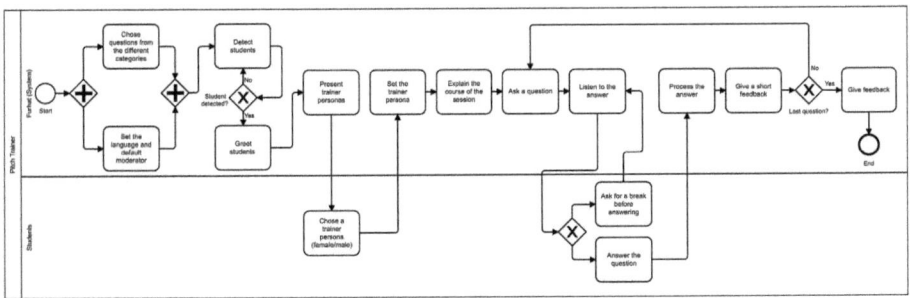

Fig. 1. System architecture with interaction flow in the pitch training simulation with Furhat.

3.2 Study Design and Participants

The study involved 27 students enrolled in an entrepreneurship course, in the Digital Business program (BSc). Students worked in teams to develop startup ideas and were required to pitch them at the end of the semester. The pitch training with Furhat was conducted two weeks before the final pitch to prepare the students for pitching in front of a jury. The pitch training used a selection of six question from pool of evaluation and due diligence criteria for startups based on the national specification DIN SPEC 90051-1, which is a German standard developed to assess the sustainability impact potential of startups [15]. The 6 questions included 3 general questions (related to due diligence) and 3questions related to sustainability-impact, all selected randomly by the system. Each pitch training session lasted 15 min. A total of 7 teams with 3–4 students each participated in 7 pitch training sessions. 63% of the study participants were 21–25 years old and 66% were female.

3.3 Research Instruments

The study applied within-subjects design with a pre- and post-intervention survey. Before the pitch training, students completed a baseline survey with questions related to socio-demographics (age and gender) and perceived preparedness for the final pitch. After the training, students completed an exit survey with a question related to perceived preparedness for the final pitch, an open question related to the choice of the persona (male or female), and items from three validated scales, i.e. 20 selected items from the Learning Experience Scale (LX) [16], 16 items from the Human-Robot Interaction Evaluation Scale (HRIES) [17], 5 selected items from the Satisfaction with Simulation Experience (SSE) scale [18]. The LX scale showed strong reliability with α = .759, as did the HRIES scale with α = .773 and the SSE learning sub-scale with α = .778), confirming that the appropriateness of the research instruments.

4 Results

4.1 Trainer Persona Choice and Gender

A statistically significant association was found between student gender and the trainer persona choice (Chi-Square p = .024; Fisher's Exact p = .039). Female students were more likely to choose the female persona, suggesting that gender congruence may play an important role in comfort or identification during interaction. Students' answers to the open question "Please briefly explain why you chose this persona" revealed key themes. First factor was voice quality, with several students noting that the chosen persona had a more pleasant, fluid, or natural-sounding voice. The second factor was the likeable and friendly appearance of a female persona. A few students described the male persona's voice sounded robotic, generic and machine-like. These results are in line with previous research showing that vocal cues play a crucial role in the attribution of gender to a robot and selection of a robot persona [19].

4.2 Preparedness for the Final Pitch

Students' self-rated preparedness for their final pitch was measured before and after the pitch training. The average rating increased from 3.30 (SD = 0.91) before the training to 3.78 (SD = 0.64) after the training. A paired samples t-test showed that this increase was statistically significant (t(26) = 4.315, p < .001), with a mean difference of 0.481 and a medium to large effect size with Cohen's d = 0.830 and Hedges' g = 0.806. These results suggest a substantial impact of pitch training and a significant gain in perceived preparedness for the final pitch after the training with Furhat.

4.3 Robot Perceptions and Learning Experiences

Furhat as pitch trainer was perceived as friendly (M = 3.67, SD = 1.00), rational (M = 3.33, SD = 1.07) and likeable (M = 3.11, SD = 1.15). Pitch training with Furhat was perceived as engaging (M = 4.0, SD = 1.00), enjoyable (M = 3.96, SD = 0.76), fun (M = 3.93, SD = 0.96), and motivating (M = 3.63, SD = 0.96). Students reported on high focus (M = 3.81, SD = 0.87) and enhanced curiosity (M = 3.52, SD = 0.97). Moreover, students rated their understanding of a pitch due to training as very high (M = 4.30, SD = 0.82). There were several significant correlations between robot perceptions and the learning experience. First, robot likeability correlated positively with the experience of fun (r = .564, p = .002), engagement (e.g., time passed quickly: r = .333, p = .090), and reduced boredom (r = −.431, p = .025). Second, likeability correlated with higher ratings of learning value (r = .451, p = .018) and ease of use (r = .583, p = .001), while, natural interaction correlated with improved understanding (r = .422, p = .028). Third, human-like qualities of the robot correlated with increased motivation (r = .417, p = .031). Finally, negative perceptions, such as perceiving the robot as "weird," correlated negatively with learning value (r = −.393, p = .043). A linear regression using the HRIES item "The robot was likeable" as a predictor showed a statistically significant effect (β = .516, p = .006), explaining 26.6% of the variance in learning experience (R^2 = .266). This shows that the perceived robot's likeability played a key role in shaping students' learning experience during pitch training with Furhat, which aligns with previous research showing that sociability and intent of interaction are positively related [17]. Furthermore, the choice of a trainer persona may have enhanced this effect [14].

5 Discussion and Conclusions

The primary goal of our study was to explore how students perceive the Furhat robot as a pitch trainer, whether gender influenced students' choice of the robot persona (male or female), how these perceptions were linked to students' learning experiences and whether the pitch training with Furhat helped to prepare for a real pitch. While the study [6] implemented automated behavioral feedback, our study used Furhat to simulate a realistic pitch scenario with questions based on the DIN SPEC 90051-1 standard and focus on the learning experience. The results of our study underscore the importance of perceived robot's sociability as a determinant of HRI quality [17]. Similar to [6], our study demonstrated positive effects of robot-assisted pitch training. Importantly, the results of our study revealed significant gains in self-perceived preparedness for a real pitch. Moreover, our results indicate that pitch training with Furhat contributed to a positive learning experience, especially in terms of engagement, enjoyment, motivation. Also, compared to previous studies, out study has also shown that student gender played an important role in selection of a robotic trainer persona (female or male), with female students' preference for a female persona more often and voice quality playing a crucial role in the persona selection. These results align with research on the importance of voice cues in HRI [19], suggesting that customisable voice features may enhance learning experience. These results demonstrate that even relatively short, structured interactions with a social robot can yield tangible learning benefits. Future research should examine whether these effects also translate into improved performance in actual pitch presentations. Furthermore, comparative studies with different approaches to pitch training could help identify optimal formats for robot-supported entrepreneurship education.

Disclosure of Interests. The authors have no competing interests to declare that are relevant to the content of this article.

References

1. He, L., Zheng, L.J., Sharma, P., Leung, T.Y.: Entrepreneurship education and established business activities: an international perspective. Int. J. Manag. Educ. **22**(1) (2024)
2. Rodrigues, A.L.: Entrepreneurship education pedagogical approaches in higher education. Educ. Sci. **13**(9), 940 (2023)
3. Clark, C.: The impact of entrepreneurs' oral 'pitch' presentation skills on business angels' initial screening investment decisions. Venture Cap. **10**(3), 257–279 (2008)
4. Grieve, R., Woodley, J., Hunt, S.E., McKay, A.: Student fears of oral presentations and public speaking in higher education. J. Further High. Educ. **45**(9), 1281–1293 (2021)
5. Bachmann, M., Subramaniam, A., Born, J., Weibel, D.: Virtual reality public speaking training: effectiveness and user technology acceptance. Front. Virtual Real **4**, (2023)
6. Trinh, H., Asadi, R., Edge, D., Bickmore, T.: RoboCOP: a robotic coach for oral presentations. Proc. ACM Interact. Mob. Wearable Ubiquitous Technol. **1**(2), 27, 1–24 (2017)
7. Darmawansah, D., Hwang, G.J.: Effects of robot-based multiple low-stakes assessments on students' oral presentation performance, collective efficacy, and learning attitude. Educ. Technol. Res. Dev. **72**, 2013–2039 (2024)
8. Song, H., Huang, S., Barakova, E., Ham, J., Markopoulos, P.: How social robots can influence motivation as motivators in learning: a scoping review. In: PETRA '23: Proc. 16th Int. Conf. Pervasive Technol. Assistive Environ., pp. 313–320. ACM, New York (2023)
9. Pai, R.Y., Shetty, A., Dinesh, T.K., Shetty, A.D., Pillai, N.: Effectiveness of social robots as a tutoring and learning companion: a bibliometric analysis. Cogent Bus. Manag. **11**(1), 2299075 (2024)
10. Serholt, S., Ekström, S., Küster, D., Ljungblad, S., Pareto, L.: Comparing a robot tutee to a human tutee in a learning-by-teaching scenario with children. Front. Robot. AI **9** (2022)
11. Buchem, I., Sostak, S., Christiansen, L.: Human–robot co-facilitation in collaborative learning: a comparative study of the effects of human and robot facilitation on learning experience and learning outcomes. J **7**(3), 236–263 (2024)
12. Yousif, J., Jiang, X.: A human-robot interaction in education: a systematic review of Furhat robots' role in student learning. Artif. Intell. Robot. Dev. J. **5**(1), 337–352 (2025)
13. González-Oliveras, P., Engwall, O., Wilde, A.: Social educational robotics and learning analytics: a scoping review of an emerging field. Int. J. Soc. Robot. **17**(2), 1235–1254 (2025)
14. Perugia, G., Lisy, D.: Robot's gendering trouble: a scoping review of gendering humanoid robots and its effects on HRI. Int. J. Soc. Robot. **15**(11), 1725–1753 (2023)
15. DIN e.V.: DIN SPEC 90051-1:2020-11 Standard für die Nachhaltigkeitsbewertung von Start ups, DIN Media, Berlin (2020)
16. Fokides, E., Kaimara, P., Deliyannis, I., Atsikpasi, P.: Development of a scale for measuring the learning experience in serious games: preliminary results. In: Digital Culture & Audiovisual Challenges, pp. 1–10. CEUR-WS, Thessaloniki (2021)
17. Spatola, N., Kühnlenz, B., Cheng, G.: Perception and evaluation in human–robot interaction: the human–robot interaction evaluation scale (HRIES)—a multicomponent approach of anthropomorphism. Int. J. Soc. Robot. **13**(7), 1517–1539 (2021)
18. Levett-Jones, T., McCoy, M., Lapkin, S., Noble, D., Hoffman, K., Dempsey, J., et al.: The development and psychometric testing of the Satisfaction with Simulation Experience Scale. Nurse Educ. Today **31**(7), 705–710 (2011)
19. Perugia, G., Rossi, A., Rossi, S.: Gender revealed: evaluating the genderedness of Furhat's predefined faces. In: Li, H., et al. (eds.) Social Robotics. ICSR 2021. Lect. Notes Comput. Sci., vol. 13086, pp. 36–47. Springer, Cham (2021)

A Progressive Multimodal Robot System for Emotional Learning in Autistic Children

Yiyi Wu[1(✉)], Maninderjit Kaur[2], and Fengpei Yuan[1]

[1] Robotics Engineering Department, Worcester Polytechnic Institute, Worcester, MA 01609, USA
{ywu16,fyuan3}@wpi.edu
[2] Department of Physical Therapy, MGH Institute of Health Professions, Boston, MA 02129, USA
mkaur1@mghihp.edu

Abstract. This research introduces an innovative social robotic system for emotion education therapy in children with autism spectrum disorder. Integrating a NAO robot with dual interfaces—one displaying emotional stimuli for children and another providing facilitator oversight—our approach implemented a progressive five-session therapeutic framework. Each session targets distinct emotions through increasingly complex multimodal exchanges, from basic dialogues to comprehensive social scenarios involving verbal, facial, bodily, and contextual emotional cues. The system harnesses advanced technologies including ChatGPT/Whisper for adaptive conversation, DeepFace for affective state recognition, and MediaPipe for postural analysis. Our holistic design incrementally increases interactional complexity across five structured activities: introductory conversation, facial emotion deciphering/expression, bodily emotion conveyance, robot-narrated stories with integrated emotional gesture demonstrations, and a concluding musical interlude. Initial findings substantiate the potential of robotic interventions to provide structured emotional literacy development for children with ASD while maintaining essential human guidance via an accessible control mechanism. This work contributes to the growing field of socially assistive robotics by demonstrating how progressive multimodal interactions can support specialized emotional learning interventions.

Keywords: Autism intervention robotics · Multimodal human-robot interaction · Emotional education therapy

1 Introduction

Socially assistive robotics (SAR) is a burgeoning domain, particularly in caring for children with autism spectrum disorder (ASD). This focus stems from their intricate care requirements and documented affinity for robotic and technological interactions [8]. For instance, the humanoid SAR, NAO, has been extensively used in ASD child-robot interaction research due to its engaging, approachable design [5,9].

Children with ASD often struggle with emotional recognition and interpretation [1,2]. Conventional emotion education typically relies on static facial expressions (e.g., through images). However, combining facial expression with body languagein conveying and understanding emotions significantly bolsters learning. Research into interventions that systematically integrate such multimodal cues, particularly dynamic bodily expressions alongside verbal and facial cues within social contexts, remains notably circumscribed.

In this work, we directly addresses this gap by designing and developing a progressive therapeutic system using a NAO robot that extends emotion education beyond conventional static facial cues to multimodal interaction and learning. By keeping stakeholders (autism care experts) in the loop throughout the development and evaluation process, we have developed a system that incrementally escalate interactional complexity through meticulously structured sessions. These sessions comprehensively employ multimodal cueswith a particular focus on dynamic bodily gestures within motivating themesencompassing verbal communication, facial expressions, and broader social contexts.

2 Methodology

This methodology details an innovative social robot system employing a progressive therapeutic protocol, the operational concept of which is illustrated in Fig. 1. Developed in collaboration with an ASD research expert (a co-aut hor), the sequence of activities within sessions are designed to feature gradually increasing interactional complexity and gradually increasing complexity of multimodal cues (verbal, facial, bodily, and social context). Its dual-interface architecture offers engaging child experiences (NAO robot, display screen) and comprehensive facilitator GUI (Graphical User Interface) control, balancing autonomous operation with human oversight.

2.1 System Architecture

Figure 2 illustrates the comprehensive robotic system architecture, integrating specialized hardware for sensing and feedback with software and algorithms for identifying the child's status and interacting with users. The NAO robot serves as the primary child interaction medium. Additionally, an external high-resolution camera with integrated microphone enhances perception and processing, overcoming NAO's native sensor limitations.

The robotic system in Fig. 2 is implemented using NAO SDK (Python 2.7) integrated with modern Python 3+ libraries for adaptive conversation and computer vision via segregated virtual environments. Core components include OpenAI ChatGPT (GPT-4o) [4] for natural language interaction, DeepFace for facial emotion analysis [7], and MediaPipe [3] for real-time body pose recognition.

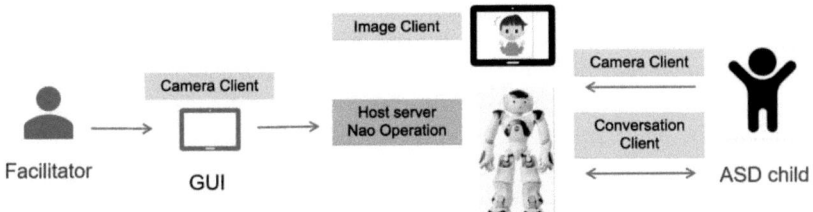

Fig. 1. Conceptual overview of the social robotic system for emotional learning in ASD children. This diagram illustrates the primary interaction pathways between *the NAO robot* (alongwith an emotion display screen), *a child with ASD*, and *a facilitator* who monitors and guides the session via a GUI. The system's modular architecture is facilitated by a central Server controlling NAO operations and various Clients (Camera Client, Conversation Client, Image Client) that enable communication and data exchange between the different components via socket connections. The overall approach effectively combines autonomous robot functionalities with essential human oversight.

Fig. 2. System architecture illustrating the workflow. Modules shaded in grey represent five activities within a therapeutic session. (Color figure online)

2.2 Therapeutic Session Protocol

The therapeutic protocol, inspired by gamified learning and progressive difficulty, aims to motivate and engage children with ASD in the interaction and learning. Each session features five structured activities targeting four core emotions (initially happy, sad, surprised, angry), with plans to introduce additional varied emotional combinations in future sessions.

Activity 1: Warm-up Conversation. Activity 1 serves as a rapport-building introduction: NAO asks two open-ended questions, "How are you today?" and "How was your day at school?". Responses are generated via the ChatGPT, configured with a prompt specifically designed to ensure ASD-friendly communication while maintaining conversational context. Turn-taking is managed through Voice activity detection: after initial vocal input is detected, the system registers turn completion if audio level falls below a set Root Mean Square (RMS) energy threshold for 3 s. If no vocal input occurs within 20 s, a timeout mechanism prompts NAO to gently re-engage.

Activity 2: Facial Emotion Deciphering and Expression. This activity focuses on educating the child in identifying and expressing facial emotions from visual stimuli (images), concluding with an emotion-related question from NAO. Four target emotion images are displayed for the child to identify. If correct, NAO provides positive confirmation. If incorrect, NAO reformulates the question as a forced-choice,provides appropriate feedback (confirming or supplying the correct answer), then prompt the child to demonstrate the facial expression. DeepFace [7] analyzes expressions, with crucial facilitator manual override for potentially attenuated/idiosyncratic ASD expressions. Successful expressions are positively reinforced; unsuccessful ones receive encouragement. NAO concludes with a related open-ended question (e.g., 'What makes you feel happy?').

Activity 3: Bodily Emotion Conveyance and Recognition. Activity 3 introduces the concept of conveying emotions via corporeal expression. NAO demonstrates four simple, pre-programmed emotion-linked movements (Fig. 3), then NAO invites the child to replicate. Real-time pose tracking is accomplished using MediaPipe, which monitors six key anatomical landmarks on the child: the left and right shoulders, elbows, and wrists. For each target emotion, a reference pose is pre-defined. Pose similarity between the child's live movement and this reference is quantified by comparing joint angles, with facilitator manual override available. If the child's initial attempt does not meet the similarity threshold, NAO offers to demonstrate the movement again. If the child agrees, the demonstration and attempt cycle repeats. If not, or if the child successfully replicates the pose, the session proceeds to the next emotion.

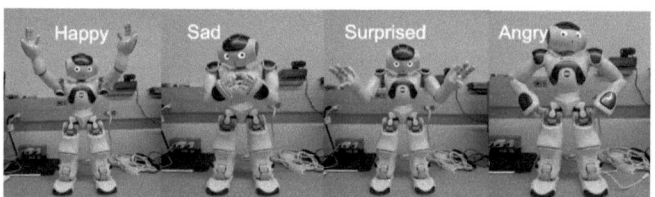

Fig. 3. Exemplar NAO robot poses representing the four target emotions: (a) Happy, (b) Sad, (c) Surprised, (d) Angry.

Activity 4: Story-Based Emotional Scenarios. Activity 4 uses robot-narrated stories incorporating the four learned emotions and associated movements, providing social context and reinforcing emotion-action links. Currently, this is primarily NAO narrative delivery for consolidated review.

Activity 5: Concluding Musical Interaction. The session culminates with a brief, calming musical interlude. The NAO robot plays a pre-selected, gentle melody and engages in simple, rhythmic swaying motions. This activity primarily serves as a positive, non-instructional session conclusion.

2.3 Facilitator Control Interface

A critical component of the system is a bespoke GUI designed for the human facilitator. This interface provides comprehensive control over the session's progression and individual activities. The GUI grants the facilitator granular command, allowing for the independent initiation, repetition, or omission of any activity component, such as specific warm-up questions, distinct emotion modules, or discrete movement demonstrations. This modular control, a design principle underscored by expert consultation (e.g., Prof. Kaur), is particularly advantageous for children with ASD who often benefit from repeated exposure to concepts and require tailored pacing.

3 Results and Discussion

An internal testing of the developed system was conducted with co-authors to assess the system's core functionality, the coherence of the therapeutic session protocol, and the performance of its key technological components.

3.1 System Performance and Functionality

Automated recognition components demonstrated variable performance. Emotion recognition (e.g., DeepFace) showed inconsistent real-time accuracy in mock interactions, performed better with pronounced expressions but struggling with subtle or idiosyncratic ASD displays. MediaPipe-based pose tracking (using joint angle similarity) promisingly identified predefined gross movements, though establishing universal recognition tolerance for all poses was challenging due to varying landmark proximity (e.g., the 'sad' pose required nuanced definition).

3.2 Discussion

Preliminary internal tests indicate our system's progressive, multimodal framework is viable: NAO autonomously executed the five-activity protocol, and its structured approach to escalating interactional complexity appears sound.

However, this initial evaluation also revealed key limitations. Automated emotion and gesture recognition showed variable accuracywhile facilitator overrides provide an interim solution, improving autonomous performance is essential. Furthermore, initial testing was confined to the authors, underscoring the critical need for future studies involving children with ASD. Qualitative feedback from Prof. Kaur, an autism care expert and co-author, also highlighted desirable refinements for overall session dynamics (e.g., adjustments to length, repetition, robot response conciseness, and voice activity timing) and for content delivery (particularly concerning NAO's story narration and the interactivity of the story module).

These identified limitations and expert recommendations guide the clear path for future iterative development. Despite current constraints, this work substantiates the system's potential for structured emotional literacy development, pending the planned enhancements and rigorous user testing.

3.3 Future Work

Future work will prioritize system enhancements: improving recognition accuracies, and refining conversational dynamics (e.g., silence timeouts, response lengths). As established, generic approaches like DeepFace struggle with the subtle or idiosyncratic emotional displays often characteristic of individuals with ASD. To address this, we plan to investigate and integrate more robust emotion and gesture recognition methodologies tailored for this population. We will consider approaches that leverage datasets specific to ASD expressions or analyze subtle facial micromovements, as general emotion recognition models may not adequately capture the nuanced emotional displays in this group [6].

More work will also be conducted to enhance content to include a highly interactive story, expressive NAO narration (e.g., voiceovers), an expanded movement repertoire, and optimized session parameters (length, repetition).

Furthermore, to gather real-world feedback and validate the system's efficacy, formal user studies with children with ASD will be conducted. These studies will incorporate a comprehensive evaluation framework, including Likert-scale assessments and other quantitative and qualitative measures, to systematically track participant progress and system performance across sessions. This will provide comprehensive assessment for iterative refinement.

Acknowledgments. Google Gemini was used to check grammar, spelling, and improve readability and language.

Disclosure of Interests. The authors have no competing interests to declare that are relevant to the content of this article.

References

1. Chaidi, I., Drigas, A.: Autism, expression, and understanding of emotions: literature review. Int. J. Online Biomed. Eng. (iJOE) **16**(02) (2020)
2. Cibralic, S., Kohlhoff, J., Wallace, N., McMahon, C., Eapen, V.: A systematic review of emotion regulation in children with Autism Spectrum Disorder. Res. Autism Spectr. Disord. **68**, 101422 (2019). https://doi.org/10.1016/j.rasd.2019.101422
3. Google: mediapipe (2023). https://developers.google.com/mediapipe. Accessed 2 Feb 2025
4. OpenAI: Gpt-4o (2023). https://api.openai.com, openAI API. Accessed 15 Mar 2025
5. Pennisi, P., et al.: Autism and social robotics: a systematic review. Autism Res. **9**(2), 165–183 (2016)
6. Rutgers university: tracking tiny facial movements can reveal subtle emotions in autistic individuals (2025). https://www.rutgers.edu/news/tracking-tiny-facial-movements-can-reveal-subtle-emotions-autistic-individuals. Accessed 9 July 2025
7. Serengil, S., Ozpinar, A.: a benchmark of facial recognition pipelines and co-usability performances of modules. J. Inf. Technol. **17**(2), 95–107 (2024). https://doi.org/10.17671/gazibtd.1399077

8. Tapus, A., et al.: Children with autism social engagement in interaction with nao, an imitative robot: a series of single case experiments. Interact. Stud. **13**(3), 315–347 (2012)
9. Yuan, F., Klavon, E., Liu, Z., Lopez, R.P., Zhao, X.: A systematic review of robotic rehabilitation for cognitive training. Front. Robot. AI **8**, 605715 (2021)

Breathe with Me: A Breathing Exercise Guided by the Robot NAO Reduces Stress

Ilona Buchem[1(✉)], Katharina Kuehne[2], Martina Mauch[1], and Niklas Baecker[1]

[1] Berlin University of Applied Sciences, Luxemburger Str. 10, 13353 Berlin, Germany
`buchem@bht-berlin.de`
[2] Cognitive Sciences Division, University of Potsdam, Potsdam, Germany

Abstract. This study investigates perceptions and effectiveness of a guided breathing exercise delivered by the prerecorded video of the robot NAO for reducing stress among university students. Drawing on research in socially assistive robotics and breathing-based stress interventions, the study examines changes in participants' stress levels before and after the exercise using the State-Trait Anxiety Inventory. Results from 42 participants showed a significant reduction in stress following the intervention. Regression analysis further revealed that participants who perceived NAO as more socially engaging experienced greater stress reduction. These findings suggest that robot-guided breathing exercises, even when delivered via video, can serve as effective tools for stress reduction in educational settings, such as university seminar rooms.

Keywords: Human-Robot Interaction (HRI) · Social Robots · Stress Reduction

1 Introduction

Stress has become a widespread challenge of modern life. In educational settings, stress has been shown to hinder memory retrieval, learning and performance in exams [1]. Stress may shift thinking from flexible to more rigid, habit-like responses, and in this way negatively impact learning and performance [1]. Students in higher education are one of the populations particularly vulnerable to mental health issues [2]. Studies indicate that a large number of university students experience symptoms of depression, anxiety, and burnout, including emotional exhaustion, feeling inhibited in daily activities, difficulties in concentrating and taking decisions [2].

As individuals seek effective and accessible methods for stress relief and psychological well-being, technology-based interventions have gained popularity due to their availability and flexibility [3, 4]. Mobile mental health (MH) apps are used for psychological support, including behavioral guidance, monitoring and relaxation [3]. However, app-based interventions have some deficits, such as a missing experience of care, connection and dialogue, which often lead to drop-out [3]. Beside apps, research also explored gaming interventions as tools to alleviate students' psychological stress [5], and virtual reality (VR) as low-risk interventions for stress management [6]. A number of studies on

VR interventions reported significant reductions in stress levels of healthy individuals facing everyday stressors [6], however, with no clear evidence for significant differences in stress reduction between VR and non-VR breathing interventions [7]. Studies have shown that socially assistive robots (SARs) can support mental well-being through personalized, embodied stress relief interventions [8]. However, most research so far has focused on the elderly and children [8, 9].

In this study, we investigate the effect of a guided breathing exercise on stress relief of students in higher education, using a pre-recorded video of the robot NAO. This study contributes to the growing body of work in HRI and psychological health support, by exploring perceptions and effects a robot-supported breathing exercise.

2 Breathing as Stress Intervention

Breathing exercises are a widely used technique for reducing psychological and physiological stress [10]. As low-cost, non-pharmacologic, self-administered interventions, breathing exercises may be applied by anyone to manage stress [11]. Studies show that breathing exercises as a synchronous, online intervention can reduce stress, improve mood and mental focus [12]. Breathing exercises (compared to watching a film), can significantly increase both the heart rate variability (HRV) and the percentage of correct answers in decision-making tasks [13]. Device-guided breathing intervention can help reduce anxiety in college students [14].

Technology-enhanced solutions used to support breathing exercises such as mobile applications [3, 4], gaming [5] and virtual reality [6, 7] often provide visual or auditory cues to guide users through slow, rhythmic breathing. Studies have shown that visualisations can enhance the efficacy of breathing practices compared to audio-only designs [15, 16]. Studies explored the effectiveness of computer-generated human-like breathing coaches in VR and found that adherence to virtual coach's instructions tends to be high due to the perceptions of the virtual coach as trustworthy and likeable [17]. This indicates that breathing exercises with anthropomorphic agents can be especially effective. Studies with social robots have indicated the effectiveness of breathing exercises supported by robots. For example, [18] applied the robot NAO as a facilitator of a breathing exercise and showed that university students enjoyed interacting with the robot, felt more relaxed and reported mood improvement after the exercise. The physical embodiment of a social robot can elicit feelings of trust and social connectedness, which are crucial in health-related contexts. For example, [19] showed that breathing exercises with a robot which combines haptic interaction with visual and audio guidance led to a significant reduction in students' stress levels.

3 Study Design and Methods

Our study aimed to examine perception and stress-reduction effects of a breathing exercise, guided by the video-recorded anthropomorphic robot NAO. We measured participants' stress levels both before and after the intervention. We hypothesized that stress levels would decrease following the breathing exercise. Additionally, we explored whether participants' perceptions of the robot, prior experience with the NAO robot, and familiarity with breathing exercises influenced the effectiveness of the intervention. The paper presents preliminary results of the study.

3.1 Participants and Video

The experiment was conducted as part of a university course on self-management. The final sample comprised 42 students (13 females, 28 males; and one with no gender disclosure (Mean age = 21 years, SD = 2.9). In addition to the video-based robot condition, the study also included two further conditions: one involving a human and another the physical NAO robot. This paper reports only on the first video condition.

We recorded a short video (5 min) of NAO guiding a breathing exercise in German. The video featured the robot standing on a white table against a white wall. NAO gave instructions, used gestures and moved the head in the rhythm of breathing. The verbatim transcript and the video are available at: https://osf.io/pr4hb, doi:https://doi.org/10.17605/OSF.IO/PR4HB.

3.2 Measures and Procedure

To assess overall stress as a transient state of tension and worry associated with autonomic arousal and anticipation of future events, we employed the short-form state scale of the Spielberger State-Trait Anxiety Inventory (STAI) [20, German version from 21] with six items, each rated on a 4-point Likert scale from "not at all" to "very much." Example items include "I feel calm" (reverse scored) and "I feel tense." Perceptions of the robot were assessed using the Human-Robot Interaction Evaluation Scale (HRIES) by [22] with 10 items rated on a 7-point Likert scale from 1 to 7. HRIES items are organised into four sub-scales: sociability, animacy, agency, and disturbance. Example items include "warm" (sociability), "alive" (animacy), "intentional" (agency), and "scary" (disturbance). The items were translated into German and presented with the original English wording. Participants' prior experience with NAO and breathing exercises were assessed with a single-item measure on a 4-point scale, from "no experience at all" to "extensive experience."

The experiment was conducted between October 2024 and January 2025. Participants were regularly enrolled first-semester students. As part of the study, students participated in the breathing exercise in the classroom. Before the exercise, participants completed a baseline survey with items related to their prior experience with NAO and breathing exercises, and the State-Trait Anxiety Inventory (STAI). After the breathing exercise, they completed the exit survey with the STAI and HRIES items.

4 Results

We calculated STAI scores for T1 (before) and T2 (after) and the HRIES scores for all 42 participants. A paired-samples t-test revealed a significant reduction in stress levels following the breathing exercise ($M = 11.43$) compared to pre-exercise levels ($M = 12.83$), $t(41) = 3.50, p < .01, d = 0.5$, indicating a moderate effect size (see Fig. 1).

To quantify stress reduction, we calculated a change score by subtracting the pre-exercise stress level from the post-exercise stress level (T2-T1). The first multiple regression analysis with the stress change score as the dependent variable, and breathing exercise experience, NAO experience, HRIES sub-scale scores, age, and gender as predictors. Among these, only the HRIES sociability sub-scale significantly predicted stress reduction ($\beta = 0.50$, $p < .05$). The second regression analysis was conducted to examine whether participants' experience with NAO moderated the effect of perceived sociability on changes in stress levels. The overall model was marginally significant, $F(3, 37) = 2.78$, $p = .055$, with $R^2 = .184$. While perceived sociability did not significantly predict stress change on its own ($p = .195$), a marginally significant interaction effect was found between sociability and NAO experience ($B = 1.368$, $p = .054$). Greater sociability was associated with increased stress reduction only among participants with higher NAO experience. Additionally, NAO experience had a significant main effect ($B = -6.684$, $p = .040$), suggesting that familiarity with the robot contributed to stress reduction. The data analysis is available at: https://osf.io/pr4hb/.

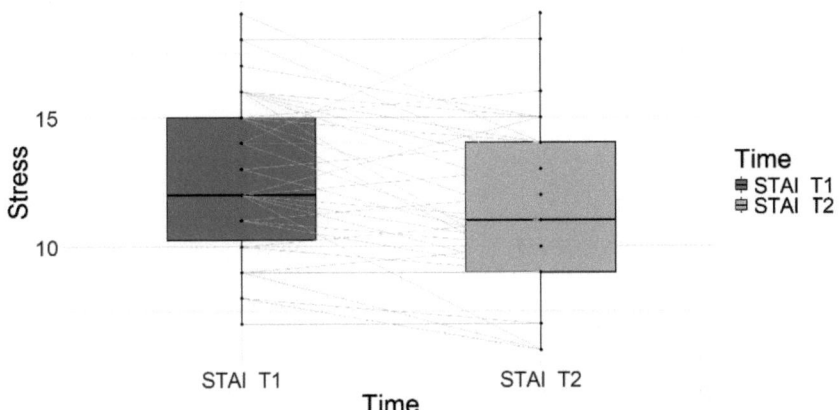

Fig. 1. Effects of the breathing exercise on stress before (T1) and after (T2) the exercise.

5 Conclusions

In our study, we investigated whether a breathing exercise guided by the video recording of the robot NAO could reduce stress. Our findings revealed a significant reduction in stress. This effect however was especially pronounced for participants with a higher level of experience with the robot. Variables such as age, gender, prior experience with breathing exercises and other perceptions of the robot did not significantly influence stress outcomes. In line with previous studies which showed that breathing exercises with social robots can effectively reduce stress [18, 19, 23–25], our study demonstrated that even a pre-recorded video of a robot delivering a breathing exercise can have a stress-reducing effect. Two interesting findings emerged from our study. First, higher perceived sociability of the robot was significantly associated with less stress reduction, and this effect depended on participants' experience with the NAO robot. Second, participants with little or no prior experience with NAO experienced no benefit or even a potential increase in stress, when the robot was perceived as more sociable. The observed stress reduction may partly stem from participants' sense of familiarity or comfort with the robot itself rather than the breathing simulation, which highlights the need for more controlled comparisons to disentangle these effects. The key limitations of the study presented in this paper include the short-term measurement of stress reduction. In our follow-up work we plan to explore the potential influence of the novelty addressed through our analysis of repeated sessions and the comparison of with two other conditions (human and real robot). We aim to explore the role of perceived robot's sociability and its interaction with prior robot experience for stress-reduction outcomes by investigating long-term effects of repeated interventions compared with two further conditions. Our research will also compare a breathing exercise with NAO, which relies on robot's arm and head movements, with robots such as the Neffy [19], which afford haptic interaction through upper body expansion. Moreover, we plan to incorporate physiological parameters as objective indicators.

Disclosure of Interests. The authors have no competing interests to declare that are relevant to the content of this article.

References

1. Vogel, S., Schwabe, L.: Learning and memory under stress: implications for the classroom. Npj Sci. Learn **1**(1), 16011 (2016)
2. Heinrichs, K., Lehnchen, J., Burian J., et al.: Mental and physical well-being among students in Germany: results from the StudiBiFra study. J. Public Health (2024)
3. Ruse, J.N., Schraube, E., Rhodes, P.: Left to their own devices: the significance of mental health apps on the construction of therapy and care. Subjectivity **4**, 410–428 (2024)
4. Almuqrin, A., Hammoud, R., Terbagou, I., Tognin, S., Mechelli, A.: Smartphone apps for mental health: systematic review of the literature and five recommendations for clinical translation. BMJ Open **15**(2), e093932 (2025)
5. Guo, T., Yan, J., Cao, C., Xiong, K., Chen, P., Yang, H:. Machine lerning-based analysis of psychological issues and game intervention for college students. In: 2024 4th International Conference on Educational Technology (ICET), pp. 141–6. IEEE, Wuhan, China (2024)
6. Meshkat, S., Edalatkhah, M., Di Luciano, C., et al.: Virtual reality and stress management: a systematic review. Cereus **16**(7), e64573 (2024)
7. Cortez-Vázquez, G., Adriaanse, M., Burchell, G.L., et al.: Virtual reality breathing interventions for mental health: a systematic review and meta-analysis of randomized controlled trials. Appl. Psychophysiol. Biofeedback **49**(1), 1–21 (2024)
8. Scoglio, A.A., Reilly, E.D., Gorman, J.A., Drebing, C.E.: Use of social robots in mental health and well-being research: systematic review. J. Med. Internet Res. 24, **21**(7), e13322 (2019)
9. Nichol, B., McCready, J., Erfani, G., et al.: Exploring the impact of socially assistive robots on health and wellbeing across the lifespan: an umbrella review and meta-analysis. Int. J. Nurs. Stud. **153**, 104730 (2024)
10. Hopper, S.I., Murray, S.L., Ferrara, L.R., Singleton, J.K.: Effectiveness of diaphragmatic breathing for reducing physiological and psychological stress in adults: a quantitative systematic review. JBI Database Syst. Rev. Implement. Rep. **17**(9), 1855–1876 (2019)

11. Morgan, S.P., Lengacher, C.A., Seo, Y.: A systematic review of breathing exercise interventions: an integrative complementary approach for anxiety and stress in adult populations. J. Holist. Nurs. **16**, 08980101241273860 (2024)
12. Gerbarg, P.L., Cruz-Cordero, Y.L., Conte, V.A., et al.: Breath–body–mind core techniques to manage medical student stress. J. Med. Educ. Curric. Dev. **10**, 23821205231212056 (2023)
13. De Couck, M., Caers, R., Musch, L., Fliegauf, J., Giangreco, A., Gidron, Y.: How breathing can help you make better decisions: Two studies on the effects of breathing patterns on heart rate variability and decision-making in business cases. Int. J. of Psychophysiology **139**, 1–9 (2019)
14. Ovadia-Blechman, Z., Tarrasch, R., Velicki, M., Chalutz, Ben-Gal, H.: Reducing test anxiety by device-guided breathing: a pilot study. Front. Psychol. **23,** 13:678098 (2022)
15. Chittaro, L., Sioni, R.: Evaluating mobile apps for breathing training: the effectiveness of visualization. Comput. Hum. Behav. **40**, 56–63 (2014)
16. Chuanromanee, T., Metoyer, R.: Evaluation and comparison of four mobile breathing training visualizations. In: 2020 IEEE International Conference on Healthcare Informatics (ICHI), pp. 1–12. IEE, Oldenburg, Germany (2020)
17. Dar, S., Ekart, A., Bernardet, U.: Usability, acceptance, and the role of realism in virtual humans for breathing exercise training. Sci. Rep. 9, 15(1), 1536 (2025)
18. Buchem, I., Thomas., E.J.: A breathing exercise with the humanoid robot NAO designed to reduce student stress during class: results from a pilot study with students in higher education. In ICERI2022 Proceedings, pp. 6545–6551. Seville, Spain (2022)
19. Thomas, E.J., Dincel, K., Buchem, I.: NEFFY – a social robot for multimodal support of slow-paced breathing exercises. In: Proceedings of the 2025 ACM/IEEE International Conference on Human-Robot Interaction, pp. 1800–2. IEEE, Melbourne, Australia (2025)
20. Marteau, T.M., Bekker, H.: The development of a six-item short-form of the state scale of the Spielberger State—Trait Anxiety Inventory (STAI). Br. J. Clin. Psychol. **31**(3), 301–306 (1992)
21. Grimm, J.: State-Trait-Anxiety Inventory nach Spielberger. Deutsche Lang- und Kurzversion.- Methodenforum der Universität Wien. MF-Working Paper 2009/02 (2009)
22. Spatola, N., Kühnlenz, B., Cheng, G.: Perception and evaluation in Human-Robot Interaction: The human–robot interaction evaluation scale (HRIES)—a multicomponent approach of anthropomorphism. Int. J. Soc. Robot. **13**(7), 1517–1539 (2021)
23. Rice, A., Klęczek, K., Alimardani, M.: The effectiveness of social robots in stress management interventions for university students. In: Ali, AA, Cabibihan, J.J., Meskin, N., Rossi, S., et al. (editors): Social Robotics. LNCS, vol. 14453, pp. 181–90. Springer, Singapore (2024)
24. Klęczek, K., Rice, A., Alimardani, M.: Robots as mental health coaches: a study of emotional responses to technology-assisted stress management tasks using physiological signals. Sensors. 21, 24(13), 4032 (2024)
25. Matheus, K., Vazquez, M., Scassellati, B.: A social robot for anxiety reduction via deep breathing. In: 2022 31st IEEE International Conference on Robot and Human Interactive Communication (RO-MAN), pp. 89–94. IEEE, Napoli, Italy (2022)

Come Closer: A Social Bench to Measure Children's Interaction with Robots

Francesca Cocchella[1,2(✉)], Sara Mongile[1], Giulia Pusceddu[3], Luca Andrighetto[4], Francesco Rea[1], and Alessandra Sciutti[1]

[1] CONTACT Unit, Italian Institute of Technology, Genoa, Italy
[2] DIBRIS, University of Genoa, Genoa, Italy
francesca.cocchella@iit.it
[3] UVIP Unit, Italian Institute of Technology, Genoa, Italy
[4] DISFOR University of Genoa, Genoa, Italy

Abstract. As social robots enter educational and public settings, understanding how children perceive and engage with them becomes crucial. This study introduces the Social Bench Tool, an interdisciplinary measure adapted from social psychology to assess children's implicit attitudes toward robots. In the task, children choose where to sit on a bench next to a humanoid robot, revealing interpersonal orientation toward it. We tested a digital version in a pilot study with adolescents and implemented a physical version during a public event with children. Preliminary results from the digital study suggest participants sat closer to the robot after interacting with it. Observations from the physical setup support the tool's potential as a behavioral measure in more naturalistic contexts. The Social Bench Tool offers a simple, intuitive way to complement self-reports in Child-Robot Interaction research.

Keywords: Children-Robot Interaction · Measure · Humanoid Robot

1 Introduction

Research on Child-Robot Interaction (CRI) is gaining traction within the broader field of social robotics, especially considering its applications in the educational field [2]. Consequently, the development of appropriate tools to interpret children's perceptions and behaviors toward robots is increasingly necessary. Conventional self-report measures, while informative, often rely on verbal and metacognitive abilities that vary widely across developmental stages. Younger participants may struggle to articulate their attitudes explicitly, which can limit data interpretability and comparability [3]. To address this issue, researchers have advocated for more accessible and developmentally appropriate techniques, such as graphic or spatial representations of constructs [12]. In this context, we propose an innovative measure: the **Social Bench Tool (SBT)**, specifically designed for CRI. This tool draws inspiration from the Social Exclusion Bench Tool [8], a social psychology self-report method, where participants indicate where they would sit on a bench already partially occupied by a member of a stigmatized group (e.g., an immigrant). This allows researchers to assess implicit prejudice through physical distance. Inspired by this, the SBT presents a bench with the humanoid robot iCub [9] seated on one side, allowing us to gather indirect indications of children's attitudes toward the robot. Participants are asked to choose where they would sit, providing a non-verbal indication of attitudes toward the robot. To validate the SBT, we ran one pilot studies during school's Open Day at the Italian Institute of Technology, in which adolescents completed the digital SBT before and after interacting with iCub. Moreover, at another Open Day, elementary kids met iCub and chose seats on a real bench, letting us observe their natural seating behavior.

2 Background

Research has consistently shown that social interactions are crucial for supporting human learning, enhancing both cognitive and emotional outcomes [7]. Recently, evidence has emerged suggesting that some of these benefits can extend to interactions between children and social robots [6]. This is largely attributed to the physical embodiment of robots [15], which sets them apart from traditional learning technologies like tablets or computers [2]. Compared to virtual agents, physically embodied robots have been found to foster greater engagement and creativity [1], potentially leading to improved learning outcomes [7]. Despite this potential, the precise impact of robot behaviors on children remains unclear [13]. Some studies indicate that social behaviors in robots support learning [10], while others suggest they may distract young users [14].

To design effective educational applications, it is crucial to consider children's expectations and how their perceptions of robots change through interaction. In a previous study [5], we showed that children's acceptance of the robot NAO before interaction predicted how pleasing they found the experience. This highlights the value of self-reports in understanding CRI in educational settings. Furthermore, Sciutti et al. [11] found that younger children initially focus on a robot's appearance, but interacting with iCub shifts their attention to its functions, while older children already prioritize functionality. This demonstrates that direct experience can reshape children's perception of robots. The field of CRI, however, still lacks standardized tools to measure how children implicitly evaluate robots, especially in naturalistic and long-term settings [4]. Most studies use self-reports or behavioral observations, which may miss children's spontaneous attitudes—especially when verbal skills are limited. To overcome this, researchers advocate for intuitive, engaging methods to assess children's perceptions and social preferences.

3 Social Bench Tool Implementation

To address the limitations outlined above, we conducted a pilot study during the School Open Days at the Italian Institute of Technology to test the digital version of the SBT. We then implemented the physical version in a similar setting. In

3.1 Experimental Study: Digital Bench Tool

Fig. 1. Digital version of the Social Bench Tool.

The study was approved by the Liguria Regional Ethics Committee. Parents or legal guardians gave informed consent. Forty-five Italian teenagers (Age: $\mu = 17.3$, $\sigma = 1.14$; gender: M = 33, F = 12) were invited to visit the experimental lab hosting the humanoid robot iCub. Before the interaction with the robot, they were asked to sit in front of a laptop displaying the SBT, with the robot iCub seated, as shown in Fig. 1. The program was implemented in HTML and displayed a static image (size: 1280 × 635 pixels), replicating the format and dimensions used in the original version of the tool. Participants were asked to respond to the following prompt: "*Imagine you are in a park. The robot iCub is seated on this bench. Please indicate where you would like to sit in the scene by clicking with the mouse.*". Afterward, they attend a 5 minute self-introduction by the robot iCub, which in the Lab explained briefly its functional capabilities and how it can interact socially with the environment. Finally, they completed the bench again.

Similarly as what was done in the previous version of the tool [8] we identified iCub's centroid ($x_{\text{icub}}, y_{\text{icub}}$) as a reference point to measure the distance from participants' positions ($x_{\text{part}}, y_{\text{part}}$). Distances were calculated using the Euclidean distance formula (Eq. 1):

$$d = \sqrt{(x_{\text{icub}} - x_{\text{part}})^2 + (y_{\text{icub}} - y_{\text{part}})^2} \qquad (1)$$

By calculating the distance between each participant's chosen position and the robot's position, we obtained a measure of physical proximity in pixels. We conducted a series of Wilcoxon Paired Sample tests over this data to test a difference between the pre- and post-interaction positions. Analyses were conducted on the open source software Jamovi[1]. Results demonstrated a significant

---

[1] https://www.jamovi.org/.

shift in participants' behavior following the interaction with the robot (Wilcoxon Signed-Rank test, $p = .0003$), with an average reduction in distance of approximately 9.08%. Participants' attitudes were categorized into five classes based on their horizontal distance from the robot, using an ordinal classification inspired by a Likert-scale structure. The observed distance ranged from 166 to 1117 pixels and was divided into five equal intervals. The distance-based categories were thus defined as follows: Distant (1): 1117âĂŞ927 pixels; Far (2): 926âĂŞ736 pixels; Intermediate (3): 735âĂŞ545 pixels; Near (4): 544âĂŞ354 pixels; Close (5): 353âĂŞ166 pixels. The mean of class distribution was 4.29±0.86 before the interaction and 4.42±0.90 after the interaction. On average, participants tended to be positioned in the near-to-close range, with a slight shift toward closer proximity after the interaction.

3.2 Physical Implementation: the Real Bench Tool

Fig. 2. Wooden version of the Social Bench Tool implemented in the lab.

A physical version of the bench was built using wood, measuring 2 meters in length, 90 cm in height, and 38 cm in depth, replicating the appearance and proportions of the digital version used in the SBT. The humanoid robot iCub was positioned on the bench using a lifting device, as shown in Fig. 2.

This physical setup was placed in our laboratory and made available during a public and Open Day event, which included a visit from local elementary schools (authorized by parents or legal guardians). Due to the nature of the event, no formal data collection was conducted, and we were not able to record detailed demographic information. However, we estimate that approximately $N = 140$ children aged between 7 and 10 visited the lab in small groups of about 15, each accompanied by teachers.

Although this initial implementation did not follow a structured observational protocol, the first author made informal observations during the school visit to explore how children spontaneously engaged with the physical bench and robot. The aim was to assess the ecological validity and potential of the tool for future studies in CRI. The following patterns were noted:

- Children generally responded with enthusiasm toward the robot: some chose to sit very close to it, while others preferred to keep a greater distance or sat on alternative chairs available in the room.
- Teachers occasionally expressed concern about the robot being touched or damaged and instructed children to avoid close proximity. This suggests that adult presence and norms may influence children's choices and should be carefully considered in future implementations.
- Differently from the digital version, children entered the room in groups, and not all could sit on the bench at once. This introduced group dynamics and spatial constraints, which may have affected behavior and should be accounted for in future designs.

While preliminary and anecdotal, these observations indicate that the physical version of the bench is a promising tool to evoke meaningful approach behaviors toward social robots. Based on this experience, we plan to design and conduct structured studies using the real bench, with appropriate methodological controls and ethical approval.

3.3 Conclusions

We presented a preliminary study showcasing the potential of a new research method. The SBT offers a simple and adaptable way to explore young users' perceptions of social robots. With both digital and physical versions, it can be used in various settings and is compatible with any robot that can (physically or *graphically*) sit on the bench. We used the digital SBT in two different contexts: a pilot study with teenagers and an exploratory implementation with younger children. These age groups were based on participants who spontaneously took part during Open Day events, where we had limited control over recruitment. In future studies, the SBT will be implemented with a more homogeneous age sample. We plan to validate the digital version by examining its correlation with established self-report measures in CRI, to strengthen its reliability. Future work will also explore different types of interactions with the robot, both in controlled laboratory settings and in more ecologically valid contexts such as schools, using video-based stimuli. Additionally, we will develop an experimental protocol for the physical bench, including systematic coding of children's behavior and measurement of their physical proximity to the robot. Overall, the SBT shows promise as a scalable and easily deployable method for assessing social distance and affinity toward robots, contributing to both research and design in CRI.

References

1. Alves-Oliveira, P., Arriaga, P., Paiva, A., Hoffman, G.: Yolo, a robot for creativity: a co-design study with children. In: Proceedings of the 2017 Conference on Interaction Design and Children, pp. 423–429 (2017)
2. Belpaeme, T., Kennedy, J., Ramachandran, A., Scassellati, B., Tanaka, F.: Social robots for education: a review. Sci. robot. **3**(21), eaat5954 (2018)

3. Borgers, N., Hox, J., Sikkel, D.: Response quality in survey research with children and adolescents: the effect of labeled response options and vague quantifiers. Int. J. Public Opinion Res. **15**(1), 83–94 (2003)
4. Charisi, V., Davison, D., Reidsma, D., Evers, V.: Evaluation methods for user-centered child-robot interaction. In: 2016 25th IEEE International Symposium on Robot and Human Interactive Communication (RO-MAN), pp. 545–550. IEEE (2016)
5. Cocchella, F., et al.: At school with a robot: Italian students' perception of robotics during an educational program. In: 2023 32nd IEEE International Conference on Robot and Human Interactive Communication (RO-MAN), pp. 1413–1419. IEEE (2023)
6. Kennedy, J., Baxter, P., Senft, E., Belpaeme, T.: Higher Nonverbal Immediacy Leads to Greater Learning Gains in Child-Robot Tutoring Interactions. Presented at the (2015). https://doi.org/10.1007/978-3-319-25554-5_33
7. Konijn, E.A., Jansen, B., Mondaca Bustos, V., Hobbelink, V.L., Preciado Vanegas, D.: Social robots for (second) language learning in (migrant) primary school children. Int. J. Soc. Robot. **14**(3), 827–843 (2022)
8. Mazzoni, D., Marinucci, M., Monzani, D., Pravettoni, G.: The social exclusion bench tool (sebt): a visual way of assessing interpersonal social exclusion. MethodsX **8**, 101495 (2021)
9. Metta, G., et al.: The icub humanoid robot: an open-systems platform for research in cognitive development. Neural Netw. **23**(8–9), 1125–1134 (2010)
10. Mubin, O., Stevens, C.J., Shahid, S., Al Mahmud, A., Dong, J.J.: A review of the applicability of robots in education. J. Tech. Educ. Learn. **1**(209–0015), 13 (2013)
11. Sciutti, A., Rea, F., Sandini, G.: When you are young,(robot's) looks matter. developmental changes in the desired properties of a robot friend. In: The 23rd IEEE international symposium on robot and human interactive communication, pp. 567–573. IEEE (2014)
12. Severson, R.L., Lemm, K.M.: Kids see human too: adapting an individual differences measure of anthropomorphism for a child sample. J. Cogn. Dev. **17**(1), 122–141 (2016)
13. Stower, R.: The role of trust and social behaviours in children's learning from social robots. In: 2019 8th International Conference on Affective Computing and Intelligent Interaction Workshops and Demos (ACIIW), pp. 1–5. IEEE (2019)
14. Vogt, P., et al.: Second language tutoring using social robots: a large-scale study. In: 2019 14th ACM/IEEE International Conference on Human-Robot Interaction (HRI), pp. 497–505. Ieee (2019)
15. Wainer, J., Feil-Seifer, D.J., Shell, D.A., Mataric, M.J.: The role of physical embodiment in human-robot interaction. In: ROMAN 2006-The 15th IEEE International Symposium on Robot and Human Interactive Communication, pp. 117–122. IEEE (2006)

Conceptual Framework for Autonomous Coaching in Orthopaedic Rehabilitation with Socially Assistive Robots

C. Tamantini[1](✉), A. Umbrico[1], A. Fabrizio[2], A. Carnevale[2],
E. Schena[2,4], U. G. Longo[2,3], and A. Orlandini[1]

[1] Institute of Cognitive Sciences and Technologies, National Research Council of Italy, Rome 00196, Italy
christian.tamantini@cnr.it
[2] Fondazione Policlinico Universitario Campus Bio-Medico, Rome 00128, Italy
g.longo@policlinicocampus.it
[3] Research Unit of Orthopaedic and Trauma Surgery, Università Campus Bio-Medico di Roma, Rome 00128, Italy
[4] Research Unit of Measurements and Biomedical Instrumentation, Università Campus Bio-Medico di Roma, Rome 00128, Italy

Abstract. Post-surgical orthopaedic rehabilitation requires personalized and adaptive therapy to restore motor function, yet current practices face challenges related to patient variability, diverse supervision needs, and limited treatment personalization. Socially Assistive Robots (SARs) offer promising support, but existing systems often rely on predefined exercise scripts and heuristic adaptation, with limited autonomy. In this paper, we propose the use of a cognitive framework to enable SARs to autonomously coach orthopaedic rehabilitation sessions through the integration of automated planning based on structured clinical knowledge with multimodal monitoring. By combining symbolic and numerical planning with closed-loop feedback, the system can adapt rehabilitation sessions in response to the patient's performance and provide feedback.

Keywords: Socially Assistive Robots · Orthopaedic Rehabilitation · Automated Planning · Multimodal Monitoring

1 Introduction

Post-surgical orthopaedic rehabilitation is fundamental to restoring patients' motor functions and independence [7]. However, this process often faces significant challenges, including patient adherence to therapy, personalization of exercise programs, and continuous supervision [8]. Standard rehabilitation protocols may not adequately address individual variations in functional recovery, requiring frequent adjustments based on patient performance and condition.

Socially Assistive Robots (SARs) have emerged as promising tools to support rehabilitation by providing patients with interactive guidance, motivation, and feedback [5]. Despite the success of SARs in facilitating movement imitation and enhancing engagement, the prevailing implementations of these systems are characterised by a reliance on pre-defined exercise scripts, thereby hindering their capacity to adapt sessions in response to the evolving requirements of orthopaedic patients [11].

This work introduces a cognitive framework that equips SARs with the ability to personalize and adapt rehabilitation sessions and long-term plans based on structured clinical knowledge and multimodal monitoring. By combining symbolic and numerical planning with reactive feedback, the system continuously adjusts therapy in response to the patient's evolving condition. Designed with a focus on orthopaedic rehabilitation, the framework supports autonomous, goal-driven coaching aligned with clinical objectives and promotes motor recovery through dynamic, patient-specific interventions.

2 Related Works

The utilisation of SARs in the domain of rehabilitation has witnessed a marked increase in research interest, particularly concerning their capacity to manage sessions, monitor performance, and provide adaptive feedback. Among the solutions proposed in literature, the NAO-therapist platform constitutes a significant contribution to the field, as evidenced by its integration of kinematic tracking and interactive support to guide therapy [3]. The system was developed through a human-centred design process involving physicians [6]. The system formalises six core functionalities: session planning, initiation, introduction, monitoring with feedback, difficulty adaptation, and session termination. Integration of these functionalities is necessary to ensure the successful execution of a rehabilitation session.

Although SAR-based systems have shown promise in rehabilitation for paediatric and elderly populations with neurological conditions [10], their use in adult orthopaedic care remains scarcely investigated. Prior studies have primarily addressed static pose imitation, which falls short for orthopaedic patients who need progressive recovery of mobility and control through targeted, phase-specific exercises. In most existing works, the primary focus has been on leveraging the robot's physical embodiment and social interaction capabilities to foster engagement and adherence. Gamified approaches have been widely adopted, aiming to increase motivation and promote active participation, especially in young users. However, from a technical standpoint, these systems are commonly based on static sequences of predefined exercises and fixed rules for difficulty modulation, which restrict their ability to tailor interventions to individual clinical needs. Furthermore, the cognitive dimension of SARs is often underutilized: most architectures do not incorporate structured models of clinical knowledge or reasoning mechanisms capable of supporting dynamic decision-making or long-term personalization of rehabilitation plans.

In this paper, we pursue a novel approach proposing a cognitive architecture that formalises the fundamental components required for SARs to support rehabilitation in orthopaedic patients. In contrast to the characteristics of previously studied populations, orthopaedic rehabilitation is characterised by specific clinical requirements. Accordingly, this contribution first outlines the potential role of SARs in addressing the distinctive needs of orthopaedic care and subsequently details the proposed cognitive architecture designed to enable autonomous, adaptive, and clinically aligned robotic coaching.

3 The Potential of Autonomous Robotic Coaches in Orthopaedic Rehabilitation

Rehabilitation for musculoskeletal disorders aims to restore strength, mobility, and motor control through personalized, high-repetition interventions [1]. In orthopaedic patients, especially post-surgery, pain, reduced capacity, and structured recovery timelines impose specific challenges [9]. These include the need for phase-based progression, personalized exercise plans, and ongoing clinical supervision, which are difficult to sustain in home-based settings due to limited staff availability [2].

Unlike neurological rehabilitation, which often focuses on re-learning basic movements, orthopaedic rehabilitation relies on varied exercise sets that must evolve in intensity and focus across healing phases. The ability to reason over patient state and adapt interventions accordingly is thus critical.

In this context, SARs can support remote or semi-supervised care by demonstrating exercises, maintaining motivation, and providing real-time multimodal feedback [1]. To be truly effective in orthopaedic care, SARs must go beyond monitoring: they must autonomously reason over clinical goals, patient conditions, and therapeutic effects to generate sessions tailored to each recovery phase.

By collecting and interpreting both performance and adherence data, SARs can also support clinicians in therapy planning and adjustment [4]. Their integration as adaptive systems into orthopaedic pathways may significantly improve the personalization and clinical effectiveness of rehabilitation programs [12,13].

4 A Framework for Autonomous SAR-Based Orthopaedic Coaching

The proposed framework, presented in Fig. 1A, is divided into two layers: a deliberative layer responsible for planning and managing clinical goals, and a reactive layer dedicated to real-time monitoring and adaptive feedback generation. The architecture was co-designed with clinicians and therapists, whose input informed the definition of therapeutic goals, adaptation logic, and interaction design, ensuring clinical relevance and applicability.

The deliberative layer governs the configuration and continuous refinement of rehabilitation sessions by replicating core aspects of human clinical reasoning. The system incorporates a *Knowledge Manager*, which formalizes structured clinical information such as patient profiles, therapeutic goals, exercise models, and session constraints into machine-readable representations. These representations

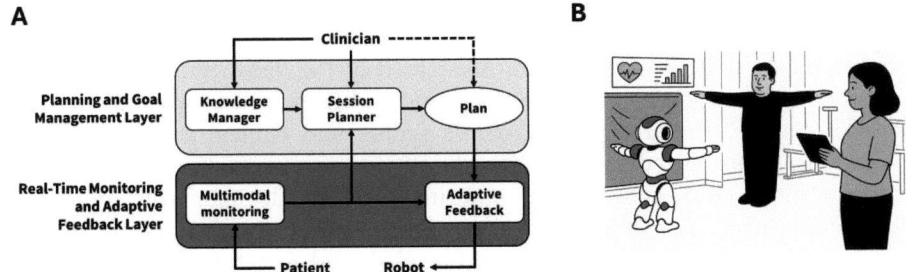

Fig. 1. A Two-layered control architecture for personalized orthopaedic robot-assisted rehabilitation. **B** Illustrative scenario.

enable the system to internally model the patient's evolving state, therapeutic needs, and intended outcomes, reflecting a form of artificial cognition. Clinical information is provided and updated by the clinician and encoded using standardized models, such as the International Classification of Functioning, Disability and Health [14]. Additionally, quantitative mappings between exercises and their expected impact on functional abilities are defined [16], allowing the robot to reason about progress toward therapeutic objectives. These cognitive representations form the basis for domain ontologies and enable the *Session Planner* to deliberate over multiple possible interventions, making decisions through symbolic reasoning and numerical estimation in a goal-oriented and patient-specific manner. Utilising this structured information, the Session Planner autonomously selects, schedules, and parametrizes exercises that are coherent with the current clinical condition of the patient. Therefore, the resulting therapy Plan is defined as a structured, adaptable sequence of exercises annotated with relevant therapeutic parameters and performance targets.

The reactive layer supports the execution of the rehabilitation session by enabling the robot to perceive, interpret, and promptly respond to the patient's ongoing performance. The system is fed by a multimodal monitoring infrastructure that includes contactless kinematic tracking, e.g., via depth cameras or computer vision-based pose estimation, to assess the correctness of movement execution without constraining the patient with wearable devices. Concurrently, it acquires physiological signals such as electromyography (EMG), heart rate (HR), and respiratory rate (RR) to estimate the muscular and cardiorespiratory workload experienced during the session [15]. These data streams update the internal representation of the patient's state and guide real-time adaptations. Based on this information, the system provides personalized feedback: corrective cues, both verbal and visual, help the patient adjust their execution in line with therapeutic goals, while motivational feedback, such as encouraging phrases or visual progress indicators, supports engagement and adherence throughout the session. The framework can also dynamically reconfigure the planned exercises; for instance, if physiological monitoring reveals excessive strain, the system may reduce the intensity or complexity of upcoming tasks to ensure safety and maintain clinical efficacy.

A typical rehabilitation session, illustrated in Fig. 1B, begins with the clinician setting therapeutic objectives (e.g., increasing range of motion) via a dedicated interface. Based on the patient's profile and clinical goals, the system generates a personalized session plan. The SAR then engages the patient, demonstrates the exercises, and provides real-time feedback during execution through its reactive layer. The clinician oversees the session through a graphical interface, validating decisions, intervening if needed, and annotating observations to refine the knowledge base. At the end, the system summarizes performance and suggests targets for future sessions.

5 Conclusions and Future Works

In this work, a cognitive framework to enhance the autonomy of SARs in rehabilitation coaching is presented. While the architecture is broadly applicable to assistive scenarios requiring personalized adaptation, its capabilities are particularly suited to orthopaedic rehabilitation. This domain is characterized by structured yet evolving therapeutic pathways, a wide set of exercises, and the need for continuous personalization based on clinical goals and patient progress. By integrating structured clinical knowledge, automated planning, and real-time multimodal monitoring, the proposed system enables dynamic session generation and closed-loop adaptation, aiming to improve engagement, safety, and functional outcomes in orthopaedic patients.

Future work will involve deploying the framework on a SAR and conducting a two-phase validation: initial testing with healthy participants to assess planning and monitoring capabilities, followed by pilot studies evaluating feasibility, usability, and therapeutic impact in orthopaedic rehabilitation.

Acknowledgments. This work was supported by the Italian Ministry of Research, under the complementary actions to the NRRP "Fit4MedRob - Fit for Medical Robotics" Grant (PNC0000007), (CUP: B53C22006990001).

Disclosure of Interests. The authors declare no conflicts of interest.

References

1. Carnevale, A., et al.: Exploring the impact of socially assistive robots in rehabilitation scenarios. Bioengineering **12**(2), 204 (2025)
2. Ehioghae, M., et al.: Effectiveness of virtual reality-based rehabilitation interventions in improving postoperative outcomes for orthopedic surgery patients. Curr. Pain Headache Rep. **28**(1), 37–45 (2024)
3. Gallego, A., Pulido, J.C., González, J.C., Fernández, F.: Design of a robotic as a service platform to perform rehabilitation therapies. In: Robot 2019: Fourth Iberian Robotics Conference: Advances in Robotics, Volume 2, pp. 681–692. Springer (2020)

4. Hakim, R.M., Tunis, B.G., Ross, M.D.: Rehabilitation robotics for the upper extremity: review with new directions for orthopaedic disorders. Disabil. Rehabil. Assist. Technol. **12**(8), 765–771 (2017)
5. Langer, A., Levy-Tzedek, S.: Emerging roles for social robots in rehabilitation: current directions. ACM Trans. Human-Robot Int. (THRI) **10**(4), 1–4 (2021)
6. Lee, M.H., Siewiorek, D.P., Smailagic, A., Bernardino, A., Badia, S.B.i.: Enabling AI and robotic coaches for physical rehabilitation therapy: iterative design and evaluation with therapists and post-stroke survivors. Int. J. Soc. Robot. **16**(1), 1–22 (2024)
7. Longo, U.G., et al.: Physical therapy and precision rehabilitation in shoulder rotator cuff disease. Int. Orthop. **44**(5), 893–903 (2020). https://doi.org/10.1007/s00264-020-04511-2
8. Longo, U.G., et al.: Conservative versus accelerated rehabilitation after rotator cuff repair: a systematic review and meta-analysis. BMC Musculoskelet. Disord. **22**, 1–22 (2021)
9. Paladugu, P., Kumar, R., Ong, J., Waisberg, E., Sporn, K.: Virtual reality-enhanced rehabilitation for improving musculoskeletal function and recovery after trauma. J. Orthop. Surg. Res. **20**(1), 404 (2025)
10. Pulido, J.C., et al.: A socially assistive robotic platform for upper-limb rehabilitation: a longitudinal study with pediatric patients. IEEE Robot. Autom. Mag. **26**(2), 24–39 (2019)
11. Raso, A., et al.: A pilot study for assessing NAO humanoid robot assistance in shoulder rehabilitation. J. Exp. Orthop. **12**(1), e70122 (2025)
12. Schmidt, D., Hedin, J., Pelegrina, A., Weyland, S., Rittmann, L.M., Jekauc, D.: Comparing the effectiveness of digital and conventional rehabilitation aftercare on work ability in orthopedic patients: a longitudinal study in germany. J. Occup. Rehabil. pp. 1–14 (2025)
13. Sobrepera, M.J., Lee, V.G., Johnson, M.J.: Therapists' opinions on telehealth, robotics, and socially assistive robot-augmented telepresence systems for rehabilitation. In: 2022 9th IEEE RAS/EMBS International Conference for Biomedical Robotics and Biomechatronics (BioRob), pp. 1–8. IEEE (2022)
14. Sorrentino, A., et al.: Personalizing care through robotic assistance and clinical supervision. Front. Robot. AI **9**, 883814 (2022)
15. Tamantini, C., Umbrico, A., Orlandini, A.: Leveraging multimodal monitoring in plan-based robot-aided rehabilitation. In: Advanced AI Methods and Interfaces for Human-Centered Assistive and Rehabilitation Robotics 2024, pp. 14–19. CEUR Workshop Proceedings, Bolzano (2024). https://ceur-ws.org/Vol-3932/paper3.pdf
16. Tamantini, C., Umbrico, A., Orlandini, A.: Repair platform: robot-aided personalized rehabilitation. In: International Conference of the Italian Association for Artificial Intelligence, pp. 301–314. Springer (2024)

HRI-Based Interview Training Using the FurHat Robot

Adam Jones and Roger K. Moore(✉)

School of Computer Science, University of Sheffield, Sheffield S1 4DP, UK
ajones29@sheffield.ac.uk ,
r.k.moore@sheffield.ac.uk
https://www.sheffield.ac.uk/cs

Abstract. Navigating the pressures of job interviews can present a significant challenge to an individual as their preparation can critically influence the outcome. While traditional face-to-face (F2F) methods for interview training are still the norm, the evolution of 'artificial intelligence' (AI) presents new opportunities, and a variety of virtual AI-based interview platforms exist to satisfy the need. However, while such platforms offer a wide range of features and broad coverage of interview-style questions, they often lack the physical presence and the capacity for real-time emotional feedback or adaptive response tailoring that is characteristic of real-world F2F scenarios. As a consequence, there is growing interest in the use of physical robots for job interview simulation. This paper presents the development of an advanced AI-based 'Interactive Interview Training System' (IITS) utilising the FurHat robot which goes beyond the feature sets of existing virtual and physical agents to create a more holistic and effective job interview simulation. In particular, FurHat has been configured to allow extensive customisation by the user, such as the ability to define job scenarios from different industry backgrounds and invoke a range of interaction styles. Also, since FurHat's Software Development Kit (SDK) incorporates a virtual animation of the robot, it has been possible to conduct a user-based evaluation which confirmed the merits of physical embodiment in HRI-based interview training.

Keywords: Interview training · FurHat robot · Virtual/physical presence

1 Introduction

Navigating the pressures of job interviews presents a significant challenge as an individual's preparation can critically influence the outcome. While traditional face-to-face (F2F) methods are still the norm, the evolution of technology – in particular, 'artificial intelligence' (AI) – presents new opportunities for interview training. For example, in a study on using AI to combine exam and interview preparation, participants reported enhanced learning and found the tool's feedback accurate in preparing them for job interviews [4].

A variety of virtual AI-based interview platforms exist (e.g. Yoodli[1] and HireVue[2]). However, while such platforms offer comprehensive features and broad coverage of interview-style questions, they often lack the physical presence and capacity for real-time emotional feedback or adaptive response tailoring that is characteristic of real-world F2F scenarios. Hence, there is interest in the use of physical robots, such as the android ERICA [5], for job interview simulation.

Although systems such as ERICA provide structured and elaborate follow-up questions, they are still relatively rigid and offer limited adaptability or opportunities for fine-tuning. This paper presents the development of an advanced AI-based interviewer based on the FurHat robot [1] that goes beyond the feature sets of virtual platforms like Yoodli and HireVue and the embodied interaction provided by physical agents such as ERICA, to create a more holistic, adaptive and effective job interview simulation. In particular, FurHat has been configured to allow extensive individual customisation by the user, such as the ability to define job scenarios from different industry backgrounds and invoke a range of interaction styles. Also, since FurHat's Software Development Kit (SDK) incorporates a virtual animation of the robot, it has been possible to conduct a short investigation into the relative merits of physical versus virtual embodiment in HRI-based interview training.

2 Motivation

The dynamics of F2F interviews are fundamentally shaped by the physical co-presence of the interviewer and interviewee [3]. This shared physical space allows an interviewer to maintain focus and exert control over the direction and flow of the interview in comparison with mediated methods. A key advantage of this in-person dynamic is the enhanced potential for building rapport; F2F settings enable interviewers to better establish the connection needed to motivate and encourage sustained and detailed engagement from the interviewee.

This personal connection is supported by the frequent use of non-verbal communication inherent in F2F interactions. Important non-verbal cues, such as facial expressions conveying emotion or nods signalling understanding, are often observable F2F but are inevitably missed in many computer-mediated interactions. These cues not only add layers of meaning to the verbal exchange but can actively encourage informants to elaborate on their thoughts.

The immediacy of F2F interaction also allows for responsive and timely probing. Interviewers can ask clarifying or follow-up questions based directly on the unfolding conversation and the interviewee's real-time verbal and non-verbal responses, a process inherently different from the potentially delayed probing in asynchronous communication. Consequently, F2F interviews often capture more spontaneous expressions, with the natural hesitations and conversational fillers (e.g., "*ums*", "*errs*") characteristic of spoken language, reflecting a less reflected stream of thought compared to carefully constructed written replies.

---

[1] https://yoodli.ai.
[2] https://www.hirevue.com/.

2.1 AI-Based Interview Platforms

To provide some form of assessment of a user's suitability for a role, AI-based interview platforms must evaluate various aspects of their behaviour. Interview practice platforms such as Yoodli provide a variety of feedback insights for the *user*, including measures such as conciseness, key points, filler words, weak words, sentence starters, pacing, eye contact, centring and pauses. In contrast, platforms such as HireVue provide analytics for the *employer*, evaluating the interviewee's hard and soft skills, as well as facial mannerisms to output a final score.

Visual and audio feature extraction is thus important in providing feedback to the user and the employer. Visual extraction can include categories such as emotion, head pose, eye contact and gestures, and audio extraction contains categories such as speaking rate, amplitude and tone [2]. Some researchers have even investigated the use of biometric data to detect subtle cues [6].

2.2 The FurHat-Based Interviewer

The FurHat-mediated 'Interactive Interview Training System' (IITS) reported here employed a state-driven approach, utilising the FurHat SDK's flow capabilities, augmented by object-oriented principles in Kotlin. Core intelligence was provided by integrating OpenAI's 'ChatGPT' via a dedicated service layer, enabling dynamic question generation and response handling, thereby overcoming the limitations inherent in static question banks [8]. The main design features were:

Bridging the Physical Presence and Rapport Gap. A primary shortcoming of virtual agent-based platforms is their inability to replicate the crucial physical co-presence fundamental to F2F interviews. The work reported here leveraged FurHat's physical embodiment to simulate this sense of shared space. The robot's capacity for realistic human-like features, including nuanced facial expressions and dynamic gaze control, replicates the vital non-verbal cues of F2F settings, aiming to create a more engaging interaction and develop a sense of connection that screen-based agents cannot achieve [7].

Enhancing Customisation. Many existing interview practice platforms offer limited scope for tailoring the scenario. FurHat was configured to address this through multi-faceted customisation. First, integration with ChatGPT enabled deep pre-prompting, allowing users to define complex interview contexts, specific roles, industry nuances, and interviewer personalities (e.g., formal, stressed, casual) far beyond typical menu-driven options. Second, FurHat's customisable facial features and voice synthesis permitted visual and auditory alignment with the desired scenario, with a view to increasing relatability and perceived realism.

Enabling Real-Time Adaptation. A significant limitation of many interview practice tools is their focus on post-session feedback rather than dynamic interaction. They may analyse gaze or speech patterns afterwards, but often fail to react during the conversation. In contrast, the system reported here is capable of adapting its questioning or non-verbal behaviour in real-time based on the user's input, creating a more dynamic and responsive dialogue akin to a human interviewer.

Incorporating Emotional Recognition and Response. Effective human interaction involves recognising and responding to emotional cues, an area often underdeveloped in interview simulation tools. This project uniquely integrated ChatGPT's inferential capabilities directly into FurHat's response generation loop. This enabled the LLM to infer the user's possible emotional state from their language, and for FurHat to respond appropriately through both tailored dialogue and synchronised, emotionally relevant facial expressions and gestures.

3 Experiment

Setup. The central aim of the experiment reported here was to investigate the differences in user perception, interaction behaviour, and perceived effectiveness between a physical robot and a virtual agent in the context of job interview training. This was facilitated by running the same IITS on either a virtual FurHat (as displayed in its SDK) or the physical robot itself – see Fig. 1.

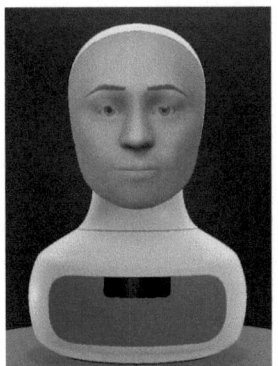
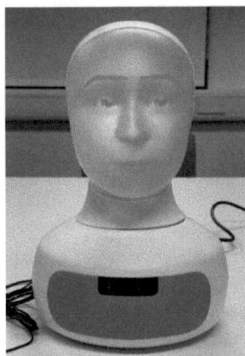

Fig. 1. Virtual FurHat display (on the left) and physical FurHat robot (on the right).

The dependent variables included (i) six *subjective* user experience metrics (measured on a 7-point Likert scale using post-condition questionnaires), (ii) five *objective* interaction measures (automatically logged by the interview system) and (iii) a 5-point 'System Usability Scale' (SUS). In addition, qualitative user feedback was gathered via an open-ended questionnaire.

Participants. The participants were aged 18 or over, primarily university students interested in improving their interview skills. The inclusion criteria were (i) an ability to participate in a mock interview conducted in English and (ii) a willingness to interact with both a virtual interface and a physical robot. A total of 10 participants were recruited in the limited time available to conduct the experiment.

3.1 Results

The results ($N = 10$) are presented in Fig. 2 and Table 1. As expected, they indicated a significantly more positive opinion for the physical robot condition compared to the virtual interface with regard to perceived realism, engagement, helpfulness, overall satisfaction, and usability (SUS score). Objective metrics also suggested participants spoke longer and used fewer fillers with the physical robot.

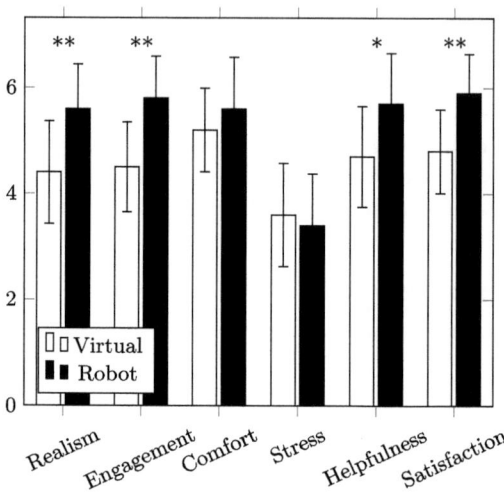

Fig. 2. Participants rated the physical robot significantly higher than the virtual interface on realism, engagement, helpfulness and satisfaction.

Table 1. Participants used significantly fewer fillers and spoke significantly longer utterances when interacting with the Physical Robot compared to the Virtual interface. The System Usability Scale (SUS) score was also significantly higher.

	Virtual	Robot
Total Fillers	9.80 (± 2.10)	8.80 (± 2.82) *
Min Duration (s)	5.30 (± 0.68)	5.21 (± 0.70)
Max Duration (s)	95.42 (± 13.48)	102.66 (± 16.25) **
Avg Duration (s)	35.86 (± 4.05)	37.62 (± 3.85) **
Total Duration (s)	295.07 (± 34.87)	312.93 (± 34.41) **
SUS Score	68.50 (± 17.05)	86.25 (± 12.43) ***

Qualitative feedback gathered from participants immediately after the experiment consistently highlighted areas for improvement in the physical robot implementation. In particular, the artificial quality of the robot's voice and occasional unnaturalness in its movements. Although, comfort and stress levels were not found to be significantly different between conditions, comments suggested the physical robot induced a slightly higher, *potentially beneficial*, level of alertness for practice.

4 Conclusion

This paper reports on the successful development of a FurHat-mediated interactive interview training system leveraging modern LLM capabilities to move beyond simpler command-based or scripted dialogues. Notwithstanding the small sample size, empirical evaluation demonstrated that physical embodiment significantly enhances user experience compared to a virtual interface. Participants found the physical robot more realistic, engaging, helpful, and ultimately more satisfying for interview practice. Hence, this work highlights the considerable potential of embodied conversational agents like FurHat as effective tools for professional skills development.

Acknowledgement. This study was conducted by A. Jones (supervised by Prof. R. K. Moore) as part of his BSc. degree in Computer Science at the University of Sheffield.

Disclosure of Interests. The authors have no competing interests to declare that are relevant to the content of this article.

References

1. Al Moubayed, S., Skantze, G., Beskow, J.: The furhat back-projected humanoid head–lip reading, gaze and multi-party interaction. Int. J. Humanoid Robot. **10**(1) (2013). https://www.furhatai.com
2. Chou, Y.C., Wongso, F.R., Chao, C.Y., Yu, H.Y.: An AI mock-interview platform for interview performance analysis. In: 10th International Conference on Information and Education Technology, pp. 37–41 (2022)
3. Curasi, C.F.: A critical exploration of face-to face interviewing vs. computer-mediated interviewing. Int. J. Market Res. **43**(4), 1–13 (2001)
4. Fulk, H.K., Dent, H.L., Kapakos, W.A., White, B.J.: Doing more with less: using AI-based big interview to combine exam preparation and interview practice. Issues Inf. Syst. **23**, 204–217 (2022)
5. Inoue, K., et al.: Job interviewer android with elaborate follow-up question generation. In: 22nd ACM International Conference on Multimodal Interaction (ICMI 2020), pp. 1–9 (2020)
6. Lee, B.C., Kim, B.Y.: Development of an ai-based interview system for remote hiring. Int. J. Adv. Res. Eng. Tech. (IJARET) **12**, 654–663 (2021)
7. Li, J.: The benefit of being physically present: a survey of experimental works comparing copresent robots, telepresent robots and virtual agents. Int. J. Hum Comput Stud. **77**, 23–37 (2015)
8. Rao S B, P., Agnihotri, M., Babu Jayagopi, D.: Improving asynchronous interview interaction with follow-up question generation. Int. J. Interact. Multimedia Artif. Intell. **6**(4), 79 (2021)

Exploring New Vitality Forms in Human-Robot Interaction

Carlesso Serena[1,2(✉)][iD], Abdul Kader Mohamed Ismail[2,3(✉)][iD],
Di Cesare Giuseppe[2,4][iD], Sciutti Alessandra[2][iD],
and Niewiadomski Radoslaw[1,2][iD]

[1] Department of Informatics, Bioengineering, Robotics and Systems Engineering (DIBRIS), University of Genoa, Genoa, Italy
[2] Cognitive Architecture for Collaborative Technologies Unit (CONTACT), Italian Institute of Technology (IIT), Genoa, Italy
serena.carlesso@iit.it, ismail.abdul-kader@port.ac.uk
[3] Department of Psychology, University of Portsmouth, Portsmouth, UK
[4] Department of Food and Drug, University of Parma, Parma, Italy

Abstract. Humans communicate their internal psychological and affective states through movement, which varies in the form with which it is performed. These forms, known as vitality forms, play a crucial role in enhancing the quality of human-robot interaction, particularly when they can be recognized by artificial agents such as humanoid robots. The present study aims to develop and validate forty short stories designed to elicit four distinct vitality forms: *fed-up*, *rude*, *gentle*, and *enthusiastic*. The stories were generated with the support of a large language model to minimize potential bias related to researchers' subjective interpretations and were validated through an online questionnaire. In the questionnaire, participants read each story and selected up to three emotional labels from a set of fifty-one. The data were analysed using two complementary methods, percentage-based and weighted frequency analyses, which yielded largely consistent results. The most effective stories for each vitality form will be used in a future human-robot interaction study to investigate the motor behaviours associated with each form during interaction with a humanoid robot such as iCub.

Keywords: Vitality Forms · Social Attitudes · Social Signal Processing · Social Robots · Data Collection · Large Language Model · iCub Robot

1 Introduction

Human beings communicate through body movements, each characterized by a distinctive form, and the repetition of the same action is never identical to its initial execution [4,5,9]. These forms were termed vitality forms (VFs) by Daniel

---

C. Serena and A. K. M. Ismail—Equal contribution.

© The Author(s), under exclusive license to Springer Nature Singapore Pte Ltd. 2026
M. Staffa et al. (Eds.): ICSR+AI 2025, LNAI 16131, pp. 590–597, 2026.
https://doi.org/10.1007/978-981-95-2379-5_51

Stern, as they express the internal psychological state of the agent performing the action [15]. Specifically, VFs can be studied by analyzing the dynamics and intensity with which actions are performed.

Recent research has begun to decode VFs [10] by examining the kinematic properties of actions directed toward others (e.g., gasping or offering an object). However, prior studies have predominantly focused on only two VFs (*gentle* and *rude*) arbitrarily selected to represent opposing ends of an intensity spectrum. These VFs have often been studied in highly controlled settings, using actors explicitly instructed to express them [6]. To support a more ecological investigation of VFs, future studies aim to guide participants in embodying specific psychological states, rather than simply imitating predefined expressions. We hypothesize that this approach will reveal not only elicit *gentle* and *rude* VFs in more naturalistic contexts, but will also enable the identification of at least two additional forms. This, in turn, will allow for a more comprehensive exploration of the kinematic features associated with VFs in social interaction. Understanding these patterns is essential in human-robot interaction (HRI), where the ability to recognize and replicate VFs based on kinematic cues can improve both the responsiveness and expressiveness of robotic agents, ultimately enhancing the quality of the interaction [7,12,14]. The present study represents a preliminary step toward this goal, focusing on the creation and validation of short narrative stimuli designed to evoke psychological states corresponding to at least four distinct VFs. Specifically, we aim to (1) design brief stories capable of eliciting empathy and inducing targeted internal states, and (2) identify, for each VF, at least two stories that most effectively convey the intended mood. These validated stories will serve as stimuli in a future HRI study investigating the kinematic expression of vitality forms.

2 Methodology

Four Vitality Forms. This study aims to investigate four VFs. In addition to the traditionally studied *gentle* and *rude* [6], we introduced two additional ones: *fed-up* and *enthusiastic*. These four labels were selected to represent a range of VF intensities and to include both positive and negative valences. Specifically, the *rude* VF reflects high intensity and negative valence, while *enthusiastic* reflects high intensity and positive valence. In contrast, *gentle* and *fed-up* VFs are characterized by low intensity, with positive and negative valence, respectively.

Stories. Ten short stories were developed for each of the four VFs, resulting in a total of forty narratives (see Supplementary Material for the full set of stories used in the study [1]). The stories were generated using a large language model (LLM) to minimize potential bias stemming from the researchers' personal experiences [3]. Specifically, the model employed was the free version of ChatGPT available as on May 2024 [11]. ChatGPT was instructed to generate brief and straightforward stories designed to express one of the four selected VFs, with the aim of reducing reader fatigue and cognitive load. An example prompt was:

"Two friends, playing cards, rude action: create a brief story". Story generation followed an iterative prompt engineering process, in which a human operator reviewed and refined outputs that did not meet predefined criteria for length, clarity, or emotional appropriateness. Below is an example of one of the ten stories developed to express the *fed-up VF*.

The Breaking Relationship
Emma, dreaming of a family and a countryside home, tried her best with Alessandro. But he focused solely on his career, neglecting her. When he forgot their anniversary again, Emma was done. She expressed her hurt and exasperation, **returning the bracelet** *he gave her at the start of their relationship. It had once meant a lot to her, but now it doesn't anymore.*

All stories featured a descriptive title, a main character, and a central event, designed to convey one of the four VFs through the character's response to the situation. In each story, the main character passed an object to another person. This gesture was highlighted in bold for two reasons: (i) to emphasize it as the central action representing the VF (e.g., "returning the bracelet"), and (ii) to draw participants' attention to the specific movement that will later serve as the basis for kinematic analysis. Importantly, the name of the targeted VFs (e.g., "rude," "gentle") were never mentioned explicitly in the stories, but were instead meant to be inferred from the narrative context.

Task. The stories were implemented in an online questionnaire using the Gorilla platform [2] and distributed via Prolific [13]. The full set of forty stories was divided into two subsets of twenty, each evenly representing the four VFs to minimize participant fatigue. Specifically, there were ten stories for every VF: *gentle*, *rude*, *fed-up* and *enthusiastic*. Participants were randomly assigned to one of the two subsets using Gorilla's built-in randomization tool. As a result, each participant read and evaluated only twenty stories. For each story, participants were instructed to read the narrative, empathize with the main character, and evaluate their behaviour. The evaluation task required participants to identify the attitude or feeling most clearly expressed by the main character through the bolded action. To allow for both interpretative flexibility and standardized data collection, participants were presented with a list of fifty-one possible attitude labels [listed in the next paragraph]. They were asked to select three labels per story that best described the character's behaviour (see Supplementary Material for a video illustrating the task [1]). The same label could not be selected more than once per story, and the order of selection was treated as meaningful: the first label was assumed to be the most representative, followed by the second and third in decreasing relevance. To monitor engagement and data quality, attention checks were included after every tenth story. In these trials, participants were asked to recall the title and main character of the story they had just read. To ensure accurate recall, the story preceding each attention check was not randomized.

Labels. Fifty-one labels were used to represent a wide range of social attitudes associated with the spectrum of VFs: *fed-up, enthusiastic, gentle* and *rude*. These labels were generated and refined using ChatGPT to ensure comprehensive and unbiased coverage of relevant emotional and interpersonal nuances. The final list of labels included: *Aggressive, Agitated, Apathetic, Arrogant, Assertive, Bored, Caring, Cautious, Collaborative, Competitive, Compassionate, Confident, Confused, Cordial, Defensive, Disdainful, Dismissive, Disrespectful, Distrustful, Dominant, Eager, Engaged, Enthusiastic, Excited, Fed-up, Friendly, Frustrated, Gentle, Hesitant, Hostile, Inclusive, Indifferent, Insecure, Intimidated, Lazy, Polite, Regretful, Relaxed, Resentful, Reserved, Resigned, Rude, Sensitive, Shy, Stressed, Submissive, Superior, Supportive, Sympathetic, Trusting,* and *Uncomfortable*.

Participants. Fifty participants, over 18 years old, were recruited via Prolific. All provided informed consent prior to participation. A custom pre-screening filter was applied to include only individuals from English-speaking countries (USA, Canada, UK, Australia, New Zealand, and EU countries) in order to minimize potential cultural or linguistic differences that could affect story comprehension and interpretation.

2.1 Data Analysis

Data were collected from two sets of stories: 24 participants completed the first questionnaire, and 20 completed the second. One participant from the second group was excluded for failing the attention check, resulting in 19 valid responses. The complete dataset is available in Supplementary Material [1]. Due to the unequal group sizes (24 vs. 19), frequency values from the second questionnaire were normalized to enable meaningful comparisons across conditions. The primary goal of the analysis was to identify which stories most consistently elicited the four target VFs. To this end, stories were grouped according to their intended VF, and for each group, only the absolute frequency of the corresponding target label was considered. For examples, the ten stories designed to evoke the *fed-up* VF were analysed exclusively based on how frequently the label "fed-up" was selected by participants. Two complementary methods were applied to determine which stories best conveyed their intended VF:

1. **Percentage Distribution.** We calculated the percentage of cases in which the expected VF was selected as the first choice.
2. **Weighted Frequency Analysis.** To account for the rank of each label selected, we applied a weighted scoring system: first choice $\times 2$, second choice $\times 1.5$, and third choice $\times 1$. This method prioritizes primary selections while still incorporating secondary and tertiary choices, providing a more nuanced view of how participants associated each story with the target VF.

3 Results and Conclusion

The two analytical methods yielded consistent results for the *fed-up* and *rude* VF conditions, clearly identifying the stories that best conveyed these forms (see Fig. 1A-B: "The Breaking Relationship" and "The Disappointing Garden" for the *fed-up VF*; "The Discriminating Shopkeeper" and "Couple Tensions" for the *rude VF*). For the *gentle VF* condition, the percentage method highlighted the story "Did you lose something?", while the weighted method was particularly helpful in identifying the most representative story among the three equally preferred ones identified by the percentage method (see Fig. 1C; among "Walking in the Park", "The Lost Balloon", and "Birthday", the story "Birthday" emerged as the most chosen). In contrast, for the *enthusiastic VF* condition, three prominent stories emerged: one was consistently selected by both methods ("An Unexpected News"), while the other two were uniquely highlighted by each method ("New Job" by the percentage method and "Traveler" by the weighted method) (Fig. 1D).

A chi-square test considering only first-choice responses confirmed a significant association between story titles and selected attitude labels (*rude VF*: $\chi^2(279) = 517.3$, p < .001; *fed-up VF*: $\chi^2(369) = 615.1$, p < .001; *gentle VF*: $\chi^2(396) = 687.4$, p < .001; *enthusiastic VF*: $\chi^2(225) = 330.1$, p < .001), indicating that responses varied systematically across narratives. While the target label was not always the most frequently selected, the most common alternatives were semantically related. This suggests that the stories evoked affective responses aligned with the intended VFs, even if expressed using different terms. For example, in the *rude VF* condition, the most frequently selected labels were *aggressive* (n = 30), followed by *rude* (n = 21) and *hostile* (n = 20). In the *fed-up VF* condition, *fed-up* (n = 35) appeared among the top labels, along with *frustrated* (n = 37) and *bored* (n = 37). In the *enthusiastic VF* condition, *excited* (n = 90) was selected more often than *enthusiastic* (n = 53), while in the *gentle VF* condition, *compassionate* (n = 30) and *caring* (n = 28) were preferred over *gentle* (n = 9).

In conclusion, at least two stories per condition consistently emerged as strong examples of their intended VFs. These findings support the idea that (1) brief, evocative narratives generated with the support of ChatGPT effectively conveyed the target VFs, and (2) at least two stories per VF were suitable candidates for use in the subsequent kinematic study.

4 Future Work

The next study will investigate VFs in participants asked to physically act the stories identified in this preliminary study as most effective in evoking the four target VFs. Specifically, we plan to select at least two of the most representative stories per condition, resulting in a total of eight narratives. For each condition, participants will read the assigned story and immerse themselves in the narrative context for a few minutes to empathize with the main character. Given that the

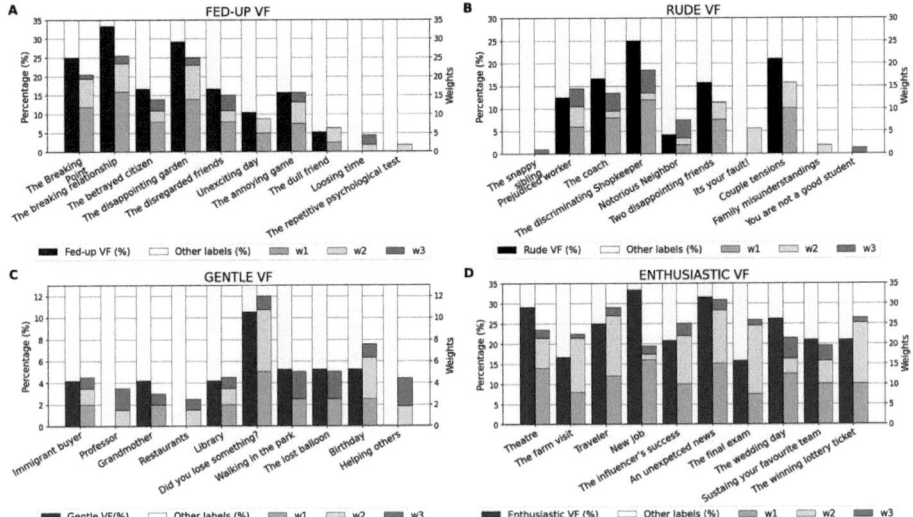

Fig. 1. Combined results for the investigated VFs. Panels A, B, C, and D show the results for the *Fed-up, Rude, Gentle,* and *Enthusiastic* VFs, respectively. For each story, the left bars (green, red, blue, orange, beige) represent the percentage of participants who selected the expected VF as their first choice. The right bars (light blue, grey, pink) indicate the weighted scores based on ranked choices (w1 = first, w2 = second, w3 = third). This comparison highlights the stories that most effectively conveyed each VF.

stories have already been validated online, we assume they are effective in eliciting the intended psychological states, prompting participants to perform actions that express the target VFs (*fed-up, enthusiastic, gentle* or *rude*). Participants will then be instructed to grasp an object and hand it over a humanoid robot (e.g., iCub [8]) (see Fig. 2 and Supplementary Material for a video illustration [1]). A motion capture system will record the kinematic parameters of these actions. Based on these data, we aim to extract meaningful kinematic features that distinguish the four VFs. We hypothesize that similar kinematic patterns will emerge across participants for the same VF, suggesting that intra-subject variability does not substantially affect VF expression. This would indicate that each VF can be reliably characterized by specific movement features. If confirmed, these features could be used to train robotic agents to recognize VFs in humans, thereby enhancing the naturalness and responsiveness of human-robot interaction.

Additionally, participants' actions will be video-recorded using a camera positioned near or behind the robot. These recordings will form a video dataset for use in a subsequent experiment, in which a new group of participants will watch the clips and evaluate the VFs expressed by the actors. Participants will be asked to select three attitude labels from the same set of fifty-one used in the present

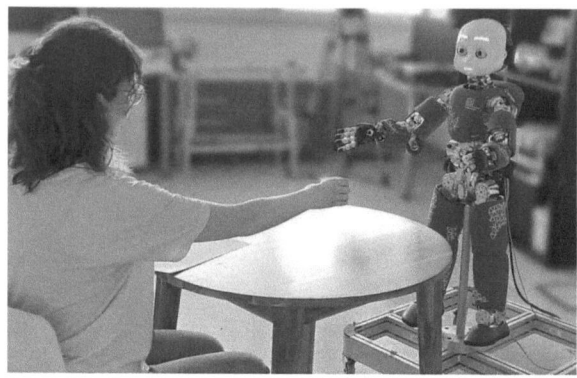

Fig. 2. Planned experimental setup. The participant reads a selected story, internalizes its associated VF, then grasp and pass an object to the humanoid robot iCub.

study. This second phase aim to assess whether VFs are recognizable not only through kinematic data, but also via human visual observation.

Acknowledgments. This work was partially supported by the PNRR MUR Project PE0000013 Future Artificial Intelligence Research (FAIR), funded by the European Union - NextGenerationEU, CUP J33C24000430007 to Radoslaw Niewiadomski.

Disclosure of Interests. The authors report no conflicts of interest.

Supplementary Material. The supplementary material includes the full set of stories and attitude labels, the collected dataset, a video illustrating the task, and a video describing the planned future experiment. All materials are available at: https://osf.io/mta2n/ [1].

References

1. Carlesso, S.: Stories for the expression of vitality forms. https://doi.org/10.17605/OSF.IO/MTA2N, https://osf.io/mta2n/
2. Cauldron Science Ltd: Gorilla experiment builder. https://www.gorilla.sc (2024)
3. Coan, J.A., Allen, J.J.: Handbook of Emotion Elicitation and Assessment. Oxford university Press (2007)
4. Czyż, S.H.: Variability of practice, information processing, and decision making–how much do we know? Front. Psychol. **12**, 639131 (2021)
5. Dael, N., Goudbeek, M., Scherer, K.R.: Perceived gesture dynamics in nonverbal expression of emotion. Perception **42**(6), 642–657 (2013)
6. Di Cesare, G., De Stefani, E., Gentilucci, M., De Marco, D.: Vitality forms expressed by others modulate our own motor response: a kinematic study. Front. Hum. Neurosci. **11**, 565 (2017)
7. Huang, P., Hu, Y., Nechyporenko, N., Kim, D., Talbott, W., Zhang, J.: Emotion: expressive motion sequence generation for humanoid robots with in-context learning. IEEE Robot. Autom. Lett. (2025)

8. Metta, G., Sandini, G., Vernon, D., Natale, L., Nori, F.: The icub humanoid robot: an open platform for research in embodied cognition. In: Proceedings of the 8th Workshop on Performance Metrics for Intelligent Systems, pp. 50–56 (2008)
9. Müller, H., Sternad, D.: Motor learning: changes in the structure of variability in a redundant task. In: Progress in Motor Control: a Multidisciplinary Perspective, pp. 439–456 (2009)
10. Niewiadomski, R., Suresh, A., Sciutti, A., Di Cesare, G.: Decoding communicative action vitality forms in social contexts. Front. Psychol. **16**, 1478875 (2025)
11. OpenAI: Chatgpt: Gpt-4o model. https://chat.openai.com/ (2024)
12. Park, S., Whang, M.: Empathy in human-robot interaction: designing for social robots. Int. J. Environ. Res. Public Health **19**(3), 1889 (2022)
13. Prolific: Prolific – trusted participant recruitment for research. https://www.prolific.com (2024)
14. Samadani, A., Gorbet, R., Kulic, D.: Affective movement generation using laban effort and shape and hidden markov models. arXiv preprint arXiv:2006.06071 (2020)
15. Stern, D.N.: Forms of Vitality: Exploring Dynamic Experience in Psychology, the Arts, Psychotherapy, and Development. Oxford University Press (UK) (2010)

Impact of Gaze-Based Interaction and Augmentation on Human-Robot Collaboration in Critical Tasks

Ayesha Jena[✉], Stefan Reitmann, and Elin Anna Topp

Department of Computer Science, Faculty of Engineering, Lund University,
Box 118, 221 00 Lund, Sweden
{ayesha.jena,stefan.reitmann,elin_a.topp}@cs.lth.se

Abstract. We present a user study with 18 participants, analyzing head-gaze-based robot control and foveated visual augmentation in a simulated search-and-rescue task. Results show that foveated augmentation significantly improves task performance, reduces cognitive load by 38%, and shortens task time by over 60%. Head-gaze patterns analysed over both the entire task duration and shorter time segments show that near and far attention capture is essential to better understand user intention in critical scenarios. Our findings highlight the potential of foveation as an augmentation technique and the need to further study gaze measures to leverage them during critical tasks.

Keywords: Human-Robot Teams · Collaboration · Human-Factors

1 Introduction

Advancements in the field of robotics have led to a need for seamless collaboration and effective communication between humans and robots in different scenarios [1]. While communication methods such as speech and gestures have been extensively studied, they require explicit commands which limits their effectiveness in dynamic real-world interaction scenarios. In such cases, methods like gaze-based interaction offer an intuitive way of communication [2]. In addition to being a method of interaction, gaze also shows operator's intentions regarding where to focus during task execution [3]. This is crucial in high-stakes scenarios, where fast recognition of user intent through gaze could enhance performance and improve collaboration.

In human-robot collaboration, gaze tracking has proved effective in combination with augmentation techniques to improve collaboration efficiency, situational awareness, and productivity [4]. While gaze is used for controlling the robot, augmentation techniques are used for visually enhancing the information provided by the system. Their effect in critical domains have been largely unexplored [5], which leads to an adoption gap in understanding operator intentions and supporting collaboration in high-stake scenarios.

Fig. 1. Left: Bird's eye view of the test environment; Right: A region of the environment showing a trapped human.

We explore this gap through a user study using our collaborative interface [6, 7]. This work is novel in its design and integration of head-gaze based interaction and real-time foveation-based visual augmentation for collaboration in a critical search-and-rescue scenario, as shown in Fig. 1. We will explain how we interpret the terms augmentation and foveation, in the context of our study in Sects. 2 and 3.

Our study explored two different interaction designs within the interface: manual head-gaze based control interface - human assisted (HA), and a dynamic foveation based interface - system assisted (SA). We found that foveation based augmentation enhances task performance, reduces cognitive load, and improves collaboration in comparison with direct gaze-based control. While head-gaze directly indicates user attention, it performed suboptimally as a primary control modality in critical scenarios. Our analysis, however, shows the usability of foveated augmentation to guide attention also in such scenarios. We further found instances of extrafoveal attention capture which would be accounted for in future studies with an adaptive system that incorporates complex gaze behavior.

2 Related Work

When human and robots collaborate in teams for critical tasks and missions, the cognitive capabilities of operators tend to decline over time. This is because of the inherent nature of such scenarios where rapid actions need to be taken while receiving, processing and combining information from multiple sources at the same time [8]. This often leads to errors which in turn can provoke catastrophic outcomes [9]. Both explicit and implicit modes of communication have been studied to minimize the operator's effort while maintaining effective information exchange during task execution. Early research focuses on explicit communication modalities such as speech, gestures, and haptic interfaces [10]. While these methods are effective in structured environments, they often lead to additional cognitive demands on operators, particularly in dynamic, high-stakes scenarios [11]. This has led to interest in implicit communication cues, such as gaze, which enable more natural and intuitive human-robot coordination [2].

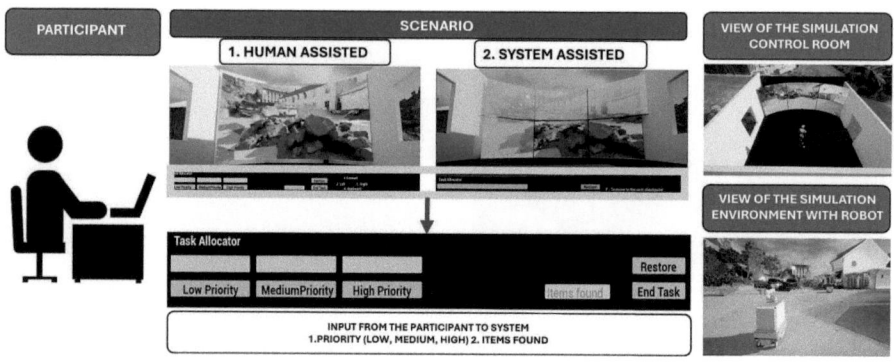

Fig. 2. The setup of the user study. Left to right: Screen view of the interface shown to participants during the experiment, View of the simulation control room which receives visual input from the robot's camera and provides inputs from the participants to the system, View of the simulation environment showing the robot in the search-and-rescue test-bed.

Gaze-only interfaces encounter challenges like the "Midas touch problem", where unintentional gaze inputs trigger undesired actions [12]. There is also the need for special hardware and software for eye tracking, and difficulties in real-world scenarios due to illumination effects, head rotations, or occlusions [13]. A similar, yet effective, approach is to use head pose instead. Studies have shown a high correlation between gaze direction and head pose in real-world scenarios, proving its effectiveness [13].

Building on methods to improve collaboration through the use of a visual interface, we explored different augmentation techniques that would enhance task performance while reducing cognitive overload [14]. Techniques like highlighting important objects seemed ineffective in our case due to clutter and background distractions. Instead, foveation seemed to be a promising approach in this regard where focused regions are rendered in high resolution and outlying areas are blurred [14]. Traditionally, this is used as a graphics-performance optimization technique, so this study is the first to apply foveation as a visual augmentation method in a search-and-rescue setting. Considering the complexities of real-world situations, this study investigates head-gaze based control and foveation based augmentation in simulation and analyzes the results using task performance metrics, subjective measurements, and gaze-based heatmaps.

3 Methodology

The study was conducted in a simulation environment where participants performed a search task with two interaction designs: HA and SA. Participants' head-gaze behavior was recorded and then analyzed to assess efficiency, cognitive workload, and task performance. Head-gaze tracking was performed using a camera-based tracking system that detected participants' head orientation and head-gaze direction. An overview and breakdown of the experimental conditions are shown in Fig. 2.

3.1 Simulation Environment

A search-and-rescue (SAR) test environment (28m x 83m) was developed from the 3D template of the real-world location provided by the WASP Research Arena for Public Safety (WARA-PS) [15] to simulate a post-disaster scenario using Unreal Engine 5.1 [16]. The primary motivation behind creating this virtual SAR test-bed was to replicate challenging and high-stake conditions in a controlled, safe environment. The added wreckage, obstacles, and people were strategically placed throughout the environment. It also had multiple other areas of interest, such as fire outbreaks and electrical hazards. Additionally, it included simulated SAR personnel to replicate realistic operational constraints and potential coordination efforts in real-time rescue missions. This was done on a collaborative interface developed earlier [6,7]. The interface sends gaze data to Unreal Engine, where it's mapped with 3D vectors to highlight screen regions in orange. A key press turns the region green, forming a dual-confirmation input. It also includes text fields and buttons for selecting priorities, and overlays foveation cues on the camera feed from the robot (Fig. 2). Some distance away from the test area, a control room, as shown in Fig. 2, was designed to replicate real-world SAR operation centers where users could interact with the disaster site by navigating a mobile robot fitted with cameras and sensors. The robot used for this setup is a combination of mobile robot platform MiR200, a Universal Robots collaborative arm UR5e, attached with an Intel Realsense D435 RGBD camera on the plate of Schunk WSG-50 parallel gripper [6].

3.2 Experiment Procedure

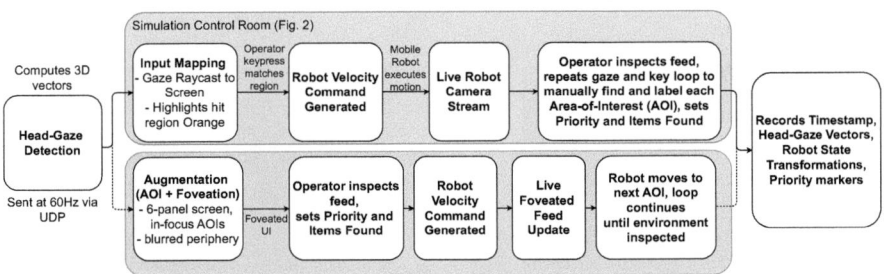

Fig. 3. The experiment procedure for both scenarios. Orange shows the HA scenario. Green shows the SA scenario. (Color figure online)

Each session lasted about 60 min and began with a system check, consent and demographic forms, and a brief training. Participants then completed two counterbalanced scenarios - HA and SA, each involving teleoperating the robot through the interface (Fig. 3). In each scenario, they navigated within the test environment to find areas that needed inspection also referred to as areas of interests (AOIs), counted and classified objects (victims, debris, hazards), and assigned priority levels (Low, Medium, High) through the interface as can be seen in Fig. 2. Before the experiment it was made sure that the ethical protocols were followed per university guidelines [17]. During each session, we recorded head-gaze, dual-confirmation key presses, robot state transformations, NASA-TLX [18], System Usability Scale (SUS) [19], post-study interview responses, and quantitative metrics (task times, AOI accuracy), all anonymized under data protection rules. A total of 18 participants (13 males, 4 females, 1 unspecified) took part in the study. 4 participants had experience in providing disaster relief. The mean age of participants was 31.29 years (SD = 9.78) excluding 1 participant who declined to report their age.

Human-Assisted (HA) Scenario In this interaction design scenario, participants controlled the robot using head-gaze for directions and keypresses for confirmations. The experimental procedure can be seen in Fig. 3.

System-Assisted (SA) Scenario In this scenario, the 6 screens shown to the participants were foveated based on the AOIs present and the density of hazard. Screens with AOIs were in focus whereas others were blurred. Although the system guided participants to prioritized regions, participants remained the final decision-makers, confirming or adjusting the importance levels of each item in AOIs (Low, Medium, High) through the interface. The six-section design was optimized to align with human visual working memory limits (5–9 chunks [20]), ensuring rapid parsing without overwhelming users during critical scenarios.

4 Results and Discussions

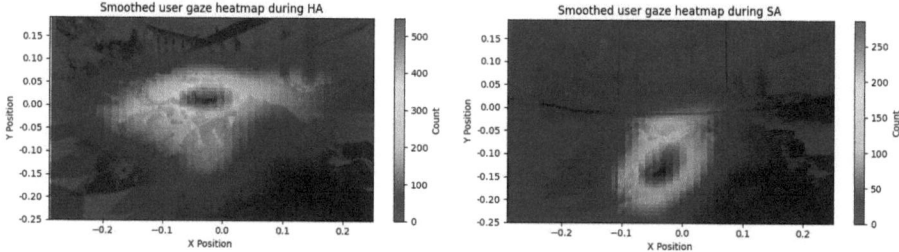

Fig. 4. Distribution of head-gaze heatmap over the 2D screen area presented to the participants.

In both the scenarios, participants were instructed to identify critical AOIs, mark them, and assign points according to their priority. The results are discussed below.

Table 1. Objective and Subjective Results for HA and SA scenarios. ∗ indicates significant result ($p < 0.001$)

Scenario	Total Time Taken (in s)	Total Humans Saved	Avg Humans Saved	NASA TLX Score	SUS
HA	678.88 ± 233.98	20 (Out of 54)	1.11 ± 0.75	53.85 ± 18.06	58.61 ± 14.80
SA	∗274.41 ± 52.95	∗47 (Out of 54)	∗2.61 ± 0.69	∗33.4 ± 15.24	∗80.13 ± 16.30

4.1 Performance Metrics

The performance of the participants was measured using task completion time and the number of humans successfully located within AOIs. There were 3 trapped humans in each scenario within AOIs, resulting in a total of 54 instances of trapped humans across all participants. From the results shown in Table 1, we can see that participants performed better with foveation. The experience of the 4 participants with disaster relief did not affect the results in any manner.

4.2 Subjective Measurements

Mental Workload The participants mental workload results (Table 1) from the NASA TLX questionnaire showed a 38% lower perceived workload in SA scenario ($M = 33.41$, $SD = 15.24$) compared to the HA scenario ($M = 53.85$, $SD = 18.07$).

System Usability Participants answered 10 questions from the system usability questionnaire using a Likert scale (1 = strongly disagree to 5 = strongly agree). Results from the Table 1 show that participants perceived foveation to have higher usability during the search task.

Subjective Questionnaire The subjective questionnaires contained long-form answers and five-point Likert scale questions. Participants provided neutral-to-positive ratings for the interface's natural intuitiveness, noting that its reliance on manual gaze-driven navigation mirrored "natural human exploration". However, this familiarity with gaze-based control came with challenges such as "slow turning" and "limited peripheral vision". On the other hand in SA, augmentation helped them streamline focus and execute the task faster, while reducing their cognitive load. However, participants also expected explainability regarding the augmentation decisions made by the system. In addition, participants wanted to be able to dynamically look at other sections of the screen to make sure the system made the correct decisions regarding foveation.

4.3 Head-Gaze Analysis

In the HA scenario, participants' head-gaze was evenly spread across the screen, looking equally to the left and right, but with a stronger focus on the upper part. This scenario required them to use their head-gaze to drive the robot, causing them to scan the screen more and focus on the upper part for forward navigation based on the interface design. In the SA scenario, participants did not need to orient their head-gaze, so they adopted a more relaxed posture and looked mostly at the lower part of the screen as can be seen in Fig. 4. Additionally, analyzing shorter time segments in this scenario during task execution highlight that gazed region and the foveated region aligned 67% of the time. In the remaining 33%, participants' gaze slightly deviated around the foveated area. Upon further analysis of view counts, view percentages, and average gaze position across the screen area, it was found that this occurred due to high-priority items and people located outside the immediate field of view. This observation can be explained by extrafoveal attention capture which is when objects or individuals in more distant areas draw the user's attention over a longer distance [21]. Similar instances of extrafoveal attention captures were also observed in the HA scenario where users verbally inquired about denoting distant AOIs in comparison to focusing on immediate AOIs.

5 Conclusion

In summary, we conducted a user study to investigate the impact of gaze-based control and foveated augmentation for human-robot teleoperation during critical task execution. The study was performed with a system designed in simulation and the effects were studied through two scenarios. Based on the results of the user study, foveation based augmentation scenario outperformed gaze-based control leading to effective human-robot collaboration. Additionally, analysis of head-gaze behavior revealed alignment between gaze and foveated regions in a majority of cases, indicating that foveation can effectively direct attention. However, deviations due to extrafoveal attention capture highlight the complexity of user attention patterns and suggest the need for systems to accommodate such behavior.

Overall, this study demonstrates that head-gaze based foveated augmentation improves performance and user experience. While head-gaze reliably conveys where the user's attention is directed, our results suggest it is not optimal as a direct control modality in critical tasks. Further analysis is required to leverage gaze measures during critical tasks. The future work includes improving the interface by combining automated scene analysis with flexible, gaze dependent foveation that operators can invoke as an explicit confirmation cue.

Acknowledgements. We would like to thank Jacek Malec and Björn Olofsson for their support during the work. This work was funded by ELLIIT - the Excellence Center at Linköping University and Lund University for Information Technology, and partially supported by the Wallenberg AI, Autonomous Systems and Software Program (WASP) funded by the Knut and Alice Wallenberg Foundation. We would also like to thank the WASP Research Arena for Public Safety (WARA-PS) for providing the 3D template.

Disclosure of Interests. The authors have no competing interests to declare that are relevant to the content of this article.

References

1. Hentout, A., Aouache, M., Maoudj, A., Akli, I.: Human–robot interaction in industrial collaborative robotics: a literature review of the decade 2008–2017. Adv. Robot. **33**(15-16) (2019)
2. Lavit Nicora, M., et al.: Gaze detection as a social cue to initiate natural human-robot collaboration in an assembly task. Front. Robot. AI **11** (2024)
3. Belcamino, V., et al.: Gaze-based intention recognition for human-robot collaboration. In: Proceedings of the 2024 International Conference on Advanced Visual Interfaces (2024)
4. Schirmer, F., Kranz, P., Rose, C.G., Willert, V., Schmitt, J., Kaupp, T.: Utilizing eye gaze for human-robot collaborative assembly. In: Proceedings of the 2025 ACM/IEEE International Conference on Human-Robot Interaction (2025)
5. Sheridan, T.B.: Human–robot interaction: status and challenges. Human factors **58**(4) (2016)
6. Jena, A., Topp, E.A.: Chaos to control: Human assisted scene inspection. In: Companion of the 2023 ACM/IEEE International Conference on Human-Robot Interaction (2023)
7. Jena, A., Topp, E.A.: Towards understanding the role of humans in collaborative tasks. In: 7th International Workshop on Virtual, Augmented, and Mixed-Reality for Human-Robot Interactions (2024)
8. Mirbabaie, M., Fromm, J.: Reducing the cognitive load of decision-makers in emergency management through augmented reality (2019)
9. Liu, Y., et al.: What affects human decision making in human–robot collaboration?: a scoping review. Robotics **13**(2) (2024)
10. Urakami, J., Seaborn, K.: Nonverbal cues in human–robot interaction: a communication studies perspective. ACM Trans. Hum.-Robot Interact. **12**(2) (2023)
11. Unhelkar, V.V., Li, S., Shah, J.A.: Decision-making for bidirectional communication in sequential human-robot collaborative tasks. In: Proceedings of the 2020 ACM/IEEE International Conference on Human-Robot Interaction (2020)
12. Velichkovsky, B., Sprenger, A., Unema, P.: Towards gaze-mediated interaction: Collecting solutions of the "midas touch problem". In: Human-Computer Interaction INTERACT'97: IFIP TC13 International Conference on Human-Computer Interaction, 14th–18th July 1997, Sydney, Australia. Springer (1997)
13. Jha, S., Busso, C.: Analyzing the relationship between head pose and gaze to model driver visual attention. In: 2016 IEEE 19th International Conference on Intelligent Transportation Systems (ITSC). IEEE (2016)
14. Su, Y.P., Chen, X.Q., Zhou, C., Pearson, L.H., Pretty, C.G., Chase, J.G.: Integrating virtual, mixed, and augmented reality into remote robotic applications: a brief review of extended reality-enhanced robotic systems for intuitive telemanipulation and telemanufacturing tasks in hazardous conditions. Appl. Sci. **13**(22) (2023)
15. WARA-PS: GitHub - wara-ps/cesium-unreal — github.com. https://github.com/wara-ps/cesium-unreal (2023), https://github.com/wara-ps/cesium-unity, Accessed 10 Feb 2024
16. Epic games: unreal engine, https://www.unrealengine.com/en-US
17. LU: ethical review — staff.lu.se. https://www.staff.lu.se/research-and-education/research-support/research-ethics-and-animal-testing-ethics/ethical-review (2023), Accessed 10 Feb 2024
18. Hart, S.G., Staveland, L.E.: Development of nasa-tlx (task load index): results of empirical and theoretical research. In: Advances in Psychology, vol. 52. Elsevier (1988)

19. Brooke, J.: Sus: a "quick and dirty'usability. Usability Eval. Ind. **189**(3) (1996)
20. Miller, G.A.: The magical number seven, plus or minus two: some limits on our capacity for processing information. Psychol. Rev. **63**(2) (1956)
21. Nuthmann, A., De Groot, F., Huettig, F., Olivers, C.N.: Extrafoveal attentional capture by object semantics. PLoS One **14**(5) (2019)

EMOROBCARE: A Low-Cost Social Robot for Supporting Children with Autism in Therapeutic Settings

Sara Cooper[1(✉)], Bartomeu Pou[1,2], Arnau Mayoral-Macau[1], Alberto Redondo[3], David Rios[3], and Raquel Ros[1]

[1] Artificial Intelligence Research Institute (IIIA-CSIC), Bellaterra 08193, Spain
{sara.cooper,bartomeu.pou,arnau.mayoral-macau,raquel.ros}@iiia.csic.es
[2] Universitat Politècnica De Catalunya (UPC), Carrer de Jordi Girona, 31, Les Corts, 08034 Barcelona, Spain
[3] Mathematical Sciences Institute (ICMAT-CSIC), Madrid 28049, Spain
{alberto.redondo,david.rios}@icmat.es

Abstract. The EMOROBCARE project aims at developing a low-cost, expressive social robot designed to support therapy for children with Autism Spectrum Disorder. This paper presents the system software design and development tools. We illustrate an example use case game that combines perception, speech, reasoning and expressive capabilities of the robot. Additional games will be developed through co-design with therapists in order to foster communication and emotional expression.

Keywords: ASD · Child–Robot Interaction · Architecture

1 Introduction

Autism Spectrum Disorder (ASD) is characterized by challenges in social communication, interaction, and behaviour. Children with ASD Level 2, in particular, often exhibit limited verbal communication and require structured, personalized therapeutic interventions. Social robots have emerged as promising tools in this domain, offering consistent, engaging, and non-judgmental interaction partners that can support therapy goals [3].

Robots such as QTrobot, NAO, and Kaspar have demonstrated effectiveness in supporting imitation, emotion recognition, and joint attention through structured and predictable interactions [7,8]. These robots are often used in clinical or educational settings, where their simplified appearance and expressive capabilities help reduce sensory overload and sustain engagement. Platforms such as Jibo and MARIA T21 have been adapted for long-term interventions, integrating serious games and real-time feedback to enhance communication and learning outcomes [9,11]. Less sophisticated robots, such as OPT and parrot-like companions, have also shown promise in emotion recognition and turn-taking activities, contributing to the development of specific social skills [12]. Despite these advances, many existing systems are limited by high costs, proprietary ecosystems.

The EMOROBCARE project is a multidisciplinary initiative aimed at designing and validating a low-cost, expressive social robot to assist therapists working with children with ASD Level 2. The project emphasizes affordability, modularity, and open-source development, leveraging technologies such as ROS2, Jetson-based hardware, and lightweight speech and vision models. Its primary goal is to evaluate the feasibility and therapeutic value of the robot in real-world therapy sessions. These sessions are structured around a triadic interaction model involving the therapist, the child, and the robot. The robot engages the child through interactive games, expressive speech, and facial animations, while the therapist guides the session and adapts the interaction based on the child's needs.

This paper presents the software architecture of EMOROBCARE, currently tested on a virtual model before deployment on the physical robot.

2 System Architecture

The 30 cm-tall EMOROBCARE robot has a spherical base, a 3-DOF head powered by affordable high-torque servos, a camera, chest-mounted microphone, side speakers, and a screen-based expressive face. A Jetson Nano handles perception, while a separate tablet displays game content, keeping the hardware simple and cost-effective.

The system architecture (Fig. 1) builds upon ROS 2-based components and a previously developed open-source architecture for situated social robots [5], which itself is based on the ROS4HRI framework [10]. This architecture provides multimodal social perception, symbolic reasoning, an LLM-based dialogue manager, intent-based controller and an interactive GUI. Additional ROS 2-based components have been incorporated: *Head controller*, which manages joint trajectories across its three joints (pan, tilt, roll); *Play motion2*, which executes predefined expressive gestures such as nodding or head shaking; *Attention manager*, to manage the robot's gaze behavior, enabling it to track objects or humans or perform random gaze shifts; and *Face interface*, which displays cartoon-like facial expressions (e.g., happy, sad, surprised).

We next outline the framework's main pipelines for autism therapy.

2.1 Vision

The goal of the vision module is to enable the robot to perceive and understand its surrounding environment in real-time during interaction with children in order to respond appropriately to children's actions and to support therapeutic games. The module builds on the ROS4HRI framework. While body detection, face detection and recognition, and gesture recognition are reused, the pipeline is extended with the following new modules:

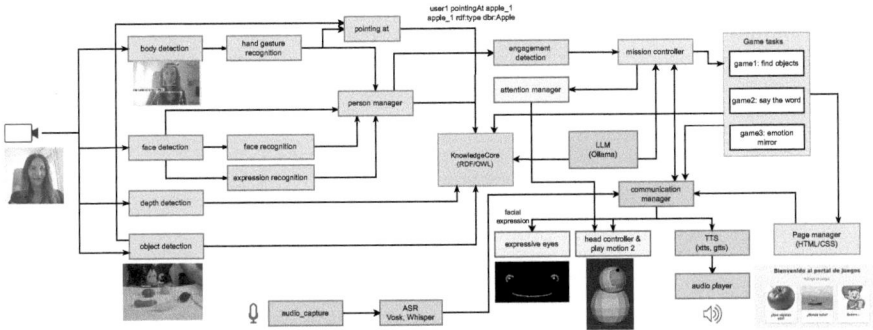

Fig. 1. EMOROBCARE software architecture: blue—perception; green—reasoning; red—speech; gray—execution; orange—supervision. (Color figure online)

- **Pointing gesture detection:** when a pointing gesture is detected, this module estimates the pointing direction by combining the orientation of the finger and the forearm. The resulting vector is intersected with detected objects or persons. This enables the robot to semantically interpret deictic gestures (e.g. john is pointing at book), allowing children to indicate objects during gameplay.
- **Object detection:** the module integrates two object-detection methods: YOLOv8[1] and YOLO-world [4] to identify objects in the world. YOLO performs best in controlled environments where objects are known in advance. YOLO-world supports open-vocabulary detection, enabling the recognition of unseen object categories, suitable for uncontrolled environments. As an example, Table 1 presents a minimal performance comparison of YOLOv8-small and YOLO-world-small on a test dataset consisting of 53 images featuring five fruit toys. The YOLO model was trained on 378 images. For YOLO-world, we evaluate two prompts: one containing only the object name (prompt 1, e.g., *pear toy*), and another including both the object and its color (prompt 2, e.g., *yellow pear toy*). As expected, YOLO-world performs worse than YOLOv8 due to the lack of task-specific fine-tuning. Interestingly, adding color to the prompt improves detection accuracy.
- **Depth estimation:** the module integrates MiDaS [2] to infer relative depth information. The aim is to symbolically represent spatial information of the world, e.g. the child is far from the robot, or the cup is in front of the child.

---

[1] https://github.com/ultralytics/ultralytics.

Table 1. YOLO vs YOLO-world comparison. Precision shows the proportion of correct positive predictions, while recall shows the proportion of actual positives correctly predicted. F1-score provides the harmonic mean of precision and recall.

Model Comparison	Precision	Recall	F1-score
YOLO	0.910	0.879	0.894
YOLO-world prompt 1	0.615	0.537	0.573
YOLO-world prompt 2	0.662	0.604	0.632

2.2 Communication

In this project, we extend the original pipeline in the following way:

- **ASR:** the robot supports both Vosk[2] and Whisper[3] at this point. To compare their performance, the Word Error Rate (WER) [1] was used on two different child audio recordings collected during therapy sessions, using Whisper's best-performing model as a reference. The results, presented in Table 2, highlight the differences in accuracy across smaller models from both Vosk and Whisper.

Table 2. Word Error Rate (WER) comparison for Whisper and Vosk on two child speech recordings. Lower values indicate better transcription quality.

Model Comparison	Audio 1	Audio 2
Whisper (best) vs Whisper (small)	0.394	0.485
Whisper (best) vs Vosk	0.535	0.781

- **TTS:** Coqui XTTS[4] enables expressive speech with emotional tones (e.g., happy, surprised, afraid, among others). Emotional speech is achieved by performing inference on the XTTS cloning model using emotional speech samples from professional voice actors. In therapeutic games, therapists often use whispering to support children's responses. The system can replicate such whispers through voice samples based on Autonomous Sensory Meridian Response (ASMR) voices. Alternatively, we have also integrated gTTS[5] as a lightweight fallback in case of limited resources in the system (e.g., if no GPU is available).
- **LLM Integration:** this module is in charge of generating a dialogue response to user inputs parsed through the communication manager. The original pipeline, based on Ollama models[6] (e.g., LLama 3.2) has been adjusted to

---

[2] https://github.com/alphacep/vosk-api.
[3] https://github.com/openai/whisper.
[4] https://github.com/coqui-ai/TTS.
[5] https://github.com/pndurette/gTTS.
[6] https://github.com/ollama/ollama.

ensure responses are predictable, supportive, and aligned with therapeutic goals. Prompts are tuned so that the robot generates friendly, peer—encouraging, patient, and age-appropriate utterances –rather than an adult or instructor outputs. Additionally, utterances include markup tags to allow expressive speech (aligning facial expression, prosodics and motions).
- **Expressive face**: consists of a mouth and two eyes, possibly adding eyebrows and color, to display different expressions (see Fig. 2).
- **Communication Manager**: it is in charge of handling the communicative acts between the robot and user processing the input from two sources: 1) from the user input (ASR), and sends it to the mission controller to process dialogue through the LLM. 2) from the mission controller, either in response to the user request, or to initiate a conversation. In this case, the response includes markup tags to allow multimodal communication based on: prosodics, facial expression and motions. For example,

```
<expression(surprise)> Such a surprise! </expression>
<do motion(shaking)> <expression(happy)> I can't believe you
are here.</expression>
```

The communication manager parsers the tags and triggers the respective modules accordingly to output the specified data. In the example above, the TTS would generate a surprised voice speaking the utterance "Such a surprise" while simultaneously displaying a surprised facial expression. Next, it triggers a shaking gesture through the head controller while speaking "I can't believe you are here" with a happy voice and facial expression. This emotional alignment across modalities enhances the robot's social presence and supports therapeutic goals by modeling expressive, context-sensitive behaviour.

2.3 Behavior Coordination

The intent-based *mission controller* processes user intents by selecting which task (in this case, games) to start. It coordinates the flow of the game, triggering the different robot skills (e.g., show game page, ask questions, provide feedback).

The symbolic *Knowledge Core*, in this context, allows for storing symbolic information of the environment, their properties and interaction events. At the moment, it keeps track of detected objects, humans, and tuples indicating which object the user is pointing to. The different components of the system can then use this information within the interaction to reason and make decisions.

2.4 Interactive GUI and Robot Model

The GUI interface[7] (Fig. 2) provides the means to visualize robot internal state and trigger actions. We have expanded its original version with the following components:

---

[7] The GUI is meant to be used for research and development of the system only.

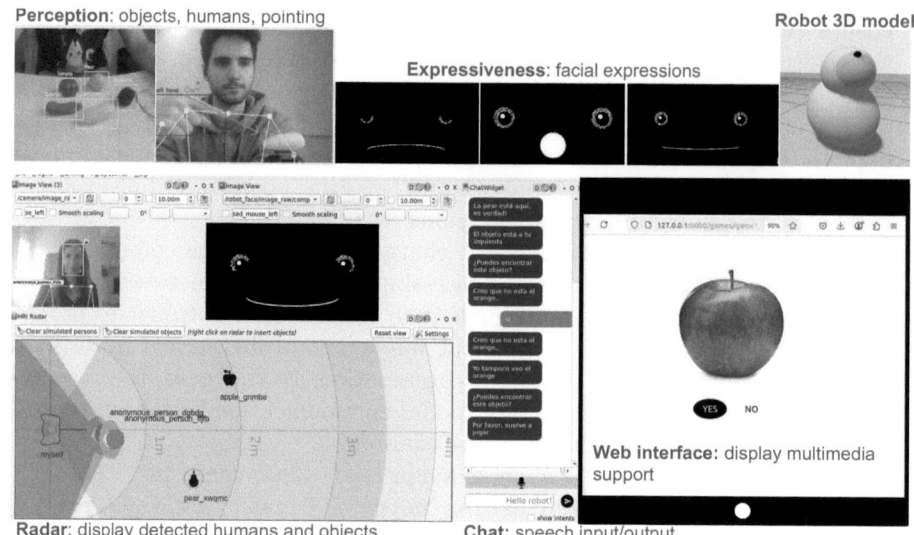

Fig. 2. Interactive GUI with perception and radar for object/human detection, facial expressions, chat for speech, web-based game content, and Gazebo robot model for testing head gestures.

- *Perception*: a visualization tool that displays vision-based detections. It extends the existing human detection to object detection and pointing gestures.
- *Radar*: a representation of the environment with spatial information of detected humans. It was also extended to include objects present in the environment and whether they are being pointed at or not.
- *Robot face*: displays the face of the robot along with transitions of facial expressions in real-time.
- *Chat*: exposes the verbal input/output of the robot. It includes a button to trigger the voice pipeline of the system whenever a user wants to verbally interact with the robot.

The system also uses a *Page manager* to show HTML/JS multimedia content on a web browser, such as images or yes/no buttons. It interfaces with ROS 2 through rosbridge to provide user input data back to the mission controller. Finally, the robot model can be loaded into Gazebo with the interactive GUI for virtual testing. The physical robot will feature the same face as the GUI and include a tablet for displaying content.

3 Use Case Demonstrator

We developed a prototype game on the virtual system, called *Finding Objects* game, to promote joint attention and vocabulary acquisition, based on input from a therapist.

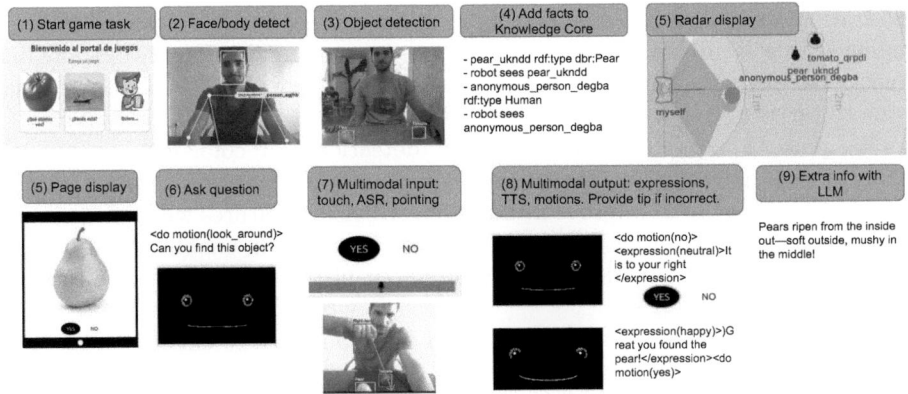

Fig. 3. Step-by-step flow of the "Finding Objects" game. The robot detects the user and objects, prompts the child with a fruit image, processes multimodal responses, provides expressive feedback and additional information using an LLM.

As illustrated in Fig. 3, the game proceeds as follows. The interaction begins with the therapist initializing the session (1) by selecting a game on the touchscreen, which triggers the `find_objects` task via the mission controller. Next, the robot detects both the user (2) and visible objects (3) such as a pear or a tomato. The system updates its knowledge base (4) and displays the objects' locations on the radar tool (5). A first round of the game starts displaying an image of one of the detected fruits (e.g., a pear) on the tablet (6). The robot asks the child "Can you find this object?" using expressive TTS, motions and facial expressions (6). The child may respond verbally, pressing the YES/NO button, or pointing at the object (7). Either input is interpreted by the communication manager and passed to the mission controller. Based on the child's response, the robot offers multimodal feedback (8): if the answer is correct, it provides positive reaction "`<expression(happy)>` Great! You found the pear!`</expression>` `<do motion(yes)>`" with a happy expression and a confirming motion; if incorrect, it might respond with a neutral expression "`<expression(neutral)>` It is on your right`</expression>` ", shift its gaze towards the object, and highlight the correct object on the screen. Finally it shares a fun fact using its LLM (9) i.e. "Pears ripen from the inside out –soft outside, mushy in the middle!". It then shows the next fruit.

4 Conclusions and Future Work

This work presents the software architecture and development tools for a low-cost social robot designed to support autism therapy in children, along with a simulated game. With core functionalities and infrastructure in place, the next steps involve refining the system and conducting a real-world pilot evaluation.

For speech, we plan to implement task-specific voices (e.g., motivational tones during games) and integrate voice emotion detection through the ASR to detect frustration, stress, or joy, enabling more adaptive responses. Advanced prompt engineering will tailor answers to therapy needs, avoiding unsuitable outputs like emoticons, offensive language, or biases. We also envision multi-robot conversations to further support therapy.

We plan to expand vision with color detection (for color-naming games), visual speech detection (to identify speakers), and head gesture recognition (for "yes" or "no" signals) to improve interaction. All vision features will be integrated into ReMap [6], a voxel-based spatial-semantic framework, enabling the robot to build 3D environment models and reason about objects and pointing directions beyond its view.

Once these tools are developed, we will build on them to enable engagement assessment by detecting emotional states (shouting, laughing), attention (e.g., child looking at the robot). Additional games will be developed with therapists on this architecture. The robot is scheduled for construction by summer 2025, with a pilot planned for autumn. User feedback will guide prototype refinements.

Acknowledgments. This research work was funded by the Ministry for Digital Transformation and the Civil Service, financed by the Recovery, Transformation and Resilience Plan through the European Union's Next Generation funds. EMOROBCARE. IASOMM24002.

Disclosure of Interests. The authors have no competing interests to declare that are relevant to the content of this article.

References

1. Ali, A., Renals, S.: Word error rate estimation for speech recognition: e-wer. In: Proceedings of Annual Meeting of the Association for Computational Linguistics (Volume 2: Short Papers), pp. 20–24 (2018)
2. Birkl, R., Wofk, D., Müller, M.: Midas v3. 1-a model zoo for robust monocular relative depth estimation. arXiv preprint arXiv:2307.14460 (2023)
3. Cabibihan, et al.: Why robots? a survey on the roles and benefits of social robots in the therapy of children with autism. Int. J. Soc. Robot. **5**(4), 593–618 (2013)
4. Cheng, et al.: Yolo-world: real-time open-vocabulary object detection. In: Proceedings of the IEEE/CVF Conference on Computer Vision and Pattern Recognition, pp. 16901–16911 (2024)
5. Cooper, et al.: Demonstration of an open-source ros 2 framework and simulator for situated interactive social robots. In: 2025 20th ACM/IEEE International Conference on Human-Robot Interaction (HRI), pp. 1770–1772 (2025)
6. Ferrini, et al.: remap: Spatially-grounded and queryable semantics for interactive robots. In: International Conference on Social Robotics, pp. 383–396. Springer (2024)
7. González-González, C.S., et al.: A long-term engagement with a social robot for autism therapy: a pilot study using user-centered design and icf-based assessment. Front. Robot. AI **8**, 669972 (2021)
8. LuxAI: Qtrobot for special needs education. https://luxai.com/assistive-tech-robot-for-special-needs-education/ (2021), Accessed 09 Jun 2025

9. Meza-Kubo, V.E., et al.: A new socially assistive robot with integrated serious games for therapies with children with autism spectrum disorder and down syndrome: A pilot study. Sensors **21**(24), 8414 (2021)
10. Mohamed, Y., Lemaignan, S.: Ros for human-robot interaction. In: 2021 IEEE/RSJ International Conference on Intelligent Robots and Systems (IROS), pp. 3020–3027. IEEE (2021)
11. Scassellati, B., et al.: Improving social skills in children with asd using a long-term, in-home social robot. Sci. Robot. **3**(21), eaat7544 (2022)
12. Silva, V., et al.: Social stories for promoting social communication with children with autism spectrum disorder using a humanoid robot: Step-by-step study. Technol. Knowl. Learn. **29**, 735–756 (2024)

When a Question Isn't Fair: Grounding Perceptions of Nonhuman Agents' (Un)Fairness in a Quiz Game Experience

August Bäckström, William Ekenberg, and Victor Kaptelinin[✉]

Umeå University, 901 87 Umeå, Sweden
victor.kaptelinin@umu.se

Abstract. If a technological agent treats people unequally, it may be perceived as "being unfair." But in what sense can fairness be considered an attribute of a nonhuman entity – a *thing*? This paper addresses this question through an exploratory study combining an experiment and a focus group. In the experiment, implemented as a quiz game hosted by an agent, two levels of participants' *Treatment* by the agent (Fair/Unfair) were combined with two levels of agents' *Anthropomorphism* (High/Low). Data about participants' perceptions of the agents were collected through Likert scales and post-session interviews. A subset of participants took part in a follow-up focus group study, in which they shared their thoughts and reflections on intelligent agents' fairness, grounded in their prior quiz game experience. The results suggest that while perceived fairness of an agent is a key aspect of human-agent interaction, operationalizing it is complicated by its ambiguity, context dependence, and entanglement with other aspects of interaction.

Keywords: Social human-agent interaction · Fairness · Anthropomorphism

1 Introduction

In various contexts, AI-based technologies emerge not just as human *tools*, but as nonhuman *agents* making "their own" situational decisions. For instance, a robotic hotel receptionist can be capable of handling guests' requests without a human supervision [1]. Studies show that people tend to perceive such artifacts as social actors (e.g., [2, 3]), to which they may assign the attribute of "fairness" [4]. Apparently, however, such artifacts are a different type of social actors compared to humans, and therefore, cannot be expected to be experienced as "fair" (or otherwise) in the same sense.

This paper aims to shed light on the meaning in which fairness can be considered an attribute of technological agents. While the issue has been addressed in existing studies (e.g., [5–7]), it arguably remains largely open.

Analyses of agents' fairness have been mostly conducted in work-related contexts, in which fairness has an objective meaning, e.g., treating people equally and making a diligent effort when contributing to shared activities [7]. In the context of teamwork, agents were found to be rewarded for being cooperative and fair and punished for being selfish, and the perception of an agent's fairness to be dependent on the agent's status and trustworthiness [5]. Analysis of fairness in resource allocation did not reveal significant differences in the assessment of human and agents' (un)fairness [6].

Studies have shown that the experience of agents and their behavior is strongly affected by anthropomorphism, and anthropomorphic qualities generally increase agents' likability and trustworthiness in a social context [8]. While anthropomorphism facilitates trust, it may, however, also result in more disappointment when agents do not meet human expectations [9]. It was also found that children are particularly positive toward certain agents' embodiments, such as child-like or dog-like robots [10], people tend to comply more with feminine intelligent agents rather than with masculine ones [3], and that there is a preference toward intelligent agents with anthropomorphic qualities and personalities matching persons' own cultures [11]. An increased human-likeness of an agent tends to positively correlate with the tendency to anthropomorphize [12] but the dependency is not linear: according to the "uncanny valley" hypothesis, too much human-likeness can be experienced negatively [13].

While existing research provides valuable insights regarding perceptions of agents' fairness, little is still known about these phenomena in non-work contexts (which are becoming increasingly central due to recent technological developments). In addition, the relation between fairness and anthropomorphism has been relatively unexplored.

To deal with these limitations, this study addressed the questions of *How is fairness experienced as an attribute of a nonhuman agent?* and *How is the experience of fairness affected by the agent's perceived level of anthropomorphism?* Accordingly, the study focused on game-like interaction, rather than interaction in a work-related context, and employed agents with the appearance of either humanoid robots or non-humanlike objects. The study comprised an experiment, implemented as a quiz game hosted by an agent, which was followed by a focus group, where the participants shared their thoughts and reflections regarding intelligent agents' fairness, grounded in their prior first-hand quiz game experience.

2 Study 1: Quiz Game Experiment

2.1 Method

Eight persons (4 females and 4 males), 18–35 y. o., with the median age group being 21–25 y. o., took part in the experiment.

The study used a two-factor within-subject design. A combination of two independent variables, "Treatment" (Fair/Unfair) of the participants and agents' "Anthropomorphism" (Low/High), produced four experimental conditions. Each participant was exposed to all four conditions, in an order determined by using the Latin Square technique.

Four agent identities corresponded to four conditions of the study. In "Unfair"—as opposed to "Fair"—conditions the agents asked the participants more difficult questions and sometimes did not reward a participant for being faster than the other player. Two "Low anthropomorphism" agents, named "XA-Q4" (the "Fair" condition) and "ZW-X3" (the "Unfair" condition), had the appearance of a regular speaker (Fig. 1a). Two "High Anthropomorphism" agents, "Sam" (the "Fair" condition) and "Kim" (the "Unfair" condition), looked like a humanoid robot having a "body", "head", rudimentary "arms", and "tracked legs" (Fig. 1b). An iPad serving as the robot's "face" displayed light-blue eyes, blinking 15–20 times per minute, and a static mouth with a neutral expression. Google Cloud Text-to-speech was used to generate two human-like voices for Sam and Kim and two mechanical voices for XA-Q4 and ZW-X3. The assignment of voices within the pairs was switched halfway through the experiment.

Fig. 1. (a) non-humanlike agents, *XA-Q4* and *ZW-X3*, (b) humanoid agents, Sam and *Kim*.

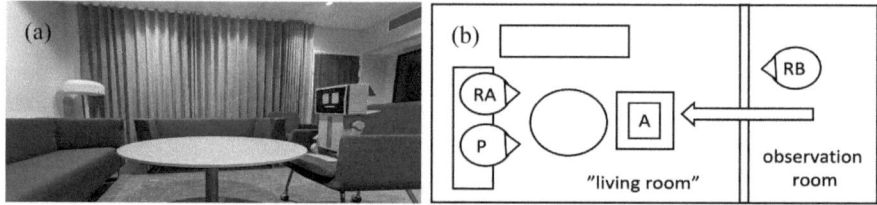

Fig. 2. The experimental setting: (a) a "living room" view, (b) the lab space floor plan (P: participant, A: agent, RA: Researcher A, RB: Researcher B)

The experiment took place at a lab space comprising a model "living room" and an adjacent observation room, separated by a one-way mirror (Fig. 2)[1].

The participants were informed about the aim of the study (which was described as assessing different types of socially aware intelligent agents) and provided their informed consent. Each participant then took part in four experimental conditions, acting as one of two players competing with one another in a quiz game "hosted" by an agent. The second player was enacted by Researcher A. The agents were controlled, using a Wizard of Oz (WoZ) technique, by Researcher B located in the observation room. Via its computer, Researcher B controlled a Bluetooth connected speaker, which was placed either on a table in front of the players or in the body of the agent. Both researchers followed a strict script designed to offer as little interactions outside of the script as possible. After each condition, the participants filled in a post-condition questionnaire. Each experimental session concluded with a semi-structured interview and debriefing. The sessions were about 60 min long.

---

[1] The first two authors conducted the experiment and focus group within their thesis work [14].

The post-condition questionnaire comprised ten attributes selected from Godspeed [15] and RoSAS [16] instruments, namely, *Happy/Feeling/Compassionate/Capable /Interactive/Reliable/Knowledgeable/Awkward/Awful/Social*, and three additional attributes, *Fair/Polite/Anthropomorphic*. All attributes were presented as 7-point Likert items. In post-interviews, the participants were asked about their experience in the study and their perception of robots' appearance and behavior. They were not explicitly prompted to talk about agents' fairness.

The study followed established guidelines for ethical research, including informed consent and confidentiality. The participants were debriefed about the use of the WoZ approach in the study.

2.2 Results

Post-condition Questionnaire. The results of post-condition questionnaire scores were analyzed using two-factor ANOVA. The "Fair" scores (Fig. 3a) showed a highly significant main effect of the "Treatment" factor ($F = 32,0627$, P-value $= 4,56E-06$, F crit $= 4,196$), and the "Anthropomorphic" scores (Fig. 3b) showed a significant main effect of the "Anthropomorphism" factor ($F = 13,5318$, P-value $= 0,001$, F crit $= 4,196$). The results served as a manipulation check: they confirm that independent variables were manipulated successfully, and differences between, respectively, "Fair vs. Unfair" and "High vs. Low Anthropomorphism" conditions were experienced by the participants as intended.

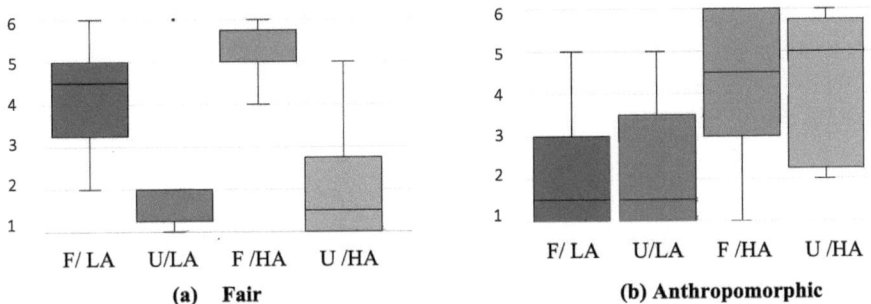

Fig. 3. "Fair" scores (a) and "Anthropomorphic" scores (b) in the conditions of the study (F: Fair, U: Unfair, LA: Low Anthropomorphism, HA: High Anthropomorphism).

There were no statistically significant interaction effects between the independent variables, and nor did we find significant main effects of the independent variables on the remaining scores. In particular, there were no significant differences between the conditions in the "Polite" scores and no significant differences between high- and low-anthropomorphism conditions in the "Social" scores.

Post-interviews. While the participants were generally positive about the experiment, finding it fun and interesting, they reported the feeling of being treated unequally. That could cause frustration, particularly because they could not appeal to an agent in the same way they would do to a human. It was emphasized that agents should treat people equally and without bias, especially in competitive or collaborative contexts.

Somewhat surprisingly, explicit references to "fairness" were rather infrequent and general. At the same time, many detailed comments were provided on the agents' appearance and behavior. The participants noted that while robots' responsiveness and social awareness (e.g., greetings, playful comments) were limited, they still positively contributed to the feeling of social engagement. The participants also stated their general preference for expressive and anthropomorphic, but distinctly non-human, agents, and noted that agent's voice is important for optimal user experience.

3 Study 2: Focus Group

3.1 Method

Five participants from Study 1 (4 females, 1 male) took part in Study 2.

The study was arranged as a face-to-face focus group session, explicitly focusing on the perception of technological agents' fairness. The session involved two researchers and five participants. During the session, the participants were asked to: (a) reflect on their experience during Study 1 (in particular, whether they were treated unequally and/or unfairly), (b) share their personal views on fairness in general, (c) comment on three fictional "unfair agent" scenarios, illustrated by storyboards: a quiz host agent being unfair to one of the players (like in Study 1), household chores being unfairly assigned by an agent to family members, and an agent unfairly taking the side of its owner in a dispute with another person, and (d) present their opinion on the social rules that should be followed by intelligent agents. The session was about 60 min long.

The study followed established ethical research guidelines, including informed consent and confidentially.

3.2 Results

The focus group discussion was recorded, transcribed, and analyzed using the thematic analysis framework [17]. The analysis produced the following main themes: *Perceived Fairness of Agents, Agents vs. Humans, Fairness vs. Politeness, Centrality of Context,* and *Fairness as a Design Objective.*

Perceived Fairness of Agents. The participants commonly described their experience in the experimental conditions in which they were treated unequally as *"it was unfair"*. They also occasionally mentioned robots *"being unfair"*. At the same time, they were hesitant to unreservedly describe the robots' (and, in general, intelligent agents') behavior in terms of "fairness". The participants mentioned alternative explanations, namely, that (a) robots' behavior was determined by how they were coded and trained rather than by the robots themselves, and (b) since *being fair* involves sympathy and empathy, and the robots lacked these qualities, they could not be considered "fair" (and, by extension, "unfair"). It was also mentioned that the experience of unfairness in the experiment could be more pronounced if "the stakes were higher".

Agents vs. Humans. A recurrent topic of the discussion was a comparison of robotic and human game hosts. The participants observed that if a human host is unfair, one can confront them, but it is not clear how, or if, one can do that when the host is a robot. It was also noted that the robotic hosts in the quiz game experiment lacked the rich nonverbal cues, which are spontaneously produced by humans (e.g., *"A human would raise an eyebrow or show something on the face"*), and it made quiz-related interactions less dynamic.

Fairness vs. Politeness. According to the participants, the relationship between fairness and another key social attribute, politeness, is not straightforward. On the one hand, fairness and politeness are two different attributes, as, for instance, *"you can be rude and fair at the same time"*. On the other hand, while different, these attributes are not completely independent from one another. In particular, if someone is unfair, their behavior may be perceived as "disingenuous" or even "sarcastic", rather than "polite".

Centrality of Context. The participants emphasized that the perception of fairness, and, more broadly, social acceptability, of agents' behavior strongly depends on the context of interaction and the agent's role in the context. The same behavior may be acceptable in one context and unacceptable in another. For instance, if an agent approaches a person with a task assignment or a reminder, it can be natural aspect of activities in a work setting, but may not be perceived well outside work, especially if it happens in front of other people. And even within the same context, what is fair and acceptable may depend on the role of the agent: e.g., a scenario in which an agent spontaneously intervened in a human-human dispute was considered by the participants particularly unacceptable because the agent in the scenario took the side of its owner.

Fairness as a Design Objective. A common position, emerging from the focus group discussion, was that fairness and equality should be important objectives when designing intelligent agents and their behavior. There were, however, also concerns about how feasible this objective is, given that what is fair is subjective and context-specific, and therefore hard to define. Main suggestions regarding how to design intelligent agents to support their perceived fairness, proposed by the participants, can be summarized as follows. First, consistent with the experiment findings, participants favored agents that were expressive and capable of rich and dynamic interaction, but also distinctly non-human. Second, agents should be able to recognize the social context of their use and adjust their behavior to the context. Third, the design of agents should be based on a transparent set of rules and explicitly support human values, such as equality.

4 Discussion

The dual nature of technological agents as, on the one hand, social actors and, on the other hand, inanimate "things", is one of the most intriguing and challenging issues in current social robotics research [18–20]. Evidence from our study highlights this duality. While the participants' rating scores and some verbal responses explicitly characterized the agents used in the study as "unfair", it also transpired that the participants were skeptical about attributing unfairness to robots' autonomous agency. Concerns about potential misunderstandings of robots as "true" agents appear to be a key reason behind the suggestion to design robots so that they are expressive but distinctly non-human.

The study highlights a particular aspect of the actor/ thing dilemma in human-agent interaction, namely, *limited possibilities for establishing a shared interpretation of the applicable social rules.* A crucial part of establishing a coherent social order in a setting is collaboratively deciding what is/ is not acceptable. If some actors disagree, they may appeal, complain, or even take the other party to court. With technological agents, it may not be possible. In our study, agents' limited communication capabilities, somewhat paradoxically, were perceived as giving them more power over people. Since the participants were effectively prevented from conveying their complaints and requests to the agents, their overall experience of unfairness included not only being treated differently than the other player but also a lack of power to influence the agent.

The finding suggests that a potential direction for the design of human-agent interaction is making it possible for humans to collaboratively establish 'house rules' with agents. This design direction, which can capitalize on recent developments in LLMs and generative AI, should, however, be explored with caution to avoid placing humans in an unfavorable negotiation position and reinforcing unfairness in subtler ways.

In addition, while quantitative data from the quiz game experiment were mostly intended as a manipulation check, they tentatively suggest that agents' "fairness" is a separate attribute, independent from both "anthropomorphism" (since we did not find a significant interaction between these factors) and "politeness" (since we did not find a significant effect of "Fairness" on the "Polite" scores). These hypotheses need to be verified in further studies.

5 Conclusion

The results of the exploratory study reported in this paper indicate that while fairness is experienced as an important aspect of human-agent interaction, operationalizing the notion of "agents' fairness" is complicated because of its ambiguous and contextual nature and entanglement with other aspects of interaction. The evidence reported in this paper may inform the choice of methodology and help shape specific, testable research questions for future studies.

6 Disclosure of Interests.

The author has no competing interests to declare that are relevant to the content of this article.

Acknowledgments. The authors would like to thank study participants for their time and insights. This study was funded by The Swedish Research Council (grant number 2021-05409).

References

1. Sevillano, E.: Custom views and reception robots: This is what hotels of the future will look like. El País, April 20, 2025. https://english.elpais.com/travel/2025-04-20/custom-views-and-reception-robots-this-is-what-hotels-of-the-future-will-look-like.html
2. Dautenhahn, K.: Socially intelligent robots: dimensions of human–robot interaction. Phil. Trans. R Soc. B Lond. B Biol. Sci. **362**(1480), 679–704 (2007)
3. Siegel, M., Breazeal, C., Norton, M.I.: Persuasive robotics: the influence of robot gender on human behavior. In: 2009 IEEE/RSJ International Conference on Intelligent Robots and Systems, pp. 2563–2568. IEEE (2009)
4. Ötting, S., Gopinathan, S., Maier, G, et al.: Why criteria of decision fairness should be considered in robot design. In: Presented at CSCW 2017 (2017). https://sites.coecis.cornell.edu/hri/files/2017/01/%C3%96tting-Gopinathan-Maier-and-Steil-2e7dua8.pdf
5. Cao, J., Chen, N.: The influence of robots' fairness on humans' reward-punishment behaviors and trust in human-robot cooperative teams. Hum. Factors **66**(4), 1103–1117 (2024)
6. Claure, H., Kim, S., Kizilcec, R.F., et al.: The social consequences of machine allocation behavior: fairness, interpersonal perceptions and performance. Comput. Hum. Behav. **146**(C) (2023)
7. Chang, M.L., Pope, Z., Short, E.S., et al.: Defining fairness in human-robot teams. In: Proceedings of RO-MAN 2020, pp. 1251–1258. IEEE (2020)
8. Roesler, E., Manzey, D., Onnasch, L.: Embodiment matters in social HRI research: effectiveness of anthropomorphism on subjective and objective outcomes. THRI **12**(1), 1–9 (2023)
9. Waytz, A., Cacioppo, J., Epley, N.: Who sees human?: the stability and importance of individual differences in anthropomorphism. Perspect. Psychol. Sci. **5**(3), 219–232 (2010)
10. Syrdal, D.S., Koay, K.L., Walters, M.L., et al.: The boy-robot should bark! – Children's impressions of agent migration into diverse embodiments. In: Proceedings New Frontiers of Human-Robot Interaction, a Symposium at AISB (2009)
11. Korn, O., Akalin, N., Gouveia, R.: Understanding cultural preferences for social robots: a study in German and Arab communities. THRI **10**(2), 1–19 (2021)
12. Rothstein, N., Kounios, J., Ayaz, H., De Visser, E.J.: Assessment of Human-Likeness and Anthropomorphism of Robots: A Literature Review. In: Advances in Neuroergonomics and Cognitive Engineering. pp. 190–196. Springer, Cham (2021). https://doi.org/10.1007/978-3-030-51041-1_26
13. Mori, M., MacDorman, K., Kageki, N.: The uncanny valley [from the field]. IEEE Robot. Automat. Mag. **19**, 98–100 (2012)
14. Bäckström, A., Ekenberg, W.: Don't be unfair, Mr Bot! An empirical study exploring the perception of fairness in non-work settings for human-agent interactions. Master's thesis. Department of Informatics, Umeå University (2023)
15. Bartneck, C., Kulić, D., Croft, E., et al.: Measurement instruments for the anthropomorphism, animacy, likeability, perceived intelligence, and perceived safety of robots. Int. J. Soc. Robot. **1**, 71–81 (2009)
16. Carpinella, C.M., Wyman, A.B., Perez, M.A., et al.: The robotic social attributes scale (RoSAS): development and validation. In: Proceedings of HRI 2017, pp. 254–262. ACM (2017)
17. Braun, V., Clarke, V.: Using thematic analysis in psychology. Qual. Res. Psychol. **3**, 77–101 (2006)
18. Clark, H.H., Fischer, K.: Social robots as depictions of social agents. Behav. Brain Sci. **46**, e21 (2023). https://doi.org/10.1017/S0140525X22000668

19. Ziemke, T.: Understanding social robots: attribution of intentional agency to artificial and biological bodies. Artif. Life **29**, 351–366 (2023). https://doi.org/10.1162/artl_a_00404
20. Kaptelinin, V., Dalli, K.C.: Understanding contextual framing: a nonessentialist perspective on social interactions with technological artifacts. In: Proceedings of HRI 2025, pp. 1121–1130. IEEE, (2025). https://doi.org/10.1109/HRI61500.2025.10974062

Open Access This chapter is licensed under the terms of the Creative Commons Attribution 4.0 International License (http://creativecommons.org/licenses/by/4.0/), which permits use, sharing, adaptation, distribution and reproduction in any medium or format, as long as you give appropriate credit to the original author(s) and the source, provide a link to the Creative Commons license and indicate if changes were made.

The images or other third party material in this chapter are included in the chapter's Creative Commons license, unless indicated otherwise in a credit line to the material. If material is not included in the chapter's Creative Commons license and your intended use is not permitted by statutory regulation or exceeds the permitted use, you will need to obtain permission directly from the copyright holder.

Diffusion of Responsibility in HRI: Reduction of Human Agency Does not Occur When Sharing a Task with a Robotic Arm

Francesca Ciardo[1(✉)], Alessandra Fava[2], Paola Ricciardelli[1], Valeria Villani[2], Cristina Iani[3], and Lorenzo Sabattini[2]

[1] Department of Psychology, University of Milan-Bicocca, Milan, Italy
Francesca.Ciardo@unimib.it
[2] Department of Sciences and Methods for Engineering, University of Modena and Reggio Emilia, Reggio Emilia, Italy
[3] Department of Surgery, Medicine, Dentistry and Morphological Sciences, University of Modena and Reggio Emilia, Reggio Emilia, Italy

Abstract. Evidence showed that when interacting with human-like or social robots, humans perceive lower agency and control over the negative outcomes of their actions, raising the Diffusion Of Responsibility (DOR) phenomenon.

In the present study, we examined whether DOR occurs when sharing a task with a robotic arm. To this end, we implemented a task in which human participants were asked to stop the inflation of a virtual balloon before it reached a pin and burst. However, every time they acted to stop the inflation of the balloon, they lost points from the starting score. Participants played the task alone or together with the Ned2 robot. Results showed that participants experienced increased responsibility over negative outcomes of their actions when sharing the task with Ned2 compared to when they performed the task alone. Together, our results showed for the first time that DOR does not occur when interacting with a non-humanoid robot.

Keywords: Human-Robot Interaction · Diffusion of Responsibility · Agency

1 Introduction

When interacting with other human beings, the phenomenon of Diffusion Of Responsibility (DOR) has been consistently reported in the psychological literature [e.g., see 3 for a review]. DOR is defined as the reduction in the perceived agency for the consequences of one's actions, especially if these are negative [3].

Two recent studies [7, 8] showed that DOR occurs also in HRI when sharing a task with a social robot, with people perceiving reduced agency and control over negative consequences of their actions. Specifically, in both studies, the authors adapted the Balloon Risk Taking Task (BART) used by Beyer and colleagues [4–6] to an HRI setting, in which human participants shared the task together with the Cozmo robot. Results showed that DOR occurred when interacting with the Cozmo robot both at implicit and explicit levels. Namely, when the task was shared with Cozmo, participants explicitly reported reduced agency and control over the negative outcome of their actions [7]. At the neurophysiological level, such evidence was supported by a reduction of the attentional resources allocated to the processing of action outcomes when also Cozmo was in charge of executing the task [8].

1.1 Aim

The present study aims to test whether the DOR over negative outcomes generated by human actions occurs when interacting with non-social robots. To this end, we replicated Ciardo and Hinz's studies [7, 8] but implemented the robotic arm Ned2 (Niryo) as a robotic co-agent. We expected agency ratings to be lower when sharing the task with Ned2 compared to when participants perform the task alone, thus confirming that participants attributed intentionality to the robotic arm.

2 Materials and Methods

2.1 Sample

Twenty-four healthy adults took part in the study. The sample included 11 males, 3 left-handed, with an age range of 19–27 years (M = 22.15, SD = 1.89). All had normal or corrected-to-normal vision. Participants provided informed written consent for taking part in the study and were debriefed at the end of it. The study was approved by the Committee for Research Evaluation (CRIP) Department of Psychology at the University of Milano-Bicocca, which operates under the supervision of the Ethics Committee of Athenaeum (Prot.RM-2023–688). The study was conducted in compliance with the ethical principles of the "Declaration of Helsinki" and of the Convention on Human Rights and Biomedicine (Oviedo Convention).

2.2 Experimental Setup

The experiment was carried out in a fully lit room. The experimental setup consisted of: (1) the Ned2 robot (Niryo); (2) a laptop connected with Ned2; (3) two QWERTY keyboards to execute a response; (4) a 24" screen (1920 ×1080) to display the task.

Participants were seated in front of a desk with a computer screen on it. The Ned2 robot (Niryo) was placed directly in front of them. Stimuli consisted of pictures of a pin and a red balloon (113 × 135 pixels). Responses during the task were executed by pressing the "SPACEBAR" for the robot, and the "K" key for the participant with right index finger. Agency ratings were collected using a mouse. Stimulus presentation, response timing, and data collection were controlled by Opensesame software [9] version 4.0.24 for Windows, which is compatible with Python 3.11.

The Ned2 robot (Niryo), is a 6-axis robotic arm designed for the educational sector, inspired by industry. Teachers from technical institutions, universities, high schools, and community colleges utilize it to practice and develop a variety of skills from the fundamentals to the expert level.

We integrated the Ned2 robot with Opensesame through a Python script to improve the performance. We connected the robot with the PC via Ethernet to guarantee stability.

To activate the robot, we sent data from Opensesame, and when this data was received by the Python script, it connected and moved the robot consequently. We have adopted this solution because it guarantees more stability and less latency (Fig. 1).

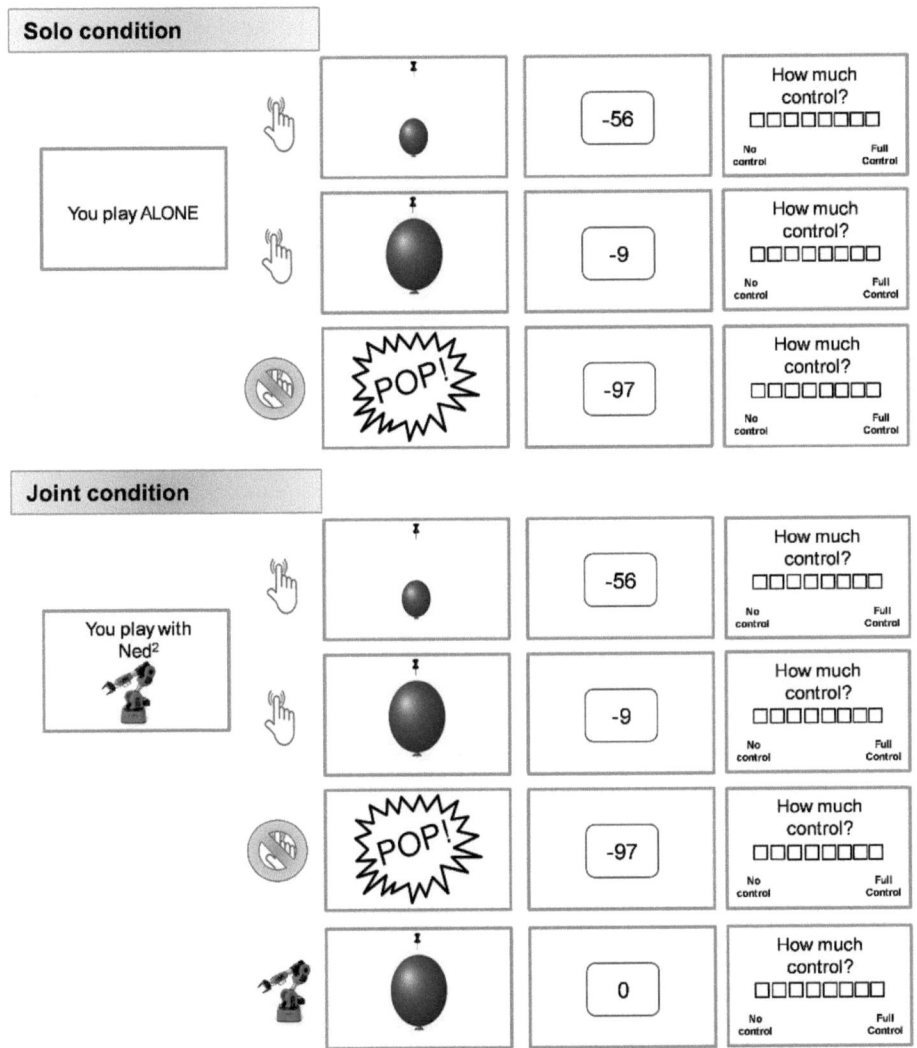

Fig. 1. Trial procedure. The task consisted of 16 blocks of 10 trials each. The order of the blocks was randomized. Half of the blocks participants played alone (Solo condition, upper panel), whereas in the other half, Ned2 was also in charge of stopping the balloon (Joint condition, lower panel). When Ned2 stopped the balloon, it would lose the respective number of points, whereas the participant would lose no points. In the event of an explosion, both agents would lose points. To prevent participants from predicting a priori when Ned2 would act, the robot was programmed to act only in 60% of joint trials. Also, Ned2 always acted only when approximately 80% of the inflation time was reached, to increase uncertainty about the intent of the robot to act.

2.3 Procedure

The task replicated the Balloon Analogous Risk Task (BART) implemented in [7, 8]. Participants were asked to stop an inflating balloon before it exploded when reaching a pin on the top of the display. In every trial, the participants would lose points from an initial amount of 5000 points. The later they stopped the balloon, the fewer points were lost. The exact number of lost points per trial was randomly chosen from a range of points, depending on four different clusters of balloon's stopped size (1–15; 16–29; 30–45; 46–60). However, if they did not stop the balloon and it exploded, the maximal number of points was lost (80–100). The game aimed to save the maximum number of points; thus, the best strategy was to wait as long as possible before stopping the balloon. Similar to previous studies [7, 8], participants were explicitly instructed that their goal was to save as many points as possible to compete against previous participants and they would not be able to compete against Ned2 since it was playing in only half of trials. At the end of each trial, after showing how many points they lost, participants rated the feeling of agency they experienced over the losses on a 8-point Likert scale. See Annex, for a detailed description of the trial procedure and for a picture of the setup.

3 Data Analysis

Each trial was classified as (i) "Self-actions" if the participant stopped the balloon; (ii) "Other agent" if Ned2 stopped the balloon (iii) "Explosions" if no one stopped the balloon and it exploded. The frequencies of the three types of trials were submitted to Pearson's chi-square test ($\chi 2$). Performance was assessed by the number of reactions in each condition (Solo vs Joint):

To evaluate DOR for self-generated outcomes, we analyzed only Human-agent trials, i.e., when the participant acted and successfully stopped the balloon. Agency ratings were analyzed using linear mixed-effects models (LMM), they were modelled as a function of Condition (Solo vs Joint), standardized Outcomes, i.e. the number of lost points for each trial, plus their interaction. Analyses were conducted using the lme4 package in R [11].

4 Results

Pearson's chi-square test ($\chi 2$) showed that participants stopped the balloon more frequently in the Solo compared to Joint condition [$\chi 2$ (2) = 1060.80, p < 0.05], as indicated by the higher percentage of Self-actions trials in the Solo (M = 37.19%,) than in the Joint condition (M = 25.75%). In the Joint condition, participants left the robot act in 20.71% of the trials. Consequently, the explosion rate in Joint decreased compared to the Solo condition (4.02% vs 12.32%, respectively). The LLM analysis showed that agency ratings differed across Condition [β = 0.44, t = 2.91, p < 0.01; 97%CI (0.14; 0.73)]. Specifically, the agency ratings were higher for the Joint (M = 6.15, SE = 0.05) compared to all the Solo condition (M = 6.00 SE = 0.05), see Fig. 2. Agency ratings were negatively predicted by the number of lost points (Outcome) [β = −0.79, t = −5.78, p < 0.01; 97%CI (−1.06; −0.52)], with smaller losses being associated with higher agency ratings. This was true for the Joint condition as indicated by the two-way interaction Condition * Outcome interaction [$\beta = 0.31, t = 2.17, p < 0.05; 97\%$CI $(0.03; 0.58)$].

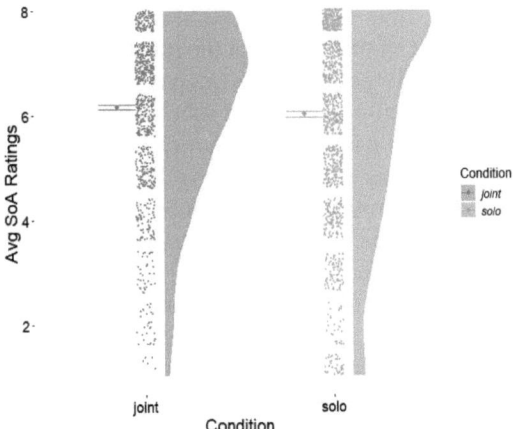

Fig. 2. Agency ratings plotted as a function of the Condition (blue = Solo; red = Joint). (Color figure online)

5 Conclusions

The present study aimed to test whether the DOR over negative outcomes generated by humans' actions occurs when interacting with non-social robots. To this end, we replicated Ciardo and Hinz's studies [7, 8] but implemented the robotic arm Ned2 (Niryo) as a co-agent. Results showed that when Ned2 was in charge of stopping the balloon, participants felt more responsible for the negative consequences of their actions, probably because they did not offload the task to the robot. This is also reflected in the average agency ratings, which resulted to be higher in the Joint compared to the Solo condition (see Fig. 2). Such a result contrasts with those of previous studies [4, 5, 7, 8], showing that when interacting with social robots, humans show a reduction in agency and DOR occurs. It could be argued that the differences in the results may be driven by variations in the task procedure compared to those implemented in [7, 8], such as a lower number of blocks (12 blocks in 7, 19 blocks in 8, and only 8 in the current experiment). However, this choice did not affect the payoff structures of the task, given that in all studies, participants played with the robot only in 50% of the blocks, and within each Joint condition block, the robot was programmed to act only in 6 out of 10 trials (60%). Thus, by reducing the number of blocks, we did not change either the payoff of the task or the optimal strategy to play. Another difference in the task procedure is the parameter set for sending the command to act to Ned2 when the inflation reached 80% of the total sequence. Such a parameter was set at 90% in previous work [7, 8]. Such a change was needed to compensate for the delay the execution of the command, which resulted to be slower with Ned2, thus by programming the robot to act at 90% of the inflation procedure as in [7, 8], it could be happened that the key press occurred after the end of the trial, see Annex.

In our study, we implemented a robotic arm that does not present any features able to elicit mental states or intentionality attribution in humans, thus participants may have perceived themselves as more responsible for the negative consequences of their actions because they perceived the robot as a tool instead of an intentional agent. Thus, the decision to act was not driven by the belief that the robot was aiming to deceive them to save more points and improve its performance, but probably by the fact that participants were less likely to offload the action to the Ned2 robot. Thus, by showing that DOR does not occur when interacting with a robotic arm, our results confirm and extend previous evidence by showing that DOR is a consequence of the need to mentalize other agents [4–6], even when the agent is a robot [7, 8]. The increased agency experienced in HRI with a robotic arm should be taken into consideration when designing the interaction of users with manipulator robots. Indeed, a higher perception of responsibility over negative consequences may lead users to experience higher anxiety and stress when interacting with a manipulator robot, resulting in negative feelings toward it and a reduction of trust.

When sharing a task with other agents, humans tend to perceive themselves as less responsible for the negative consequences of their actions (i.e., diffusion of responsibility). This study showed that, in contrast to previous studies reporting DOR in HRI with social robots [7, 8], this phenomenon does not occur in HRI in which the partner is a robotic arm. We propose that in HRI, the DOR is not due only to the human ability to perceive robots as active agents irrespective of their physical appearance, but it may result from a complex interplay between intentionality attribution and partners' action representation. Future work could benefit from incorporating implicit measures and manipulation checks, in order to further assess the potential role of intentionality attribution when interacting with a non-social robot.

References

1. Flughafen München GmbH: Hi! I'm Josie Pepper. https://www.munich-airport.com/hi-i-mjosie-pepper-3613413. Accessed Jun 2025
2. Chen, W.-K.: Linear Networks and Systems, pp. 123–135. Wadsworth, Belmont (1993)
3. Liu, D., Liu, X., Wu, S.: A literature review of diffusion of responsibility phenomenon. In: Proceedings 8th International Conference on Humanities and Social Science Research (ICHSSR 2022), pp. 1806–1810. Atlantis Press (2022)
4. Beyer, F., Sidarus, N., Fleming, S., Haggard, P.: Losing control in social situations: How the presence of others affects neural processes related to sense of agency. eNeuro 5(1), ENEURO-0336 (2018)
5. Beyer, F., Sidarus, N., Bonicalzi, S., Haggard, P.: Beyond self-serving bias: diffusion of responsibility reduces sense of agency and outcome monitoring. Soc. Cogn. Affect. Neurosci. **12**(1), 138–145 (2017)
6. Chambon, V., Sidarus, N., Haggard, P.: From action intentions to action effects: how does the sense of agency come about? Front. Hum. Neurosci. **8**, 320 (2014)
7. Ciardo, F., De Tommaso, D., Beyer, F., Wykowska, A.: Attribution of intentional agency toward robots reduces one's own sense of agency. Cognition **194**, 1–11 (2020)
8. Hinz, N.-A., Ciardo, F., Wykowska, A.: ERP markers of action planning and outcome monitoring in human-robot interaction. Acta Physiol. (Oxf) **212**, 1–11 (2021)

9. Mathôt, S., Schreij, D., Theeuwes, J.: OpenSesame: an open-source, graphical experiment builder for the social sciences. Behav. Res. **44**, 314–324 (2012)
10. Lejuez, C.W., et al.: Evaluation of a behavioral measure of risk taking: the balloon analogue risk task (BART). J. Exp. Psychol. Appl. **8**, 75–84 (2002)
11. R Core Team: R: A Language and Environment for Statistical Computing. R Foundation for Statistical Computing, Vienna (2018)

Exploring Emotional Support Through Interaction with a Social Robot for Individuals with a Visual and Cognitive Impairment: a Pilot Study

Veerle L. N. F. Hobbelink[1,2](✉), Dustin Lischer[1], Martijn van Zeeland[1], Rick Gevaert[1], Victor van der Hout[1], and Matthijs H.J. Smakman[1]

[1] HU University of Applied Sciences Utrecht, Utrecht, The Netherlands
veerle.hobbelink@hu.nl
[2] VU University Amsterdam, Amsterdam, The Netherlands

Abstract. While social robots are increasingly used to support people with disabilities, their potential for adults with both cognitive and visual impairments remains understudied. This exploratory study first identified the emotional support needs and robot design requirements of these individuals and their caregivers. A small user study with three participants revealed positive engagement with the social robot, particularly appreciation for its soft exterior and personalized content. Participants expressed a desire for longer interactions, but also encountered operational difficulties due to the robot's design. Overall, their positive responses and willingness to continue use suggest the potential of social robots to support this population.

Keywords: Social Robots · Emotional Support · Visual Impairment · Cognitive Impairment · Participatory Design

1 Introduction

Globally, 2.2 billion people are visually impaired in some capacity [14]. Individuals with visual impairments often struggle to navigate their environment and remain socially connected, which can result in loneliness and depression [4]. Similarly, those with cognitive impairments, such as dementia or intellectual disabilities, face unique challenges that increase the prevalence of depression and loneliness within this group [10]. Approximately 25% of individuals with cognitive impairments also have visual impairments, compounding their difficulties [6]. Research indicates a high prevalence of depression among individuals with both visual and cognitive impairments [11].

Social robots are increasingly used to support people with disabilities, enhancing both autonomy and social interaction [2]. Previous research has explored the use of social robots in different domains of caregiving, such as elderly care [3] and support for people with cognitive disabilities [5]. These robots are reported to be able to provide companionship, reduce loneliness, support cognitive stimulation, assist with movement, structure daily activities, and promote mental well-being through emotional support (e.g., [3,5]). Given these supportive features of social robots, they may hold potential for people with visual and cognitive impairments. However, accessibility of social robots for people with visual impairments remains limited [7], and support for individuals with both visual and cognitive impairments is understudied.

This study uses qualitative participatory design to explore to potential of social robots to support the emotional well-being of individuals with visual and cognitive impairments. We will report on the design requirements elicited from interviews and observations and on two consecutive sessions with three participants, both with visual and cognitive impairments, wherein the robot was implemented to support emotional well-being.

2 Materials and Methods

2.1 Expectations and Requirements Methodology

To explore expectations and requirements for social robots, we conducted semi-structured interviews with three individuals with visual and cognitive impairments and two of their caregivers. Interviews focused on four themes: (1) social interaction, (2) expectations of technology, (3) activities and preferences, and (4) daily routines. Additionally, we observed each client-caregiver pair for a day to identify moments in the daily schedule where a social robot could provide support.

Requirements (r) and Robot Selection. Participants expressed a need for a *soft exterior* (r1) *talking companion* (r2), the *ability to personalize* (r3), a *clear voice* (r4), and *autonomous use* (r5). Observations indicated that participants preferred to use the social robot *after their daytime activities* (r6). Based on the requirements (r) elicited, we selected the most suitable robot at our disposal, the SAMbuddy robot. SAMbuddy, developed originally as a buddy for children [9], is a stuffed plush animal with a soft exterior and was perceived as accessible and pleasant (see Fig. 1a). SAMbuddy allows caregivers to upload audio fragments via a simple local network by holding the "circle" button, ensuring data is stored privately and securely. These audio fragments are activated by pressing the triangle "play" button.

2.2 User Testing Methodology

We tested the social robot with the participants in two consecutive sessions, where there was room for alterations based on participants' suggestions between sessions.

 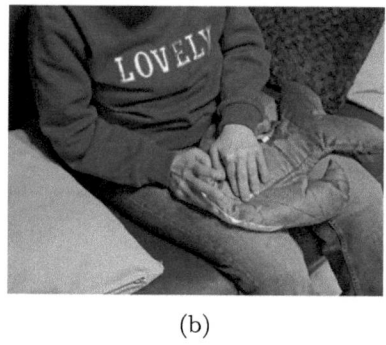

Fig. 1. (a) Social robot SAMbuddy [9]. (b) Social robot SAMbuddy on one of the participants' laps.

Participants. Three adult clients ($N = 3$) from a Dutch care facility participated in this study. All had both cognitive and visual impairments, and informed consent was obtained from participants and their caregivers. To protect anonymity, we withhold the age and gender of the participants. Diagnoses follow the International Classification of Functioning, Disability and Health (ICF). Participant one is blind with no light perception (NPL) [13] and has a mild cognitive impairment, with a developmental age of 7–12 years. Participant two is also blind NPL, with a moderate cognitive impairment and a developmental age of 4–7 years. Participant three is visually impaired (visual acuity –0.16, or 16% vision loss per WHO standards) and has a mild cognitive impairment with a developmental age of 7–12 years.

Observations. After each interaction, participants were asked reflective questions to gather their impressions of SAMbuddy (adapted from [8]; see Appendix B). Questions such as "Can you tell us what you just did?" and "How did it feel talking to SAMbuddy?" were adjusted to match participants' abilities. Semi-structured interviews were transcribed using Amberscript (Oct/Nov 2024), reviewed for accuracy, and independently coded by two researchers. The data were then thematically analyzed [1].

Interview. Following each interaction, participants were asked reflective questions to elicit their impressions of the SAMbuddy (adapted from [8], see Appendix B). The questions included 'Can you tell us what you just did?' and 'How did it feel talking to the SAMbuddy?' These questions were adjusted to align with the participants' abilities. Semi-structured interviews were conducted and transcribed using Amberscript (OCT/NOV 2024). The precision of the transcriptions was reviewed, coded separately by two researchers, and thematically analyzed [1].

Robot Interaction. The robot was personalized for each participant using pre-recorded audio files featuring a male AI voice. These included questions about the participant's day (e.g., "What did you do today?") and bird sounds. The robot addressed participants by name and, in one case, referenced a personal interest. Audio content was tailored based on input from both participants and their caregivers to ensure relevance and suitability.

Procedure. Participants first took part in an introductory session to explore the robot's buttons and functions, ask questions, and suggest features they would like implemented. This was followed by two interaction sessions, held in participants' homes to ensure a naturalistic setting (see Fig. 1b). Each session lasted five to fifteen minutes, with the robot using pre-programmed audio files tailored to individual needs. The second session was adapted based on participant feedback, For example, questions about previous activities for one participant ('Do you still remember what bird sounds you recognized last time?'), or about future activities for another. Researchers made observations throughout, and interviews were conducted after both sessions.

3 Results

In session one, participant one responded to all of SAMbuddy's questions with one-word answers, maintaining a calm demeanor, smiled at the robot's sounds, and described the bird sounds as "funny" and "relaxing." Despite slight frustration when operating the robot, as its buttons were hard to find based on touch, they held it throughout and were reluctant to let go. They expressed a desire for more questions and longer interactions, stating the robot would need to stay all day to provide support. Participant two maintained a focused demeanor, gave short, direct responses, and smiled throughout. They gave a longer 30-second answer to "What did you do today?" and reacted enthusiastically to the bird sounds, naming each bird. Operating the robot's buttons caused minor confusion, but they expressed particular joy in naming the birds. Participant three gave concise (1–10 word) answers, stayed silent and focused, and held the robot close while using its buttons. They answered a typically difficult question, appeared calm and smiling, and expressed post-session feelings of relaxation, despite slight difficulty with the buttons.

In session two, participant one gave more elaborate answers based on feedback, again found the bird sounds "relaxing," and experienced fewer difficulties operating the robot. They placed it on their lap, commented on its softness, and reiterated a desire for longer conversations. Participant two greeted the robot warmly and gave longer responses. A technical error required a restart, which caused some frustration. During the new bird sounds fragment, they remained engaged and enthusiastic, named all birds, and suggested adding animal sounds like dogs or horses. They reported enjoying the entire interaction. Participant three again gave brief (1–5 word) responses, with occasional longer answers. They stayed focused, held the robot close, and operated its buttons. Afterward, they expressed relaxation and calmness, appreciated the robot overall, but preferred live responses. They also noted they would have liked to use the robot on a previous difficult day.

4 Discussion

This study examined how social robots can support individuals with both visual and cognitive impairments by identifying user requirements and conducting an exploratory case study with SAMbuddy. Participants and caregivers emphasized the need for a talkative, tactilely pleasant, and personalized robot. Despite minor frustrations with operation, all participants responded positively, showing signs of comfort or excitement, suggesting the potential of social robots for this understudied group. These results align with prior research on the emotional support capabilities of social robots [3,8].

Personalization emerged as a key factor: tailored questions in session two led to more detailed responses and engagement. All participants expressed interest in longer interactions and offered suggestions for improvement, underscoring the need for adaptive, user-centred design. The robot's physical comfort also contributed to positive experiences; participants described SAMbuddy as "nice and soft," pointing to the role of social touch in initial bonding [12]. These suggestions highlight the importance of continuous improvement and user-centred design in the development of emotional support robots.

4.1 Limitations and Future Work

This study had several limitations, including a small sample size ($N = 3$), lack of control conditions, and only two interaction sessions per participant. Usability was also affected by technical issues, as SAMbuddy's buttons were difficult to locate through touch alone. Future research should improve the robot's conversational abilities and explore features such as haptic feedback, auditory cues, and expanded adaptive responses to better support users with visual and cognitive impairments. Including control conditions and incorporating physical indicators, such as measures of stress or relaxation, could provide a deeper insight into the user experience. Long-term use and larger participant groups will also be important to assess effectiveness and sustained engagement.

4.2 Conclusion

This study explored the potential use of social robots to support people with both visual and cognitive impairments. Initial positive reactions and willingness to use the robot showed potential for a social robot to provide support to these individuals. Further research on social robots as care companions for individuals with visual and cognitive impairments needs to be conducted to validate these findings.

Acknowledgments. We would like to thank the clients and caregivers of Visio't Hoge Veen who voluntarily agreed to take part in our research.

Disclosure of Interests. The authors have no competing interests to declare that are relevant to the content of this article.

A Observation Schemes

A.1 Dutch (original)

(Tables 1, 2, 3, 4, 5 and 6).

Table 1. Observatieschema over de mate van interactie

Gedrag	Ja/Nee	Frequentie	Opmerkingen
Reageert verbaal op vragen van de robot			
Reageert non-verbaal (lichaamsbewegingen, bewegingen naar de robot)			
Reageert kort en direct (betrokkenheid interactie)			
Reageert uitgebreid (hoe lang/aantal woorden)			
Luistert stil/aandachtig naar het geluid of vraag (focus)			
Aanraking van de robot tijdens interactie (letten op goed vasthouden, knuffelen)			

Table 2. Observatieschema over de emotionele expressie

Reactie	Ja/Nee	Frequentie	Opmerkingen
Lacht of glimlacht			
Toont frustratie (onrustig bewegen, zuchten, irritatie tonen)			
Toont verwarring (stil, fronsen, aarzelen)			
Toont spanning/angst (onrustige bewegingen, verandering stem)			

Table 3. Observatieschema over de emotionele interactie

Indicator	Ja/Nee	Frequentie	Opmerkingen
Ontspannen houding tijdens interactie			
Lijkt getroost of gerustgesteld			
Vertelt of reageert met positieve gevoelens			

A.2 English (translated)

Table 4. Observation scheme for the degree of interaction

Behavior	Yes/No	Frequency	Notes
Responds verbally to questions from the robot			
Responds non-verbally (body movements, movements toward the robot)			
Responds briefly and directly (engagement interaction)			
Responds extensively (how long/number of words)			
Listens quietly/attentively to the sound or question (focus)			
Touches the robot during interaction (pay attention to good holding, hugging)			

B Questionnaire

B.1 Dutch (original)

Post-interactie questionnaire (mondeling afgenomen)

1. Kun je vertellen wat je net hebt gedaan? (omschrijven pilot en testen van geheugen)
2. Hoe vond je het om te praten met de robot? (open vraag, doorvragen)

Emotionele staat (eerst vraag stellen, daarna cijfer vragen)

1. Hoe voelde je je voor het gesprek met de robot? (1.Heel slecht, 2. Slecht, 3. Tussenin, 4. Goed, 5. Heel goed)
2. Hoe voelde je je toen je met de robot praatte? (1. Zeer ongemakkelijk, 2. Ongemakkelijk, 3. Tussenin, 4. Prettig, 5. Heel prettig)
3. Hoe voel je je nu? (is er een verandering in emotie na de interactie?) (1. Veel slechter, 2.slechter, 3.hetzelfde, 4.beter, 5.veel beter)

Table 5. Observation scheme for emotional expression

Behavior	Yes/No	Frequency	Notes
Smiles			
Shows frustration (moving restlessly, sighing, showing irritation)			
Shows confusion (silent, frowning, hesitating)			
Shows tension/anxiety (restless movements, change in voice)			

Table 6. Observation scheme for emotional support

Indicator	Yes/No	Frequency	Notes
Relaxed posture during interaction			
Appears comforted or reassured			
Talks or responds with positive feelings			

4. Denk je dat je nog een keer met Sam zou willen praten? (1. Helemaal niet. 2. Liever niet. 3. Misschien. 4. Leuk. 5 lijkt me heel leuk)

Vragen ter verbetering van de robot

1. Wat zou de robot beter moeten kunnen doen? Waarom?
2. Hoe heeft de robot je ondersteuning kunnen bieden?

B.2 English (translated)

Post-interaction questionnaire (orally administered)

1. Can you tell what you just did? (describe pilot and test memory)
2. How did you like talking to the robot (open question, ask additional questions)

Emotional state (ask question first, then ask grade)

1. How did you feel before talking to the robot? (1.Very bad, 2. Bad, 3. In between, 4. Good, 5. Very good)
2. How did you feel when talking to the robot? (1. Very uncomfortable, 2. Uncomfortable, 3. In between, 4. Pleasant, 5. Very pleasant)
3. How do you feel now (is there a change in emotion after the interaction?) (1. Much worse, 2. Worse, 3. Same, 4. Better, 5. Much better)
4. Do you think you would like to talk to Sam again? (1. Not at all. 2. Rather not. 3. Maybe. 4. Nice. 5 Seems very nice)

Questions to improve the robot

1. What should the robot be able to do better? Why?
2. How did the robot provide you with support?

References

1. Braun, V., Clarke, V.: Using thematic analysis in psychology. Qual. Res. Psychol. **3**(2), 77–101 (2006)
2. Broadbent, E.: Interactions with robots: the truths we reveal about ourselves. Ann. Rev. Psychol. **68**, 627–652 (2017). https://doi.org/10.1146/annurev-psych-010416-043958
3. Broekens, J., Heerink, M., Rosendal, H., et al.: Assistive social robots in elderly care: a review. Gerontechnology **8**(2), 94–103 (2009). https://doi.org/10.4017/gt.2009.08.02.002.00
4. Brunes, A., B. Hansen, M., Heir, T.: Loneliness among adults with visual impairment: prevalence, associated factors, and relationship to life satisfaction. Health Qual. Life Cutcomes **17**, 1–7 (2019).https://doi.org/10.1186/s12955-019-1096-y
5. Guemghar, I., et al.: Social robot interventions in mental health care and their outcomes, barriers, and facilitators: scoping review. JMIR Ment Health **9**(4), e36094 (2022). https://doi.org/10.2196/36094
6. Koninklijke Visio: https://www.visio.org/nl-nl/expertise/meervoudige-beperking
7. Pivin-Bachler, J., Gomez, R., Van Den Broek, E.L.: "One for all, all for one". a first step towards universal access with a social robot. In: Workshop Proceedings of the 19th International Conference on Intelligent Environments (IE2023), pp. 186–195. IOS Press (2023). https://doi.org/10.3233/AISE230031
8. Rodríguez-Domínguez, M.T., et al.: Interaction assessment of a social-care robot in day center patients with mild to moderate cognitive impairment: a pilot study. Int. J. Soc. Robot. **16**(3), 513–528 (2024). https://doi.org/10.1007/s12369-024-01106-4
9. Smakman, M.H., et al.: A trustworthy robot buddy for primary school children. Multimodal Technol. Interact. **6**(4), 29 (2022)
10. Victor, C.R., et al.: Prevalence and determinants of loneliness in people living with dementia: findings from the ideal programme. Int. J. Geriatric Psychiatry **35**(8), 851–858 (2020). https://doi.org/10.1002/gps.5305
11. Whitson, H.E., Cousins, S.W., Burchett, B.M., Hybels, C.F., Pieper, C.F., Cohen, H.J.: The combined effect of visual impairment and cognitive impairment on disability in older people. J. Am. Geriatr. Soc. **55**(6), 885–891 (2007). https://doi.org/10.1111/j.1532-5415.2007.01093.x
12. Willemse, C.J.A.M., van Erp, J.B.F.: Social touch in human–robot interaction: robot-initiated touches can induce positive responses without extensive prior bonding. Int. J. Soc. Robot. **11**(2), 285–304 (2018). https://doi.org/10.1007/s12369-018-0500-9
13. World Health Organizaition: World Report on Vision, October 2019, https://www.who.int/publications/i/item/9789241516570
14. World Health Organization: (Aug 2023), https://www.who.int/news-room/fact-sheets/detail/blindness-and-visual-impairment

A Path to Gradual Individual Experience and Recollection for Social Robots Based on a Cognitive Architecture

Thomas Sievers(✉) and Nele Russwinkel

Institute of Information Systems, University of Lübeck, 23562 Lübeck, Germany
{t.sievers,nele.russwinkel}@uni-luebeck.de

Abstract. Many attempts are aiming to provide social robots with human-like cognitive abilities such as memory, language comprehension and visual and spatial processing. Cognitive architectures in combination with Large Language Models (LLMs) have the potential to act as basic components for such a system. We demonstrate the use of an Adaptive Control of Thought-Rational (ACT-R) model in combination with an LLM to store experiences from human-robot interaction (HRI) in the declarative memory of the cognitive architecture for a humanoid social robot. These experiences can be retrieved from memory as associated recollections and used for the robot's actions and for prompt augmentation of the LLM. This type of memory also allows the creation, storage and updating of person models from interactions with different people, which enables the robot to get to know these people better through temporally unrelated interactions and to respond to them individually.

Keywords: Social robots · Cognitive architecture · Large language model

1 Introduction

Social robots must be designed and developed to meet the needs of their social environment and be able to respond appropriately and comprehensibly [9]. Their understanding of social norms and expectations should guide their decision-making, and they are required produce mental simulations to understand and predict the thoughts, feelings and intentions of others in a broader social context. When it comes to developing truly human-like cognitive abilities, individual experiences, mediated by social interactions between humans and machines, are essential for an AI agent [14].

In order to interact naturally with a robot, we would expect it to be able to remember and relate to what we have already experienced or discussed with it in the past within a contextual framework. This requires an episodic memory for the robot that is consistent and able to recall recollections associated with us, representing a kind of "narrative self" that includes identity and continuity over time [4]. A long-term memory analogous to human memory, with storage of individual facts and experiences, recollection through associations of current experiences with stored experiences, and functionalities such as forgetting or reinforcing memories, would be a useful cognitive capability for a robot in HRI.

But how can a robot store individual experiences in interaction with humans, remember them later and learn from them? If this is to happen in a way that is comparable to human abilities, a cognitive architecture that has been tried and tested in cognitive psychology is likely to be essential. For this reason, we chose the Adaptive Control of Thought-Rational (ACT-R) as the cognitive architecture to develop human-like memory functionalities for the robot [1]. A Large Language Model (LLM) was used to formulate the dialog parts of the robot and the recollections to be stored. The associated recollections were in turn provided to the LLM via prompt augmentation for consideration in its utterances.

2 Related Work

With the recent successes of language models in various fields, interest in the interplay between LLMs and cognitive architectures has also increased, and ways of integrating LLMs with cognitive architectures have been discussed [2,3,7,11]. Insights from human cognition and psychology that underlie cognitive architectures can contribute to the development of systems that are more efficient, reliable and human-like [17]. The storage of episodic recollections has long been studied in simulation models of human memory [6]. Paplu et al. investigated the use of long-term memory to generate context for customized interactions and the connection with the interaction partner on an emotional level in a personalized HRI [13]. They employed a MySQL database to store the memory content.

In previous work, we have shown in principle that an ACT-R cognitive architecture connected to a social robot can store and process recollections using an LLM [15]. However, studies on the use of different types of memory chunks for different purposes (e.g., memory and person model) have been lacking. In addition, we had not yet tested our system idea with memories of interactions that occurred several weeks or longer ago.

An integration of ACT-R with LLMs was applied for human-centered decision making by using knowledge from the decision process of the cognitive model as neural representations in trainable layers of the LLM [19]. Sumers et al. proposed a language agent with a framework for modular memory components and a generalized decision making process that combines insights from symbolic artificial intelligence and cognitive science [16].

3 Methods

Our approach to generate and utilize individual experiences for a robot combines the memory capabilities of the ACT-R cognitive architecture with the linguistic capabilities of an LLM to both formulate recollections and refer to those recollections in utterances during a subsequent interaction. In addition, individual characteristics of the interaction partner (e.g. preferences, interests, etc.) are stored in a person model so that they can be referred to later.

3.1 Cognitive Model

Cognitive architectures like ACT-R refer both to a theory about the structure of the human mind and to a computer-based implementation of such a theory. They are particularly suitable for human cognitive modeling [8]. Cognitive architectures attempt to describe and integrate the basic mechanisms of human cognition. In doing so, they rely on empirically supported assumptions from cognitive psychology. Their formalized models can be used to react flexibly to actions in a human-like manner and to develop a situational understanding regarding human behavior for adequate reactions. ACT-R comprises a declarative and a procedural memory, whereby the declarative memory supports lexical knowledge by encoding, storing and retrieving semantic knowledge, as in humans, while the procedural memory enables the learning of habits and skills [18].

Creating Recollections. In ACT-R, declarative knowledge is represented in the form of chunks, i.e. representations of individual properties as strings, each of which can be accessed via a labeled slot. The cognitive model we developed should receive chunks with the name of the person speaking and keywords for the memory association as well as the actual memory fact as a phrase from the robot application. Then it had to check whether there were already any memory chunks with this same name indicating an existing recollection for this person. Given the name, the model also searched for matching chunks already stored in the declarative memory for the specified keywords. For simplicity reasons we assumed the transfer of not more than three keywords. The model's productions of the procedural memory checked all combinations of the sequence of keywords for a match with memory content and generated a hit if at least one of the keywords were matching. In this case, the associated recollection was called up and returned to the robot application for LLM prompt augmentation. Generally, the new chunk was stored in the declarative memory.

Person Model. According to Person Model Theory (PMT), we generally understand others based on specific background knowledge that we accumulate over the course of our lives and use to develop "person models" of ourselves and other people [10]. These person models are the basis on which we recognize and evaluate people with both mental and physical characteristics. To enable the robot to remember individual characteristics of the people it has dealt with, we stored them in a person model linked to the person's name in ACT-R's declarative memory. A memory chunk was to be created for each person with slots such as interest, hobby, task in the organization and special sensitivities. One of the robot's goals in the interaction was to fill these slots with relevant content by asking specific questions and updating the person model chunk.

3.2 Prompting the LLM

We applied OpenAI's Generative Pretrained Transformer (GPT) language model to generate speech and process the dialog and memory content of an interaction [12]. The system prompts for the LLM differed depending on the task. In the event that a person model needed to be completed, the LLM was instructed to specifically ask for missing characteristics such as the interests of the human interlocutor and to generate a term from the answer, which was then saved in the corresponding slot of the person model. Otherwise, in addition to formulating an answer in the dialog, the LLM had the task of creating the fact phrase to be stored as a recollection and three suitable keywords from the facts just discussed.

4 Interaction Process Comprising Individual Experiences

We tested our proposed system with the social robot Navel [5]. Figure 1 schematically shows the course of an interaction between the robot and a human. At the very beginning, the application loads all previous contents of the declarative memory from a text file saved for this purpose so that they are available to the cognitive model even after a restart. The robot also waits until a person appears in its field of vision and looks at it. If it perceives a person, it greets them.

Now it is important whether the robot can determine the identity of this person. Since it is currently not possible to access Navel's camera recordings for a visual detection, we use speaker recognition, i.e. we check whether the robot recognizes the speaker's voice by comparing it with audio samples of already known speakers. If the recognition fails, the robot asks for the name of the speaker, creates voice samples for recognition and generates a person model for later completion. Once a person has been recognized, the declarative memory of the ACT-R model is searched for recollections concerning this person and information from the associated person model. If the person model is incomplete, an attempt is made to complete it. Content from recollections and the person model is fed to the LLM via the prompt for consideration and reference in the conversation. As described in Chap. 3.2, the LLM generates a response as well as keywords and fact phrases for storage in memory, whereby the name of the interaction partner and the date and time of the interaction are also stored for possible later reference. If the person responds to the robot's answer, a new turn begins, otherwise the interaction ends.

5 Discussion and Initial Findings

Our investigations into the optimal use of the ACT-R cognitive architecture to generate a long-term memory for a social robot are still in their infancy. In particular, meaningful comparative studies on the perception of the described memory capabilities of the robot in interaction with humans are lacking.

However, as a proof-of-concept for technical feasibility, we can confirm both the generation and storage of recollections of events during a dialog interaction

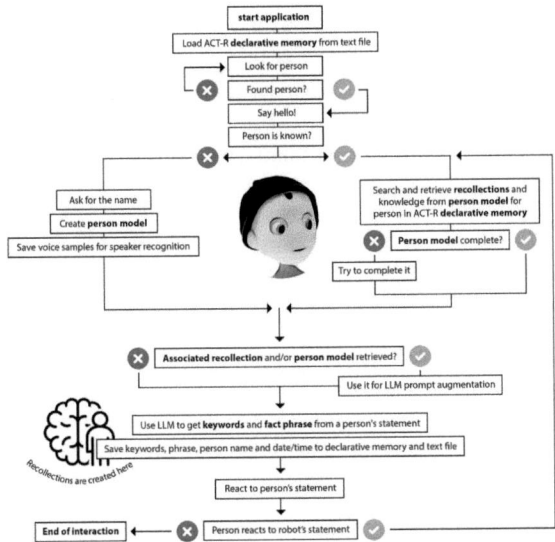

Fig. 1. Interaction process with access to individual previous experiences

as well as retrieval and reference during the conversation. Individual recollections can be combined into a chain of episodic memory and used for prompt augmentation. Actual retrieval is influenced by the productions of procedural memory in the ACT-R model as well as by settings such as noise, utility for the subsymbolic processes and the like. Eventually, the effectiveness of the process depends very much on the exact formulation of the prompts for the LLM, especially if the robot's task changes during the ongoing interaction (e.g., completing the person model vs. conversation considering remembered knowledge). In addition, the basic possibility of referring to recollections available in plain text is also feasible with regard to the explanatory or black box problem of AI.

6 Conclusion and Future Work

Our idea that individual recollections of a robot retrieved by a model of the ACT-R cognitive architecture create an enriched, more human-like personalized interaction experience between a robot and a human has yet to be proven. Progress along this path could lead to a memory system that supports the accumulation of knowledge at ever higher levels of abstraction, and would possibly also be capable of prospection, i.e. the mental simulation of actions. This would require a significantly expanded ACT-R model. However, the collection of personal information when dealing with humans requires responsible handling of this data. Although the recollections are stored directly on the robot, the use of an external LLM could represent a flaw in terms of data protection.

References

1. Anderson, J.R., Bothell, D., Byrne, M.D., Douglass, S., Lebiere, C., Qin, Y.: An integrated theory of the mind **111**(4), 1036–1060 (2004), https://doi.org/10.1037/0033-295X.111.4.1036
2. Binz, M., Schulz, E.: Turning large language models into cognitive models (2023), https://arxiv.org/abs/2306.03917
3. Dubey, S., Ghosh, R., Dubey, M., Chatterjee, S., Das, S., Benito-León, J.: Redefining cognitive domains in the era of chatgpt: a comprehensive analysis of artificial intelligence's influence and future implications. Med. Res. Arch. **12** (2024), https://doi.org/10.18103/mra.v12i6.5383
4. Gallagher, S.: Philosophical conceptions of the self: implications for cognitive science. Trends Cogn. Sci. **4**(1), 14–21 (2000). https://doi.org/10.1016/S1364-6613(99)01417-5
5. navel robotics GmbH: navel. Technical Report (2025), https://navelrobotics.com
6. Hintzman, D.L.: Minerva 2: a simulation model of human memory. Behav. Res. Methods Instrum. Comput. **16**(2), 96–101 (1984). https://doi.org/10.3758/BF03202365
7. Knowles, K., Witbrock, M., Dobbie, G., Yogarajan, V.: A proposal for a language model based cognitive architecture. In: Proceedings of the AAAI Symposium Series (2024), https://api.semanticscholar.org/CorpusID:267206594
8. Kurup, U., Lebiere, C.: What can cognitive architectures do for robotics? Biologically Inspired Cogn. Archit. **2**, 88–99 (2012). https://doi.org/10.1016/j.bica.2012.07.004
9. Mahdi, H., Akgun, S.A., Saleh, S., Dautenhahn, K.: A survey on the design and evolution of social robots — past, present and future. Robot. Auton. Syst. **156** (2022). https://doi.org/10.1016/j.robot.2022.104193
10. Newen, A.: The person model theory and the question of situatedness of social understanding. In: The Oxford Handbook of 4E Cognition. Oxford University Press, September 2018. https://doi.org/10.1093/oxfordhb/9780198735410.013.25
11. Niu, Q., et al.: Large language models and cognitive science: a comprehensive review of similarities, differences, and challenges (2024), https://arxiv.org/abs/2409.02387
12. OpenAI: the most powerful platform for building ai products. Technical Report (2025), https://openai.com/api/
13. Paplu, S., Navarro, R.F., Berns, K.: Harnessing long-term memory for personalized human-robot interactions. In: 2022 IEEE-RAS 21st International Conference on Humanoid Robots (Humanoids), pp. 377–382 (2022). https://doi.org/10.1109/Humanoids53995.2022.10000213
14. Sandini, G., Sciutti, A., Morasso, P.: Artificial cognition vs. artificial intelligence for next-generation autonomous robotic agents. Front. Comput. Neurosci. **18** (2024). https://doi.org/10.3389/fncom.2024.1349408
15. Sievers, T., Russwinkel, N.: Retrieving memory content from a cognitive architecture by impressions from language models for use in a social robot. Appl. Sci. **15**(10) (2025). https://doi.org/10.3390/app15105778
16. Sumers, T.R., Yao, S., Narasimhan, K., Griffiths, T.L.: Cognitive architectures for language agents (2024), https://arxiv.org/abs/2309.02427
17. Sun, R.: Can a cognitive architecture fundamentally enhance llms? or vice versa? (2024), https://arxiv.org/abs/2401.10444

18. Whitehill, J.: Understanding act-r - an outsider's perspective (2013), https://arxiv.org/abs/1306.0125
19. Wu, S., Oltramari, A., Francis, J., Giles, C.L., Ritter, F.E.: Cognitive llms: Towards integrating cognitive architectures and large language models for manufacturing decision-making (2024), https://arxiv.org/abs/2408.09176

SitBot: A Posture-Mimicking Robot to Reduce Slouching

Chia-An Wang[✉], Adam Wikström, Linus Pettersson, Anasha Sarker, Martina De Cet, Georgios Diapoulis, Mohammad Obaid, and Ilaria Torre

Chalmers University of Technology and University of Gothenburg, Gothenburg, Sweden
{chiaan,adamwi,pelinus,anashas,demart,geodia,mobaid,ilariat}@chalmers.se

Abstract. Poor posture is a common issue in modern sedentary lifestyles and can lead to long-term musculoskeletal problems. This study explores whether a robot can improve human posture through mimicry. We designed a teddy bear robot that mimics people's slouching behaviour, and alerts the person to return to an upright posture. The prototype was tested in a controlled user study involving 20 participants. Results indicate that the inclusion of slouch mimicry tends to make people correct their posture and increases their posture awareness, without being perceived as more distracting than a baseline condition. These initial results suggest that slouch mimicry can be an effective solution to improve people's posture while working at a desk.

Keywords: Human-Robot Interaction (HRI) · Posture · Mimicry

1 Introduction and Related Work

The increasing use of technology and prolonged sedentary behaviours have been linked to poor postural habits and musculoskeletal issues [10], as well as emotional disturbances including stress, anxiety and depression [8]. Given the central role of technology in education, such issues are increasingly common among university students [3]. Various technological solutions have been proposed to help people maintain a healthy posture, such as reminder systems, wearables to monitor posture, and other desktop tools (e.g., [1,13]). While effective to some extent, these systems are often perceived as intrusive or easy to ignore, thus limiting their long-term engagement. Design research suggests that more embodied, interactive technologies such as robots may offer a more engaging and acceptable alternative [18]. In particular, Socially Assistive Robotics (SAR) has shown promise in encouraging healthy behaviours in sedentary contexts. For example, robots that prompt users to take breaks have been found to be more engaging and motivating than traditional alarms [7,18,20]. However, most robotic applications rely on explicit cues or predefined prompts (e.g. [7]).

To the best of our knowledge, little has been done to integrate human social norms, such as mimicry, into an embodied technology as a motivator to improve one's posture while working or studying. Mimicry, or alignment, is a widespread phenomenon in human-human interaction, whereby people tend to unconsciously imitate each other's gestures, facial expressions, speech patterns, mannerisms, and more, to signal affiliation and promote positive rapport [4]. This phenomenon has been studied in the field of Human-Robot Interaction (HRI), both in terms of whether people mimic a robot, thus unconsciously signalling that they are positively aligned towards it (e.g. [12]), and in terms of robots mimicking people, with the aim of improving the interaction. Researchers have studied the effect of robots mimicking e.g. human speech features [9], gestures [15], and facial expressions [17]. Robot mimicry has generally been shown to have positive effects on people in several aspects, including mood improvement [2] and likeability [14]. However, the question of whether mimicry can be used to nudge people to change an undesired behaviour remains underexplored within the context of HRI. Kucharski et al. [7] developed a robot that encourages office workers to take breaks by slowly changing its posture; however, in this case the robot did not mimic the workers' posture, but simply changed posture at pre-defined intervals.

We propose a novel solution to support individuals sitting at a desk by developing a social robotic platform that encourages proper sitting habits through subtle mimicry-based embodiment cues. With this social robot, we investigate the following research question: How does a robot's posture-mimicking behaviour affect a user's sitting posture during desk work? Here, we present a study that addresses this question by examining whether robots, by mimicking people's slouching behaviours, can improve people's posture and posture awareness.

2 Method

We used a rapid prototyping process [5] to develop a teddy bear-shaped robot that mimics slouching. The animal-like form was chosen to encourage empathy [5], and the teddy bear specifically due to its anatomical similarity to humans, particularly the ability to sit upright with a bent back, enabling posture mimicry.
Robot Prototype: Given the intended use case (a robot companion for desk work), we incorporated soft textures and a friendly appearance to enhance user acceptance. The prototype was built using a 28 cm tall IKEA stuffed teddy bear and a custom skeleton composed of three foam segments representing the head, chest, and lower body. These segments were connected via servo motors to enable posture control. Figure 1 illustrates the design stages of the prototype. The waist servo could shift between two positions (100° and 50°), representing upright and slouched postures. A speaker was used to play a sighing sound when the robot slouched. This was meant to alert people to pay attention to the robot. All the code and data are available here.
Study Setup and Procedure: To test the effect of robot posture mimicry, we conducted a between-subjects study with two experimental conditions: one where the robot would slouch and sigh (condition SM), and one where the robot would only sigh (condition S) whenever the participant slouched at the desk[1].

---

[1] Link to a video showcasing the teddy bear robot's movement and sound.

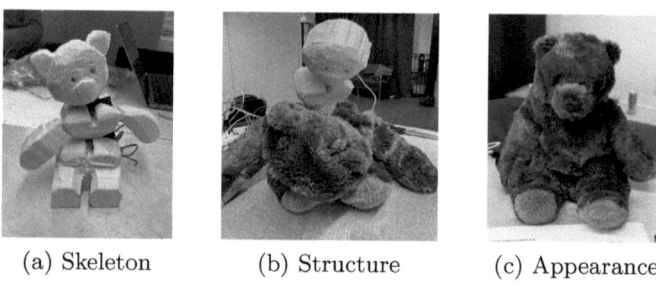

(a) Skeleton   (b) Structure   (c) Appearance

Fig. 1. Final teddy bear robot prototype. (a) shows the foam skeleton, (b) the structure inside the bear, and (c) the completed appearance.

Participants were asked to read a long technical research paper while seated on a tall chair at a high table. Each session began with signing an informed consent form and reading a cover story describing the robot as a "companion teddy bear". Participants were told to "keep posture in mind" without revealing the role of the robot. The robot's response was triggered through Wizard-of-Oz: a researcher prompted the robot to react whenever a participant was observed to be slouching (here, we defined slouching as leaning forward with a bent back or drooping shoulders, based on previous field observations). Participants' posture was noted down throughout the reading task. After 10 min of reading, participants were asked to complete a short survey with two 7-point Likert questions on robot awareness and perceived distraction, and a semi-structured interview assessing people's general perceptions of the robot, and how they interpreted the robot's nonverbal communication. Each session lasted approximately 20 min.

Participants: We recruited 20 participants (age = 19–58; 12 women, 7 men, 1 preferred not to say), who were randomly assigned to one of the conditions. The experiment followed ethical guidelines from Chalmers University of Technology.

3 Results

Descriptive statistics of the ratings and posture corrections can be seen in Fig. 2. A Bayesian ordinal regression model was fitted for both robot awareness and perceived distraction to estimate the effect of mimicry, using the rethinking R package. Compared to Frequentist methods, Bayesian models provide full uncertainty estimates and allow intuitive probability statements about effects. They are particularly well suited for small samples and ordinal data, making them ideal for analysing the subjective ratings and behaviour in this study. For behavioural observations, a separate Bayesian logistic regression model was used, where each slouch event was treated as a trial and each posture correction as a binary outcome. All code, data and equations used in this study are publicly available at the project's GitHub repository linked earlier.

Regarding robot awareness, people in the SM condition reported slightly higher ratings than in the S condition. The posterior probability that SM rated higher awareness was 70.3%, with a mean group effect b = 0.30 and a 90% credible interval of [−0.62, 1.22]. For perceived distraction, the posterior probability that SM found the robot more distracting was 65.3%. The estimated mean group effect b = 0.21, with a 90% credible interval of [−0.68, 1.12].

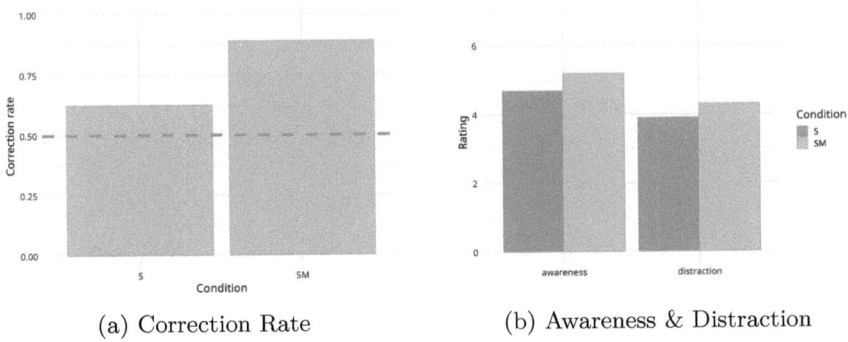

(a) Correction Rate   (b) Awareness & Distraction

Fig. 2. Comparison between conditions. (a) shows correction rates (dashed line = 50% chance). (b) shows awareness and distraction ratings.

The effect on posture was analysed by looking at whether people corrected their posture after the robot alerted or mimicked them. The Bayesian model estimated a posterior probability of 97.4% that posture correction was more likely in the SM condition compared to S. The estimated group intercept was $a = 1.37$, corresponding to a baseline correction rate of approximately 80% for S ($\text{logit}^{-1}(1.37) \approx 0.80$). The group effect was $b = 0.91$, which translates to an increase in correction rate of about 91% in the SM group ($\text{logit}^{-1}(1.40+0.91) \approx 0.91$). The 90% credible interval for b was $[0.13, 1.72]$.

To facilitate comparisons within the HRI community, we also fitted corresponding frequentist regression models to both the Likert scale ratings and the posture correction data. For the ratings, an ordinal logistic regression found small, non-significant group effects for robot awareness ($b = 0.35 \pm 0.80$, $t = 0.44$, odds ratio = 1.43) and perceived distraction ($b = 0.64 \pm 0.82t = 0.77$, odds ratio = 1.89). For the posture correction, a binomial logistic regression model estimated the baseline correction rate for the S condition as 80% ($\text{logit}^{-1}(1.42)$), with a significant intercept of 1.42 ($p < 0.001$), meaning that people in the S group corrected their posture significantly more than chance. The group effect was estimated at $b = 1.00$, corresponding to an odds ratio of 2.72 ($p = 0.12$), meaning that there was no statistically significant difference in the posture correction rates between the two groups.

Finally, we conducted a thematic analysis on the open-ended questions. The results revealed four key themes: participants generally considered the robot's behaviour as either posture-corrective or emotionally expressive. In the SM condition, the participants understood the corrective function better than in the S condition. The robot sounds were effective in drawing attention to the robot, but five people found them distracting. Mimicry was reported to increase posture awareness (one participant saw it as a "mini version" of themselves). Lastly, two participants wished for personalisation in the robot's embodiment.

4 Discussion and Conclusion

We developed and evaluated a prototype robot that mimics users' posture to encourage them to sit correctly at a desk. Our preliminary results provide initial evidence that mimicking tends to increase people's posture correction and posture awareness, compared to simply drawing attention with auditory cues, as demonstrated by both the Bayesian analysis of participants' behaviour and thematic analysis of the post-interaction interviews. Interestingly, this behavioural change occurred with a very small, not-significant increase in perceived distraction or awareness of the robot. On the contrary, the interview data suggest that the auditory cue alone was sometimes confusing to participants, whereas posture mimicry appeared to clarify the robot's intended message.

To our knowledge, this is the first study in HRI to explore posture-mimicking as a form of implicit feedback to promote behaviour change. While mimicry has been studied in social affiliation and imitation in HRI (e.g. [12,14,15]), its use to signal (un)desired behaviour is novel and holds promising results.

Another interesting finding is that adding mimicry to the auditory cue did not significantly increase perceived distractions or awareness of the robot as shown in Fig. 2. This suggests that postural mimicry can enhance behavioural compliance without introducing additional cognitive load. This also aligns with previous research showing that multimodal cues are more effective at conveying information than unimodal cues (e.g. [16]). Previous studies suggested that embodied agents such as robots should be more engaging and effective than disembodied computer applications [18], and smartphone-based applications are also known for inducing distractions [6]; still, an experimental comparison between a robot application such as ours and, for example, a mimicking virtual avatar remains to be conducted. In sum, we suggest that posture mimicry is most effective when used as part of a multimodal feedback system rather than as a standalone cue.

While our study did not directly measure perceived engagement or likeability, it is possible that the mimicking gesture contributed to a greater sense of affiliation with the robot, as this is one of the goals of unconscious mimicry [4]. Although our data cannot confirm this interpretation, the increased posture correction observed in the SM condition may reflect increased affiliation with the robot. This can also be linked to participants' comments indicating a desire for more robot personalisation. Previous work on desktop companion robots allowed people to personalise their robot, and this was found to be a positive design feature [7]. Future studies should explicitly measure perceptions such as likeability and engagement, and investigate how personalisation and mimicry might jointly contribute to the effectiveness of socially assistive robots. Another open question for future work is what other human behaviours could be mimicked by robots to support or nudge positive change. Researchers have begun to explore ideas such as yawn contagion in HRI [11], and mirroring or contrasting user behaviour at a desk to influence attention and productivity [19].

Our findings should be viewed in light of some limitations. First, the small sample size (N = 20) limits generalisability and statistical power. While frequentist analyses found no significant effects, Bayesian analyses suggest tentative support for postural mimicry. These results are preliminary and require validation with larger, more diverse samples. Second, the study used a Wizard-of-Oz setup, with manually controlled robot behaviour. Though this ensured consistency, it may not reflect real-world responses to an autonomous system. Future studies should include an autonomous version to assess ecological validity. Third, we did not test a mimicking-only condition without sound, due to pilot results showing that movement alone often went unnoticed. Still, future work should include this for completeness. Fourth, the robot's ability to mimic posture was limited to a single slouching pose, although bad sitting posture can vary between individuals. More advanced prototypes with a more sophisticated anatomy should replicate a wider range of postures and use sensors and cameras for autonomous and real-time detection. Fifth, while our results show promising positive results of using mimicry as a way to make people slouch less, mimicry might actually also have the reverse effect of making people slouch more. This is an ethical concern that should be investigated before similar persuasive technologies are adopted more widely. Lastly, we did not measure other aspects of user perception, such as engagement, likability, or long-term adherence, which should be explored in future work to better understand the persuasive robot's overall impact.

In sum, with our teddy bear prototype, we suggest that posture-mimicking by a robot is a novel and promising strategy to implicitly encourage users to correct their posture, without adding cognitive load or being perceived as distracting.

References

1. Bootsman, R., Markopoulos, P., Qi, Q., Wang, Q., Timmermans, A.A.: Wearable technology for posture monitoring at the workplace. Int. J. Hum Comput Stud. **132**, 99–111 (2019)
2. Burns, R., Jeon, M., Park, C.H.: Robotic motion learning framework to promote social engagement. Appl. Sci. **8**(2) (2018)
3. Castro, O., Bennie, J., Vergeer, I., Bosselut, G., Biddle, S.J.H.: How sedentary are university students? a systematic review and meta-analysis. Prev. Sci. **21**(3), 332–343 (2020)
4. Chartrand, T.L., Bargh, J.A.: The chameleon effect: the perception-behavior link and social interaction. J. Pers. Soc. Psychol. **76**(6), 893 (1999)
5. Deneke, J., Lehane, D., Kandler, A., Menchini, T., Laaksoharju, M., Obaid, M.: Using rapid prototyping to explore design implications for a pill-dispensing social agent. In: Proceedings of the 5th International Conference on Human Agent Interaction, HAI 2017, pp. 53–59. ACM, New York, NY, USA (2017)
6. Kaminske, A., Brown, A., Aylward, A., Haller, M.: Cell phone notifications harm attention: an exploration of the factors that contribute to distraction. Eur. J. Educ. Res. **11**(3), 1487–1494 (2022)

7. Kucharski, P., et al.: Apeow: a personal persuasive avatar for encouraging breaks in office work. In: Annals of Computer Science and Information Systems, October 2016
8. Lee, E., Kim, Y.: Effect of university students' sedentary behavior on stress, anxiety, and depression. Perspect. Psychiatr. Care **55**(2), 164–169 (2019)
9. Molenaar, B., Soliño Fernández, B., Polimeno, A., Barakova, E., Chen, A.: Pitch it right: using prosodic entrainment to improve robot-assisted foreign language learning in school-aged children. Multimodal Technol. Interact. **5**(12), 76 (2021)
10. Montuori, P., et al.: Assessment on practicing correct body posture and determinant analyses in a large population of a metropolitan area. Behav. Sci. **13**(2) (2023)
11. Obaid, M., Kuchenbrandt, D., Bartneck, C.: Empathy and yawn contagion: can we (humans) catch yawns from robots? In: Proceedings of the 2014 ACM/IEEE International Conference on Human-Robot Interaction, HRI 2014, pp. 260–261. ACM, New York, NY, USA (2014)
12. Paetzel, M., Varni, G., Hupont, I., Chetouani, M., Peters, C., Castellano, G.: Investigating the influence of embodiment on facial mimicry in hri using computer vision-based measures. In: 2017 26th IEEE International Symposium on Robot and Human Interactive Communication (RO-MAN), pp. 579–586. IEEE (2017)
13. Robbins, M., Johnson, I., Cunliffe, C.: Encouraging good posture in school children using computers. Clin. Chiropr. **12**(1), 35–44 (2009)
14. Shinohara, Y., Mitsukuni, K., Yoneda, T., Ichikawa, J., Nishizaki, Y., Oka, N.: A humanoid robot can use mimicry to increase likability and motivation for helping. In: Proceedings of the 6th International Conference on Human-Agent Interaction, HAI 2018, pp. 122–128. ACM, New York, NY, USA (2018)
15. Stolzenwald, J., Bremner, P.: Gesture mimicry in social human-robot interaction. In: 2017 26th IEEE International Symposium on Robot and Human Interactive Communication (RO-MAN), pp. 430–436. IEEE (2017)
16. Torre, I., Holk, S., Yadollahi, E., Leite, I., McDonnell, R., Harte, N.: Smiling in the face and voice of avatars and robots: Evidence for a 'smiling mcgurk effect'. IEEE Trans. Affect. Comput. (2022)
17. Tscherepanow, M., Hillebrand, M., Hegel, F., Wrede, B., Kummert, F.: Direct imitation of human facial expressions by a user-interface robot. In: 2009 9th IEEE-RAS International Conference on Humanoid Robots, pp. 154–160. IEEE (2009)
18. Šabanović, S., Reeder, S.M., Kechavarzi, B.: Designing robots in the wild: in situ prototype evaluation for a break management robot. J. Hum.-Robot Interact. **3**(1), 70–88 (2014)
19. Yoon, S., Kim, S., Park, G., Lim, H.: Evaluating how desktop companion robot behaviors influence work experience and robot perception. In: Extended Abstracts of the CHI Conference on Human Factors in Computing Systems. CHI EA 2024, ACM, New York, NY, USA (2024)
20. Zhang, B.J., Quick, R., Helmi, A., Fitter, N.T.: Socially assistive robots at work: making break-taking interventions more pleasant, enjoyable, and engaging. In: 2020 IEEE/RSJ International Conference on Intelligent Robots and Systems (IROS), pp. 11292–11299. IEEE Press (2020)

Author Index

A

Ahmed, Eshtiak 159
Ahmed, Mahmoud Mohamed Hussien 83
Ahtinen, Aino 311
Al Krad, Ibrahim 96
Álvarez-Arias, Sofía 413
Alessandra, Sciutti 590
Amirabdollahian, Farshid 46, 490
Anastasiou, Dimitra 547
Andrighetto, Luca 572
Annese, Luca 508
Antonj, Matilde 499
Arlinghaus, Clarissa Sabrina 194

B

Baber, Chris 424
Bäckström, August 616
Baecker, Niklas 566
Barnard, Pepita 456
Bekier, Piotr 387
Belpaeme, Tony 211
Bendel, Oliver 462
Bergmann, Felix 331
Biagi, Federico 531
Biagiotti, Luigi 531
Blum, Kai M. 96
Bodenhagen, Leon 439
Bonga, Georges Arnaud Kouayim 553
Borghi, Guido 531
Boribun, Wisanukorn 482
Buchem, Ilona 553, 566
Burdman, Roni 372
Buruk, Oğuz 'Oz' 159

C

Caldiroli, Cristina Liviana 399
Calebsolly, Praminda 456
Caleb-Solly, Praminda 490, 516
Camara, Fanta 539
Cameron, Alfie 456
Carnevale, A. 578

Carrasco, Ana 311
Carrasco-Martínez, Sara 413
Castro-González, Álvaro 413
Catalini, Riccardo 531
Chen, Yang 356
Chowdhury, Aparajita 311
Ciardo, Francesca 625
Cocchella, Francesca 572
Cooper, Sara 607
Craigon, Peter 456

D

Dao, Mai 343
Datteri, Edoardo 399
De Cet, Martina 648
Desmet, Pieter M. A. 59
Di Nuovo, Alessandro 490
Diapoulis, Georgios 648
Doernbach, Tobias 96
Dogangün, Aysegül 126
Downs, Charles 476
Dragone, Mauro 490

E

Edan, Yael 372
Ekenberg, William 616
Elara, Mohan Rajesh 269, 281
Eyssel, Friederike 224

F

Fabrizio, A. 578
Faria, Diego Resende 46
Farić, Ana 499
Farkaš, Igor 499
Fava, Alessandra 625
Ficuciello, Fanny 243, 256
Fong, Hunter 16
Foronda, Cynthia 476
Fujii, Koyo 516

G

Gaffinet, Ben 547
Ganal, Elisabeth 174
Gerndt, Reinhard 96
Gevaert, Rick 632
Giuseppe, Di Cesare 590
Gohari, Mohammad 243, 256
Gomez, Randy 356
Gosala, Bethany 111
Grando, Ricardo Bedin 96
Gupta, Manjari 111

H

Hamari, Juho 159
Hasnine, Mohammad Nehal 83
Hawley, Mark 490
Heidari, Hamidreza 256
Heidmann, Frank 482
Higgins, Angela 490
Hirokawa, Masakazu 33
Hobbelink, Veerle L. N. F. 632
Hommel, Bernhard 295
Hornáčková, Hana 499
Hout, Victor van der 632
Hu, Jun 59
Hu, Mingyang 356
Huang, Zijun 424
Hunt, Edmund R. 424
Hunt, Joseph 516

I

Iani, Cristina 625
Indurkhya, Bipin 33, 83, 141
Ismail, Abdul Kader Mohamed 590
Iwata, Kenji 331

J

Jair, Patrick Houman 3
Jansen, Nadine 126
Jena, Ayesha 598
Jokinen, Kristiina 524
Jones, Adam 584

K

Kamińska, Alicja 33
Kappas, Arvid 295
Kaptelinin, Victor 616
Kaur, Maninderjit 559
Kobayashi, Yoshinori 331
Kołbasa, Anna 33
Kolks, Laurens A. G. 59
Koyuturk, Cansu 508
Kubullek, Ann-Kathrin 126
Kuehne, Katharina 566
Kukier, Tymon 33

L

Lancaster, Karen 456
Lapomarda, Leonardo 399
Larghi, Silvia 399
Le, Anh Vu 281
Leusmann, Jan 311
Li, Guangliang 356
Li, Yifei 16
Lischer, Dustin 632
Longo, U. G. 578
Lúčny, Andrej 499
Lugrin, Birgit 174
Łukasik, Albert 387

M

Magassouba, Aly 516
Maier, Günter W. 194
Maj, Konrad 387
Malinovská, Kristína 499
Mambilla, Kennedy 194
Mancini, Maurizio 16
Maroto-Gómez, Marcos 413
Mauch, Martina 566
Maurelli, Francesco 295
Mayoral-Macau, Arnau 607
Mazzola, Carlo 499
McCarthy, Mark 343
Mcclaughlin, Emma 456
Milivojevic, Sanja 424
Mishra, Deepti 111
Mongile, Sara 572
Moore, Roger K. 584
Moraes, Pablo 96
Müller, Florian 311
Muthugala, M. A. Viraj J. 269

N

Nahum, Ehud 372
Naudet, Yannick 547
Nichols, Eric 356
Niebling, Florian 174
Niewiadomski, Radoslaw 16

Nikolovska, Kristina 295
Nunez, Eleuda 33

O

Obaid, Mohammad 648
Ognibene, Dimitri 508
Øllgaard, John Allan 439
Olteanu, Yasmin 553
Orlandini, A. 578
Oron-Gilad, Tal 372

P

Palinko, Oskar 439
Pande, Akshara 111
Park, Chung Hyuk 3
Pasternak, Katarzyna 476
Patania, Sabrina 508
Peng, Zhuochao 59
Peters, Christopher 96
Pettersson, Linus 648
Pitsch, Karola 331
Pohl, Jan 295
Potter, Stephen 490
Prabakaran, Veerajagadheswar 281
Pou, Bartomeu 607
Pusceddu, Giulia 572

R

Radhakrishnan, Gayathri Girijadevi 46
Radoslaw, Niewiadomski 590
Radosz-Knawa, Zuzanna 33
Rasmussen, Ricki Kenn 439
Rea, Francesco 572
Redondo, Alberto 607
Reed, Darren 539
Reitmann, Stefan 598
Ren, Qiaoqiao 211
Ricciardelli, Paola 625
Rios, David 607
Rodríguez-Huelves, Juan 413
Ros, Raquel 607
Ruggeri, Azzurra 508
Russwinkel, Nele 641

S

Sabattini, Lorenzo 625
Sachinthana, W. K. R. 269
Salici, Giacomo 531
Samarakoon, S. M. Bhagya P. 269

Sang, Ash Yaw 281
Sarker, Anasha 648
Sato, Yuya 83
Satoh, Tomomi 331
Satoh, Yutaka 331
Schena, E. 578
Schetter, Francesco 243
Schmidt, Albrecht 311
Schmiedel, Theresa 224
Schneider, Sebastian 450
Sciutti, Alessandra 572
Segura-Bencomo, Arecia 413
Serena, Carlesso 590
Shino, Kosei 331
Siegmann, Tamara 462
Sievers, Thomas 641
Simon, Markus 224
Smakman, Matthijs H. J. 632
Soufargi, Selim 16
Steinhaeusser, Sophia C. 174
Sudermann, Tabea 439
Sulaiman, Shifa 243
Suzuki, Kenji 33
Suzuki, Ryota 331
Syvänen, Antti 470

T

Takao, Mina 331
Tamantini, C. 578
Tanhua-Piiroinen, Erika 470
Thankachan, Biju 524
Tian, Liu 356
Topp, Elin Anna 598
Torre, Ilaria 648
Turunen, Markku 524
Tveretina, Olga 46

U

Uchida, Naoki 331
Umbrico, A. 578

V

Vänni, Kimmo J. 470
Väänänen, Kaisa 311
Valls, Pol Barrera 439
van Zeeland, Martijn 632
Vavrečka, Ana 499
Vezzani, Roberto 531
Villani, Valeria 625

Visser, Ubbo 476
Viteli, Jarmo 470
Vonschallen, Stephan 224

W
Wang, Chia-An 648
Wang, Tianyuan 539
Wang, Yuhuan 83
Webb, Helena 456
Webb, Nicola 424
Wikström, Adam 648
Wilcock, Graham 524
Wolf, Angelina Stoyanova 439
Woolley, Robert 539
Wróbel, Alicja 141

Wu, Yiyi 559

X
Xu, Jiaxin 59
Xue, Haian 59

Y
Yamazaki, Akiko 331
Yamazaki, Keiichi 331
Yan, Fujian 343
Yuan, Fengpei 559

Z
Zguda, Paulina 33, 141
Zumthor, Ennio 224

MIX
Papier aus verantwortungsvollen Quellen
Paper from responsible sources
FSC® C105338

If you have any concerns about our products,
you can contact us on
ProductSafety@springernature.com

In case Publisher is established outside the EU,
the EU authorized representative is:
**Springer Nature Customer Service Center GmbH
Europaplatz 3, 69115 Heidelberg, Germany**

Printed by Libri Plureos GmbH
in Hamburg, Germany